Contemporary Perspectives on Interpersonal Communication

Contemporary Perspectives on Interpersonal Communication

Sandra Petronio
Arizona State University

❖

Jess K. Alberts
Arizona State University

❖

Michael L. Hecht
Arizona State University

❖

Jerry Buley
Arizona State University

WCB **Brown &**
Benchmark
PUBLISHERS

Madison, Wisconsin•Dubuque, Iowa•Indianapolis, Indiana
Melbourne, Australia•Oxford, England

Book Team

Editor *Stan Stoga*
Developmental Editor *Mary E. Rossa*
Production Editor *Carla D. Kipper*
Visuals/Design Developmental Consultant *Marilyn A. Phelps*
Visuals/Design Freelance Specialist *Mary L. Christianson*
Publishing Services Specialist *Sherry Padden*
Marketing Manager *Carla J. Aspelmeier*
Advertising Manager *Jodi Rymer*

WCB Brown & Benchmark

A Division of Wm. C. Brown Communications, Inc.

Vice President and General Manager *Thomas E. Doran*
Editor in Chief *Edgar J. Laube*
Executive Editor *Ed Bartell*
Executive Editor *Stan Stoga*
National Sales Manager *Eric Ziegler*
Director of CourseResource *Kathy Law Laube*
Director of CourseSystems *Chris Rogers*

Director of Marketing *Sue Simon*
Director of Production *Vickie Putman Caughron*
Imaging Group Manager *Chuck Carpenter*
Manager of Visuals and Design *Faye M. Schilling*
Design Manager *Jac Tilton*
Art Manager *Janice Roerig*
Permissions/Records Manager *Connie Allendorf*

Wm. C. Brown Communications, Inc.

President and Chief Executive Officer *G. Franklin Lewis*
Corporate Vice President, President of WCB Manufacturing *Roger Meyer*
Vice President and Chief Financial Officer *Robert Chesterman*

Cover and interior design by Kay D. Fulton

Copyedited by Karen Dorman

A Times Mirror Company

Library of Congress Catalog Card Number: 92–70463

ISBN 0–697–13356–7

Printed in the United States of America by Wm. C. Brown Communications, Inc.,
2460 Kerper Boulevard, Dubuque, IA 52001

10 9 8 7 6 5 4 3 2 1

"This is dedicated to the ones we love."

Contents

Preface

This reader focuses on issues in relational interpersonal communication. We have synthesized the traditional interpersonal perspectives with the more current relational orientation in the field of communication. The book is comprised of eight chapters and an extensive bibliography. There are several features that will help the student better understand the scholarly articles included in this book.

First, the introductory section is composed of two original chapters which present *a theoretical overview* (chapter 1) discussing significant models and theories used as underpinnings for the articles in this reader, and *a methodological overview* (chapter 2) focusing on the major approaches used in the articles found in this reader. These two chapters provide some needed background information to help the student understand the articles included in this book.

Second, in addition to the actual statistical summaries presented in the published articles, the authors of this reader have included a simplified presentation of the statistical analyses. Because many of the articles are not written for the general population, the statistical analyses are sometimes difficult to understand. Thus, we have inserted one or more side boxes in the original articles that explain the procedures.

Third, this reader is organized according to two overarching principles that represent theory and research in the area of interpersonal communication. We contend that interpersonal communication is often defined in terms of the individual, where research and theorizing focuses on *strategic processes* the person uses to interact with others. In this research tradition, we study how individuals understand communication, create messages, and achieve their goals or influence others.

We also propose that interpersonal communication focuses on *developmental processes* in communicative relationships. Here we are concerned with how relationships are formed, changed, and ended through communicative acts. Whereas the strategic processes approach is concerned with the behaviors and thoughts of individuals, the developmental approach looks at how communication is a factor in the way relationships change over time.

There are times when these two orientations overlap, but in order to provide a framework for organizing research literature, the approaches of strategic processes and developmental processes are used as separate structures for the chapters in this book.

There are four sections to this book. Section I contains the two original chapters on theory and methods. Section II contains articles written from interpersonal perspectives. These sections include articles which focus on strategic processes and articles which focus on developmental processes. Section III contains only articles which deal with strategic processes. It is divided into two chapters. The first contains articles on interpersonal influence. The second contains articles on interpersonal politics and conversational management. Finally, Section IV is dedicated to developmental processes. It, too, is divided into two chapters. The first contains articles on interpersonal bonding. The second contains articles on interpersonal competence.

Fourth, this reader includes approximately 200 citations of articles relating to the areas of focus within the book. Thus, students have an available pool of information with which to extend their knowledge about the issues addressed in the book. With these citations, this reader has the capacity to function as a major resource for the student and instructor.

We want to thank the people who reviewed portions of the manuscript for their useful and insightful comments: Kevin Barge, Baylor University; Melanie Booth-Butterfield, West Virginia University; Steven Duck, University of Iowa; Randall Koper, University of the Pacific; Larry Nadler, Miami University; and Mark Redmond, Iowa State University.

We also deeply appreciate the special assistance that Robert Krizek, Eric Snider, James Stiff, and the people at the Auxiliary Resource Center—Marian Buckley, Fran Mularski, and Janet Soper—gave to the project.

SECTION I

Overview

CHAPTER 1

Interpersonal Communication Theory

Jerry Buley, Sandra Petronio, Michael L. Hecht, Jess K. Alberts

*One thing I have learned in a long life: That all our science,
measured against reality, is primitive and childlike—and yet it
is the most precious thing we have.*

Albert Einstein (Hoffman, 1972)

INTRODUCTION

Today, interpersonal communication is one of the largest areas within the field of communication. There are entire journals reserved for research in this area. Only a few years ago interpersonal communication research had to fight for space in the scholarly journals as "the new kid on the block." The broadening of the communication field from its original focus on the source orientation of a message (e.g., public speaking) to include an interpersonal orientation has not been without the pain of paradigms lost.

The study of communication as a social science is quite young compared to such social sciences as sociology and psychology. In many ways we are still in the infant stage of theory development. Unlike psychology which has tended to focus on the psyche and its inputs and outputs, and unlike sociology which has tended to focus on groups of people as they exist in society, we in communication focus on the messages exchanged between people and how those messages affect other aspects of their lives. In interpersonal communication, we further limit

this to focus our research on how the messages people exchange affect the relationships between them.

Research in communication is both similar to research in other fields and very different from it. It is similar in that scholars of communication want to learn more about their phenomenon. However, researchers in other areas develop symbolic structures as tools to help them understand the phenomenon they wish to study. That phenomenon is logically separate from the created symbolic structure. For example, Einstein used complicated mathematical representations along with interesting verbal models to help him understand and explain his theory of relativity. His symbolic structures, whether they were made up of words or numbers, were not the thing itself.

In communication, the tool is the phenomenon and the phenomenon is the tool. The words and symbols we use to describe what we study are the very thing we study. This reflexivity increases the complexity of doing research in communication. We have to use symbols, numbers, and words to develop theories to understand how people use symbols.

3

You, as a student of interpersonal communication, are coming in contact with the field at a time of very rapid change. To understand the complexities of interpersonal communication theory, you must grasp the language and approaches of the professionals who also pursue such an understanding.

In order to do research, a scholar first must make two kinds of assumptions. One of these is about how do we know we know. The second is about what it means to be human. These assumptions affect the way we do research, but more importantly, they affect the questions we ask. This chapter is our attempt to show you the assumptions that communication researchers have made and introduce you to the theoretical perspectives found in interpersonal communication.

EPISTEMOLOGY AND ONTOLOGY

Epistemology

The first question every researcher must answer regardless of his/her field is that of epistemology: "How do we know?" This question deals with such issues as "Where do I look?" and "When I look, what constitutes data?"

In the first portion of this chapter we will look at how scholars have attempted to answer these questions. In answering them, a scholar makes a commitment to a given direction, which makes it difficult to see other things. It is very much like putting on a pair of magnifying glasses. A given pair of epistemological glasses allows you to see some things much more clearly than if you did not have them on. However, as with magnifying glasses, the limitation of an epistemology is that it also prevents you from seeing, or distorts other things.

Even those who are not professionals in the social sciences can make significant contributions. These are often people who have little vested interest in a particular way of thinking and have no position to lose. They have not yet learned what can and cannot be done. Among you, the readers of our book, are the future scholars of our field. You, who are motivated to

do so, will make your way by taking risks, by looking beyond what others have seen. Or, as Sir Isaac Newton has said, "If I have seen further, it is by standing on the shoulders of giants" (Bartlett, 1968, p. 379).

There are many ways we can answer the question "How do we know?" One is to suggest, as did Plato over 2,500 years ago, that since our perceptions are always flawed they are not to be trusted as the basis of knowledge (Stumpf, 1966). Instead, we must use rationality—clear, reasoned, enlightened ideas. Plato's perspective may seem primitive to us today because he believed that perceptions are mapped into our brains at birth. Thus how we know is a function of using rationality to discover the truth existing in our own minds.

Centuries later, Descartes pursued a rationalistic epistemology based on the idea that if we carefully deduce from one clear idea to another we will eventually construct an all-encompassing body of knowledge (Durant & Durant, 1963). Descartes also believed that our minds are separate from our bodies spiritually. This belief has been pervasive even in contemporary times and has had a significant impact on research and theory in the social sciences.

Aristotle, Plato's student, felt scholars would never be able to go significantly beyond what we already know if we are limited to our own thoughts (Stumpf, 1966). What was needed, Aristotle believed, was a logic which suggested a natural relationship between what is going on in our minds and what is going on in the world around us. This logic would be informed by our observations of the world. The tool of this logic would be the syllogism (e.g., "All men are mortal. Aristotle is a man. Therefore, Aristotle is mortal."). Theory results when we use logic to form a premise out of what we observe. Aristotle limited what is now called Rational Empiricism by arguing that there is no way that the result of this logical reasoning could be changed by further observation. Thus, the route between reality and knowledge is one-way.

To this point we have the extreme position which says that reality is primarily known by thinking about it. As you might expect, someone might come along to argue that it is our reasoning, not our perceptions, which cannot be trusted, and only observation will inform us about reality. Sir Isaac Newton made this argument. He suggested that anything which is not a direct result of an observation of the phenomenon is merely hypothesis and hypotheses were, according to Newton, fallacious arguments. He believed that the perceivable world was "real" and ordered by knowable forces. Knowledge, said Newton, consists of our ability to predict, describe, understand, and control. Ultimately, for Newton, the world is like a machine, and our job is to discover the organizing principles and express them as mathematical relationships. Newton's empiricism guided many scholars up to the beginning of this century, and some to this day.

Newton presented four Rules for Reasoning in Philosophy as a description of his methods (Durant & Durant, 1963). These rules functioned as assumptions. The first rule or assumption is that if we have a simple theory and a complex theory which produce the same results, then we should accept the simple theory over the complex one. A second assumption is that the same causes produce the same effects. The third is that we can generalize from experiment to similar situations. The last assumption is that all results of research are subject to future disconfirmation.

The social sciences, for the most part, began in the middle of the last century. Many of the earliest scholars of human behavior, interaction, and society were guided by Rationalism. They believed that in order to learn about humans they had to look inside themselves. They were roused from their introspective musings by Watson (1913), an early behaviorist, who told them that if they were ever going to learn about human behavior they would have to look beyond themselves.

In rejecting rationalistically-based introspection, many of these scholars were ready for a new epistemology. At the same time a group of scholars came together to "unify" science by specifying the process of knowing that should be followed by all disciplines. This group, referred to as the Vienna Circle, put together Logical Positivism (also known as scientific empiricism and, incorrectly, as positivism). They argued that to know about a phenomenon we have to reduce it to its smallest elements (called Reductionism) and describe the relationships among these elements as accurately as possible. They also argued that while we may find relationships between elements, we cannot know which is a cause and which is an effect. The final test of all knowledge is observation. Reason alone, say the proponents of this epistemology, cannot produce knowledge. Thus was born Scientific Empiricism, or what has since become known as Logical Positivism.

In Logical Positivism, the elements of a given phenomenon are defined by specifying the operations that we performed to observe them (called Operationalization). Any other meanings, including common-sense knowledge, are, for the purposes of developing theory, ignored. If our research is concerned with love, then love consists only of the data we acquired using the operations we performed. In sum, a research statement is one in which all terms are operationally defined and their relationship empirically demonstrated. Logical Positivism has been one of the more pervasive epistemologies in the social sciences, especially communication, in the first three quarters of this century. Articles in this book which are clearly based on Logical Positivism include Berger and Calabrese; Dillard; and Daly, Vangelisti, and Daughton.

General Systems Theory (GST) is a perspective that scholars from a variety of fields have developed on how we know we know. The result is not only a theory but a way of thinking. While not entirely an epistemology, many of its assumptions directly challenge critical assumptions of Logical Positivism. In the early 1940s, scholars in a variety of fields saw similarities between the phenomena in their different fields. They believed that this similarity might form the basis for a way to integrate knowledge (Berren, 1968).

A major starting point for GST is Einstein's concept of relativity—that everything in the universe is related to everything else in some way.

GST suggests that if we want to know how something works we cannot look at its components in isolation from one another—that is, the whole is greater than the sum of its parts.

Another major assumption made by GST is that everything is in process, that change is inevitable. Under this assumption scholars see relationships as changing and evolving through stages of development (Boulding, 1968).

GST was developed by way of analogy. Similarities across different fields were abstracted into a set of generalized semantic concepts. These concepts described systems in general (thus, *General* Systems Theory), not a specific system. There are several important concepts in GST. One is the notion that the components of an open system must be in dynamic balance (homeostasis), in order to survive. Another important concept is that open systems are interactive with their environment, both putting information and energy into the environment and receiving feedback from the environment. Another is that components of a system must balance their inputs and outputs of information and energy exchanged with the other components over time.

Using GST a researcher can understand how the human digestive system is like an automobile assembly plant, which is like a human relationship. At its most simplistic, GST is a list of concepts which describe functions of any system. At this level it is a theory "skeleton" onto which a researcher hangs the meaningful components of a phenomenon from his or her own field. At a more complex level, GST is an epistemology that makes assumptions about how we know we know.

One thing which is made clear by GST is the importance of understanding what is the unit of analysis. Using Logical Positivism we look at the phenomenon and attempt to break it down into smaller and smaller pieces, believing that by doing so we can better understand it. GST assumes that if we want to understand a phenomenon we have to study that phenomenon in its entirety. We can, for example, study cellular structure if we are a microbiologist. The cell is a unit of analysis and its components might be various proteins and acids. As an endocrinologist,

we might study human glands and ducts, and cells among the components. Knowing something about how cells operate may or may not help us in understanding specific aspects of glands and ducts (Boulding, 1968).

Similarly, we can study individual human beings by looking at the information they receive and transmit. This can help us understand something about what it means to be human. However, if our interest is in human relationships, then the unit of analysis is the relationship, and people are the components. If we want to understand how attitudes are formed, maintained, or changed, then the appropriate unit of analysis is the individual. On the other hand, if we want to know about how relationships are formed, maintained, or changed, then the relationship is the unit of analysis.

Probably the first scholar in communication to use GST was Berlo (1960), when he discussed the concept of process. However, the model of communication he presented at that time duplicated others dating back to Aristotle which posit the linear movement of information from source to receiver, but with the addition of feedback. Adding feedback to this model did not make it more reflective of a process in the way Berlo described the concept or more in line with GST. A more correct conceptualization from the GST point of view suggests reciprocity of information flow. But even that is not the most representative conceptualization.

What is needed is a model which allows us to see that both people in any interaction are at all times both receiving and transmitting information simultaneously. It allows us to understand that when we see one person as the source and the other as the receiver we are taking a biased perspective on the system of interest, the dyad. The linear model presented by Berlo (1960) and earlier scholars is an accurate description only when the individual is the system of interest.

Little research has been done in interpersonal communication using GST. However, we have included several articles based on some of its assumptions. Among those which are closer to this perspective are Pearce; Planalp; Knapp, Ellis, and Williams; Baxter and Bullis; and Petronio.

Ontology

In addition to making assumptions about how we know we know, a scholar must also make assumptions about what it means to *be*. More specifically, ontology deals with our assumptions as scholars about what behavior means and the nature of people. We had a difficult time deciding whether to put this section in this chapter on theory or the chapter on methods. It relates to both. We have included it here to help you understand how it impacts on theory and theory development.

We see two major ontological issues with several subissues. One major ontological issue has to do with free will. Questioned here are intent, choice making, creating goals, and planning how to meet them. Philosophical debate on this issue ranges from determinism to teleology. The deterministic position is that humans do not initiate behavior but merely react to events around them. A more extreme position is that everything is preordained. While we may perceive that we have free choice, that we exist in the world, that we are independent of other people, this is simply an illusion. A less extreme position suggests that people are basically passive, their behavior and their thoughts determined by prior events. These events might be biologically determined (a position taken by sociobiologists), a function of religion (if you are a theologian), or a result of your past experiences (if you are a behavioral psychologist).

The teleological position suggests that people are active decision makers, that people make plans and act on them. They are truly free agents, if they choose to be. If a scholar takes the teleological position to an extreme, she/he is likely to believe that human behavior is not very predictable, or perhaps that it is not at all predictable. The scholar who takes the extreme deterministic position, of course, believes that human behavior is highly if not perfectly predictable, if we know all the prior events, or if we somehow get a hint of the *Master Plan*.

Littlejohn (1989) groups theoretical speculations based on these perspectives into two groups: actional and nonactional theories. The actional theorists believe that humans are proactive in their interpretation of what is going on around them. Littlejohn (1989) states:

> *Actional theory* assumes that individuals create meanings, they have intentions, they make real choices. The actional view rests on the teleological base, which says that people make decisions that are designed to achieve goals. (p. 27)

"*Nonactional theory*," according to Littlejohn (1989), is much more deterministic in that it "assumes that behavior is determined by and is responsive to past pressures" (p. 27).

A second ontological issue essentially starts with the assumption that human behavior exists and that our understanding of it is important, whether people choose how they will behave or not. This issue has to do with the interpretation of that behavior. There are several issues subsumed here.

First, given that people do behave, do we believe that behavior is highly predictable in a given person across time, that a person's behavior changes greatly throughout a given day, or do we believe that some of a given person's behavior is predictable, while some of it is dynamic? Researchers who take the more deterministic position tend to develop trait theories. They see people as predictable, static beings who change only very slowly. Those who take the teleological position tend to develop state theories. They believe an individual's behavior is variable and can be changed quickly. Of course, a middle position would suggest that some of a person's behavior can be quite predictable while some is variable.

Again, given that behavior exists, on what aspect of human behavior do we place our primary focus? Littlejohn (1989) asks it this way: "To what extent is human experience basically individual versus social?" (p. 27). We in the United States tend to be more individually oriented and consequently are more protective of our independence than some other cultures. This cultural disposition might tend to cause scholars to focus on individuals and the individual experience in our theory development. At the same time, much of who we are, much of how we feel, is the result of our relationships with others. To focus on individuals precludes us from seeing relationships between people (except as a peripheral aspect of a given individual; see Duck's article for a more complete discussion). In interpersonal communication we are interested in relationships. However, much of the research in interpersonal communication has focused on the individual.

Many communication scholars are concerned with communication as it is affected by culture. Some suggest that a relationship is a culture. These scholars believe that it is impossible to understand communication outside of the context of the culture in which it occurred; they argue that every assertion of knowledge about communication should come attached to a statement as to the culture in which the assertion was tested. Taken to its extreme, this position would suggest that it is either difficult or impossible to develop general theories of interpersonal communication.

This brings up an ontological subissue concerning whether we should interpret human behavior in a universal or in a situational context. Is the behavior which occurs in a given situation generalizable in any way to any other situation? If we believe that behavior is very situation specific, then we also believe that it cannot be generalized to other situations. If we are willing to assume the universality of behavior, then we believe that when people in a specific situation behave in a specific way, other people will behave in much the same way in similar situations in the future.

Still other scholars are beginning to argue that some behavior is biologically determined. The more extreme among these scholars would argue that the most important human behaviors (e.g., finding a mate) are driven by DNA in its attempt to ensure that it reproduces itself into the future. Thus, to understand interpersonal communication these scholars would suggest we must look at it in terms of this biological imperative.

We can all see that at least some of our behavior is culturally constrained. And, there is evidence that at least some of our behavior is biologically constrained. This would suggest that the extremes of both positions are probably not accurate descriptions of human behavior. It also suggests that the task of the scholar of interpersonal communication is made even more difficult because it entails understanding everything it means to be human ranging from biological roots which make us all alike, to the overlay of complex cultural differentiation making us all different.

THEORETICAL PERSPECTIVES AND ORIENTATIONS INFLUENCING COMMUNICATION

There are many ways that one might categorize the attempts to develop theory in interpersonal communication. Unfortunately, it is impossible to develop mutually exclusive categories for such theories since there is so much overlap among them. Nevertheless, in order to deal with them efficiently, we have had to categorize them in this presentation. Therefore, please understand that the categories we have chosen are as much based on convenience as they are on logic. We have attempted, in this section, to give you an overview of some of the theories used in the study of interpersonal communication.

Many of the theories presented in this chapter are applied to issues in interpersonal communication research from other disciplines. In addition a number of perspectives included here are representative of theory development in our own field.

Our survey is by no means complete. In the description of each theory we have also noted the articles in this book which use that theory. For each theory we have described, we have attempted to give you the name of the person in communication who has been most closely associated with that theory. Finally, because of space limitations, we have only been able to give you cursory overviews of each theory. We leave it up to you to explore these theories in more depth.

Cognitive Theories

Cognitive theories are those which focus on the attitudes, beliefs, opinions, thoughts, and the structures of thought. Most generally, these theories have looked at how (or whether) people alter their cognitive states correspondent to the messages they receive. Typically, such theories have the individual as the point of focus. (See Planalp's article on relational schemata for one perspective on cognitive theory). Several articles deal with aspects of cognitive theory. For example, Miller, Boster, Roloff, and Seibold and Witteman and Fitzpatrick look at compliance gaining strategies, Dillard looks at the influence goals that people have in personal relationships, and Roloff et al. go beyond persuasion to look at how obligation works in acquiring resources from intimates.

Social Cognition

This theory attempts to explain how people process the information they receive and how they construct messages from their cognitive structures. Thus, it emphasizes both the structures and processes involved in thought. The central structures are *schema, prototypes,* and *scripts.* Schema is the overarching concept and refers to a general framework for understanding a class of events, objects, or people. For example, you have a schema for books that allows you to know when something is a book. Related to the schema is the prototype, an exemplar or representative of the class of things. For some people, John Kennedy is the prototypical president, and for others Ronald Reagan is. We judge specific objects and people against the prototype (Littlejohn, 1989).

Finally, having a schema allows you to know how events typically occur. This typical model of an event is called a script. For example, you probably expect that the teacher will go to the front of the room and start talking when class begins. If the class were in elementary school you would also expect the teacher to take attendance. Scripts allow you to anticipate what will happen next in a situation. Without a script for baseball, you would not know what the second baseman does during a double play after the shortstop throws her/him the ball. The processes of social cognition includes social judgment and uncertainty reduction described below.

Social Judgment Theory (e.g., Sheriff & Hovland, 1959)

Suppose you have your eye on a fantastic new camcorder. If someone offered to give you an 8mm movie camera, you would probably not be very impressed. On the other hand, the 8mm camera would be a miracle gift to someone from a third-world country where camcorders have not arrived. In other words, how you evaluate something depends on some point of reference. How you evaluate aspects of your social interaction depends on your previous experience. The more important an issue is to you (ego involvement) the greater the influence your point of reference has. For any given issue you have a *latitude of acceptance* and a *latitude of rejection.* According to the theory, when a message is relatively close to your own attitude, you will see it as being closer to your position than it actually is (*assimilation*). When a message is relatively distant from your attitude, you will see it as further from your position than it actually is (*contrast*).

Constructivism (e.g., Delia, O'Keefe, & O'Keefe, 1982)

Like social judgment theory, constructivism suggests that people respond to the messages in their environment according to previously established cognitive states. It is based on the idea that people sort incoming information according to such bipolar dimensions as hot/cold, good/bad, honest/dishonest. These dimensions, called *constructs,* are organized into more or less complex structures called *interpretive systems.* More complex systems include a greater number of constructs and are more abstract. An individual gives meaning to experience through assignment of experience to his/her cognitive structures. People with more complex systems are said to more effectively understand their environment and interaction, and create more effective messages. They are also assumed to better take the perspective of the other (understand another point of view), and adapt messages to their views.

Consistency Theories (e.g., Newcomb, 1953; Festinger, 1957)

Perhaps the largest body of research in interpersonal communication is in the area of social influence. Several examples are included below. The theory suggests that each person's attitudes, opinions, beliefs, perceptions, and knowledge are *cognitive elements*. Consistency theory centers on the processes by which messages change a person's cognitive elements (predisposition to act positively or negatively toward something). Consistency theories start with the assumption that people are uncomfortable with inconsistency between and among their cognitive elements. These theories predict that your behavior will change when you receive information which upsets the consistency of your cognitive elements.

The Uncertainty Reduction Theory in the field of communication was developed by Berger and Calabrese (1975). The basic theoretic perspective focuses attention on the initial interaction (the *entry phase* of this developmental paradigm) between strangers with the expectation that it would be extended to explain later stages of relationships. When two strangers meet neither knows much about the other. The central assumption of this theory is that the primary concern of parties in an initial interaction is to reduce the uncertainty they have about the behavior of both themselves and others in the interaction. Uncertainty is reduced by using verbal and nonverbal communication. Thus, the level of uncertainty stimulates the need to communicate.

Uncertainty reduction theory might be the most formal communication theory we have at this time in that it stipulates six axioms positing relationships between communication variables and uncertainty reduction. These axioms are then used syllogistically to arrive at 21 theorems.

Though this places uncertainty reduction theory in the realm of rationalism, as described in the epistemology section above, the theory continues to be informed and changed by observation. Thus, it is better described as rational empiricism.

Uncertainty reduction theory assumes that uncertainty is an aversive condition. Recent studies (e.g., Bavelas, Black, Clovil, & Mullett, 1990) have indicated that there are times when uncertainty is actually desired. Sunnafrank suggests an adjustment to Berger and Calabrese's theory in predicting outcomes to initial interaction. Sunnafrank suggests that a person's predicted outcome for the interaction is more important than the impetus to reduce uncertainty. It is clear, however, that cognitive processing is a key process in uncertainty reduction.

Attribution Theory (e.g., Kelley, 1967)

Kelley (1967) defined attribution as the process of perceiving the dispositional properties of self (*internal* attribution) and/or an entity in the environment (*external* attribution). For example, if a person enjoys playing a computer game, does the person attribute the enjoyment of that game to himself or herself, or to the game itself? In answer to this question Kelley proposes that the person will attribute enjoyment of the game to the game if the person does not enjoy all computer games (*differential response*), if the person enjoys it a second time (*consistency over time*), if the person enjoys it in a variety of places and times (*consistency over modalities*), and if others enjoy it as well (*consensual agreement*). Kelley argues that to the degree that these conditions are not met, the person will attribute the enjoyment to self. Kelley proposed that the less stable a person's attributions are, the more persuadable by others that person is. Attribution instability stems from a lack of or little social support, inadequate prior information, or experiences which lower a person's self-confidence. Further, Kelley argues that person A will be successful in influencing person B if B's communication enables A to increase the distinctiveness and stability of his/her attributions.

The Heuristic Model of Persuasion (e.g., Chaiken, 1987)

Chaiken (1987) notes that most prior models of persuasion have assumed that people engage in a significant amount of information processing when deciding whether to accept the premise of a persuasive attempt. This he calls the systematic approach. Chaiken proposes instead a heuristic model which suggests that "opinion change in response to persuasive communications is often the outcome of only a minimal amount of information processing" (Chaiken, 1987, p. 3). According to this notion, people may decide on the basis of such less relevant features as source credibility, likability, and physical attractiveness, among other things. According to the heuristic model, when people process persuasive messages in this way they are using cognitive heuristics, decision rules learned earlier in life.

An example of such a decision rule might be, "People who know what they are talking about can talk faster without making mistakes than can people who do not know." Thus, a person who talks fast is more likely to be believed than a person who does not. Another example might be that people who know more can make more arguments than can people who do not know as much. Therefore, persuasive attempts with several arguments are more believable than those with only a few.

Whether people will process persuasive messages systematically or heuristically depends on several factors. The less involved people are with the topic the more likely they will use the simple decision rules rather than to process the semantic content of that message. People who are less skilled in processing persuasive messages systematically are more likely to process the message heuristically. Heuristic processing is also more likely to be used when the message is delivered with high salience or vividness.

The Conversation Memory Organization Packet (MOP) (Kellerman & Lim, 1990)

Noting that while the process of getting to know another person is relatively routine, Kellerman and Lim (1990) suggest that how that process is implemented varies with a person's goals for the outcome of the specific interaction. Kellerman and Lim propose a model of conversation called Memory Organization Packet (MOP) which suggests that conversation is a series of relatively small routines which people use to accomplish their goals in a specific conversation. MOPs are "knowledge structures that organize behavioral sequences appropriate to a given situation to achieve one's goal" (Kellerman & Lim, 1990, p. 1163). Kellerman and Lim note that what we talk about in initial conversations with others is organized into topics (called scenes) ranging from greeting to goodbye. At any particular point in the conversation there may be many different scenes available to an interactant. There are categories of scenes which are more likely to occur during the beginning stages and others which are more likely to occur in later stages. At any given moment in time, any scene in a given category is likely to be the next used as long as the two persons are continuing to converse in that category of scenes. The result is a predictable sequence of scenes across people in initial interaction.

There are three ways that a person may introduce variability into the conversation MOP. The specific scenes chosen is one way. The second is the choice to stay on the same subject or switch to another one. The last has to do with how long one stays in a particular category of scenes. A person may select more or less scenes, avoid or choose bridge scenes, or accept/refuse scenes offered by one's partner. The last two of these three ways to introduce variability affect the timing of the conversation. Through astute use, these interactants may slow down or speed up the process consistent with their goals for the interaction.

Elastic Capacity Model of Persuasive Cue Processing (e.g., Stiff, 1986)

Stiff (1986), drawing on Kahneman (1973), presents the elastic capacity model of persuasive cue processing. In this model humans are seen as being multichannel processors of communication capable of processing parallel stimuli. Up to a certain limit, the amount of information processing capacity available to a person expands with the difficulty of the processing task. While working on a difficult task a person exerts more effort and thus has more capacity available than a person working on simpler tasks. People divide this capacity between primary and secondary tasks. When the task demand is low, the amount of capacity used for a primary task is far less than total capacity. This leaves a significant amount of capacity for processing secondary tasks (or parallel processing). When the task demand is high the capacity required for the primary task approaches the total capacity, leaving little room for performing secondary tasks (or sequential processing).

Planning Theory (e.g., Berger, in press; Dillard, 1990)

Planning theory is concerned with the cognitive processes that are involved in the development and production of communicative messages. This theory proposes that in order to understand communicative processes we must not only study exchange of symbols, we must also understand the cognitive processes underlying the interpretation and generation of those symbols. The perspective relies upon the constructs of goals and plans for its conceptual underpinnings. Goals are descriptions of what the person anticipates for the future. As Dillard, Segrin, and Harden (1989) suggest, there are two kinds of goals, primary and secondary. Primary goals instigate the plan and are more immediate and explicit whereas secondary goals shape the plan, function as a superordinate structure guiding the overall development of the plan, and are more implicit (i.e., social appropriateness, efficiency).

As Berger (in press) notes, plans are cognitive representations that specify a set of actions necessary for the attainment of a goal. We do not have a specific plan for every possible human interaction. We may, however, have an abstract plan that can be modified for the specific situation. Plans are characterized differentially on three dimensions: (1) hierarchy—plans vary in levels of abstraction; (2) complexity—plans are differentiated by the number of elements and contingencies of a plan; (3) completeness—refers to the extent to which elements of a plan are fleshed out (Dillard, 1990).

The generation and production of plans entails devising action sequences, anticipating the outcomes, adjusting the outcomes according to the projections, and realizing the plan in action. When individuals are trying to achieve a goal, their first inclination is to search their long-term memory, by using situational cues, for plans that have been previously used. Another means of generating a message is through instruction. A plan of action can be taught for immediate or later use.

Once a plan has been devised it may be selected by the person to be carried out. The outcome of the plan can be fulfilled or thwarted (Berger, in press). In the event that a goal is not accomplished, the individual can either generate a new plan or use a contingency plan which is an option of the original plan.

Self-Focus Theories (e.g., Berger & Douglas, 1982)

These are among the newest theories to be applied in interpersonal communication. Most of the theories we describe in this chapter assume that intent motivates the behavior which people perform; that is, they are conscious of what they are doing as they are doing it. What we are calling self-focus theories are concerned with the degree to which people are conscious of the behaviors they are performing. These theories suggest that we perform at least some of our behavior at a semiconscious or unconscious level. One can argue that intent is a much less viable concept if the behavior in question is being performed at a low level of consciousness. Thus, we have a point of controversy in the field.

Some self-focus theories represent people as being consistently more (or less) conscious of their own behaviors, that it is a trait. Other theories represent people as being variable in the degree to which they are conscious of their own behaviors as they are performing them, that it is a state. The impetus for change in the degree to which we are aware of our own behavior according to some theories is environmentally induced, and in other theories is internally induced. We will present only two self-focus theories in this chapter, one trait theory and one state theory.

Self-Monitoring (Snyder, 1974) suggests that people differ in terms of their degree of awareness of their own behavior. Some people are higher on measures of self-monitoring and are more aware of their own behavior in the presence of others and adjust their behavior according to environmental influences. Other people are lower on the same measure and are less aware of their behavior in the presence of others.

Scripts and Self-Awareness (e.g., Abelson, 1976) is a more complex phenomenon. Abelson suggests that the human brain has difficulty attending to everything going on in its environment, and taking care of all cognitive processes at the same time. One of the ways it handles this is by turning regularly performed sequences of behaviors into scripts which are generalizable across similar situations. While a person performs scripted behavior, the person's mind is actively performing other activities.

Both of these theories suggest that while an individual's communicative behavior "may have the appearance of flowing from a set of highly conscious cognitive processes, the fact may be that the individual is enacting the communicative behavior at a low level of awareness" (Berger and Douglas, 1982, p. 54). Please note that many communication theories assume a high degree of consciousness while communication occurs. Self-focus theories suggest that at some point in time a person may be more or less conscious of what he/she is doing and/or saying. If the self-focus theories are true, then the efficacy of a given communication theory will vary with the degree of an individual's self-focus.

Some self-focus theories place emphasis on the degree to which a person pays more attention to his or her own values and attitudes, or more attention to social cues when deciding how to behave. People who are less self-focused are more likely to follow the crowd, while those who are more self-focused are more likely to follow

their own attitudes, values and beliefs. This suggests that if the self-focus theories are true, then most of the communication theories which posit attitudes, values, and beliefs as central to the explanation of communication behavior will vary in explanatory efficacy depending on the degree of an individual's focus on self.

Behavior Theories (e.g., Watson, 1913; Pavlov, 1927; Skinner, 1938)

Behavior theories center on the notion that if we want to be able to explain behavior, then we must observe and develop theories about behavior. These range from classical conditioning, which forms the basis for much of our language learning, to operant conditioning which has been used predominantly in education (e.g., Watson, 1913, Pavlov, 1927, and Skinner, 1938). Included in behaviorism is social learning theory. Behavior theories tend toward being trait theories because they imply that how a person behaves is determined by her/his reward/punishment history. These theories are not deterministic, however, because they usually imply that a person's behavior can be changed by additional learning.

Social Learning Theory (e.g., Miller & Dollard, 1941; Bandura, 1962) begins with the idea that behavior is learned. Given this, we must learn the principles involved in its learning and the social conditions in which it occurs. The four principles seen as fundamental to learning are *drive, cue, response,* and *reward.* In addition to its clear interpersonal application, this theory has also been used to test the notion that people, especially children, imitate the behaviors they have seen performed on television.

Drive is any strong stimulus which impels the organism to behave. *Primary* drives are biological in nature; hunger is an example. *Secondary* drives are learned. One of these secondary drives is the *drive to imitate,* i.e., the matching of the responses of others becomes a rewarded response in its own right. Thus, according to Miller and Dollard (1941) when there is imitation (1) the behavior of another serves as a cue; (2) leading to an internal response; (3) producing a drive to imitate, the strength of which is based upon previously rewarded imitation trials; (4) which activates imitative responding; (5) leading to a reward which in turn leads to the reduction of the drive.

Bandura (1962) argued against several aspects of the theory as presented by Miller and Dollard (1941). They suggested that the observer of the model did not have to have the model's response in his/her response repertoire, that neither the observer nor the model had to be reinforced for modeling to occur, that an observer's responses may be shaped to match those of a model by successive approximations. Further, they argued that we must separate the processes involved in mentally acquiring the knowledge of the behavior and actually performing the behavior. They argued that reinforcement only serves to activate the previously learned response into performed behavior.

In presenting his theory, Bandura (1962) argued that exposure to a model creates a mental image of a behavioral alternative which can be used when the person finds himself/herself in circumstance similar to the model's. The observer's ability to add verbal labels to the model's behavior greatly increases the observer's ability to accomplish the imaging state of imitation.

Social Process Theories of Interpersonal Communication

Many theories which are useful in interpersonal communication deal with the information people exchange with one another to reveal themselves to others and come to know the persons with whom they interact.

Social Exchange Theory (e.g., Homans, 1961) is based on a combination of behavioristic psychology and economics. While the theory is much more complex than we can present here, a simple description is that the exchange of rewards and costs in a relationship, as perceived by its participants, determines the relationship. Homans (1961) describes three descriptive terms and two variables. Activity, sentiment, and interaction are the descriptive terms. Activities are voluntary behaviors. Sentiments are the subclass of social behaviors. Interaction is the exchange of sentiments.

Quantity (i.e., frequency of activity or sentiment) and value (degree of reinforcement or punishment of a given activity or sentiment) are the variables of Homans' theory. Homans saw two components to value. One is a constant and refers to the value a person has for a particular social activity regardless of where/when she/he performs it. The other is the value a person has for a social activity depending on that person's current state (e.g., deprivation of social activity).

Homans developed several propositions, several corollaries and what he called the Rule of Distributive Justice. The central assumption is the formula that Profit = Reward minus Cost. We will not go into all propositions, but will present two corollaries to give the flavor of the theory. The first is "The more cost Person incurs in emitting an activity, the less often he [or she] will emit it." The second is "the more often Person has emitted a costly activity, the more costly he [or she] finds any further unit of that activity" (Homans, 1961, p. 60).

Self-Disclosure (e.g., Altman & Taylor, 1973)

A large body of research has examined how people reveal themselves to one another, much of it atheoretical. Altman and Taylor (1973), drawing on concepts from social exchange theory, developed a "theoretical approach" which they called *Social Penetration*. They put forward two hypotheses. The first suggests that "interpersonal exchange gradually progresses from superficial, nonintimate areas to more intimate, deeper layers of the selves of the social actors" (Altman & Taylor, 1973, p. 6). The second states that "people assess interpersonal rewards and costs, satisfaction and dissatisfaction, gained from interaction with others, and that the advancement of the relationship is heavily dependent on the amount and nature of the rewards and costs" (Altman & Taylor, 1973, p. 6).

Social penetration assumes that people have many levels of information structured inside themselves ranging from very public to very private. Imagine an onion. Layers near the surface of the onion represent less private information. Those closer to the center are much more private. Social penetration refers to the peeling away of the onion, layer by layer, as the participants interact with one another. The movement to successively more private information is initiated by profiting by the interaction which occurred on the present level.

There are some new approaches to disclosure, reframing the concept as revealing of private information (see Petronio, 1991, in this book).

Interpretive Theories

Symbolic Interactionism (e.g., Mead, 1934; Blumer, 1969)

The term "Symbolic Interactionism" was coined by Herbert Blumer (1969) while he was expanding upon a theory developed by George Herbert Mead. Mead developed the original theory as a reaction to Watsonian Behaviorism (Mead, 1934). The theory was one of the first attempts to systematically study communicative interaction, and it suggests a major theoretical proposal outlining communicative principles used in research and theorizing in the field of communication today. We present below three premises upon which the theory of symbolic interaction is based. These principles have been presented by Blumer (1969) and represent his interpretation of Mead's theory. There are two approaches to symbolic interactionism, the Iowa school and the Chicago school. Blumer's perspective is representative of the Chicago school.

The first premise suggests that meanings are in people, not objects, and when we have constructed such meanings, we act toward the event or object based on the meaning we have ascribed. For example, the U.S. flag, in itself, does not have meaning; it consists of cotton cloth and dye. But we as individuals attribute meaning to the flag.

When that occurs, we may hold this cloth in reverence or use it symbolically to show our disapproval of some events, such as war.

The second premise suggests that we derive meanings for the things in our environment out of our communication with others. Communication is the mechanism through which we are social, and our meanings for communicative symbols arise out of our talking with others.

The third premise suggests that these meanings are handled in and modified through interpretative processes we use in dealing with our environment. The person is an active participant in the interaction. He/she uses an interpretative process (i.e., perceptions and cognitions) to filter the information and construct meanings based on his/her understandings of the world.

The theory of symbolic interaction was influential in developing a concern for the notion of "self," for contributing a focus on the notion of "roles," and linking the issue of perceptions to the study of communicative interaction.

Rules (e.g., Pearce, 1976, 1980)

For two people to be able to communicate, the participants must share rules for using symbols; for example, who gets to talk when and what should be said. To say that "meanings are in people" ignores the fact that in order to communicate we have to have the same rule associating a particular symbol with a particular meaning. Further, we typically have rules that are associated with social environments, and those rules help us decide on appropriate behavior for the situation (See Pearce's article on rules).

Systems

The Palo Alto Group (e.g., Watzlawick, Bavelas, & Jackson, 1967)

General Systems Theory probably finds its best representation in this perspective. This theory has been extended by Millar and Rogers (1976) in communication. Watzlawick et al. argue that relationships are the product of communication between people. They present five concepts and axioms about communication in relationships. The first axiom is that we cannot *not* communicate. Even when we are not talking, our non-verbal behaviors are communicating. A second axiom says that every communication has both a content and a relationship message. There is ''what it says,'' and ''what it says about the relationship.''

An uninvolved party observing an interaction will see it as a series of exchanged behaviors. Each participant in the interaction has a perspective. One might say, ''I yell at you because you never *do* anything around here!'' The other says, ''I never do anything around here because you are always *yelling* at me!'' Both are defining the relationship individualistically rather than relationally, and thus see it in terms of cause and effect rather than an ongoing process. This is the concept of punctuation.

Watzlawick et al. (1967) suggest that we communicate both digitally and analogically. Verbal communication tends to be digital in that it represents something but bears no relationship to it (e.g., words). Analogical communication has a direct and inseparable link with the thing it represents (e.g., lips upturned at the ends is not only a sign of a particular feeling, it is also a part of that feeling). Digital communication is primarily used to carry the content message of communication. Analogic communication primarily carries the relationship's messages.

The final concept from the Palo Alto Group has to do with symmetrical and complementary interaction. When two people in a relationship behave very similarly, they have a symmetrical relationship. A negative example of this might occur when both partners are trying to control the other. A positive example would occur when both are riding a two-person bicycle. When their behaviors are quite different, they are said to have a complementary relationship. A negative example occurs when one marital partner behaves in ways which allow the alcoholic other to continue drinking. A positive example is when one person wants to lead and the other wants to follow in some area.

SUMMARY

These theoretical perspectives provide a basis for research in interpersonal communication. Many of the readings found in this book rely upon the assumptions and principles outlined in this theory chapter. While we did not have the room to go into lengthy explanations, we hope that the information provided gives some insights into the issues found in the perspectives discussed in this chapter.

REFERENCES

Abelson, R. P. (1976). Script processing in attitude formation and decision making. In J. S. Carroll & J. W. Payne (Eds.), *Cognition and social behavior.* Hillsdale, NJ: Erlbaum.

Altman, I., & Taylor, D. A. (1973). *Social penetration: The development of interpersonal relationships.* New York: Holt, Rinehart and Winston.

Bandura, A. (1962). Social learning through imitation. In M. R. Jones (Ed.), *Nebraska symposium on motivation.* Lincoln: University of Nebraska Press.

Bartlett, J. (1968). *Familiar quotations* (14th ed.). Boston: Little, Brown and Company.

Bavelas, J. B., Black, A., Clovil, N., & Mullett, J. (1990). *Equivocal communication.* Newbury Park, CA: Sage Publications.

Berger, C. R. (in press). A plan-based approach to strategic communication. In D. E. Hewes (Ed.), *Cognitive bases of interpersonal communication.* Hillsdale, NJ: Erlbaum.

Berger, C. R., & Calabrese, R. J. (1975). Some explorations in initial interaction and beyond: Toward a developmental theory of interpersonal communication. *Human Communication Research, 1,* 99–112.

Berger, C. R., & Douglas, W. (1982). Thought and talk: ''Excuse me, but have I been talking to myself?'' In F. E. X. Dance (Ed.), *Human communication theory.* New York: Harper & Row.

Berlo, D. K. (1960). *The process of communication: An introduction to theory and practice.* New York: Holt, Rinehart and Winston.

Berrien, F. K. (1968). *General and social systems.* New Brunswick, NJ: Rutgers University Press.

Blumer, H. (1969). *Symbolic interactionism: Perspective and method.* Englewood Cliffs, NJ: Prentice-Hall.

Boulding, K. E. (1968). General systems theory—The skeleton of science. In W. Buckley (Ed.), *Modern systems research for the behavioral scientist: A source book* (pp. 3–10). Chicago: Aldine Publishing.

Chaiken, S. (1987). The heuristic model of persuasion. In M. P. Sanna, J. M. Olson, & C. P. Herman (Eds.), *Social influence: The Ontario symposium* (vol. 5, pp. 3–39). Hillsdale, NJ: Erlbaum.

Delia, J. G., O'Keefe, B. J., & O'Keefe, D. J. (1982). The constructivist approach to communication. In F. E. X. Dance (Ed.), *Human communication theory: Comparative essays*. New York: Harper & Row.

Dillard, J. P. (1990). A goal-driven model of interpersonal influence. In J. P. Dillard (Ed.), *Seeking compliance: The production of interpersonal influence messages* (pp. 41–56). Scottsdale, AZ: Gorsuch.

Dillard, J. P., Segrin, C., & Harden, J. M. (1989). Primary and secondary goals in the production of interpersonal influence messages. *Communication Monographs, 56,* 199–238.

Durant, W., & Durant, A. (1963). *The story of civilization: Part VIII. The age of Louis XIV.* New York: Simon and Schuster.

Festinger, L. (1957). *A theory of cognitive dissonance.* Stanford, CA: Stanford University Press.

Hoffman, B. (1972). *Albert Einstein: Creator and rebel.* New York: Viking Press.

Homans, G. C. (1961). *Social behavior: Its elementary forms.* New York: Harcourt, Brace.

Kahneman, D. (1973). *Attention and effort.* Englewood Cliffs, NJ: Prentice-Hall.

Kellerman, K., & Lim, T. (1990). The conversion MOP: III. Timing of scenes in discourse. *Journal of Personality and Social Psychology, 59*(6), 1163–1179.

Kelley, H. H. (1967). Attribution theory in social psychology. In D. Levine (Ed.), *Nebraska symposium on motivation* (pp. 192–238). Lincoln: University of Nebraska Press.

Littlejohn, S. W. (1989). *Theories of human communication* (3rd ed.). Belmont, CA: Wadsworth Publishing Company.

Mead, G. H. (1934). *Mind, self and society: From the standpoint of a social behaviorist* (edited with an introduction by Charles Morris). Chicago: University of Chicago Press.

Millar, F. E., & Rogers, L. E. (1976). A relational approach to interpersonal communication. In G. R. Miller (Ed.), *Explorations in interpersonal communication*. Beverly Hills, CA: Sage Publications.

Miller, N. E., & Dollard, J. (1941). *Social learning and imitation.* New Haven, CT: Yale University Press.

Newcomb, T. M. (1953). An approach to the study of communication acts. *Psychological Review, 11,* 575–586.

Pavlov, I. P. (1927). *Conditioned reflexes.* New York: Oxford University Press.

Pearce, W. B. (1976). The coordinated management of meaning: A rules-based theory of interpersonal communication. In G. R. Miller (Ed.), *Explorations in interpersonal communication*. Beverly Hills, CA: Sage Publications.

———. (1980). *Rules theories of communication varieties, limitations, and potentials.* Paper presented at the Speech Communication Association Convention, New York.

Sheriff, M., & Hovland, C. (1959). *Social judgment.* New Haven, CT: Yale University Press.

Skinner, B. F. (1938). *The behavior of organisms.* Englewood Cliffs, NJ: Prentice-Hall.

Snyder, M. (1974). Self-monitoring of expressive behavior. *Journal of Personality and Social Psychology, 30,* 528.

Stiff, J. B. (1986). Cognitive processing of persuasive messages cues: A meta-analytic review of the effects of supporting information on attitudes. *Communication Monographs, 55,* 77–89.

Stumpf, S. (1966). *Socrates in Sartre.* New York: McGraw-Hill Co.

Watson, J. B. (1913). Psychology as the behaviorist views it. *Psychological Review, 20,* 158–177.

Watzlawick, P., Bavelas, J., & Jackson, D. (1967). *Pragmatics of human communication: A study of interactional patterns, pathologies, and paradoxes.* New York: Norton.

CHAPTER 2

Methods for Studying Interpersonal Communication Research

Jess K. Alberts, Michael L. Hecht, Jerry Buley, Sandra Petronio

This chapter presents a brief introduction to the various methods one might use to study interpersonal communication. It is intended to introduce you to some of the ways researchers attempt to answer questions about the communication behavior of individuals and dyads.

Research is a part of the daily conduct of everyone's life. Anytime you collect information in order to make a decision, you are engaging in research. If you want to find out which manufacturer makes the best, most economical compact disc player or which professor gives the fairest (or easiest) exams, you are engaging in methods of research.

In addition to conducting research, we use the research of others to make judgments about issues we encounter. For example, in a recent advertisement for a computer, the company stated that their battery pack runs for more than three and a half hours, which, the ad points out, is more than any other. However, the ad does not provide enough information for us to judge the accuracy of this claim. By what method did this company arrive at this conclusion? What type of research was conducted to determine the length of the battery life? In addition to needing more information about this ad, when we read articles in magazines about how to time-proof your face, ways to interest your man or woman, or how to cope with money problems, we need some idea of the dependability of the information. One way to evaluate whether the information is to be believed is through learning about research methods. The communication research in this book should provide insight into the ways dependable research is to be conducted.

Communication researchers' methods are necessarily systematic. That is, dependable research is planned, organized, orderly, and methodical. Such research always begins with a question. A question helps guide the study to a particular end. Typically people attempt to answer questions in order to describe, explain, and/or predict interpersonal communication behavior. For example, Baxter and Bullis (1986) describe the turning points dating partners see as causing positive and negative changes in their relationships. Roloff, Janiszewski, Burns, and Manrai (1988) attempt to explain the associations between intimacy level and the obligation to offer and provide resources to others in times of need. And Stiff, Dillard, Somera, Kin and Sleight (1988) attempt to identify which personality and communication characteristics motivate people to volunteer. Once a question has been chosen, the researcher has to develop a plan to answer the question. Dependable research is planned from start to finish. The research plan is like the script for a movie or a recipe for cooking.

Before we begin discussing research methods, there are three terms you need to be familiar with: variable, independent variable, and dependent variable. A variable is a concept, often but not always quantitatively measured, that contains two or more values or categories that can vary over time or over a given sample (e.g., age). An independent variable is a variable that can affect change in the other (the dependent variable) but can not itself be affected by changes in the dependent variable. For example, gender is an independent variable which tends to affect height, (that is, men tend to be taller than women). However, height cannot affect gender (that is, being tall cannot affect or determine your gender).

TWO APPROACHES TO RESEARCH

There are two general research approaches: the grounded approach and the hypothesis-testing approach. Using a grounded approach, the researcher begins with general assumptions about interpersonal communication, formulates questions, and observes interpersonal communication, obtaining detailed information. These observations most often are then categorized and interpreted.[1] For example, the Dillard (1989) study examines the types of influence goals that individuals use in personal relationships. A group of respondents described their goals in interpersonal influence attempts, and the researcher then categorized these goals into six groups.

The hypothesis-testing approach is somewhat different. In this instance, the researcher uses theory to hypothesize or make predictions about what is expected. Hypotheses are informed guesses about how two or more things relate to one another. The researcher then observes interpersonal communication to determine if the prediction is accurate. Wiemann (1977) hypothesized that a person's interaction management skills would be related to others' perceptions of that person's communication competence. He then had respondents evaluate participants' communication competence and found that his hypothesis was supported.

One important difference between these two approaches is how specific the predictions are before the study. In the grounded approach, the researcher has general goals and questions. The specific conclusions emerge out of the study itself and are guided and shaped by what is observed.

For example, in the Baxter and Bullis (1986) study on turning points, they did not try to predict what the turning points in relationship development would be, but asked, ''What phenomena comprise relationship turning points in the perceptions of romantic relationship partners?'' They then interviewed 80 people about their relationships and extracted the turning point types from the resulting data.

In the hypothesis-testing approach, the researcher decides beforehand in very specific terms what to look for and examines only the hypothesis proposed. For example, in Daly, Vangelisti, and Daughton's (1988) study of conversational sensitivity, the researchers predicted that people with greater conversational sensitivity would be more empathic and would pay more attention to others. They then had 230 respondents complete a variety of measures which assessed conversational sensitivity, self-monitoring, empathy, communication apprehension, and social anxiety. The resulting data were then used to test the validity of the prediction.

After deciding on a research question or hypothesis, the researcher must decide how to collect the information necessary to answer the research question or test the hypothesis. This is called the method. In choosing a method, there are a number of decisions the researcher makes. First, the researcher must choose a setting for the study. Some researchers examine interpersonal communication in an experimental setting while others study it as it occurs naturally, and some combine the two.

METHODS OF DATA COLLECTION

Two important issues any researcher must consider when selecting methods for conducting research are validity and reliability. Validity represents the degree to which the method one uses to measure something actually measures it. For example, height is not a valid measure of intelligence while a balance scale is a valid measure of one's weight. Reliability represents how accurate a measure is. For instance, scales in doctors' offices tend to be more reliable in measuring a person's weight than are the scales most people have in their homes. In terms of communication measures, reliability indicates how accurate the scores on the measures are. If a measure is highly reliable, then one can be confident that the scores are very accurate.

Experiments

The experiment is a highly controlled method of attempting to demonstrate the existence of a relationship between one or more independent variables and one or more dependent variables. During an experiment the researcher arranges for events to occur and then measures the effects. In an experiment, the researcher attempts to control the environment in order to minimize the influence of extraneous variables; that is, things that might influence the effects being researched. For example, in Witteman and Fitzpatrick's (1986) study of the use of compliance-gaining strategies by marital couples, the researchers had 50 couples participate in a laboratory study. Each of the couples engaged in two role plays in which they tried to persuade one another to change a behavior. The interactions were videotaped and recorded, and the information was later coded and analyzed to determine the influence of couple type on compliance-gaining strategy type. This study was more effectively conducted in an experimental setting, because if the researchers had had to wait and observe 50 couples until they spontaneously engaged in compliance-gaining behavior, they may have had a very long wait.

There are advantages and disadvantages to using an experimental setting. It is the best method in social science for establishing causality, and experiments typically offer more control. Control often allows one to be more efficient (as in the Witteman and Fitzpatrick [1986] study) and offers less chance for error. However, experiments tend to occur in artificial environments, and much of social behavior may be altered or may not occur in this situation. As well, the presence of the experimenter can affect the behavior of the participants, which will then affect the results. Finally, certain groups may be impossible

to study in the laboratory, either because of their size (a cross-section of the American public) or their nature (gang members).

An exception to the controlled, laboratory experiment is the natural experiment. A natural experiment occurs when one observes a situation before, during and/or after some change occurs naturally. For instance, one could conduct observations in an airport and record the verbal interactions of passengers and airline personnel during the course of a "normal" flight day. Then one could observe the same situation during a time when there were numerous flight delays due to bad weather. In this way, the researcher could compare verbal interaction patterns between airline personnel and passengers under both conditions.

Observations

A number of researchers prefer to observe naturally occurring behavior. These researchers pick an interactional setting, watch for interpersonal communication behavior to occur, and then record it. Examples of such settings could include lines at movie theatre box offices, grocery stores, classrooms, or doctors' waiting rooms. The researcher merely records the behavior and its effects. For example, if you wished to analyze the greeting behavior of sales clerks in department stores serving different socioeconomic classes, you would observe clerks greeting customers at (perhaps) a Sears, a Dillard's and a Saks Fifth Avenue. There are two primary types of observation: participant and nonparticipant. The participant observer is a regular participant in the activities being observed. For example, if one wished to observe children's persuasive strategies with their parents at grocery stores, the researcher would go to a grocery store and act as a shopper while conducting the observation. The nonparticipant observer, on the other hand, does not participate in group activities in the particular setting. A researcher who wished to observe children's interactions with their peers at recess would simply observe the children at play.

The strongest advantage of observational research is the naturalness of the setting and the greater likelihood that people will act and communicate as they typically would. Another advantage of such research is that it allows the researcher to see communication behavior in context and thus allows him or her to focus on a greater variety of issues or to change the focus of the research as different, perhaps unanticipated, behaviors arise. The disadvantage of observational research is that the researcher has little or no control over the situation, may have difficulty gaining entry into the situation, and such research is often quite time-consuming, as one must wait for the variable of interest to occur naturally.

RECORDING INTERPERSONAL COMMUNICATION

No matter what setting is relied upon to answer the research question/hypothesis, the researcher has to record the interpersonal communication behavior or reactions to it. Recording refers to the manner in which the researcher describes what is observed. The three most common methods for recording communication behavior are surveys, video or tape recordings, and field notes.

Surveys

Most people are familiar with surveys; they are used by market researchers in shopping malls and by educational institutions, among others. Surveys use written or oral questions which are designed to gather information. There are two primary types of questions used: open- and closed-ended questions. The difference is whether or not the survey specifies the range of answers available to the respondent. Open-ended questions do not specify the answers. For example, in the Metts and Cupach (1989) study on the influence of situation on the type of remedial strategy people are likely to use in response to embarrassment, they asked the respondents to describe a situation in which they were significantly

embarrassed. The respondents then generated their own answers. An example of a closed-ended question occurs in the Petronio and Martin (1986) study of the effects of revealing private information. These researchers asked their respondents to indicate on a scale from one to four the degree to which they would predict negative and positive outcomes of disclosure. One represented that such an outcome was "never true" and four represented the belief that such an outcome was "always true."

Whether one wishes to use open-ended or closed-ended questions depends upon several factors. Essentially, open-ended questions provide more information and allow for topics or answers the researcher did not anticipate, while closed-ended questions are easier to interpret.

There are two ways in which surveys may be used to study interpersonal communication. First, and less common, is the sample survey. This consists of drawing a random sample of people and administering a questionnaire to this sample of individuals. The sample is representative of a given population and is generalizable to that population. Thus, if we took a random sample of seniors at Arizona State University and asked them questions about student life, the information we learn from these data are representative of seniors at ASU (Arizona State University), and the findings may be generalized only to that population.

The second type of survey is more loosely based on survey research principles and is more often referred to as a "questionnaire" study. This type is not typically administered to a random sample of a population, but rather data are collected from accidental samples or convenience samples of individuals. The difference is that the data collected from such sources may not be generalized to any population, nor are the data representative of anyone except the individuals involved in the study. This is an important point because the information we learn from this type of an approach is limited in scope.

With both types of surveys, there are three ways in which the survey may be administered. First is the face-to-face method; it is most frequently used by those conducting a questionnaire study. This method entails asking the respondents, in a face-to-face setting, questions and recording their responses or having the respondents record their own responses. A second way to administer a survey is over the telephone, a method more frequently used in sample surveys. In this case, respondents are asked survey questions over the phone and are asked to provide responses to the researcher. The third method uses mail or postal surveys. As one might expect, the respondent is sent a questionnaire to complete and mail back to the researcher.

With a sample survey, these different methods for administering the survey influence the way a sample is drawn, and each has its limitations in terms of the percentage of people who will respond to the survey.

The advantages of surveys include the fact that they are generally easy to administer; thus, one can often sample larger groups of people. However, a major disadvantage is that one is relying upon the respondents' ability to be aware of and to have memory of their own behavior. Some communication behaviors are so ''mindless'' that one either is not aware of them and/or does not remember them later. For example, if one asked people how they know when it is their turn to talk in a conversation, many of them would be unable to tell you. Related to this is the fact that people may be more likely to remember information that is important or unusual, rather than typical. As well, there is a tendency for people to respond in ways that are socially desirable. Thus, when using surveys, one must study communication behavior which people are more likely to remember and which is less subject to social desirability biases.

Video and Tape Recordings

Video and tape recordings are yet another way in which researchers collect data. They have the advantage of permanence, and they may be collected in either experimental or naturalistic settings. Tape recordings are easier to collect because the equipment is less expensive, more portable, and more unobtrusive. However, video

recordings are often preferable because they are able to record not only the spoken word but nonverbal cues that extend, replace, or contradict the spoken word. Typically, once video or audio tapes have been recorded, the researcher reduces them to written transcripts for in-depth analysis. Alberts' (1988) analysis of couples' conversational complaints is an example of a study which used audio recordings for data collection.

Field Notes

A final recording method is called field notes. Essentially, field notes are a written record of one's observations. Typically, the researcher enters a setting, then writes down descriptions of the communication behavior observed. It is usually best to record one's observations as they occur, but if this is not possible, the researcher may jot down a few notes during the observation and write full notes after having left the scene. Or, if even this is not possible, one may choose to record the observations as soon after the observation as possible. The clearest and most descriptive notes tend to be those that are recorded in the setting, but recording the notes later does allow the researcher greater freedom to observe all that is occurring. Sometimes audio tape recorders are used to record the researcher's observation, if this can be accomplished discreetly.

METHODS OF DATA ANALYSIS

Once data are collected, they are subjected to one or more forms of analysis. During this process the researcher attempts to bring order and understanding to the data which have been observed, recorded, or written down. Three general methods of data analysis are content analysis, coding systems, and statistical analyses.

Content Analysis

Content analysis is a method for describing and inferring characteristics of messages. Often, content analysis is used to take a verbal, nonquantitative document (such as answers to open-ended questions or transcripts of tapes) and transform it into quantitative data. The results of content analysis generally can then be presented in tables containing frequencies or percentages. In content analysis, the researcher examines the data collected and looks for recurring patterns to emerge. These recurring characteristics are placed into categories based on similarity and then are labeled. In this way, the categories "emerge" from the data. Baxter and Bullis' (1986) analysis of relational turning points provides an example of content analysis. The researchers collected audio tapes of interviews with 80 subjects who described the histories of their relationships. They then examined transcripts of those interviews and developed 14 categories of types of turning points which occur during romantic relationship development.

Coding Systems

Coding systems allow researchers to observe and categorize communication behavior. They can be used to analyze data that have been collected in naturalistic or experimental settings, and they may be used for communication behavior which has been recorded through video and audio tapes, surveys, or during field research. First, one lists various types of communication behavior, then one checks off the behavior when it is observed (in the setting, on the survey, in the video recording, or in transcripts of the audio tapes). For example, a researcher may have a checklist of compliance-gaining strategies to use for observing children's attempts to influence their parents' purchases at grocery stores. Each time the researcher observes one of the behaviors occurring, a check is recorded next to the category. An example of a study which used a coding system for analyzing data is Alberts' (1988) study of couples' complaints. She developed a coding system of five complaint types and five complaint response types. Then, as she examined the transcripts of the couples' talk, she put a checkmark beside each complaint or response type as it occurred.

Statistical Analysis

Statistics are used to analyze numerical data. Statistical analyses are generally conducted for two purposes: description and inference. Descriptive data analysis summarizes the information in the data, often by tabulating and graphing it. Inferential data analysis may be conducted for two purposes: to estimate the characteristics of a population from data gathered on a sample, and to test for significant differences between groups and significant relationships between variables. The Knapp, Ellis, and Williams (1980) study of communication behavior associated with relationship terms provides examples of both descriptive and inferential statistics. In the study, the authors provide a list of 62 relationship terms and respondents' evaluations of the degree of intimacy associated with those terms. These findings are represented in a table of the mean scores given for each term by the 100 respondents. These are descriptive statistics; that is, the mean value summarizes the scores for all of the 100 respondents. In this study, the authors also analyze which communication behaviors are associated with the different types of relationship terms. Here they attempt to determine significant relationships among the variables (such as relationship term, communication behavior, sex of respondent, etc.). In this case, the authors used inferential statistics.

There are many types of statistical analyses. Some are used to analyze categorical data, that is, categories of things such as types of complaints or types of turning points. Other forms of statistical analyses are used to analyze quantitative data, such as scores on measures of conversational sensitivity or loneliness. In Appendix A we have included brief explanations of some of the various ways one can analyze data.

SUMMARY

This chapter provided a brief overview of the process of studying interpersonal communication. Research was defined as the use of systematic methods to answer questions. Also, it was shown that the goals of answering questions were description, explanation, and prediction.

Systematic methods were then described. Grounded and hypothesis-testing approaches to research were differentiated based on the specificity of their predictions: hypothesis-testing approaches make specific predictions while grounded approaches make more general ones. Next we examined two settings for studying interpersonal communication: experimental and naturalistic. Then we described three methods for recording interpersonal communication: surveys, video and audio recordings, and field notes. Finally, we discussed three methods for analyzing data: content analysis, coding systems, and statistical analysis.

NOTES

1. Many of these ideas as they relate to nonverbal communication are discussed in ''Researching Nonverbal Communication,'' in J. A. DeVito and M. L. Hecht (Eds.), *Nonverbal Communication Reader* (pp. 413–435), Prospect Heights, IL: Waveland Press, 1990.

REFERENCES

Bailey, K. D. (1982). *Methods of social research.* New York: The Free Press.

Hecht, M. L. (1990). Researching nonverbal communication. In J. A. DeVito & M. L. Hecht (Eds.), *Nonverbal communication reader.* Prospect Heights, IL: Waveland Press.

Smith, M. J. (1988). *Contemporary communication research methods.* Belmont, CA: Wadsworth.

SECTION II

Interpersonal Perspectives

CHAPTER 3 ⊙

Interpersonal Communication Perspectives on Strategic Processes

INTRODUCTION

Three perspectives are presented in this chapter representing strategic processes. The first is Pearce's rules perspective. Pearce rejects much of what has counted for theory in interpersonal communication as being "based on a mechanistic model of humanity, a Humean conception of cause, and a logical positivist methodology." In its place he sponsors a rules perspective. He argues that this perspective requires pluralistic and naturalistic methods which allow for both teleological as well as causal explanation.

The second perspective is the uncertainty reduction theory (URT) from Berger and Calabrese. Their theory also rejects much of prior theoretical speculation in order to develop one which is more centrally based on communication constructs.

Sunnafrank's article represents a third perspective. He proposes that individuals function from a predicted outcome model in initial interactions. His model also addresses the relationship between communication and the need to reduce uncertainty.

THE COORDINATED MANAGEMENT OF MEANING: A RULES-BASED THEORY OF INTERPERSONAL COMMUNICATION

W. Barnett Pearce

THIS PAPER DESCRIBES continuing development of a theory of interpersonal communication. The focus of the theory is on the ability of two persons to engage in conversation.[1]

An analysis of conversations provides a convenient entry point into the study of human experience generally. The social sciences have traditionally been concerned more with the bizarre than with the normal, more with the improbable than with the commonplace. Of course,

events three standard deviations from the mean are inherently interesting—a journalist sees news value in "man bites dog" but not in "dog bites man"—but the glamour of studies of genius or depravity may mask the importance of accounting for what usually happens. Recalling the old adage about the fish being the last to discover the existence of water, the social sciences have only recently developed an explicit interest in the development and function of social routines, talk, and the formation of interpersonal relationships (Douglas, 1970). The study of everyday life quickly focuses on interpersonal communication—the sequencing of messages in conversations and the sequencing of conversations into relationships—as the primary activity in human sociation and has demonstrated that apparently simple acts of conversation are in fact incredibly complex feats which even social scientists can perform better than they can explain.

For quite different reasons, persons in a number of disciplines have felt it in their interest to develop an understanding of some phase of interpersonal communication. A patient detective could find fingerprints enough to indict half of academe for improper fondling (see Budd and Ruben, 1972), but explanations of human ability to participate in conversations are unsatisfactory.

Theoretic offerings are based on different orienting assumptions, vary in scope, and possess quite different amounts and types of explanatory power.

This theory is identified by the phrase "the coordinated management of meaning," which is offered both as an ancestral term under which the fuller explication of the theory may be subsumed and as a useful descriptor of what persons do when they communicate. The coordinated management of meaning differs from other treatments of interpersonal communication largely because it is avowedly general, unabashedly theoretical, deliberately based on a set of assumptions differing from recent orthodoxy, and self-consciously two levels of abstraction away from observable exchanges of messages. The theory was briefly described in Pearce (1976) for an undergraduate audience. In this paper, the assumptions behind the theory are articulated, some conceptual problems are solved, and the methodological implications of the theory are described. If the coordinated management of meaning meets the usual criteria for a theory, I will make this rather extravagant claim[2]: it

provides an integrating perspective which forces the inclusion of concerns traditionally associated with anthropology, sociology, and psychology, as well as communication studies, and structures an explanatory framework which indicates how the different contributions of each of these disciplines function in an adequate explanation of human sociation.

ASSUMPTIONS

The term "preparadigmatic" well describes the current condition of the social sciences (Kuhn, 1970). Normal science occurs when there is relatively full communication among scientists and they render relatively unanimous professional judgments. This happy state is attained when scientists share a common socialization and adhere to a common disciplinary matrix involving "symbolic generalizations," beliefs in particular models, common values, and acceptance of particular exemplars of how to do research. (Kuhn, 1970:177–187). This is far from the state of the social sciences today.[3]

According to Harré and Secord (1973:27–28), the recent orthodoxy is based on (1) a mechanistic model of man, (2) a Humean conception of cause, and (3) a logical positivist methodology. Although the radical behaviorism which consistently follows from these premises has been successively revised (Koch, 1964), only recently have coherent packages of alternative assumptions been offered, and none has been widely accepted as a new paradigm.[4] As a result, current research on human sociation lurches about, unguided by theory and frequently based on unstated and untenable premises (Harré and Secord, 1973:27–83).

Source: The article is taken from *Explorations in interpersonal communication* by Gerald R. Miller. (c) 1976 Sage Publications, Beverly Hills, CA, USA. Reprinted by permission of Sage Publications, Inc.

The assumptions of the coordinated management of meaning may be summarized as stipulating (1) a diverse set of models for man, (2) a set of alternative modes of explanation for human action, and (3) a social science characterized as pluralistic and naturalistic.

The theory stipulates that human action is diverse, being both proactive and reactive, caused and purposive, and that each form of action requires a different explanatory model. A useful typology differentiates between *controlled, influenced,* and *creative* action in such a way that the appropriate explanatory mode for each can be determined (Harris, 1975). Controlled behavior is reactive or "caused" (in a Humean sense) and is appropriately explained by identifying antecedents and subsuming the particular instance under a nomothetic law (Hempel, 1966). A person's meanings or volition have no effect on controlled behavior: if a person steps from a curb and is hit by a speeding Mack truck, none of these will change the distance, direction, and trajectory of his body. Influenced behavior is structured by socialization and is appropriately explained by describing the rules which persons follow as they conduct purposive action. This explanation follows the form of a somewhat modified practical syllogism (Von Wright, 1971). Influenced behavior varies as a function of the actor's meanings and volition. For example, a person probably would not step from a curb to pick up a dime from the street (or would reinterpret this act of basic greed) if he self-consciously weighed the gain of the dime against the danger of being hit by a truck or if he followed a rule which specified a scramble in the gutter for a dime as indecorous. Examples of influenced behavior include kneeling in the presence of royalty, using a "demand ticket" to get into a conversation (Nofsinger, 1975), or employing turn-taking cues to manage interaction while conversing (S. Duncan, 1972). Finally, creative behavior is a product of individual choice which is not the normal, expected meaning or movement. Creativity may involve following rules in a novel way or acting independently of the rules. It is not clear what explanatory mode is appropriate for creative be-

havior. Perhaps no more can be done than an explicative history.

Interpersonal communication probably includes elements of all three types of action, but for the most part it consists of influenced behavior in which individuals allow their actions to be governed and guided by rules (Cushman and Whiting, 1972; Pearce, 1973). But the transactive nature of human communication (Rossiter and Pearce, 1975) requires an explanatory procedure which goes beyond a listing of the rules or a description of how individuals follow rules. Since the outcome is the result of a frequently nonsummative input of both persons, the conversation which actually occurs may not resemble the rule-governed behaviors of either person independently. As a result, an explanation must be able to account for the effect of each person on the other as well as each person's rule-governed behavior.

The assumptions that human action is diverse and that each type of behavior necessitates a different form of explanation have significant implications for the nature of social science. Specifically, a science which is appropriate for studying interpersonal communication must be pluralistic and naturalistic. It must be pluralistic in that it grants legitimacy to a variety of forms of research and theoretic formulations and—most importantly—in that the decisions about how to do research and how to frame explanations are determined by the characteristics of the phenomena being studied. For example, it must admit teleological as well as causal explanatory frameworks and must contain criteria by which to determine when each is appropriate. It must be naturalistic [5] in that it is at least sometimes based on actor-defined variables rather than exclusively on observer definition. Meanings as well as movements must be understood to account for actions, and in influenced behavior an observer must elicit the actor's meanings rather than superimpose his own.

These assumptions are to an extent the direct denial of yesterday's orthodoxy and are consistent with what I view as an emerging consensus on an "anthropomorphic" concept of man (Harré and Secord, 1973). However, there is little agreement about the shape of a coherent theory and a viable methodology built on these assumptions. The following sections present a new attempt to work out the implications of these assumptions.

THE COORDINATED MANAGEMENT OF MEANING

These paragraphs present a perspective from which to think about interpersonal communication. The picture is of persons who have learned a set of rules which describe how they and others should behave in conversation and who make strategic choices about which rules to follow and which persons to converse with in order to achieve a satisfactory mode of sociation. The joke is that the rules frequently contradict each other and fail to cover some situations and that everybody learns a different set of rules. Keeping score in the resulting confusion is difficult for both communicators and social scientists. The coordination problems in the management of meaning are like those of five musicians suddenly thrust before an audience, who must simultaneously perform and collectively decide what numbers to play, how fast to play them, and who should play what parts. The element of surprise in the joke is that people so frequently produce such good music.

Meaning

Since communication must be understood as action (interpreted movement) rather than simply as movements, an explanation of communication must account for the communicators' meanings as well as the messages they exchange. Without attempting to construct a comprehensive theory of meaning, this theory specifies meaning in interpersonal communication as *episodic.*

Communicators do not perceive their conversations as an undifferentiated stream of experience. Rather, they punctuate them into units, each of which situates particular interpretations of messages *synchronically,* by locating them within a context of related meanings (e.g., "this

comment was made during a brainstorming session"), and *diachronically,* by providing an interpretation of past messages and a prediction of future ones (e.g., "we are trying to generate as many ideas as possible regardless of merit; we'll evaluate them later"). These units of meaning have been variously described, but the concept of episode is perhaps the most useful.

The definition of episode—"any part of human life, involving one or more people, in which some internal structure can be determined" (Harré and Secord, 1973:153)—is useful because it is purposefully imprecise, being determined by the actors rather than an observer; because it indicates that episodes may vary widely in scope (from "having coffee with" to "having an affair with"); and because it defines episodes interpersonally.

A description of an episode answers the question, "What does he think he is doing?" Whether or not a particular lexicon has an appropriate word for it, the enactment of an episode constitutes a sequence of actions which are perceived as entities and thus are "noun-able." Particular conversations may be described as "having a fight," "making up," "culturally appropriate greeting rituals," "bull sessions," etc. But notice that the rules in each of these differ: behaviors which are expected and legitimate in making up do not exist in greeting ritual, and those appropriate in bull session do not exist in church.

A cluster of rules which specify legitimate and expected behaviors and meanings may be considered an operational definition of an episode, with the implicit instruction: "to enact episode X, do this. . . ." Actually, the task confronting communicators is usually the other way around: they are presented with behavior and must reason "if he is doing this, he must be enacting episode X, and given episode X, I should do this. . . ." This mental process is comparable to abstraction and generalization in concept-formation (Bruner et al., 1956) and explains the process behind H.D. Duncan's (1968:32) insistence on the interrelation between form (*how* we communicate) and content (*what* we communicate).

Specifying meaning as episodic orients analysis to integrated patterns of meaning with behavioral implications, but there is still considerable equivocation in the use of the term. To avoid paralyzing confusion in the explanation of communication, it is necessary to differentiate three referents for episode, designated by subscripts.

$Episodes_1$ consist of patterns of meanings and behaviors which are culturally sanctioned and which exist independently of any particular individual or dyad. These are the public symbols necessary for meaning to be shared and seem identical with the concept of "significant symbols" described by Mead (1934) and H.D. Duncan (1968). Traditionally studied by anthropologists and sociologists, $Episodes_1$ include social institutions and related rituals such as marriage and rites of passage, and ritualized ways of dealing with particular situations such as greeting rituals, patterns of social deference, and treatments of humor or sarcasm.

$Episodes_2$ consist of patterns of meanings and behaviors in the minds of individuals and are similar to discussions of images (Boulding, 1956), plans (Miller et al., 1960), acts (Morris, 1946), or definitions of situations (McHugh, 1968). These are private symbols which express individuals' understanding of the forms of social interaction in which they are participating, or in which they want to participate. To the extent that a person's $Episodes_2$ resemble society's $Episodes_1$, the person will be able to converse easily, understanding and being understood. To the extent that the $Episodes_2$ are idiosyncratic, the person will have greater coordination problems.

$Episodes_3$ consist of the communicators' interpretation of the actual sequence of messages which they jointly produced. Episodes-as-coenacted have been studied by Cicoural (1974) and Garfinkel (1967) among others, but explanations of conversations are barren unless they are integrated with analysis of $Episodes_1$ and $Episodes_2$.

When two people communicate, the $Episodes_1$ which they have learned from their cultures provide them with a repertoire of patterns of actions which they may assume are common to both (the "assumption of reciprocal perspectives," Cicourel, 1974, or "background expectancies," Garfinkel, 1967). From this repertoire, both persons select and/or construct the $Episode_2$ which reflects their particular interpretation of what they want to enact or what they feel is appropriate. As each person begins to enact his $Episode_2$, the combination of both their actions structure $Episode_3$. A coordinated management of meaning can easily be achieved when both persons share an $Episode_1$, when both want to enact the same $Episode_2$, and when the structure of the $Episode_1$ equals $Episode_2$. In this instance, both know the rules for enacting the $Episode_3$; they understand what to expect and what is expected of them. When heads of state meet for a summit conference, it is mutually desirable that at least their public conversations proceed smoothly. The function of protocol officers is to identify an $Episode_1$ common to both and to get their principals to internalize it as their $Episodes_2$ so that the $Episode_3$ will proceed smoothly. In these contexts, statesmen sacrifice spontaneity and individuality for a performance which looks good for the cameras.

Most people must muddle through life deprived of the services of protocol officers, however, and their conversations may be expected to flow smoothly if they and their conversational partners are willing to take complementary roles and if they share definitions of $Episodes_1$. This is why communication within tribal society is easy: everyone knows his roles, and there is a ritualized pattern for handling all of the usual interactions (Albert, 1972). Modern Western society is not like that: it is characterized by an acceptance of change, recognized interdependency, and a celebration of heterogeneity. This frequently leads to communication between persons who do not have a common repertoire of $Episodes_1$ or who have conflicting $Episodes_2$, and coordination problems in their management of meanings is the result.

Management

Kelly (1955) forcefully argued that persons are the prisoners of neither their history nor their heredity. They can manage their meanings even though they cannot change their environment or themselves. People are "always free to reconstrue what they cannot deny." This ability accounts for the fact that people can transcend their cultures (their Episodes$_2$ $\neq$ their Episodes$_1$) and that people can produce and understand an Episode$_3$ which may differ from either communicator's Episodes$_1$ or Episodes$_2$.

Management of meaning may take several forms, an observation which itself bodes ill for methodology. In the simplest case, a person might shift from one episode to another as that which best identifies a particular sequence of behaviors. Alternatively, a person might redefine the structure of an episode by changing the cluster of rules comprising it or by changing the perception of its boundaries or internal structure. The most complex form of management of meaning involves shifting the level of abstraction. As Russell demonstrated with the theory of types, it is impossible to perceive the world without paradox unless levels of abstraction are granted such that one statement will be seen as describing a class of others without itself being a part of that class. In much the same way, persons manage their meanings by changing level of reflexive self-awareness.[6]

An adequate explanation of interpersonal communication must account for the fact that people not only can but regularly do manage their meanings. Discussion of meaning management is facilitated by two analytic devices: an adaptation [7] of the process model of coorientation (Pearce and Stamm, 1973) and the concept of enigmatic episodes (Harré and Secord, 1973).

The process model of coorientation assumes that persons interact with others on the basis of perceived agreement or disagreement about what episode is being enacted and that these expectations are subject to confirmation or disconfirmation by the other person's subsequent acts. The model identifies four coorientational states: pre-dicted agreement confirmed (PAC), predicted agreement disconfirmed (PAD), predicted disagreement confirmed (PDC), and predicted disagreement disconfirmed (PDD). The hypothesis on which the model is built states that persons communicate differently depending on what their expectation is and whether it is confirmed or disconfirmed. The management of meaning is of particular importance in the two states in which the expectation is disconfirmed. In each instance, persons must reevaluate the meanings of previous messages and change their expectations for the meanings and behaviors which will occur subsequently.

The explanatory power of this concept of the management of meaning may be demonstrated by contrasting Rogerian client-centered therapy with gestalt counseling. Rogers employs "unconditional positive regard" and reflective statements which in effect support the client's definition of his Episode$_2$ (by inducing the agreement states of PAC or PDD) and encourage him to explore it. Gestalt therapists deliberately refuse to enact the Episode$_3$ (inducing the disagreement states of PAD and PDC) requested by the patient, forcing the patient to reconstrue his Episodes$_2$. These distinctions clearly demonstrate the different strategies and objectives (exploration versus reconstruction of Episodes$_2$) of the two approaches. (Based on the model, one would expect a difference between Rogerian clients in PAC and those in PDD and between Gestalt clients in PAD and those in PDC.)

The enactment of enigmatic episodes also necessitates the management of meaning. An episode is enigmatic if its expression in the form of rules is inadequate as a guide for action. There are two forms of enigmatic episodes. *Equivocal* episodes are those in which a particular pattern of behaviors is interpretable in two or more contradictory ways or in which a particular interpretation fits two or more patterns of behavior. Episodes in which the rules do not describe appropriate behaviors specifically or completely enough to guide actions or interpretations are designated as *ambiguous*.

For most people, communicating with the terminally ill is an enigmatic (ambiguous) episode. Partly because we institutionalize seriously ill patients, most people have not learned an $Episode_1$ which could guide them. Thrown into relying on their own ingenuity, these conversations are more troublesome and require more management of meanings than the enactment of a nonenigmatic episode.

Coordination

The study of communication properly centers on the coordination procedures by which individuals intermesh their own actions with those of someone else to produce $Episodes_3$. Just as five virtuoso musicians cannot play together unless they achieve some system of tacit agreements which enables them to coordinate their performance, so the success of a conversation depends on the coordination achieved by both persons, as well as their individual merits.

Coordination is achieved when the communicators "contract" (Carson, 1969) with each other to enact a particular episode. The early phases of conversations frequently are best understood as negotiations in which each requests the other to enact his preferred $Episode_2$, and these requests are either accepted or rejected, usually with a counterrequest. Once a request is accepted, each knows what to expect and what is expected—*if* their understandings of the rules of the episode are similar.[8]

Coordinating the management of meaning becomes quite a problem when the communicators have different $Episodes_2$ which they need/want to enact or when their definition of an $Episode_2$ is similar enough that they think that they share rules which in fact differ. (This is, of course, the origin of the plot line of many TV situation comedies.)

The essential condition of coordination is consensual rules. Given a set of rules common to both communicators, each can accurately predict what the reaction to his behaviors will be and can reliably interpret the significance of what the other does. Without consensual rules, conversational chaos and frustration result. One important

topic for communication theory is the manner in which consensual rules are developed in particular conversations. A tentative taxonomy identifies three coordination strategies: *casting, mirroring,* and *negotiation.*

Coordinating conversations by casting occurs when a person has a preferred $Episode_2$ (or repertoire of $Episodes_2$) and he develops or terminates interpersonal relationships depending on the other person's ability to participate in the $Episode_3$ that he wants to enact. A useful analogy is that of an actor who has found a script with a part in it which he wants to play but who must find a stage upon which to perform and a group of people to fill the other roles. When coordinating by casting, a person communicates by recruiting others to enact particular roles and training them for the part. Casting has an imperative tone: others are offered an opportunity to interact with the caster only if they are willing to play the game, but there may be a wide range of stylistic variations. Sophisticated casting may be subtle, humorous, or deliberately blatant.

Coordinating conversations by mirroring is just the opposite of casting. Desiring above all else participation in an interaction with other people or with a particular other, a mirrorer is willing to take any role in an $Episode_3$ proposed by the other person. When coordinating by mirroring, persons communicate by seeking to discover what the other person wants them to do and eliciting feedback to see if they are doing well. Mirroring has a dependent, acquiescent tone and may perhaps best be detected by observing chameleonlike changes as the person moves between various relationships and situations.

Coordinating conversations by negotiation is more complicated than doing so by either mirroring or casting. In negotiation, a person is willing to compromise between his $Episode_2$ and that of the other person. Successful negotiations frequently result in an $Episode_3$ unlike either of the $Episodes_2$. Four negotiation strategies have been described at some length (Pearce, 1976). *Invocation* occurs when a person begins to enact an $Episode_3$, inviting the other to take the complementary role. *Ingratiation* (better described as bargaining) occurs when a person enacts an episode which the other person finds desirable with the assumption that the other will then reciprocate. Negotiation by *creating shared experiences* is a way of structuring a common background which provides a pattern for future interactions. *Metacommunicating* consists of talking explicitly about the episodes which are or might be enacted.

All these coordination strategies comprise a repertoire of techniques by which people can manage each other and their own meanings. Sometimes it works well and usually well enough for people to get by, but these successes do not disguise the fact that good communication is a highly sophisticated form of action requiring considerable competency to perform or to study.

METHODOLOGICAL ISSUES

The assumptions on which this theory is based necessitate a pluralistic and naturalistic methodology, but the precise shape of a research program which would be appropriate for this theory is far from clear. In fact, one of the highest prices paid for abandoning the positivist paradigm is that one must renounce a comfortably elaborated methodology for which laudable virtues—objectivity, replicability, etc.—are claimed.

There have been many calls for a nonpositivist research program in the last 15 years, and social scientists are rightly impatient with self-selected sirens whose songs do not describe how to get to work. Before this theory or any other can claim to be a viable alternative way of studying communication scientifically, it must at least show that it is possible to do legitimate research consistent with its premises.

Type of Behavior

Since the methodology required by this theory is pluralistic, researchers must choose between various models for the appropriate description of the phenomena they want to study. This choice may be expressed as a hypothesis that the phenomena possess the criterial attributes of controlled, influenced, or creative behavior. For several reasons (space, author's interests, applicability to conversations), this discussion will deal only with influenced behavior.

The hypothesis that a particular aspect of conversation consists of influenced behavior implies that the behavior is rule-governed. The hypothesis may be tested by answering five questions based on the characteristics of rules.

1. Is there a logically or empirically necessary relationship between antecedents and consequents? This question must be answered "no" by demonstrating the possibility of alternative sequences. An affirmative answer would suggest that the behavior be conceptualized as controlled and would be explained very differently.
2. Is the observed pattern a recurring one? This question must be answered "yes" by demonstrating a statistical regularity. In the absence of any necessary relationship, this regularity attests to the presence and function of rules which account for structure, differentiating it from creative behavior.
3. Can the communicators generate these sequences? This question must be answered "yes" by demonstrating that informants can interpolate and extrapolate to complete fragments of the pattern. For example, if presented a transcript in which some messages have been deleted, the informants could supply the missing messages or variants of them which they and others will perceive as functionally synonymous. This ability demonstrates that the actors perceive the internal structure of the episode.
4. Can the communicators perceive alternative sequences of messages which are inappropriate? This question is another attempt to tap into the internal structure of the episode, this time by negation, and must be answered "yes."
5. Are sanctions (positive or negative) applied to deviations from the pattern? Although the existence of observable sanctions is not a necessary condition,[9] the presence of negative sanctions is one indication that a rule has been violated (see Garfinkel, 1967).

If each of these questions is answered in the indicated way, the researcher can conclude that the conversation in question is rule-governed, and this decision determines the rest of his procedure.

Description

A naturalistic methodology stresses the importance of describing the phenomena. The ultimate descriptive phrase for influenced behavior in conversations is to say that "they enacted an Episode$_3$ of ritualized insults" where the episode named can be described in at least two ways. The first description is external to the episode and may follow an organizing scheme similar to Burke's dramatistic pentad. The five terms in the pentad can be adapted to social action by specifying the *scene* as the socially defined interpersonal context, the *act* as the effect of what is done in the social institutions, the *agency* as the medium in which communication takes place, and the *purpose* as the struggle to achieve the consensus necessary to integrate social action (this is slightly revised from H.D. Duncan, 1968:19). Duncan correctly identified the pentad as a way of accounting for the structure of social action but not its function. For that, episodes must also be defined by describing the cluster of rules which translate between the symbolic meaning and the patterns of inferences and behaviors which constitute the episode.

Rules may be stated in a number of ways, but should be reducible to a form such as "If we are enacting Episode$_3$ A, and he does Act B, then I am expected to or legitimately may do Act C" (this is an adaptation of Gottlieb, 1968). The first phrase establishes a boundary condition; the second ties into the particular structure of the Episode$_3$ as it is being enacted; and the third expresses the role of rules in establishing acts/meanings which are required for the episode to be enacted (*constitutive* rules) and the array of allowable acts from which the person may choose (*regulative* rules). Both descriptions may be validated by comparing them with the actors' perceptions and behavior (although the actors should not be expected to be fully aware of or able to articulate either rules or symbolic meanings).

If the communicators are following the same rules, their coordination problems are easy and an observer can readily describe their conversation by identifying the rules. Both coordinating the management of meaning and describing the ensuing conversation are more difficult when the communicators follow different rules (e.g., their Episodes$_2$ are different) or when Episode$_3$ is enigmatic (e.g., the rules do not adequately specify meanings and behaviors). In these instances, a researcher must identify those sequences of messages which are based on a consensually shared rule and those which are not. The latter may be described in terms of each communicator's Episode$_2$ and his use of coordination strategies. For example, this conversational excerpt shows a quickly corrected coordination problem:

> TOM: Hey, did you hear what happened downtown today?
>
> DICK: Tell me.
>
> TOM: No, I was asking you.
>
> DICK: Oh, well, there was a demonstration at the post office. . . .

To describe this sequence of messages, it is necessary to contrast Tom's and Dick's Episodes$_2$. Tom wanted to enact a *question-answer* sequence based on an Episode$_1$ which legitimates this pattern (Schlegloff, 1968). Dick interpreted what Tom and he were doing as a three-message sequence which functions to give Tom an extended speaking turn during which he can play newscaster. This interpretation is also based on a common Episode$_1$ (Sacks, 1967, 1972). Tom's second message acknowledged the coordination problem and used the negotiation strategy of meta-communication (Pearce, 1976). Dick's second statement is an appropriate response to Tom's first remark, indicating his awareness of and willingness to follow the rules of a question-answer episode.

For some purposes, additional descriptors can be used. For example, the Episodes$_1$ may be identified as enigmatic because the opening for each is the same. The question "Did you hear . . . ?"

does not differentiate between "question-answer" and "three utterance turn-request." Further, Dick's first response put Tom in a coorientation state of predicted agreement disconfirmed, and Tom's second message put Dick in the same state, while Dick's second response put Tom in a state of predicted agreement confirmed, which shows that his coordination strategy was successful. Of course, a description may be more or less detailed depending on the researcher's purpose, but the apparatus necessary for a highly detailed description should be included in a theory which is based on the assumptions articulated above and which will be tested by naturalistic research.

Explanation

A two-step explanation is necessary for conversations. First, each person's behavior must be explained in answer to the question, "Why did he do that?" But conversations are transactive and cannot be explained adequately even by a full explication of each person's actions individually. The second step in explanation is to account for the Episode$_3$.

The practical syllogism (Von Wright, 1971) is a viable explanatory model for each person's rule-governed actions. Two characteristics of the model make it particularly appropriate: it explains actions teleologically, in terms of reasons or goals to be achieved rather than in terms of antecedent causes, and it explains an action by showing that it is a reasonable choice without assuming that it was logically or empirically necessary.

The practical syllogism takes this form:

>A wishes B to occur;
>
>A knows/believes that he must do X if B is to occur;
>
>Therefore, A does X.

where: A is a person,

B is an episode, and

X is a particular behavior given meaning by its location in the episode.

The first premise poses a statement of purpose ("He wanted to do B") as a "final" explanatory principle for the observed behavior.[10] As any five-year-old child can demonstrate, a series of "why" questions may be extended beyond anyone's ability to answer. Certainly it can be asked, "Why does he want B to occur?" Although this is an interesting question, it is external to the theory of the coordinated management of meaning; rather, it is more suitable to the mythology of motivation, reinforcement schedules, needs, etc. The more appropriate question is, "How do you know that A wishes B to occur?" which is answered with reference to interview and observational techniques.

The second premise links the occurrence of the desired episode to the production of the observed behavior. As stated in the syllogism, however, the connection between B and X is simply assumed. The warrant which justifies the second premise is a statement of the rules which comprise the episode. These rules are generated by the descriptive procedures discussed in the previous section.

Given the ability to specify the statements which function as the first and second premises of the practical syllogism and to state the rules which are the warrant for the second premise, the observed behavior can be explained by demonstrating that it logically follows. An explanation of a well-coordinated conversation—such as the enactment of a "Hi, how are you?" greeting ritual—is straightforward. A poorly coordinated conversation, however, is more difficult, in part because the same syllogism cannot be used for both communicators. The coordination problem may be traced to a difference in one or both of the premises, and the communication problem may be explained by contrasting the syllogisms which explain the behavior of each individual.

Note the difference between explaining an instance of an actor's behavior, which requires a single syllogistic form, and explaining a conversation. Unless the communicators have achieved a high degree of coordination, explaining a conversation requires constructing a practical syllogism for each person and comparing them. The appropriate explanatory terms for uncoordinated conversations are those which describe the fit between the syllogisms, such as "One person was enacting Episode$_2$ B and the other Episode$_2$ C" or "Their understanding of the rules for Episode$_1$ D differed." Ultimately, it will be desirable to develop a set of terms describing different kinds of coordination problems and to determine which coordination strategies are most frequent and most effective in each.

Prediction and Control

In addition to description and explanation, potential for prediction and control are frequently cited as criteria for scientific theory. In fact, those in the positivist tradition sometimes argue that prediction and control are essential for a theory to be considered scientific (Kaplan, 1964; Rudner, 1966), and several audiences have criticized preliminary statements of this theory because of its supposed inability to predict or control. These criticisms may be responded to in two ways. The weaker reply—albeit a valid one—is that prediction and control are neither necessary nor sufficient conditions of a scientific theory (as Toulmin, 1961, has lucidly demonstrated). The stronger reply is that this theory does have the capacity to predict and confers at least some ability to control, but in a special way, consistent with its own assumptions.

A theory of rules-based social action is necessarily two steps removed from behavior. This type of theory will not predict behavior with any consistency because the actors' interpretive activities and choices intervene between the observer's theoretical postulates and the observable behaviors. However, the theory may well predict the way actors engage in interpretive activities and make choices.

The concept of a theory two steps removed from the actual exchanges of messages can be clarified by contrasting it with a one-level theory (see Bergmann, 1954). In the dream world of a naive positivist, there is no "slippage" between the world of things and the symbolic system which represents them. A necessary, consistent, one-to-one relationship between concepts and variables is structured by the alchemy of operational definitions and other magic potions. Prediction and control are possible, in part, because symbolic manipulations of concepts are considered isomorphic with operational manipulations of things.

The assumptions of isomorphism between observed and theoretic terms cannot be sustained when dealing with rule-governed human action. A given behavior may mean many things depending on how the actor construes its signification and significance (Morris, 1964), and quite different behaviors may be interpreted by the actor as functionally synonymous. But slippage occurs even in these actor-defined relations between events and their interpretation as the actors "manage" their meanings.

However, a theory of social action can develop predictive utility about the way persons construe their experience. Specifically, the theory of the coordinated management of meaning may develop propositions about communication situations in which coordination problems are likely, about persons who will be more or less able to coordinate their management of meanings with specific others, and about the effect of using particular coordination strategies.

Consistent with the principle of methodological pluralism, some of these propositions may invoke a causal explanatory model and some a rules-based model. For example, it may be argued that ongoing patterns of interpersonal relationships and communication are systemic in nature (Watzlawick et al., 1967). If so, the network of interrelationships necessitates that a given system-state precludes some alternatives and that a given input will have certain kinds of effects. This proposition (based on Pearce, 1976) is based on a systemic view of communication: the use of metacommunication as a negotiation strategy in the coordinated management of meaning inevitably leads to an alteration in the relationship between the communicators by introducing an irreversible increase in the level of their self-awareness. The explication of such propositions depends on an assumption of causality (or necessary interdependency) among the components of the communication system.

Other propositions assume a structure of meta-rules which describe rule-utilizing action. Consider the problem of sequencing a set of episodes during the course of an evening or a lifetime. One negotiation strategy is bargaining (called "ingratiation" in Pearce, 1976) according to a meta-rule of equity. The problem is solved by enacting a sequence of episodes such that every second one is preferred by each person. The selection of episodes is explained by stipulating that the persons wanted a continuing relationship; they each believed that they had to enact some episodes which "favored" the other person if the relationship was to succeed (because of the meta-rule of equity); therefore they acted as they did.

Propositions based on assumptions of necessary relations among components of a system confer ability to predict and control based on an understanding of the structure of the phenomena. Propositions based on an explication of meta-rules allow an observer to develop better than chance expectancies about what will happen by reconstructing at least part of the person's decision making procedure, but they do not permit confident predictions or the ability to control.

The difference between the two is best illustrated by the observer's response if the unexpected occurs. If a prediction based on causal or structural assumptions is wrong, this constitutes an anomaly and the observer must rethink the theory. If an expectation based on meta-rules is wrong, this may require a reworking of the theory or may indicate that the person is engaging in creative action—which cannot be predicted but might be understood.

The value of predictive and controlling ability is obvious, but there is also value in propositions based on meta-rules. For one, an analysis of meta-rules permits the theory to be extended to a level permitting symbolic manipulation and hypothesis development. Consider the hypothesis that interpersonal relationships in Western society are governed by two meta-rules, one which specifies an equitable distribution of values

(Brittan, 1973) and the other which legitimates a hierarchical order (H.D. Duncan, 1968). Assuming that these are rules which warrant inferences about particular behaviors in specific situations, various patterns of expected behavior can be hypothesized. Further, these hypotheses may be contrasted with those drawn from intellectually constructed societies based on other rules such as inequity (unabashed exploitation) and egalitarianism. This symbolic manipulation permits nonempirical construction of alternative societies and empirical tests of the goodness-of-fit between various constructions and the actual structure of interpersonal relationships.

CONCLUSION

The theory described in this report differs significantly from conventional orthodoxy because it is explicitly based on a set of assumptions unlike those of the still-dominant paradigm. One claim for the value of the theory rests on the judgment that its assumptions are better: they admit the diversity of human actions; they stress the importance of actors' meanings; and they structure teleological as well as causal explanatory models. A second claim for the value of the theory rests on its ability to integrate into one coherent framework many strands of social science without imposing a doctrine of conceptual or methodological monism. Rather than amalgamating the social sciences, it demonstrates the relations between them. Specifically, the methodology of studying rule-governed action requires an understanding of culturally sanctioned $Episodes_1$ and individual choice of $Episodes_2$ as well as the coordination strategies used in a particular conversation. A third claim for the value of the theory is that it is heuristic. The theory sensitizes an observer to aspects of communication which were not previously identified and poses questions not previously asked. The question remains, however, whether this perspective is more useful than others. Ultimately, this will be answered with data rather than by argument. Research presently being conducted is designed to test some of the implications of the theory.[11]

NOTES

1. Although interpersonal communication is not limited to dyads, my discussion will be, primarily for syntactical reasons.

2. . . . he said, somewhat nervously. (See Rossiter and Pearce, 1975:60.)

3. Full communication among scientists is certainly not the norm, as evidenced by the frustrating public exchange between Westley (1973) and Darnell (1971, 1973), neither of whom could understand or would grant even provisional legitimacy to the perspective of the other. And professional judgments are hardly uniform, as evidenced by the pointed exchange between critics and authors of the "Top Three" competitively selected papers in the Interpersonal and Small Group Division of SCA at its 1975 convention. At issue were disagreements about whether data are inevitably theory-laden, the function of concepts in research, and the most productive forms of research.

4. Harré and Secord (1973) are no exception. In my judgment, their attack on the old paradigm is brilliant and their discussion of ethogeny as a research program is provocative, but their work does not achieve the status of a viable alternative. This is due to at least three factors. First, the admitted (p. 9) overemphasis on self-directed behavior and the decision to use this as a prototype limits their ability to account for a variety of behavior and in particular masks the role of self-awareness in rule-following. Second, the discussion of episode is equivocal (Harré, 1974, and Toulmin, 1974, do better, but choose the wrong bases to make distinctions). Third, the discussion of methodology is admittedly incomplete (pp. 295–296) and unsatisfying. More disturbing, in a small lecture-discussion in November 1975, Secord was unwilling or unable to go beyond the suggestions in the book.

5. I hesitate to use the term "naturalistic" because of its vagueness. I do *not* mean field studies as opposed to lab studies, because location is not the criterion; nor do I mean a theoretic exploration, because there is no such thing as non-theory-laden observation. The proper reference for naturalistic inquiry is that which studies entities and variables defined by the actors in an attempt to account for their experience. Thus defined, naturalistic inquiry gains the advantage of forcing observers to respect the experience of the actors and draws on their tacit knowledge as a source of information.

6. Because of its reflexive nature, self-awareness is a difficult concept. Consider this schema:

meta meta awareness:	He was aware of being aware of being aware of hitting the ball.
meta awareness:	He was aware of being aware of hitting the ball.
awareness:	He was aware of hitting the ball.
direct action:	He hit the ball.

These propositions follow: (1) There is a possibility of an infinite regress (at least far enough to disrupt the ability to act). (2) A person can volitionally move to the next higher level of awareness, but cannot move to the next lower. The problem is like that of deciding to forget the number 9; one must remember what it is that he is trying to forget. (3) A person cannot choose to act at a particular level. That choice itself is at the next higher level. (4) All levels of awareness are potentially available to a person, but most behavior is somnambulant, in which higher levels are disattended to. The procedure by which this is accomplished is an important area of study. (5) The level of awareness at which a person acts makes an important difference in the meaning of the action. For example, a person may be proud to have hit the ball (direct action), ashamed of himself for being proud (awareness), proud of himself for feeling ashamed to be proud (meta awareness), and ashamed for feeling proud for feeling ashamed for feeling proud (meta meta awareness). Now ask him, "How do you feel about hitting the ball?"

7. The adaptation consists of substituting episodes for attitudes or beliefs as the object toward which the persons are simultaneously oriented while retaining the basic structure of the model. Although this introduces some difficult methodological problems, it brings the coorientation paradigm into line with the assumptions of the theory of the coordinated management of meaning.

8. . . . and if both are willing to abide by the contract. I have not included in this report a discussion of "fraudulent contracts" in which a person proposes a coenactment of a particular episode just so that he can "set up" and exploit the other (see Carson, 1969). This topic presents no insurmountable problems, but does create complications with levels of self-awareness.

9. Among other reasons, sanctions are not necessary conditions of episode enactment because (1) sanctions vary as a function of the importance/significance of the episode and (2) sanctions are applied when a negatively evaluated episode is enacted as well as when a person fails to enact a positively evaluated episode . . .

10. The fact that the person participates in the episode is sufficient to say that he "wishes" it to occur since he could refuse the enactment if he chose. To say that he did not really "want" to enact the episode or that it was the only alternative available to him is irrelevant for explanatory purposes since "wishes" carries the meaning of *purposeful intent* rather than *evaluation*.

11. I refuse to end this paper by saying that more research needs to be done, but it does, and I hope that others will find this theoretic framework useful for their own work.

REFERENCES

Albert, E.M. (1972). "Culture patterning of speech behavior in Burundi." Pp. 72–105 in J. Gumperz and D. Hymes (eds.), Directions in sociolinguistics. New York: Holt, Rinehart and Winston.

Bergmann, G. (1954). The metaphysics of logical positivism. New York: Longmans, Green.

Boulding, K. (1956). The image. Ann Arbor: University of Michigan Press.

Brittan, A. (1973). Meanings and situations. Boston: Routledge and Kegan Paul.

Bruner, J., Goodnow, J., and Austin, G. (1956). A study of thinking. New York: John Wiley.

Budd, R., and Ruben, B. (1972). Approaches to human communication. New York: Spartan.

Carson, R. (1969). Interaction concepts of personality. Chicago: Aldine.

Cicourel, A. (1974). Cognitive sociology. New York: Free Press.

Cushman, D., and Whiting, G. (1972). "An approach to communication theory: Toward consensus on rules." Journal of Communication, 22:217–238.

Darnell, D. (1971). "Toward a reconceptualization of communication." Journal of Communication, 21:5–16.

——— (1973). "To Bruce Westley, with love." Journal of Communication, 23:476–478.

Douglas, J. (1970). Understanding everyday life. Chicago: Aldine.

Duncan, H.D. (1968). Symbols and society. New York: Oxford University Press.

Duncan, S., Jr. (1972). "Some signals and rules for taking speaking turns in conversations." Journal of Personality and Social Psychology, 23:283–292.

Garfinkel, H. (1967). Studies in ethnomethodology. Englewood Cliffs, N.J.: Prentice-Hall.

Gottlieb, G. (1968). The logic of choice. New York: Macmillan.

Harre, R. (1974). "Some remarks on 'rule' as a scientific concept." In T. Mischel (ed.), Understanding other people. Oxford: Basil Blackwell.

Harre, R., and Secord, P. (1973). The explanation of social behavior. Totowa, N.J.: Littlefield, Adams.

Harris, L. (1975). "Construction and preliminary testing of a behavior continuum." Unpublished paper.

Hempel, C. (1966). Philosophy of natural science. Englewood Cliffs, N.J.: Prentice-Hall.

Kaplan, A. (1964). The conduct of inquiry. San Francisco: Chandler.

Kelly, G. (1955). The psychology of personal constructs. New York: Norton.

Koch, S. (1964). "Psychology and emerging conceptions of knowledge as unitary." Pp. 1–41 in T.W. Wann (ed.), Behaviorism and phenomenology. Chicago: University of Chicago Press.

Kuhn, T. (1970). The structure of scientific revolutions (2nd ed.). Chicago: University of Chicago Press.

McHugh, P. (1968). Defining the situation. Indianapolis: Bobbs-Merrill.

Mead, G.H. (1934). Mind, self and society. Chicago: University of Chicago Press.

Miller, G., Galanter, E., and Pribram, K. (1960). Plans and the structure of behavior. New York: Holt, Rinehart and Winston.

Morris, C. (1946). Signs, language and behavior. New York: George Braziller.

——— (1964). Signification and significance. Cambridge, Mass.: Massachusetts Institute of Technology Press.

Nofsinger, R., Jr. (1975). "The demand ticket: A conversational device for getting the floor." Speech Monographs, 42:1–9.

Pearce, W.B. (1973). "Consensual rules in interpersonal communications: A reply to Cushman and Whiting." Journal of Communication, 23:160–168.

——— (1976). An overview of communication and interpersonal relationships. Palo Alto, Calif.: Science Research Associates.

Pearce, W.B., and Stamm, K. (1973). "Coorientational states and interpersonal communication." Pp. 177–204 in P. Clarke (ed.), New models for communication research. Beverly Hills, Calif.: Sage.

Rossiter, C., and Pearce, W.B. (1975). Communicating personally. Indianapolis: Bobbs-Merrill.

Rudner, R. (1966). Philosophy of social science. Englewood Cliffs, N.J.: Prentice-Hall.

Sacks, H. (1967, 1972). "Mimeographed lecture notes." University of California, Berkeley.

Schegloff, E. (1968). "Sequencing in conversational openings." American Anthropologist, 70:1075–1095.

Toulmin, S. (1961). Foresight and understanding. Bloomington: Indiana University Press.

——— (1974). "Rules and their relevance for understanding human behavior." Pp. 185–215 in T. Mischel (ed.), Understanding other people. Oxford: Basil Blackwell.

Von Wright, G.H. (1971). Explanation and understanding. Ithaca, N.Y.: Cornell University Press.

Watzlawick, P., Beavin, J., and Jackson, D. (1967). Pragmatics of human communication. New York: Norton.

Westley, B. (1973). "Darnell reconceptualized." Journal of Communication, 23:187–194.

SOME EXPLORATIONS IN INITIAL INTERACTION AND BEYOND: TOWARD A DEVELOPMENTAL THEORY OF INTERPERSONAL COMMUNICATION

Charles R. Berger and Richard J. Calabrese

This paper provides a theoretical perspective for dealing with the initial entry stage of interpersonal interaction. The seven axioms and 21 theorems presented suggest a set of research priorities for studying the development of interpersonal relationships. The paper concludes with a discussion of some of the problems to be considered if the theory is to be extended beyond the initial stages of interaction.

When communication researchers have conducted empirical research on the interpersonal communication process, they have tended to employ social psychological theories as starting points. Theories relevant to such areas as person perception, social exchange, and interpersonal balance have frequently been employed as frameworks from which to derive testable hypotheses about the interpersonal communication process. While it is true that Newcomb's (1953) balance formulation and subsequent research on the acquaintance process (Newcomb, 1961) do include communication-relevant constructs, his theory does not focus on several important aspects of interpersonal communication. Obviously, Asch's (1946) work in the area of person perception and subsequent developments in that area (Kaplan & Anderson, 1973) are also relevant to the study of interpersonal communication. However, here too we find that these formulations do not directly focus upon the interpersonal communication process.

Source: The article is taken from *Human Communication Research* [1: 99–112, 1975]. (c) 1975 International Communication Association, 8140 Burnet Rd., Austin, TX 78766. Reprinted by permission of Sage Publications, Inc. and ICA.

The present model seeks to remedy this situation by employing communication-relevant constructs which, in turn, lead to the formation of hypotheses which directly involve communication behavior. In constructing the theory, we have elected to focus our attention on the initial phases of interaction between strangers. Our hope is that through subsequent research and theoretical extension, the model can be used to make predictions about and explain interpersonal communication phenomena which occur later in relationships. In our explication of the model, we have attempted to include previous research findings which lend support to our axioms and theorems.

DEVELOPMENTAL STAGES

Before we consider specific constructs and their relationships with each other, we feel it useful to provide some idea of the *possible stages* by which the communication transaction might be viewed. For purposes of the discussion, it is assumed that the persons involved in the communication transaction are strangers. We have labeled the first stage of the transaction the *entry phase*. One reason for the use of the term "entry" is that when strangers are faced with each other in a particular situation, their communication behaviors are, in part, determined by a set of communication rules or norms. Some rules are implicit; persons may not be able to verbalize them or indicate where they acquired them. Other rules are quite explicit and the individual might be able to indicate verbally what the rule is and where he acquired his knowledge of the rule. For example, two persons might both say "please" when asking someone to pass them something. One person might indicate that he said "please" because it "is the polite thing to do," while the other person might indicate that he said "please" because it is "natural" and not necessarily "polite." From this example it would seem that the first person is more *aware* of the "rule" which guided his behavior. Of course, it would also be possible for a person to be more or less certain about the appropriateness of a particular behavior. Some persons consistently have to concern themselves about the "appropriateness" of their behavior in particular situations, while others do not. These individual differences would suggest that the *learning* of rules and norms appropriate to situations, whether through direct instruction or social modeling, is not uniform for all individuals.

Findings to be discussed later indicate that during the entry phase, communication content is somewhat structured. For example, message content tends to be focused on demographic kinds of information. The amount of information asked for and given by the interactants tends to be symmetric. During the latter phases of the entry stage, persons begin to explore each other's attitudes and opinions. The kinds of attitude issues explored are of rather low consequence or low involvement. By the end of the entry phase, the interactants have a fairly confident estimate of whether or not they will develop their relationship toward a more intimate level.

The second phase of the communication transaction we have labeled the *personal phase*. This phase begins when the interactants engage in communication about central attitudinal issues, personal problems, and basic values. This phase could begin after a few minutes of interaction; however, in most informal communication situations, the personal phase does not appear until the individuals involved have interacted on repeated occasions. While there are almost always rules and norms which regulate communication behavior in most situations, when interactants have moved to the personal phase, communication is more spontaneous and less constrained by social desirability norms. During this phase, per-

sons may talk about socially undesirable aspects of their personalities and social relations. In the entry phase, such information is not usually sought or given.

The final phase of the transaction we have called the *exit phase*. During this phase decisions are made concerning the desirability of future interaction. Frequently, these decisions are discussed and plans for future interaction made. At a more macroscopic level of analysis, the exit phase of a relationship may occur over several interactions. Divorce is probably a good example. In most instances, it is probably the case that the final physical act of parting is preceded in time by a series of interactions and decisions which produce the final behavior. Knapp, Hart, Friedrich, and Shulman (1973) have begun to study the kinds of non-verbal behaviors which occur during the exit phase of a particular communication transaction. Their data suggest several behaviors which signal the end of a particular encounter.

By employing these descriptive categories we do not mean to imply that the phases are exhaustive or necessarily exclusive. Moreover, there are probably conditions under which the entry phase will be of relatively short duration and the interactants will move rapidly to the personal phase. Of course, it is also possible that because of certain information gained during the entry phase, the interaction will be terminated and the personal phase skipped entirely. All of these possibilities will be discussed in greater detail. By employing certain constructs, we feel that we can provide adequate explanations for these kinds of phenomena.

AXIOMS

Verbal Communication and Uncertainty

Central to the present theory is the assumption that when strangers meet, their primary concern is one of uncertainty reduction or increasing predictability about the behavior of both themselves and others in the interaction. This assumption is consistent with Heider's (1958) notion that man seeks to "make sense" out of events he perceives in his environment. By uncertainty we mean at least two things. First, at the very beginning of a particular encounter, there are a number of alternative ways in which each interactant *might behave*. Thus, one task for each interactant is to attempt to *predict* the most likely alternative actions the other person might take. Moreover, the individual interactant must then select from his own available response alternatives those which might be most appropriate to the predicted action of the other. However, before such response selection can occur, the individual must reduce his uncertainty about the other; that is, narrow the range of alternatives about the other's probable future behavior. He must attempt to develop predictions about the other *before* the other acts. In the first sense of uncertainty reduction, the individual is engaged in a *proactive* process of creating predictions.

The second sense of uncertainty concerns the problem of *retroactively* explaining the other's behavior. For example, a target person might say something or act in a particular way which induces the other interactant to ask himself or others, "I wonder what he meant by that?" In almost any situation, there are a number of plausible alternative attributions one might make for a particular communicative act. The problem here is for the individual to reduce the number of plausible alternative explanations for the other person's behavior. Thus, in our view, uncertainty involves both prediction and explanation components.

The view of uncertainty explicated above follows from Heider's (1958) seminal attribution work and is consistent with later attribution formulations. Jones, Kanouse, Kelley, Nisbett, Valins, and Weiner (1972), Kelley (1967), and Kelley (1973) generally take the view that we strive to make our own behavior and the behavior of others *predictable,* and we try to develop causal structures which provide *explanations* for our own behavior as well as the behavior of others. Within this framework, interpersonal communication behavior plays at least two different roles. First, we must attempt to develop

predictions about and explanations for our own and others' communication behavior; that is, communication behavior itself is something which we endeavor to predict and explain. Second, communication behavior is one vehicle through which such predictions and explanations are themselves formulated. Attribution theorists have been quick to point out that such predictions and explanations generally yield *imperfect knowledge* of ourselves and others. However, it is significant that such imperfect knowledge does *guide our total behavior toward others*. Thus, crucial to an understanding of a given individual's communication behavior is a knowledge of the kinds of predictions and explanations the individual has for the behavior of the person with whom he is interacting.

Such theorists as Adams (1965), Altman and Taylor (1973), Homans (1961), and Thibaut and Kelley (1959) have argued that reward/cost ratios determine whether or not an interaction will continue. Following from their position, one might argue that since uncertainty reduction is rewarding, the notion of rewards/costs is coterminous with the uncertainty construct. This analysis is somewhat faulty for the following reasons. While uncertainty may be rewarding up to a point, the ability to completely predict another's behavior might lead to boredom. Boredom in an interpersonal relationship might well be a cost rather than a reward. Moreover, since it is difficult to stipulate on an *a priori* basis just what is likely to be rewarding in a particular relationship, we feel that the reward/cost notion is of limited value in the construction of theory designed to predict rather than to retrodict interaction outcomes. Thus, we feel that uncertainty reduction is a more fruitful organizing construct than is reward/cost.

There are data which support the assertion that at the beginning of the entry phase uncertainty is relatively high and is subsequently reduced as a function of time. For example, Lalljee and Cook (1973) found that as interactions between strangers progressed, filled pause rate decreased while speech rate increased. Pause rate and speech rate were employed as two empirical indicators of uncertainty. In addition, it was found that a measure of anxiety, the non-ah speech disturbance ratio, did not decrease as the interaction progressed. This latter finding was interpreted as lowering the plausibility of the rival hypothesis that the decrease in pause rate was directly related to anxiety reduction.

The preceding discussion of the uncertainty construct and the empirical evidence provided by Lalljee and Cook (1973) suggests the following axiom:[1]

> **AXIOM 1:**   *Given the high level of uncertainty present at the onset of the entry phase, as the amount of verbal communication between strangers increases, the level of uncertainty for each interactant in the relationship will decrease. As uncertainty is further reduced, the amount of verbal communication will increase.*

This axiom posits a reciprocal causal relationship between the amount of verbal communication and the level of uncertainty reduction; i.e., reduction in uncertainty level feeds back to determine the amount of verbal communication. The previously cited Lalljee and Cook study *which allowed for two-way exchange* found that the number of words per minute uttered by interactants *increased* significantly over a nine minute period. However, a study by Berger and Larimer (1974) revealed that when *feedback was not allowed* between strangers, the number of words per minute uttered *decreased* significantly over a four minute period. In this study, subjects were led to believe that they were talking to a person in another room whose picture they possessed. Actually, the pictures had been previously scaled for physical attractiveness (high, moderate, or low). While no differential effects were found for the physical attractiveness variable, across all conditions there were significant decreases in verbal output over time. The present formulation would suggest that since the subjects did not receive any feedback from the targets, the subjects' levels of uncertainty about the targets remained at a high level. The persistent high level of uncertainty about the target persons reduced the amount of communication directed toward them.

The Communication Environment and Uncertainty

The basal level of uncertainty a person has about a stranger can be modulated by the communication situation itself. For example, the street of a large city provides an observer with relatively little information about the persons walking along it. By contrast, an observer at a political rally for a particular candidate may be able to infer, with a high probability of being correct, the political attitudes of those present at the rally. In situations where uncertainty levels are reduced by the situation itself, conversations are likely to begin by focusing on content areas related to the situation. Two persons meeting for the first time at a political rally might well open a conversation by discussing the particular candidate and expressing their views about him. In other circumstances, the same two persons might begin a conversation by focusing upon each other's backgrounds. Thus, we recognize that uncertainty level may be influenced by the communication situation itself.

Nonverbal Affiliative Expressiveness and Uncertainty

For the same reason that high uncertainty levels at the beginning of the encounter lower the amount of verbal communication during that period, uncertainty also acts to lower nonverbal expressions of affiliation. There are a number of empirical indicators of nonverbal affiliative behavior which have been shown to be positively correlated with each other. For example, in a factor analytic study of various verbal and nonverbal dimensions in an initial interaction situation, Mehrabian (1971a) found significant positive correlations between such variables as total statements per minute, percent duration of eye contact, head nods per minute, positive verbal content, head and arm gestures per minute, and pleasantness of vocal expressions. These and other variables loaded on a factor labeled *affiliative behavior*. A second study by Mehrabian and Ksionzky (1971) found much the same pattern of factor loadings for the same variables as those used in the Mehrabian study. It is interesting to note that in both of these factor analyses, distance between the interactants was not associated with the affiliative behavior factor.

In comparing the results of these two studies with the results of other prior research on the distance-liking relationship, Mehrabian (1971b) points out that several experimental studies have supported an inverse relationship between liking and physical distance; persons who like each other tend to stand closer to each other. Mehrabian explains this apparent inconsistency by arguing that in both the factor analytic studies cited above, the distance between the interactants was averaged over the duration of the interaction. Studies which show liking to be associated with smaller interaction distances usually use *initial* distance between interactants as the primary dependent variable.

The above discussion of the nature of the nonverbal affiliative expressiveness dimension and its relationship to level of uncertainty suggests the following axiom:

> **AXIOM 2:** *As nonverbal affiliative expressiveness increases, uncertainty levels will decrease in an initial interaction situation. In addition, decreases in uncertainty level will cause increases in nonverbal affiliative expressiveness.*

Uncertainty and Information Seeking

Given the relatively high level of uncertainty existing at the onset of the entry phase, one would expect persons in the situation to interrogate each other in order to gain information which might be instrumental in uncertainty reduction. Thus, one might expect interactants to engage in more question asking in the initial phases of the interaction. Moreover, the kinds of questions asked during the beginning of the entry phase might be ones which demand relatively short answers. For example, requests for such information as one's occupation, hometown, places of prior residence, and so on, generally call for relatively short responses. It seems that if an individual gives a relatively long response to such questions, he is generally judged somewhat negatively, especially when a detailed answer to the question was not explicitly called for. The predominance of short-answer questions during the early stages of the entry phase allows interactants to sample a number of different attributes in a relatively short time.

The preceding line of argument leads to the following axiom:

> **AXIOM 3:** *High levels of uncertainty cause increases in information seeking behavior. As uncertainty levels decline, information seeking behavior decreases.*

Data reported by Frankfurt (1965) support the relationship posited in Axiom 3. In this study, the number of questions asked to another in a simulated communication situation declined through time.

Uncertainty and Intimacy Level of Communication Content

We assume, as does Goffman (1959), that persons generally prefer to have smoothly running interpersonal relationships. Goffman argues that persons frequently assist each other in their performances so that each performer will maintain "face." Given this assumption and the relatively high level of uncertainty existing at the beginning of the entry phase, we might ask what is the least disruptive way of reducing uncertainty about the other? One strategy might be to ask the other how he feels about a variety of political and social issues. The problem with this strategy is that persons may disagree on such issues which, in turn, may lead to disruptions of their relationship. A better strategy would be to ask for and give biographical and demographic information during the entry phase. Dissimilarities along these dimensions probably have a relatively trivial negative impact on the interaction system. However, *similarities and dissimilarities in background characteristics might lead to the development of predictions of similarity or dissimilarity on more crucial attitudinal issues.* Thus, not only might uncertainty be reduced, predicted similarities or differences might also determine: (1) whether or not the interaction system will continue to exist and/or (2) whether or not the interactants will engage in a discussion of more intimate issues. For if two persons predict that they have widely differing beliefs on intimate and consequential issues and if they wish to have a smoothly running interaction, they will probably choose to avoid discussions of the issues of potential conflict.

The preceding discussion suggests the following axiom concerning the relationship between uncertainty and intimacy level.

AXIOM 4: *High levels of uncertainty in a relationship cause decreases in the intimacy level of communication content. Low levels of uncertainty produce high levels of intimacy.*

In their discussion of social penetration theory, Altman and Taylor (1973) argue that intimacy level of communication content tends to increase through time. However, their explanation of this phenomenon rests on the notion that as a relationship becomes more rewarding and less costly, persons will become more intimate. Our explanation of the same phenomenon is that as persons continue to communicate with each other, their uncertainty about each other decreases. Decreases in uncertainty lead to increases in intimacy level of communication.

Taylor and Altman (1966) had both college students and navy recruits sort 671 conversational topics along an intimacy continuum. Generally it was found that topics falling into such categories as biographical, hobbies and interests, and current events received low intimacy ratings, while topics falling into the categories of religion, sex, and personal attitudes received higher intimacy ratings. Taylor and Altman suggest that the statements scaled in their study can be used as guidelines for developing rating systems to score the intimacy level of communication content. Sermat and Smyth (1973) followed Taylor and Altman's recommendation and were able to obtain acceptable interjudge reliabilities of content intimacy in their study. However, Cozby (1973) has pointed out that the kinds of topics

which Taylor and Altman scaled for intimacy value may be quite different from the kinds of communication content actually passed during an interaction. For example, according to the Taylor and Altman scaling study, talking about movies is a relatively low intimacy communication topic. However, there is probably a great deal of difference in perceived intimacy between a conversation in which the interactants talk about the movie "Mary Poppins" and one in which they exchange their views on "Deep Throat." Thus, although the Taylor and Altman study may provide us with rather general guidelines about the intimacy level of communication content, more specific kinds of content within general topic areas must be assessed for intimacy value.

A study by Berger (1973) revealed that during the course of interaction between strangers, the amount of demographic (low intimacy) information asked for and given was highest during the first minute of interaction. After the first minute, statistically significant decreases in the amount of demographic information exchanged were observed; while the amounts of information asked for and given in such more intimate categories as "attitudes and opinions" and "other persons" increased. Studies by Cozby (1972), Ehrlich and Graeven (1971), Sermat and Smyth (1973), Taylor, Altman, and Sorrentino (1969), and Taylor, Altman, and Wheeler (1973) also support the development of intimacy through time.

These outcomes are in agreement with the observations of Altman and Taylor (1973) who suggest that the early stages of the development of a relationship are characterized by exchanges of "superficial" information. While we agree that most observers would tend to judge a conversation consisting of exchanges of biographical information "superficial," we feel that the kinds of information asked for and given during the initial phases of the entry stage are crucial for the development of inferences about the persons rendering the information.

As Jones and Goethals (1972) have pointed out, primacy effects are more the rule than the exception in person perception research. There are conditions under which recency effects will obtain, but because of the prevalence of primacy effects, we are forced to conclude that information exchanged early in the interaction has functional significance for the actors involved. Knowing that a given individual is a college professor may well help to reduce uncertainty about his political and social attitudes. Obviously, many of the inferences drawn may be inaccurate. Nevertheless, persons do encode messages on the basis of such "imperfect knowledge."

Uncertainty and Reciprocity Rate

The notion that a reciprocity norm acts to control information exchange in an interaction has been advanced by Gouldner (1960). Research in the area of interviewer-interviewee speech behavior suggests that interviewees tend to match variations in the rate of interviewer speech behavior (Matarazzo, Wiens & Saslow, 1965). Furthermore, evidence supporting the proposition that the amount of information exchanged in an interaction tends to be reciprocal has been reported by Worthy, Gary, and Kahn (1969). While these studies support the existence of a reciprocity norm in interaction, the underlying explanation for the phenomenon is not clear.

In view of the present formulation and the previous argument that persons prefer smoothly running interactions to ones in which there is great stress (Goffman, 1959), it seems reasonable to assume that the easiest way in which to reduce mutual uncertainty would be to ask for and give the same kinds of information at the same rate of exchange. In this way, no one interactant in the system would be able to gain *information power* over the other. Moreover, it also seems reasonable to assume that as uncertainty is reduced, there is less need for symmetric exchanges of information at a rapid rate. That is, it becomes more possible for greater time lags to occur between speaking and listening. Once uncertainty is at relatively low levels, one person might be able to talk to another for long periods of time without fear of being accused of "dominating the conversation." However, if a given individual plays the speaker for long periods of time during the entry phase, he would most probably be accused

of dominating the conversation and the probability that the interaction would continue would be reduced. Thus, when uncertainty is high, reciprocity rate will also be high. As uncertainty is reduced, reciprocity rate decreases. Formally stated:

AXIOM 5: *High levels of uncertainty produce high rates of reciprocity. Low levels of uncertainty produce low reciprocity rates.*

Altman and Taylor (1973) have argued that the reciprocity construct is of limited value in the development of a theory of interaction development since there has been little in the way of *explanation* provided for the reciprocity phenomenon; i.e., merely asserting that a particular norm exists does not ipso facto explain its existence. However, we feel that the requirement for even uncertainty reduction in order to avoid asymmetries in information power distribution provides an explanation for the reciprocity norm's appearance during initial interaction.

Jourard (1960) found evidence suggestive of a "dyadic effect" concerning the intimacy level of self-disclosure. In this study he found that persons who disclosed more to others reported that they also received high amounts of disclosure from others. Subsequent experimental evidence (Worthy, Gary & Kahn, 1969; Ehrlich and Greaven, 1971; Cozby, 1972; Sermat & Smyth, 1973) suggests that when an individual discloses intimate information to another, the other tends to reciprocate at that level of intimacy. Moreover, Sermat and Smyth (1973) found that when a confederate continued to demand higher levels of disclosure through the questions he asked the subject, while at the same time refusing to disclose intimate information about himself, the subject tended to lower his level of liking for the confederate. However, when the confederate matched the subject's level of disclosure and then demanded disclosure at a higher intimacy level, the subject was more willing to meet the confederate's disclosure request. These studies together with Axiom 5 suggest that early in a relationship it is crucial for the interactants to convey information evenly and at a fairly rapid rate and to disclose information which is at about the same intimacy level. Violations of one or more of these rules raise the probability of dissolution of the relationship.

Similarity and Uncertainty

Most social psychological theories concerned with friendship formation have employed the notion of *similarity* of some sort as an antecedent of liking. Byrne (1971), Duck (1973), Homans (1961), Newcomb (1953), and Newcomb (1961) have argued that similarities along such dimensions as attitudes and conceptual structure produce interpersonal attraction, while dissimilarity produces negative interpersonal affect. Byrne employs a reinforcement framework to explain the similarity-attraction relationship. He argues that attitude agreements are rewarding and that such rewards lead to liking. By contrast, balance theorists (Heider, 1958) explain the similarity-liking relationship by arguing that shared affect toward an object will result in pressures toward liking. Recently, Duck (1973) has developed a "filter hypothesis" which asserts that different kinds of similarity are important for liking at different phases of the relationship. He suggests that at the early stages of a relationship, similarity of attitudes tends to be a strong determinant of liking; however, as the relationship progresses, *conceptual similarity* along both content and structural dimensions becomes the significant determinant of attraction. Duck employs Kelly's (1955) theory of personal constructs as a conceptual basis for his predictions. He reports several studies, employing a modified version of the Role Rep Test, which show that friends do have significantly higher levels of conceptual similarity than randomly formed dyads.

There is an impressive amount of evidence (Berscheid & Walster, 1969; Byrne, 1971) to demonstrate a positive relationship between attitude similarity and interpersonal attraction. Moreover, Duck's (1973) research supports a positive relationship between similarity of conceptual structure and friendship formation. In our view, both types of similarity act to reduce the level of uncertainty in a relationship; i.e., similarity of attitudes and conceptual structure produces decreases in uncertainty, while dissimilarities along attitude and conceptual dimensions raise uncertainty levels. Why do disagreements along attitude dimensions tend to raise uncertainty? After all, if a person holds an opinion opposed to mine, does that not reduce my uncertainty about him?

In order to answer the above question, we must consider the influence of affect direction on the number of alternative attributions generated about a person. Koenig (1971) has argued that when we dislike another person, social norms demand that we provide explanations for our dislike. When we like someone, however, we do not have to provide explanations for our liking. This phenomenon Koenig has labeled "justification"; i.e., we must justify our negative affect toward others. Koenig presents data which lend support to his justification hypothesis. Moreover, in research currently being conducted by Berger, a tendency has been found for persons to make more causal attributions for a disagreement between two persons than when the two persons show agreement. In these studies, subjects are presented with alleged conversations in which persons show either attitude agreement or attitude disagreement. Some studies have involved tape recorded conversations while others have used transcriptions of conversations. After the subjects read through or listen to the conversations, they are asked to list as many reasons (attributions) as they can for the agreement or disagreement shown by the persons in the conversation. Data from one of the studies indicate that subjects who were presented with a conversation in which disagreement occurred make more attributions than do subjects who are presented with agreeable conversations. These data suggest that as dissimilarity between persons increases, uncertainty in terms of number of alternative explanations for behavior also increases. Similarity reduces the necessity for the generation of a large number of alternatives for explaining behavior. The preceding line of argument suggests the following axiom:

AXIOM 6: *Similarities between persons reduce uncertainty, while dissimilarities produce increases in uncertainty.*

Uncertainty and Liking

As we noted in the previous section, a number of social psychologists have adduced evidence supportive of a positive relationship between similarity and liking. Furthermore, two main theoretical positions have been employed to explain this relationship: (1) reinforcement theory and (2) cognitive consistency theories. Earlier in this paper we suggested some inadequacies of the reinforcement approach to the study of interaction development. We have also argued that similarity-dissimilarity is connected to uncertainty level. By making such a connection, we are subsuming the notion of similarity-dissimilarity and the related notions of balance under the broader conceptual umbrella of uncertainty. This formulation is consistent with the suggestion made by Berkowitz (1969) that "the striving for cognitive balance may actually only be a special case of a desire for certainty" (p. 96).

When persons are unable to make sense out of their environment, they usually become anxious. Moreover, Festinger (1954) has suggested that persons seek out similar others who are proximate when they experience a high level of uncertainty regarding the appropriateness of their behavior and/or opinions in a particular situation. Schachter's (1959) research on anxiety and affiliation tends to confirm this social comparison theory prediction for first born children. In view of the tendency to seek out similar others in order to reduce uncertainty, reduction of uncertainty by such means should tend to produce liking. This line of reasoning leads to the following axiom regarding the relationship between uncertainty and liking:

> **AXIOM 7:** *Increases in uncertainty level produce decreases in liking; decreases in uncertainty level produce increases in liking.*

Taken together, Axioms 6 and 7 suggest that uncertainty level mediates between similarity and liking. It should be clear, however, that variables other than similarity-dissimilarity influence uncertainty level. Thus, an observed relationship between uncertainty level and liking may be due to similarity and/or the amount of communication that two persons have had with each other.

THEOREMS

From the preceding seven axioms, it is possible to deduce the following 21 theorems. Existing evidence relevant to the relationship posited by the theorem will be cited.

> **THEOREM 1:** *Amount of verbal communication and nonverbal affiliative expressiveness are positively related.*

The relationship suggested by Theorem 1 has been verified in at least two factor analytic studies (Mehrabian, 1971a; Mehrabian & Ksionzky, 1971). In both studies such variables as total number of statements per minute and number of declarative statements per minute were found to correlate positively and significantly with such indices of nonverbal behavior as percent duration of eye contact, head nods per minute, hand and arm gestures per minute, and pleasantness of vocal expressions. The observed correlations among these empirical indicators of the amount of verbal communication and the amount of nonverbal affiliative expressiveness lend support to Theorem 1.

> **THEOREM 2:** *Amount of communication and intimacy level of communication are positively related.*

While no study has directly related these two variables, the Lalljee and Cook (1973) finding that as an interaction progresses the number of words uttered per unit of time increases and the finding that intimacy levels of communication content increase with passage of time would suggest the relationship posited by Theorem 2.

> **THEOREM 3:** *Amount of communication and information seeking behavior are inversely related.*

Indirect support for Theorem 3 can be derived from the Lalljee and Cook (1973) and the Frankfurt (1965) studies. As we noted above, Lalljee and Cook found significant increases in speech rate over a nine minute initial interaction period. Frankfurt reported data which supported the proposition that as an interaction progresses, the number of questions asked decreases. Taken together, these findings would suggest an inverse relationship between the amount of communication and the amount of information seeking behavior.

THEOREM 4: *Amount of communication and reciprocity rate are inversely related.*

While there are no data bearing directly upon the veracity of Theorem 4, the suggestions that as the relationship continues the amount of communication will increase and that greater time lags in reciprocity will be tolerated as the relationship continues both lend support to Theorem 4. However, the notion that reciprocity rate will decrease through time is one which needs to be verified empirically.

THEOREM 5: *Amount of communication and liking are positively related.*

Empirical support for the above proposition has been obtained by Lott and Lott (1961) and Moran (1966). In both of these studies it was found that persons who expressed liking for each other communicated more than persons who were strangers or persons who did not work together well. In his discussion of group cohesiveness and quantity of interaction, Shaw (1971) concludes that cohesiveness and amount of verbal interaction are positively related.

THEOREM 6: *Amount of communication and similarity are positively related.*

Data supportive of Theorem 6 have been presented by Schachter (1959). Following from Festinger's (1954) social comparison theory, Schachter found that persons preferred to affiliate with similar others. While Theorem 6 would seem to hold for initial interaction situations, there is some evidence that under certain conditions, dissimilarities between persons will produce increases in the amount of communication. Schachter (1951) found that the amount of communication directed toward a deviant in a group tended to increase through time. In highly cohesive groups to which the group task was highly relevant, the amount of communication directed toward the deviant tended to increase at first then to decrease. The discrepancy between these findings and the social comparison theory findings

seems to involve the nature of the interaction situation. Schachter's (1951) deviation-rejection study involved a *group* of persons interacting for the purpose of producing solutions to a problem; i.e., the group was explicitly *task oriented*. By contrast, the findings related to social comparison theory seem to be more relevant to situations in which the "task" confronting the *individual* is one of establishing the appropriateness of his opinions and behavior. For purposes of the formulation, the relationship between amount of communication and similarity suggested by the data relevant to social comparison theory would seem to be most appropriate, since the present theory deals with initial interaction situations between strangers.

THEOREM 7: *Nonverbal affiliative expressiveness and intimacy level of communication content are positively related.*

THEOREM 8: *Nonverbal affiliative expressiveness and information seeking are inversely related.*

THEOREM 9: *Nonverbal affiliative expressiveness and reciprocity rate are inversely related.*

There is little, if any, direct or indirect empirical evidence bearing upon the above three theorems. Studies involving intimacy level of communication content, information seeking, and reciprocity rate have not related these variables to nonverbal indices of affiliative behavior. Thus, research is needed to determine whether empirical hypotheses derived from the above three theorems hold.

THEOREM 10: *Nonverbal affiliative expressiveness and liking are positively related.*

The previously cited Mehrabian factor analytic studies as well as the research in the area of visual interaction summarized by Exline (1971) tend to support the above theorem. Persons who are attracted to each other have higher levels of eye contact, greater numbers of head nods and hand gestures per unit of time, and more frequent displays of pleasant facial expressions than persons who dislike each other.

THEOREM 11:   *Nonverbal affiliative expressiveness and similarity are positively related.*

We know of no studies which provide direct support for Theorem 11, although it seems reasonable to assume that since liking and nonverbal affiliative expressiveness have been found to be positively related, similarity and nonverbal affiliative expressiveness should also be found to be positively related.

THEOREM 12:   *Intimacy level of communication content and information seeking are inversely related.*

THEOREM 13:   *Intimacy level of communication content and reciprocity rate are inversely related.*

There are no data which provide direct support for these two theorems. Altman and Taylor's (1973) social penetration theory and research suggest, however, that intimacy levels of communication increase through time, while information seeking attempts decrease. These tendencies lend some support to Theorem 12.

THEOREM 14:   *Intimacy level of communication content and liking are positively related.*

One implication of Theorem 14 is that persons tend to disclose intimacy information to persons they like and withhold intimate information from persons whom they do not like. In a review of self-disclosure literature relevant to this issue, Pearce and Sharp (1973) concluded that self-disclosure generally occurs within the context of positive relationships. However, these authors caution that there is some contradictory evidence which suggests that the relationship between disclosure and liking is probably a complex one.

THEOREM 15:   *Intimacy level of communication content and similarity are positively related.*

THEOREM 16:   *Information seeking and reciprocity rate are positively related.*

THEOREM 17:   *Information seeking and liking are negatively related.*

THEOREM 18:   *Information seeking and similarity are negatively related.*

There is no evidence that bears directly upon the above four theorems. However, since Theorems 17 and 18 appear to be non-commensensical predictions, further comment is in order. First, Theorem 17 suggests that as liking increases in a relationship, the amount of information seeking behavior will decrease. One operational indicator of information seeking suggested earlier was the number of questions asked per unit of time. It would seem reasonable to suggest that as a relationship develops through time, there is less need for questions to be asked. Frankfurt's (1965) findings support his suggestion. As the relationship develops, persons are more willing to proffer information about themselves without specifically being asked for it. Thus, if positive affect does develop in a relationship through the reduction of uncertainty then the necessity for extensive interrogation would also tend to decrease, thus producing a negative relationship between information seeking and liking. In the case of Theorem 18, we have suggested that similarity tends to reduce uncertainty and that reductions of uncertainty obviate the necessity for extensive verbal interrogation. Thus, we would expect to find that similarity and information seeking are negatively related.

THEOREM 19:   *Reciprocity rate and liking are negatively related.*

THEOREM 20:   *Reciprocity rate and similarity are negatively related.*

THEOREM 21:   *Similarity and liking are positively related.*

While there appears to be little evidence bearing on Theorems 19 and 20, there is an incredible amount of support for the similarity-attraction relationship. Byrne's (1971) research relevant to the attraction paradigm not only demonstrates that attitude similarity produces attraction, Byrne, Clore, and Worchel (1966) found that persons are more attracted to others who are perceived to be from economic backgrounds similar to their own. In addition, Duck (1973) has found that *conceptual similarity* is positively related to friendship formation. It should be kept in mind, however, that the present theory explains the above empirical findings by employing the uncertainty construct as a mediating variable. This implies that if the effects of uncertainty were statistically removed from the similarity-attraction relationship, the similarity-attraction relationship would weaken significantly.

BEYOND INITIAL INTERACTION

For the present time, we have elected to confine our theory to the initial stages of interaction between strangers. Obviously, a full blown theory of interaction development would have to stipulate broader boundary conditions than the present one. We feel that one critical construct which might be part of such an extension is *frequency of contact.* The reason for our view is simply that in all probability, persons who do not have frequent contact with each other become uncertain about each other; i.e., as the time between contacts increases, persons' opinions, beliefs, and behaviors can change due to the influence of other persons and events. When two persons face each other after a long period of separation, they may have to go through a certain amount of biographic-demographic scanning behavior in order to "update" their "knowledge" of each other. Thus, because of the possible strong link between contact frequency and uncertainty level, an extension of the present formulation would have to take into account this relationship.

In a broader social perspective, Toffler (1970) has suggested that the rate of social change in the United States is increasing. One ingredient in the accelerated rate of change is the high level of mobility experienced by both individuals and families. If the rate of social change is indeed increasing and persons are becoming more mobile, then the necessity for going through the process explicated by the present model increases. Persons who experience frequent moves and the necessity of making new friends must go through the uncertainty reduction process more frequently than less mobile persons. The crucial

social question is whether there is an upper limit of uncertainty that the individual can tolerate. If there is, then it would seem imperative that techniques be developed to help highly mobile persons form stable relationships with others as quickly as possible. For example, perhaps information about new neighbors could be provided to a family about to move into a new neighborhood. Advanced information about neighbors might aid the new family in their adaptation to the new environment. While this process may seem "artificial" and not very "spontaneous," it could help the highly mobile family anchor themselves more quickly in their new environment.

We believe that the present formulation serves to bring together a diverse body of findings as well as to generate predictions for future research. Some of the theorems generated by the model have already received strong empirical support while others have not been subjected to direct test. Obviously, there are other relevant constructs which might be explicitly incorporated into the model. Some of these constructs will no doubt be derived from the failure of the present model to predict particular relationships. Thus, our view is that the present formulation is a first effort. Hopefully, subsequent research and reformulation will result in a more general theory of the developmental aspects of interpersonal communication.

NOTES

1. The procedure for explicating the axioms and theorems of the present theory is taken from Blalock (1969). Blalock suggests that assumed causal relationships be stated as axioms and statements of covariation stated as theorems.

REFERENCES

Adams, J. S. Inequity in social exchange. In L. Berkowitz (Ed.), *Advances in experimental social psychology,* Vol. 2. New York: Academic Press, 1965, 267–299.

Altman, I., & Taylor, D. A. *Social penetration: The development of interpersonal relationships.* New York: Holt, Rinehart and Winston, 1973.

Asch, S. E. Forming impressions of personality. *Journal of Abnormal and Social Psychology,* 1946, 41, 258–290.

Berger, C. R. The acquaintance process revisited: Explorations in initial interaction. Paper presented at the annual convention of the Speech Communication Association, New York, November, 1973.

Berger, C. R., & Larimer, M. W. When beauty is only skin deep: The effects of physical attractiveness, sex and time on initial interaction. Paper presented at the annual convention of the International Communication Association, New Orleans, April, 1974.

Berkowitz, L. Social motivation. In G. Lindzey and E. Aronson (Eds.), *The handbook of social psychology,* Vol. 3. Reading, Mass: Addison-Wesley, 1969, 50–135.

Berscheid, E., & Walster, E. H. *Interpersonal attraction.* Reading, Mass: Addison-Wesley, 1969.

Blalock, H. M. *Theory construction: From verbal to mathematical formulations.* Englewood Cliffs, N.J.: Prentice-Hall, 1969.

Byrne, D. *The attraction paradigm.* New York: Academic Press, 1971.

Byrne, D., Clore, G. L., & Worchel, P. The effect of economic similarity-dissimilarity on interpersonal attraction. *Journal of Personality and Social Psychology,* 1966, 4, 220–224.

Cozby, P. C. Self-disclosure, reciprocity and liking. *Sociometry,* 1972, 35, 151–160.

Cozby, P. C. Self-disclosure: A literature review. *Psychological Bulletin,* 1973, 79, 73–89.

Duck, S. W. *Personal relationships and personal constructs: A study of friendship formation.* New York: Wiley, 1973.

Ehrlich, H. J., & Graeven, D. B. Reciprocal self-disclosure in a dyad. *Journal of Experimental Social Psychology,* 1971, 7, 389–400.

Exline, R. V. Visual interaction: The glances of power and preference. In J. K. Cole (Ed.), *Nebraska symposium on motivation.* Lincoln: University of Nebraska Press, 1971, 163–206.

Festinger, L. A theory of social comparison processes. *Human Relations,* 1954, 7, 117–140.

Frankfurt, L. P. The role of some individual and interpersonal factors on the acquaintance process. Unpublished doctoral dissertation, The American University, 1965.

Goffman, E. *The presentation of self in everyday life.* New York: Doubleday Press, 1959.

Gouldner, A. W. The norm of reciprocity: A preliminary statement. *American Sociological Review,* 1960, 25, 161–178.

Heider, F. *The psychology of interpersonal relations.* New York: Wiley, 1958.

Homans, G. C. *Social behavior: Its elementary forms.* New York: Harcourt, Brace and World, Inc., 1961.

Jones, E. E., & Goethals, G. R. Order effects in impression formation: Attribution context and the nature of the entity. In E. E. Jones, D. E. Kanouse, H. H. Kelley, R. E. Nesbitt, S. Valins, and B. Weiner, *Attribution: Perceiving the causes of behavior.* Morristown: General Learning Press, 1972.

Jones, E. E., Kanouse, D. E., Kelley, H. H., Nisbett, R. E., Valins, S., & Weiner, B. *Attribution: Perceiving the causes of behavior.* Morristown: General Learning Press, 1972.

Jourard, S. Knowing, liking, and the "dyadic effect" in men's self-disclosure. *Merrill Palmer Quarterly of Behavior and Development,* 1960, 6, 178–186.

Kaplan, M. F., & Anderson, N. H. Information integration theory and reinforcement theory as approaches to interpersonal attraction. *Journal of Personality and Social Psychology,* 1973, 28, 301–312.

Kelley, H. H. Attribution theory in social psychology. In D. Levine (Ed.), *Nebraska symposium on motivation.* Lincoln: University of Nebraska Press, 1967, 192–240.

Kelley, H. H. The processes of causal attribution. *American Psychologist,* 1973, 28, 107–128.

Kelly, G. A. *The psychology of personal constructs.* New York: Norton, 1955.

Knapp, M. L., Hart, R. P., Friedrich, G. W., & Shulman, G. M. The rhetoric of goodbye: Verbal and nonverbal correlates of human leave taking. *Speech Monographs,* 1973, 40, 182–198.

Koenig, F. Positive affective stimulus value and accuracy of role perception. *British Journal of Social and Clinical Psychology,* 1971, 10, 385–386.

Lalljee, M., & Cook, M. Uncertainty in first encounters. *Journal of Personality and Social Psychology,* 1973, 26, 137–141.

Lott, A. J., & Lott, B. E. Group cohesiveness, communication level, and conformity. *Journal of Abnormal and Social Psychology,* 1961, 62, 408–412.

Matarazzo, J. D., Wiens, A. N., & Saslow, G. Studies of interview speech behavior. In L. Krasner and L. P. Ullman (Eds.), *Research in behavior modification: New developments and implications.* New York: Holt, Rinehart and Winston, 1965, 179–210.

Mehrabian, A. Verbal and nonverbal interaction of strangers in a waiting situation. *Journal of Experimental Research in Personality,* 1971, 5, 127–138. (a)

Mehrabian, A. Nonverbal communication. In J.K. Cole (Ed.), *Nebraska symposium on motivation.* Lincoln: University of Nebraska Press, 1971. (b)

Mehrabian, A., & Ksionzky, S. Factors of interpersonal behavior and judgment in social groups. *Psychological Reports,* 1971, 28, 483–492.

Moran, G. Dyadic interaction and orientational consensus. *Journal of Personality and Social Psychology,* 1966, 4, 94–99.

Newcomb, T. An approach to the study of communicative acts. *Psychological Review,* 1953, 60, 393–404.

Newcomb, T. *The acquaintance process.* New York: Holt, Rinehart and Winston, 1961.

Pearce, W. B., & Sharp, S. M. Self-disclosing communication. *Journal of Communication,* 1973, 23, 409–425.

Sermat, V., & Smyth, M. Content analysis of verbal communication in the development of a relationship: Conditions influencing self-disclosure. *Journal of Personality and Social Psychology,* 1973, 26, 332–346.

Schachter, S. Deviation, rejection, and communication. *Journal of Abnormal and Social Psychology,* 1951, 46, 190–207.

Schachter, S. *The psychology of affiliation: Experimental studies of the sources of gregariousness.* Stanford: Stanford University Press, 1959.

Shaw, M. E. *Group dynamics: The psychology of small group behavior.* New York: McGraw-Hill, 1971.

Taylor, D. A., & Altman, I. Intimacy-scaled stimuli for use in studies of interpersonal relationships. Bethesda: Naval Medical Research Institute, 1966, Tech. Report No. 9, MF022. 01.03–1002.

Taylor, D. A, Altman, I., & Sorrentino, R. Interpersonal exchange as a function of rewards and costs and situational factors: Expectancy confirmation-disconfirmation. *Journal of Experimental Social Psychology,* 1969, 5, 324–339.

Taylor, D. A., Altman, I., & Wheeler, L. Self-disclosure in isolated groups. *Journal of Personality and Social Psychology,* 1973, 26, 39–47.

Thibaut, J. W., & Kelley, H. H. *The social psychology of groups.* New York: Wiley, 1959.

Toffler, A. *Future shock.* New York: Random House, 1970.

Worthy, M., Gary, A. L., & Kahn, G. M. Self-disclosure as an exchange process. *Journal of Personality and Social Psychology,* 1969, 13, 59–64.

PREDICTED OUTCOME VALUE DURING INITIAL INTERACTIONS: A REFORMULATION OF UNCERTAINTY REDUCTION THEORY

Michael Sunnafrank

This article presents an expansion and reformulation of uncertainty reduction theory. Past research indicates that support for the basic axioms of the uncertainty perspective is weak, especially with regard to initial interaction processes. It is suggested that uncertainty reduction is not the primary concern of individuals during this entry phase, as previously posited. Rather, uncertainty reduction is cast as subordinate to the more central concern of increasing positive relational outcomes. During initial interactions, uncertainty reduction is expected to enhance individuals' perceived ability to forecast future relational outcomes. Important initial interaction behaviors and decisions are presumed to follow from the values these forecasted outcomes take. Several major revisions of uncertainty axioms and theorems are generated.

Several theoretical perspectives on human behavior in general and communicative behavior in particular assume that individuals attempt to increase predictability or reduce uncertainty about their relationships with others (Heider, 1958; Kelly, 1973; Miller & Steinberg, 1975). Uncertainty reduction theory (Berger, 1979; Berger & Bradac, 1982; Berger & Calabrese, 1975), the most formally articulated theoretical treatment of this position in communication, proposes that a key element in relational development is individuals' uncertainty level concerning knowledge and understanding of selves and others. The original uncertainty perspective (Berger & Calabrese, 1975) focused exclusively on potential influences of uncertainty and uncertainty reduction during beginning acquaintance. More recent revisions attempt to extend the theory to include later relational stages, as well as adding new variables and propositions (Berger, 1979; Berger & Bradac, 1982; Gudykunst, Yang, & Nishida, 1985; Parks & Adelman, 1983).

Source: The article is taken from *Human Communication Research* [13. 3–33, 1986]. 1986 International Communication Association, 8140 Burnet Rd., Austin, TX 78766. Reprinted by permission of Sage Publications, Inc. and ICA.

This perspective generates a unifying explanation for previously diverse research findings. Although this ability to explain past results is a desirable characteristic, the crucial test of uncertainty reduction theory is the predictive accuracy of its unique proposals. Novel propositions and implications from this perspective have generated a substantial amount of research on the antecedents and consequents of uncertainty. However, research results have provided only mixed support for the theory. Some of this research examines aspects of uncertainty reduction theory in a manner that does not entail direct tests of its basic axioms and theorems and, therefore, produces only implicit support for these propositions (Berger & Douglas, 1981; Berger & Perkins, 1978; Sherblom & Van Rheenan, 1984). Works that do involve relatively direct tests of theoretic relationships normally provide only partial and weak support (Clatterbuck, 1979; Gudykunst & Nishida, 1984; Gudykunst, Yang, & Nishida, 1985).

Mixed support justifies neither a complete acceptance nor rejection of uncertainty reduction theory. Rather, findings indicate that both more critical tests and theoretical modifications may be in order. This article proposes one such modification in an effort to increase the uncertainty perspective's explanatory and predictive utility. This change involves altering the theory to reflect a potentially important relationship between uncertainty about another and individuals' perceptions of future relational rewards and costs to be obtained with the other. Recent revisions of Berger and Calabrese's (1975) perspective acknowledge that a relationship between uncertainty and the perceived outcome value of relations with others may exist, but give it only a minor role in the theory. Both Berger (1979) and Berger and Bradac (1982) propose that incentives provided by rewards and costs controlled by another may trigger or increase individuals' attempts to reduce uncertainty, while leaving the original theoretical propositions intact.

The present proposal accords individuals' perceptions of future relational reward and cost outcomes a more encompassing role. Several perspectives assume that individuals make predictions to increase the potential for achieving positive relational outcomes (Altman, 1974; Lott & Lott, 1974; Miller & Steinberg, 1975). Within these perspectives uncertainty reduction would not be the primary concern of individuals, but only a means to achieving the more central goal of maximizing outcomes. The major focus of this article involves incorporating individuals' perceptions of these relational outcomes into the uncertainty framework. Prior to examining this position, it is necessary to review previous uncertainty formulations and research results.

UNCERTAINTY REDUCTION THEORY

Berger and Calabrese (1975) propose seven axioms detailing the relationship of uncertainty level to amount of verbal communication, nonverbal affiliative expressiveness, information seeking, intimacy level of communicative content, reciprocity rate, similarity, and liking. Also specified are 21 theorems concerning the interrelation of these variables through uncertainty. Consistent with various attribution perspectives (Heider, 1958; Jones & Davis, 1965; Kelley, 1973), Berger and Calabrese propose that uncertainty regards both prediction of future behaviors and explanation of present and past behaviors. Prediction involves a proactive process of determining the most likely future relational behavior of partners, and selecting appropriate self-behavior given this prediction. Explanation involves a retroactive process of determining the perceived causes of the observed behaviors of self and others.

Berger (1979) and Berger and Bradac (1982) propose a further distinction between two types of uncertainty: cognitive and behavioral. Cognitive uncertainty encompasses uncertainty that individuals have about their own and relational others' beliefs and attitudes. Behavioral uncertainty refers to predictability of behavior in particular circumstances. These two types of uncertainty may often be highly related, especially when behavioral predictions are rooted in perceived knowledge of the relating individuals' cognitions. However, in some circumstances behavioral uncertainty may be strongly influenced by knowledge of situational constraints on behavior that have little relation to cognitive uncertainty. In ritualized communicative encounters, such as those occurring in the beginning of initial interactions or in formal role relationships, behavior may be highly predictable due to situation-relevant norms and rules. Knowledge of these behavioral constraints would likely reduce behavioral uncertainty in the immediate situation, but should be little related to cognitive uncertainty about the beliefs and attitudes of the interaction partners, although information exchanged during the encounter may influence these cognitive uncertainty levels. Uncertainty reduction theory is primarily concerned with how we come to know others as individuals; as such, uncertainty formulations focus on the cognitive element of uncertainty.

Berger and Calabrese (1975) originally proposed that uncertainty-reduction processes apply to all initial interaction situations. Later formulations add three conditions, any of which should increase the likelihood of activating the reduction of uncertainty (Berger, 1979; Berger & Bradac, 1982). First, individuals are more likely to engage in uncertainty reduction when others have high incentive value; that is, if others are perceived as likely to provide rewards or costs to them. Second, if the behavior of others deviates from what is normally expected, increased uncertainty-reduction efforts are expected. Third, uncertainty-reduction efforts should become more pronounced as the perceived probability of future interaction increases.

These elaborations of uncertainty reduction theory also propose three general categories of information-seeking strategies individuals employ to reduce uncertainty: passive, active, and interactive. Passive strategies involve unobtrusive observation of target individuals to obtain information about them. Active strategies necessitate intervention in the form of seeking information from third parties or through manipulation of the target person's environment. Interactive strategies involve obtaining information directly from the target person through such communicative methods as interrogation and self-disclosure.

Research on uncertainty reduction has advanced along three main related lines within this general conceptual framework. One line of research examines the use of information-seeking strategies, but generally does not directly test basic uncertainty axioms and theorems. Other research focuses on extending and modifying Berger and Calabrese's (1975) original theory to include relational stages beyond early acquaintance. Finally, some research directly tests Berger and Calabrese's propositions in beginning relationships.

Research on information-seeking strategies generally supports uncertainty expectations. Research on the use of passive strategies provides support for the expectation that individuals prefer to observe strangers in those situations that provide greater potential for gathering uncertainty-reducing information (Berger & Douglas, 1981; Berger & Perkins, 1978). However, these investigations do not directly examine the relation of passive-strategy use to uncertainty level, nor do they test uncertainty-reduction axioms and theorems.

Gudykunst et al. (1985) report research including more direct evidence on theoretic propositions regarding information seeking, as well as other variables related to uncertainty reduction. These researchers applied an uncertainty model to acquaintance, friend, and dating relationships in three cultures, and found that the overall model provided an acceptable description of the data. However, tests of several hypotheses resulted in mixed support of specific uncertainty-reduction predictions. Only one of seven hypotheses regarding information-seeking strategies received consistent support. Little support was provided for Berger and Bradac's (1982) proposals regarding the influence of self-monitoring and self-consciousness on information seeking. Tests of four axioms and four theorems, beyond those employed to derive hypotheses concerning interactive strategy use, resulted in consistent support for one axiom, no support for one theorem, and various degrees of partial support in the remaining cases.

Further investigations of uncertainty propositions in established relationships have resulted in inconsistent support. Parks and Adelman (1983) tested an expansion of uncertainty reduction theory with premarital partners, and found support for several predictions regarding communication networks that were unique to their expansion. However, only partial support was provided for the uncertainty axioms tested in this research. Prisbell and Anderson's (1980) examination of uncertainty in established relationships produced partial support for one uncertainty-reduction axiom and equivocal support for one axiom and one theorem. Overall, research examining uncertainty reduction theory within established relationships provides mixed support for uncertainty-reduction propositions, with partial and weak support being the typical finding.

A few studies have examined uncertainty propositions in the entry-level relationships addressed by the original theory. Gudykunst and Nishida (1984) asked participants from Japan and the United States how they would behave in an imagined meeting with a stranger. Results provided consistent support for only one axiom out of the four axioms and six theorems tested. Clatterbuck (1979) reports a reanalysis of seventeen studies employing attributional confidence measures of uncertainty level, including several that appear to involve beginning relationships. The results of this reanalysis produced partial support for three uncertainty axioms. In short, research on the entry phase has provided only limited support for uncertainty reduction theory.

Two general conclusions can be drawn from a review of uncertainty-reduction research. First, uncertainty axioms and theorems have yet to be tested under optimal conditions specified by the theory. Studies clearly meeting the incentive condition, deviance condition, or probability of future interaction condition proposed by Berger (1979) and Berger and Bradac (1982) all appear to involve relationships beyond the early acquaintance stage that is the theory's initial scope. Conversely, studies focusing on beginning relationships do not explicitly address the incentive, deviance, and future interaction probability conditions. It seems reasonable that the initial encounters employed in most of these studies should produce uncertainty concerns even in the absence of these conditions, though these concerns might be minimized. Still, these antecedents should be included in future tests to provide maximum likelihood of detecting uncertainty-related processes, if present.

Second, the low level of support for uncertainty propositions, even under these less than optimal conditions, requires further explanation. Tests of 16 of the 28 axioms and theorems proposed by Berger and Calabrese (1975) have been conducted in the research reviewed above. Well over 100 individual tests have been performed in this research, with only approximately half resulting in theoretical support. With few exceptions, this support has been in the form of weak associations between the variables examined. Though future research employing more optimal conditions may produce greater consistency and strength of support, the current pattern of results suggests that theoretic modifications may also be required.

The remainder of this article attempts to supply such modifications. The focus is limited to the initial interactions addressed by the original theory, though some implications for later relational stages are discussed. Given the weak support thus far obtained for uncertainty reduction theory in early-acquaintance research, this limitation appears to be justified. Moreover, the present formulation is restricted to initial interaction situations involving individuals who will or can, with minimal effort, be in physically proximate settings in the future. Most established relationships begin in such initial contact situations. It is also apparent that these proximate situations produce a broad range of communicative relationships, from relations involving no further or very restricted contact through highly developed social relationships. Given the focus of this inquiry on beginning relational development, the present formulation examines the possible role of initial interactions in producing this relational variation.

PREDICTED OUTCOME VALUE

Berger and Calabrese (1975) propose that the central concern of strangers upon meeting is the reduction of uncertainty about the self and other in the relationship. The predicted-outcome-value perspective posits that a more primary goal is the maximization of relational outcomes. These two goals may be complementary: The reduction of uncertainty may aid individuals to achieve more positive experiences in the relationship. Prior to exploring this possible connection and the resultant modifications of uncertainty reduction theory, it is necessary to outline the predicted-outcome-value position.

Various theoretical perspectives and related research programs support the view that individuals seek to increase the positiveness of their outcomes in relationships with others. Several communication perspectives posit that an individual's experience with outcome values during interactions is a primary factor in relational development processes (Miller & Steinberg, 1975; Roloff, 1981; Sunnafrank & Miller, 1981). Related social psychological orientations on social exchange (Homans, 1961, 1974; Kelley & Thibaut, 1978; Thibaut & Kelley, 1959), social penetration (Altman & Taylor, 1973), social reinforcement (Byrne, 1961, 1971; Byrne & Nelson, 1965), and equity (Adams, 1963; Walster, Berscheid, & Walster, 1973, 1976; Walster, Walster, & Berscheid, 1978) take similar positions on the centrality of outcome values in social relationships. These perspectives share the assumptions that individuals desire to maximize their outcomes and are more likely to form relationships with available others who enable them to do so.

The typical outcome-value explanation of relational development concentrates on individuals' past and present relational experiences. However, some perspectives discuss the potential influence of the value of forecasted outcomes on this process, especially during the beginning stages of relationships. Altman and Taylor (1973) posit that relationships develop because partners expect that the rewards of this development will outweigh the costs. Although the social exchange perspective is largely based on experienced outcome values, Thibaut and Kelley (1959) do propose that individuals employ experienced outcomes to predict future outcome potential for relationships. Sunnafrank and Miller (1981) propose that a major determinant of attraction between relative strangers is the perception of how future interactions will proceed.

The importance of predicted outcome value in beginning relationships is due to the limited outcome experiences typically available during initial interactions, and the tendency for these experiences to be markedly similar across relationships. Berger and Bradac (1982) note that communication during this stage is highly structured and routinized: Individuals normally exchange limited demographic information, followed by conversations on topics with little likelihood of producing obvious relational or personal consequences. As Altman and Taylor (1973) note, rewards and costs obtained at this beginning level are relatively low in magnitude. Moreover, the routinized nature of initial interactions would appear to produce somewhat similar outcome-value experiences in most relationships.

Although relatively little variance in outcome-value experiences should be evident in beginning relationships, differences in the demographic and low-consequence information provided through this conversational routine would distinguish between the interaction partners individuals meet. Berger's (1975) research demonstrates that this information strongly influences individuals' perceptions of the cognitive disposition of others, suggesting that impressions of partners will vary greatly as a result of information available during initial interactions. This view is consistent with uncertainty positions (Berger, 1979; Berger & Bradac, 1982; Berger & Calabrese, 1975), as well as with the attribution formulations from which they are derived (Heider, 1958; Jones & Davis, 1965; Kelley, 1973).

The current perspective assumes that these impressions are employed to forecast outcomes likely to be obtained in the future, an assumption shared with other perspectives on relational development (Altman & Taylor, 1973; Miller & Steinberg, 1975). Obviously, these varying impressions would produce different estimates of future outcome values. Given the relatively minor outcome differences from initial interaction experiences, these forecasted values should be of critical importance to relational-development decisions. Individuals should employ these predictions in making decisions about whether to avoid, restrict, or seek further relational contact, as well as how to proceed with the interaction given these predictions. The primary consideration in such decisions should be the individual's desire to maximize future outcomes.

Given this framework, several propositions regarding beginning relationships are possible. Those introduced here have relatively direct implications for uncertainty reduction theory, as is detailed in the following section. First, individuals should be more attracted to partners and relationships when greater predicted outcome values are expected in the relational future. Second, increasingly positive predicted outcomes will produce more communicative attempts to extend initial interactions and establish future contact. Conversely, increasingly negative predicted outcomes will result in communicative attempts to terminate or curtail the conversation and future contact. Finally, individuals will attempt to guide conversations toward topics expected to result in the most positive predicted outcomes.

PREDICTED OUTCOME VALUE AND UNCERTAINTY

Both uncertainty-reduction and predicted-outcome-value processes may have important, related roles in beginning communicative relationships. Exploring the affinity between these perspectives should produce a more complete understanding of relational development. This connection rests on the assumption that uncertainty reduction increases individuals' perceived outcome-maximization potential, an assumption that leads to several alterations in basic uncertainty-reduction axioms (Berger & Calabrese, 1975).

Berger (1979) and Berger and Bradac (1982) acknowledge a possible uncertainty-outcome value association in proposing that another person's incentive value influences uncertainty-reduction efforts. Additionally, increased deviance and probability of future interaction, proposed by these authors as also increasing uncertainty, should be related to outcome-value concerns: Deviant behavior by others indicates that future outcomes will be difficult to determine, whereas increased probability of future interaction increases the relevance of future outcomes. Increased uncertainty concerns under these conditions may reflect perceptions that reduced uncertainty is required to determine future outcome values.

Further support for this association may be derived from the posited relationship between cognitive and behavioral uncertainty. Though uncertainty reduction theory explicitly focuses on cognitive uncertainty, key connections to the behavioral component are provided by most formulations. Berger (1975) and Berger and Bradac (1982) propose that reduced uncertainty about the cognitive dispositions of others should reduce behavioral uncertainty in nonroutine situations. The behavioral predictions arrived at in this process may be used to estimate the value of outcomes to be received in the relational future.

Given the highly routinized structure of initial interaction, it might appear that the relation between cognitive and behavioral uncertainty would not apply to this relational stage. Although the structure and general behaviors of partners during beginning communicative contact are largely governed by external guidelines, conversational behavior and topics beyond the first, brief, demographic exchanges are increasingly determined by partners' cognitive dispositions.

This suggests that even during initial interactions, cognitive uncertainty levels are related to uncertainty about the behavioral reactions of others to the introduction of conversational topics. Cognitive uncertainty reduction should also provide a basis for predicting future behaviors of others in even less routine encounters beyond this beginning phase. Both of these possibilities support the view that an important function of cognitive uncertainty reduction during initial interactions is the reduction of future behavioral uncertainty.

From the predicted-outcome-value perspective, these uncertainty-reduction efforts would result from individuals' desires to maximize relational outcomes. Reducing uncertainty concerning future behaviors allows individuals to determine likely outcome-value alternatives for the relationship. These behavioral predictions and associated outcome values provide a means of determining how to proceed with the interaction and relationship to realize the most positive outcomes.

At a general level, these projections should allow individuals to determine if the most positive course of action would be to continue the interaction and relationship at the entry level, attempt to terminate or restrict the interaction and relationship, or seek to escalate the interaction and relationship. At a more specific level, predictions regarding likely future behavioral alternatives and associated outcome values should allow individuals to determine how to communicate in attempting to realize the most positive results. Given this goal, individuals presumably would introduce conversational behaviors and topics expected to produce these positive outcomes. Several such communicative strategies are addressed under individual axioms below.

This proposed outcome-value function of reducing cognitive and future behavioral uncertainty provides the foundation for modifying uncertainty-reduction axioms. The relationships formulated in the original axioms generally postulate a linear association between uncertainty and specified variables (Berger and Calabrese, 1975). Although there may be a linear component

to these relationships, the predicted-outcome-value perspective suggests greater complexity. If individuals are motivated to reduce uncertainty in order to increase the value of their outcomes, reduced uncertainty with regard to either negative or positive outcomes should be useful to those individuals, though these outcome differences would result in substantially different relational consequences. For example, decreased uncertainty that future behavior will result in generally negative outcomes should produce attempts to terminate or restrict the relationship. Conversely, more attempts to continue or increase contact with the relational partner should be produced by decreased uncertainty that future behavior will result in generally positive outcomes. This indicates that the linear relationships specified by uncertainty axioms require modification based on predicted-outcome-value levels: Decreased uncertainty may produce one set of results when predicted outcome values are positive, and an opposite set when the values are negative. The specific modifications regarding each of the axioms are discussed below.

MODIFICATION OF AXIOMS

Amount of Verbal Communication

Axiom 1 of uncertainty reduction theory posits a reciprocal causal relationship between amount of verbal communication and uncertainty:

> **AXIOM 1:**   *Given the high levels of uncertainty present at the outset of the entry phase, as amount of verbal communication increases, the level of uncertainty for each interactant in the relationship will decrease. As uncertainty is further reduced, the amount of verbal communication will increase (Berger & Calabrese, 1975).*

Berger and Calabrese (1975) draw empirical support for this relationship from Lalljee and Cook (1973) and Berger and Larimer (1974). Lalljee and Cook found that as initial interactions proceed, the number of words uttered per minute increases. This research also demonstrated that uncertainty, as indicated by filled pause and speech rates, decreases during these interactions. No direct evidence of a positive association between uncertainty reduction and amount of verbal communication is provided by these findings, as the measure of uncertainty employed verbal indicators that were also used to assess amount of verbal communication. However, these results are consistent with Axiom 1. Berger and Larimer found that amount of verbal communication decreases when feedback between partners is not allowed. Berger and Calabrese suggest this lack of feedback maintains high uncertainty levels producing decreases in amount of verbal communication. Although no measure of uncertainty was provided, these results appear consistent with Axiom 1.

Subsequent tests provide mixed support for the posited relationship between uncertainty and amount of verbal communication. Only four of eleven tests involving relationships beyond the entry stage are consistent with Axiom 1 (Gudykunst et al., 1985; Parks & Adelman, 1983). Initial interaction tests are limited to Clatterbuck's (1979) reanalysis, which provides consistent support for a weak, positive association between amount of time spent together and uncertainty reduction. Overall, empirical evidence provides only indirect support for Axiom 1 during initial interactions, and more direct, but weak and inconsistent, support beyond this relational state. No evidence concerning the reciprocal causal nature of this relationship has been provided.

The predicted-outcome-value perspective leads to a modified verbal communication-uncertainty relationship. This perspective is in general agreement with Berger and Calabrese's (1975) expectation that uncertainty reduction and amount of verbal communication are positively related in the beginning phase of initial interactions, though these perspectives differ substantially on the relation of uncertainty and verbal communication subsequent to this period. The current perspective assumes that during initial interactions individuals attempt to acquire information about partners to enable them to predict future outcome values. Information-seeking strategies likely to be employed in these situations, such as interrogation and self-disclosure,

involve verbal communication. Information-seeking and intimacy processes (to be discussed later) indicate that these strategies produce increasingly lengthy speaking turns with fewer speaker and topic switches as initial interactions proceed. This would result in a more constant flow of verbal communication during the course of the conversation, and reduced uncertainty as more information is made known.

Uncertainty reduction allows individuals to form tentative judgments of the outcomes to be obtained from partners' likely future behaviors. When associated predicted outcome values are positive, individuals should seek continued interaction to realize these outcomes. The more positive the predicted outcome values, the greater the likelihood of attempted continuation. When successful, these attempts should lead to further increases in the rate of verbal communication and in uncertainty reduction through the above processes. In addition, the lengthened interaction period would produce an increase in the total amount of verbal communication during the conversation.

When behavioral uncertainty reduction produces tentative judgments that future outcomes will be negative, individuals should attempt to terminate or restrict the interaction. The more negative predicted outcome values, the more likely these attempts. One method of attempting termination or restriction would be to reduce the amount of verbal communication. Individuals should produce briefer comments and ask fewer questions requiring briefer answers as they seek to curtail the conversation. Unless partners respond by engaging in substantially longer speaking turns, this would result in reduced amounts of verbal communication. In addition, when attempts to end the conversation are successful, the overall amount of verbal communication during the conversation will be lower as a result of early termination.

The expected relationship between amount of verbal communication (both rate and total quantity), uncertainty reduction, and predicted outcome value is summarized in the following proposition.

PROPOSITION 1:   *During the beginning stage of initial interactions, both the amount of verbal communication and uncertainty reduction increase. Further increases in amount of verbal communication occur when uncertainty reduction results in positive predicted outcome values, whereas decreases in amount of verbal communication follow from negative predicted outcome values.*

The apparent contradiction between this proposition and the results reported by Lalljee and Cook (1973) and Clatterbuck (1979) can perhaps be explained: Both of these studies indicate that amount of verbal communication may increase as initial interactions proceed. It may be that initial interactions more typically produce positive than negative predicted outcomes. This would produce an overall pattern of increasing verbalization when predicted outcome value is not considered. Because neither of these studies provides a measure of predicted outcome value, the present explanation remains speculative.

The methods employed in these studies may also explain the apparent inconsistency. As Clatterbuck (1979) indicates, the validity of his use of time in a relationship as a measure of amount of verbal communication is problematic. Rates of verbal communication could vary widely in conversations, but length of relational time would not necessarily measure such variation. Additionally, many of the initial interaction studies analyzed by Clatterbuck (1979), as well as Lalljee and Cook's (1973) research, employ conversational time periods set by the experimenters, which effective eliminates participants' opportunities to terminate the interaction. It also seems likely that participants' abilities to curtail the conversation may be restricted in such experimentally produced situations. Participants generally find themselves in dyadic situations with little to do but converse with their assigned partner. Conversation is experimentally induced, no alternative conversational partners are available, and participants are generally unable to engage in other activities. Typical initial interaction situations enable individuals to make choices in these areas, providing acceptable options for curtailing the conversation. All of the above procedures indicate that the results of these studies cannot be applied to the current proposition, which assumes normal termination and curtailment possibilities. Clearly, future research employing adequate measures and procedures is needed to test Proposition 1.

Nonverbal Affiliative Expressiveness

Axiom 2 of uncertainty reduction theory posits a reciprocal causal relationship between nonverbal affiliative expressiveness and uncertainty levels:

AXIOM 2:   *As nonverbal affiliative expressiveness increases, uncertainty levels will decrease in an initial interaction situation. In addition, decreases in uncertainty level will cause increases in nonverbal affiliative expressiveness (Berger & Calabrese, 1975).*

The empirical base Berger and Calabrese (1975) provide for this axiom rests on the work of Mehrabian (1971) and Mehrabian and Ksionzky (1971). These studies indicate that a number of nonverbal affiliative behaviors are related to amount of verbal communication. These findings coupled with Axiom 1 suggest an association between nonverbal affiliative expressiveness and uncertainty. Gudykunst and Nishida's (1984) research tested this association directly, with results providing no support in one test and support for a weak association in another. No tests of the reciprocal causal nature of this relationship have been reported.

If nonverbal affiliative expressiveness and amount of verbal communication are positively related, the earlier proposed alteration of the verbal communication-uncertainty relationship suggests changes in Axiom 2. Aside from Mehrabian's (1971) and Mehrabian and Ksionzky's (1971) findings, there are grounds for expecting a positive association between nonverbal affiliative expressiveness and amount of verbal communication. Speakers regularly employ nonverbal affiliative cues, such as head nods and arm gestures, to compliment and emphasize verbal messages. Listeners generally provide nonverbal feedback or backchanneling (Duncan, 1975), including head nods and smiling, during partners' speaking turns. This backchanneling may provide reinforcement to the speaker that induces longer speaking turns and greater self-disclosure (Burgoon & Saine, 1978). These tendencies to provide nonverbal affiliative cues during verbal exchanges support the view that amounts of these variables should be positively related. This association alone should provide sufficient reason to expect an uncertainty-nonverbal affiliation relationship similar to the posited relationship regarding amount of verbal communication.

A more direct relation between uncertainty and nonverbal affiliative expressiveness is suggested by the predicted-outcome-value perspective. During initial interactions, uncertainty reduction may be related to the reinforcement properties of nonverbal expressions of affiliation from listeners. Increasingly lengthy speaker turns and self-disclosures in response to this nonverbal reinforcement would provide interactants with substantially more information about one another, with associated reduction in uncertainty levels. Individuals may employ such cues in an attempt to acquire information, though this reinforcement may often just represent an attempt to appear agreeable. As McLaughlin, Cody, and Rosenstein (1983) note, partners prefer to convey such agreement during initial interactions. In either case, the result would be increased information acquisition and reduced uncertainty.

When predictions of positive outcomes are arrived at through this process, further increases in nonverbal affiliative expressions are likely. This increase would be partially due to the increases in amount of verbal communication expected in these positive situations. Moreover, partners should employ these expressions of affiliation to attempt to continue the interaction and potential relationship. The more positive predicted outcome values, the greater the increase of nonverbal affiliative expressiveness should be.

Conversely, when negative predicted outcomes result from cognitive and behavioral uncertainty reduction, decreases in nonverbal affiliative expressiveness should occur. The expected decrease in amount of verbal communication in negative situations would suggest this. Additionally, decreased affiliative cues are likely when individuals attempt to terminate or curtail interactions with negative predicted outcome values. The more negative these values, the more pronounced this reduction should be.

The proposed relationship between nonverbal affiliative expressiveness, uncertainty reduction, and predicted outcome value leads to the following proposition.

PROPOSITION 2: *During the beginning stages of initial interactions, increases in listeners' nonverbal affiliative expressiveness produce reduction in their uncertainty levels. When this uncertainty results in positive predicted outcome values, further increases in nonverbal affiliative expressiveness occur. Uncertainty reduction associated with negative predicted outcome values produces decreases in nonverbal affiliative expressiveness.*

Information Seeking

Uncertainty reduction theory proposes a reciprocal causal relationship between information seeking and uncertainty, partially reflected in the following axiom:

AXIOM 3: *High levels of uncertainty cause increases in information seeking behavior. As uncertainty levels decline, information seeking behavior decreases (Berger & Calabrese, 1975).*

Berger and Calabrese (1975) derive empirical support for this formulation from Frankfurt's (1965) finding that the number of questions asked during simulated conversations declined over time. Berger and Calabrese also suggest that several demographic questions, likely to produce brief responses, occur in the beginning of initial interactions. The resulting rapid exchange of speaking roles should produce a high number of questions relative to later stages of initial interaction involving more prolonged responses. Although this axiom is based primarily on the use of interrogation as an information-seeking technique, Berger's (1979) introduction of self-disclosure as a strategy to obtain information about partners appears compatible with Axiom 3.

Direct tests of this relationship are limited to the two performed in Gudykunst and Nishida's (1984) study of hypothetical conversations: one test resulted in support for a weak association and the other produced no support. Gudykunst, Yang, and Nishida's (1985) work with developed relationships provided mixed support for a derivative of this axiom. No tests of the reciprocal causal nature of this relationship have been reported.

Prior to examining the predicted-outcome-value perspective on information seeking, a few relevant points concerning this variable need to be addressed. First, it should be clear that individuals may both seek information without receiving it and obtain information that is not sought. It seems reasonable to expect that individuals will provide more unsolicited information as positive interactions proceed, reducing the need for the use of interrogation and self-disclosure as information-seeking methods. Second, information-seeking attempts may be directed at soliciting differing amounts of information. A request for demographic information may by expected to produce rather limited information, but subsequent questions may require more extensive information from partners. Just considering the number of questions asked ignores the amount of information requested. It may well be that as initial interactions proceed, explicit information-seeking requests may decrease in number but increase in the amount of information that is sought. Finally, the earlier discussion of nonverbal affiliative expressiveness suggests that these cues may be used as an additional information-seeking strategy. The use of this strategy should increase as positive initial interactions progress toward longer speaking turns, perhaps replacing interrogation and self-disclosure strategies to a degree. The inclusion of

this potential strategy indicates that the type of information-seeking behavior may change in the course of initial interactions.

Within this broadened conceptual framework, information-seeking behavior is viewed as occupying a central position in outcome-maximization processes. Given the highly limited information possessed about others at the outset of initial interactions, explicit information-seeking behavior should begin almost immediately. The rapid exchange of speaker and listener roles at this stage may reflect a high rate of demographically directed information-seeking attempts. This information should reduce uncertainty to a degree, but only lead to tentative impressions of future outcome values. In order to increase the perceived accuracy and validity of these impressions, individuals should begin to seek more detailed information about the cognitive dispositions of partners. Demographic information obtained earlier may suggest topics likely to produce such information. This more detailed information should result in further uncertainty reduction and more stable predictions of future outcome values.

When this uncertainty reduction is associated with positive predicted outcomes, continued information-seeking attempts to further test these predictions and possibly achieve the positive outcomes seem likely: The more positive predicted outcome values, the more likely such attempts. Conversely, uncertainty reduction associated with negative predicted outcomes should result in decreased information-seeking behavior. Because individuals are expected to terminate or curtail these interactions, further information seeking that would produce prolonged conversation should be avoided. The more negative the predicted outcome values, the more pronounced the reduction in information-seeking behavior.

The predicted-outcome-value perspective thus leads to the following proposition regarding the relation of uncertainty to information-seeking behavior:

PROPOSITION 3:   *High levels of uncertainty produce increased information-seeking behavior in beginning initial* *interactions. Decreased uncertainty, when associated with positive outcome values, produces increased information-seeking behavior. When associated with negative predicted outcome values, reduced uncertainty produces decreased information-seeking behavior.*

Intimacy Level of Communication Content

Uncertainty reduction theory predicts that uncertainty level has a negative influence on intimacy level of communication content.

> **AXIOM 4:** *High levels of uncertainty in a relationship cause decreases in intimacy level of communication content. Low levels of uncertainty produce high levels of intimacy (Berger & Calabrese, 1975).*

Berger and Calabrese (1975) review several studies supporting the position that as initial interactions and relationships proceed, intimacy level of communication content increases (Berger, 1973; Cozby, 1972; Ehrlich & Graeven, 1971; Sermat & Smyth, 1973; Taylor, Altman & Sorrentino, 1969; Taylor, Altman & Wheeler, 1973). Subsequent research by Berger, Gardner, Clatterbuck, and Shulman (1976) provides further support for increased topic intimacy as initial interactions proceed. Together, these studies indicate that initial interactions begin with conversations focused on demographic topics that are followed by discussions of more intimate but peripheral ''attitudinal'' information. Further relational development is associated with generally increasing levels of content intimacy. If uncertainty level generally decreases while intimacy level increases over time in a relationship, a negative association between these variables should be observed.

Gudykunst et al.'s (1985) study of established relationships provides evidence for this negative association. This study indicates that higher levels of uncertainty are associated with either lower levels of own self-disclosures or partners' self-disclosures. Berger, Gardner,

Parks, Schulman, and Miller (1976) report results indicating that level of content intimacy in initial interactions has no influence on uncertainty. However, no direct evidence regarding Axiom 4 is provided by this research because the posited influence of uncertainty level on content intimacy was unexamined.

Berger and Calabrese (1975) note that the results of past intimacy studies are generally interpreted as supporting Altman and Taylor's (1973) position that as relationships become more rewarding, increasingly intimate discussions occur. Altman and Taylor stipulate that these more intimate discussions will focus on topics projected to produce further rewards. Berger and Calabrese propose a different explanation of this phenomena, reflected in Axiom 4. The predicted-outcome-value perspective suggests that a composit of these positions may produce the most useful view of changes in intimacy level during initial interactions.

The current explanation of the movement of the content of initial interaction from general demographic information to more detailed information about individual partners is addressed in the previous section. This movement can be conceptualized as proceeding along an intimacy continuum: Demographic exchanges provide highly superficial information about group membership, whereas subsequent exchanges produce more intimate information about partners' cognitive dispositions. This change is expected to increase individuals' perceived ability to accurately predict outcome-value alternatives through cognitive and behavioral uncertainty reduction.

Increasing content intimacy should involve topics related to demographic information acquired in the beginning interaction phase. Cognitive and future behavioral uncertainty regarding these topics should be high. However, uncertainty regarding topics unrelated to known demographic categories should be higher still. Given this, individuals should perceive greater accuracy in predicting outcomes for demographically suggested topic areas. When the discussion of some such topics is expected to result in positive outcomes, more intimate conversations on these topics should occur. This discussion would further reduce uncertainty and increase the perceived accuracy of predicting future outcomes. If continued predictions of positive outcomes result, increasingly intimate content should be exchanged. The more positive the predicted outcome values, the more likely the attempts at increasing intimacy level.

Conversely, it is possible that none of the topics suggested by early demographic exchanges leads to acceptable outcome values. This should result in either continued demographic and superficial exchanges or attempts to terminate the conversation. A similar process should occur when more intimate conversations result in negative predicted outcomes. Individuals should attempt to terminate these interactions, move the content of discussion back to less intimate levels, or attempt to discuss other topics suggested by known demographic categories. In any case, increasing content intimacy would not result from negative outcome-value predictions. The more negative these values, the more likely attempts at conversational termination or restriction to low intimacy levels.

The expected relationship between content intimacy, predicted outcome value, and uncertainty is summarized in the following proposition:

> **PROPOSITION 4:** *Given high uncertainty levels at the onset of interactions, communication content is low in intimacy. When subsequent uncertainty reduction is associated with positive predicted outcome values, intimacy level of communicative content increases. When uncertainty reduction is associated with negative predicted outcome values, intimacy level is maintained at or decreases to low levels.*

Reciprocity Rate

Uncertainty reduction theory posits a positive causal relationship between uncertainty levels and reciprocity rates:

> **AXIOM 5:** *High levels of uncertainty produce high rates of reciprocity. Low levels of uncertainty produce low reciprocity rates (Berger & Calabrese, 1975).*

Several studies demonstrate that conversational exchanges between equal status partners are reciprocal in nature. Partners generally match speech rates (Matarazzo, Wiens & Saslow, 1965), amount of information disclosed (Worthy, Gary & Kahn, 1969), and intimacy level of communicative content (Jourard, 1960). Violating this norm of reciprocity tends to reduce attraction to violators during initial contact situations (Sermat & Smyth, 1973). In subsequent research, Berger, Gardner, Parks, Shulman, and Miller (1976) report that reciprocity of content intimacy in initial interactions leads to lower uncertainty levels than nonreciprocity. However, research has yet to test the relationship between uncertainty level and reciprocity rates.

Berger and Calabrese (1975) propose that reciprocal behavior is due to concerns about the distribution of informational power in relationships: Reciprocal exchanges help assure that neither interaction partner will obtain an informational advantage over the other. Given the relative lack of partner information available during beginning initial interactions, even moderate differences in amount or intimacy of information could lead to large power imbalances. Only small amounts of information should be provided in beginning speaking turns to avoid such imbalances. The result of this should be the brief comments and rapid exchanges of speaking roles which characterize this stage. As the information base about partners increases, relative balance could be maintained with greater amounts of information provided during individual speaking turns.

Alternatively, the predicted-outcome-value perspective explains reciprocal information exchange during initial interactions as due to partners' mutual attempts to maximize their outcomes. The central role of possessing information about partners in producing outcome maximization has been discussed extensively. Partner cooperation in providing the needed information is clearly required in these beginning interactions. In order to solicit such behavior from partners, individuals should demonstrate their own willingness to cooperate. When mutual decisions to cooperate are coupled with the information-seeking and intimacy-level processes discussed earlier, a general matching on amount and intimacy of information would be expected.

This reciprocal *behavior* should continue as long as partners choose to cooperate. Continued cooperation would result from uncertainty reduction associated with positive predicted outcome values, though reciprocity *rates* should decline as a result of increasing length of speaking turns. Such continued cooperation should convey the individual's desire to maintain the interaction and relationship. When negative predicted outcome values are associated with reduced uncertainty, attempts to reciprocate should be discontinued or severely curtailed as a method of terminating or restricting the conversation and relationship.

The following proposition reflects this predicted-outcome-value view of the uncertainty-reciprocity rate relationship.

PROPOSITION 5:   *During the beginning stage of initial interactions, high uncertainty levels are associated with high rates of reciprocity. When uncertainty reduction is associated with positive predicted outcome values, reciprocity rate declines. When uncertainty reduction is associated with negative predicted outcome values, greater decreases in reciprocity rate occur.*

Similarity

Uncertainty reduction theory posits a positive causal relationship between similarity and uncertainty reduction:

AXIOM 6:   *Similarities between persons reduce uncertainty, whereas dissimilarities produce increases in uncertainty (Berger & Calabrese, 1975).*

Berger and Calabrese (1975) propose that uncertainty level mediates between similarity and liking. Much of their empirical evidence for Axiom 6 is drawn from studies demonstrating a positive attitude-similarity/attraction association (Berscheid & Walster, 1969; Byrne, 1971). In addition, Berger and Calabrese cite evidence demonstrating that individuals provide more explanations for not liking others than for liking them (Koenig, 1971), and more explanations for dissimilarities between people than for similarities (Berger, 1975). These differences in number of explanations are taken as an indication that uncertainty levels are higher under conditions of dissimilarity or disliking than of similarity or liking.

Subsequent tests of the uncertainty-similarity relationship have yielded mixed support for Axiom 6. In studies of established relationships, Parks and Adelman (1983) report weak support for the uncertainty-similarity association, Prisbell and Anderson (1980) report support with some forms of similarity but not with others, and Gudykunst et al.'s (1985) research indicates support in only four of nine tests. Studies of initial interactions find equally ambiguous support. Clatterbuck's (1979) reanalysis of several studies consistently supports a weak perceived similarity-uncertainty relationship though providing no support for actual similarity. Gudykunst and Nishida (1984) report to relationship between the uncertainty and similarity variables.

Contrary to the uncertainty reduction position, initial interaction information indicating either similarity or dissimilarity should generally reduce cognitive and future behavioral uncertainty, as long as individuals have previous knowledge of others who display these same similarities or dissimilarities. When individuals have formed impressions of others from certain demographic groups or who hold particular low risk cognitive dispositions, information indicating their partner is aligned with that group or disposition would reduce uncertainty. As Miller and Steinberg (1975) indicate, individuals are likely to apply these impressions to early-acquaintance partners through a process of stimulus generalization. This stimulus generalization should reduce uncertainty levels, regardless of whether the information employed indicates similarity or dissimilarity. In some cases, individuals may have greater familiarity with and, therefore, more well-formed impressions of others from similar demographic groups than from dissimilar ones. Information indicating similarity should result in greater uncertainty reduction in such situations, though dissimilar information would still reduce uncertainty.

This perspective on the similarity-uncertainty association is summarized in the following proposition:

PROPOSITION 6: *Both similarities and dissimilarities between persons reduce uncertainty. Greater uncertainty reduction will result from similarities when dissimilarities reflect groupings that are not highly familiar to individuals.*

Liking

Uncertainty reduction theory proposes a negative causal relationship between uncertainty level and liking:

AXIOM 7: *Increases in uncertainty level produce decreases in liking; decreases in uncertainty level produce increases in liking (Berger & Calabrese, 1975).*

Berger and Calabrese (1975) base this axiom primarily on the assumption that uncertainty mediates between similarity and liking. Gudykunst et al. (1985) report consistent support for the uncertainty-attraction relationship from nine tests on developed relationships. However, research on the initial interaction stage provides inconsistent support. Clatterbuck (1979) reports support for an uncertainty-attraction relationship in some studies but not in others. Gudykunst and Nishida's (1984) research provides no support for this relationship. In addition, recent work indicates that the previously accepted positive attitude similarity-attraction relationship does not apply to normal initial interactions (Sunnafrank, 1983, 1984, 1985; Sunnafrank & Miller, 1981), suggesting that the basis of Axiom 7 may be in error.

The predicted-outcome-value perspective expects that higher forecasted outcome values will produce higher levels of attraction. The current application of this perspective to uncertainty-related variables makes it clear that uncertainty reduction could be associated with either negative or positive predicted outcome values. When

cognitive and future behavioral uncertainty reduction leads to positive predicted outcome values, increased liking should result. However, uncertainty reduction associated with negative predicted outcome values should produce opposite attraction influences. The relationship between uncertainty, liking, and predicted outcome value is formally stated in the following proposition.

PROPOSITION 7: *When decreased uncertainty is associated with positive predicted outcome values, liking increases. When associated with negative predicted outcome values, liking decreases.*

HYPOTHESES

Berger and Calabrese (1975) deduce 21 theorems from their original seven axioms. To further clarify differences between uncertainty reduction and predicted-outcome-value theories, corresponding hypotheses are derived from the current propositions. Fifteen such hypotheses are presented below. The derivation of these hypotheses is based on the assumption that predicted outcome value is influencing the consequent variables, as indicated in six of the above propositions. (Because Proposition 6 does not specify a relationship involving predicted outcome value, it was not employed in this process.) Nine of these hypotheses predict different associations from those expected by uncertainty-reduction theorems. These hypotheses are presented first, along with the corresponding theorems. Critical comparisons of the two theories will require investigation of these conflicting predictions, as well as those present in the seven pairs of axioms and propositions. Given this, a brief discussion of empirical evidence relevant to these hypotheses is provided. Finally, the six hypotheses that are in agreement with uncertainty-reduction theorems are presented.

Conflicting Predictions

- *Hypothesis* 1 (POV): Amount of verbal communication and information-seeking behavior are positively related.

- *Theorem* 3 (URT): Amount of communication and information seeking behavior are inversely related (Berger & Calabrese, 1975).
- *Hypothesis* 2 (POV): Nonverbal affiliative expressiveness and information-seeking behavior are positively related.
- *Theorem* 8 (URT): Nonverbal affiliative expressiveness and information seeking are inversely related (Berger & Calabrese, 1975).
- *Hypothesis* 3 (POV): Intimacy level of communication content and information-seeking behavior are positively related.
- *Theorem* 12 (URT): Intimacy level of communication content and information seeking are inversely related (Berger & Calabrese, 1975).
- *Hypothesis* 4 (POV): Information-seeking behavior and reciprocity rate are inversely related when predicted outcome values are positive, and positively related when predicted outcome values are negative.
- *Theorem* 16 (URT): Information seeking and reciprocity rate are positively related (Berger & Calabrese, 1975).
- *Hypothesis* 5 (POV): Information-seeking behavior and liking are positively related.
- *Theorem* 17 (URT): Information seeking and liking are negatively related (Berger & Calabrese, 1975).
- *Hypothesis* 6 (POV): Amount of verbal communication and reciprocity rate are inversely related when predicted outcome values are positive, and positively related when predicted outcome values are negative.
- *Theorem* 4 (URT): Amount of communication and reciprocity rate are inversely related (Berger & Calabrese, 1975).
- *Hypothesis* 7 (POV): Nonverbal affiliative expressiveness and reciprocity rate are inversely related when predicted outcome values are positive, and positively related when predicted outcome values are negative.
- *Theorem* 9 (URT): Nonverbal affiliative expressiveness and reciprocity rate are inversely related (Berger and Calabrese, 1975).
- *Hypothesis* 8 (POV): Intimacy level of communication content and reciprocity rate are inversely related when predicted outcome values are positive, and positively related when predicted outcome values are negative.
- *Theorem* 13 (URT): Intimacy level of communication content and reciprocity rate are inversely related (Berger & Calabrese, 1975).
- *Hypothesis* 9 (POV): Reciprocity rate and liking are inversely related when predicted outcome values are positive, and positively related when predicted outcome values are negative.
- *Theorem* 19 (URT): Reciprocity rate and liking are negatively related (Berger & Calabrese, 1975).

All of these conflicting hypothesis/theorem pairs involve reciprocity rate, information-seeking behavior, or both. Currently, there is no empirical basis for assessing the relative accuracy of reciprocity-rate hypotheses and theorems. Direct comparisons will require inclusion of the predicted-outcome variable in future research. Lack of research on reciprocity-rate theorems renders even an indirect evaluation of the contrasting prediction impossible. Though some uncertainty-reduction research examines various aspects of reciprocity (for example, see Berger, Gardner, Parks, Schulman, & Miller, 1976), none directly tests these theorems.

However, research evidence does allow a direct comparison of two information-seeking hypothesis/theorem pairs. Gudykunst and Nishida's (1984) research on the initial interaction situations addressed by both theories provides support for predicted-outcome-value predictions. Their results demonstrate a positive association between information seeking and nonverbal affiliative expressiveness, as well as between information seeking and liking. These findings are consistent with Hypotheses 2 and 5 respectively, and in opposition to Theorems 8 and 17. This limited evidence suggests that future research on conflicting uncertainty-reduction and predicted-outcome-value predictions will prove useful.

Concordant Predictions

- *Hypothesis* 10 (POV): Amount of verbal communication and nonverbal affiliative expressiveness are positively related (URT Theorem 1).
- *Hypothesis* 11 (POV): Amount of verbal communication and intimacy level of communication content are positively related (URT Theorem 2).
- *Hypothesis* 12 (POV): Amount of verbal communication and liking are positively related (URT Theorem 5).
- *Hypothesis* 13 (POV): Nonverbal affiliative expressiveness and intimacy level of communication content are positively related (URT Theorem 7).
- *Hypothesis* 14 (POV): Nonverbal affiliative expressiveness and liking are positively related (URT Theorem 10).
- *Hypothesis* 15 (POV): Intimacy level of communication content and liking are positively related (URT Theorem 14).

CONCLUSION

Prior to the development of uncertainty reduction theory, the primary frameworks for studying interpersonal communication were generally provided by various social psychological theories of interpersonal relations. Berger and Calabrese (1975) note that although such frameworks are relevant to interpersonal communication, they rarely focus directly on important communication concerns. Uncertainty reduction theory responded to this shortcoming by making communication processes and constructs its central focus. Their formulation rejected the dominant rewards-costs analysis of interpersonal relations, and proposed uncertainty reduction as the major explanatory factor in interpersonal communication processes. The focus of uncertainty re-

duction theory on communication clearly represented a major theoretical advance. However, empirical evidence provides inconsistent and generally weak support for the posited role of uncertainty reduction, suggesting that major theoretical modifications are needed.

Predicted-outcome-value theory attempts to provide these modifications, though maintaining Berger and Calabrese's (1975) focus on communication processes. This perspective acknowledges the potential complementary nature of uncertainty-reduction and rewards-costs orientations. The resulting theoretical integration assumes that uncertainty is not the central goal of individuals in beginning relationships, but only an important vehicle for the primary goal of achieving positive relational outcomes.

Predicted-outcome-value theory proposes 22 propositions and hypotheses; the preponderance conflict with corresponding uncertainty-reduction predictions. These propositions and hypotheses have the potential to resolve many inconsistent uncertainty-reduction findings. In the few cases in which direct empirical evidence exists, findings support predicted-outcome-value expectations over those of uncertainty-reduction theory. Given this, research designed to test these contrary predictions seems warranted. This testing process will obviously require research methods that adequately reflect the current perspective. Developing valid measures and manipulations of predicted outcome value will be particularly crucial. Such attempts might initially concentrate on individuals' global perceptions of predicted-outcome-value levels, an approach that would be sufficient to test the formal relationships posited here.

In addition to research on the formal predicted-outcome-value propositions and hypotheses, several other potentially fruitful research possibilities are suggested by the current perspective. Research questions concerning the use of nonverbal affiliative expressiveness as an information-seeking strategy, and the relationship of predicted outcome value to reciprocal communication behavior (other than reciprocity rate), among other questions, are clearly raised by predicted-outcome-value theory. This formulation may also have the potential to help explain theoretically inconsistent results from uncertainty-reduction research on communication-network variables (Parks & Adelman, 1983), cultural context (Gudykunst & Nishida, 1984), as well as self-consciousness and self-monitoring (Gudykunst et al., 1985). Finally, potential connections between predicted-outcome-value theory and several seemingly compatible perspectives should be explored. For example, work on account sequences in initial interactions (McLaughlin, Cody, & Rosenstein, 1983), affinity-seeking strategies (Bell & Daly, 1984), and interpersonal goals (Sunnafrank & Miller, 1981) all address communication variables and processes that appear to be particularly relevant to the predicted-outcome-value perspective. Research that explicitly examines these potential connections may prove highly useful.

In closing, it should be noted that if tests of predicted-outcome-value theory are sufficiently supportive, attempts to expand the theory to include relational stages beyond initial interactions would be reasonable. Such attempts must confront several issues raised by critiques of relational development perspectives (for example, see Bochner, 1978). Although it is not within the scope of the present article to address all of these concerns, the issue of specifying causal mechanisms of relational change is particularly relevant, given the current formulation. Predicted-outcome-value theory proposes that predicted-outcome-value levels are the primary determinant of change in initial interactions. However, when relational contact continues beyond beginning interactions, further change may be more influenced by how these levels compare to those projected for alternative relationships, when such alternatives are readily available. For example, highly positive predicted outcome values should not result in further relational escalation when more positive alternative relationships exist. (For a more complete development of the idea of comparing outcomes for alternative relationships see Thibaut and Kelley, 1959, Chapter 6.) Future expansions of predicted-outcome-value theory should give serious consideration to this comparison process as a component of relational change in continuing relationships.

Further speculation on possible expansions of predicted-outcome-value theory would be premature at this point. The immediate task is to begin empirical examination of the current perspective. At a minimum, these tests will lead to theoretical modifications. It is hoped that the present formulation provides both an adequate conceptual grounding and sufficient justification for beginning this testing process.

REFERENCES

Adams, J. S. (1963). Toward an understanding of inequity. *Journal of Abnormal and Social Psychology, 67,* 422–436.

Altman, I. (1974). The communication of interpersonal attitudes. In T. E. Huston (Ed.), *Foundations of interpersonal attraction* (pp. 121–142). New York: Academic Press.

Altman, I., & Taylor, D. A. (1973). *Social penetration: The development of interpersonal relationships.* New York: Holt, Rinehart & Winston.

Bell, R. A., & Daly, J. A. (1984). The affinity-seeking function of communication. *Communication Monographs, 51,* 91–115.

Berger, C. R. (1973, November). *The acquaintance process revisited: Explorations in initial interaction.* Paper presented at the annual convention of the Speech Communication Association, New York.

Berger, C. R. (1975). Proactive and retroactive attribution processes. *Human Communication Research, 2,* 33–50.

Berger, C. R. (1979). Beyond initial interaction: Uncertainty, understanding, and the development of interpersonal relationships. In H. Giles & R. N. St. Clair (Eds.), *Language and social psychology* (pp. 122–144). Oxford: Basil Blackwell.

Berger, C. R., & Bradac, J. J. (1982). *Language and social knowledge: Uncertainty in interpersonal relations.* London: Edward Arnold.

Berger, C. R., & Calabrese, R. J. (1975). Some explorations in initial interaction and beyond: Toward a developmental theory of interpersonal communication. *Human Communication Research, 1,* 99–112.

Berger, C. R., & Douglas, W. (1981). Studies in interpersonal epistemology III: Anticipated interaction, self-monitoring, and observational context selection. *Communication Monographs, 48,* 183–196.

Berger, C. R., Gardner, R. R., Clatterbuck, G. W., & Schulman, L. S. (1976). Perceptions of information sequencing in relationship development. *Human Communication Research, 3,* 29–46.

Berger, C. R., Gardner, R. R., Parks, M. P., Schulman, L., & Miller, G. R. (1976). Interpersonal epistemology and interpersonal communication. In G. R. Miller (Ed.), *Explorations in interpersonal communication* (pp. 149–172). Beverly Hills, CA: Sage.

Berger, C. R., & Larimer, M. W. (1974, April). *When beauty is only skin deep: The effects of physical attractiveness, sex and time on initial interaction.* Paper presented at the annual convention of the International Communication Association, New Orleans.

Berger, C. R., & Perkins, J. W. (1978). Studies in interpersonal epistemology I: Situational attributes in observational context selection. In B. D. Rubin (Ed.), *Communication yearbook 2* (pp. 171–184). New Brunswick, NJ: Transaction.

Berscheid, E., & Walster, E. H. (1969). *Interpersonal attraction.* Reading, MA: Addison-Wesley.

Bochner, A. (1978). On taking ourselves seriously: An analysis of some persistent problems and promising directions in interpersonal research. *Human Communication Research, 4,* 179–191.

Burgoon, J. K., & Saine, T. (1978). *The unspoken dialogue: An introduction to nonverbal communication.* Boston: Houghton Mifflin.

Byrne, D. (1961). Interpersonal attraction and attitude similarity. *Journal of Abnormal and Social Psychology, 62,* 713–715.

Byrne, D. (1971). *The attraction paradigm.* New York: Academic Press.

Byrne, D., & Nelson, D. (1965). Attraction as a linear function of proportion of positive reinforcements. *Journal of Personality and Social Psychology, 1,* 659–663.

Clatterbuck, G. W. (1979). Attributional confidence and uncertainty in initial interaction. *Human Communication Research, 5,* 147–157.

Cozby, P. C. (1972). Self-disclosure, reciprocity and liking. *Sociometry, 35,* 151–160.

Duncan, S. (1975). Interaction units during speaking turns in dyadic, face-to-face conversations. In A. Kendon, R. Harris, & M. Key (Eds.), *Organization of behavior in face-to-face interaction* (pp. 199–213). The Hague: Mouton.

Ehrlich, H. J., & Graeven, D. B. (1971). Reciprocal self-disclosure in a dyad. *Journal of Experimental Social Psychology, 7,* 389–400.

Frankfurt, L. P. (1965). *The role of some individual and interpersonal factors on the acquaintance process.* Unpublished doctoral dissertation, American University.

Gudykunst, W. B., & Nishida, T. (1984). Individual and cultural influences on uncertainty reduction. *Communication Monographs, 51,* 23–36.

Gudykunst, W. B., Yang, S. M., & Nishida, T. (1985). A cross-cultural test of uncertainty reduction theory: Comparisons of acquaintance, friends, and dating relationships in Japan, Korea, and the United States. *Human Communication Research, 11,* 407–455.

Heider, F. (1958). *The psychology of interpersonal relations.* New York: John Wiley.

Homans, G. C. (1974). *Social behavior: Its elementary forms* (2nd ed.). New York: Harcourt Brace Jovanovich.

Jones, E. E., & Davis, K. E. (1965). From acts to dispositions. In L. Berkowitz (Ed.), *Advances in experimental social psychology* (Vol. 2, pp. 219–266). New York: Academic Press.

Jourard, S. (1960). Knowing, liking, and the "dyadic effect" in men's self-disclosure. *Merrill Palmer Quarterly of Behavior and Development, 6,* 178–186.

Kelley, H. H. (1973). The process of causal attribution. *American Psychologist, 28,* 107–128.

Kelley, H. H., & Thibaut, J. W. (1978). *Interpersonal relations: A theory of interdependence.* New York: John Wiley.

Koenig, F. (1971). Positive affective stimulus value and accuracy of role perception. *British Journal of Social and Clinical Psychology, 10,* 385–386.

Lalljee, M., & Cook, M. (1973). Uncertainty in first encounters. *Journal of Personality and Social Psychology, 26,* 137–141.

Lott, A. J., & Lott, B. E. (1974). The role of reward in the formation of positive interpersonal attitudes. In T. E. Huston (Ed.), *Foundations of interpersonal attraction* (pp. 171–192). New York: Academic Press.

Matarazzo, J. D., Wiens, A. N., & Saslow, G. (1965). Studies of interview speech behavior. In L. Krasner & L. P. Ullman (Eds.), *Research in behavior modification: New developments and implications* (pp. 179–210). New York: Holt, Rinehart & Winston.

McLaughlin, M. L., Cody, M. J., & Rosenstein, N. E. (1983). Account sequences in conversations between strangers. *Communication Monographs, 50,* 102–125.

Mehrabian, A. (1971). Verbal and nonverbal interaction of strangers in a waiting situation. *Journal of Experimental Research in Personality, 5,* 127–138.

Mehrabian, A., & Ksionzky, S. (1971). Factors of interpersonal behavior and judgment in social groups. *Psychological Reports, 28,* 483–492.

Miller, G. R., & Steinberg, M. (1975). *Between people.* Chicago: Science Research Associates.

Parks, M. R., & Adelman, M. B. (1983). Communication networks and the development of romantic relationships: An expansion of uncertainty reduction theory. *Human Communication Research, 10,* 55–79.

Prisbell, M., & Anderson, J. F. (1980). The importance of perceived homophily, level of uncertainty, feeling good, safety, and self-disclosure in interpersonal relationships. *Communication Quarterly, 28,* 22–33.

Roloff, M. E. (1981). *Interpersonal communication: The social exchange approach.* Beverly Hills, CA: Sage.

Sermat, V., & Smyth, M. (1973). Content analysis of verbal communication in the development of a relationship: Conditions influencing self-disclosure. *Journal of Personality and Social Psychology, 26,* 332–346.

Sherblom, J., & Van Rheenen, D. D. (1984). Spoken language indices of uncertainty. *Human Communication Research, 11,* 221–230.

Sunnafrank, M. (1983). Attitude similarity and interpersonal attraction in communication processes: In pursuit of an ephemeral influence. *Communication Monographs, 50,* 273–284.

Sunnafrank, M. (1984). A communication-based perspective on attitude similarity and interpersonal attraction in early acquaintance. *Communication Monographs, 51,* 372–380.

Sunnafrank, M. (1985). Attitude similarity and interpersonal attraction during early communicative relationships: A research note on the generalizability of findings to opposite-sex relationships. *Western Journal of Speech Communication, 49,* 73–80.

Sunnafrank, M., & Miller, G. R. (1981). The role of initial conversations in determining attraction to similar and dissimilar strangers. *Human Communication Research, 8,* 16–25.

Taylor, D. A., Altman, I., & Sorrentino, R. (1969). Interpersonal exchange as a function of rewards and costs and situational factors: Expectancy confirmation-disconfirmation. *Journal of Experimental Social Psychology, 5,* 324–339.

Taylor, D. A., Altman, I., & Wheeler, L. (1973). Self-disclosure in isolated groups. *Journal of Personality and Social Psychology, 26,* 39–47.

Thibaut, J. W., & Kelley, H. H. (1959). *The social psychology of groups.* New York: John Wiley.

Walster, E., Berscheid, E., & Walster, G. W. (1973). New directions in equity research. *Journal of Personality and Social Psychology, 25,* 151–176.

Walster, E., Walster, G. W., & Berscheid, E. (1978). *Equity: Theory and research.* Boston: Allyn & Bacon.

Worthy, M., Gary, A. L., & Kahn, G. M. (1969). Self-disclosure as an exchange process. *Journal of Personality and Social Psychology, 13,* 59–64.

CHAPTER 4

Interpersonal Communication Perspectives on Developmental Processes

There are three perspectives that represent the notion of developmental processes. The first example is found in the article by Duck, editor of the *Journal of Social and Personal Relationships*. He argues that most prior theories of relationships ". . . are focused at an individual level of analysis . . ." and goes on to suggest that future research should focus on the relational level.

The second perspective in this chapter is given to us by Leslie A. Baxter. Baxter breaks new ground by proposing three contradictions which she maintains constitute the primary dialectical forces which parties experience in their interpersonal relationships.

Third, Planalp attempts to link relational knowledge (our understanding of other relationships) to how we will communicate in a future relationship.

Finally, the last perspective in this chapter is presented by Trost and Kenrick who describe the evolutionary influences on interpersonal relationships.

RELATIONSHIPS AS UNFINISHED BUSINESS: OUT OF THE FRYING PAN AND INTO THE 1990s

Steve Duck

This paper outlines three problems that are foreseen to face us as we enter the 1990s. These are: (1) defining the nature of relationships in the face of discrepancies between the reports of partners and outsiders about the events that occur in the relationship; (2) clarifying the nature of claims that relationships are 'processes'; and (3) providing a better understanding of the everyday conduct and routines of relationships, particularly the role of everyday talk. It is argued that longitudinal work and work capturing the experiences and reports of both members of a dyad must solve the first problem at a theoretical level before they can be helpful. It is suggested that, after Billig's (1987) argument that thinking and arguing characterize social behavior, relationships are best conceived phenomenally as unfinished business, just as research usually is. Several suggestions are made about the nature of relationships and, in the course of the paper, some suggestions are made for future work on social and personal relationships, loneliness, social support, children's friendship and process models of relating.

The research decade of the 1990s begins for us with this issue of *JSPR*. The past decade has been a remarkable time of birth and growth for the field of social and personal relationships—and one that promises great opportunities for the 1990s as we consolidate our work. It is a time for continued optimism; nonetheless, this should be cautious optimism. Landmark years such as those ending in a 9 or in a 0 are beguiling and tend to make us think, unrealistically, that eras are ending or that we are suddenly moving into new ways of doing things, or, worse, to fall into the trap of unrestrained self-congratulatory decade reviews and 'an orgy of mutual-back-slapping' (Hinde, 1982).

By contrast, I believe that the 1980s, valuable though they have been in many respects and clearly the decade where the field of social and personal relationships was brought to birth, leave us with many remaining challenges and opportunities for resolving conceptual problems. Not only is this true at the 'micro level' of such research areas as love, maintenance of relationships and social support (see forthcoming 1990 Special Issue of *JSPR*), but also at the 'macro level' of broad-scale conceptualization of the phenomena that we study and the ways in which they should be envisioned. Most 'theories of relationships'— and there are not many—are focussed at an individual level of analysis and deal with individual attributions about relational events, individual processing of information about others, individual characteristics and their effect on relational partners, or individual strategies and plans for or about relationships. The 1990s should be the decade of expansion to a relational level of theory and analysis.

In this article I will spell out some of the implications of such a level of analysis, first focussing on persons as essentially future-oriented and then raising some fundamental issues about the

characterization of 'process' in relationships in that light. I will also weave into the argument some discussion of the roles of relaters' different perspectives on relational phenomena and the significance of everyday activity in the conduct of relationships. In particular, I shall emphasize the role of talk—not of language as a system, but of talk as a daily enacted relational adhesive that modifies and embodies relational forms. These arguments will lead to the specification of a number of objectives as we move inexorably towards the even more unrealistic 'milepost' of AD 2000, when we can expect calls for decade, centurial and even millenial reviews of our work.

THE DEVELOPING STYLE OF WORK IN SOCIAL AND PERSONAL RELATIONSHIPS

The titles of the last three Annual Review chapters on our field are testament to the subtly changing *Zeitgeist*. The first (Byrne & Griffitt, 1973) was entitled 'Interpersonal Attraction,' the next 'Interpersonal Attraction and Relationships' (Huston & Levinger, 1978) and the most recent 'Interpersonal Processes in Close Relationships' (Clark & Reis, 1988). A parallel change has been attached to the *style* of work as well as its focus. Thus, the recent battle-cry has been for work on process and transaction (Duck & Sants, 1983; Cutrona et al., 1990; Kelley et al., 1983; Clark & Reis, 1988; Duck, 1988; Reis & Shaver, 1988). What does it mean, how is it different, and what bridges must first be crossed before we reconceptualize relationships in this way?

One important element may be some reconceptualization of the ascendancy of cognition or judgement, pure and simple, in relating. Hinde (1979, 1981), from whose work some date the start of this field, urged attention to the patterning of interaction and, in various ways, this emphasis

Source: The article is taken from *Journal of Social and Personal Relationships* [7: 5–28, 1990]. (c) 1990 Sage Publications Ltd., 6 Bonhill St., London EC24A 4PU, UK. Reprinted by permission of Sage Publications Ltd.

on behavioral description has proved especially fruitful. Kelley et al. (1983), Planalp (1985, 1987) and Gottman (1989) have all shown us the importance of accounting for regularities in the patterns of such behavior as marital interaction, conflict, commitment or relationships between close associates. However, the observance of patterns of behavior is where the research begins, not where it ends. Although others (for example, Duck, 1986; Duck & Pond, 1989) have propounded a fuller description of the patterns of everyday behavior and everyday talk (rather than de-contextualized situations of conflict, for instance), it is the accounting for such patterns rather than their description alone which the above theorists urge upon us. While some approaches argue for attention to causal conditions surrounding patterns of interaction (Kelley et al., 1983), others (Planalp, 1987) have argued for an explanation in terms of schemata that produce patterns of behavior. Yet others have argued in different ways and at different levels that social forces, relational forces or individual forces influence relationships through complex dialectics that will indicate and create patterns across time as individuals attempt to resolve contradictory elements pulling them here or there. Thus, Rawlins (for example, Rawlins & Holl, 1988) seems to argue for study of dialectical forces *within an individual* as that person struggles to relate to others; Baxter (1988) seems to place the dialectical force *between people* as they contend with personal needs for, say, privacy, versus the other's needs for information; and Hinde (1981) notes the dialectics *between relationships and other forces,* whether individual or societal. These are important differences of emphasis within the same general school of thought.

An interesting notion in such a tradition is that individuals, dyads or relationships resolve their dilemmas and establish patterns of response or behavior over time as a consequence of resolving dialectical tensions. An equally challenging notion, however, has been proposed in an entirely different corner of the academic world by Billig (1987) when he argues that human thought is essentially dialogic and continuous so that resolution of dilemmas is a perpetual task and not one that is necessarily dealt with for ever by any particular apparent resolution. For Billig, thinking is always unfinished business carried out through argument with oneself and with others. In a recent book advocating a rhetorical approach to social psychology, Billig (1987) thus argues that the deliberative, contemplative, dialectical, argumentative—essentially dialogic—side of human life has been neglected in our theorizing. For Billig, a major part of our thinking is not making minor or major decisions as product, but reaching them as process. As thinkers, people are in constant dialog with themselves (and others), considering arguments and counter-arguments, proposing or imagining one possible future as against another, or speculating about the likelihood of this outcome and its ramifications rather than that. For Billig, we argue both with other people and with ourselves, weighing up alternatives, considering possibilities and dealing with different ways of resolving such discrepancies (cf. Rawlins's view of dialectics). Just as common sense, as has often been noted in textbooks, simultaneously confronts a culture with different and conflicting ways of viewing particular issues (cf. Hinde's view of dialectics), so people too reflect and confront arguments for and against particular viewpoints without always being able to decide between them (cf. Baxter's view of dialectics). For Billig, much of our thinking is unfinished business that *never* ends: while we are alive we are always persons with a future, the future is always somewhat uncertain, and we contemplate or discuss the alternative possible futures reflectively and can always reach new conclusions.

It is easy to see how this applies not only to research but also to relationships. (Indeed, a point that runs through the present paper is the reflexive point that researchers are also human beings and act in many of the same ways as other human beings whose behavior we try to explain. Thus, the parallel here is unsurprising but nonetheless important and ramified.) One of the most common conclusions reached in research papers is that reported findings leave more to be discovered or that 'more research needs to be done'. The quest for answers is often described as leading to more questions than answers, and, indeed, 'good research' is sometimes defined as that which leads to the best questions rather than the best answers (Reiss, 1988).

I believe that this type of analysis can be applied to the conduct of relationships also, for new apparent certainties or new levels of intimacy in relationships can lead to new problems or leaves others untouched. No interaction resolves all issues; every interaction has the potential for changing the relationship. In Shotter's (1987) words, relaters ever face 'a ceaselessly unforeseen originality' in their relating. Thus, negotiating a relationship to the point of reaching the agreement to marry evidently does not solve all of a related couple's problems, for example, but presents them instead with new ones. There is always more relating that needs to be done, in short, and even apparently stable relationships can be shown to be essentially open-ended by some catastrophe, crisis, development or declaration. In this sense, Billig's argument can be taken to generalize normal human processes of thought to the specific case of relationships since these, too, are also unfinished business—as marrying couples looking at the recent divorce figures may all too dramatically suspect. His argument suggests that we could usefully explore the possibility that, psychologically, relationships are at least not permanent stations or states so much as temporary transitions, or, as Duck & Sants (1983) argue, continuous processes. What this proposal requires is that we make closer consideration of the nature of processes in relationships. This seems to suggest that we consider the inherent tensions of relationships that prompt continual balancing (namely, the forces created in and for relationships by the obvious but often ignored fact that partners, even in well established relationships, have different perspectives upon it). It also suggests to me that we consider the role of talk in everyday life as a carrier or instrument for resolving discrepancies or dialogs that arise between alternative perspectives. This argument is simple in form, but complex in detail: it is that relationships are unfinished business conducted through resolution of and dialog about personal, dyadic or relational dilemmas,

through talk. It requires us, however, to explore the underlying philosophies of work on relationships and to challenge the 'objective' stance that is often presumed for an observer, especially a scientific one, in our scholarly discussions. It also requires us to consider the relative roles of individual, dyadic and relational levels of analysis.

How then, is our unfinished business to progress? Let us consider some lines of development presently achieving greater recognition in this field and try to pick out these underlying themes in each of them. Recent claims identify topics felt to be especially needful of correction in our field and these provide a guide. Thus, calls for a process orientation to relationships have become increasingly fashionable (Duck & Sants, 1983; Clark & Reis, 1988), as are calls for longitudinal research and for collection of data from both partners in the dyad (Lloyd, forthcoming). The advantages of these emphases were in fact spelled out in the very first pages of the opening issue of this Journal in 1984 (Duck et al., 1984). It is true that longitudinal work is under-strength in this field (and Griffin & Sparks [1990] provide an interesting exemplar of such work over a 4-year span). It is also true that most research seeks to understand punctate reaction rather than longitudinal change, and that most papers sample the thinking of one member of a dyad, couple or pair. It can only be to the good of the field if such work is matched by a new focus of research on broader perspectival and temporal issues.

Nonetheless, these calls need to be thought through. The study of a problem longitudinally brings its own special difficulties (for instance, Griffin & Sparks [1990] report the first study we have published where one subject died between treatments!). Furthermore, the study of a problem longitudinally does not automatically make the work good, interesting or useful unless conceptual, theoretical work has been done beforehand to depict the nature of the phenomenon ('a relationship') that is being studied diachronically and how changes in its path affect the whole. To argue that we will understand 'a relationship' by studying it across time precisely begs the question, in the true meaning of that phrase: In order to reach a definition of a relationship, we need to study it across time, but the 'it' is what we are trying to define in the first place. Therefore, in order to define it and study it over time, we have to presume that it had already been defined. Thus, we assume the conclusion in the proof. Likewise, the adoption of a process approach does not solve problems until the nature of the process itself is clearly understood and built into theory in an intelligible or testable way, and distinguished from a mere synonym for the word 'operation' (cf. Cutrona et al., 1990; Eckenrode & Wethington, 1990; Leatham & Duck, 1990).

It is too readily assumed that the data of 'a relationship' are definite and that what we are tracking through time is the way in which such agreed data move along a pathway, rather than, for instance, utterly transform themselves as insects do at various points in their lives (Duck, 1984). Thus, when Kelley et al. (1983: 13) argue that 'descriptive analysis necessarily precedes the clarification of relationships,' we should note that the claim assumes that there will necessarily be agreement about the items to be classified and described. Nonetheless, for each disciplinary branch of the scholarly tree of relationship science, some elements count as data and some as error term or as irrelevant, and yet one researcher's 'error term' can easily be the very topic of another's Life's Work (Duck & Sants, 1983). The choice of data—of what is to *count* as data—precedes even the description of 'what is occurring in an interaction.' The time has now come for us to adopt more critical awareness of the different ways in which members of this interdisciplinary community slice the conceptual pie. Some research focuses on the attributions made in relationships and therefore presumes, as it were, that what goes on in the head comes out of the mouth in ways that do not need to be researched (Ross & McFarland, 1988). Others in our scholarly community focus on the style and structure of talk itself, without focusing much on the attributions that may precede it (for example, Hopper et al., 1981). Some may explore the *effects* of a sense of social support on health, while others seek to explain where the sense of social support comes from and how it is daily transacted

(Gottlieb, 1985; Cutrona et al., 1990). Such diversity is all to the good and this Journal has taken a strong position of support for multiplicity and diversity of styles of research. However, it is useful to pause and explore our assumptions here and to notice that each researcher's focus implicitly redraws a very, very complex map of relational phenomena. The decision to count certain phenomena as data and not to count others is an implicit theoretical statement about processes in relationships. Our eventual task as researchers is not to argue for this or that style of data gathering, but to compile a sensible composite picture from the jigsaw pieces that different research strategies ultimately create.

Paradoxically, this point can be well illustrated by the parallel problem of dyadic data and how they should be treated, parallel in the sense that just as different scientific observers of relationship phenomena make different decisions about the data that are to be accounted, so do partners in relationships. Gottman (1979, 1989) has shown the latter in his extensive program study of conflict in married couples, where disagreement about the starting-point, structure and course of the disagreement is as likely as is conflict about the topic of the disagreement itself.

DYADIC DATA

Some authors (for example, Berscheid & Peplau, 1983: 12) lament the fact that 'when investigators cannot agree on an issue so fundamental as when two people are in a "relationship" with each other . . . [it is] . . . problematic indeed.' Others have argued (for example, Olson, 1977; Duck & Sants, 1983) that differences in perspectives on relationships are endemic to the nature of the concept. It is time, I believe, for this field to move from the level of analysis that expects agreement on terminology and towards an understanding of the higher-order question of the *meaning* of differences in terminology for, or perspectives on, relationships. We should stop treating differences between observers, methods and data sets as merely irritating annoyances involving some form of measurement error and we should start to realize that the differences are grounds for theoretical work, in several senses. What do differences in perspectives mean for theory? Why and in what circumstances do they occur? How should they be dealt with in our future work?

Relationships can be studied and represented, sometimes implicitly, as purely objective entities without consideration of the ways in which subjects actually experience them day to day (except insofar as such experiences indicate a partial, 'inaccurate' or 'biased' understanding of the relationship that the objective observer is studying). Thus, Kelley et al. (1983: 23) define 'properties of relationships' very carefully as 'any summary description of interaction that an investigator may choose to devise.' (Note that the responsibility for creating a useful terminology of properties lies with the investigator/describer in this definition.) Later in the argument, however, properties are discussed not as descriptive impositions but as real properties of relationships about which participants' reports may differ, in complexity or awareness from those made by the, by now, 'impartial objective observer,' as if such observers do not also have perspectives. In brief, the claim shifts from one based on *attributed* properties to one based on *revealed* properties, and from the role of the observer as creator of labels to one based on the observer as privy to the truth, from the Rhetoric of Power Codes to the Rhetoric of Truth Codes (McGee & Lyne, 1987). This is an important logical shift, and a frequent one in this field, whose subtlety and importance to the discourse of researchers is easily missed. In brief, a problem that faces researchers in the 1990s is to grasp the *phenomenal nature* of relationships as well as those factors that 'objectively' ought to influence them to develop, stabilize or decline. This problem will entail us understanding more about what we mean by 'a process.' It will also entail us tackling the theoretical question of whether a relationship exists independently of the two partners' views and experiences of it or somehow is created from their views. One thing we do not yet know is the way in which partners' perspectives on the relationship grow and change

individually but also come to converge over time into a combined history of the relationship, for example.

Berscheid & Peplau (1983: 13) acknowledge that

> the degree of correspondence between the participants' beliefs about the relationship and an investigator's description of the properties of the actual [sic] relationship activity encompasses a huge set of interesting questions. However, to be useful, relationship descriptors must ultimately be true to the properties of the interconnected activity patterns that can be recorded and agreed upon by impartial investigators.

Work published before and since that statement has indicated the inadvisability of too great a degree of optimism about the agreement of either impartial observers or relationship participants on the activity patterns within the relationship (Olson, 1977; Gottman, 1979; Surra et al., 1988). Nor, even if such evidence did not exist, should we too readily assume that impartial observers will agree about the defining content of 'a relationship'—at least we know how the researchers do not. My point is that such disagreement can be treated in one of two ways: one way treats it as an irritation that makes the work of science difficult; the other treats disagreements as data and tries to explain *why* they occur and what it means that they do.

Equally, the Kelley et al. (1983) analysis begins (p. 22) by stating that 'causation is never observed directly; it is always inferred' or, in terms of the previous points, it is an attribution or an inference or a proposition posed by an observer. Later in the argument, however, the causal links and causal connections are given objective status taken away from the activity of an observer; thus (p. 25) the authors write of "the operative causal conditions,' 'multiple causation is the rule rather than the exception,' and 'the contributing cause.' Thus, the argument again subtly shifts from descriptive terms found phenomenally useful by an observer seeking to create regularity and understanding, to the case where the regularities *are there* and are revealed to the right persons using the right methods.

This is an extremely important point in the study of relationships. Its importance is not just that it is difficult to grasp but that it cuts to the roots of the philosophy of science that presently pervades the area. It is only if we assume that relationships exist independently of the participants themselves that we as outside observers can ever claim that a relater's reports are biased, for instance (since bias, by definition, necessarily presumes a discrepancy from an objectively determinable standard). It is also only if such objective assumptions are made that we can raise questions as to the 'accuracy' of people's claims about their numbers of friends (since this again presumes that there are true numbers, independently of the subject's beliefs and reports, that we can use as a basis for assessing 'the validity' of subjects' reports). (Yet in other sections of a report [usually the Methods and Procedures section], researchers allow subjects to define friendship, dating, . . . and so on for themselves and tell *us* if they qualify as subjects for our study!) It is only if such assumptions are made that we can talk of 'the size' of someone's social network as a permanent feature of their social world and consequently get perturbed about the differences between 'actual' and 'perceived' social support. On the 'objective' model, discrepancies or conflict between parties are special puzzles that lead us to explore their emotions about, but rarely their different views of, an argument; on the 'phenomenal model' it is to be expected that partners will disagree about conflict as about anything else, and the interest centers on the communicative mechanisms by which they resolve or fail to resolve such differences. It is not, then, that we cannot ask about the relationships between subjective reports and 'objective data'; rather, we should be clear about what it means to make the comparison.

If, for example, we relate the person's sense of the size of his or her perceived network, or nominations of friends, or assignments to friendship categories, to such other variables as daily fluctuation and change as mood, we may find that fluctuations can be understood to define something of the character of friendship. Barbee's

(1990), work for instance, shows that a person's mood affects the performance of friendship roles. Equally, a person whose friendship nominations remain stable through trouble and difficulty just may be a different sort of person from those whose nominations change and shift somewhat. Just as children's friendship nominations are notably unstable in the child's earlier years (Asher & Gottman, 1982), so too as adults we experience feeling warmer or colder about other persons as we continue to experience them day to day. It is not that one of the views of the friendship is 'more accurate' than the other; it is that friendship is experienced differently at different times and under different circumstances; it is not a stable, average experience, but rather one that varies round the average. In other contexts we all know that mean and variance *together* provide more useful information about phenomena than does either measure alone. For this reason, researchers should begin not only to collect as data, but also to report, variabilities in the friendship status claims/reports of subjects, and then should begin the work of explaining any discovered patterns in such variability.

The same issue lies at the root of the problem of dyadic data. If we do as some urge and collect the beliefs about friendship or personal relationships from both partners in a dyad, then we may learn little more than that two persons disagree. There is already stunning evidence from Surra et al. (1988) that some couples can disagree by *more than one year* on the date of their first sexual intercourse together. So what do we learn from such dyadic data? It could be that the different persons use different definitions of what 'intercourse' means, or it could be that persons differ in their recall of relationship events (itself an interesting research issue), or it could be that they experience the relationship differently, or it could all be due to the problems of memory and retrospection, or to measurement error. These are *all* implicit 'theories' about the data and although one of them is routinely preferred over the others in scientific reports, the basis for so doing is often mere habit. So-called (but, let it be noted, unresearched—Duck, 1988) biases, errors, perspectival shifts and retrospective rewriting of history or attributional realignments probably evidence processes that are important in the development, maintenance and even existence of relationships.

I have dwelt on two types of perspective difference, one between the participants in a relationship and the other between the different disciplines that make up our field. Consider now a third: that provided by the passage of time. Researchers' own view of our field is different today from the view that reviewers took of it 10 years ago. Much has changed. Equally, partners in a relationship are faced with substantial changes to their experiences as their relationships continue across time. Each day is filled with somewhat different events that give somewhat different opportunities for experiencing success and failure, seeing one's limitations, experiencing the benefits and costs of a given friendship or of friendship in general, or developing, maintaining or dissolving relationships. Therefore, reactions differ even within a given type of 'state' of relationship. Relationships are not driven just by constant unidirectional forces but are subject to volatile interior psychological psychodynamics · and to other unstable elements exterior to the relationship, as a variety of scholars has shown.

How would our work be different if we were to build into our models of relationships and relationshipping that which subjective experience tells us, namely that human beings are occasionally inconsistent, and responsive to the daily events and changes that occur in their lives? For one thing, we would focus to some extent—not entirely, but to some extent—on the ways in which daily events affect a person's perceptions of alternative futures for a relationship (develop it?, stabilize it?, maintain it?, dissolve it?). We might even get interested in the ways in which they *talk* about the future of the relationship.

At present we take perhaps too little notice of the temporal and perspectival fluctuations that probably affect our subjects as much as they evidently affect ourselves as scholars and as human beings. On some days they, too, may feel anxieties about the relationship's future that are not felt on other days; such alternative forms and futures for the relationship would occupy their decisions about how to act (How would partner react if I did this as opposed to that?). Sometimes persons are the victims of genuine doubt, changes of mind and heart, repentance or uncertainty (Billig, 1987). On some days people feel happy and on others sad (Barbee, 1990). How then are we to conceptualize the fluctuations in feelings about a friend that this discussive and debating rhetorical model of human behavior predicts?

As researchers we have typically assumed that feelings about a friend are important reflections of a given stage or level of relationship. Such a position is roundly criticized at length by Acitelli & Duck (1987) and by Reis & Shaver (1988). Only rarely and in 'process models' is the possibility suggested that expressed feelings reflect some state of the person's larger inner life instead. Thus, Reis & Shaver (1988: 376) argue that 'a [process] model of intimacy must include fluctuating motives, needs and strategic concerns. . . . [I]t is unsafe to assume that [a person] has perpetual, constant tendencies towards intimacy that are independent of specific desires, fears, and goals.' Thus, we can theoretically accommodate the experience of being irritated by a friend one day and exhilarated the next; or the indecisiveness of how to ask someone out for a date, propose marriage or lead up to an intensification of involvement or seriousness. Indeed, as Billig (1987) contends, human beings debate or discuss with others; we often get involved in the long-term effort of *making* plans rather than just having them; and in the course of so doing we choose between possibilities that in some sense are equally considerable, at least for a moment. Thus, we also define for ourselves and for our partners some aspect of our relationship with them, by selecting those choices and alternatives that, for example, define the power balance in the relationship, set up the notion of caring about the other's feelings, or are consistent with a future together rather than apart. Minor changes of feeling and focus about a given relationship are daily experiences yet are hardly ever studied.

Once researchers have captured 'a relationship' by asking subjects some questions, it is all too easy to treat it as forever stable.

PROCESS

Such considerations bring us into confrontation with the rather large but crucial question for the 1990s: How do we theorize the *processes* of relationships and day-to-day life?

Some authors (for example, Huston et al., 1981) write of 'interpersonal processes' which are grasped nonetheless only indirectly by study of individual or dyadic retrospective reports of transactions; others (for example, Reis & Shaver, 1988) write of 'relational processes' and seem to mean the cognitive operations that are not directly observable, but whose products interest us, and also transactive interaction; at other times the word 'process' is used as something of a handy but misleading synonym for 'operations' (as in 'the process of social support,' studied as an outcome consequent upon a behavior such as requesting help). Several other writers (too numerous to cite fairly) offer 'process models' of relating in the form of black boxes with arrows between them, or circles with differing degrees of overlap, describing the black boxes or diagrams as the process when it is really the *arrows* or the *movements* of the circles that should be so characterized. I think we in this field should begin to have a standard question for all producers of such models and the question should be: 'How do you propose to conceptualize the arrows or the movement?' Let me give a facetious caricature, represented by Figure 1 and its model of cooking, along similar lines. The really interesting bit—the process, the part we want to comprehend—is consigned to the status of an arrow.

FIGURE 1   The 'Process model' of cooking.

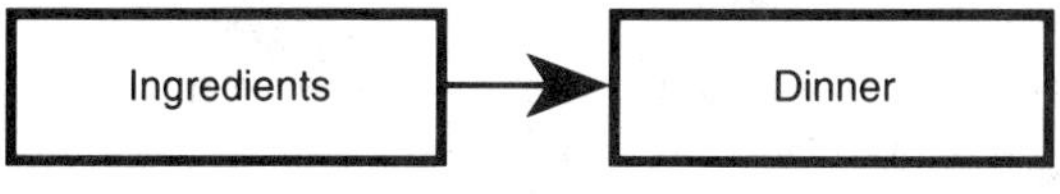

Despite the loose ways in which 'process' is often used, there is one key feature to a process: The essence of a process is *time,* and the recognition that time modifies detail is never far from a true process model. However, there are two things to bear in mind here: one deals with the ways in which process is to be conceptualized by the researchers and the other with the ways in which it is reported by the subjects. Processes are transitions between states which are clearly recognized and easily definable end-points. Here lies the trap: it is easier to diagram the end-points than the movement that is continuous. This trap, identified by Proust, William James and Wittgenstein, is, namely, that however much we know that time flows by, and things change imperceptibly, nevertheless human beings, including scientific speculators, have a tendency to think and perceive in 'stills' rather than in 'movies.' For this reason, explored by social-cognition researchers (Ross & McFarland, 1988), humans find it easier to look for change-*points* than change itself in their relationships and identify days, times, and even minutes when they saw things changing. Continuous transitions are thus most often summarized in convenient but dangerously misleading ways that provide useful simplifications of unimaginable complexity and so assist subsequent thinking. Thus, researchers in the past have often characterized divorce as an event rather than a process, something that happened the day the partners actually split up or the day the court papers were signed—or official agencies may require dates to be assigned to relationship change (such as official marriage dates) when the psychological and communicative momentum to reach that 'turning-point' is concealed at points in history well before the event itself 'occurs.' Handy mnemonics though such diagrammatic forms are, they nevertheless lead even thoughtful scientists into the same serious trap: 'we describe incomplete [or continuous] processes by their supposed final product' (Shotter, 1987: 227). This is, however, a general human tendency: what we are dealing with here is a tendency to report things in a particular way rather than an accurate report of the events themselves, far less of the processes behind them. Just as our diagrams to explain change often conspicuously omit true process from the diagram in favor of antecedents or results of change, so too existing models and theories offered to account for process are often, as described above, schematic representations of beginning and end-points alone. Our task as relationship researchers, however, is to conceptualize process—the arrow part, not the end-points alone—and to bear in mind the human tendency, which applies to us also, of thinking in terms of stages or easily characterizable end-points of processes rather than the processes themselves.

TALK AND EVERYDAY ROUTINES

Such thinking and focussing on states and end-points has led us to overlook daily behavior, since this is essentially rather fluid and protean and hence difficult to fit into neat categories. The call for focus on such work is now, however, beginning to be answered in the area of social support, and is doing so by drawing on the literature of the previously separated field of personal relationships. Thus, Gottlieb (1985) and Pierce et al. (1990) argue for a process approach to the transactions of social support as they are carried out in other psychological and environmental contexts. Also, Cutrona et al. (1990) argue for closer attention to the actual transactions of social support and elucidation not only of the verbal content of the act of delivering support but also its nonverbal context. Leatham & Duck (1990) extend this argument to a call for attention, by social-support researchers and personal-relationship workers alike, to the routine relational contexts that provide background for management of sudden stress—a context provided by daily conversation and interaction between people in long-term relationships. From such regular and previously unremarked activity spring the sense of support that has nevertheless been so often shown to be correlated only moderately with the actual delivery of support at the time of crisis (Cutrona, 1986).

Important here is the idea that daily transactions, behavior and conversation influence some of the global cognitive and psychological forces that have been previously assumed to be stable, monolithic influences on relational behavior, such as 'emotion' or 'cognition.' Daily transactions are *joint* activity between people which, since they are conjointly constructed, cannot be attributed safely to one particular source of causation (Shotter, 1987). To the extent that we fail to comprehend the role of talk in the everyday experience of subjects, in their relationships and in their everyday social activity, we fail also to understand a relational level of analysis. Equally, many items that we treat as independent variables, when we cut the conceptual pie at one point in the process, are themselves likely to be dependent variables at other points, and many features that can be seen from one perspective as 'individual' become 'relational' when we attend to truly joint action or transaction, as more complex analytic procedures for relational data are making all too plain (Kenny, 1988).

Just as we researchers have arguments as to the objectivity of relational phenomena, so we tend to assume that relational events are perceived in unmediated form by our subjects, but of course they are not. Attitude similarity, if it is to have any effect, must be *revealed,* and is likely to be discovered through talk; desires for intimacy have to be *communicated* if they are to influence anyone else; self-disclosure has, most often, to be *conveyed through talk* if it is to play its part in relationship development or change. In short, the time has come for researchers on relationships to explore the ways in which gross psychological variables have their effects through communication, the ways in which people talk to one another about their relationship to achieve relational goals, and the role of everyday talk in the broad area of personal-relationship conduct.

A Case for Talk

We could extend such an argument to make the claim that much social interaction and communication serve the purpose not of ratifying the past but of proposing a future or offering a view of what is to come, out of the many views that can be proposed. One element in our field at present is the belief that once we can define the form of a relationship, it takes on a definite and predictable character and, as such, its dynamic potential for change may be forgotten until it becomes one of those Dissolving Relationships to which we attend anew, usually but possibly incorrectly, using somewhat different explanatory principles (compare and contrast Duck, 1982).

In this respect the role of everyday talk in the daily conduct of relationships is undervalued as a mechanism for change, which is most often explained in terms of exterior 'events' or internal attitudinal or cognitive, attributional catastrophes (see chapters in Duck & Gilmour, 1981). Talk is often not of direct interest to the workers in our field and is sometimes operationalized as a mere medium for the transmission of thought. If we, by contrast, hypothesize that talk in relationships is not just a simple medium for exposure of feelings or psychological states, or at the very least is more complex in its functions than a mere vessel for cognition, then some exciting new ideas emerge. We can characterize talk as something that serves creative, *instrumental* functions (for example, it serves to promote intimacy or argument or the exertion of power [cf. the Huston et al. (1981) work indicating the importance of negotiation over leisure time and activity]) or as a provider of *indexical* functions (such as showing intimacy—for example, the work by Hopper et al. [1981] on personal idioms in relationships), but thirdly, also as something that actually *embodies the relationship* (Duck & Pond, 1989) and defines it. Talk should not be excluded from our considerations in the study of relationships, nor should it be studied just as a vehicle for the enactment of strategies although the field is in need of more work on that, too. Yet even in significant methodological developments in our approach to social participation, such as the Rochester Interaction Record (Wheeler &

Nezlek, 1977), it is *thoughts about* interaction that are assessed and not a single question assesses either the content or the style of participants' talk—the ways in which they *interact* rather than just participate or, as it were, merely sample social activity. Yet those measures that assess satisfaction with an interaction are presumably (and are presumed to be) tapping effects created in the mind by other minds through joint activity. In real social life, these effects are created not by the disembodied collisions of thoughts, attitudes or opinions, but by transactions usually involving talk that transmits those thoughts to the outside world and has effects of the type studied for so long by communication researchers. Thus, the transacted *inter*action of social participation does not consist of thoughts and evaluations moving at random through the air, but is built substantially on talk in all its complexity.

Although Billig's argument for a rhetorical approach to social science can be applied to relationships, then, it can be buttressed by further concepts from a more traditional background provided by rhetorical theory. Rhetoric typically (for example, Hauser, 1986) examines communicative *actions* of an agent exercising choice, as distinguished from natural *motion* in the physical world. Action is broken down into five modes. *Situated action* is action that takes place in a specific place at a specific time and whose characteristics jointly influence the meaningfulness and relevance of the communication that occurs. Relational theorists such as Ginsburg (1988) have used a similar concept. *Symbolic action* is action using symbols with a meaning to the participants. Several examples of such human abilities to create and manipulate symbols in relationships have been identified directly by Baxter (1987) in her intriguing work on relational symbols, and indirectly by Hopper et al. (1981) in their work on the development of personal idioms of speech by persons forming relationships. *Transaction* refers to the dynamic symbolic exchanges that occur among communicating partners. It is important that rhetorical theory does not, as so many studies in our own field presently do, conceptualize (or at least conduct studies as if) social behavior consisted of one active person doing 'social things' *to* another, passive, person. Older and now discredited studies of propaganda took such an active–passive perspective, whereas recent studies of interpersonal communication (for example, Cappella, 1988) concern themselves with transaction. Regrettably too few studies in the field of personal relationships actually study the transaction that the authors are nevertheless likely to infer towards in their discussion sections. By contrast, Gottman (Gottman & Parker, 1988) has done work that notably focuses on transactions and shows many profitable and distinctive future directions for such ideas (Gottman, 1989). *Social action* involves one person attempting to engage another person (through symbols). Thus, although events can be seen to occur, the significance of the events, the ways in which they are understood and perceived, and the ways in which they are resolved, are essentially social constructs. Thus, although individuals may reflect on the past, it is the 'reflection' part, not the 'part' part, that has greatest effect on their subsequent behavior, their mental activity, not the 'objective reality' that creates effects on their thinking (G. Kelly, 1969). *Strategic action* is evident in, and is often singled out for study by, research on social and personal relationships. It is clear that *some* relationship activity is strategic and much attention has been devoted to secret tests (Baxter & Wilmot, 1984), affinity testing (Douglas, 1987) and plan making (Berger, 1988). This is all to the good. However, it is also evident that much relationship activity is *not* strategic in this sense (Duck & Rutt, 1989) and that by focussing mostly on the thoughtful, often punctate, aspects of relating we run the risk of overlooking the routines that are clearly evident in most of our lives and which are often conducted through and as talk with others.

In other words, it would help us greatly if we were to explore the implications (for the present and the future of relationships) of the narratives and accounts that individuals construct about the past. Interesting recent work indicates both that the creation of stories about, for instance, 'our first meeting' tend as much to reflect the person's particular needs and to embody the relationship's present in their eyes, as it does to capture the relationship's first encounter 'accurately' (Duck & Miell, 1986). Furthermore, a person's reconstruction of the last 3 days of a relationship are as significant a force in indicating the subject's expectations about the future as is the rest of the relationship's history (Miell, 1987). A relationship's history—that is, the emotional and constructive bits that matter, its meaning rather than the historical 'facts' of its date and so on—is in our heads or hearts, not on paper.

In sum, then, a needed development in the field of social and personal relationships is a focus on the ways in which talk itself serves to mediate, energize and embody some of the operations which we have learned more about in this last decade. For instance, how do different love styles or attachment styles get transmitted into the world through styles of talk? They cannot be merely mental frameworks but must have some influence on the ways in which subjects talk to each other to convey their emotions. How do subjects talk intimately? What is the role of 'Future talk' in setting the trajectory for developing relationships? How do the transactions of social support actually convey comfort, support or assistance? How do the conversations of children relate to their friendship interaction and their expression of changing capacities for friendship with age? How do lonely people represent their worlds in their talk and how does such talk construct their loneliness?

I do not advocate the closer study of talk in a vacuum, since it is clearly only one large but missing part of the meaning of the term 'process in relationships.' Other elements are 'participant perspectives' and 'time' as factors. However, the points are all related since to take a 'process view' of relationships is to adopt a different pattern of discourse about research, to focus on different elements in the puzzle of relationships, and to empower the study of phenomena in different ways from those currently pursued. Each testifies to the fact that relational events are perceived not in a direct way but in mediated ways, through memory, recall, dialog and conversation. Everyday conversation is our window on these processes as they affect real-life relationships.

However, these points about the talk of our subjects in their relationships are paralleled by the need for researchers also to 'watch their language' and the ways in which our thinking about the phenomena is guided by it. Rhetoricians are not the only reviewers who recognize that persons reveal their thinking through the nature of their discourse, not only in respect of particular words and content (Duck, 1987), but also through the higher-order structure in which discourse is constructed (McGee & Lyne, 1987). Thus, scientists use a form of discourse as well as a content that is recognizably 'scientific.' In such discourse, appeals are made to certain sorts of symbols that empower a scientific description and increase the *ethos* or personal credibility of the person making the claims. In scientific reports, for instance, a large part is devoted to description of method and the Rhetoric of Method adds credibility to the inferences that are claimed in the discourse itself, thus bolstering the claims made there (McGee & Lyne, 1987). The Rhetoric of Enquiry studies the ways in which scholars communicate amongst themselves and the ways in which the *structure* of their discourse influences its content and the very methods used, a point that I have alluded to here already by commenting on the dominance of the trajectory metaphor in conceptualizing relationship growth. Indeed, in analysis of the ways in which changes to the APA style manual have been precedent to new views of the work of psychologists, Bazerman (1987) argues that 'to treat scientific style as fixed and

epistemologically neutral is rhetorically naive and historically wrong.' Thus, we should be aware of researchers' styles of language and metaphors as much as we need to pay attention to the talk of our subjects of study. These points about talk here have implications not only for study of participants' reports in relationships—in so far as it would urge us to attend to the structure of their discourse in relationships—but also for the way in which we view our own activity as scientists studying relationships.

I have dwelt on these issues not with a purpose of being negative about our impressive and promising past in this field, but with the hope of showing the exciting challenges that lie ahead and some fruitful directions for going to meet them. If we wrestle satisfactorily with these opportunities for theoretical development, then we will build on the base established in the 1980s and prove it to have been an entrancing threshold into the rich house of research understanding that stands in this fascinating, absorbing and vibrant field.

I have tried to show that in order to expand the theoretical approach to relationships to a satisfactory dyadic or relational level of analysis, we must first grapple with the problems of discrepancies in perspective and conceptualization of process. There is plenty of good thinking in the present field on which to build, but the transacted nature of relationships, seen from a dyadic level, presents us with our greatest and most rewarding theoretical challenges. These must be tackled if we are not to look back on the 1990s as a time of disappointment and retrenched analysis of individual cognition's contribution to relationships as if that were all there is to relating.

REFERENCES

Acitelli, L. K. & Duck, S. W. (1987) 'Intimacy as the Proverbial Elephant,' in D. Perlman & S. W. Duck (eds) *Intimate Relationships.* Newbury Park: Sage.

Asher, S. R. & Gottman, J. M. (1982) *The Development of Children's Friendship.* Cambridge: Cambridge University Press.

Barbee, A. (1990). 'Interactive Coping: The Cheering up Process in Close Relationships,' in S. W. Duck (ed.) *Personal Relationships and Social Support*. London: Sage.

Baxter, L. A. (1987) 'Symbols of Relationship Identity in Relationship Cultures,' *Journal of Social and Personal Relationships* 4: 261–80.

Baxter, L. A. (1988) 'A Dialectical Perspective on Communication Strategies in Relationship Development,' in S. W. Duck et al. (eds) *Handbook of Personal Relationships*. Chichester: Wiley.

Baxter, L. A. & Wilmot, W. (1984) 'Secret Tests: Social Strategies for Acquiring Information about the State of the Relationship,' *Human Communication Research* 11: 171–201.

Bazerman, C. (1987) 'Codifying the Social Scientific Style: The APA Publications Manual as a Behaviorist Rhetoric,' in J. S. Nelson, A. Megill & D. N. McCloskey (eds) *The Rhetoric of the Human Sciences: Language and Argument in Scholarship and Public Affairs*. Madison: U Wisc Press.

Berger, C. R. (1988) 'Uncertainty and Information Exchange in Developing Relationships,' in S. W. Duck et al. (eds) *Handbook of Personal Relationships*. Chichester: Wiley.

Berscheid, E. & Peplau, L. A. (1983) 'The Emerging Science of Relationships,' in H. H. Kelley, E. Berscheid, A. Christensen, J. H. Harvey, T. L. Huston, G. Levinger, E. M. McClintock, L. A. Peplau & D. R. Peterson. *Close Relationships*. New York: W. H. Freeman.

Billig, M. (1987) *Arguing and Thinking: A Rhetorical Approach to Social Psychology*. Cambridge: Cambridge University Press.

Burnett, R., McGhee, P. & Clarke, D. (1987) *Accounting for Relationships*. London: Methuen.

Byrne, D. & Griffitt, W. (1973) 'Interpersonal Attraction,' *Annual Reviews of Psychology* 24: 317–36.

Cappella, J. N. (1988) 'Personal Relationships, Social Relationships and Patterns of Interaction,' in S. W. Duck et al. (eds) *Handbook of Personal Relationships*.

Clark, M. S. & Reis, H. T. (1988). 'Interpersonal Processes in Close Relationships,' *Annual Reviews of Psychology* 39: 609–72.

Cutrona, C. E. (1986) 'Objective Determinants of Perceived Social Support,' *Journal of Personality and Social Psychology* 50: 349–55.

Cutrona, C. E., Suhr, J. & McFarlane, R. (1990) 'Interpersonal Transactions and the Psychological Sense of Support,' in S. W. Duck (ed.) *Personal Relationships and Social Support*. London: Sage.

Douglas, W. (1987) 'Affinity Testing in Initial Interaction,' *Journal of Social and Personal Relationships* 4: 3–16.

Duck, S. W. (1982) 'A Topography of Relationship Disengagement and Dissolution,' in S. W. Duck (ed.) *Personal Relationships 4: Dissolving Personal Relationships*. London: Academic Press.

Duck, S. W. (1984). 'A Perspective on the Repair of Personal Relationships: Repair of What, When?,' in S.W. Duck (ed.) *Personal Relationships 5: Repairing Personal Relationships*. London: Academic Press.

Duck, S. W. (1986) *Human Relationships*. London: Sage.

Duck, S. W. (1987) 'Adding Apples and Oranges: Investigators' Implicit Theories about Relationships,' in R. Burnett, P. McGhee & D. Clarke (eds) *Accounting for Relationships*. London: Methuen.

Duck, S. W. (1988) *Relating to Others*. Milton Keynes, UK: Open University/Dorsey Press.

Duck, S. W. & Gilmour, R. (eds) (1981) *Personal Relationships 2: Developing Personal Relationships*. London: Academic Press.

Duck, S. W. & Miell, D. E. (1986) 'Charting the Development of Relationships,' in R. Gilmour & S. W. Duck (eds) *The Emerging Field of Personal Relationships*. Hillsdale, NJ: LEA.

Duck, S. W. & Pond, K. (1989) 'Friends, Romans, Countrymen, Lend Me Your Retrospective Data: Rhetoric and Reality in Personal Relationships,' in C. Hendrick (ed.) *Review of Personality and Social Psychology, Vol. 10: Close Relationships*. Newbury Park: Sage.

Duck, S. W. & Rutt, D. J. (1989) 'Everyday Experience of Relational Communication: Are All Communications Created Equal?' paper presented at the Annual Convention of the Speech Communication Association, New Orleans, November.

Duck, S. W. & Sants, H. K. A. (1983). On the Origins of the Specious: Are Interpersonal Relationships Really Interpersonal States?,' *Journal of Social and Clinical Psychology* 1: 27–41.

Duck, S. W., Fitzpatrick, M., Lock, A. & McCall, G. J. (1984) 'Social and Personal Relationships: A Joint Editorial,' *Journal of Social and Personal Relationships* 1: 1–10.

Eckenrode, J. & Wethington, E. (1990) 'The Process and Outcome of Mobilizing Social Support,' in S. W. Duck (ed.) *Personal Relationships and Social Support*. London: Sage.

Ginsburg, G. P. (1988) 'Rules, Scripts and Prototypes in Personal Relationships,' in S. W. Duck et al. (eds) *Handbook of Personal Relationships*. Chichester: Wiley.

Gottlieb, B. H. (1985) 'Social Support and the Study of Personal Relationships,' *Journal of Social and Personal Relationships* 2: 351–75.

Gottman, J. M. (1979) *Marital Interaction: Experimental Investigations*. New York: Academic Press.

Gottman, J. M. (1989) 'Berscheid-Hatfield Award Address,' *Iowa/International Network on Personal Relationships Newsletter* 8: 7–13.

Gottman, J. M. & Parker, J. (eds) (1988) *Conversations with Friends*. Cambridge: Cambridge University Press.

Griffin, E. & Sparks, G. (1990) 'Friends Forever: A Longitudinal Exploration of Intimacy in Same Sex Friends and Platonic Pairs,' *Journal of Social and Personal Relationships* 7: 29–46.

Hauser. G. A. (1986) *Introduction to Rhetorical Theory*. New York: Harper & Row.

Hinde. R. A. (1979) *Towards Understanding Relationships*. London: Academic Press.

Hinde, R. A. (1981) 'The Bases of a Science of Interpersonal Relationships,' in S. W. Duck & R. Gilmour (eds) *Personal Relationships 1: Studying Personal Relationships*. London: Academic Press.

Hinde, R. A. (1982) 'Closing Remarks,' First International Conference on Personal Relationships, Madison, WI.

Hopper, R., Knapp, M. L. & Scott, L. (1981) 'Couples' Personal Idioms: Exploring Intimate Talk,' *Journal of Communication* 31: 23–33.

Huston, T. L. & Levinger, G. (1978) 'Interpersonal Attraction and Relationships,' *Annual Review of Psychology* 29: 115–56.

Huston, T. L., Surra, C. A., Fitzgerald, N. M. & Cate, R. M. (1981) 'From Courtship to Marriage: Mate Selection as an Interpersonal Process,' in S. W. Duck & R. Gilmour (eds) *Personal Relationships 2: Developing Personal Relationships*. London: Academic Press.

Kelley, H. K., Berscheid, E., Christensen, A., Harvey, J. H., Huston, T. L., Levinger, G., McClintock, E. M., Peplau. L. A. & Peterson, D. R. (1983) *Close Relationships*. New York: W. H. Freeman.

Kelly, G. A. (1969) 'Ontological Acceleration,' in B. Maher (ed.) *Clinical Psychology and Personality: The Collected Papers of George Kelly*. New York: Wiley.

Kenny, D. A. (1988) 'The Analysis of Data from Two Person Relationships,' in S. W. Duck et al. (eds) *Handbook of Personal Relationships*. Chichester: Wiley.

Leatham, G. & Duck, S. W. (1990) 'Conversations with Friends and the Dynamics of Social Support,' in S. W. Duck (ed.) *Personal Relationships and Social Support*. London: Sage.

Lloyd, S. A. (forthcoming) 'A Behavioral Self-report Technique for Assessing Conflict in Close Relationships,' *Journal of Social and Personal Relationships* 7.

McGee, M. C. & Lyne, J. (1987) 'What Are Nice Folks Like You Doing in a Place Like This? Some Entailments of Treating Knowledge Claims Rhetorically,' in J.S. Nelson, A. Megill & D. N. McCloskey (eds) *The Rhetoric of the Human-Sciences: Language and Argument in Scholarship and Public Affairs*. Madison: UWisc Press.

Miell, D. E. (1987) 'Remembering Relationship Development: Constructing a Context for Interactions,' in R. Burnett, P. McGee & D. Clarke (eds) *Accounting for Relationships*. London: Methuen.

Olson, D. H. (1977) 'Insiders' and Outsiders' Views of Relationships: Research Studies,' in G. Levinger & H. Raush (eds) *Close Relationships: Perspectives on the Meaning of Intimacy*. Amherst: UMass Press.

Pierce, G., Sarason, B. R. & Sarason, I. G. (1990) 'Integrating Social Support Perspectives: Working Models, Personal Relationships and Situational Factors,' in S. W. Duck (ed.) *Personal Relationships and Social Support*. London: Sage.

Planalp, S. (1985) 'Relational Schemata: A Test of Alternative Forms of Relational Knowledge as Guides to Communication,' *Human Communication Research* 12: 3–29.

Planalp, S. (1987) 'Interplay between Relational Knowledge and Events,' in R. Burnett, P. McGee & D. Clarke (eds) *Accounting for Relationships*. London: Methuen.

Rawlins, W. & Holl, M. (1988) 'Adolescents' Interaction with Parents and Friends: Dialectics of Temporal Perspective and Evaluation,' *Journal of Social and Personal Relationships* 5: 27–46.

Reis, H. T. & Shaver, P. (1988) 'Intimacy as an Interpersonal Process,' in S. W. Duck et al. (eds), *Handbook of Personal Relationships*, pp. 367–90. Chichester: Wiley.

Reiss, D. (1988) Foreword to *Between Husbands and Wives* by M. A. Fitzpatrick. Newbury Park: Sage.

Ross, M. D. & McFarland, C. (1988) 'Constructing the Past: Biasses in Personal Memory,' in D. Bar-Tal & A. Kruglanski (eds) *Social Psychology of Knowledge*. Cambridge: Cambridge University Press.

Shotter, J. (1987) 'Accounting for Relationship Growth,' in R. Burnett, P. McGhee & D. Clarke (eds) *Accounting for Relationships*. London: Methuen.

Surra, C. A., Arizzi, P. & Asmussen, L. (1988) 'The Association between Reasons for Commitment and the Development and Outcome of Marital Relationships,' *Journal of Social and Personal Relationships* 5: 47–63.

Wheeler, L. & Nezlek, J. (1977) 'Sex Differences in Social Participation,' *Journal of Personality and Social Psychology* 35: 742–54.

DIALECTICAL CONTRADICTIONS IN RELATIONSHIP DEVELOPMENT

Leslie A. Baxter

Three fundamental contradictions were examined in the stages of development identified retrospectively by 106 romantic relationship parties: autonomy–connection, openness–closedness, and predictability–novelty. The contradictions were reported to be present in approximately three-quarters of all identified stages. The openness-closedness contradiction was more likely than the other two contradictions to be reported during the initial stage of development; autonomy–connection and predicta-bility–novelty contradictions were reported with increased frequency in subsequent developmental stages. Relationship parties reported that they managed the contradictions with six basic types of responses. These response forms were not reported with equal frequency across the contradictions and the stages of development. Current relationship satisfaction did not correlate significantly with the reported presence of the contradictions but did correlate with the ways in which the contradictions were managed.

> *The test of a first-rate intelligence is the ability to hold two opposed ideas in the mind at the same time and still retain the ability to function.*

F. Scott Fitzgerald

Although F. Scott Fitzgerald's quotation refers to the individual person's ability to function with contradiction, it might well have been made with reference to interpersonal relationships. An increasing number of scholars have recently pointed to the presence of opposing, or contradictory, tendencies which underlie relationship dynamics (for example, Altman, et al., 1981; Baxter, 1988; Bochner, 1984; Rawlins, 1983a, b, 1989). Despite the growing call for a dialectical perspective on the study of relationships, the corpus of empirically based work is still quite limited. The purpose of this study is to explore descriptively several of the issues suggested in Baxter's (1988) recent theoretical statement on the nature of dialectical contradictions in relationship development.

The term 'dialectic' evokes many meanings. Although many equate the term with dialectical materialism, Marx's theory is but one example of dialectical thinking. Cornforth (1968) identifies two root concepts which qualify a theory as dialectical: *process* and *contradiction*. The centrality of the process concept mandates a theoretical domain focused on developmental change. Such change is the result of the struggle and tension of contradiction from a dialectical

Source: The author wishes to thank Barbara Montgomery, reviewers Bill Cupach and Michael Hecht (the last two of whom acted as the Journal's reviewers) for their helpful comments on an earlier version of this article. The article is taken from the *Journal of Social and Personal Relationships* [*7:* 69–88, 1990]. (c) 1990 Sage Publications Ltd., 6 Bonhill St., London EC24A 4PU, UK. Reprinted by permission of Sage Publications Ltd.

perspective. A contradiction is present whenever two tendencies or forces are interdependent (the dialectical principle of unity) yet mutually negate one another (the dialectical principle of negation). To a dialectical thinker, the presence of paired opposites, or contradictions, is essential to change and growth; the struggle of opposites thus is not evaluated negatively by dialectical thinkers. Further, contradictions themselves can undergo change over time.

Altman et al. (1981) have noted the non-dialectical bias of existing relationship theory and research. Relationships are typically conceived as homeostatic social systems which develop uni-directionally toward the states of interdependent connection, openness and uncertainty reduction or predictability. Only limited research examines the opposite states of independence or autonomy, information closedness and uncertainty or novelty (for example, Baxter & Wilmot, 1985), and this work is typically insular in its failure to examine the simultaneous interplay of these states with their dialectically opposite conditions. By contrast, a dialectical perspective would find meaning in connection, openness and predictability only by examining the broader contradictions of which they are a part.

Baxter (1988) posits that three contradictions constitute the primary dialectical forces which parties experience in their interpersonal relationships: autonomy–connection, openness–closedness and predictability–novelty. Of these three, the autonomy–connection contradiction is probably the most central (Cupach & Metts, 1988; Rawlins, 1983a). No relationship can exist unless the parties forsake individual autonomy. However, too much connection paradoxically destroys the relationship because the individual entities become lost. Simultaneously, autonomy can be conceptualized only in terms of separation from others. But too much autonomy paradoxically destroys the individual's identity, because connections with others are necessary to identity formation and maintenance.

Baxter (1988) identifies openness–closedness as a second significant dialectical contradiction

experienced by relationship parties. Relationships need both information openness and information closedness. On the one hand, open disclosure between relationship parties is a necessary condition for intimacy; but on the other hand, openness creates vulnerabilities for self, other and the relationship that necessitate information closedness (Rawlins, 1983b).

The third dialectical contradiction posited by Baxter is predictability–novelty. Just as relationships need predictability, they also need novelty (Altman et al., 1981). Pragmatic systems theorists refer to a dysfunctional condition known as 'schismogenesis' which can result from overly rigidified (i.e. predictable) interaction (Fisher, 1978). Learning theorists similarly recognize the emotional deadening that can result from excessive repetition (Kelvin, 1977).

These three contradictions can function at several levels in interpersonal relationships. Dialectical theorists who assume an objective reality would appropriately focus on how the contradictions function, regardless of whether the parties are consciously aware of them. By contrast, dialectical theorists of the social reality tradition would concentrate on contradictions as subjectively experienced by the relationship parties. This study adopts the latter perspective, defining the domain of contradictions as those subjectively experienced and reported by relationship parties.

If the contradictory pairs of autonomy–connection, openness–closedness and predictability–novelty are to be examined in a fully dialectical manner, research must not only document that they are subjectively experienced but must address this experience as embedded in the process of relationship development. The first two research questions address this issue.

The first research question (RQ1) addresses the reported presence of autonomy–connection, openness–closedness and predictability–novelty contradictions in relationship parties' retrospective accounts of the stages of their relationships' development. Are these three contradictions perceived as present throughout a relationship's reported development stages? Only during later reported stages of development? Only during earlier reported stages? Baxter (1988) argues that the existence of a relationship implies the existence in some form of the three basic dialectical contradictions; thus, we would expect these contradictions to be perceived as present across a relationship's stages of development. However, this claim needs to be examined empirically, Thus,

> **RQ1:**   *To what extent are the autonomy–connection, openness–closedness and predictability–novelty contradictions retrospectively reported across the stages of a relationship's development?*

The second research question poses a cross-sectional variation on the issue of perceived contradictions and relationship development. Relationship parties may recall their relationship's development in a manner biased toward the simplified 'smoothing out' of unstable fluctuations (Miell, 1987). This potential bias toward simplification could produce an underestimation of the reported dialectical contradictions in the retrospectively constructed stage accounts examined in the first research question. As a way of offsetting this possible bias, relationship development is approached cross-sectionally, using relationship duration as an alternative measure of developmental stage. Employing relationship parties' accounts of their current relationship status, a cross-sectional approach can address whether the contradictions are equally likely to be reported in relationships of varying developmental length:

> **RQ2:**   *To what extent are the autonomy–connection, openness–closedness and predictability–novelty contradictions reported in relationships of varying length?*

After establishing at a general level the reported presence of the three contradictions in the developmental stages of relationships, the next logical point of inquiry is an elaboration of the ways in which the relationship parties cope with the contradictions. Baxter (1988) has posited six fundamental types of response strategies that relationship parties enact with regard to the autonomy–connection, openness–closedness and predictability–novelty contradictions. For purposes of presentation, these six can be grouped into four more basic types:

1. *Selection.* The relationship parties perceive the co-existence of both elements of a given contradiction and seek to transcend the contradiction by making one condition or pole dominant to the exclusion of the other condition. Thus, for example, in grappling with simultaneous pulls in the directions of autonomy and connection, the parties may opt to break up, thereby making autonomy the dominant state.

2. *Separation.* Rather than legitimating one pole and thereby extinguishing the other, separation involves the continued co-existence of both poles. However, the parties seek to deny the interdependence of the contrasting elements by 'uncoupling' or separating them temporally or topically. Two types of separation can be identified: (a) *cyclic alternation* between the contrasting poles from one point in time to another; and (b) *topical segmentation* through the separation of content or activity domains into those for which one contrasting pole is appropriate and those for which the other contrasting pole is appropriate. For example, if one party defines his or her sports involvement as an autonomy domain, it is inappropriately a target for connection.

3. *Neutralization.* Like separation, neutralization features the perceived presence of both contrasting poles. However, unlike separation, in which each contrasting element is enacted in its full intensity some of the time or in some domains of activity, neutralization is characterized by the dilution of intensity of the contrasting elements. Basically, the elements are neutralized through compromise in which a portion

of each contrasting condition is perceived to be sacrificed. Two types of neutralization are posited:
(1) *moderation,* for example small talk which evidences both diluted openness and diluted closedness; and
(b) *disqualification,* in which the contrasting elements are handled indirectly, ambiguously or 'off-the-record.'

4. *Reframing.* Unlike the first three categories of response in which the contrasting elements are regarded as zero-summed opposites, reframing is characterized by a perceptual transformation of the elements along different dimensions of meaning such that the two contrasts are no longer regarded as opposites. For example, the party who ceases to regard autonomy as the opposite of connection and instead views it as an enhancement to connection has succeeded in reframing the contradiction.

Although Baxter (1988) posited that the six response strategies are conceptually relevant to all three of the basic contradictions, they may not be equally distributed in practice. On the face of it, some response strategies appear to require more cooperative negotiation between the parties for certain of the contradictions and thus may be less frequent in reported use. Coping with the autonomy–connection contradiction through topical segmentation, for example, implies that both parties accept the demarcation of domains appropriately associated with autonomy and connection, respectively. By contrast, the same type of response strategy for the openness–closedness contradiction requires limited negotiation between the parties; one party can silently define certain topics as 'off limits' to open disclosure and the other party will have no basis for challenging this decision. The third research question considers the reported ways in which the three contradictions are managed:

RQ3: *What are the reported coping strategies used in response to the autonomy–connection, openness–closedness and predictability–novelty contradictions?*

It further seems useful to determine the extent to which the contradictions are treated in similar ways as a function of developmental stage. Some coping strategies appear more complex than others, thereby limiting their reported use to later developmental stages when the parties have developed a substantial relational history together. In particular, Baxter (1988) suggests that reframing is a sophisticated and complex phenomenon likely to emerge only later in a relationship's developmental history. The extent to which this is the case with regard to each of the contradictions merits examination.

Research questions four and five parallel the first two, above, in addressing the developmental-stage issue both retrospectively and cross-sectionally:

RQ4: *To what extent are the response strategies employed with equal frequency for the three contradictions across the retrospectively identified stages of relationship development?*

RQ5: *To what extent are the response strategies employed with equal frequency for the three contradictions in relationships of varying length?*

The sixth and final research question examines satisfaction with the relationship as it may relate to the perceived presence of the dialectical contradictions and how they are managed. On the one hand, the perceived presence of contradictions may be a source of relationship dissatisfaction. Contradictions, by their very nature, make it problematic for relationship parties to fulfill both contrasting elements at once, thereby resulting in frustration and tension. On the other hand, dialectical theorists argue that contradictions are essential to relationship change and growth and thus constitute sources of relational satisfaction. The key to whether perceived contradictions are sources of dissatisfaction or satisfaction may rest more with the way in which the parties cope with the contradictions than in their presence or absence per se. In summary,

> **RQ6:** *Is relationship satisfaction correlated with the perceived presence of the autonomy–connection, openness–closedness and predictability–novelty contradictions and with the reported ways in which those contradictions are managed?*

METHODS

Participants in the study were 106 undergraduates at a private university who were selected through a stratified random sampling of all enrolled undergraduate students. The stratification variable was the gender of the participant to insure a corpus of relationship accounts lacking a gender sampling bias. If a student's name surfaced in the random procedure, a member of the trained interview team contacted the prospective participant by telephone to screen his or her eligibility for participation and to solicit cooperation in arranging a time and place for the actual interview. Interviewers could not conduct interviews with someone with whom they had prior familiarity. All prospective participants were informed that the purpose of the interview was to hear about people's relationship experiences, and they were given assurance that their identity would be kept confidential. Prospective participants were not eligible for participation unless they were currently in a romantic opposite-sex relationship of at least 1 month's duration.

Interviewer Preparation

The interviewing team was composed of three male and nine female advanced undergraduates who had successfully completed at least one methodology course which involved interviewing. The team members were hand-picked by the principal investigator based on the perception that they were skilled in interacting with others.

In the 5 weeks prior to actual data collection, the team met with the principal investigator to develop and pilot test an interview schedule and to receive additional training and practice in how to conduct focused interviews.

Throughout the period of actual data collection, interviewers were required to submit an audio tape and a written transcript of each interview as it was completed. However, only the written transcripts were used in data analysis because they were less cumbersome. The principal investigator read each transcript and listened to the corresponding tape as they were submitted in order to check for accuracy in the transcription. All interviewers were given copies of the written transcripts, and time was reserved at each week's team meeting to clarify points of perceived confusion or ambiguity in the interview contents.

Data-Collection Procedures

After an initial introduction in which participants were reminded of the study's focus on 'how relationships develop' and that every relationship is different with no right or wrong answers, participants were given a piece of paper upon which to record and label the stages of their relationship from time of first meeting to the present. Participants were asked to imagine that their relationship was a book and that they were constructing a 'table of contents' of the book's chapters; a chapter was defined as 'a stage or period in the relationship's history different from other stages or periods.' Participants were asked to create a title for each chapter which captured the essence of the relationship during that chapter. Participants were told that they could have as many chapters as they found necessary in describing the 'book' of their relationship.

The 'table of contents' was used to structure the interview proper. After the participant completed the 'table of contents,' he or she was provided with an introduction to the three contradictions as follows:

> Many people at some point or other in their relationship experience certain 'pulls' or 'tugs' within themselves in different directions. The first of these 'pulls' I will label the ME-WE Pull. On the one hand, a person is attracted to the relationship with the other person and wants to be

with that person, yet he or she also wants autonomy, separation or independence to be their own person and do their own thing. The second 'pull' I will label the TO TALK OR NOT TO TALK Pull. On the one hand, a person wants to tell it all and disclose in a totally open manner to their partner about everything, but they also feel a 'tug' toward discretion and not talking about everything. The last 'pull' I will label the NOVELTY–PREDICTABILITY Pull. On the one hand, a person wants a little mystery, spontaneity, surprise or uncertainty in their relationship. On the other hand, a person wants to know what is coming off in the relationship with some degree of predictability. Are these three 'pulls' clear? What is really important to understand is that people may experience these sorts of things in relationships where they are both satisfied or dissatisfied—these 'pulls' do not say anything about how well or poorly the relationship is doing. You may or may not have experienced any of these 'pulls'—that is what we are interested in discussing for each of the chapters you have written down.

For each chapter, participants were first asked to elaborate on what their chapter title meant. Then the interviewer asked a series of questions designed to solicit the following information: (1) whether each pole of a given contrasting pair was desired during that chapter; and (2) in instances in which a co-existence of desire for both elements of a contrasting pair was reported, an accounting of what the experience was like and how the parties responded.

After completing the chapter-by-chapter review, participants were asked to fill out Norton's (1983) 6-item survey on their current level of relationship satisfaction. Although this instrument was designed for use with marital couples, it has been used successfully with non-married romantic pairs as well (Baxter & Bullis, 1986).

Data-Coding Procedures

The principal investigator performed the data coding, with a second independent coder, who was unaware of the study's purposes, coding twenty-five of the transcripts selected at random

as a reliability check. The twenty-five transcripts that were double-coded involved a total of 134 relationship stages. For each relationship stage ('chapter'), two data codes were generated for each of the three contradictions: (1) presence or absence of the contradiction: and (2) the type of coping response enacted by the parties. (In instances in which more than one coping response was evident from the transcript text, coders were instructed to code the strategy type discussed first by the respondent.) For the autonomy–connection, openness–closedness and predictability–novelty contradictions, respectively, the percent- age coding agreement and kappa value (Cohen, 1960) were as follows for the respective coding decisions: (1) autonomy–connection: 0.95 ($k = 0.88$) and 0.88 ($k = 0.80$); (2) openness–closedness: 0.91 ($k = 0.77$) and 0.93 ($k = 0.89$); and (3) predictability–novelty: 0.84 ($k = 0.67$) and 0.83 ($k = 0.71$). These values were deemed sufficiently high to proceed. To be conservative, however, all coding discrepancies in the double-coded subsample were resolved by using the second coder's decisions given this person's lack of knowledge of the research questions.

RESULTS

The relationship duration for the fifty-three male and fifty-three female participants in the study ranged from 1 to 192 months with a mean of 20.2 months and a median of 16 months. Two of the participants reported on their marital relationship. The number of reported 'chapter' stages ranged from two to eleven, with a mean of 5.61 and a median of five stages. For the sample as a whole, a total of 595 'chapter' stages was generated by the participants. No significant difference was found between males and females on relationship length ($t = 1.16$, d.f. $= 104$), and on reported number of relationship stages ($t = 0.90$, d.f. $= 104$). The correlation between reported relationship duration and reported number of stages was moderate and significant ($r = 0.25$, d.f. $= 104$, $p < 0.01$).

STATISTICAL SUMMARY 1

Preliminary Analyses

A t-test was calculated to compare males and females. T-tests tell you if there is a difference between two groups. For example, you might want to see if one group (e.g., males) had more eye contact than a second group (e.g., females). In this study males and females did not differ in the length of their relationships nor in the number of stages of relationship they described.

The internal reliability check for the satisfaction measure produced a Cronbach's alpha value of 0.95. Relationship satisfaction was not correlated with relationship length ($r = 0.08$, d.f. $= 104$, $p = 0.40$), nor with the reported number of stages ($r = 0.04$, d.f. $= 104$, $p = 0.70$).

STATISTICAL SUMMARY 2

Reliability is a measure of how accurate and consistent the scores are. If a measure is highly reliable then you can be confident that the scores are very accurate, and that the items or indicators that are part of the measure are consistent with each other or consistent over time. The satisfaction measure proved to be very accurate and consistent.

A correlation is a measure of the association between two or more variables. A high correlation shows that two variables are very much related to each other. A zero correlation may mean that they are independent of each other or unrelated. A positive correlation means that as the scores of one variable increase, the scores on the second variable increase as well. Thus if someone scores high on one variable (e.g., talkativeness), they are likely to also score high on the other variable (e.g., number of friends). Relationship satisfaction was not related to or influenced by how long the relationship had lasted nor the number of stages of relationship described.

The three contradictions were reported in a large proportion of the identified stages. The autonomy–connection contradiction was present in 79 percent of all relationship stages. Illustrative of the contradiction's presence is this account by a male participant:

> I wasn't really sure which way I wanted to go. There were a lot of things that were real attractive about being in a partnership with [partner]. But I was still trying to figure out exactly who I was, as well. . . . I guess I was sort of worried that I would lose some of my self-identity, especially with my group that I hang out with. There were some things that I didn't want to give up, and I was afraid I would have to.

The openness–closedness contradiction was reported for 72 percent of all relationship stages. The following statement of the contradiction by a male respondent is interesting because it illustrates the interdependence between the autonomy–connection and openness–closedness contradictions:

> I needed my space and one of the ways to get that space was to keep things that I was thinking to myself. But again, to try to have the relationship and have the relationship go strongly you have to communicate openly. . . .

The predictability–novelty contradiction was present in 69 percent of the reported relationship stages. A female account of the dilemma is representative:

> It was all kind of novel. In that first stage you shouldn't have to depend on somebody to be there at fixed times and places. If a first stage is predictable, the relationship dies off real fast. . . . But it's really bad when you wait on Friday night and don't go out with your friends because you want him to come over, only he doesn't show up. In a relationship, I want someone I can depend on and that will be predictable and be there when I need him.

This response also illustrates the interdependence of contradictions, in this instance autonomy–connection with predictability–novelty. The respondent appears to link her partner's autonomy with

TABLE 1
Proportion of Relationships of Varying Stage Differentiation Characterized by Dialectical Contradictions in Each Stage

Rel. Stage Differentiation	Contradiction	Relationship Stage										
		1	2	3	4	5	6	7	8	9	10	11
	A/C	0.58	0.77	0.87	0.96	—	—	—	—	—	—	—
Low[a]	O/C	0.84	0.74	0.67	0.79	—	—	—	—	—	—	—
	P/N	0.48	0.71	0.90	0.96	—	—	—	—	—	—	—
Cochran's	Q	13.7*	0.36	6.14*	4.60							
	n	31	31	30	24							
	A/C	0.53	0.79	0.79	0.86	0.91	0.93	1.00	—	—	—	—
Medium[b]	O/C	0.74	0.76	0.71	0.69	0.64	0.75	0.50	—	—	—	—
	P/N	0.36	0.53	0.69	0.72	0.85	0.71	0.80	—	—	—	—
Cochran's	Q	19.16*	11.06*	2.76	5.25	16.0*	6.20*	6.33*				
	n	58	58	58	58	58	28	10				
	A/C	0.53	0.76	0.76	0.88	0.82	0.82	0.88	0.71	0.75	1.00	1.00
High[c]	O/C	0.59	0.88	0.94	0.77	0.59	0.59	0.65	0.71	0.63	0.80	1.00
	P/N	0.47	0.65	0.71	0.82	0.88	0.59	0.82	0.88	0.88	1.00	1.00
Cochran's	Q	0.43	3.43	4.33	2.00	4.20	2.29	4.75	2.00	3.00	2.00	—
	n	17	17	17	17	17	17	17	17	8	5	2

[a]Relationships with a total number of stages equal to 2, 3, or 4.
[b]Relationships with a total number of stages equal to 5, 6, or 7.
[c]Relationships with 8–11 total stages.
*Significant at $p < 0.05$.

novelty and establishes her own autonomy based on perceived predictability in the relationship.

Research Question 1 Table 1 provides a summary of the proportion of times the basic contradictions were reported in the identified stages of development. Because the range in the number of identified stages was so large (2–11), relationship accounts were grouped into three clusters of stage differentiation: low (2–4 identified stages); medium (5–7 identified stages); and high (8–11 identified stages). For each cluster of relationships, Cochran's Q (Siegel, 1956) was employed at each stage to determine whether the three contradictions were significantly different from one another in their reported presence.

STATISTICAL SUMMARY 3

Research Question 1

Cochran's Q, like the t-test, is used to compare groups to each other. Here, the stages of relationship were compared to each other (i.e., early vs. middle vs. later). Results showed that openness–closedness was more likely to be found in the beginning of a relationship than autonomy–connection and predictability–novelty. As the relationship progressed, autonomy–connection and predictability–novelty issues appeared more frequently, and openness–closedness appeared less frequently.

TABLE 2
Presence of Dialectical Contradictions by Relationship Length

Contradiction	Relationship-Length Quartiles				
	1–7 mos.	8–15 mos.	16–22 mos.	23–192 mos.	Total
Autonomy/connection	0.76[a]	0.92	0.88	0.93	0.88
Openness/closedness	0.80	0.69	0.65	0.72	0.72
Predictability/novelty	0.72	0.85	0.77	0.83	0.79
Total no. of relationships	25	26	26	29	106
Cochran's Q	0.66	8.00[b]	6.75[b]	5.40[c]	

[a]Values represent percentage of column *n*.
[b]Significant at 0.05 level with 2 d.f.
[c]Significant at 0.10 level with 2 d.f.

The three dialectical contradictions were not equally prevalent across the stages of relationship development. For relationships of low- and medium-stage differentiation, the openness–closedness contradiction was significantly more likely to be experienced in the initial developmental stage than were the autonomy–connection and predictability–novelty contradictions. The direction of differences among the proportions supports a pattern of convergence in the reported presence of the three contradictions, with the increased presence of the autonomy–connection and predictability–novelty contradictions in subsequent stages and a stabilization or slight decline in the reported presence of the openness–closedness contradiction in subsequent stages. Relationships of high stage differentiation did not differ significantly at any stage in the reported presence of the contradictions; however, the direction of the differences paralleled, albeit more modestly, the pattern evident in low- and medium-stage differentiation relationships.

Research Question 2.   Table 2 presents a breakdown of the proportions of relationships of varying length in which respondents reported the presence of the contradictions in their accounts of current relationship status. Cochran's Q test was again employed, to compare the extent to which the three contradictions were present for relationships grouped by developmental length into four quartiles. The results are similar to those reported for the first research question. Reported experiencing of the autonomy–connection and predictability–novelty contradictions was lowest for relationships of shortest duration, with increased presence of these two contradictions in relationships of longer duration. Experience with the openness–closedness contradiction was greatest in relationships of shortest duration with a slight decline in reported presence for relationships of greater length.

STATISTICAL SUMMARY 4

Research Question 2

Cochran's Q was used again to compare longer and shorter relationships. In shorter relationships autonomy–connection and predictability–novelty were less likely to be an issue, and in longer relationships openness–closedness was less likely to be an issue.

Research Question 3.   Table 3 provides an overall summary of the frequency of reported response strategies for each contradiction. Because these data are collapsed across relationship

TABLE 3
Frequency of Response Strategies by Contradiction Type

Strategy[a]	Contradiction		
	Autonomy–Connection	Openness–Closedness	Novelty–Predictability
Selection	107 (0.23)[b]	72 (0.17)	75 (0.19)
Separation/cyclic altern.	277 (0.60)	53 (0.13)	106 (0.27)
Separation/segmentation	7 (0.02)	194 (0.46)	190 (0.48)
Neutralization/moderation	27 (0.06)	76 (0.18)	2 (0.005)
Neutralization/disqualif.	8 (0.02)	18 (0.04)	1 (0.003)
Reframing	34 (0.07)	6 (0.01)	21 (0.05)

[a]2.3 percent of the autonomy–connection strategies were not codable; 1.9 percent of the strategies for openness–closedness were not codable; and 3.9 percent of the strategies for predictability–novelty were not codable.
[b]Values in parentheses represent the proportion of column totals.

stages, the independence assumption for a chi-square test is precluded in the multiple instances reported by a given respondent. However, the tabled values suggest at a descriptive level that the response strategies were not reported equally for the three contradictions.

Of the 471 stages in which the autonomy–connection contradiction was present, the most commonly reported response strategy was Separation in the form of cyclic alternation. A female respondent expressed succinctly what this enactment was like: '. . . we kind of kept floundering around together . . . drifting towards each other and drifting apart again . . . kind of a cycle.' The reference to 'drifting' in this example captures the passive, reactive manner in which many parties managed the contradiction through cyclic alternation; much more rare was an explicitly negotiated alternation of autonomy with connection.

The second most frequent response strategy with regard to the autonomy–connection dilemma was Selection. Usually a proactive, not reactive, response, relationship parties experienced opposing pulls and legitimated only one of the contrasts. Typical is this account by a male respondent:

We did want both [autonomy and connection].
We decided, well, we're going to give this a shot.
We just kind of thought, if it doesn't work out, it doesn't work out. If it does, then all the better.

Of the 427 chapter stages in which the openness–closedness contradiction was present, Separation through segmentation was the dominant response strategy, followed by Neutralization through moderation and Selection. Segmentation involved a differentiation of topic domains into those for which disclosure was appropriate and those regarded as 'taboo topics' (Baxter & Wilmot, 1985). Rarely were the 'taboos' a source of explicit negotiation between the parties. Neutralization through moderation typically manifested itself in the proverbial 'small-talk ritual' in which respondents engaged in superficial to modest disclosure yet maintained moderate discretion. Depending on what else was transpiring in a given chapter, Selection could take the form of 'total openness' (more common) or the total withholding of information from the other (less common).

In coping with the predictability–novelty contradiction the relationship parties were most likely to employ Separation through segmentation, followed in turn by Separation through cyclic alternation and Selection.

Segmentation involved a distinction between relational predictability on the one hand and interactional predictability on the other hand. Parties desired maximum predictability about the state of the relationship, but they enjoyed the spontaneity and excitement of not being able to predict what was going to occur in the interaction episode. A male respondent articulated segmentation particularly well as follows:

> I guess novelty and predictability in my mind can't be mixed because they are for different things. Predictability is the confidence that she's not going to leave tomorrow and go out with another guy. That's what I wanted confidence in. And for the novelty, I just wanted . . . well, spunk or whatever. I wanted our times together to be fun and exciting.

Cyclic alternation for this sample of respondents was very much driven by the school calendar. Equating predictability with the routines brought about through classes, sports and studying, relationship parties punctuated the academic term with the novelty of vacations and the summers. As one female expressed it:

> Especially toward the end of the term when 'we' was really getting on our nerves, I would long for the break when we would have the time to do what we wanted whenever we wanted to. The vacations were like a shot in the arm for our relationship.

The Selection response involved concerted efforts either to enhance predictability or to enhance novelty, depending on where the relationship was at the time. Efforts to create predictability generally involved talking explicitly about issues such as the state of the relationship. Parties attempted to increase their novelty in one of two basic ways. Some parties achieved novelty through greater autonomous, individual activity. As one female respondent indicated, 'The predictability is us; the novelty is me. That's why I decided to go back to school after out kids were old enough.' Other parties achieved novelty by undertaking joint activities that were new and different for the pair. As one male respondent indicated,

> We were caught in the school rut—get up, go to classes, go to dinner together, study together, sleep together, get up, go to classes. . . . In the middle of the term we just decided to bag the rut and do things on impulse that we felt like doing. We just took off to the beach in the middle of the week. We'd go out dancing and partyin' a lot. Both of our grades suffered for what we did but I don't have any regrets.

Research Question 4. In determining whether the response types were equally likely to emerge across the reported stages of relationship development, relationships were initially divided into groups, each group comprised of relationships reporting an equal number of stages (relationships with two reported stages were collapsed with three-stage relationships because of small ns, as were relationships with ten and eleven reported stages). Within each group and for each contradiction, a 'mean stage rank' was derived for each response strategy by assigning all strategies reported in the first stage a rank of '1,' all strategies reported in the second stage a rank of '2,' and so on. These mean stage ranks represented a summary index of placement across stages for each response-strategy type. In turn, these mean stage rank scores were ranked from '1' to '6' to capture the relative temporal placements of the six response strategies. Table 4 presents the temporal placement rank-orders of the response strategies for each contradiction. Higher rank values within a given column for a specific contradiction indicate reported use in a later, as opposed to an earlier, developmental stage. Thus, for example, in relationships of nine-stage differentiation the autonomy–connection contradiction was managed through relatively early use of moderation (rank of '1') and relatively late use of reframing (rank of '4').

Although Neutralization through moderation and through disqualification were infrequently reported strategies in coping with the autonomy–connection contradiction, they were employed earlier than other strategies when employed. By contrast, Reframing was likely to be used later than other strategies when respondents reported its use.

Similar placement findings emerged for the openness–closedness contradiction. Neutralization through moderation was a strategy whose reported use was earlier than other strategies, in contrast to the Reframing strategy which was likely to emerge later than other strategies when reported in use.

Parallel findings emerged with respect to the predictability–novelty contradiction. For all three contradictions, the infrequently reported strategies of Neutralization through moderation and dis-

TABLE 4
Rank Order of Reported Strategies by Type of Contradiction
and Relationship Stage Differentiation

Contradiction	Type of Strategy	Relationship Stage Differentiation							
		2/3	4	5	6	7	8	9	10/11
Autonomy–connection									
	Selection	2	2	3	4	6	4	3	3
	Cyclic alt.	3	5	4	3	3	5	2	2
	Segmentation	—	3	5	5	4	—	—	—
	Moderation	1	1	2	1	2	2	1	1
	Disqual.	—	4	1	2	1	1	—	4
	Reframing	4	6	6	6	5	3	4	—
Openness–closedness									
	Selection	2	4	3	5	6	5	2	4
	Cyclic alt.	—	3	5	3	5	4	—	2
	Segmentation	3	2	4	2	3	3	3	3
	Moderation	1	1	1	1	2	1	1	1
	Disqual.	—	5	2	4	1	2	—	5
	Reframing	—	6	6	6	4	—	—	—
Predictability–novelty									
	Selection	2.5	4	3	3	1	3	1	3
	Cyclic alt.	1	3	1	1	3	2	3	4
	Segmentation	2.5	2	4.5	2	2	1	4	2
	Moderation	—	1	—	—	—	—	—	1
	Disqual.	—	—	2	—	—	—	—	—
	Reframing	4	5	4.5	—	4	4	2	5

qualification and Reframing had distinct temporal placements. Neutralization strategies, when reported, were likely to be used in early stage development. By contrast, Reframing, when reported, was likely to be used in later stages of development.

Research Question 5.   Table 5 presents a cross-sectional portrait for relationships of varying length of the reported use of the response strategies for each contradiction. Unfortunately, small cell sizes jeopardize a meaningful interpretation. However, to the extent that the Neutralization and Reframing strategies were reported, the temporal placement of their use is largely consistent with that found in the retrospective stage accounts.

Research Question 6.   Overall satisfaction with the relationship was operationalized as the mean score on the 6-item satisfaction survey. Spearman correlations were computed between this score and the overall proportion of stages in which a respondent reported the presence of each of the three contradictions. Satisfaction with the relationship did not correlate significantly with the proportion of stages in which the autonomy–connection contradiction was perceived to be present ($r_s = 0.09$, d.f. = 104), the proportion of stages in which the openness–closedness contradiction was perceived to be present ($r_s = -0.18$, d.f. = 104) and the proportion of stages in which the predictability–novelty was perceived to be present ($r_s = 0.15$, d.f. = 104).

STATISTICAL SUMMARY 5

Research Question 6

Satisfaction was not related to how often the three issues occurred. However, satisfaction was related to the strategies used, increasing when Segmentation and Reframing were used to cope with predictability–novelty or Reframing was used to cope with autonomy–connection, and decreasing when Selection was used to cope with predictability–novelty or when Disqualification was used to cope with openness-closedness.

Satisfaction was significantly, but modestly, correlated with proportional reliance on certain of the response strategy types. Satisfaction was positively correlated with use of Segmentation ($r_s = 0.29$, d.f. $= 104$, $p < 0.05$) and Reframing ($r_s = 0.26$, d.f. $= 104$, $p < 0.05$) in coping with the predictability–novelty contradiction and negatively correlated with use of Selection ($r_s = -0.20$, d.f. $= 104$, $p < 0.05$). Satisfaction was negatively correlated with use of Disqualification ($r_s = -0.21$, d.f. $= 104$, $p < 0.05$) in coping with the openness–closedness contradiction. Reframing was positively correlated with satisfaction ($r_s = 0.30$, d.f. $= 104$, $p < 0.05$) for the autonomy–connection contradiction, and Selection was negatively correlated ($r_s = -0.25$, d.f. $= 104$, $p < 0.05$).

DISCUSSION

The autonomy–connection, openness–closedness and predictability–novelty contradictions were reported in approximately three-quarters of the relationship stages which were retrospectively identified by romantic relationship parties. The prevalence of contradiction in these data may simply reflect a method artefact in that the interview schedule focused respondent attention on the possibility of these contradictions. However, other research using more oblique interview methods (for example, Rawlins, 1983a, b) has similarly found contradiction to be a salient theme in relationship development. Dialectical theorists of an objectivist view might even argue that this study underestimated the force of contradiction in relationship development by examining only those contradictions of which respondents were aware.

These data are also limited in their reliance on only one party's perceptions of the contradictions and how they were managed and on retrospective accounts of relationship development. Future research needs to gather longitudinal data from both relationship parties in order to provide a richer portrait of the dialectical dynamics of relationship development. For example, the relative absence in these data of the autonomy–connection and predictability–novelty contradictions in the initial reported stage of relationship development may reflect nothing more than respondents' implicit relationship theories about the excitement and joy characteristic of 'falling in love.'

Notwithstanding these caveats, the results of this study present interesting implications for our understanding of relationship development. If these three contradictions are as prevalent in relationship development as the results suggest, theories such as social penetration (Altman & Taylor, 1973) and uncertainty reduction (Berger & Calabrese, 1975) which posit unidirectional development toward increased connection, openness and predictability may need revision in order to capture the reverse pulls toward autonomy, closedness and novelty. Indeed, social penetration has already been subject to such a dialectical revision (Altman et al., 1981).

Based on the accounts provided by these respondents, relationship parties are quite active in coping with the presence of dialectical tensions. Although instances of all of Baxter's (1988) posited strategic response types were reported, respondent repertoires appear to be dominated by two coping responses: Separation through cyclic alternation for the autonomy–connection contradiction and Separation through segmentation for the openness–closedness and predictability–novelty contradictions. Management of the openness–closedness contradiction through seg-

TABLE 5
Proportion of Strategic Responses by Contradiction and Relationship Length

Contradiction	Strategy Type	Relationship Length in Quartiles			
		1	2	3	4
Autonomy–connection					
	Selection	0.21	0.17	0.22	0.15
	Cyclic alt.	0.42	0.71	0.74	0.70
	Segmentation	0.11	0.04	0	0
	Moderation	0.16	0.04	0	0
	Disqual.	0	0.04	0	0
	Reframing	0.05	0	0.04	0.11
	Uncoded	0.05	0	0	0.04
	n	19	24	23	27
Openness–closedness					
	Selection	0.20	0.28	0.12	0.10
	Cyclic alt.	0.15	0.17	0.24	0.14
	Segmentation	0.45	0.39	0.47	0.62
	Moderation	0.10	0.11	0.06	0
	Disqual.	0.10	0	0.06	0.05
	Reframing	0	0	0	0.05
	Uncoded	0	0.06	0.06	0.05
	n	20	18	17	21
Predictability–novelty					
	Selection	0.22	0.23	0.05	0.21
	Cyclic alt.	0.11	0.27	0.60	0.33
	Segmentation	0.56	0.50	0.30	0.38
	Moderation	0	0	0	0
	Disqual.	0	0	0	0
	Reframing	0	0	0.05	0.04
	Uncoded	0.11	0	0	0.04
	n	18	22	20	24

mentation is similar to the finding of Baxter & Wilmot (1985) concerning the distinction between 'taboo' topics as opposed to disclosive topics. Management of the predictability–novelty contradiction through segmentation involves the differentiation of relationship predictability from episodic novelty, a distinction noted by Berger & Bradac (1982) and by Baxter & Wilmot (1984).

The strategies most frequently reported are not necessarily those associated with overall relationship satisfaction, with the exception of the segmentation response in coping with the predictability–novelty contradiction. Reframing, positively associated with relationship satisfaction for the autonomy–connection and predictability–novelty contradictions, appears to be an under-utilized coping strategy. Complex in nature, Reframing requires transformation of meaning in which the contrasting elements of a given contradiction cease to be regarded as antithetical to one another. The relative infrequency of the Reframing strategy may be the result of the short relationship histories reflected in this sample. Reframing may be more prevalent among relationship parties in longer relationships such as marriage.

The relative infrequency of Neutralization through both moderation and disqualification is a surprising finding given other research in interpersonal communication (for example, Tannen, 1984). Neutralization would probably appear more frequently in a finer grained method of data collection such as recorded discourse. However, to the extent that respondents are aware of Neutralization through disqualification and report its use in coping with the openness–closedness contradiction, overall relationship satisfaction appears to be damaged.

Relationship satisfaction appears to be moderately damaged, as well, in the use of Selection to manage both the autonomy–connection and predictability–novelty contradictions. In attempting to extinguish these contradictions by ignoring one of their respective dialectical aspects, relationship parties are likely to grow frustrated with the unmet need for the ignored aspect. This finding supports a dialectical revision of uncertainty-reduction theory to encompass the management of both certainty and uncertainty in relational life. The finding also challenges the assumption that positive relationships are those of maximum connection with the other and minimal autonomy from the other.

Many unanswered questions merit research attention from a dialectical perspective. This study focused primarily on one type of interpersonal relationship—the pre-marital romantic relationship. Whether the three contradictions under investigation in this study are present in other relationships such as friendships awaits research attention. The coping responses of the parties in other relationship types also deserve attention. Because meaning is culturally determined, elements perceived as contradictory in one culture may not generalize to other cultural groups, suggesting the need for cross-cultural replication of the particular contradictions under investigation in this study. Finally, the contradictions of autonomy–connection, openness–closedness and

predictability–novelty doubtless do not exhaust the domain of contradictions which parties experience in their relationships and which researchers may observe in relationships.

REFERENCES

Altman, I. & Taylor, D. (1973) *Social Penetration: The Development of Interpersonal Relationships.* New York: Holt, Rinehart & Winston.

Altman, I., Vinsel, A. & Brown, B. (1981) 'Dialectic Conceptions in Social Psychology,' in L. Berkowitz (ed.) *Advances in Experimental Social Psychology: 14.* New York: Academic Press.

Baxter, L. A. (1988) 'A Dialectical Perspective on Communication Strategies in Relationship Development,' in S. W Duck, D. F. Hay, S. E. Hobfoll, W. Iches & B. Montgomery (eds) *Handbook of Personal Relationships.* London: Wiley.

Baxter, L. A. & Bullis, C. (1986) 'Turning Points in Developing Romantic Relationships,' *Human Communication Research* 12: 469–93.

Baxter, L. A. & Wilmot, W. (1984) 'Secret Tests: Social Strategies for Acquiring Information about the State of the Relationship,' *Human Communication Research* 11: 171–201.

Baxter, L. A. & Wilmot, W. (1985) 'Taboo Topics in Romantic Relationships,' *Journal of Social and Personal Relationships* 2: 253–69.

Berger, C. R. & Bradac, J. J. (1982) *Language and Social Identity.* London: Arnold.

Berger, C. R. & Calabrese, R. J. (1975) 'Some Explorations in Initial Interaction and Beyond: Toward a Developmental Theory of Interpersonal Communication,' *Human Communication Research* 1: 99–112.

Bochner, A. (1984) 'The Functions of Human Communication in Interpersonal Bonding,' in C. Arnold & J. Bowers (eds) *Handbook of Rhetorical and Communication Theory.* Boston: Allyn & Bacon.

Cohen, J. (1960) 'A Coefficient of Agreement for Nominal Scales,' *Educational and Psychological Measurement* 20: 37–48.

Cornforth, M. (1968) *Materialism and the Dialectical Method.* New York: International Publishers.

Cupach, W. & Metts, S. (1988) 'Perceptions of the Occurrence and Management of Dialectics in Romantic Relationships,' unpublished paper presented at the Fourth International Conference on Personal Relationships, Vancouver, Canada.

Fisher, B. A. (1978) *Perspectives on Human Communication.* New York: Macmillan.

Kelvin, P. (1977) 'Predictability, Power and Vulnerability in Interpersonal Attraction,' in S. W. Duck (ed.) *Theory and Practice in Interpersonal Attraction.* London: Academic Press.

Miell, D. (1987) 'Remembering Relationship Development: Constructing a Context for Interactions,' in R. Burnett, P. McGhee & D. Clarke (eds) *Accounting for Relationships: Explanation, Representation and Knowledge.* London & New York: Methuen.

Norton, R. (1983) 'Measuring Marital Quality: A Critical Look at the Dependent Variable,' *Journal of Marriage and the Family* 45: 141–51.

Rawlins, W. K. (1983a) 'Negotiating Close Friendship: The Dialectic of Conjunctive Freedoms,' *Human Communication Research* 9: 255–66.

Rawlins, W. K. (1983b) 'Openness as Problematic in Ongoing Friendships: Two Conversational Dilemmas,' *Communication Monographs* 50: 1–13.

Rawlins, W. K. (1989) 'A Dialectical Analysis of the Tensions, Functions and Strategic Challenges of Communication in Young Adult Friendships,' in J. A. Anderson (ed.) *Communication Yearbook 2.* Newbury Park: Sage Publications.

Siegel, S. (1956) *Nonparametric Statistics for the Behavioral Sciences.* New York & London: McGraw-Hill.

Tannen, D. (1984) *Conversational Style: Analyzing Talk Among Friends.* Norwood, NJ: Ablex Publishing Corporation.

RELATIONAL SCHEMATA:
A TEST OF ALTERNATIVE FORMS OF RELATIONAL KNOWLEDGE AS GUIDES TO COMMUNICATION

Sally Planalp

One key task of research in relational communication is to understand how relational knowledge guides communicative processes. A necessary step in that direction is to determine what form of relational knowledge guides the cognitive processes involved in producing and comprehending messages. Based on tests of other forms of social knowledge, the best unobtrusive indicator of relational knowledge was determined to be systematic distortions in memory. Three forms of relational knowledge—general dimensional knowledge, situation-specific knowledge, and behavior-specific knowledge—were contrasted for their ability to account for biases in memory for relational implications of remarks in conversations. Two sets of results were noteworthy. First, very strong effects on both accuracy and direction of memory were found, indicating that some form of relational knowledge guided memory for conversations. Second, when the three forms of relational knowledge were contrasted, only one—behavior-specific knowledge—accounted for a significant proportion of those memory effects (83 % for accuracy and 85% for errors). The findings challenge the validity of well-established dimension- and situation-based approaches to relational knowledge and suggest alternative approaches that may be more compatible with the uses to which relational knowledge is put in communication.

In its broadest sense, relational communication can be thought of as the process by which people define their relationships through communication and how, in turn, communication reflects those definitions. People enter initial interactions with some sense of what communicative behaviors are appropriate for the type of relationship they anticipate; they interact, gleaning information about their relationship from the interaction; they use that information to guide further interaction, then update their knowledge of the relationship based on it, and so on. It is a continual process of using

Source: The article is taken from *Human Communication Research* (12: 3–29, 1985). (c) International Communication Association, 8140 Burnet Rd., Austin, TX 78766. Reprinted by permission of Sage Publications, Inc. and ICA.

relational knowledge to guide interaction and using interaction to modify relational knowledge.

Current research in the area of relational communication reflects both directions of the interplay between knowledge and interaction. One line of work is composed of systems for coding interaction that translate from concrete properties of messages to general properties of relationships (Courtright, Millar, & Rogers, 1979; Fisher & Drecksel, 1983). A second line of work is designed to translate from relational terms (friend, coworker, spouse) to communication patterns associated with those relationships (Berger, Weber, Munley, & Dixon, 1977; Bochner, Kaminski, & Fitzpatrick, 1977; Knapp, Ellis, & Williams, 1980). The two lines of research should meet to complete the cycle of interplay between relational knowledge and interaction, but they have developed as if they were independent aspects of relational communication instead of two complementary parts of an ongoing process. This article was motivated by three goals: to analyze how each line of research is limited by its failure to consider the complete process of relational communication, to address the issue of links between relational knowledge and communication more directly, and to investigate what form of relational knowledge might guide communication.

TWO SIDES OF RELATIONAL COMMUNICATION

Relational Coding

The study of relational communication is most strongly identified with systems for coding the relational meanings of messages (Fisher & Drecksel, 1983; Rogers & Farace, 1975). Consistent with the assumptions of the "Palo Alto Group," whose work served as a major impetus for relational coding, the focus of research has been on *what* patterns of interaction could be observed rather than on *why* they occurred (Wilder, 1979, p. 173). The general research tactic has been to record interactions, to develop systematic coding schemes for assigning relational meanings to remarks (usually dominance values assigned to adjacent remarks), and to describe the

nature of the relationship between the interactants based on summaries of codes assigned to remarks throughout the interaction. Although no one would argue against grounding the study of relational communication in observable patterns of interaction, many would argue that the work should not stop there. If consistent patterns of interaction are observed, one might reasonably ask why they occur, recur, and change. As Harré (1977) suggested, we should look for the mechanisms that generate regularities observed in interaction.

A number of relational communication scholars have argued that the mechanism that guides relational communication consists of structures of relational knowledge and the cognitive processes by which they are used to produce and interpret messages. For example, Wilmot and Baxter (1984) argued that relational communication requires complex interpretive processes that involve expectations and beliefs about relationships. Berger (1983) looked to social cognitive mechanisms as explanations for patterns of interaction and theoretical principles that could save research on relational communication from an avalanche of descriptive data. Finally, Planalp and Hewes (1982) indicated that cognitive mechanisms are needed to retain relational information from interaction to interaction and serve as a basis for guiding the course of future interactions.

Explaining patterns of interaction by appeal to relational knowledge makes it possible to address two specific issues that cannot be answered by coding approaches as they exist currently. The first concerns how messages are adapted to relationships. People communicate differently with supervisors, spouses, salesmen, and second cousins even though they may not have any direct experience with relationships of each type to draw on for guidance. They are able to communicate appropriately by drawing on stereotyped knowledge of relationships. Furthermore, when relationships are already established, knowledge of past interactions and anticipated future interactions guides communication in the present (Hinde, 1979, p. 14). Similarly, if people want to redefine their relationships, they are able to use subtle changes of interaction patterns to indicate bids for changing from friend to lover, from student to colleague, or from opponent to teammate because they know what interaction patterns characterize different relationships. Thus, studying the link between relational knowledge and interaction can improve our understanding of how communication is adapted to novel, established, and changing relationships.

Just as one might ask how relational knowledge influences interaction patterns, one might also ask how interaction patterns influence relational knowledge. In other words, how does interaction affect people's conceptions of their relationships? This is a second issue that has not been addressed adequately by studies of relational coding. Instead the implicit assumption has been made that all messages have equal and constant relational impact, an assumption that has been challenged on several fronts. For example, Planalp and Hewes (1982) challenged it using evidence that people are incapable of processing information based on such subtle and constant variation occurring over entire lifetimes in some cases. They argued that relational knowledge must guide what messages are attended to, what relational meanings are inferred, and how that information is integrated with prior knowledge. King and Sereno (1984) also proposed that the amount of impact remarks have on overall relational definitions depends on whether they are consistent or inconsistent with expectations. Remarks that conform to expectations have little impact because they are not informative; those that violate expectations have stronger impact. In both cases, interpretive links between messages and relational expectations or knowledge are considered substantive problems rather than foregone conclusions.

Relationship Terms

A second major strain of research is less strongly associated with the label *relational communication* than is work on relational coding, but it deals with the same issues from a different angle. This work complements work on relational coding in the sense that the focus is on definitions of relationships rather than on interaction. The question that guides research is what characteristics of communication or behavior people associate with different types of relationships (Berger, Weber, Munley, & Dixon, 1977; Knapp, Ellis, & Williams, 1980; Rands & Levinger, 1979; Wish, Deutsch, & Kaplan, 1976). Studies typically involve generating several different types of relationships, asking subjects to judge them either in direct comparison to one another or on a battery of rating scales, and using techniques such as factor analysis or multidimensional scaling to reduce the results to underlying bases of judgment. Its major weaknesses involve the use of data reduction techniques to tap relational knowledge and the lack of explicit ties between relational labels and interaction.

There are several reasons to question whether data reduction techniques (such as factor analysis and multidimensional scaling) tap the relational knowledge that people use to interact appropriately. One is that judgments based on differences among types of relationships may not reflect accurately the knowledge needed to produce different interaction patterns. Just as judgments of the differences between apples and oranges may tell us little about the genetic mechanisms needed to produce them, judgments of the differences between interaction patterns of liked and disliked others (Bochner, Kaminski, & Fitzpatrick, 1977) may tell us little about the mechanisms that produce them. To compound the problem, the results of data reduction studies vary depending on which relationships are being judged. A striking example is the difference in results found by Wish, Deutsch, and Kaplan (1976) and by Rands and Levinger (1979). In the former, 44 diverse relationships were found to be judged along four primary dimensions (friendliness, equality, intensity, and formality). In the latter, four much more similar relationships (casual acquaintances, good friends, close relationships, and spouses) were found to be judged along two primary dimensions (affective interdependence and behavioral interdependence). As this example illustrates, dimensions or factors derived from studies that contrast relationships cannot be presumed to reflect relational knowledge directly because they depend on which relationships are contrasted. To extend the criticism further, one might question the validity of using any contrastive study to uncover the relational knowledge that guides interaction. Normally interaction is guided by knowledge of the particular relationship at hand, not knowledge of the differences between it and 43 or even 3 other relationships.

More important, these studies have been limited to assessing associations between relational terms and dimensions of judgment rather than going on to establish how those dimensions translate into the kinds of concrete communicative behaviors used every day (conversations, for instance). Certainly behavioral indicants can be found for almost any dimension or factor of judgment (Knapp, Ellis, & Williams, 1980, p. 169; Rands & Levinger, 1979, p. 650), but how knowledge of relationships based on dimensions guides choices and judgments of appropriate behaviors (if at all) is not clear. It is possible that people locate a given relationship on a dimension and judge any behavior that falls roughly at the same point on the dimension as appropriate. For example, the professor-student relationship falls at the unequal end of the equality/inequality dimension (Wish, Deutsch, & Kaplan, 1976). For professors and students to behave appropriately, one person (presumably the professor) should make domineering remarks and other person (presumably the student) should make submissive remarks. Similarly, interactions in which this pattern is observed should have relatively little impact on relational definitions because they are typical, whereas interactions in which professors are submissive and students are dominant should have greater impact (King & Sereno, 1984). On the other hand, it is equally possible that relationships are associated with behaviors in other ways that produce dimensions as artifacts. The point is that there is no direct evidence concerning the form of relational knowledge that guides interactions, and there is reason to question whether dimensions or factors are able to play that role.

To summarize the criticisms of current work on relational communication, neither of the two major lines of research has been able to answer two key questions: What is the source of patterned interaction, and how do interaction patterns influence overall definitions of relationships? Work on relational coding of messages has focused on describing interaction patterns rather than on explaining where they come from or what impact they have on overall definitions of relationships. Work on the meaning of relational labels has focused on judgments among different types of relationships on underlying dimensions rather than on how knowledge of a particular relationship affects interaction or vice versa. Each line of work in its own way has failed to complete the link between relational knowledge and interaction that would make it possible to understand how relational knowledge guides interaction and how interaction impacts on relational knowledge. What is necessary is to consider interaction and relational knowledge *together* to discover how the two are related. To avoid the same criticisms leveled at current research, a valid measure of relational knowledge that is grounded in messages must be found. Toward that end, literature in social cognition was consulted for guidelines.

RELATIONAL SCHEMATA

Although the influence of relational knowledge on interaction has not been studied extensively from the point of view of cognitive psychology, the influence of similar structures on the processing of information about action, discourse, persons, and social entities has received extensive study and provides guidelines for studying relational knowledge (Craik, 1979; Hastie, 1981). By general consensus, the term used to denote generic structures of world knowledge that guide processing of information is *schema*. Craik (1979, p. 64) defines schemata as "coherent conceptual frameworks, built on the basis of experience, which allow interpretation and comprehension of novel events." Such a structure for relational knowledge would be termed a "relational schema." Relational schemata, then, are coherent frameworks of relational knowledge that are used to derive relational implications of messages and are modified in accord with ongoing experience with relationships. They provide the cognitive equivalent of "definitions of relationship" that guide message interpretation and production. The notion of schema thus provides a foothold for studying how relational knowledge is represented and used in processing relational information, especially information in conversations.

Several theorists have discussed entities like relational schemata. Housel and Acker (1979, pp. 15–16) proposed the relational schema as a complement to the content schema. They defined relational schemata as "receivers' expectations for the different ways people relate to one another (e.g., seduction, one-upmanship, competition, love, and hate)." Winograd (1977, p. 81) proposed "interpersonal schemas" as "conventions for interactions between the participants in the communication." Although Tesser (1978) did not refer to "relational schemata" explicitly, he tied his work on the effects of thought on attitudes toward the other person to the literature on schemata. Raush, Barry, Hertel, and Swain (1974, p. 49) referred to schemata that "develop from experience with others; they organize images of oneself and others and the relations between oneself and others." Each of these conceptions reflects a type of framework for representing knowledge about the relationship between two people.

Yet the question still remains of how evidence for relational schemata might be gathered. Here work in cognitive science provides explicit guidelines. Most important, social knowledge is presumed *not* to be directly observable, because it is implicit knowledge that is not accessible to awareness (Wegner & Vallacher, 1977, Chap. 1). Even if it were accessible, the reporting would be intrusive during interaction and direct reports would not be trustworthy due to experimental demand and to people's tendency to "tell more than they know" (Nisbett & Wilson, 1977). Instead, schemata are assumed to be entities that can be observed only indirectly but like any

unobservable entity (an electron for example) its existence can be demonstrated by what it *does*, in this case, by how it influences cognitive processes.

Schemata have long been used to explain systematic effects on attention (Cohen & Ebbesen, 1979; Neisser, 1976), inference (Bower, Black, & Turner, 1979; Kant, 1902), and judgment (Oldfield & Zangwill, 1942a, 1942b; Taylor, Crocker, & D'Agostino, 1978), but the effects that are most strongly grounded in theory, well documented, and broadly based are systematic effects on memory (Hastie, 1981; Rumelhart & Ortony, 1977; Taylor & Crocker, 1981). In fact Bartlett, the currently acknowledged forefather of modern notions of schema, introduced the schema as the keystone of a reconstructive, as opposed to a purely reproductive, theory of memory (Bartlett, 1932; Oldfield & Zangwill, 1942c). According to Bartlett, schemata produce systematic influence on memory because people do not *reproduce* from memory what *was* but at least partly *reconstruct* what was based on what *must have been*. For example, the actual forms of address used in a conversation between friends might not be reproduced from verbatim memory as much as reconstructed under the presumption that friends call one another by their first names (Argyle & Henderson, 1984). Systematic memory errors such as this have been found based on schemata for texts (Bower, Black, & Turner, 1979; Stein & Glenn, 1979), persons (Cantor & Mischel, 1979), and social structures (Picek, Sherman, & Shiffrin, 1975; Spiro, 1980).

In addition, the influence of schemata on accuracy of memory has been widely studied. Hastie (1981) reviewed a large body of work encompassing the areas of verbal learning, visual schemata, social group schemata, and points of view for the influence of schema-event congruence on accuracy of memory. He concluded that memory for schema-congruent events and for schema-incongruent events is more accurate than memory for events that are moderately congruent with or irrelevant to the schema. Although the advantage of schema-congruent events can be explained by accurate reconstruction, explanations for the memory advantage of schema-incongruent events are not so obvious and are sources of further speculation and investigation. Unlike schema-congruent events, schema-incongruent events seem to be remembered well only under certain conditions—such as when there are only a few or when there is sufficient time to think about them (Fiske & Linville, 1980; Graesser, Gordon, & Sawyer, 1979; Hastie & Kumar, 1979).

In short, research on schemata across a variety of content domains indicates that to investigate the effects of relational schemata on cognitive processes, one should first look to memory. Concretely, what people remember about interactions (whether accurately or inaccurately) is indicative of what they believe to be true and thus serves as an unobtrusive measure of their knowledge. When aspects of an interaction having to do with the relationship between the interactors are targeted, indirect evidence for relational schemata can be gathered.

CANDIDATES FOR RELATIONAL SCHEMATA

It is impossible to specify in advance all the possible forms that relational schemata might take, but rather than analyze patterns of accuracy and error of memory completely inductively, three plausible alternatives were considered. Relational schemata might take the form of general dimensions of a relationship; they might consist of general expectations for appropriate behavior in particular situations, or they might consist of concrete behaviors that are expected.

There are several reasons to believe that dimension-based knowledge guides relational communication. Representations consisting of a small number of dimensions that recur across a large number of relationships (Wish, Deutsch, & Kaplan, 1976) are both parsimonious and broadly applicable. The empirical evidence supporting a dimension-based representation is also very strong. The same dimensions have been found repeatedly in a large number of studies across a variety of research settings and subject populations (for reviews see Swenson, 1973, Chap. 7;

Triandis, 1977). Even those that challenge the number of basic dimensions of relationships call for more dimensions rather than a fundamentally different form of representation (Burgoon & Hale, 1984). More important, most of the current work on relational communication either uses one of the well-established dimensions as a basis for coding interaction (dominance or affect) or moves from relational labels to dimensions, as discussed earlier.

Situation-based knowledge is a second possibility. Theorists such as Cantor, Mischel, and Schwartz (1982), Forgas (1979), Goffman (1974) and Harré (1977) have drawn attention to the importance of the social situations in which roles are enacted and relationships realized. As a plausible form of relational knowledge, situation-specific knowledge has two points in its favor. First, variations in the same relationship from situation to situation are undeniable. People relate to one another differently in public than in private, at work and at play, in sickness and in health. Relational knowledge represented at this level would be an effective guide to appropriate interpretations and action. Situational knowledge also strikes a balance between abstract dimensions and concrete behaviors. Wish and Kaplan (1977) uncovered the same dimensions for communicative situations that were found for relationships, and in addition, significant associations between situations and relationships. Moreover, the situations they used—such as settling a trivial misunderstanding, working for a common goal with one person directing the other, or talking to each other at a large social gathering—were more directly tied to concrete behavior than the relationships with which they were associated. Situations seemed to link abstract dimensions with concrete behaviors.

The third possibility is that relational knowledge is represented as expectations about concrete behaviors. A great deal of work has connected roles and personal relationships with types of behaviors (e.g., Benajamin, 1974; Horowitz, 1979; Leary, 1957; Phillips & Thompson, 1977; Rands & Levinger, 1979) because ultimately relational knowledge must be used to interpret and produce behaviors. If relational knowledge were represented as the behaviors expected of participants in relationships, it would be in a form compatible with its uses. Unlike more abstract forms, knowledge represented as concrete behaviors could guide behavior without the need for higher-level inferential processes.

Because a case can be made for all three levels of relational knowledge, the only way to choose among them is by direct tests contrasting their effects on memory. Specifically, the level that is able to account for systematic patterns of accuracy and error in memory (if any) would meet the criterion established earlier as the most valid test for relational schemata.

METHODS

Briefly, the experimental tests were done as follows. Three conversations were constructed, each containing approximately thirty remarks. For each remark, three paraphrases were constructed that had essentially the same content but varied in the degree to which they expressed dominance or submissiveness. Subjects were then asked to read a conversation made up of some combination of those paraphrases and to answer several irrelevant distractor questions. One week later, they were given all three paraphrases of each remark and asked to designate which paraphrase occurred in the conversation they had read earlier. Accuracy and error patterns were then analyzed to determine whether there were systematic errors and if so, what form of relational knowledge guided them.

Stimuli.   Although there were no theoretical constraints on the type of relationship to be used, the professor-student relationship was chosen for several reasons. First, role relationships provide clear examples of relational knowledge held by the typical social actor.[1] Second, of the role relationships that might have been tested, those varying along the dimension of dominance were of greatest interest because of the implications for work on relational coding cited earlier. Third, the college students used as subjects were sure to be familiar with professor-student relationships.

Three conversations were constructed based on what subjects in a prior study reported to be typical topics of discussion between professors and students (Planalp, 1983). In one (Conversation A), a student asked to add the professor's class, in another (Conversation E), a student asked to make up an exam that was missed, and in the third (Conversation G), a student requested a change of grade for the professor's course. Each conversation was approximately 1 ½ typed pages long. For nearly every remark in each of the three conversations (34 in A, 30 in E, 26 in G), three paraphrases varying in dominance were constructed.[2] Examples of the 90 remarks are shown in Table 1.

Levels of relational knowledge were operationalized in the following ways. General, dimension-based dominance was measured by asking subjects to choose which of the three paraphrases for each remark was dominant (D), submissive (S), and neutral (N) (for examples of codes assigned, see Table 1). On average, 70.1% of subjects agreed on the code assigned.[3] Dominant paraphrases were considered most consistent with dimension-based knowledge for professors whereas submissive paraphrases were least consistent; the reverse was considered true for students. Thus the first prediction was that dominant paraphrases should produce greater accuracy and more intrusions for professors (followed by neutral, followed by submissive). The second was that submissive paraphrases by students would produce greater accuracy and intrusions than neutral ones, and neutral more than dominant.

Situation-based dominance was determined using a somewhat different procedure. To assess the degree to which each of the three paraphrases fit situational expectations, it was necessary first to assess what the expectation was for the situation and then to assess how close each paraphrase came to it. A different, but comparable group of subjects was asked to indicate on three 9-point scales[4] expected dominance values for professors in general, students in general, and professors and students in each of the three situations (adding a course, making up an exam, changing

	Spk	Paraphrases	Dom	Beh	Sit
		TABLE 1 **Examples of Paraphrase Pretests**			
E1	S	I could come back later if you can't talk now.	S	M	M
		I have to talk to you right now.	D	L	D
		Do you have time to talk right now?	N	H	F
		I missed the exam on Friday, I had to go to the clinic.			
E2	P	Do you have a note for a medical excuse?	S	H	F
		I require a note for medical excuses.	D	L	M
		I'd like to see a note for medical excuses.	N	M	D
E3	S	I didn't need it for other classes.	D	L	F
		I didn't realize I needed it for this class.	S	H	D
		I didn't think I needed it for this class.	N	M	M
E4	P	Well, you do need it for this class.	D	M	F
		Well, I would like to see one.	N	H	M
		Well, it would help me to see one.	S	L	D
E5	P	Students often exaggerate their excuses.	S	H	D
		Students often don't have good excuses.	N	M	M
		Students often lie about their excuses.	D	L	F
E6	S	I don't have a note. You could call the clinic to verify.	N	M	F
		I don't have a note. Call over to the clinic if you don't believe me.	D	L	D
		I don't have a note. Maybe I could have the clinic call you.	S	H	M

Source: Spk is speaker (S = student, P = professor); Dom is dominance (D = dominant, N = neutral, S = submissive); Beh is likelihood of behavior occurring (H = high, M = moderate, L = low); Sit is consistency with situational expectations (F = fits, M = moderately fits, D = deviates).

a grade). After those judgments were made, subjects were then asked to rate one of the three paraphrases for each remark on the same scales (for a total of 90). T-tests comparing mean differences indicated that in all cases, situational means differed from general means, and those for professors differed from their counterparts for students (Table 2). That is, professors and students were expected to exhibit different levels of dominance from one situation to the next. All effects were large (approximately one standard deviation; Cohen, 1977) except for contrasts between general expectations and expectations for Conversations E and G for professors, which were small to moderate (.4 S.D.). The directions of all t-tests were as predicted except in the case of Conversation A, where it was found that subjects expected students to be substantially *more* dominant than professors. Then situation-specific codes were assigned to the paraphrases by determining which of the three best fit the situational

expectation (F), which deviated from it the most (D), and which fit to a moderate degree (M) by computing differences between means for each paraphrase and the appropriate situational mean.[5] The situation-based prediction, then, was that accuracy of memory and intrusions of memory would be greater for paraphrases that came closer to situational expectations (F > M > D).

Behavior-specific expectations were measured by asking subjects to judge which of the three paraphrases was most likely to occur in conversation (H for highly likely), which was least likely to occur (L), and which was moderately likely (M) (see Table 1). On average, 58.3% of subjects agreed with the codes assigned.[6] For both professors and students, it was predicted that highly likely paraphrases would be more accurately remembered and produce more memory intrusions than moderately likely ones, and moderately likely ones more than unlikely ones.

T A B L E 2
T-Tests for Differences between General and Situation-Specific Expectations

	General Expectation	Conversation A (Adding Course)	Conversation E (Making up Exam)	Conversation G (Changing Grade)
Professor	6.65	4.90	7.05	7.06
	(1.09)	(1.41)	(1.15)	(1.00)
Student	4.03	6.28	5.43	5.97
	(1.22)	(1.26)	(1.70)	(1.46)

Source: Higher values indicate greater dominance. Upper figure is mean; lower is standard deviation. All means for situation-specific expectations differ from the general expectation for both students and professors ($p < .01$). Means for professors and students also differ from each other within each situation and in general ($p < .01$). For all means, n = 83.

T A B L E 3
Measures of Association between Three Levels of Relational Knowledge

	Professors		Students	
	Situational Dominance	Behavioral Likelihood	Situational Dominance	Behavioral Likelihood
General dominance	+.079	−.091	−.269	−.525
	12.8	12.8	15.9	30.1
Situational dominance		−.181		+.381
		9.8		24.4

Source: Measures are based on frequencies of remarks across all three conversations; upper figure is Goodman-Kruskal gamma; lower figure is percentage reduction error in column measure given row measure.

Finally, after all paraphrases had been assigned general dominance, situational dominance, and likelihood codes, associations between the three measures were computed (Table 3). Associations were weak to moderate, ranging from 9.8% of behavior-specific codes being predictable from situational codes for professors to 30.1% of behavior-specific codes being predictable from general dominance codes for students. The three measures were more strongly associated for students than for professors. For professors, general and situational dominance were positively associated with each other and negatively associated with the likelihood that the paraphrase would occur. For students, situational dominance and behavioral likelihood were positively associated with each other and negatively associated with general dominance.

These findings indicate that the three measures tapped forms of relational knowledge that overlapped slightly. Table 3 indicates that judgments of how well a given paraphrase fit the expected level of dominance for the situation could be predicted in part by its overall level of dominance. Similarly, judgments of the likelihood of a paraphrase occurring could be predicted in part by its general dominance level and by how well it fit the expected level of dominance for the situation, although more strongly by the former. For example, the judged likelihood of a student choosing a given paraphrase could be predicted 30.1% of the time by knowing how dominant the remark was (the more dominant, the less likely).

Before memory effects could be tested, all paraphrases had to be arranged into conversations to be presented to subjects. Because memory for any paraphrase might be influenced by those that surround it, five configurations of each conversation were constructed. The configurations varied according to their consistency with situation-specific expectations ranging from conversations containing 80% of remarks that fit situational expectations to ones where 80% deviated from them. In principle, configurations could have been constructed using general dominance or behavior-specific knowledge as well, but using all three was not feasible because of the large number of subjects required. Situation-specific knowledge was chosen because it struck the balance between the other two.

Procedures.   To test for memory effects, 202 students in a beginning public speaking class at a large midwestern university read through one of five configurations of all three conversations and answered six questions concerning his or her ability to imagine the conversations realistically. The purpose of the six questions was only to lead subjects to believe they had finished the experiment after the first phase so they would not rehearse the material during the interval between phases. The second phase took place one week later. Subjects then identified which of the three paraphrases of each remark they had read the week before. If subjects had no idea which remark they had read, they were instructed to leave the item blank. The actual occurrence of missing data was negligible.

The choice to use a recognition memory task at a relatively long time interval was made because the goal was to discover what knowledge guided systematic memory effects. The recognition task made it possible to have more confidence in systematic biases based on relational implications of remarks by (a) generating alternatives that were similar in content but different in relational implications, (b) pretesting the relational implications of alternatives using naive judges, and (c) presenting the alternatives in the context of the complete conversations so that all remarks could be cued. Recall responses would have been difficult to match to the correct stimulus remark and would have required post hoc judgments of dominance values for all responses given by subjects. A relatively long time interval was used so that enough errors would be found to determine if there was a systematic pattern to them. Theories of reconstructive memory indicate that time interval should effect only the amount of error, not the knowledge that produces systematic biases.

Methods of Analysis.   Log-linear analysis of the complete data matrix indicated that the configuration of the conversation in which remarks occurred did not influence memory. The simplest log-linear model that fit the data did not include any effect of configuration (p = .35, residual chi-square = .5% of total; Planalp, 1983). Memory effects could therefore be analyzed on a remark-by-remark basis. First, accuracy of memory was assessed. For 80% of remarks, some configurations of the conversation contained the paraphrase that fit situational expectations while other configurations contained the paraphrase that deviated from them. Because the basic content of the remark was the same in both cases, comparisons between the two paraphrases constituted the best test of the influence of relational implications on accuracy. A series of chi-square tests were performed contrasting frequencies of accurate identification for the two paraphrases. Of the 71 tests performed, 29 were significantly different at the p < .005 level. Each of the 29 pairs of paraphrases was then recoded according to the general dominance and behavior-specific implications and direction of greatest accuracy in memory was assessed for the complete set by sign test.

STATISTICAL SUMMARY 1

Log-linear analysis tests whether three or more variables are associated or related to each other. It is used with variables that have categories (e.g., ethnicity might have African American, white American, Mexican American; gender includes male and female; and income might have high, medium, and low) and shows you if the category of each variable tends to occur more frequently together (e.g., African American, female, middle income). This analysis showed that the arrangement or order of the conversation did not influence memory.

Chi-square analysis is like log-linear analysis except it is only used with two variables at a time. It tells you if two variables that have categories (e.g., ethnicity might have African American, white American, Mexican American; and income might have high, medium, and low) are related to each other. With Chi-square you can see if a category of one variable (e.g., African American) tends to occur more frequently with a category of a second variable (e.g., middle income). Here Chi-square tests were used to see if the type of statement (general dominance, situational dominance, behavioral likelihood) influenced the accuracy of memory. These analyses showed that behavior-specific knowledge had the greatest impact on memory.

Direction of memory error was assessed in a comparable way. For each remark presented, a chi-square test was performed to determine if one distractor paraphrase was more likely to be chosen than the other. If the difference was statistically significant at the .005 level, there was a memory bias for that item. Biases were found for 96 of the 163 remarks analyzed. Each paraphrase, again, was recoded according to general dominance and behavior-specific knowledge, and the direction of error for remarks as a set was determined by sign test.

RESULTS

The first set of results addressed the question of whether accuracy of memory differed for remarks with essentially the same content but different relational implications. It clearly did. Nearly half the paraphrases compared (41%) showed differential accuracy at the $p < .005$ level of statistical significance. To determine why such strong differences occurred, the three bases of relational implications—general dominance, situation-based dominance, and behavior-specific knowledge—were then contrasted for their abilities to account for the *direction* of differential accuracy. The comparisons were very clear (Table 4). Across all three conversations, behavior-specific knowledge predicted 23 of the 27 significantly different pairs (14 of 27 expected by chance alone, $p < .001$). In contrast, general dominance accounted for 17 of 28 (compared to 14 of 28 by chance, $p > .10$) and situation-based dominance accounted for slightly fewer remarks than chance (14 of 29, $p > .10$). When the remarks were divided by conversation, the same pattern was found except that general dominance predicted well in Conversation G (7 of 8, $p < .05$).

The second set of results addressed the question of whether remarks were remembered *differently* depending on their relational implications. Again, they clearly were. When remarks were analyzed for the direction in which memory errors occurred, the identical pattern of results was found. Over half (59%) of the remarks showed a memory bias significant at $p < .005$. When levels of relational knowledge were pitted against one another to account for memory biases, behavior-specific knowledge was again clearly superior. It accounted for biases in 79 of 95 remarks (48 expected by chance alone, $p < .001$) whereas general dominance accounted for slightly fewer than chance (44 of 91, $p > .10$) and situation-based dominance accounted for only as many as chance (48 of 96, $p > .10$). When errors were divided by conversation and by type of remark presented (hence types of distractors), the identical pattern was found across all subdivisions.

TABLE 4
Summary of Sign Tests for Predictions of Memory Accuracy and Errors

Conversation	General Dominance[a]		Situational Dominance		Behavioral Likelihood	
A	A:[b]	4:6 (p = .38)[c]	A:	4:7 (p = .28)	A:	9:1 (p = .02)
	E:	15:26 (p = .07)	E:	14:27 (p = .03)	E:	33:7 (p < .00)
E	A:	6:4 (p = .38)	A:	6:4 (p = .38)	A:	8:2 (p = .05)
	E:	16:9 (p = .12)	E:	18:10 (p = .10)	E:	24:4 (p < .00)
G	A:	7:1 (p = .04)	A:	4:4 (p = .5)	A:	6:1 (p = .07)
	E:	13:12 (p = .5)	E:	16:11 (p = .19)	E:	22:5 (p < .00)
Total	A:	17:11 (p = .19)	A:	14:15 (p = .5)	A:	23:4 (p < .00)
	E:	44:47 (p = .43)	E:	48:48 (p = .5)	E:	79:16 (p < .00)

[a]Predictions based on general dominance for professors were that dominant remarks would be better remembered than neutral, which in turn would be better than submissive and just the reverse for students; predictions based on situational dominance were that the closer the mean dominance value for each remark was to the expected mean value for the professor or student in that situation, the more accurate memory would be; predictions based on behavioral likelihood were that the more likely the remark was to occur, the better it would be remembered.
[b]A refers to accuracy; E to errors. The ratio reported is correctly predicted remarks to incorrect ones: chance = 1:1.
[c]Probabilities are adjusted for the sign test itself being based on a sample of the population of relevant remarks, following Maxwell (1961, p. 130). The test is appropriate for samples larger than 20, but unadjusted figures for those tests with n < 20 show only two substantial differences. Accuracy for behavioral likelihood predictions for conversations E (8:2) and G (6:1) are both approximately .25 based on tabulated probabilities.

DISCUSSION

What evidence do these findings provide for or against relational schemata? First, memory for remarks in conversations was not random but rather showed strong systematic biases. Because memory biases are the hallmark of schemata, they indicate that some schema (or schemata) guided memory for conversations. Second, because the paraphrases that showed systematic biases differed only in subtle changes of phrasing indicating degrees of dominance or submissiveness, relational schemata are a likely candidate. Third, schema-based memory involves reconstructing what did occur, at least in part, from knowledge of what was most likely to have occurred. Thus intrusion in memory of paraphrases with highly likely relational implications is consistent with the existence of relational schemata.

In addition, the findings give clues to what form professor-student schemata take. They clearly do *not* take the form of simple knowledge that professors are dominant and students are submissive or of knowledge of appropriate levels of dominance for professors and students in different situations. What form they *do* take is not so clear. The findings implicate knowledge of the specific behaviors that are appropriate for professors and students, yet the sheer number of memory effects predicted by likelihood judgments (79 of 95) makes an explanation based on behavioral expectations implausible. People are simply incapable of remembering long lists of data without some organizing principle (Lachman, Lachman, & Butterfield, 1979, Chaps. 7 & 8; Miller, 1956).

The remaining question, then, is what organizing principle accounts for the effects of likelihood judgments on memory. One possibility is that some phrasings were simply more memorable than others, regardless of their implications for dominance. Two considerations make this explanation implausible. First, the distinctions between paraphrases were produced using commonly used words, none of which seemed to be inherently more memorable without considering professor and student roles. Second, the same phrasings were found to be the preferred memory option in one case and the dispreferred option in another.

A second possibility is that some other relational dimension intruded and produced the memory effects, the most obvious candidate being affect (cooperativeness or friendliness). In a post hoc check, a new group of subjects was asked to make ratings of liking (or friendliness) for all paraphrases in the same way they made dominance and likelihood ratings.[7] Affect alone also failed to account for memory effects consistently beyond chance levels. Although the overall trend for memory errors was toward paraphrases that expressed liking (54 of 90 remarks, p < .05), it was attributable to only one subset (when remarks consistent with situational expectations were presented in Conversation A). Affect did not predict accuracy of memory beyond chance (14 of 27 remarks, p = .5). Nevertheless, affect was found to be associated with behavioral likelihood judgments (.528 gamma, 31.3% PRE for

professors; 884 gamma, 60.7% PRE for students) and dominance (−.845 gamma, 60.7% PRE for professors, −.858 gamma, 58.0% PRE for students).

The more plausible explanation is that memory errors were guided by some form of relational knowledge associated with likelihood judgments. The fact that moderate to high associations were found between dominance, affect, and likelihood judgments—even though only likelihood predicted memory errors—suggests that the principle guiding memory is associated with dominance and affect but is not reducible to them. In order to understand better why likelihood judgments predicted memory effects so well, the conversations were examined for clues to the bases for choosing one paraphrase as more likely than another.

All three situations used in this study involved negotiations between professors and students. The general pattern of choices seemed to reflect subjects' knowledge of their respective rights and obligations. For example, when the topic is adding a course (Conversation A), professors' most likely remarks reflect their obligation to admit students if sufficient need is demonstrated and students' most likely remarks reflect an obligation to demonstrate need. When make-up exams are discussed (Conversation E), the most likely remarks for students are those that recognize their right to make up exams and their obligation to provide legitimate excuses. Professors' most likely remarks reflect the complementary right to determine legitimacy of excuses and the obligation to give a make-up exam if the excuse is legitimate. Finally, when students ask professors to change grades (Conversation G), they are likely to indicate that they recognize their right to a fair grade, but that professors hold the right to determine what is fair. In all three situations, both parties' most likely remarks hold the assumption that the ultimate decision lies in the hands of the professor. (For a detailed remark-by-remark analysis, see Planalp, 1983, pp. 253–257).

The overall view of student-professor interactions gleaned from these three conversations is that remarks are chosen based on each party's understanding of their mutual rights and obligations. Professors may not have to be dominant all the time because their rights are recognized; students may not have to be submissive because they have rights as well. Instead, professors and students choose remarks that reflect their knowledge of what to expect of others and what others expect of them. Viewing relational knowledge as a system of mutual rights and obligations, although not predominant in communication studies, is by no means new; it is a staple of role theory (Biddle, 1979, p. 210) and symbolic interactionism (McCall & Simmons, 1978). One can further argue that social actors not only recognize their respective rights and obligations, but also choose messages that presume them or present messages so that the other will recognize them (Baumeister, 1982; Goffman, 1959). Labov and Fanshel (1977) found presumptions about the rights and obligations of mother-daughter roles to be fruitful in explicating the richer meanings of therapeutic discourse. Brown and Levinson (1978) have also offered an account of how message strategies reflect both parties' self-presentation needs that might include their respective rights and obligations. The pattern of results found in this study suggests that pursuing relational knowledge in terms of rights and obligations might prove more fruitful in understanding how relational knowledge interacts with messages better than dimensional or situational approaches.

Although it would be premature to argue that a system of rights and obligations is the form of relational schema that links definitions of relationships and interaction, it is instructive to consider how it might do so. Two key questions were posed earlier: What is the source of patterned interactions, and how do interaction patterns influence overall definitions of relationships? Rights and obligations might serve as the source of patterned interactions if participants choose their remarks based on whether they think they have the right to ask a question, make a statement, make a certain presumption, and so on. Knowledge of the rights and obligations that govern different

relationships would provide a basis for making remarks appropriate to the relationship. Bids for redefining the relationship could be made by remarks that deny the legitimacy of certain rights and obligations or assert the legitimacy of new ones. Ultimately the set of rights and obligations may evolve into one that characterizes a different relationship (e.g., colleagues rather than professor and student). Again, rights and obligations are used here only for purposes of illustrating how relational schemata might function in communication; any other form of relational schema might function in the same way.

CONCLUSIONS

The most basic contribution this study makes to work on relational communication is to demonstrate how relational knowledge can be studied in the context of interaction. The same methods that have been used to gather evidence for scripts, story grammars, and person schemata were used here to uncover evidence for relational schemata in conversations. Because evidence for relational schemata was found using those techniques, the ways we have often viewed and studied relational communication must be reevaluated. Rather than viewing relational communication as a property of messages (especially as interacts), we are led to view it as the interplay between messages and relational schemata.

Even though the main purpose of this study was to uncover relational knowledge using memory, possible implications of the memory effects themselves should not be overlooked. The relational implications of remarks in conversations were strongly and systematically biased to be consistent with prior expectations. In particular, remarks that fit expectations were more likely to be remembered accurately than those that did not, and when errors were made they were likely to be consistent with expectations. The long-run result of such biases may be that variability in the relational implications of messages is "smoothed" by assimilation into the expectation, thus imposing continuity among messages and interactions. This may be one way people are able to maintain stable conceptions of their relationships despite fluctuations in the relational implications of messages.

Most important, these findings challenge the validity of dimension- and situation-based approaches to relational knowledge. Many studies of relational communication have assumed that dimensional representations are the bridge between definitions of relationships and actual interaction. The findings of this study indicate otherwise. Because previous studies relied on data reduction techniques, no representation other than one based on dimensions or factors was possible; if less restrictive techniques had been available, a different form of representation might have been found. The dimensions or factors found in those studies may have been abstract surrogates for more complex forms of knowledge such as those found here. Furthermore, preliminary analyses suggest that a possible alternative to dimensional representations, at least for role relationships, may be relational partners' knowledge of their mutual rights and obligations. Professors and students were not expected to maintain characteristic levels of dominance in their interactions, but rather to produce messages that reflected socially accepted operating rules for the relationship. Although this alternative awaits further testing in different situations and different relationships, it may more accurately capture forms of relational knowledge used in producing, comprehending, and remembering social interaction.

NOTES

1. Following the distinctions made by Miller and Steinberg (1975) and Hinde (1979), we assume that knowledge of interpersonal relationships contains basic knowledge of social roles that is elaborated by incorporating knowledge of the unique individuals filling those roles. The property of embeddedness of schemata (Rumelhart & Ortony, 1977) provides the mechanism for interplay between role and interpersonal relationships. Role relationships were chosen as a simpler and more tractable starting point for this research.
2. The tactic used to manipulate consistency between schema and event (in this case relationship and conversation) was to hold the relationship constant and vary relational properties of conversations. For purposes of experimental control it would have been preferable to hold the conversation constant and vary the relationship, but the results of a prior experiment indicated that the same conversation was not equally plausible for different types of relationships (Planalp, 1983, Chap. 3). The paraphrases used to vary the dominance of remarks were generated by the experimenter, but post hoc checks indicated that naive subjects generated similar kinds of paraphrases.
3. Codes were assigned using two criteria. First, codes for dominance, neutrality, and submissiveness were assigned when the majority of subjects gave the same designation and when each set of three paraphrases contained one paraphrase for each code. Most remarks (81 of 90) met that criterion. if they did not, dominant and submissive remarks were assigned using majority rule and neutral paraphrases were assigned by default (an additional 7 remarks). Two remarks met neither criterion, were not assigned codes, and were excluded from all analyses. Using these assignment rules, percentage agreement varied between conversations and between paraphrases from a low of 57.8% (neutral, Conversation E) to 80.8% (dominant, Conversation G) where chance was 33.3%.
4. The scales used were dominant-submissive, controlling-yielding, assertive-deferential (Folger & Sillars, 1980). Separate reliabilities were computed for all judgments made that ranged from a low of .56 to a high of .97. Fewer than 4% had Cronbach's alphas < .70. Because reliabilities were so high, the three scales were subsequently averaged to produce a composite index of dominance.
5. For example, the first remark shown in Table 1 had paraphrases judged as 3.48, 7.81, and 5.02, respectively. The appropriate situational anchor was students making up an exam (5.43 from Table 2). Thus paraphrase 1 was designated as a moderate deviation (5.43 − 3.48 = 1.95), paraphrase 2 as deviating the most (7.81 − 5.43 = 2.38), and 3 as best fitting situational expectations (5.43 − 5.02 = .41).
6. Codes were assigned using the majority criterion (56 of 90) and the moderate code default option (11 of 90) as used for dominance (see note 3). In some cases (17 of 90) the skew of the distribution of judgments was considered as well. Using these three rules, 6 of 90 remarks could not be assigned codes. Percentage agreement ranged from 47.4% (moderate, Conv G) to 67.5% (low likelihood, Conv E) where chance was 33.3%.
7. Affect codes were assigned using exactly the same procedures as used to assign dominance codes. Of the 90 remarks, 79 were assigned by simple majority rule and an additional 8 by majority plus moderate liking default, leaving four uncoded. Average reliability was 68.4% ranging from 57.6% (moderate liking, Conv G) to 81.6% (disliking, Conv E).

REFERENCES

Argyle, M., & Henderson, M. (1984). The rules of friendship. *Journal of Social and Personal Relationships, 1,* 211–237.

Bartlett, F. C. (1932). *Remembering.* New York: Cambridge University Press.

Baumeister, R. F. (1982). A self-presentational view of social phenomena. *Psychological Bulletin, 91,* 3–26.

Benjamin, L. S. (1974). Structural analysis of social behavior. *Psychological Review, 31,* 392–425.

Berger, C. R. (1983). *Thinking and relating: Social cognition and relational control.* Paper presented at the Speech Communication Association Convention, Washington, DC.

Berger, C. R., Weber, M. D., Munley, M. E., & Dixon, J. T. (1977). Interpersonal relationship levels and interpersonal attraction. In B. Ruben (Ed.), *Communication yearbook 1.* New Brunswick, NJ: Transaction-International Communication Association.

Biddle, B. J. (1979). *Role theory: Expectations, identities and behaviors.* New York: Academic Press.

Bochner, A. P., Kaminski, E. P., & Fitzpatrick, M. A. (1977). The conceptual domain of interpersonal communication behavior: A factor-analytic study. *Human Communication Research, 3,* 291–302.

Bower, G. H., Black, J. B., & Turner, T. (1979) Scripts in memory for text. *Cognitive Psychology, 11,* 177–220.

Brown, P., & Levinson, S. (1978). Universals in language usage: Politeness phenomena. In E. N. Goody (Ed.), *Questions and politeness.* New York: Cambridge University Press.

Burgoon, J. K., & Hale, J. L. (1984). The fundamental topoi of relational communication. *Communication Monographs, 51,* 193–214.

Cantor, N., & Mischel, W. (1979). Prototypes in person perception. In L. Berkowitz (Ed.), *Advances in experimental social psychology* (Vol. 12). New York: Academic Press.

Cantor, N., Mischel, W., & Schwartz, J. C. (1982). A prototype analysis of psychological situations. *Cognitive Psychology, 14,* 45–77.

Cohen, C. E., & Ebbesen, E. B. (1979). Observational goals and schema activation: A theoretical framework for behavior perception. *Journal of Experimental Social Psychology, 15,* 305–329.

Cohen, J. (1977). *Statistical power analysis for the behavioral sciences* (2nd Ed.). New York: Academic Press.

Courtright, J. A., Millar, F. E., & Rogers-Millar, L. E. (1979). Domineeringness and dominance: Replication and expansion. *Communication Monographs, 46,* 179–192.

Craik, F. I. M. (1979). Human memory. *Annual Review of Psychology, 30,* 63–102.

Fisher, B. A., & Drecksel, G. L. (1983). A clinical model of developing relationships: A study of relational control interaction. *Communication Monographs, 50,* 66–78.

Fiske, S. T., & Linville, P. (1980). What does the schema concept buy us? *Personality and Social Psychology Bulletin, 6,* 543–557.

Folger, J. P., & Sillars, A. (1980). Relational coding and perceptions of dominance. In B. Morse & L. Phelps (Eds.), *Interpersonal communication: A relational perspective.* Minneapolis, MN: Burgess.

Forgas, J. P. (1979). *Social episodes: The study of interaction routines.* New York: Academic Press.

Goffman, E. (1959). *The presentation of self in everyday life.* Garden City, NY: Doubleday.

Goffman, E. (1974). *Frame analysis.* New York: Harper & Row.

Graesser, A. C., Gordon, S. E., & Sawyer, J. D. (1979). Recognition memory for typical and atypical actions in scripted activities: Tests of a script pointer + tag hypothesis. *Journal of Verbal Learning and Verbal Behavior, 18,* 319–332.

Harré, R. (1977). The ethogenic approach: Theory and practice. In L. Berkowitz (Ed.), *Advances in experimental social psychology* (Vol. 10). New York: Academic Press.

Hastie, R. (1981). Schematic principles in human memory. In E. T. Higgins, C. P. Herman, & M. P. Zanna (Eds.), *Social cognition: The Ontario symposium* (Vol. 1). Hillsdale, NJ: Lawrence Erlbaum.

Hastie, R., & Kumar, P. A. (1979). Person memory: Personality traits as organizing principles in memory for behaviors. *Journal of Personality and Social Psychology, 37,* 25–38.

Hinde, R. A. (1979). *Towards understanding relationships.* New York: Academic Press.

Horowitz, L. M. (1979). On the cognitive structure of interpersonal problems treated in psychotherapy. *Journal of Consulting and Clinical Psychology, 47,* 5–15.

Housel, T. J., & Acker, S. R. (1979). *Schema theory: Can it connect communication's discourse?* Paper presented to the International Communication Association Convention, Philadelphia.

Kant, I. (1902). *Critique of pure reason* (J.M.D. Meiklejohn, Trans.). New York: Collier.

King, S. W., & Sereno, K. K. (1984). Conversational appropriateness as a conversational imperative. *Quarterly Journal of Speech, 70,* 264–273.

Knapp, M. L., Ellis, D. G., & Williams, B. A. (1980). Perceptions of communication behavior associated with relationship terms. *Communication Monographs, 47,* 262–278.

Labov, W., & Fanshel, D. (1977). *Therapeutic discourse.* New York: Academic Press.

Lachman, R., Lachman, J. L., & Butterfield, E. C. (1979). *Cognitive psychology and information processing.* New York: Lawrence Erlbaum.

Leary, T. (1957). *Interpersonal diagnosis of personality.* New York: Ronald Press.

McCall, G. J., & Simmons, J. L. (1978). *Identities and interactions* (2nd ed.). New York: Free Press.

Miller, G. A. (1956). The magical number seven plus or minus two: Some limits on our capacity for processing information. *Psychological Review, 63,* 81–96.

Miller, G. R., & Steinberg, M. (1975). *Between people: A new analysis of interpersonal communication.* Palo Alto, CA: Science Research Associates.

Neisser, U. (1976). *Cognition and reality.* San Francisco: W. H. Freeman.

Nisbett, R. E., & Wilson, T. D. (1977). Telling more than we can know: Verbal reports on mental processes. *Psychological Review, 84,* 231–259.

Oldfield, R. C., & Zangwill, O. L. (1942a). Head's concept of the schema and its application in contemporary British psychology: Part I. Head's concept of the schema. *British Journal of Psychology, 32,* 267–286.

Oldfield, R. C., & Zangwill, O. L. (1942b). Head's concept of the schema and its application in contemporary British Psychology: Part II. Critical analysis of Head's theory. *British Journal of Psychology, 33,* 58–64.

Oldfield, R. C., & Zangwill, O. L. (1942c). Head's concept of the schema and its application in contemporary British psychology: Part III. Bartlett's theory of memory. *British Journal of Psychology, 33,* 113–129.

Phillips, J. L., & Thompson, E. G. (1977). An analysis of the conceptual representations: Components in a network model of cognitive organization. *Journal for the Theory of Social Behavior, 7,* 161–184.

Picek, J. S., Sherman, S. J., & Shiffrin, R. M. (1975). Cognitive organization and coding of social structures. *Journal of Personality and Social Psychology, 31,* 758–768.

Planalp, S. (1983). *Relational schemata: An interpretive approach to relationships.* Unpublished doctoral dissertation, University of Wisconsin.

Planalp, S., & Hewes, D. E. (1982). A cognitive approach to communication theory: *Cogito ergo dico?* In M. Burgoon (Ed.), *Communication yearbook 5.* New Brunswick, NJ: Transaction-International Communication Association.

Rands, M., & Levinger, G. (1979). Implicit theories of relationship: An intergenerational study. *Journal of Personality and Social Psychology, 37,* 645–661.

Rausch, H. L., Barry, W. A., Hertel, R. K., & Swain, M. A. (1974). *Communication, conflict and marriage.* San Francisco: Jossey-Bass.

Rogers, L. E., & Farace, R. V. (1975). An analysis of relational communication in dyads: New measurement procedures. *Human Communication Research, 1,* 222–239.

Rumelhart, D. E., & Ortony, A. (1977). The representation of knowledge in memory. In R. Anderson, J. Spiro, & W. Montague (Eds.), *Schooling and the acquisition of knowledge.* Hillsdale, NJ: Lawrence Erlbaum.

Spiro, R. (1980). Accomodative reconstruction in prose recall. *Journal of Verbal Learning and Verbal Behavior, 19,* 84–85.

Stein, N. L., & Glenn, C. G. (1979). An analysis of story comprehension in elementary school children. In R. Freedle (Ed.), *New directions in discourse processing* (Vol. II). Norwood, NJ: ABLEX.

Swenson, C. H., Jr. (1973). *Introduction to interpersonal relationships.* Glenview, IL: Scott, Foresman.

Taylor, S. E., & Crocker, J. (1981). Schematic bases of social information processing. In E. T. Higgins, C. P. Herman, & M. P. Zanna (Eds.), *Social cognition: The Ontario symposium* (Vol. 1). Hilsdale, NJ: Lawrence Erlbaum.

Taylor, S. E., Crocker, J., & D'Agostino, J. (1978). Schematic bases of social problem-solving. *Personality and Social Psychology Bulletin, 4,* 447–451.

Tesser, A. (1978). Self-generated attitude change. In L. Berkowitz (Ed.), *Advances in experimental social psychology* (Vol. 11). New York: Academic Press.

Triandis, H. C. (1977). *Interpersonal behavior.* Monterey, CA: Brooks/Cole.

Wegner, D. M., & Vallacher, R. R. (1977). *Implicit psychology.* New York: Oxford University Press.

Wilder, C. (1979). The Palo Alto group: Difficulties and directions of the interactional view for human communication research. *Human Communication Research, 5,* 171–186.

Wilmot, W. W., & Baxter, L. A. (1984). *Defining relationships: The interplay of cognitive schemata and communication.* Paper presented at the Western Speech Communication Association Convention, Seattle.

Winograd, T. (1977). A framework for understanding discourse. In M. A. Just & P. Carpenter (Eds.), *Cognitive processes in comprehension.* New York: John Wiley.

Wish, M., Deutsch, M., & Kaplan, S. J. (1976). Perceived dimensions of interpersonal relations. *Journal of Personality and Social Psychology, 33,* 409–420.

Wish, M., & Kaplan, S. J. (1977). Toward an implicit theory of interpersonal communication. *Sociometry, 40,* 234–246.

AN EVOLUTIONARY PERSPECTIVE ON INTERPERSONAL COMMUNICATION

Melanie R. Trost
Douglas T. Kenrick

Social scientists often put evolutionary theory into a mental category that includes loose connections to chimpanzee social behavior, eugenics, and bones in the Olduvai Gorge. Evolution is regarded by many social scientists as the domain of biologists and ethologists, with little to say about human behavior. On the other hand, communication patterns are a basic area of study for animal behaviorists, and books on animal behavior may include more than one chapter on communication (e.g., Wilson, 1975). Darwin (1872) himself began to spell out the implications of evolutionary theory for human social interaction in The Expression of Emotions in Man and Animals. *However, the Darwinian approach was largely rejected in the 1920's when social scientists began to adopt the related assumptions of anthropologists committed to cultural relativism and psychologists committed to behaviorism (Freeman, 1983). As a discipline, communication has historically relied upon explanations of human behavior other than biological predispositions. However, Darwin's original predictions about the cross-cultural universality of certain emotional expressions in humans have received strong support in recent years (Ekman, 1972; Ekman et al., 1987), and interest in applying evolutionary theory to the study of human communication is growing (Capella, 1991; Harkness, 1990). This paper will present a short overview of how evolutionary principles may enrich research on interpersonal communication.*

THE PRINCIPLES OF EVOLUTION

In his earlier classic, *Origin of Species,* Darwin (1859) outlined a compelling argument for the evolution of physical features. The argument has three basic assumptions. First, animals reproduce so rapidly that any one species would quickly overrun the world, if not for competition from other animals using the same resources. Second, animals within species vary in ways that can be passed from one generation to the next. Third, any variations that assist in the struggle for survival and reproduction will therefore be naturally selected. It is relatively easy to understand how physical characteristics can be passed from one generation to the next. But, it makes no sense for an animal to inherit a body without also inheriting a program to run that body. If a bat inherited the program to run a giraffe's body, or vice-versa, the results would be catastrophic. Very few researchers who study the social behaviors of animals doubt that they inherit programs to run their bodies (Wilson, 1975). Peacocks inherit not only a lovely set of tailfeathers, but also a brain programmed to display those feathers at the correct season of the year and in the presence of a peahen's flirtatious glances. Modern evolutionary biologists assume that the same principles apply to human beings: we inherited not only an upright posture, a set of vocal cords, and a large brain, but also a brain programmed to run a human body within a human social group (e.g. Kenrick & Hogan, 1991; Lumsden & Wilson, 1981).

The implications of these assumptions for human communication are clear. The ability to communicate with others has always been a central task of daily human living (Lancaster, 1975). Therefore, communication strategies that have provided a survival advantage should be naturally selected. Consider mother-infant interactions. Infants are helpless and, for most of our evolutionary history, have depended upon their mothers for protection. Thus, mother-infant pairs that were able to synchronize their emotional expressiveness would be more likely to survive (and those infants to subsequently reproduce) than would mother-infant pairs that were not able to recognize each other's emotional states. Capella (1991) reviews evidence that an infant will recognize and mimic the emotional expressions of his or her mother immediately after birth, arguing against a social learning explanation and supporting the notion that this is an adaptive characteristic which has been naturally selected.

In addition to innate behavioral dispositions, researchers may look for evidence of evolutionarily stable characteristics by (a) comparing behavior patterns across cultures, and (b) comparing human behaviors with those of other primates. Behavior patterns that are the same among the inhabitants of the United States, Japan, and the remote regions of New Guinea are difficult to explain in terms of similar cultural influences. Therefore, one common strategy for uncovering the biological bases of behavior is to look for such universalities in human behavior across a variety of cultures. For example, Eibl-Eibesfeldt (1975) has found similar sequences of nonverbal movements in flirting females from Samoa, Papua, France, Japan, Africa, and South America. Another approach is to look for similarities in the behavior patterns of humans and other primates, patterns that may have evolved from our common ancestry. For example, researchers have observed a number of similarities between humans and other primates in their use of social deception (Whiten & Byrne, 1988). We will now describe a program of research that has taken an evolutionary perspective on one area of interpersonal communication, heterosexual relationships.

INTERPERSONALLY RELATING IN EVOLUTIONARY TERMS

The evolutionary perspective would seem to be of special relevance to heterosexual mating behavior. If our ancestors had succeeded in every other aspect of their fight for survival, but did not care about reproduction, we would not be here to talk about it. Many social science theories view intimate relationships in terms of social exchange models (e.g., Clark & Reis, 1988; Huston & Levinger, 1978). These models portray potential partners looking for an equitable bargain in a marketplace of mate competition. According to these theories, any sex differences in the commodities bartered by males and females are shaped by cultural norms. Evolutionary theory focuses directly on sex differences in social exchange, and explains those differences in terms of the principles of differential parental investment and sexual selection.

Differential parental investment refers to the discrepancy between males and females in the amount and type of resources expended on offspring (Trivers, 1972). In mammals, females provide direct physical resources: the offspring grow inside the female's body, and need to be nursed after birth. This limits the maximum number of progeny of any female, resulting in a greater investment in any single offspring. Females therefore need to be careful to choose a mate whose genes will result in the birth of a healthy infant. Males, on the other hand, contribute less in the way of direct physical resources to any given offspring. They provide the initial fertilization and, in many mammalian species, that is all. This leaves males free to mate more frequently than females. Males, therefore, have less to lose from mating with any available female. If females have an inherently greater parental investment, which leads them to be more selective than males, how do they exercise their greater choosiness? As part of a process he called sexual selection, Darwin (1859) suggested that females are more likely to prefer males who display obvious signs of superiority over their competitors. Thus, females should choose males who are dominant and re-source-laden, whereas males should prefer females who appear to be reproductively healthy.

Trait Preferences

An evolutionary perspective on heterosexual relationships needs to consider not only the evolutionary force of sex differences in partner preferences, but the amount of time and resources invested, as well (Kenrick & Trost, 1989). As predicted by the economic models, males and females do exchange resources, and the amount of goods exchanged will change as the relationship becomes more involved. What is bartered, however, is not due to random cultural norms, but rather to the forces of differential parental investment and sexual selection. From an evolutionary perspective, females will value males who show evidence of dominance, status, and wealth—characteristics related directly to superiority over other males, and indirectly to the potential to provide resources for offspring. Males, on the other hand, should value females who show evidence of youth and physical attractiveness—characteristics related to physical health and the ability to bear and nurture offspring (Buss & Barnes, 1986; Symons, 1979). In addition, because of the difference in parental investment, females should be more selective when considering partners for a low commitment sexual relationship such as a "one-night stand."

Support for these expectations has been found in a number of recent empirical investigations. In one series of studies, college students rated their minimum acceptable levels of 24 characteristics in a partner at several levels of involvement, from dating to marriage (Kenrick, Sadalla, Groth, & Trost, 1990; Kenrick, Groth, Trost, & Sadalla, 1991). Consistent with the economic models, both males and females became more selective as the relationship increased in commitment. Consistent with the evolutionary model, however, females were typically more selective than males. This difference was most exaggerated when considering partners for a sexual relationship, especially a one-night stand. In addition, females were more selective at all levels of involvement

when considering variables related to status and earning capacity. The only variable on which males showed greater selectivity than females was the minimum acceptable level of physical attractiveness.

Age Preferences

Researchers have long noted a discrepancy in the ages of partners sought by males and females in "lonely hearts advertisements." In essence, males advertise for females who are significantly younger than the females looking for them (Cameron, Oskamp, & Sparks, 1977). Economic models explain this difference in terms of gender discrepancies in cultural norms: a woman exchanges youth and physical attractiveness for a man's economic resources. An alternative evolutionary model suggests that males and females follow different reproductive strategies, and that these should change over the life-span (Kenrick & Keefe, in press). Female fertility peaks at approximately age 24, and declines steadily thereafter until menopause ends reproductive capabilities. Although males decline in health with age, they do not undergo menopause. On the other hand, males tend to accrue additional resources with age. These differences lead to the expectation that the desired age of partners should change differently for the two sexes as they age. Teenage males should seek similar or slightly older females (who are more fertile than younger females), whereas males in their twenties should be interested in females their own age. As males age beyond their twenties, they should seek younger females. Females, on the other hand, need to maximize their available resources, and can best accomplish this by marrying a man who is old enough to be resourceful, but not so old that he will be likely to die before they have raised their offspring (Leonard, 1989).

Kenrick and Keefe (in press) studied age preferences in both personal advertisements and marriages across a wide variety of cultures and generations and found striking consistencies in female and male specifications. Females at all ages and in all cultures were interested in partners their own age and older. Males in all cultures, on the other hand, systematically lowered their age preferences as their own age increased. Males in their teens and twenties were interested in partners around their own age, with no particular aversion to older women. By the time males reached their fifties and sixties, however, the oldest female age desired was several years below their own age, and the minimum specified was almost a generation younger. These findings are not consistent with the normative assumption that men should prefer younger women. Any normative pressures should be strongest in younger men, who tend to be more stereotypically sex-typed (Deutsch, Zalenski, & Clark, 1986). However, younger men were equally interested in women above and below their own ages. The data are consistent with the evolutionarily adaptive strategy for both sexes, however.

CONCLUSIONS

This short exposition on human relationships has attempted to show how communication scholars can frame and interpret questions about interpersonal communication by considering an evolutionary perspective. It seems reasonable to assume that some human patterns of interaction have evolved through natural selection: behaviors that helped our ancestors to survive and reproduce were passed to subsequent generations, and the strategies for successful survival varied with the individual's sex and age, with their genetic relationship to the person with whom he or she was interacting, and so on.

Although we have focused primarily on heterosexual relationships, other areas of communication have been studied from an evolutionary perspective. Recent work in the area of social influence has examined children's acquisition and use of manipulative messages to gain resources (Harkness, 1990). People appear to be quick to deceive under circumstances that would have gained a genetic advantage for our ancestors. In addition, studies of social cognition suggest that our thought processes are particularly well designed to detect cheaters (Cosmides & Tooby, 1989). As noted earlier, there is a long tradition

of research which shows that certain nonverbal expressions of emotion are the same around the world (Ekman, 1972; Ekman et al., 1987). Given the obvious survival value of recognizing a threatening face as opposed to a friendly face, it is perhaps not surprising that an angry face in a crowd of happy faces tends to ''pop out,'' grabbing the viewer's visual attention (Hansen & Hansen, 1988).

In line with the differential parental investment model, there is evidence that females may control the mating process in subtle, nonverbal ways. Although males initiate sexual behavior across all cultures, regardless of the local norms regarding sexual intercourse (Marshall & Suggs, 1971), females consciously signal their ''proceptivity'' through various nonverbal and verbal strategies (Perper & Weiss, 1987). These are just a few areas in which evolutionary theory has already led researchers to make novel predictions that are not possible using traditional learning or cognitive theories, and numerous other hypotheses could be generated based on variables such as sex, genetic relatedness, and social dominance position. Contrary to some opinions, an evolutionary perspective does not eliminate the need for cultural approaches to understanding behavior; indeed, culture is an important force in shaping how we interact. However, culture can only operate within the constraints placed upon it by biological limitations (Kenrick, 1987). Our future understanding of how and why we communicate may be best explored by investigating the interaction between the forces of culture and the limitations of evolution.

REFERENCES

Buss, D. M., & Barnes, M. F. (1986). Preferences in human mate selection. *Journal of Personality & Social Psychology, 50,* 559–70.

Cameron, C., Oskamp, S., & Sparks, W. (1977). Courtship American style—newspaper ads. *Family Coordinator, 26,* 27–30.

Capella, J. N. (1991). The biological origins of automated patterns of human interaction. *Communication Theory, 1,* 4–35.

Clark, M. S. & Reis, H. T. (1988). Interpersonal processes in close relationships. *Annual Review of Psychology, 39,* 609–672.

Cosmides, L., & Tooby, J. (1989). Evolutionary psychology and the generation of culture, Part II. *Ethology and Sociobiology, 10,* 51–97.

Darwin, C. (1859). *The origin of species.* London: Murray.

Darwin, C. (1872). *The expression of the emotions in man and animals.* London.

Deutsch, F. M., Zalenski, C. M., & Clark, M. E. (1986). Is there a double standard of aging? *Journal of Applied Social Psychology, 16,* 771–775.

Eibl-Eibesfeldt, I. (1975). *Ethology: The biology of behavior* (2nd Ed.). New York: Holt, Rinehart, & Winston.

Ekman, P. (1972). *Darwin and the human face.* New York: Academic Press.

Ekman, P., & Friesen, W. V., et al. (1987). Universals and cultural differences in the judgments of facial expressions of emotion. *Journal of Personality and Social Psychology, 53,* 711–717.

Freeman, D. (1983). *Margaret Mead and Samoa.* Cambridge, MA: Harvard University.

Hansen, C. H., & Hansen, R. D. (1988). Finding the face in the crowd: An anger superiority effect. *Journal of Personality and Social Psychology, 54,* 917–924.

Harkness, C. D. (1990). Competition for resources and the origins of manipulative language. In J. P. Dillard (Ed.), Seeking compliance: The production of interpersonal influence messages (pp. 21–39). Scottsdale, AZ: Gorsuch Scarisbrick.

Huston, T. L. & Levinger, G. (1978). Interpersonal attraction and relationships. *Annual Review of Psychology. 29,* 115–156.

Kenrick, D. T., Groth, G., Trost, M. R., & Sadalla, E. K. (1991). *Integrating evolutionary and social exchange perspectives on relationships: Effects of gender, self-appraisal, and involvement level on mate selection.* Unpublished manuscript. Arizona State University.

Kenrick, D. T., & Hogan, R. (1991). Cognitive psychology. In M. Maxwell (Ed.), *The sociobiological imagination.* Albany, NY: SUNY Press.

Kenrick, D. T. & Keefe, R. C. (in press). Age preferences in mates reflect sex differences in human reproductive strategies. *Behavioral and Brain Sciences.*

Kenrick, D. T., Sadalla, E. K., Groth, G., & Trost, M. R. (1990). Evolution, traits, and the stages of human courtship: Qualifying the parental investment model. *Journal of Personality, 58,* 97–116.

Kenrick, D. T., & Trost, M. R. (1989). A reproductive exchange model of heterosexual relationships. In C. Hendrick (Ed.), *Review of personality and social psychology: Close relationships* (Vol. 10, pp. 92–118). Newbury Park, CA: Sage.

Lancaster, J. (1975). *Primate behavior and the emergence of human culture.* New York: Holt, Rinehart, & Winston.

Leonard, J. L. (1989). Homo sapiens: A good fit to theory, but posing some enigmas. *Behavioral & Brain Sciences, 12,* 26–27.

Lumsden, C. & Wilson, E. O. (1981). *Genes, mind, and culture: The coevolutionary process.* Cambridge, MA: Harvard University.

Marshall, D. S., & Suggs, R. C. (1971). *Human sexual behavior: Variations in the ethnographic spectrum.* New York: Basic Books.

Perper, T., & Weis, D. L. (1987). Proceptive and rejective strategies of U.S. and Canadian college women. *Journal of Sex Research, 23,* 455–480.

Symons, D. (1979). *The evolution of human sexuality.* Oxford University Press.

Trivers, R. (1985). *Social evolution.* Menlo Park, CA: Benjamin/Cummings.

Whiten, A., & Byrne, R. (1988). Tactical deception in primates. *Behavioral and Brain Sciences, 11,* 233–274.

Wilson, E. O. (1975). *Sociobiology.* Cambridge, MA: Harvard University.

Strategic Processes

CHAPTER 5 ○

Interpersonal Influence

INTRODUCTION

How do people persuade friends, coworkers, and lovers to do things for them? Four articles in this chapter present perspectives on social influence. Most research on social influence has examined the use of messages to change others. In their seminal study, Miller, Boster, Roloff, and Seibold, in what has now become known as the "MBRS" model, examine the strategies people select for compliance gaining.

In the second article, Roloff, Janiszewski, McGrath, Burns, and Manrai present a perspective which suggests that obligation may substitute for persuasion in intimate relationships.

Finally, two articles examine aspects of social influence in close interpersonal relationships. Dillard deviates from the norm of research on social influence by focusing on influence goals people have in their close relationships. Witteman and Fitzpatrick analyze compliance-gaining strategies in marital interaction.

COMPLIANCE-GAINING MESSAGE STRATEGIES: A TYPOLOGY AND SOME FINDINGS CONCERNING EFFECTS OF SITUATIONAL DIFFERENCES

Gerald Miller, Frank Boster, Michael Roloff and David Seibold

Students of persuasion have devoted considerable research energy to questions dealing with the influence of message sources on persuasive effectiveness. Typically, however, such research has sought to identify characteristics of sources which either heighten or diminish their persuasive impact. Thus, the Aristotelian concept of *ethos* evolved into a mid-twentieth century concern for sets of source dimensions commonly termed *credibility*. More recently, several writers have argued for the greater utility of a construct labeled *source valence,* a construct that includes not only the dimensions commonly associated with credibility but also embraces aspects of interpersonal attraction and the degree of homophily present between the source and receiver of the message.[1]

As a grand strategy for exploring the many issues associated with the role of the message sender in the persuasive process, this source characteristics approach is limited by its relative lack of concern with the *message choices* made by the potential persuader. Stated differently, when people seek to exert communicative control over certain areas of their social environments (or to

Source: The article is taken from *Communication Monographs* [44: 37–51, 1977]. Reprinted by permission of the Speech Communication Association, 5105 Backlick Rd., Annandale, VA 22003.

purposively affect the behaviors of others, or however one wishes to put it), they must select from among a set of symbolic alternatives of their disposal. For example, the statements, ''Any fair and ethical businessman should honor his product warranties,'' and, ''If you don't fix my brakes, I'll sue!'' seek the same persuasive end, but the strategic assumptions underlying them differ markedly. Choice of the former message assumes the likely persuasive efficacy of a strategy based on moral appeal, while selection of the later implies the expectation that a strategy based on threats and potential punishment is most likely to result in persuasive success.

To be sure, message choices are probably directly related to the characteristics of the potential persuader. If a person is regarded as highly knowledgeable in a particular area, communicative attempts to control the attitudes and behaviors of others regarding this area are likely to lean heavily on expertise strategies. Similarly, physical and/or social prowess may predispose a communicator to make frequent recourse to threats and punishment strategies. Although reasonable, such suggested relationships are largely speculative, since little research has systematically examined the relationship of source characteristics to subsequent choices of particular compliance-gaining strategies. One exception is the work of Christie and his associates on the manipulative techniques of the Machiavellian, but their research is limited by its concern with a particular personality type.[2]

In addition to source characteristics, situational, or context variables probably exert a strong influence on selection of persuasive strategies. For example, Miller and Steinberg have recently suggested a conceptual distinction between noninterpersonal and interpersonal communication transactions based on the kinds of data that communicators use to make predictions about the probable outcomes of alternative message strategies.[3] These writers liken prediction-making in noninterpersonal transactions to a process of stimulus generalization, with predictions about message outcomes based primarily on cultural and sociological data. Conversely, interpersonal transactions involve predictions based on stimulus discrimination, with the primary source of data being psychological.

Miller and Steinberg's conceptual distinction has at least two implications for the study of choice of compliance-gaining strategies. First, persons involved in interpersonal transactions might be expected to be more successful in their choices of message strategies, since their predictions would be based on discriminating differences between the intended persuadee and others with similar sociological and cultural characteristics. In other words, the strategy chosen would be tailored to the particular person from whom compliant behavior is desired.

Second, one might expect that some strategies used in noninterpersonal transactions would be chosen, at most, infrequently in interpersonal relationships. For instance, strategies grounded in punishment are a fairly common persuasive commodity in brief noninterpersonal confrontations. By contrast, choice of such strategies in ongoing interpersonal transactions could result in emotional scars which would threaten the stability and health of the relationship. Hence, communicators involved in interpersonal relationships should be reluctant to resort to punishment strategies when seeking compliant behavior—unless, of course, the personal characteristics of the intended persuadee are conducive to the success of such strategies.

Issues such as the ones posed in the preceding paragraphs have led us to embark on a program of research aimed at dealing with the following questions:

1. What are the control strategies available to potential persuaders and how can these strategies be grouped and classified most usefully?
2. How is the choice of control strategies influenced by certain situational differences associated with the persuasive transaction?
3. How do relevant individual differences of potential persuaders affect the choice of control strategies?

The research reported in this paper deals primarily with Questions one and two. Concern with Question one stems from the fact that careful empirical definition of a taxonomy of control strategies is a necessary first step for investigating Questions two and three. Moreover, the ability to specify unambiguously the various compliance-gaining strategies that may be invoked by communicators could aid researchers interested in studying a wide variety of persuasive problems.

Not surprisingly, the literature provides some clues that assist in the development of a taxonomy of control strategies. French and Raven conceptually delineate five bases of social power: reward power, coercive power, expert power, legitimate power, and referent power.[4] Each of these bases of power suggests a counterpart control strategy; e.g., successful use of reward power hinges on the persuader's ability to trigger the persuadee's perception that the persuader has the power to mediate rewards and to confer these rewards on the persuadee in return for the latter's compliant behavior.

Similar, though shorter lists of strategies are implied by the writings of Etzioni and Kelman.[5] Etzioni distinguishes three types of organizational power: coercive, remunerative, and normative; while Kelman focuses on the social influence processes of compliance, identification, and internalization. Finally, Skinner articulates yet another list of compliance-gaining techniques growing out of a radical behavioristic conception of social control.[6]

It should be emphasized that all of the conceptual treatments described above center on characteristics of the potential persuader or on persuadee outcomes resulting from compliance with persuasive recommendations, rather than on the content of message strategies per se. In other words, the translation of a specific basis of power—e.g., coercive power—into a specific "package" of message content—e.g., "Failure to produce 30 units hourly will result in loss of your job."—is a necessary step for developing operational message indicants of the various strategies.

A beginning step in this translation process has been accomplished by Marwell and Schmitt.[7] Using many of the conceptual schemes mentioned above, these researchers generated a list of sixteen compliance-gaining strategies. These strategies are summarized in Table 1, using as an example a persuasive transaction in which a father attempts to persuade his son to study more conscientiously.

Marwell and Schmitt go on to report the results of a factor analysis of these 16 compliance-gaining strategies, with college undergraduates used as respondents. This analysis yielded a five-factor solution. The results are summarized in Table 2 along with the labels assigned to each of the factors by Marwell and Schmitt.

Three considerations caused us to extend the taxonomical work of Marwell and Schmitt rather than relying upon their classification of control strategies. First, all of their respondents were drawn from undergraduate sociology classes in a major Midwestern university. We deemed it desirable to sample from a somewhat broader population of respondents. Second, although Marwell and Schmitt presented their respondents with four hypothetical persuasive situations, the criteria for selecting the particular situations were not articulated clearly. In the present study, we elicited responses about preferences in control strategies for each of the following situations: a noninterpersonal, short-term consequences situation (NI/STC); a noninterpersonal, long-term consequences situation (NI/LTC); an interpersonal, short-term consequences situation (I/STC); and an interpersonal, long-term consequences situation (I/LTC).[8] This approach permitted us to generate data relevant to Question two. Finally, we felt that a classification of control strategies based on factor analysis suffers from methodological limitations. Consequently, the taxonomy reported in this study is derived from what we will term a cluster analysis, rather than from the more typically employed factor analytic procedures. Our reasons for choosing this approach are detailed more fully in the next section of this paper.

T A B L E 1
Sixteen Compliance-Gaining Techniques with Examples from Family Situations.*

1. Promise	(If you comply, I will reward you.) "You offer to increase Dick's allowance if he increases his studying."
2. Threat	(If you do not comply, I will punish you.) "You threaten to forbid Dick the use of the car if he does not increase his studying."
3. Expertise (Positive)	(If you comply, you will be rewarded because of "the nature of things.") "You point out to Dick that if he gets good grades he will be able to get into a good college and get a good job."
4. Expertise (Negative)	(If you do not comply, you will be punished because of "the nature of things.") "You point out to Dick that if he does not get good grades he will not be able to get into a good college or get a good job."
5. Liking	(Actor is friendly and helpful to get target in "good frame of mind" so that he will comply with request.) "You try to be as friendly and pleasant as possible to get Dick in the 'right frame of mind' before asking him to study."
6. Pre-Giving	(Actor rewards target before requesting compliance.) "You raise Dick's allowance and tell him you now expect him to study."
7. Aversive Stimulation	(Actor continuously punishes target making cessation contingent on compliance.) "You forbid Dick the use of the car and tell him he will not be allowed to drive until he studies more."
8. Debt	(You owe me compliance because of past favors.) "You point out that you have sacrificed and saved to pay for Dick's education and that he owes it to you to get good enough grades to get into a good college."
9. Moral Appeal	(You are immoral if you do not comply.) "You tell Dick that it is morally wrong for anyone not to get as good grades as he can and that he should study more."
10. Self-Feeling (Positive)	(You will feel better about yourself if you comply.) "You tell Dick he will feel proud if he gets himself to study more."
11. Self-Feeling (Negative)	(You will feel worse about yourself if you do not comply.) "You tell Dick he will feel ashamed of himself if he gets bad grades."
12. Altercasting (Positive)	(A person with "good" qualities would comply.) "You tell Dick that since he is a mature and intelligent boy he naturally will want to study more and get good grades."
13. Altercasting (Negative)	(Only a person with "bad" qualities would not comply.) "You tell Dick that only someone very childish does not study as he should."
14. Altruism	(I need your compliance very badly, so do it for me.) "You tell Dick that you really want very badly for him to get into a good college and that you wish he should study more as a personal favor to you."
15. Esteem (Positive)	(People you value will think better of you if you comply.) "You tell Dick that the whole family will be very proud of him if he gets good grades."
16. Esteem (Negative)	(People you value will think worse of you if you do not comply.) "You tell Dick that the whole family will be very disappointed in him if he gets poor grades."

*From Marwell and Schmitt, pp. 357–58.

T A B L E   2
Factor Loadings: Oblique Rotation, Sixteen Compliance-Gaining Techniques.**

Technique	Factor I	Factor II	Factor III	Factor IV	Factor V
Promise	.507*	.210	.023	.035	.010
Threat	.056	.566*	.034	.024	.219
Expertise (positive)	.010	.002	.521	.259	−.002
Expertise (negative)	.101	.118	.488*	.070	.195
Liking	.563*	−.030	.150	.142	−.017
Pre-Giving	.663*	.041	.021	.111	.074
Aversive Stimulation	.126	.560*	.062	.071	.095
Debt	.023	.210	.070	.037	.486*
Moral Appeal	−.111	.150	.103	.363*	.286
Self-Feeling (positive)	.121	.011	.047	.732*	.042
Self-Feeling (negative)	−.031	.149	−.012	.556*	.289
Altercasting (positive)	.117	.009	.175	.599*	−.090
Altercasting (negative)	−.010	.209	−.059	.371*	.343*
Altruism	.217	.013	.116	−.018	.530*
Esteem (positive)	.135	−.066	.118	.557*	.182
Esteem (negative)	.010	.099	−.008	.345*	.526*

*Items used to define the five factors.
**From Marwell and Schmitt, p. 360. They name the five factors as follows: Factor I, Rewarding Activity; Factor II, Punishing Activity; Factor III, Expertise; Factor IV, Activation of Impersonal Commitments; Factor V, Activation of Personal Commitments.

PROCEDURES

Samples

Data were collected from three separate samples: 81 students from communication classes in a large Midwestern university, 82 students from speech and theatre classes at a two-year community college, and 21 career Army recruiters enrolled in extension classes of a Midwestern liberal arts college. Elimination of nonusable responses reduced these sample sizes to 75 university students, 76 community college students, and 17 Army recruiters (N = 168). All subsequent findings are based on these figures.

Analysis of demographic data provided by respondents revealed a sex ratio of 40% female and 51% male (9% declined to answer). The median age for the entire sample was 19.6 years (mean = 22 years). Seventeen percent of the respondents were married and 83% were single (including 4% divorced, separated, or widowed).

Although nearly all of the university students reported full-time student status, the community college respondents listed occupations including farmer, clerk, police officer, secretary, waitress, factory worker, nurse, and truck driver (in fact, 48% of that sample indicated present occupations other than "student"). Twenty percent of respondents were majoring in the physical sciences and technology, 18% in the humanities, 14% in education, 12% in the social sciences, and 30% in other diverse disciplines ranging from life sciences to business administration. Eighty percent of participants came from the Central United States; 8% were from the East; 4% from the West; and 2% from foreign countries (6% could not be classified). The average number of siblings for each respondent was three, and each was an average of second in birth order rank. Analysis of responses to optional questions on political and religious affiliation, as well as racial background, revealed the following profile: 69% of the sample were Christian (3% were Jewish and the remainder listed ''Other''); 82% were White (6% were Black and the rest ''Other''); and 27% classified themselves as Democrats (24% called themselves Republicans; the rest checked ''Other'').

Although this research sought primarily to isolate the major dimensions of compliance-gaining behaviors in interpersonal and noninterpersonal situations, rather than to describe the distribution of such behaviors in the population, we believe the characteristics of the overall sample are not overly restrictive. Indeed, we believe our results generalize considerably beyond those of Marwell and Schmitt and even those involving mostly ''college sophomores.'' Nevertheless, other populations may produce results different from those presented below. Children or the aged, for example, may differ from our young and middle-aged respondents in their tactics for gaining compliance from others, or racial differences may obtain within our culture. Hence, any suggestive results stemming from this research will need to be tested with other populations.

Questionnaire Construction

To distinguish dimensions of compliance-gaining strategies, a questionnaire was constructed to elicit respondents' judgments of their own likelihood of using specific strategies in different situations. Questionnaires were completed by participants during regularly scheduled classes throughout the months of September and October, 1974. The technique employed in this research was similar to the one used by Marwell and Schmitt to study compliance-gaining behaviors.

To minimize respondent-researcher interaction, detailed instructions on the cover sheet of the questionnaire informed participants that four situations in which persons might find themselves would be described in the booklet and that:

> Every situation has something in common. They are all situations in which one person is trying to induce another to do something. That is, they are

situations in which one person is trying to influence, or gain the compliance of, another. Imagine that, in each situation, *you* are the individual who is trying to persuade the other.

Participants were then informed that a list of ''methods which persons commonly use to get another to do something'' would follow each situation. For each situation, they were asked to rate how likely they would be to use each of the sixteen message-oriented behaviors (each representing a strategy) to gain compliance from the other hypothetical person described in *that* situation, to suggest any strategies other than the sixteen provided which they might use in such a situation, and to indicate how likely they would be to use each strategy.

Situations

Consistent with the conceptualizations developed by Miller and Steinberg, two *interpersonal* and two *noninterpersonal* situational stimuli were constructed, cross-cut by the short term and long-term nature of the consequences. Three criteria were used for the selection of specific situations: (1) each had to permit the use of all sixteen strategies; (2) each had to be a situation that respondents in the samples had faced or could see themselves facing; (3) two were to deal with short-term relational consequences and two were to deal with long-term relational consequences. The last criterion reflected an attempt to further extend the Marwell and Schmitt findings, which were based only on situational stimuli involving short-term relational consequences. To be sure, the situations selected in no way represent a systematic sample of all compliance-gaining situations. We make no apology for this fact, but do note two points. First, it is doubtful that the parameters of a ''population'' of such situations are known at this stage. Second, the situations selected are theoretically meaningful to the extent that they permit applications of theoretic conceptions presented by Miller and Steinberg.

The four situations used in this study were described as follows, without reference to the kind of situation:

Situation #1 (Noninterpersonal; short-term consequences)

The car that you presently own is beginning to require large maintenance cost, and you would like to trade it on a new car. You are interested in getting the best deal that you can on a new Chevrolet. You want Mr. Buckley, the Chevrolet dealer with whom you are only slightly acquainted, to give you $1,000, as a trade-in, for your old car. How likely would you be to employ each of the following strategies in order to get a $1,000 trade-in on your old car?

Situation #2 (Noninterpersonal; long-term consequences)

You have been living six months in a house that you purchased. You learn that your next-door neighbors (the Smiths—persons with whom you have had only limited contact since moving in) plan to cut down a large shade tree that stands near your property in order to construct their new two-car garage. However, in the long run, loss of the shade tree will adversely affect the beauty of your home, your comfort, and perhaps the value of your home. How likely would you be to employ each of the following strategies in order to get the Smiths to leave the tree standing?

Situation #3 (Interpersonal; short-term consequences)

You have been carrying on a close relationship with a woman (man) for the past two years. On this particular evening an old acquaintance unexpectedly passes through town. You want to visit with your acquaintance, but you have already promised to go to the movies with your friend and she (he) has made it clear that she (he) is counting on it very much. How likely would

you be to employ each of the following strategies in order to get your friend to allow you to visit your acquaintance?

Situation #4 (Interpersonal; long-term consequences)

You have been carrying on a close relationship with a woman (man) for the past two years. You have recently received two employment offers: one in the immediate vicinity and one in the Southwest United States, over 1,000 miles away. Although both of you wish to stay together and to continue the relationship, you find the latter position much more challenging and attractive while she (he) wants you to take the local position so that she (he) can remain close to friends and relatives. How likely would you be to employ each of the following strategies in order to get your friend to accompany you to the job in the Southwest U.S.?

Strategies and Measurement

Each of the situations above was followed by a brief description of the 16 compliance-gaining techniques listed earlier in Table 1. Eight-interval Likert scales, ranging from "Extremely likely" to "Extremely unlikely," were used to assess respondents' willingness to use each of the sixteen strategies provided for each stimulus situation. Scale polarity was reversed after every few questions to prevent response set by participants.[9]

Analysis

The structure of the data was analyzed using a clustering procedure.[10] As indicated above, Marwell and Schmitt employed factor analysis with an oblique rotation: the reduced item correlation matrix, $\tilde{R}$, is reproduced by taking the product of the factor loading matrix (A), the matrix correlations between factors Φ, and A', thus

$$\tilde{R} = A \Phi A'$$

STATISTICAL SUMMARY 1

Cluster analysis was used by Miller et al. to determine if the strategies could be grouped into a smaller number of categories. This analysis is useful if you have a large number of variables and you want to see if two or more of them actually combine or work together. A type of "confirmatory" analysis was used in which the groupings were judged to see if they were internally consistent (all items in the group are highly related to each other) and parallel (items within the group have the same relationship with variables not in the group—e.g., they all have a strong relationship with another variable or they all have a weak relationship with that variable).

Analysis of variance (ANOVA) is a technique for seeing if three or more groups differ from each other. For example, if you have three groups, you may want to know which one talks the most. Analysis of variance was used by Miller et al. to show that different strategies were used in the four different situations (short-term consequences and noninterpersonal relationship, short-term consequences and interpersonal relationship, long-term consequences and noninterpersonal relationship, and long-term consequences and interpersonal relationship).

Next, the cluster analyses were computed separately for each of the four situations. This was done to see if the same clusters or groupings of strategies would appear in each of the situations. These analyses showed minor variations for each situation. Thus there were minor differences in the ways the strategies grouped in each of the situations. However, most groupings were based on the likelihood of using a group of strategies (e.g., grouping all low likelihood strategies together). Other strategy groupings reflected reward or punishment.

Finally, a cluster analysis was computed across all four situations. This analysis ignored the differences between the situations and grouped the strategies based on their likelihood of use in all of the situations.

In the present study a factoring procedure was initially utilized to obtain provisional clusters. Principal components were extracted from $\tilde{R}$; the communalities being estimated using an iterative procedure. The principal components were then rotated, using a varimax criterion. Hence, $\tilde{R}$ was reproduced by taking the product of the factor loading matrix and its transpose

$$\tilde{R} = AA'$$

Subsequent to this preliminary cluster analysis, the correlation matrix, R, was reassessed. Two criteria were applied to these correlations. First, if a set of items $X_1, X_2, \ldots, X_n$ are to be said to measure some underlying variable T, then the correlation matrix defined by the items $X_1, X_2, \ldots, X_n$ must form a Spearman rank one matrix. That is, the intercorrelations of $X_1, X_2, \ldots, X_n$ must satisfy the following product rule to within sampling error

$$^rX_1X_2 = {}^rX_1T{}^rX_2T$$

if they are alternate measures of T.

Second, if a set of items $X_1, X_2, \ldots, X_n$ are to be said to measure some underlying variable T, and if Y is some variable other than $X_1, X_2, \ldots, X_n$ then Y must have the same correlation with $X_1, X_2, \ldots, X_n$, to within sampling error. Thus

$$\frac{^rX_1y = {}^rX_1T}{{}^rX_2y{}^rX_2T}$$

which follows from applying the previously-mentioned product rule, if

$$^rX_1y = {}^rX_1T{}^ryT$$

and

$$^rX_2y = {}^rX_2T{}^ryT$$

Only those strategies which met both these criteria were considered to be defining a given cluster. Following Campbell and Fiske's argument, if a strategy is to be said to be a valid indicator of an underlying variable, then it must: (1) exhibit internal consistency, i.e., correlate highly with other indicators of that underlying variable, and (2) exhibit parallelism, i.e., correlate to the same degree as other indicants of that underlying variable, with indicators of other underlying variables.[11] Marwell and Schmitt give no indication that they applied these criteria to their data. Hence, the analytic procedure used here should produce a more accurate structural representation of the data.

RESULTS

The results are reported by first considering how the various situations influenced the likelihood of strategy use; second, examining how each specific strategy varied across situations; third, considering the structure of strategy use in each situation; and finally, examining the structure of all strategies over all situations.

Table 3 lists the strategies that respondents indicated they would be likely to use (strategies with a mean likelihood of use of greater than five) and unlikely to use (strategies with a mean likelihood of use of less than three) in each of the four situations. Two strategies, positive altercasting and altruism, were highly likely to be used across interpersonal situations and both were also likely to be used in the noninterpersonal, long-term consequences situation. Two strategies, negative esteem and aversive stimulation, were unlikely to be used in the interpersonal situations.

In noninterpersonal situations positive expertise and promise were consistently likely to be used, although the latter was also likely to be used in the interpersonal, long-term consequences situation. Noninterpersonal situations are also characterized by the fact that none of the strategies were consistently unlikely to be used.

Long-term consequences situations are marked by the consistently high probability of

---

T A B L E   3
Strategies Likely and Unlikely to be Used in Each of the Four Situations

	Interpersonal	
	Short-term	Long-term
Likely Strategies	Altruism ($M = 5.95$) Altercasting+ ($M = 5.81$) Liking ($M = 5.29$)	Threat ($M = 5.88$) Altercasting+ ($M = 5.82$) Altruism ($M = 5.59$) Liking ($M = 5.45$) Promise ($M = 5.28$)
Unlikely Strategies	Moral appeal ($M = 2.42$) Aversive Stimulation ($M = 2.42$) Esteem– ($M = 2.45$) Threat ($M = 2.51$) Pre-giving ($M = 2.85$)	Esteem– ($M = 2.17$) Self-feeling– ($M = 2.25$) Aversive Stimulation ($M = 2.51$) Debt ($M = 2.74$) Esteem+ ($M = 2.94$)
	Noninterpersonal	
	Short-term	Long-term
Likely Strategies	Threat ($M = 5.83$) Promise ($M = 5.79$) Liking ($M = 5.62$) Expertise+ ($M = 5.36$)	Expertise+ ($M = 6.15$) Expertise– ($M = 5.86$) Altruism ($M = 5.52$) Promise ($M = 5.23$) Liking ($M = 5.21$) Debt ($M = 5.17$) Altercasting+ ($M = 5.08$)
Unlikely Strategies	Moral appeal ($M = 2.98$)	Aversive Stimulation ($M = 2.28$)

use of promises, positive altercasting, and altruism, although each is also likely to be used in certain short-term consequences situations. Aversive stimulation is the sole strategy that is consistently unlikely to be used in long-term consequences situations, although it is also unlikely to be used in the interpersonal, short-term consequences situation.

Short-term consequences situations are characterized by the inconsistency of a high likelihood of use strategy. Moral appeal was the sole strategy that was consistently unlikely to be used.

Only the debt strategy seemed to enter into a possible interaction between the type and duration of the situation. Specifically, debt was likely to be used in the noninterpersonal, long-term consequences situation but unlikely to be used in the interpersonal, long-term consequences situation. In other situations, its likelihood of use was rated consistently moderate. Finally, only the liking strategy was likely to be used in all four situations, whereas positive self-feeling and negative altercasting were neither likely nor unlikely to be used in all four situations.

To ascertain how particular strategies varied across situations, a one-way analysis of variance for repeated measures was performed. The results suggested that the probability of strategy use varied considerably for all strategies across situations (with the exception of "liking" [$p = .0191$], the significance level was zero to four decimal places for each strategy).

To determine the structure of strategy use in the various situations, cluster analyses were performed. A one-cluster structure best represented the data for the noninterpersonal, short-term consequences situation (Table 4). All strategies with the exception of promise, pregiving, aversive stimulation, and threat met the criteria for fit on this cluster. The strategies deleted from the solution were of moderate to high likelihood of use, while the strategies defining the cluster cover a wide range of likelihood of use.

The noninterpersonal, long-term consequences situation produced a two-cluster solution (Table 5). Cluster I is primarily defined by the following strategies: promise, positive expertise,

TABLE 4
The Cluster Structure for the Noninterpersonal Short-Term Consequences Situation

	Cluster I
Expertise (+)	.61
Self-feeling (−)	.66
Altercasting (−)	.66
Debt	.57
Altercasting (+)	.65
Moral appeal	.60
Altruism	.42
Liking	.41
Esteem (+)	.61
Esteem (−)	.62
Self-feeling (+)	.55
Expertise (−)	.62

TABLE 5
The Cluster Structure for the Noninterpersonal, Long-Term Consequences Situation

	Cluster I	Cluster II
Self-feeling (+)	.71	.05
Expertise (+)	.64	.07
Esteem (+)	.62	.40
Altercasting (+)	.60	.30
Debt	.56	.28
Altruism	.54	.10
Esteem (−)	.51	.50
Promise	.46	.09
Self-feeling (−)	.43	.37
Altercasting (−)	.30	.57
Moral appeal	.25	.50
Pre-giving	.18	.38

$r_{12} = .48$

positive and negative self-feeling, positive esteem, positive altercasting, negative esteem, debt, and altruism. There are several similarities in these strategies. First, they have a relatively high likelihood of being used in this situation. Second, all strategies in this cluster are nonpunishing strategies, and additionally, they tend to involve the activation of commitments, with only promise and positive expertise as exceptions.

The three strategies that primarily define Cluster II for the noninterpersonal, long-term consequences situation are negative altercasting, moral appeal, and pre-giving. This cluster is similar in composition to Cluster I, the primary distinction being that the Cluster II strategies have a lower likelihood of use. This may perhaps be accounted for by the greater contribution of the activation of personal commitments strategies to the first cluster, since these strategies are among the most likely to be used in the noninterpersonal, long-term consequences situation.

Analysis of the structure of the interpersonal, short-term consequences situation yielded a three-cluster solution (Table 6). Cluster I is primarily defined by the following strategies: liking, positive expertise, positive and negative self-feeling, and debt. Cluster I might be construed as a nonpunishing activity cluster, although the inclusion of debt in this cluster makes this interpretation somewhat less crisp than one would like. Generally, Cluster I may be characterized as consisting of strategies ranging from moderate to high likelihood of use in which the individual to be persuaded is the primary focus of the influence attempt and in which nonpunishing strategies are emphasized.

Cluster II is primarily defined by the following strategies: threat, negative expertise, and moral appeal. Cluster II may be characterized as being composed of strategies which are unlikely to be used in this situation, with the primary focus on the individual to be persuaded and the emphasis on nonrewarding strategies.

The strategies comprising Cluster III are promise, pre-giving, positive esteem, and negative esteem. This cluster is made up of strategies that range from moderate to low likelihood of use and that focus on persons other than the individual to be persuaded; i.e., the consequence of noncompliance is activation of certain behaviors or opinions of the persuader and/or other relevant persons.

TABLE 6
The Cluster Structure for the Interpersonal, Short-Term Consequences Situation

	Cluster I	Cluster II	Cluster III
Debt	.69	.23	.17
Expertise (+)	.58	.20	.20
Self-feeling (−)	.57	.51	.61
Liking	.57	−.01	.32
Self-feeling (+)	.54	.33	.17
Expertise (−)	.39	.51	−.05
Moral appeal	.33	.48	.20
Promise	.02	.02	.65
Esteem (+)	.09	.10	.63
Esteem (−)	.04	.43	.51
Pre-giving	.26	−.15	.48

$r_{12} = .63$
$r_{13} = .41$
$r_{23} = .30$

TABLE 7
The Cluster Structure for the Interpersonal, Short-Term Consequences Situation

	Cluster I	Cluster II
Aversive Stimulation	.60	.12
Esteem (+)	.56	.31
Esteem (−)	.52	.11
Self-feeling	.52	.12
Debt	.49	.32
Promise	.12	.58
Liking	.19	.57
Self-feeling (+)	.42	.48

$r_{12} = .45$

The solution for the interpersonal, long-term situation produced two clusters (Table 7). Cluster I consists of the following strategies: aversive stimulation, positive and negative esteem, negative self-feeling, and debt; while Cluster II is primarily defined by the promise, liking, and positive self-feeling strategies.

Cluster I is composed of strategies that were unlikely to be used as persuasive inducements in an interpersonal, long-term consequences situation, and Cluster II is composed of strategies that had a relatively high likelihood of use in this situation.

Consideration of each strategy in each situation yields a total of sixty-four variables. These variables were clustered to ascertain the overall structure of the strategies. Perhaps the use of certain strategies is consistent regardless of the situation, but for others, the type and/or duration of the situation are the primary determinants of strategy use.

The overall analysis, which produced eight clusters, reflects the situation-specific nature of strategy use.[12] Cluster I reflects the moderate to low likelihood of use of activation of impersonal commitment strategies in short-term situations. Cluster II is primarily a strategy, rather than a situational cluster, and reflects the moderate to high likelihood of use of the altruism strategy in all situations and the promise strategy in both long-term consequences situations. Cluster III illustrates the moderate degree to which activation of commitment strategies are likely to be used in noninterpersonal, long-term consequences situations. In a similar vein, Cluster IV shows that activation of commitment strategies are unlikely to be used in interpersonal, long-term consequences situations. Cluster V is primarily a strategy cluster, reflecting the high likelihood of use of liking across all four situations. Cluster VI exhibits the low likelihood of using esteem strategies in interpersonal, short-term consequences situations. Finally, Cluster VII displays the low likelihood of use of socially unacceptable strategies in interpersonal, short-term consequences situations, whereas Cluster VIII indicates that such strategies are more likely to be used in noninterpersonal situations.

DISCUSSION

One major goal of the present study was to develop a smaller, more abstract typology of compliance-gaining strategies which could be employed by persuasion researchers and which

could replace the rather cumbersome set of sixteen strategies developed by Marwell and Schmitt. Instead, inadequacies of the Marwell and Schmitt study were underscored by the finding that, as we had expected, the strategies are highly situationally bound. This conclusion is supported by several pieces of evidence. First, the cluster structure in each of the various situations is drastically different. Structures range from a three-cluster solution to a one-cluster solution, and the composition of the clusters varies considerably across situations. Second, the results of the analysis of variance show that each strategy varied significantly across situations. Finally, in the overall cluster solution, six of the eight clusters obtained are highly situationally bound. Only the liking and altruism strategies, tend to have similar likelihoods of use regardless of situation type.

Although some of the cluster grouping and strategy preferences for the various situations defy explanation, a number of them conform with general social expectations about the nature of the persuasion process as well as with the conceptual distinctions between noninterpersonal and interpersonal and short-term and long-term consequences developed by Miller and Steinberg. For instance, our analysis revealed that only liking was assigned a high probability of use across the four situations. In other words, respondents apparently had a general preference for a strategy that places the intended persuadee in a positive frame of mind—to borrow from the title of a popular novel, ''friendly persuasion'' is superior to unfriendly persuasion.

Moreover, this tendency is somewhat more pronounced in interpersonal situations. Reward-oriented strategies and activation of commitment strategies with positive connotations are predominantly rated as being highly likely to be used in these situations. The presence of threat as a high likelihood of use strategy in the interpersonal, long-term consequences situation is the only exception. Additionally, in interpersonal situations, punishing activities such as aversive stimulation are rated as being of low likelihood of use, along with activation of commitments strategies which have a negative connotation. The presence of pre-giving as an unlikely strategy to be used in interpersonal situations is the only exception to this case.

Noninterpersonal situations vary from interpersonal situations in that different strategies are rated as having a high likelihood of use. The primary source of variance is the increase in the likelihood of use of the expertise strategies. Reward-oriented and activation of commitment with positive connotation strategies still exhibit high likelihoods of use, thus reflecting the general trend of the results. However, a greater emphasis is placed upon strategies which involve logical argument, the success of which, in turn, is aided by certain characteristics of the source of the strategy. This is an expected shift; in noninterpersonal situations, the persuader is often unable to provide a great deal of reward for the persuadee, control the persuadee sufficiently to punish, and/or have any commitments to activate in the persuadee as a result of not having a strongly developed relationship.

Two other interesting findings may be noted concerning noninterpersonal situations. When compared with interpersonal situations, noninterpersonal situations may be characterized as containing more strategies that have a high likelihood of use. Second, the cluster solutions in the noninterpersonal situations produce smaller structures. This is particularly true in the noninterpersonal, short-term consequences situation in which a one-cluster structure is the best solution. Considering both findings jointly, it is plausible to conclude that in the noninterpersonal situations persons are somewhat more uncertain as to what type of strategy to employ and, hence, tend to rate more strategies as highly likely to be used. This interpretation follows closely from Miller and Steinberg's argument that interpersonal relationships, which are based upon psychological data, facilitate one's ability to predict the other's behavior. This ability to predict, in turn, produces the ability to control by choosing an appropriate persuasive strategy to produce the desired behavioral effect. But in noninterpersonal situations such data on others are lacking, and prediction

and, hence, control become somewhat more tenuous processes. In response to their uncertainty, persons may grab at any strategic straw which promises to produce some measure of control over an uncertain environment.

Long-term consequences situations are characterized by the commonality of the high probability of use of reward-oriented and activation of commitment with positive connotation strategies such as positive altercasting, altruism, liking, and promise. The likelihood of using threat in the interpersonal situation and debt in the noninterpersonal situation are anomalous; however, these situations are oriented toward reward and activation of positive commitment strategies and toward avoiding punishing strategies—which may be noted from the low likelihood of use of aversive stimulation in these situations.

The short-term situations are extremely variable. The only commonalities in these situations are the high probability of use of liking, which is likely to be used in all situations and is not something common only to short-term situations, and the low likelihood of use of moral appeal. Threat is a pronounced anomaly in these situations: it has a high likelihood of use in the noninterpersonal situation but a low likelihood of use in the interpersonal situation. This finding has considerable intuitive value, but it illustrates the lack of consensus in the short-term situations. Generally, then, these situations seem to be predominantly affected by the type of situation rather than the duration of the relational consequences. More generally, the effect of the type of situation seems to be greater than the effect of the duration of consequences variable. This is exemplified by the previous discussion and the high likelihood of use of threat in the noninterpersonal, long-term consequences situation.

We began by proposing that persuasion research can profit from continued scrutiny of the role of *source* characteristics in message selection, but that such scrutiny should be couched within study of the relevance of *situational* contexts. The results presented here underscore the importance of a situational emphasis in examining personal influence attempts. Respondents' choices of compliance-gaining strategies in this study tended to be situation-specific. These findings are consistent with a number of articles indicating that situations differ among themselves in the extent to which they typically determine the behavior of persons in those situations.[13]

Interpretation of these results must also be considered in light of possible subject perceptions of the stimulus materials. For example, attribution theory research has emphasized that we tend to attribute our own action to the situations in which we find ourselves, while attributions to others are based more on perceptions of personal proclivities and inferences concerning dispositional traits.[14] A corollary to this point is that we scrutinize situations in considering our own behaviors, while we scrutinize others' traits in interpreting their behaviors. It may be, then, that the situational prominence revealed in this study was also a function of respondent orientation. Stated differently, given attribution findings, respondents faced with assessing the likelihood of their own choice of compliance-gaining strategies may have cued to situational differences in answering, responses not reflective of more stable (i.e., across situations) personal tendencies they might normally exhibit in their usual influence attempts. Subsequent research, therefore, will need to parse situational and personal characteristics affecting message choice more carefully.

Finally, by both emphasizing and identifying situational and individual difference variables affecting persuasive strategies, we anticipate that future research will bear out our emphasis upon examining the interaction of source and situational variables in control strategy choices. Abundant empirical research has shown that interactions between persons, situations, and behaviors account for at least as much or more total variation than does any of these sources considered alone.[15] To state the importance of this point more generally, the scope of future research on persuasive influence must be expanded from predominantly source-oriented or message-centered conceptualizations to perspectives which account for the domains of source traits, message choices,

situational effects, and their interactions. As a beginning step, investigators could delve more deeply into the adequacy of our interpersonal-noninterpersonal long-term consequences/short-term consequences situational typology by initially generating a larger sample of situations of each of the four types. If the structures of each of the situations within one of the four types are similar, then it may be concluded that the typology is reasonable. If not, then further conceptualization will need to be undertaken in order to develop a more adequate situational typology.

NOTES

1. See, James C. McCroskey and Thomas McCain, "The Measurement of Interpersonal Attraction," paper read at the Annual Convention of the Western States Speech Communication Association, Honolulu, Hawaii, November, 1972; James C. McCroskey, Thomas Jensen and Cynthia Valencia, "Measurement of Credibility of Peers and Spouses," paper read at the Annual Convention of the International Communication Association, Montreal, Canada, April, 1973; Velma J. Lashbrook, "Leadership Emergence and Source Valence: Concepts in Support of Interaction Theory and Measurement," *Human Communication Research,* 1 (1975), 308–15.

2. Richard Cristie and Florence L. Geis, *Studies in Machiavellianism* (New York: Academic Press, 1970).

3. Gerald R. Miller and Mark Steinberg, *Between People: A New Analysis of Interpersonal Communication* (Palo Alto: Science Research Associates, 1975).

4. John R. P. French, Jr. and Bertram Raven, "The Bases of Social Power," in *Group Dynamics,* ed. Dorwin Cartwright and Alvin Zander, 2nd ed. (New York: Harper and Row, 1960), pp. 607–23.

5. See, Amitai Etzioni, *A Comparative Analysis of Complex Organizations,* rev. ed. (New York: The Free Press, 1975); Herbert C. Kelman, "Processes of Opinion Change," *Public Opinion Quarterly,* 25 (1961), 57–78.

6. B. F. Skinner, *Science and Human Behavior* (New York: MacMillan, 1953).

7. Gerald Marwell and David R. Schmitt, "Dimensions of Compliance-Gaining Behavior: An Empirical Analysis," *Sociometry,* 30 (1967), 350–64.

8. Our use of the terms "long-term consequences" and "short-term consequences" may be ambiguous and invites clarification. We are speaking here of the longevity of the relational effects created by successful or unsuccessful social influence. Contrast the following two situations: one member of a relationship persuades the other to attend a movie on a particular evening, rather than going to a basketball game. Unless there are other areas of relational conflict, the long-term

consequences of successful compliance-gaining are likely to be minimal. But suppose one member of a relationship persuades the other to take a job in Chicago instead of Seattle. Here compliance-gaining carries with it a number of long-term consequences (e.g., living in Chicago rather than Seattle) which could profoundly influence the relationship. Conversely, failure to persuade the other to accept the Chicago position implies a similar, though reversed, set of long-term consequences (e.g., living in Seattle rather than Chicago).

9. Copies of the questionnaire may be obtained from the authors.

10. The specific routine used in this study is contained in a set of computer programs developed by John E. Hunter and Stanley H. Cohen for the Computer Institute for Social Science Research, Michigan State University.

11. Donald T. Campbell and Donald W. Fiske, ''Convergent and Discriminant Validation by the Multitrait-Multimethod Matrix,'' *Psychological Bulletin*, 56 (1959), 81–105.

12. Because of limitations of space, we have chosen not to table the overall analysis. Copies are available from the first author.

13. See for example, Roger G. Barker, *Ecological Psychology: Concepts and Methods for Studying the Environment and Human Behavior* (Stanford, California: Stanford Univ. Press, 1968); and Allan W. Wicker, ''Processes Which Mediate Behavior-Environment Congruence,'' *Behavioral Science,* 17 (1972), 265–77.

14. Edward Jones and Richard Nisbett, *The Actor and the Observer: Divergent Perceptions of the Causes of Behavior* (New York: General Learning Press, 1971).

15. For a review of this literature see Richard H. Price and Dennis L. Bouffard, ''Behavioral Appropriateness and Situational Constraint as Dimensions of Social Behavior,'' *Journal of Personality and Social Psychology*, 30 (1974), 579–86.

ACQUIRING RESOURCES FROM INTIMATES: WHEN OBLIGATION SUBSTITUTES FOR PERSUASION

Michael E. Roloff
Northwestern University
Chris A. Janiszewski
University of Florida
Mary Anne McGrath
Loyola University
Cynthia S. Burns
Northwestern University
Lalita A. Manrai
University of Delaware

*The acquisition of needed resources is a necessary part of human activity. Persuasion is a tool that can be used to acquire commodities. However, because of obligations inherent in intimate relationships, the necessity of elaborated persuasive messages is lessened. Furthermore, when an intimate's request is rejected, negative responses and counterpersuasion are likely. This article presents the results of a study in which three measures of intimacy are related to the obligation to grant requests for resources, the obligation to **offer** resources in a time of need, characteristics of requests for resources, and characteristics of responses to rejection. Although not all three measures yielded identical results, increasing intimacy with a potential*

Source: The article is taken from *Human Communication Research* [14: 364–396, 1988]. © International Communication Association, 8140 Burnet Rd., Austin, TX 78766. Reprinted by permission of Sage Publications, Inc. and ICA.

helper increased obligations to grant requests for resources, and obligation to offer resources in a time of need. Moreover, increasing intimacy was negatively associated with request elaboration, frequency of explanations, and inducements. When responding to rejection, increasing intimacy was negatively related to forgiving statements and positively related to counter-persuasion. Finally, after rejection, intimates composed messages, judged to be less polite than those that contained their initial request. The politeness of postrejection messages created by nonintimates was not perceived to differ from that of their initial requests.

Beginning at birth, humans need the assistance of others. Beyond material resources, such as food and shelter, individuals require symbolic commodities such as information, status, deference, sympathy, and affection (e.g., Buss, 1983; Foa & Foa, 1974). While resources may be sought from several providers, family and close friends are especially important suppliers of needed commodities. Individuals rely upon intimates for social support in areas such as problems at work (Burke & Weir, 1975), physical ailments (Finlayson, 1976), mental illnesses (Horowitz, 1978), personal problems (Griffith, 1985), task completion (Shapiro, 1980), and general assistance (Rule, Bisanz, & Kohn, 1985). Moreover, satisfaction with received support is positively correlated with the degree of relational intimacy shared with the helper (Hobfoll, Nadler, & Leiberman, 1986).

Communication serves two functions in the acquisition of needed commodities: (1) communication may itself convey valued resources, and (2) communication may be a medium through which the exchange of resources is negotiated (Roloff, 1981). There is evidence that individuals interpret their interactions as exchanges of symbolic resources such as information, love, and status (Dailey & Roloff, 1987), and these processes conform to principles of reciprocity (Roloff & Campion, 1985). Consistent with the second function, people report that 57% of their everyday persuasion attempts involve seeking resources such as information, objects, assistance,

and companionship and that 64% of all persuasive messages are aimed at targets classified as close friends and immediate or extended family members (Rule et al., 1985).

This article focuses on the relationship among intimacy, obligation to provide needed resources, and the degree of elaboration evidenced in commodity-seeking messages. Specifically, three arguments will be advanced: (1) As the degree of intimacy with a potential helper increases, obligations to accommodate requests for and to volunteer needed resources increase and converge; (2) as the degree of intimacy with potential provider increases, commodity-seeking messages will be less elaborated; and (3) as the degree of intimacy with a potential helper increases, messages in response to a rejected request will be less forgiving, less polite, and more coercive.

INTIMACY AND OBLIGATIONS TO PROVIDE NEEDED RESOURCES

Research indicates that when in need, individuals turn to their intimates for commodities. One might argue that this pattern results from simple propinquity. Presumably, one is in more frequent contact with intimates than nonintimates and, therefore, they are more available targets. Although we found no research directly testing this possibility, Griffith (1985) discovered that 52% of typical support providers were communicated with on a weekly basis or less frequently. Moreover, DePaulo (1978) found that when given a choice between receiving assistance from a stranger, acquaintance, or friend, individuals expressed a significant preference for the friend's help. These results suggest that the desirability of intimate providers results from more than proximity.

An alternative perspective posits that intimates may be chosen because of greater likelihood that they will comply with the request. For example, Shapiro (1980) reported that individuals needing help on a task were significantly more likely to seek assistance from a friend than from a stranger, and believed that the friend was significantly more likely to accommodate the request. Interestingly, persons were willing to seek assistance from friends and expected them to comply regardless of how costly the help would be to the target. On the other hand, help seeking among strangers was negatively related to the costs of compliance to the target. Similarly, Bar-Tal, Bar-Zohar, Greenberg, and Hermon (1977) found that individuals believed that their intimates (e.g., parents, close friends) were under greater obligation to provide them with requested assistance than were nonintimates (e.g., strangers). In that study, respondents attributed compliance by their intimate partners to role obligation, while compliance by nonintimates was ascribed to a norm of social responsibility.

A basis for these expectations may be the communal nature of intimate relations (Clark, 1983a; 1983b; 1984; Clark & Mills, 1979; Mills & Clark, 1982). Clark and Mills have argued that relationships differ in the extent to which they are guided by exchange or communal norms. Exchange relationships are based upon an equity or contribution rule. Partners promptly repay favors and are under no special obligation to provide needed assistance. Communal relations are need based. Individuals are obligated to engage in behavior that promote each other's welfare, and expectations for repayment are relaxed. Persons expecting or desiring an exchange relationship are more attracted to partners who reciprocate benefits (Clark & Mills, 1979), feel exploited if a request for aid is not followed with a promise of reciprocation (Clark & Waddell, 1985), and keep records of individual contributions to a joint task (Clark, 1984). In contrast, communal partners feel less attraction when a request for reciprocation occurs (Clark & Mills, 1979), do not feel greater exploitation when no reciprocation is offered (Clark & Waddell, 1985), and do not keep records of each other's needs in a joint activity (Clark, Mills, & Powell, 1986).

Consistent with this analysis, Roloff (1987) has suggested that intimates are expected not only to comply with requests for assistance but to *anticipate* and *enact* behaviors that reduce a partner's needs. For example, Argyle and Henderson (1984) identified a rule of friendship that dictates that partners are obligated to *volunteer*

help in a time of need. Respondents in their study indicated that this rule was important to friendships, was more operative in current than in lapsed friendships, and its violation was a significant cause of relational breakups. An implication of this rule is that intimate partners need not provide detailed accounting of their needs nor should they have to overly justify their requests. The partners are obligated to monitor each other's needs and be responsive to them.[1] Consistent with this rule, Clark and Ouellette (1983) discovered that communal partners offered *unrequested* assistance when they perceived the facial expression of their partner to be sad rather than normal while exchange partners were unaffected by the apparent mood of the partners.

Based upon prior research, we offer the following hypothesis: (H1) As intimacy with a potential helper increases, the dual obligations to comply with a request and to offer assistance in the absence of a request increase. Although untested in the aforementioned studies, the obligation to comply with a request and the obligation to volunteer assistance may be of equal strength within intimate relationships. In essence, the communal nature of intimate relationships demands sensitivity to needs as well as willingness to act so as to meet them. Hence we propose the following hypothesis: (H2) The strength of the two obligations will converge across increasing levels of intimacy.

INTIMACY AND MESSAGE ELABORATION

In a sense, obligation reduces the role of communication and persuasion in the acquisition of resources from intimate partners. Obviously, resource-seeking messages are sent to intimates, but the inclusion of material designed to motivate the recipient to comply is less necessary.[2] Presumption is in the direction of a favorable response to the request because the *obligation* inherent in relational expectations satisfies an important felicity condition for granting requests (Jacobs & Jackson, 1981).

However, the situation is quite different should an individual be required to seek resources from a nonintimate partner. There is limited inherent presumption of obligation to help. Consequently, the help seeker should experience greater uncertainty as to the probability of compliance. Communication and persuasion become critical for successful acquisition of commodities. They are tools that must motivate the target to comply.

In response to this uncertainty, nonintimate relative to intimate help seekers will communicate more elaborate messages. By elaboration, we mean the number of clauses contained in the message will be greater when the target is a nonintimate rather than an intimate partner. In particular, four persuasive elements will be more evident in nonintimate help-seeking messages: apologies, explanations, inducements, and contingencies.

Apologies are clauses that acknowledge the potential inappropriateness of the request and express regret for its occurrence (Goffman, 1971; Schlenker, 1980). Examples of apologies include clauses such as "I hate to bother you . . . ," "I normally wouldn't ask you . . . ," "Excuse me . . . ," and "I know you are busy. . . ." When communicating an apology, the help seeker appears to be minimizing impressions of presumptuousness and insensitivity to the costs being requested from the target (Brown & Levinson, 1978). Since nonintimates are under less inherent obligation to provide assistance, the absence of such linguistic devices might engender reactance (Brehm, 1966). When the request is portrayed as legitimate and, by implication, the target is under some obligation to provide assistance, nonintimates may reject the request due to the feeling that it poses an unjustified threat to their freedom of decision making (Langer & Abelson, 1972). Compliance without such apologies might even imply passive acknowledgment of a willingness to comply in similar domains in the future, something that the target may wish to avoid (Jones, 1970).

Explanations are clauses that justify the request (Wiseman & Schenck-Hamlin, 1981).

When seeking resources, they communicate the basis for the need. Examples include the following: "I have been sick recently . . . ," "I can't find . . . ," and "Someone took my. . . ." Including such items are critical to gaining assistance in nonintimate relationships (Bostrom, Humphreys, & Roloff, 1981). Compliance is greater when the need results from causes external rather than internal to the requester (Berkowitz, 1969; Horowitz, 1968) and if the basis of the need is an uncontrollable factor such as illness rather than a controllable one such as inadequate effort or choice (Barnes, Ickes, & Kidd, 1979; Folkes, 1985; Langer & Ableson, 1972; Meyer & Mulherin, 1980). It should be noted that the quality of explanation may be a better predictor of compliance when the request is large rather than small (Langer, Blank, & Chanowitz, 1978). Regardless, we expect that more explanations will be communicated by nonintimate help seekers than by intimates.

Inducements are clauses that offer a reward for compliance (Tedeschi, Schlenker, & Bonoma, 1973) or express the requester's indebtedness toward the target should he or she respond favorably (Greenberg, 1980). They include promises (e.g., "if you help, I will do something for you"), compliments (e.g., "you are so good at this, could you help me?"), and expressions of gratitude (e.g., "I will be most appreciative if you help"). If norms of social responsibility are weak, the help seeker will find explanations of need ineffective and may provide some inducement as a motivator. By acknowledging a debt or offering compensation for compliance, an additional reason is provided. Moreover, expressing deference to the target or acknowledging a future debt may minimize impressions of presumptuousness (Brown & Levinson, 1978). Research indicates that among strangers, verbal reinforcements, such as complements, increase the likelihood of assistance (Bostrom et al., 1981) as do promises of rewards (Harris, Liguori, & Stack, 1973).

Finally, *contingencies* are clauses indicating limits to the request. For example, help seekers may specify when they will return a borrowed resource, express the precise amount of resource needed, and state exactly for what the resource will be used. Each constitutes an assurance or implicit contract that the commodity will not be wasted (Brickman et al., 1983) and, in the case of lending, the resource will not be damaged or become unreasonably inaccessible to the lender. Presumably, such devices are attempts to reduce the target's feelings of uncertainty or risk associated with helping a relatively unfamiliar other.

Based upon this analysis, we advance the following hypothesis: (H3) As intimacy with a potential helper increases, commodity-seeking messages will become less elaborated (i.e., fewer clauses); and (H4) as intimacy with a potential helper increases, requests for resources will contain fewer apologies, explanations, inducements, and contingencies.[3]

INTIMACY AND RESPONSE TO REJECTION

Our analysis suggests that obligations to provide assistance increase with intimacy. Consequently, when a request is made to an intimate, a positive response is expected. When such requests are rejected, expectations are disconfirmed. As a result of these unexpected responses, the requester may experience anger and resentment toward the intimate. Alternatively, the lower expectations for helping among nonintimates should result in muted negative reactions.

Research provides support for this reasoning. Bar-Tal et al. (1977) found that after a rejection, requesters felt greater resentment toward an intimate (e.g., parent, sibling, friend) than a nonintimate (e.g., acquaintance, stranger). Furthermore, Clark and Waddell (1985) discovered greater increases in felt exploitation when communal partners (e.g., parents, romantic partners) knew about, but did not respond to their partners' needs than when similar nonresponsiveness occurred between exchange partners (e.g., coworker, fellow student, landlord).

The aforementioned studies do not indicate whether such negative reactions are explicitly *communicated* after rejection. If so, reactions

from intimates should evidence more elaboration as the communicators express their dissatisfaction and apply pressure to comply. The greater degree of elaboration in intimate relative to nonintimate responses should be apparent in cues such as counterpersuasion and coercion.

Counterpersuasion attempts are clauses that (1) repeat the initial request, (2) make a revised and often reduced counteroffer (e.g., "If you can't help now, how about later?"), (3) amplify upon the need for compliance (e.g., "I am desperate!"), or (4) indicate the ease with which the assistance might be provided (e.g., "This really won't take long"). Because nonintimates are under less initial obligation to provide assistance, a rejection may be followed by fewer additional attempts at persuasion. In essence, after a strong initial attempt, the failure to gain compliance may suggest that additional effort is likely to be unsuccessful and may be perceived as inappropriate. For intimates, the initial attempt included minimal persuasive appeals and subsequent messages might express the help seeker's legitimate need resulting in success.

Coercive reactions are clauses that (1) threaten the target, or (2) insult the target. They include expressions such as "Don't ask me for a favor ever again," or "You're selfish." These are the most overt expressions of the resentment felt by rejected help seekers. Because nonintimates are under limited obligation to provide assistance, the requester may be unlikely to threaten or insult the target. Among intimates, the unexpected denial might result in anger and coercive expressions. For example, spouses report utilizing more coercive conflict resolutions tactics than do dating couples (Fitzpatrick & Winke, 1979).

While the preceding message cues flow directly from increased elaboration among intimates, *forgiving responses* should increase as the level of intimacy decreases. Forgiving expressions are clauses that indicate that (1) the requester understands the right of the target to say no, (2) the requester feels no resentment toward the target, or (3) the requester appreciates the target's consideration of the request. Examples include the following: "That's okay," "Don't worry about it," "Thanks anyway," and "I understand." In essence, the communicator is retreating from the request. Since nonintimates were under less obligation, their rejection may be viewed as legitimate, and forgiving statements should be in greater evidence.

Given the configuration of cues within the requests and responses, perceived politeness of the messages may vary across levels of intimacy. Nonintimates may be aware that their targets are under less inherent obligation to help. Consequently, their requests should contain more apologies, explanations, inducements, and contingencies. When rejected, they forgive the target and tactfully drop the issue. Intimates communicate brief but not necessarily impolite messages. However, they respond to rejection with increased pressure or with direct expressions of anger. The refusal of help seekers to forgive or to discontinue the request after rejection may be perceived as impolite and inappropriate.

Based upon this theorizing, we posit the following hypotheses: (H5) As intimacy with a potential partner increases, responses to rejection will contain more counterpersuasion attempts and coercive reactions; (H6) as intimacy with a potential partner increases, responses to rejection will contain fewer expressions of forgiveness; and (H7) compared with initial requests for resources, responses to rejection by intimates will be perceived to be less polite than the initial request while the perceived politeness of nonintimate requests and responses will not differ.[4]

METHODS

Participants

In total, 60 undergraduates enrolled in communication classes at a medium-sized midwestern university participated in this study. Each received credit toward class assignments for their cooperation. The responses from 1 participant were deleted from the analyses due to significant missing data. Of the remaining 59 participants, 33 were female, 25 male, and 1 person did not respond to the gender item. Most of the participants were freshmen and sophomores (61%).

Procedures

Recruits were sought during class sessions. After indicating interest, respondents were asked to complete a questionnaire assessing their feelings about lending personal items to other members of the class. The questionnaire was composed of three sections: (1) an intimacy manipulation used to guide selection of the target, (2) a series of target-related measures, and (3) a section to record the actual elaboration evident within one of two specific requests (borrow class notes for a half hour or three days) and responses to a rejection of the requests. The second and third sections of the questionnaire were counterbalanced.

Each participant was randomly assigned booklets containing one of three relational instructions. Individuals were asked to select a member of the class whom they considered a stranger, acquaintance, or friend. They were encouraged to look at and think of this target throughout the exercise. After selecting the target, the respondent completed the target-related measures and the request/response elaborations. Target-related measures included an assessment of the relationship between the respondent and the target, the respondent's obligation to provide assistance to the target, the amount of prior help seeking by the target, and the demographic characteristics of the respondent and target.

In the elaboration section, respondents' request and response elaborations were assessed. Elaborations were measured under one of six conditions: (1) whether the target was a stranger, acquaintance, or friend, and (2) whether the request was to borrow the notes for a half hour or for three days. The second independent variable (length of request) served as a control variable and will be discussed in more detail later. Therefore, to measure request elaboration, respondents were asked to "imagine that in the next few minutes you will walk up to the stranger (acquaintance, friend) and ask him or her to lend you his or her class notes for a half hour (three days). Please write down what you would say." On the next page, subjects were instructed: "Imagine that the stranger (acquaintance, friend) *says no* to your request. Write down exactly *what, if anything, you would say to him or her after your request was denied.''*

At the end of the questionnaire, items assessing the demographics of the respondent were included. After the last questionnaire was finished, respondents were debriefed and thanked.

Design

The experiment used a three (level of intimacy with target) by two (size of request) full factorial design. Level of intimacy was the independent variable of interest while the size of request manipulation was included as a control variable.

Although level of intimacy was directly manipulated, there may be reason to expect substantial variance among respondents' definitions of a stranger, acquaintance, or friend. Because intimacy labels are *culturally* based, they may be somewhat imprecise. Miller and Steinberg (1975) argued that significant variation in intimacy may exist within a given type of cultural relationship (e.g., spouse). In essence, friendships may differ in intimacy and, for some people, may actually overlap with acquaintances. This potential problem may have been accentuated because the sample was drawn from a classroom, a setting in which some may not have had close friends to choose as targets. Consequently, while the cultural labels imply different degrees of intimacy, slippage across the categories may have occurred. This implies that more direct measures of intimacy may be better predictors of obligation and elaboration. Accordingly, two direct indicators of intimacy were created: communication and relational intimacy.

Communication intimacy. Communication intimacy focuses on the frequency with which certain types of interactions take place or will occur in the future. Intimate relationships involve a high degree of shared understanding, presumably arising from frequent prior disclosures (Chelune, Robinson, & Kommor, 1984; Hatfield, 1984). Our measure consisted of eleven, self-report items assessed on seven-point scales. They included (1) frequency of communication with the

target, (2) amount of leisure time spent with target, (3) frequency of working together on class projects, (4) frequency of socializing together outside of class, (5) frequency of discussing personal problems with target, (6) frequency of target's discussion of personal problems with respondent, (7) likelihood of keeping in contact after the end of the academic term, (8) anticipated frequency of seeing the person after the end of the academic term, (9) comfort with disclosing personal problems to the target, (10) degree of knowledge of target, and (11) degree of knowledge the target has of respondent. A coefficient *alpha* of .88 resulted.

Relational intimacy. This measure is a broader-based assessment and arises from prior research and theorizing about dimensions that differentiate among types of relationships. Research identifying implicit theories of relationships suggests that people may differentiate intimate from nonintimate relationships on a variety of general dimensions. For example, Wish, Deutsch, and Kaplan (1976) found that relationships are perceived to vary along four dimensions: cooperative and friendly versus competitive and hostile, equal versus unequal, intense versus superficial, and socioemotional and informal versus task-oriented and formal. An examination of their plots of relational types indicates close friends, casual acquaintances, and classmates are differentiated on all four dimensions, although most strongly on the intensity one. In addition, Marwell and Hage (1970) reported that friendships and family relationships are perceptually differentiated from other role relations by their low visibility and regulation. Moreover, Argyle and Henderson (1984) discovered that individuals expected their close friends to be more caring and supportive than their casual acquaintances. Beyond empirically determined dimensions, Hinde (1979) has argued that people perceive their more intimate relationships to have an extensive history and anticipated an extended future.

Based upon this work, a 14-item scale measured on seven-point semantic differentials was created. Respondents evaluated their relationship with the target on the extent (7 to 1) to which it was cooperative-competitive, informal-formal, superficial-intense, equal-unequal, involving-indifferent, caring-uncaring, amiable-hostile, socioemotional-task-oriented, private-public, close-distant, old-new, permanent-temporary, desirable-undesirable, and good-bad. A coefficient *alpha* of .86 was obtained.

The second independent variable, size of request, was a control variable. Prior research has not explored the limits of obligation arising from excessive requests across levels of intimacy. Roloff (1987) hypothesized that obligations in intimate relationships do have some limits such that requests beyond a certain amount force help seekers to motivate intimate targets to provide assistance. While plausible, this speculation must be tempered by Shapiro's (1980) research suggesting that individuals are willing to ask and expect that their friends will comply regardless of the cost of compliance to the target. Hence, we chose not to advance a hypothesis but instead examine whether level of intimacy influenced elaboration within different magnitudes of request size. Failure to find an interaction between intimacy and request size on elaboration would simply attest to the robustness of the intimacy variable. Alternatively, an interaction would suggest that size of request may constitute an important qualifier for our approach. To add realism to the request, the study was conducted in classes three to four days before the actual midterm exam. In each class, more than 50% of the exam material came from lecture material contained in class notes.

Dependent Variables

A series of dependent measures was designed to assess respondents' feelings of obligation (hypotheses 1 and 2), request message elaboration (hypotheses 3 and 4), and response message elaboration politeness (hypotheses 5, 6, and 7). In order to perform manipulation checks, additional measures on the normativeness of a request to borrow class notes and the adequacy of the request size manipulation were included.

Obligation measures. Respondents were asked a series of questions about the degree of obligation that existed in their relationship with the target. The first set of items focused on obligations related to class notes. Participants indicated on seven-point scales the extent to which they would be obligated to lend their class notes to the target if asked. On a separate item, they rated the extent to which they would feel obligated to offer their class notes if they knew the target needed them. Similar questions assessed the obligation of lending money when requested and offering it when having knowledge of the target's need.

The money questions are a means of determining whether the obligations extend into other resource domains. Although not strictly comparable in our operationalizations, Brinberg and Castell (1982) discovered that college students viewed spending money on a friend as considerably different than telling a friend about a lecture or book. Spending money on a friend was similar to loving behaviors. The authors speculated that this may stem from the relative impoverishment of college students and their desire to expend scarce resources only on intimate others. In any case, an additional resource tests the generalizability of the hypotheses.

Communication codes. Both the requests and responses to rejection were unitized by two coders into clauses using grammatical definitions (Perrin, 1959).[5] Of a combined total of 623 units in the requests, only 5 disagreements were evidenced. In total, 100% agreement occurred in the unitization of the responses.

Each unit in the request was placed by two coders into one of 12 categories. Six of the categories stemmed from the hypotheses: apologies, explanations, promise inducements, compliment inducements, gratitude inducements, and contingencies. The same definitions given earlier were used for the categorization. Six additional codes were made for supplementary analyses (e.g., manipulation checks): (1) introductory cues (clauses that identify the communicator, including name, enrollment in the class, or seat), (2) qualifiers (clauses that try to determine whether the target could provide the resources such as asking if the person was in class or has complete notes), (3) requests (clauses that sought the class notes), (4) greetings (clauses that acknowledge the beginning of the interaction such as "Hello," "How are you?"), (5) substitutions (clauses that imply the requester has alternative source of class notes such as "I can get them elsewhere"), and (6) uncodable units. Both coders were blind as to the experimental conditions.

Cohen's *kappa* evidenced adequate agreement between the coders (.84), and across all categories combined, 88% of the codes agreed. Although we originally intended to analyze each of three inducement forms independently, their occurrence on an individual basis was too low for adequate tests. Consequently, we collapsed promises, exchange statements, and expressions of gratitude into an inducement category. The percentage agreement for the codes contained in the hypotheses was 77% for apologies, 91% for explanations, 93% for inducements, and 80% for contingencies. Disagreements were settled by discussion.

Each unit in the responses to rejection was placed by two coders into one of eleven categories. Seven of the categories were related to the hypotheses: forgiving statements, pleading statements (counterpersuasion), repeated requests (counterpersuasion), counteroffers (counterpersuasion), ease of compliance statements (counterpersuasion), insults (coercion), and threats (coercion). Definitions presented earlier were used for these categories. In addition to a miscellaneous code, three others were utilized: inquiries (questions about the basis for rejection), substitution statements (clauses indicating an available alternative source of class notes), and departure signals (clauses terminating the interaction such as "See you tomorrow" or "Good Bye").

Cohen's *kappa* was .88 and, across all categories combined, 91% of the judgments agreed. However, examination of the frequencies suggested alterations were necessary. First, because of low individual frequencies, the four counterpersuasion measures (pleading, repeated requests, counteroffers, ease of compliance statements) were combined into a single index. Second, the use of insults and threats was so low that they could not be combined into a usable measure of coercion. Therefore, they were not analyzed. So few inquiries about the basis for rejection was made that this variable was also dropped. Of the two remaining variables related to the hypotheses, the coders evidenced a 94% agreement rate when using the forgiving code and 86% for the counterpersuasion code.

Finally, two coders rated the perceived politeness (hypothesis 7) of each request and response message on a seven-point scale. The coders were within one scale unit in 87% of the cases and were off by more than two scale units in only one of the judgments. The correlation between the politeness judgments was .76. Disagreements were resolved through discussion.

Manipulation Check Measures

To assess the appropriateness of a request to borrow class notes, respondents were asked to indicate on a seven-point scale how frequently students made such requests. The adequacy of the request size manipulation was determined by asking participants on open-ended items what they considered a reasonable amount of time and the maximum amount of time they would lend notes to the target.

RESULTS

Manipulation Checks

First, the interrelationship among the three indicators of intimacy was examined. Relational and communication intimacy are significantly correlated ($r = .75$, $p < .001$). A one-way ANOVA indicated significant differences in relational intimacy across levels of manipulation intimacy ($F = 32$, df = 2/56, $p < .001$, $eta^2 = .54$). Higher mean relational intimacy was reported in the friend condition (M = 68.95, SD = 8.69) followed by the acquaintance (M = 65.84, SD = 8.34) and stranger conditions (M = 48.90, SD = 8.50). A similar significant pattern occurred for communication intimacy across levels of manipulated intimacy ($F = 56.6$, df = 2/56, $p < .001$, $eta^2 = .84$). Again, higher mean communication intimacy was evidenced in the friend condition (M = 50.00, SD = 12.84) followed by the acquaintance (M = 34.21, SD = 11.87) and stranger conditions (M = 15.60, SD = 3.34).

STATISTICAL SUMMARY 1

Manipulation Checks

A correlation is computed to see if two or more variables are related to each other. A high correlation shows that two variables are very much related to each other. A zero correlation may mean that they are independent of each other or unrelated. A positive correlation means that as the scores of one variable increase, the scores on the second variable increase as well. Thus if someone scores high on one variable (e.g., talkativeness), they are likely to also score high on the other variable (e.g., number of friends). The correlation analysis showed that relational intimacy and communication intimacy were related to each other.

Next, an analysis of variance was computed to see if the groups differed from each other. For example, if you have three groups, you may want to know which one talks the most. In this study, the analysis of variance showed that the experiment was successful in creating difference levels of intimacy and request sizes.

Examination of the standard deviations in the latter test indicates substantial variation across cells. As previously theorized, greater variation

in communication intimacy occurred in the acquaintance and friend conditions than in the stranger cell ($F\mathrm{max} = 14.78$, df = 3/18, $p < .01$). Although the mean values and explained variance estimate indicates a strong relationship, slippage is evident in the more intimate conditions.

In addition, the three intimacy measures were related in a predictable fashion to the frequency of qualifying codes in the requests. More intimate partners should have greater information about the target and should not have to determine whether they were in class or had complete notes. Consequently, intimacy should be negatively related to the frequency of the qualifying codes. Although the main effect for manipulated intimacy was only marginally significant ($F = 2.59$, df = 2/53, $p < .08$, $eta^2 = .09$), the cell means evidence decreasing frequency from the stranger condition (M = .71, SD = .71) to acquaintance (M = .19, SD = .40) through friend condition (M = .14, SD = .36). Negative correlations were also found between communication intimacy ($r = -.26$, $p < .05$), relational intimacy ($r = .38$, $p < .01$) and the frequency of qualifying codes.

The indicator of the appropriateness of the class note request indicates such requests were common among the population (mean of 5.6 on seven-point scale, SD = 1.16). Therefore, the topic was normative within this social system.

Finally, the adequacy of the request size manipulation was assessed. Enough participants made specific time responses so that we could statistically compare reasonable (friend = 15; acquaintance = 19; stranger = 19) and maximum (friend = 13; acquaintance = 19; stranger = 19) amounts of time individuals were willing to lend notes.[6] Responses were coded into the number of days. Significant differences were observed across levels of intimacy for both a reasonable ($F = 4.37$, df = 2/50, $p < .05$, $eta^2 = .15$) and maximum ($F = 3.99$, df = 2/47, $p < .05$, $eta^2 = .14$) amount of lending time. Friends indicated longer reasonable (M = 1.87, SD = 1.12) and maximum lending times (M = 5.31, SD = 2.03), followed by acquaintances (reasonable: M

T A B L E 1
Means and Standard Deviations for Obligation Measures by Manipulated Intimacy

	Stranger n = 20	Acquaintance n = 19	Friend n = 20
Obligation to Grant Request for Class Notes	3.37[a] (2.14)	5.21[b] (1.65)	6.10[c] (.91)
Obligation to Offer Class Notes	1.63[a] (1.01)	3.42[b] (1.46)	4.65[c] (1.72)
Obligation to Grant Request for Money	1.42[a] (1.17)	2.58[b] (1.71)	4.00[c] (1.86)
Obligation to Offer Money	1.47[a] (1.02)	1.95[b] (1.31)	3.55[c] (1.88)

Source: Row means with common superscripts do not differ at $p < .01$. Standard deviations are in the parentheses.

= 1.84, SD = .83; maximum: M = 4.68, SD = 3.94) and strangers (reasonable: M = 1.10, SD = .65; maximum: M = 2.2, SD = 1.70). The half hour request was well within the parameters of being a reasonable amount. The three day request was greater than the average reasonable amount across the levels of intimacy, but within the maximum personal limit set by acquaintances and friends. Therefore, the two request sizes fell in different areas of reasonableness, but both fell within the maximum permissible amount for intimates.

Hypotheses 1 and 2

The first two hypotheses predicted differences in obligation across levels of intimacy. Table 1 contains means and standard deviations for the obligation measures. Separate two factor mixed ANOVAs using level of intimacy as a between-subject factor and type of obligation (obligated to grant a request versus obligation to offer) as a within-subjects factor were computed. Because within-subject factors are more sensitive to a variety of violated assumptions (Winer, 1971), an alpha level of .01 was chosen for these results. When examining the obligation to lend class notes, significant main effects for level of intimacy ($F = 24.9$, df = 2/54, $p < .01$, $eta^2 = .32$) and type of obligation ($F = 51.9$, df = 1/54, $p < .01$, $eta^2 = .16$) were found, but no signifi-

cant interaction. As predicted in hypothesis 1, obligations to grant requests and to offer resources increased across levels of intimacy. Contrary to hypothesis 2, the obligation to grant a request remained higher than the obligation to offer a resource across all levels of intimacy.

STATISTICAL SUMMARY 2

Hypotheses 1 and 2

Analyses of variance (ANOVA) were used to test the hypotheses. Each tested whether intimacy and type of obligation affected amount of obligation. There was a greater feeling of obligation in more intimate relationships and when the obligation was to grant a request.

When examining the obligations to grant a request for, or to offer needed money, only a significant main effect for intimacy ($F = 13.9$, df = 2/54, $p < .01$, $eta^2 = .30$) was found. Again, obligations to grant requests and to offer resources increased across levels of intimacy.

Table 2 contains correlations among communication intimacy and relational intimacy and the obligation measures. In support of hypothesis 1, the correlations are all positive and statistically significant. Overall, there is substantial support for the first hypothesis and none for the second.

TABLE 2
Correlations Between Communication, Relational Intimacy, and Obligation Measures

	Communication Intimacy	Relational Intimacy
Obligation to Grant Request for Class Notes	.44	.48
Obligation to Offer Class Notes	.57	.50
Obligation to Grant Request for Money	.67	.58
Obligation to Offer Money	.57	.41

Source: All correlations > .32, $p < .01$; n = 59.

TABLE 3
Means and Standard Deviations for Request Codes by
Manipulated Intimacy and Size of Request

	Stranger		Acquaintance		Friend	
	Half Hour $n = 10$	Three Days $n = 10$	Half Hour $n = 10$	Three Days $n = 9$	Half Hour $n = 11$	Three Days $n = 9$
Request Elaboration	5.60 (2.06)	7.00 (3.65)	4.20 (1.81)	5.67 (2.82)	3.73 (1.19)	5.00 (1.50)
Apologies	.48 (.64)	.30 (.48)	.20 (.42)	.38 (.58)	.09 (.30)	.66 (.79)
Explanations	1.20 (.92)	1.20 (.92)	.80 (.42)	.78 (.44)	.54 (.52)	1.22 (.61)
Inducements	.20 (.42)	.54 (.75)	.20 (.42)	.16 (.47)	.09 (.30)	.16 (.47)
Contingencies	.80 (.92)	.87 (.92)	.50 (.53)	1.44 (.73)	.54 (.52)	.99 (.50)

Source: In order to correct for severe heterogeneity of variance, the raw scores of apologies and inducements have been transformed into square roots. Standard deviations are in the parentheses.

Hypotheses 3 and 4

Table 3 displays the means and standard deviations related to elaboration of requests. Hypotheses 3 and 4 explicitly predict a *bivariate* relationship of a particular form between intimacy and measures of elaboration. Although we did not advance an interaction hypothesis, we examined the form of the bivariate relationship across magnitude of request size.

Our analysis included four tests. First, the results of 3 × 2 (intimacy by size of request)

ANOVAs utilizing manipulated intimacy (stranger, acquaintance, friend) will be reported. Second, we computed bivariate correlations among communication and relational intimacy and each elaboration measure. Third, regressions employing the communication intimacy measure, size of request, and their interactions will be described (Cohen & Cohen, 1975).[7] Finally, similar regressions using the relational intimacy measure will be included. Table 4 contains the results of the two sets of regressions.

STATISTICAL SUMMARY 3

Hypotheses 3 and 4

ANOVAs, correlations, and multiple regressions were computed to examine the effects of intimacy and size of request on the amount of elaboration and the number of apologies, explanations, inducements, and contingencies.

Correlations are used to see if two or more variables are related to each other. A high correlation shows that two variables are very much related to each other. A zero correlation may mean that they are independent of each other or unrelated. A positive correlation means that as the scores of one variable increase, the scores on the second variable increase as well. Thus if someone scores high on one variable (e.g., talkativeness), they are likely to also score high on the other variable (e.g., number of friends).

Multiple regression is like correlation except here you want to see if a single outcome or criterion variable is related to a group of variables. For example, you might want to know how someone obtains high satisfaction from a conversation. Using multiple regression you can see if the factors of topic, length of conversation, nonverbal contact, and empathy affect satisfaction.

In this study, people were found to elaborate their request less with more intimate relationships and with smaller requests. Neither the number of apologies nor the number of explanations nor the number of contingencies were affected by intimacy or size of request. Fewer inducements were offered to friends or in intimate conversations.

First, the degree of elaboration (*i.e.,* number of clauses) contained in the requests were analyzed. The ANOVA yielded significant main effects for manipulated intimacy ($F = 3.07$, df = 2/53, $p < .05$, $eta^2 = .093$) and size of request ($F = 6.01$, df = 1/53, $p < .02$, $eta^2 = .091$) and no interaction between the two. Less elaboration occurred across levels of intimacy and with smaller requests.[8] Moreover, we found significant and negative bivariate correlations among elaboration and both communication intimacy ($r = -.40$, $p < .001$) and relational intimacy ($r = -.41$, $p < .001$).

Neither set of regression analyses yielded evidence of an interaction among the two intimacy measures and magnitude of request. In the first set of regressions, a significant negative *beta* was observed for communication intimacy ($-.36$, $p < .004$) and a positive *beta* occurred for size of request ($.25$, $p < .03$). Similarly, the second set of regressions yielded a significant negative *beta* for relational intimacy ($-.38$, $p < .001$) and a positive one for request size ($.26$, $p < .03$).

Second, the number of apologies contained in the requests were examined. This time, the ANOVA identified no significant main effects and the interaction between manipulated intimacy and request size only approached significance ($F = 2.35$, df = 2/53, $p < .10$, $eta^2 = .08$). The bivariate correlations among communication intimacy, relational intimacy, and number of apologies were not significant.

Although the communication intimacy measure was not significantly related to apologies, an interaction was observed in the regression analysis involving relational intimacy and request size. The addition of the interaction term contributed significant variance (R^2 change = .10) beyond that of the two main effects (final regression: $R = .37$, $R^2 = .14$, $F = 3.02$, df = 3/55, $p < .03$). In order to examine the form of the interaction, separate regressions were computed between relational intimacy and apologies with each of the two request size conditions. For the small request size, as relational intimacy increased, the frequency of apologies decreased ($beta = -.48$, $p < .01$). A nonsignificant, positive association was observed in the large request size condition ($beta = .20$, NSD). Thus the hypothesized relationship held only when request size was small.[9]

Third, an ANOVA indicated that manipulated intimacy and request size were not significantly related to the number of explanations as either main effects or interaction. However, the hypothesized negative association was observed between the number of explanations and both

TABLE 4
Hierarchical Regressions of Request Codes on
Intimacy Measures, Request Size, and Their Interaction

	Intimacy	Request Size	Interaction Term		
	Beta	Beta	Beta	R	R²
Relational Intimacy					
Request Elaboration	−.38*	.26*	NSD	.49*	.24
Apologies	−1.01*	−1.42*	1.72*	.37*	.14
Explanations	−.37*	.12	NSD	.40*	.16
Inducements	−.26*	.10	NSD	.29 (*p* < .08)	.08
Contingencies	−.07	.23 (*p* < .09)	NSD	.25	.06
Communication Intimacy					
Request Elaboration	−.36*	.25*	NSD	.47*	.22
Apologies	−.08	.16	NSD	.19	.04
Explanations	−.26*	.12	NSD	.31 (*p* < .06)	.09
Inducements	−.26*	.09	NSD	.29 (*p* < .08)	.08
Contingencies	−.06	.23 (*p* < .09)	NSD	.24	.06

Source: Unless the interaction term was significant, the *beta* weights and *R*s were derived from step one of the regression.
* = *p* < .05.

communication intimacy ($r = -.28$, $p < .05$) and relational intimacy ($r = -.38$, $p < .01$).

Neither of the regression analyses identified significant interactions between communication or relational intimacy and request size on the number of explanations. Again, request size was not related to the number of explanations as a main effect. As predicted, communication intimacy was significantly and negatively related to the number of explanations (*beta* = −.26, $p < .05$).[10] Similarly, relational intimacy was negatively related to the number of explanations (*beta* = −.37, $p < .01$).

Fourth, when examining the number of inducements, significant effects are found only for communication and relational intimacy. As hypothesized, the number of inducements was negatively correlated with communication intimacy ($r = -.27$, $p < .05$) and relational intimacy

($r = -.27$, $p < .05$). The regression analyses yielded no evidence of a main effect for request size or an interaction between communication or relational intimacy and request size. In the first set of regressions, a significant *beta* for communication intimacy was observed (−.26, $p < .05$) as was the case for relational intimacy in the second set (−.26, $p < .05$).[11]

Finally, no support is found for the hypothesized relationship with contingencies. The ANOVA yielded a marginally significant main effect for request size ($F = 3.61$, df = 1/53, $p < .06$, $eta^2 = .06$ and the interaction between manipulated intimacy and request size only approached significance ($F = 2.52$, df = 2/53, $p < .09$, $eta^2 = .08$). Furthermore, neither the bivariate correlations nor the two sets of regressions yielded significant associations.

TABLE 5
Means and Standard Deviations of Response Codes by
Manipulated Intimacy and Request Size

	Stranger		Acquaintance		Friend	
	Half Hour $n = 9$	Three Days $n = 10$	Half Hour $n = 10$	Three Days $n = 7$	Half Hour $n = 10$	Three Days $n = 9$
Response	2.44	3.00	2.50	2.43	2.50	2.78
Elaboration	(1.24)	(1.33)	(1.27)	(.79)	(1.43)	(1.48)
Forgiving	1.78	1.50	1.50	.86	1.00	.78
Statements	(.67)	(1.08)	(1.08)	(.90)	(.67)	(1.09)
Counter-	.11	.40	.20	.49	.34	.99
persuasion	(.33)	(.70)	(.63)	(.62)	(.56)	(.95)

Source: Due to serve heterogeneity of variance, the counterpersuasion raw scores have been transformed into square roots. Standard deviations are in parentheses.

TABLE 6
Hierarchical Regressions of Response Codes on
Intimacy Measures, Request Size, and the Interaction Term

	Intimacy	Request Size	Interaction Term		
	Beta	Beta	Beta	R	R^2
Relational Intimacy					
Response Elaboration	−.12	−.07	NSD	.12	.01
Counter-persuasion	.16	.32*	NSD	.34*	.11
Forgiving Statements	−.22	−.21	NSD	.28	.08
Communication Intimacy					
Response Elaboration	.04	.12	NSD	.12	.01
Counter-persuasion	.41*	.36*	NSD	.50*	.25
Forgiving Statements	−.37*	−.24	NSD	.41*	.17
		($p < .07$)			

Source: In all cases, the *betas* and *R*s were derived from step one of the regressions.
* = $p < .05$.

Thus there is support for the notion that elaboration will be influenced by the level of intimacy with the target. Although not always significant across the three intimacy measures, the frequency of apologies, explanations, and inducements tend to decrease with increasing intimacy.

Hypotheses 5, 6, and 7

Again, ANOVAs, bivariate correlations, and regressions were used to test hypotheses 5 and 6. Table 5 contains the relevant means and standard deviations related to these hypotheses and Table

6 displays the results of the regressions. Four subjects did not make valid responses to this portion of the questionnaire and their data were deleted. Instead of writing exactly what they would say, they described their general reaction.

STATISTICAL SUMMARY 4

Hypotheses 5, 6, and 7

ANOVAs, correlations, and multiple regressions were used to test the effect of intimacy and request size on response elaboration, counterpersuasion, and forgiving. Response elaboration and forgiving were not affected, and larger requests produced more counterpersuasion. However, friends were less polite in their responses than in their initial requests while strangers were equally polite in both.

No support is found for the prediction that response elaboration would be affected by intimacy. None of the measures of intimacy, size of request, or their interaction was related to that variable.

The ANOVA yielded only a significant main effect of request size on the frequency of counterpersuasion ($F = 5.32$, df $= 1/49$, $p < 0.3$, $eta^2 = .09$). Larger requests produced more counterpersuasion. Of the two bivariate correlations, only the one between communication intimacy and frequency of counterpersuasion was significant ($r = .35, p < .01$). Neither set of regressions yielded a significant interaction between communication or relational intimacy and request size. However, a positive *beta* was observed between communication intimacy and frequency of counterpersuasion ($.41, p < .001$). Also, a positive *beta* was found for request size in the first ($.32, p < .02$) and second ($.36, p < .001$) sets of regressions.

The frequency of forgiving codes was related to intimacy. The ANOVA yielded a nearly significant main effect for manipulated intimacy ($F = 2.95$, df $= 1/49$, $p < .06$, $eta^2 = .04$) and no other significant effects. The means indicate that intimacy was negatively related to expressed forgiveness.[12] Only the bivariate correlation between communication intimacy and frequency of forgiving cues was statistically significant ($r = -.33, p < .01$). Neither of the sets of regressions identified significant interactions. However, communication intimacy was negatively related to the frequency of forgiving codes ($beta = -.37, p < .01$).

Finally, Table 7 displays the means and standard deviations of perceived politeness. There is support for hypothesis 7. When combining the request size conditions, friends encoded response messages that were perceived to be less polite than their initial requests ($t = 2.82$, df $= 18$, $p < .02$). A similar result held for acquaintances ($t = 2.40$, df $= 17$, $p < .05$). The request and response messages encoded by strangers were perceived to be of similar politeness.[13]

Thus, while the total number of clauses is unrelated to intimacy, forgiving statements and perceived politeness decrease with greater intimacy. Moreover, the degree of communication intimacy is positively related to counterpersuasion.

TABLE 7
Means and Standard Deviations of Perceived Politeness by Manipulated Intimacy, Request Size, and Request/Response

	Stranger	Acquaintance	Friend
Request	4.79	4.72	4.74
	(1.27)	(.83)	(.87)
Response	4.05	4.00	3.78
	(1.81)	(1.14)	(1.39)

Source: Standard deviations are in parentheses.

DISCUSSION

These data provide empirical support for our initial thesis that obligations inherent in intimate relations may substitute for elaborated persuasion when seeking resources. Intimates report greater obligations to provide class notes and money, regardless of whether requested to do so or simply upon discovering a partner's need. The requests of intimates are relatively less elaborate, containing fewer apologies (at least for small requests), explanations, and inducements. Rejections from intimate partners prompted fewer forgiving statements and greater counterpersuasion from individuals scoring high in communication intimacy. Finally, the responses of friends and acquaintances were perceived to be less polite than were their initial requests. The requests and responses of strangers were not perceived to differ.

However, several discrepancies should be highlighted. First, the obligations to comply or to volunteer assistance did not converge with increasing intimacy. Across levels of intimacy, individuals saw the obligation to comply to be greater than the obligation to act spontaneously upon mere observation of a need. Perhaps uninvited assistance is perceived to be more presumptuous regardless of level of intimacy. Nadler and Fisher (1984) reviewed evidence that receiving help from a similar other can be threatening to one's self-worth. If help is *imposed* rather than *invited,* the recipient may perceive it to be a claim of superior status by the help provider. If this perception is widely shared, felt obligation to volunteer help may be moderated.

Contrary to our hypotheses, the frequency of request contingencies and overall response elaborations were unrelated to any measure of intimacy. Perhaps the setting for the request reduced the necessity of stating contingencies such as when the class notes would be returned. Regardless of intimacy level, the respondents would likely see the target in class again. It might be assumed that all borrowers would return the notes the next class period. Hence, less externally imposed regular contact might have stimulated more stated contingencies.

The absence of an association with response elaboration may be a function of two conflicting relationships between intimacy and individual response codes. Communication intimacy was positively associated with counterpersuasion and negatively correlated with forgiving codes. Nonsignificant correlations of similar direction were observed for relational intimacy. This implies that messages constructed by intimates and nonintimates contain similar numbers of clauses but the content of the clauses are different.

In all but one case, the relationship between intimacy and elaboration measures held across the two request sizes. The frequency of apologies decreased only with greater relational intimacy for small requests while a nonsignificant relationship was observed for the larger request. This implies that intimates and nonintimates engage in a similar degree of facework when making larger requests (Brown & Levinson, 1978). However, it is curious that the same tendency is not manifested in the other codes. Perhaps apologies are sufficient to reduce any perceived impoliteness and other codes need not be elaborated.

Finally, while the three intimacy measures yielded similar results for the obligation and likelihood assessments, their relative degree of influence varied in the tests of elaboration. The results did not differ dramatically in direction but in magnitude. Typically, relational and/or communication intimacy produced results of greater magnitude and significance than manipulated intimacy. This may have arisen from the selection process or from actual variations within culturally ascribed labels of intimacy. While significantly related, variance in relational and communication intimacy occurred within each condition. Hence relational and communication intimacy measures may have provided more individuated assessments of intimacy than the manipulation and provided a more powerful test of the hypotheses.

The lack of correspondence between communication and relational intimacy was most evident among the response measures. Examination of Table 6 indicates that both relational and communication intimacy are related in the same direction to counterpersuasion and forgiving statements but only the *betas* for communication intimacy are statistically significant. Since the two intimacy measures have similar levels of reliability and are significantly intercorrelated, the different patterns of significance are perplexing. Apparently, the communication intimacy measure better taps orientation toward interaction than does our assessment of relational intimacy. This might constitute further evidence that behavior-specific relational knowledge influences communication processes to a greater extent than does general relational dimensions (Planalp, 1985). Thus both scales assess intimacy but one is more directly tied to communication.

Before discussing future research directions, certain limitations must be addressed. First, intimacy in this study ranged only as high as friendship. While we expect that greater obligation and less elaboration will be found in even more intimate relations, this study cannot demonstrate such. For example, Dillard and Fitzpatrick (1985) found that the most frequent compliance-gaining strategy observed in marital interaction is direct request, and Witteman and Fitzpatrick (1986) reported that use of direct requests resulted in the target's compliance or a mutual resolution to a problem. This implies that lack of elaboration may extend to even more intimate relations than studied here.

Second, this study did not employ a variety of needed resources. While the class note stimulus was realistic, it is possible that it differed in important ways from other resources. For example, would individuals seek more abstract resources such as affection or status in the same fashion? Blau (1964) has argued that some resources are valuable only if given spontaneously without negotiation. Thus asking for another's respect may be unsatisfying regardless of the level of intimacy shared with the target. Future research should explore commodity seeking for both abstract and concrete resources.

Third, although every effort was made to enhance the realism of the situation, respondents were still role playing. It is plausible that actual help-seeking messages may be different. However, it is difficult to explain how the results were influenced by low involvement. Why would low-involved intimates be different from low-involved nonintimates in either obligations or message elaboration? Presumably, low involvement might result in less effort and elaboration in all conditions rather than a decreasing pattern. If anything, we would anticipate greater differences (especially in negative responses to rejection) would occur in actual help seeking. Again, future research should explore this possibility.

With these limitations in mind, the results may have important implications for future research. First, this approach offers an alternative to the study of generic compliance gaining. A variety of studies have focused on intimacy and general compliance-gaining activity (Cody, McLaughlin, & Schneider, 1981; Dillard & Burgoon, 1985; Fitzpatrick & Winke, 1979; McLaughlin, Cody, & Robey, 1980; Miller, 1980; Miller et al., 1977; Roloff & Barnicott, 1978, 1979; Sillars, 1980) and research indicates that intimacy is a dimension differentiating compliance-gaining situations (Cody & McLaughlin, 1980; Cody, Woelfel, & McLaughlin, 1983). While some of these studies have found significant intimacy effects on the selection of compliance-gaining strategies, much of the research is conducted on an atheoretical basis. As a result, when explanations for effects are advanced, they appear post hoc and do not appear to be derived from any particular perspective. Although our research is at an early stage, intimacy and concurrent obligation may provide both an explanatory and predictive base from which to view such effects.

Moreover, the lack of theorizing has retarded exploration of the entire compliance-gaining situation. When people experience a resource deficit, they must first identify someone from whom to seek the commodity. This preliminary step has important impact upon the kinds of commodity-seeking messages people ordinarily enact. Most individuals are inclined to seek resources from intimate partners. Therefore, our research suggests that typical messages may be far less elaborated and sophisticated than many of the compliance-gaining strategies contained in taxonomies currently used by researchers (Marwell & Schmitt, 1967; Wiseman & Schenck-Hamlin,

1981). This is not to say that people may never use these strategies, but that they may be unnecessary. Such persuasive devices tend to be used when an individual is forced to seek compliance from nonintimates, when refused compliance by an intimate, or when the request size exceeds the normal amount for the intimate relationship. In essence, elaboration occurs only when the individual anticipates or encounters resistance to the message. Otherwise, interactants produce "arguments which are minimally sufficient to gain agreement" (Jackson & Jacobs, 1980, p. 262).

If so, elaboration may not always occur even when seeking resources from nonintimates. Nonintimates who are indebted to each other may substitute the reciprocity norm for persuasion (Gouldner, 1960). Individuals receiving a resource from nonintimates are compelled to be friendly or at least not hostile toward benefactors until reciprocation occurs. Greenberg (1980) argues that indebtedness is sufficiently aversive that individuals are motivated to find ways to repay favors. Thus a request from a nonintimate to whom a debt is owed need not be elaborated to motivate the debtor. The prior obligation substitutes. For example, authority figures in organizations may perceive they are under little compulsion to elaborate their directives to employees. The acceptance of a wage or salary obligates the employees to obey certain commands regardless of an expressed rationale, and, ordinarily, employees do obey these minimal messages (Barnard, 1938; Langer, Blank, & Chanowitz, 1978). Questioning the legitimacy of the superior's method of transmitting directives might create even greater negative reaction than denying a request from an intimate.

Overall, this research indicates that intimate relations have greater obligations associated with them and that requests from intimates are less elaborated. To the extent that such requests are ordinarily complied with, persuasive messages in intimate relationships may be relatively simple. Only when noncompliance is anticipated or occurs will elaborated persuasive appeals be encoded.

NOTES

1. We do acknowledge that the desire to monitor and care for intimates may partly result from other sources. For example, altruism, affection, and the desire to stimulate attraction toward self may also prompt such caring behavior. These sources are worthy of future consideration. However, at this juncture, we are primarily interested in obligations arising from social norms.

2. Our use of the term *persuasion* implies two things. First, intimate relationships are associated with obligations that imply that requests will meet minimal resistance. Hence, people may not expect they will have to persuade or convince their intimate partners to comply. Second, as a result, the number of persuasive cues contained within their requests may be lessened.

3. At face value, hypothesis 4 may seem redundant with hypothesis 3. If messages have fewer clauses or simple statements then it follows that fewer message cues of all variety may be found. However, we do not expect that to be true. Our analysis suggests that only those cues related to persuasion should be affected by intimacy. Consequently, ritualistic forms of speech (e.g., greetings) or requests should not vary across levels of intimacy. Indeed, analysis of the data to be reported later indicated no relationship among intimacy and the number of request statements and greetings contained in commodity-seeking messages.

4. Because the requests of nonintimates contain greater numbers of cues considered to be polite (Brown & Levinson, 1978), one might be tempted to hypothesize that the requests of nonintimates will be judged to be more polite than those of intimates. We believe that such a hypothesis may be unwise for the following reason. Brown and Levinson (1978) note that in encoding a politeness strategy, one might be perceived as "too polite" and, paradoxically, judged to be insulting and rude. Hence the elaborated requests composed by nonintimates could be perceived as too much. Consequently, we have no basis upon which to predict that the greater number of cues in nonintimate messages will result in greater or lesser perceived politeness.

5. This standard permitted complex and compound sentences to be subdivided. Simple sentences were also included as single clauses.

6. Two individuals did not complete the items. Of the remaining responses, four persons in the friend condition indicated that they could be reasonably expected to lend their class notes as long a period of time as the target needed them. Only one person outside of the friend condition was willing to lend the class notes for an indefinite period.

7. For this analysis, request size was dummy coded (0 = half hour; 1 = three days) and entered along with communication intimacy on the first step of a hierarchical multiple regression. On the second step, the interaction of communication intimacy and request size was entered. A similar procedure was conducted using relational intimacy rather than communication intimacy.

8. Examination of cell means collapsed across request size suggested that elaboration decreased from a high in the stranger cell (M = 6.15, SD = 3.01) through the acquaintance condition (M = 4.89, SD = 2.40) to a low in the friendship cell (M = 4.30, SD = 1.45). A one-way ANOVA performed on those data verified the means differed significantly (F = 3.15, df = 2/56, p < .05, *eta* = .32) and also identified a significant linear trend among them (F = 6.05, df = 1/56, p < .017, r = −.31). Moreover, a trend analysis yielded no significant departure from linearity (F < 1).

9. Although only marginally significant, the aforementioned interaction between manipulated intimacy and request size was of a similar form. The weak interaction resulted from different trends within the time condition. For the small request, the frequency of apologies decreased with greater intimacy while the opposite occurred for the large request size. Among friends, the number of apologies was significantly greater (F = 4.08, df = 1/53, p < .05) when the request was large rather than small.

10. Examination of Table 4 indicates that the overall multiple correlation was only marginally significant (p < .06). Because we advanced a priori hypotheses, we believe it is legitimate to report the significant *beta* (p < .05) for communication intimacy. The lack of statistical significance may have resulted from the weak relationship between request size and the number of explanations. Also, low statistical power for detecting a relationship of this magnitude (R^2 = .09) was afforded by this sample size (power = .56).

11. Examination of Table 4 indicates that both multiple correlations were only marginally significant (p < .08). Because we posited a priori hypotheses, we believe it is legitimate to report the significant *beta* (p < .05) for both communication and relational intimacy. Again, request size made a minimal contribution to the overall regression. Also, this sample size allowed for low power for detecting a relationship of this magnitude (power = .48).

12. As hypothesized, the cell means indicate that the frequency of forgiving cues decreased from a high in the stranger cell (M = 1.63, SD = 1.03) through the acquaintance condition (M = 1.23, SD = 1.03) to a low in the friendship cell (M = .89, SD = .87). A one-way ANOVA yielded a nearly significant difference (F = 2.97, df = 2/52, p < .06, *eta* = .32) and a significant linear trend (F = 5.16, df = 1/52, p < .018, r = −.31). No significant departure from linearity was observed (F < 1).

13. We also conducted a supplementary analysis on the politeness judgments. We computed a three-factor mixed ANOVA using manipulated intimacy and request size as between group factors and type of message (request versus response to rejection) as a within group factor. Only the main effect for message types was significant (F = 12.6, df = 1/50, p < .001). In general, requests were perceived to be more polite (M = 4.75) than responses (M = 3.95). However, the t-tests reported in the text indicated that, as predicted, only the requests and responses constructed by intimates differed significantly from each other.

REFERENCES

Argyle, M., & Henderson, M. (1984). The rules of friendship. *Journal of Social and Personal Relationships, 1*, 211–237.

Barnard, C. I. (1938). *The functions of the executive.* Cambridge, MA: Harvard University Press.

Barnes, R. D., Ickes, W., & Kidd, R. F. (1979). Effects of the perceived intentionality and stability of another's dependency on helping behavior. *Personality and Social Psychology Bulletin, 5*, 367–372.

Bar-Tal, D., Bar-Zohar, Y., Greenberg, M. S., & Hermon, M. (1977). Reciprocity behavior in the relationship between donor and recipient and between harm-doer and victim. *Sociometry, 40*, 293–298.

Berkowitz, L. (1969). Resistance to improper dependency relationships. *Journal of Experimental Social Psychology, 5*, 283–294.

Blau, P. (1964). *Exchange and power in everyday life.* New York: John Wiley.

Bostrom, R. N., Humphreys, R. J., & Roloff, M. E. (1981). Communication and helping behavior: The effects of information, reinforcement, and sex, on helping responses. *Communication Quarterly, 29*, 147–155.

Brehm, J. W. (1966). *A theory of psychological reactance.* New York: Academic Press.

Brickman, P, Kidder, L. H., Coates, D., Rabinowitz, V., Cohn, E., & Karuza, J. (1983). The dilemmas of helping: Making aid fair and effective. In J. D. Fisher, A. Nadler, & B. M. DePaulo (Eds.), *New directions in helping* (Vol. 1, pp. 17–49). New York: Academic Press.

Brinberg, D., & Castell, P. (1982). A resource exchange theory approach to interpersonal interactions: A test of Foa's theory. *Journal of Personality and Social Psychology, 43*, 260–269.

Brown, P., & Levinson, S. (1978). Universals in language usage: Politeness phenomena. In E. N. Goody (Ed.), *Questions and politeness: Strategies in social interaction* (pp. 56–289). London: Cambridge University Press.

Burke, R. J., & Weir, T. (1975). Giving and receiving help with work and non-work related problems. *Journal of Business Administration, 6*, 59–78.

Buss, A. H. (1983). Social rewards and personality. *Journal of Personality and Social Psychology, 44*, 553–563.

Chelune, G. J., Robinson, J. T., & Kommor, M. J. (1984). A cognitive interactional model of intimate relationships. In V. J. Derlega (Ed.), *Communication, intimacy, and close relationships* (pp. 11–40). New York: Academic Press.

Clark, M. S. (1983a). Reactions to aid in communal and exchange relationships. In J. D. Fisher, A. Nadler, & B. M. DePaulo (Eds.), *New directions in helping* (Vol. 1, pp. 281–304). New York: Academic Press.

Clark, M. S. (1983b). Some implications of close social bonds for help-seeking. In B. M. DePaulo, A. Nadler, & J. D. Fisher (Eds.), *New directions in helping* (Vol. 2, pp. 205–229). New York: Academic Press.

Clark, M. S. (1984). Record keeping in two types of relationships. *Journal of Personality and Social Psychology, 47,* 549–557.

Clark, M. S., & Mills, J. (1979). Interpersonal attraction in exchange and communal relationships. *Journal of Personality and Social Psychology, 37,* 12–24.

Clark, M. S., Mills, J., & Powell, M. C. (1986). Keeping track of needs in communal and exchange relationships. *Journal of Personality and Social Psychology, 51,* 333–338.

Clark, M. S., & Ouellette, R. (1983). *The impact of relationship type and the potential recipient's mood on helping.* Unpublished manuscript, Carnegie-Mellon University.

Clark, M. S., & Waddell, B. (1985). Perceptions of exploitation in communal and exchange relationships. *Journal of Social and Personal Relationships, 2,* 403–418.

Cody, M. J., & McLaughlin, M. L. (1980). Perceptions of compliance-gaining situations: A dimensional analysis. *Communication Monographs, 47,* 132–148.

Cody, M. J., McLaughlin, M. L., & Schneider, M. J. (1981). The impact of relational consequences and intimacy on the selection of interpersonal persuasion tactics: A reanalysis. *Communication Quarterly, 29,* 91–106.

Cody, M. J., Woelfel, M. L., & Jordan, W. J. (1983). Dimensions of compliance-gaining situations. *Human Communication Research, 9,* 99–113.

Cohen, J., & Cohen, P. (1975). *Applied multiple regression/correlation analysis for the behavioral sciences.* Hillsdale, NJ: Erlbaum.

Dailey, W. O., & Roloff, M. E. (1987). *What do we want from information exchange? Profit? Equity? Neither?* Paper presented at the annual meetings of the International Communication Association, Montreal.

DePaulo, B. M. (1978). Help-seeking from the recipient's point of view. *JSAS Catalog of Selected Documents in Psychology, 8,* 62.

Dillard, J. P., & Burgoon, M. (1985). Situational influences on the selection of compliance-gaining messages: Two tests of the predictive utility of the Cody-McLaughlin typology. *Communication Monographs, 52,* 289–394.

Dillard, J. P., & Fitzpatrick, M. A. (1985). Compliance-gaining in martial interaction. *Personality and Social Psychology Bulletin, 11,* 419–433.

Finlayson, A. (1976). Social networks as coping resources: Lay help and consultation patterns used by women in husbands' post-infarction career. *Social Science and Medicine, 10,* 97–108.

Fitzpatrick, M. A., & Winke, J. (1979). You always hurt the one you love: Strategies and tactics in interpersonal conflict. *Communication Quarterly, 27,* 3–11.

Foa, U. G., & Foa, E. B. (1974). *Societal structures of the mind.* Springfield, IL: Charles C. Thomas.

Folkes, V. S. (1985). Mindlessness of mindfulness: A partial replication and extension of Langer, Blank, and Chanowitz. *Journal of Personality and Social Psychology, 48,* 600–604.

Goffman, E. (1971). *Relations in public.* New York: Harper Colophon.

Gouldner, A. W. (1960). The norm of reciprocity: A preliminary statement. *American Sociological Review, 25,* 161–178.

Greenberg, M. S. (1980). A theory of indebtedness. In K. Gergen, M. Greenberg, & R. Willis (Eds.), *Social exchange: Advances in theory and research* (pp. 3–26). New York: Plenum.

Griffith, J. (1985). Social support providers: Who are they? where are they met? and the relationship of network characteristics to psychology distress. *Basic and Applied Social Psychology, 6,* 41–60.

Harris, M. B., Liguori, R. A., & Stack, C. (1973). Favors, bribes, and altruism. *Journal of Social Psychology, 89,* 47–54.

Hatfield, E. (1984). The dangers of intimacy. In V. J. Derlega (Ed.), *Communication, intimacy, and close relationships* (pp. 207–220). New York: Academic Press.

Hinde, R. A. (1979). *Toward understanding relationships.* New York: Academic Press.

Hobfoll, S. E., Nadler, A., & Leiberman, J. (1986). Satisfaction with social support during crisis: Intimacy and self-esteem as critical determinants. *Journal of Personality and Social Psychology, 51,* 296–304.

Horowitz, A. (1978). Family, kin, and friend networks in psychiatric help-seeking. *Social Science and Medicine, 12,* 297–304.

Horowitz, I. A. (1968). Effect of choice and locus of dependence on helping behavior. *Journal of Personality and Social Psychology, 8,* 373–376.

Jackson, S., & Jacobs, J. (1980). Structure of conversational argument: Pragmatic bases for the enthymeme. *Quarterly Journal of Speech, 66,* 251–265.

Jacobs, J., & Jackson, S. (1981). Argument as a natural category: The routine grounds for arguing in conversation. *Western Journal of Speech Communication, 45,* 118–132.

Jones, R. A. (1970). Volunteering to help: The effects of choice, dependence, and anticipated dependence. *Journal of Personality and Social Psychology, 14,* 121–129.

Langer, E. J., & Abelson, R.P. (1972). The semantics of asking a favor: How to succeed in getting help without really dying. *Journal of Personality and Social Psychology, 24,* 26–32.

Langer, E. J., Blank, A., & Chanowitz, B. (1978). The mindlessness of ostensibly thoughtful action. *Journal of Personality and Social Psychology, 36,* 635–642.

Marwell, G., & Hage, J. (1970). The organization of role relationships: A systematic description. *American Sociological Review, 35,* 884–900.

Marwell, G., & Schmidt, D. R. (1967). Dimensions of compliance-gaining behavior: An empirical analysis. *Sociometry, 30,* 350–364.

McLaughlin, M. L., Cody, M. J., & Robey, C. S. (1980). Situational influences on the selection of strategies to resist compliance-gaining attempts. *Human Communication Research, 7,* 14–36.

Meyer, J. P., & Mulherin, A. (1980). From attribution to helping: An analysis of the mediating effects of affect and expectancy. *Journal of Personality and Social Psychology, 39,* 201–210.

Miller, G. R., Boster, F., Roloff, M., & Seibold, D. (1977). Compliance-gaining message strategies: A typology and some findings concerning effects of situational differences. *Communication Monographs, 44,* 37–51.

Miller, G. R., & Steinberg, M. (1975). *Between people.* Chicago: Science Research Associates.

Miller, M. D. (1982). Power and relationship type as predictors of compliance-gaining strategy use. *Journal of Language and Social Psychology, 1,* 111–121.

Mills, J., & Clark, M. S. (1982). Exchange and communal relationships. In L. Wheeler (Eds.), *Review of personality and social psychology, 3* (pp. 121–144). Beverly Hills, CA: Sage.

Nadler, A., & Fisher, J. D. (1984). Effects of donor-recipient relationships on recipients' reactions to aid. In E. Staub, D. Bar-Tal, J. Karylowski, & J. Reykowski (Eds.), *Development and maintenance of prosocial behavior: International perspective on positive morality* (pp. 397–417). New York: Plenum.

Perrin, P. G. (1959). *Writer's guide and index to English.* Glenview, IL: Scott, Foresman.

Planalp, S. (1985). Relational schemata: A test of alternative forms of relational knowledge as guides to communication. *Human Communication Research, 12,* 3–29.

Roloff, M. E. (1981). *Interpersonal communication: The social exchange approach.* Beverly Hills, CA: Sage.

Roloff, M. E. (1987). Communication and reciprocity within intimate relationships. In M. E. Roloff & G. R. Miller (Eds.), *Interpersonal processes: New directions in communication research* (pp. 11–38). Newbury Park, CA: Sage.

Roloff, M. E., & Barnicott, E. F. (1978). The situational use of pro- and antisocial compliance-gaining strategies by high and low Machiavellians. In B. D. Ruben (Ed.), *Communication yearbook 2* (pp. 193–205). New Brunswick, NJ: Transaction.

Roloff, M. E., & Barnicott, E. F. (1979). The influence of dogmatism on the situational use of pro- and anti-social compliance-gaining strategies. *Southern Speech Communication Journal, 45,* 37–54.

Roloff, M. E., & Campion, D. E. (1985). Conversational profit-seeking: Interaction as social exchange. In R. L. Street, Jr. & J. N. Cappella (Eds.), *Sequence and pattern in communicative behaviour* (pp. 161–189). London: Arnold.

Rule, B. G., Bisanz, G. L., & Kohn, M. (1985). Anatomy of a persuasion schema: Targets, goals, and strategies. *Journal of Personality and Social Psychology, 48,* 1127–1140.

Schlenker, B. R. (1980). *Impression management.* Monterey, CA: Brooks/Cole.

Shapiro, E. G. (1980). Is seeking help from a friend like seeking help from a stranger? *Social Psychology Quarterly, 43,* 259–263.

Sillars, A. L. (1980). The stranger and the spouse as target persons for compliance-gaining strategies: A subjective expected utility model. *Human Communication Research, 6,* 265–279.

Tedeschi, J., Schlenker, B., & Bonoma, T. (1973). *Conflict, power, and games: The experimental study of interpersonal relations.* Chicago: AVC.

Waddell, B., & Clark, (1982). *Feelings of exploitation in communal and exchange relationships.* Paper presented at the meetings of the Eastern Psychological Association, Baltimore.

Winer, B. J. (1971). *Statistical principles in experimental design* (2nd ed.). New York: McGraw-Hill.

Wiseman, R. L., & Schenck-Hamlin, W. (1981). A multidimensional scaling validation of an inductively-derived set of compliance-gaining strategies. *Communication Monographs, 48,* 251–270.

Wish, M. Deutsch, M., & Kaplan, S. J. (1976). Perceived dimensions of interpersonal relations. *Journal of Personality and Social Psychology, 33,* 409–420.

Witteman, H. & Fitzpatrick, M. A. (1986). Compliance-gaining in marital interaction: Power bases, processes, and outcomes. *Communication Monographs, 53,* 130–143.

TYPES OF INFLUENCE GOALS IN PERSONAL RELATIONSHIPS

James Price Dillard

This study was designed to address three issues: (1) What types of influence goals do people see as typical in their close relationships? (2) How can these goals best be interpreted empirically and theoretically? (3) How do different types of influence goals correspond to action? Cluster analytic methods were applied to a sample of goals generated by people who were asked to recall their goal in an interpersonal influence event of their own initiation. A six-group solution was retained whose clusters were labeled Give Advice (Lifestyle), Gain Assistance, Share Activity, Change Political Stance, Give Advice (Health), and Change Relationship. These clusters differed significantly on each of nine variables used to validate the cluster solution. In addition, goal types were differentially associated with three aspects of compliance-gaining messages. These results provide some of the foundational material that is prerequisite to the development of theory in the area of interpersonal influence in personal relationships.

Acts of interpersonal influence are inherent in all types of relationships. However, close, personal relationships may be the social arena that is most active in terms of sheer frequency of influence attempts. One central feature of efforts at producing behavioral change is the goal of the source. The goal provides the impetus for action and defines what the interaction episode is about. Thus, goals are fundamental to the study of influence. It is, therefore, surprising that there is not more empirical research directed at basic concerns such as identifying types of influence goals. This paper moves toward filling that gap. The purpose of the investigation reported here was to begin to carve out the descriptive building blocks necessary to the construction of a theory of interpersonal influence.

The process of interpersonal influence may be conceptualized as a sequence beginning with an actor's goals. Goals are construed to be 'any desired state of affairs that the individual is committed to bringing about or maintaining' (Klinger, 1985: 312). Goals engender plans and, in turn, plans guide behavior. When plans are disrupted, or particular courses of action prove ineffective, goals may be altered or discarded. Though brief, this account gives some theoretical structure to the present undertaking. One implication of this structure is that research on interpersonal influence should begin at the beginning—that is, with the study of goals.

Although many theorists have argued that people possess and act on multiple goals (e.g. Tracy, 1984), the focus in this investigation was solely on social influence goals. Influence goals were conceptualized as the motivations underlying attempts to produce behavioral change in a target person. This narrow focus was adopted in order to make the findings relevant to research on compliance-gaining attempts, and because of Reither's (1981) data which show that people tend to resist forming specific goals. It was reasoned that articulation of concrete, behavior-change goals would force specificity of goal descriptions that would, in turn, enhance the reliability of judgments made concerning those goal descriptions.

I would like to express my gratitude to Scott Broetzmann for his valuable contributions to phases one and two, and to Pam Miner for her help with data collection in phase three. The preparation of this paper was supported, in part, by a grant from the Wisconsin Alumni Research Fund, #135–3356.

Probably the most comprehensive theoretical treatment of influence goals comes from Schank & Abelson's (1977) work on story comprehension. They suggest the existence of a set of persuasive techniques, called a *persuade package,* which are called on to serve *delta* (i.e. change) goals (pp. 83–8). Five types are specified in their scheme, four of which are relevant to this paper: (1) D-KNOW, whose purpose is to acquire information, (2) D-CONT, whose purpose is to gain control of an object, (3) D-SOCCONT, which represents a desire for social control, i.e. power or authority, and (4) D-AGENCY, whose purpose is to get a target person to act on behalf of the source.

Unfortunately, few data are available to permit an assessment of Schank & Abelson's (1977) theorizing. The scant empirical base that does exist casts doubt on the adequacy of their classification scheme. One study which briefly considered the substance of interpersonal influence goals is Hecht (1984). His content analysis indicated the existence of goals concerned with altering target behavior on social issues, matters of relational growth, self-improvement, and entertainment (joining in fun activities). Another study, conducted by Kipnis et al. (1980), describes five influence goals specific to supervisor–subordinate relationships.

A third empirical effort is reported by Rule et al. (1985), who gathered goal data from sixty-four men and women by asking, 'What kind of things do people persuade other people/their friends/their fathers/their enemies to do?' Their content analysis indicated that only 23 percent of the data were classifiable using the Schank & Abelson categories. They hypothesized the existence of four additional goals (to change target's opinion, to change target's activity, to change a state of ownership, and to change a role relationship) which accounted for another 58 percent of the data. Four more goal categories, which accounted for the remaining 19 percent of their sample, emerged from the data: to get target to alter a personal habit, to assist the source, to help or harm a third party, and to engage in self-harmful activities. These findings suggest the need to expand the Schank & Abelson scheme.

One other data-based effort, which leads to much the same conclusion, is Cody et al. (in press). Their cluster analysis of the Cody et al. (1986) data on perceptions of compliance-gaining situations led them to adopt a twelve-group solution which they later modified to an eleven-group typology. It is of interest to the present endeavor that further reduction of the goal types resulted in three superordinate categories which Cody et al. (in press) distinguish as pro-relational/co-operative, non-intimate, and role- or self-related. Those lines of conceptual cleavage underscore the importance of studying influence in close relationships as distinct from persuasive activities in other contexts.

As the preceding review shows, there has been relatively little systematic, empirical research on types of influence goals or the interrelationships among them. The paucity of research on this topic is all the more evident when the focus is narrowed to influence goals in close relationships. In light of the well-known importance of personal relationships to individual actors, the apparent frequency of compliance-gaining attempts in those relationships (Rule et al., 1985), and the impact of influence activities on relational happiness and satisfaction (Dillard & Fitzpatrick, 1985), it is evident that this lack of research attention is undeserved.

In view of these issues, the present study sought to provide answers to several questions: (1) What types of influence goals do persons see as typical in their close relationships? (2) How can these goals best be interpreted empirically and theoretically? (3) How do various types of influence goals correspond to action?

Method and results

Phase One: Generating a Sample of Goals

Self-report data concerning goals in interpersonal influence attempts were collected from 152 people enrolled in undergraduate communication courses at a large midwestern university. The sample was 59 percent female. The average age was 23.05 years.

Additional data were gathered from people employed in local retail and service businesses ($n = 49$). The business sample was 71 percent female. The average age was 27.47. The data from the two samples were pooled for a total n of 201.

Participants were provided with a brief questionnaire that asked them to give a written description of a situation in which they had tried to persuade someone to do something and to describe their goal in that influence attempt. The instructions called for participants to select a situation which met the following three criteria:

1. It should involve someone that you know well. That might be a good friend, a lover, a spouse, a parent, a sibling, a boss, an employee, or a co-worker.
2. It should be an instance in which you tried to change that person's behavior, i.e. not simply an attitude, opinion, or belief. For example, convincing someone to vote one way or the other in an election would be OK. Convincing someone that a painting was beautiful would not.
3. Finally, it should be a situation in which you were (un)successful at persuading this person to do what you wanted— (you tried but he or she didn't do what you wanted) you tried and he or she did what you wanted.

All told, 87 people reported on successful influence attempts and 104 described unsuccessful attempts.

Three judges examined the pool of goal descriptions for the purpose of drawing a representative sample. They used an iterative, inductive procedure that required each judge independently to consider all of the goals, develop candidate criteria for framing the sample, and then to present his or her reasoning to the other judges. After several meetings, three criteria were deemed adequate: content, structure, and clarity.

The content criterion was developed by a close examination of the data and of previous reports. Ten content categories emerged: social relations,

companionship, entertainment, political activity, health, values and morality, financial matters, career, tasks/labor, and changes in locale. Six goals were chosen to represent each category except political activity. For the latter category, only five instances were found in the sample.

The structure criterion addressed the question of who would benefit from the influence. This feature of influence situations has been shown to be perceptually salient in other exploratory work (Hertzog & Bradac, 1984). Whereas previous studies (e.g. Boster & Stiff, 1984) have tended to focus only on self- and other-benefit, that scope was expanded in this study to include goals which would benefit both parties as well as a third party. Due to the makeup of the sample, it was not possible to achieve numerical balance across the four categories. Instead the number of goals in each benefit category roughly corresponds to their frequency of occurrence in the pool of statements: self-benefit (30 percent), other-benefit (46 percent), mutual benefit (12 percent), third-party benefit (12 percent).

The clarity criterion required that the goal description be stated clearly and that only one goal be mentioned. Hence, statements such as 'I wanted him to take me to the shoe store and then to go over my mother's house' were eliminated. After several meetings, a total of fifty-nine goals were settled on for use as stimuli in the next segment of the investigation.

Phase Two: Developing Goal Clusters

One hundred people, enrolled in undergraduate classes at a large, midwestern university, served as judges in this portion of the study. Their mean age was 23.26 and 54 percent were female.

Each participant was given a deck of goals in random order and was instructed to sort the fifty-nine stimuli into categories based on their similarity to one another. Although no upper or lower limit on the number of categories was specified, participants were told that single-goal categories were not permissible. Respondents were instructed to make at least two passes through the deck. In the first pass, they were to familiarize themselves with the goals and to form prelimi- nary categories. They were provided with a page in the instruction booklet entitled 'Possible Cat- egories' on which to record their initial ideas. In the second (or later) pass, they were to do the actual sorting. The instructions read: 'Beginning with the first card in the deck, you should care- fully read each goal statement and begin to create piles. Remember, the idea here is that all the goals within one pile are to be alike, and are to be different from the goals which you have put into other piles.'

Participant groups ranged in size from three to seventeen people. The amount of time required to complete the sorting task varied from 30 minutes to an hour.

Data from individual respondents were com- piled to form a summary matrix of similarities. This matrix was then analyzed using the Quick Cluster program available through SPSS/PC (Norusis, 1986). This program requires that the user specify the number of clusters a priori. One pass is made through the data to develop maxi- mally discrepant initial cluster centers. A second pass is made through the data using those esti- mates to classify the cases into clusters.

STATISTICAL SUMMARY 1

Phase 2

Cluster analysis was used to determine how to group the goals. Cluster analysis helps you group variables together into a smaller number of categories. If you have a large number of variables, you may want to see if two or more of them actually combine or work together. This analysis suggested that there were six types of goals: give advice (lifestyle), gain assistance, share activity, change political stance, give advice (health), and change relationship.

The question faced by the cluster analyst is that of how many groups to retain. In order to limit the range of choices, a mean and standard deviation were computed on the number of groups formed by participants in the Q-sort task

in phase two. The average number of groups was 7.87. The standard deviation was 2.85. After rounding these values to whole numbers, the de- cision was made to consider the average number of groups plus and minus one standard deviation in the cluster analysis. Thus, analyses were con- ducted so as to produce cluster solutions of five through eleven groups.

The next task was to choose the optimal so- lution from that set of candidates. Several criteria for making this decision are discussed in the lit- erature on cluster analysis. One is parsimony and another is interpretability. However, both of those criteria require only that the analyst com- pare one solution to another. An alternative, less subjective, method is to assess the various solu- tions against some external criteria. It is possible to form predictions concerning the ways in which the groups differ and then to have a separate set of judges rate the stimuli judgment (the goals) on scales that are reflective of those predictions. Such a procedure is commonly used to validate multidimensional scaling solutions (e.g. Kruskal & Wish, 1978). The variables tapped by the judges' ratings can then be used in a discriminant analysis as a means of placing individual stimuli into groups. The classification efficiency of the discriminant equation provides a somewhat more objective means of selecting the optimal cluster solution. However, prior to understanding such an analysis it is necessary to have ratings of the stimuli in hand. The next segment of the inves- tigation was conducted in order to obtain those ratings.

Phase Three: Goals in Context

This phase involved developing scales which re- flected potential interpretations of the differences between the groups. Since it was unlikely that the groups differed on a single dimension only, two methods were used in developing expectations about the ways in which the goals might be dif- ferentiated from one another. First, prior work on influence goals and on compliance-gaining situ- ations was examined. Second, multidimensional scaling analyses were conducted on the present data set for two through six dimensional solutions. The stress values for those solutions were 0.24, 0.18, 0.14, 0.12, and 0.10 respectively. The corresponding R-squared values were 0.71, 0.76, 0.81, 0.84, and 0.87. On this basis, it was anticipated that the following dimensions might prove valuable in discriminating among clusters: degree of source benefit, target benefit, and group benefit, 'publicness' of the influence act, normative pressure to acquiesce to the request, desire for improvement of an adequate situation (versus remedying a bad situation), type of relationship with target of the request (voluntary versus nonvoluntary), desire for relational growth/maintenance, and specificity (versus globality) of the influence issue.

For phase three of the investigation, 240 students enrolled in undergraduate courses at a large, midwestern university served as respondents to one of twelve different forms of a questionnaire. In other words, twelve groups composed of twenty students each responded to one version of the questionnaire. Their mean age was 21.7 and 56 percent were female.

In total, thirty-six items were developed to tap the nine variables that were expected to distinguish the goal types. To fill out the data matrix required to conduct the planned discriminant analysis, it was necessary that each of the fifty-nine goals be judged on each of the thirty-six scales. Because of the large number of judgments involved in constructing this matrix, a strategy was employed whereby groups of individuals would make a more limited number of evaluations. First, six forms of a questionnaire were developed which differed in terms of the goals to be judged. Five of the forms contained ten goals, whereas the sixth contained nine. Initially, the goal statements were randomly assigned to questionnaires and randomly ordered within questionnaires. When two nearly identical statements occurred within the same version, one was reassigned to another questionnaire.

Second, the thirty-six rating items were broken down into two subsets and crossed with the existing breakdown of goals. This procedure

yielded twelve versions of a questionnaire which differed in terms of both goals and rating scales. Thus, twelve subgroups, each $n = 20$, rated either nine or ten goals on eighteen scales.

Each version of the questionnaire consisted of a cover page, a list of goal statements, and a series of pages which showed a goal statement followed by eighteen Likert-type rating scales. The cover page described the study and gave instructions regarding the use of a five-point Likert scale: 1 = Strongly disagree, 2 = Disagree, 3 = Neutral, 4 = Agree, 5 = Strongly agree.

The second page provided a complete list of the goals in that particular version of the questionnaire. In order to minimize order effects that might occur from using the first goal in the series as a perceptual anchor, participants were instructed to read over the entire set of goal statements prior to making any judgments. The remaining pages provided a single goal statement at the top of each page followed by eighteen rating scales designed to tap the expected content of the goal dimensions.

Responses to each rating scale were collapsed across subjects and within questionnaires. This resulted in thirty-six mean ratings for each goal, i.e. one mean rating per item based on the combined judgments of twenty respondents. Through the use of confirmatory factor analysis, the individual items were combined to form unidimensional composite scales. The particular procedure used was that advocated by Hunter (1980). The final, composite scales are given in Table 1.

STATISTICAL SUMMARY 2

Phase 3

Confirmatory factor analysis is used to validate the groupings of items. For example, if you have twenty items on a survey and you think they will group into four variables, you can use confirmatory factor analysis to test this. In this study the items did group into six types of goals.

TABLE 1
Scales Used to Aid in Interpreting the Cluster Solutions

Source Benefit (alpha = 0.73)

1. . . . would be very beneficial to the source.

2. . . . is purely in the interest of the source.

Target Benefit (alpha = 0.94)

3. . . . would be very beneficial to the target.

4. . . . is for the good of the *individual* target person.

Group Benefit (alpha = 0.68)

5. . . . is an activity that should be done for the good of some larger group, e.g. community, society, etc.

6. . . . benefits some third person or group, i.e. not the source or target.

Publicness (alpha = 0.90)

7. . . . pertains to a very public activity.

8. . . . represents an activity that involves many other people.

Normative Pressure (alpha = 0.82)

9. . . . emphasizes an obligation.

10. . . . refers to something that 'should' be done because of social norms.

Improvement (alpha = 0.80)

11. . . . tries to remedy an important problem.

12. . . . is concerned with making things better.

13. . . . focuses on trying to prevent something bad from happening (R).

Voluntary—Nonvoluntary Relationship (alpha = 0.93)

14. . . . focuses on friends or lovers (as opposed to family).

15. . . . involves a person with whom the source chose to have a relationship.

Relational Growth/Maintenance (alpha = 0.95)

16. . . . concerns how often the source and target can or will interact with one another.

17. . . . has to do with the potential for two people in a relationship to become closer to one another.

18. . . . reflects a concern for building/maintaining a relationship.

Specificity (alpha = 0.72)

19. . . . is concerned with specific issues in how a relationship will work rather than global matters (like will the relationship continue).

20. . . . refers to a concrete, material problem (e.g. money).

Note: Items followed by (R) were reflected.

A series of seven discriminant analyses was performed using the composite rating scales as predictors and the goal groupings as criterion variables. These analyses revealed that 68 percent of the cases were correctly classified for the five-group solution, 73 percent for the six-group, 73 percent for the seven-group, 70 percent for the eight-group, 71 percent for the nine-group, 73 percent for the ten-group, and 68 percent for the eleven-group. Inspection of the clusters in the various solutions showed that the seven-, eight-, nine-, and eleven-group solutions had at least one cluster which contained only one member. Since single-member clusters are undesirable because of the dangers inherent in generalizing from a single instance, attention was focused on the five- and six-group solutions. Although both were interpretable, classification efficiency was maximized in the six-group solution (73 percent). Hence, it was retained. Table 2 gives the results of that analysis. For each cluster, its component goal statements are listed along with their Euclidean distances from the cluster center.

T A B L E 2
Results of the Cluster Analyses: The Six-Group Solution

Cluster/Label	Euclidean Distance	Goal Statement (I Wanted . . .)
I. Give Advice (Lifestyle)	61.08	. . . the person to quit trying to pick a fight with my friends.
	62.14	. . . the person to buy a computer for the family.
	66.60	. . . my mother to start buying light salt instead of regular salt.
	69.20	. . . a close female friend to terminate a struggling relationship with her boyfriend.
	69.96	. . . my mom to relax, enjoy the sunshine, and sit and talk for awhile.
	70.19	. . . to convince my brother not to move to Texas to find a job.
	72.16	. . . to persuade my daughter to select a certain college.
	73.75	. . . my room-mate to go to summer school.
	77.84	. . . my younger sister to stop seeing her boyfriend.
	78.50	. . . the person to start an IRA (Individual Retirement Account).
	79.52	. . . to convince my younger brother not to drop out of high school, and to stay and earn his diploma.
	79.82	. . . Dave to be more realistic about his financial situation by moving into a less expensive apartment.
	79.89	. . . my father to reconcile his differences with my first cousin.
	79.90	. . . my son to pick up his room.
	80.98	. . . the person to run in a 5-mile run.
	82.10	. . . to convince someone to change majors.
	82.69	. . . him to take Spanish 4 in high school instead of starting another language.
	84.29	. . . my room-mate to return to her employer $30 which was accidentally paid to her.
II. Gain Assistance	60.66	. . . the person to stop giving me advice about my love life.
	64.89	. . . my girlfriend to type my paper.
	66.09	. . . the person to make an announcement over a PA system.

Cluster/Label	Euclidean Distance	Goal Statement (I Wanted . . .)
	67.29	. . . the person to leave a party and take me to another city so I could see my boyfriend.
	72.94	. . . to borrow $100 from my ex-boyfriend.
	74.55	. . . this person to fill out a questionnaire.
	78.58	. . . the person to give me a ride to the supermarket.
	78.89	. . . the Dean of Engineering to readmit me after I had been dropped.
III. Share Activity	45.61	. . . this person to call more often.
	56.13	. . . her to go to the restaurant of my choice.
	69.92	. . . this person to walk to the store with me.
	76.07	. . . this person to attend a movie.
	77.62	. . . the person to go to a party with me.
	78.59	. . . the person to go out to a bar with me for a few beers on the evening before her exam.
	79.22	. . . them to come over to my apartment to visit me.
	80.74	. . . the person to go out with me on a Thursday night.
IV. Change Political Stance	60.83	. . . the person not to participate in political demonstrations on campus.
	79.49	. . . the person to vote in a certain way.
	77.72	. . . the person to vote in the WSA elections, specifically for the High Tide party.
	84.81	. . . the person to vote for Reagan.
	85.84	. . . the person to vote for me in the fraternity's presidential election.
V. Give Advice (Health)	52.05	. . . my friend not to see someone because it was bad for my friend's mental health.
	61.17	. . . my room-mate to use some form of birth control because she is sexually active.
	64.40	. . . the person to stop smoking.
	65.60	. . . the person to see a doctor.
	73.13	. . . my room-mate to conform to a cleaner lifestyle.
	74.59	. . . my room-mate to stop drinking so much.
	79.26	. . . the person to stop using cocaine on such a heavy basis.
	76.96	. . . the person to stop smoking pot.
VI. Change Relationship	51.89	. . . the person to attend church with me on a regular basis.
	55.75	. . . two good friends to live with me next year in the apartment we are living in now.
	60.63	. . . my boyfriend to dress up more.
	63.64	. . . the person to go to Florida.
	71.42	. . . my room-mate to go out for a couple of beers
	76.09	. . . the person to buy something.
	78.58	. . . the person to stay in Madison this summer.
	79.66	. . . this person to stay in Madison for the summer of 1986.
	80.59	. . . my room-mate to stay in Madison for the summer rather than go home to Boston.
	80.60	. . . my father to approve of my idea to live in a different city this summer.
	81.55	. . . my room-mate to pay the utility bills on time so the service wouldn't be interrupted.

TABLE 3
Z-Scores of the Validation Scales by Goal Cluster

Scale	Goal Clusters					
	I	II	III	IV	V	VI
Source Benefit	−0.80	0.93	0.79	0.53	−0.66	0.36
Target Benefit	0.48	−1.25	−0.63	−0.81	1.34	−0.07
Group Benefit	0.07	−0.32	−0.89	1.28	0.62	−0.29
Publicness	−0.23	−0.44	0.35	1.25	−0.41	0.19
Normative Pressure	0.08	−0.69	−0.43	0.06	0.96	−0.04
Improvement	0.11	−0.34	−0.96	−0.19	1.52	−0.26
Voluntary Relationship	−0.70	0.09	0.81	−0.59	0.59	0.40
Relational Growth	−0.32	−0.69	0.69	−0.74	0.41	0.59
Specificity	0.01	−0.52	−0.14	−1.18	0.44	0.65
Proportion of Goals Sample (%)	32	14	14	9	14	19

Note: Table entries are *z*-scores. Labels for goal clusters are I = Give Advice (Lifestyle), II = Gain Assistance, III = Share Activity, IV = Change Political Stance, V = Give Advice (Health), and VI = Change Relationship.

> ### STATISTICAL SUMMARY 3
>
> Discriminant analysis is a statistical technique for describing group differences. If you have two or more groups and want to know if they differ on a series of variables, you might use discriminant analysis. For example, discriminant analysis can tell you if effective and ineffective groups differ in the amount of times they meet, the number of members, and the type of leadership. In Dillard's study, the analysis demonstrated that there were differences among the goal types.

Univariate analyses of variance were conducted using cluster membership as the independent variable and each of the nine validation variables as dependent variables. These analyses showed significant differences (at $p < 0.05$) across clusters for each of the nine variables. These latter findings are consistent with the expectation that people can, and probably do, distinguish goals on multiple dimensions.

To assist in interpretation of the clusters, each group's z-score on each of those nine variables

was computed. The results are presented in Table 3. Inspection of the z-scores in column one shows that the goals in Cluster I are low in source-benefit ($z = -0.80$), above average in target benefit ($z = 0.48$), and primarily directed at family members (voluntary relationship $= -0.70$). Because of the emphasis on how one should live, the cluster was given the name *Give Advice (Lifestyle)*.

Cluster II is characterized by the highest degree of source benefit of any of the clusters ($z = 0.93$) and the lowest degree of target benefit ($z = -1.25$). As the examples in Table 2 also show, goals in this group were oriented entirely toward gain for the source. Since this collection of goals appeared to be conceptually similar to Cody et al.'s (in press) *Gain Assistance* category, it was given the same label.

The set of goals in Cluster III is also high in source benefit ($z = 0.79$). However, in contrast to the previous cluster, this group focuses exclusively on targets in a voluntary relationship with the source, i.e. non-kin ($z = 0.81$), and on topics concerned with how to manage the shared activities in that relationship (relational growth, $z = 0.69$). In line with earlier work, this cluster was named *Share Activity*.

Two characteristics of Cluster IV set it off from the other clusters. It is high in group benefit ($z = 1.28$) and in publicness ($z = 1.25$). An examination of the content of the cluster shows that every one of the goals is concerned with convincing the target to engage in some politically related behavior. Cluster IV was given the label *Change Political Stance.*

The goals grouped into Cluster V are unique in their focus on convincing the target to eliminate some self-harmful behavior. They mention convincing the target to stop drinking, to stop smoking pot, and to stop using cocaine; all of which are health-related issues. In light of these features, it is not surprising that target benefit was perceived as high ($z = 1.34$), normative pressure as high ($z = 0.96$), and improvement as high ($z = 1.52$). This cluster was labeled *Give Advice (Health).*

The sixth and final cluster was similar to *Share Activity* in that its three highest, positive z-scores were on source benefit ($z = 0.36$), voluntary relationship ($z = 0.40$), and relational growth ($z = 0.59$). The difference between the two clusters appears to lie in the type of change that is sought. Whereas Cluster III goals focus on joint, short-term activities, the Cluster VI goals primarily represent longer-term matters that require continuous effort or one-time, major effort. Consequently, the last cluster was named *Change Relationship.*

When considering the names given to the clusters it is apparent that not every goal statement (item) is a perfect exemplar of the label, which should come as no surprise. Individual items are subject to a high degree of measurement error and may be 'incorrectly' assigned to clusters for that reason alone. Inspection of the clusters tends to confirm this—the items which pose the greatest difficulty in interpretation are generally those that are furthest from the cluster centers. Thus, labels for the clusters were *not* chosen purely on the basis of cluster content. Rather, the general theme was considered as well as the information provided by the ratings and the insights present in earlier studies.

Phase Four: Goals and Influence Messages

One of the assumptions laid out at the beginning of this paper was that goals cause planning to take place and that planning in turn guides action. With that in mind, the task of isolating different types of goals was undertaken. Implicit in such an activity is the claim that different types of goals engender different types of plans which then bring about different sorts of action, i.e. goals are related to actions. In the context of interpersonal influence, it is reasonable to expect that variations in goal type might show corresponding variations in the means used to achieve those goals.

Several investigations have attempted to uncover the perceptual dimensions that naive actors use to classify compliance-gaining messages (e.g. Falbo, 1977). Although the findings are not perfectly consistent across studies, there are some strong similarities which indicate the existence of at least three perceptual dimensions of influence messages: directness, positivity, and logic. *Directness* refers to the extent to which a message makes explicit the change that the source is seeking in the target. *Positivity* is the degree to which the positive outcomes associated with compliance or negative outcomes associated with noncompliance are specified. The third dimension, *logic,* reflects the presence of evidence and reason in the influence message. Each of these three aspects of influence messages were examined. It was predicted that variations in the form of influence messages would occur as a function of goal type.

Students enrolled in undergraduate classes at a large, midwestern university provided data for use in this study ($n = 295$). Outside of regularly scheduled class time, students responded to a questionnaire that asked them to focus on an influence attempt of their own initiation. Criteria for selecting the attempt were the same as those used in phase one. Participants provided open-ended descriptions of (1) their influence goal and (2) of the content of the interaction. They were

T A B L E 4
Z-Scores of the Message Variables by Goal Type

Message Variables	Goal Type					
	I	II	III	IV	V	VI
Directness	0.11	−0.25	−0.17	−0.47	0.22	0.34
Positivity	0.03	−0.28	−0.03	−0.30	0.10	0.45
Logic	0.07	−0.12	−0.23	−0.09	0.17	0.27
Proportion of Sample (%)	17	22	22	4	24	11

Note: Table entries are *z*-scores. Labels for goal types are I = Give Advice (Lifestyle), II = Gain Assistance, III = Share Activity, IV = Change Political Stance, V = Give Advice (Health), and VI = Change Relationship.

instructed to unitize their reports of the interaction by following an alternating series of prompts; 'First, you said:', 'Then, s/he said:', 'Next, you said:', and so on. Each prompt was followed by several blank lines for recording the actions of each interactant. Respondents were encouraged to be as descriptive as possible. Half of the questionnaires asked the participants to report on successful influence attempts ($n = 148$), while the other half asked for unsuccessful attempts ($n = 147$).

Each of the goal descriptions was coded by two of three trained judges into one of the six goal types isolated in the previous phase. Each judge coded two-thirds of the data set and each judge worked in tandem with the other judges on one-third of the data set. Cohen's kappas for the three pairings were 0.94, 0.97, and 0.87, indicating a very high degree of reliability among the judges. Disagreements were resolved by discussion. This procedure yielded a relative frequency distribution of goal types which is given in Table 4.

The interaction descriptions were each rated by three trained judges for directness, positivity, and logic. Each rater read the entire interaction description on three separate occasions, and after each reading, rendered a global judgment about the source's behavior for one of the variables. All judgments were made on five-point scales.

The directness rating reflected the extent to which the source was explicit in his or her request for behavioral change. If a source made a direct request immediately in the interaction it was rated as very direct. Interactions in which the source never made an explicit request, but only hinted at it, were judged low in directness. Cronbach's alpha for this dimension was 0.84.

Positivity judgments were made on the degree to which the source alluded to the positive or negative consequences which would result from the target's compliance (or lack thereof). References to desirable material or relational consequences were rated as positive, whereas references to aversive, unpleasant outcomes were rated as negative (i.e. low in positivity). Instances in which there were few or no references to any outcomes were judged as neutral. Cronbach's alpha for this dimension was 0.78.

Judgments regarding the use of logic were made on the degree to which the source employed plausible and compelling reasons in his or her influence attempt. Hints and direct requests exemplify a minimal use of logic, while offering several realistic and compelling reasons demonstrates a high degree of logic. Cronbach's alpha for this set of ratings was 0.86.

To provide an omnibus test of the extent to which variations in goal type predicted the three features of compliance-gaining messages, a multivariate multiple regression analysis was conducted. The six goal types were dummy coded and treated as predictors. The dependent variables were directness, positivity, and logic. Consistent with expectations, the analysis revealed a statistically reliable relationship between the two sets of variables. Wilks' lambda = 0.90, $F = 1.92$, d.f. = 15,792, $p < 0.05$. Multiple correlation coefficients for the univariate equations were 0.23 ($F = 3.47$, d.f. = 5,289, $p < 0.01$) for directness, 0.21 ($F = 2.87$, d.f. = 5,289, $p < 0.05$) for positivity, and 0.18 ($F = 1.96$, d.f. = 5,289, $p < 0.10$) for logic. A more finely grained picture of the variations in message use as a function of goal type emerges from the pattern of z-scores in Table 4.

STATISTICAL SUMMARY 4

Phase 4

Finally, multiple regression analyses were used. Multiple regression can be used to see if an outcome or criterion variable is related to a group of variables. For example, you might want to know how someone obtains high satisfaction from a conversation. Using multiple regression you can see if the factors of topic, length of conversation, nonverbal contact, and empathy affect satisfaction. The type of multiple regression used in this article, multivariate regression, shows the relationship between two different sets of variables. This analysis showed that the goals were related to the dependent variables (directness, positivity, and logic).

DISCUSSION

The first two research questions driving this investigation concerned the isolation and interpretation of types of influence goals common to close relationships. One heartening observation is that there is considerable convergence between the results of this study and previous efforts. Four of the six goal clusters are conceptually similar to groupings reported in Cody et al. (in press) and in Rule et al. (1985). In an attempt to prevent the proliferation of names/categories in the literature, Cody et al.'s labels for those four clusters have been adopted or slightly modified: Gain Assistance, Change Relationship, Give Advice (Health), and Share Activity. In contrast to these near-perfect matches is the Give Advice (Lifestyle) category. It is somewhat similar to Cody et al.'s Obtain Permission in its focus on family members, but has no apparent mate in the Rule et al. scheme. Finally, Change Political Stance is unique to the present study. Such differences as exist between the present findings and earlier work may be the result of this study's emphasis on close relationships or the focus on behavior change goals rather than persuasion goals. Further work, which broadened the sampling frame of both goals and people in close relationships, would provide even greater confidence that the goal types found in this and earlier studies are firmly grounded in the phenomenology of naive actors.

The third research question focused on the relationship between goals and action. Hence, the final phase of the investigation attempted to establish a link between the various goal types and three aspects of influence messages: directness, positivity, and logic. The data did, in fact, show reliable associations between communication behavior and different goal types. Such findings bring additional validation to the cluster analytic results as well as support to the general claim that goals impact the production of influence messages.

Attention to the specifics of the relationships between the goal types and the message variables is also warranted. As Table 4 shows, a Change Relationship goal produced messages that were relatively high on all three message variables: directness, positivity, and logic. The reliance on logic no doubt reflects the fact that this type of goal is important to the actor and consequently engenders relatively well-planned persuasive discourse. The high values of positivity and directness may be accounted for by noting that the desired change is in the direction of escalating the relationship rather than de-escalating. The presence of a Give Advice (Health) goal also corresponded to messages that were above average in directness, positivity, and logic. On this point, people apparently prefer to phrase their health-related advice positively (e.g. You'll live longer if you stop smoking) than negatively (e.g. You'll die if you don't stop smoking). The Gain Assistance, Change Political Stance, and Share Activity goals yielded messages that were below average in directness, positivity, and logic. This pattern implies that people attempt to realize these goals through the use of hints and other 'nonconventional instrumental requests' (Gordon & Ervin-Tripp, 1984). Often such messages are motivated by the desire to avoid the appearance of interfering with the autonomy of the target or by a concern for maintaining the source-target relationship. Understanding the substance of these and other concerns, and how they act in conjunction with influence goals to shape the message production process, is the next logical step in elaborating a goals–planning–action account of interpersonal influence.

Although the contribution of any single study is necessarily small, the present empirically driven effort has made a clear step towards illuminating the substance of influence goals in personal relationships. The isolation of perceptually based goal types, consideration of their attributes, and the examination of their linkage to communication provide some of the foundational material upon which a more theoretical account of interpersonal influence may be erected.

REFERENCES

Boster, F. J. & Stiff, J. B. (1984) 'Compliance-Gaining Message Selection Behavior', *Human Communication Research* 10: 539–56.

Cody, M. J., Canary, D. J. & Smith, S. W. (in press) 'Compliance-gaining Goals: An Inductive Analysis of Actors' Goal Types, Strategies, and Successes', in J. Daly & J. Wiemann (eds) *Communicating Strategically.* Hillsdale, NJ: Erlbaum.

Cody, M. J., Greene, J. O., Marston, P. J., O'Hair, H. D., Baaske, K. T., & Schneider, M. J. (1986) 'Situation Perception and Message Strategy Selection', in M. L. McLaughlin (ed.) *Communication Yearbook 9.* Beverly Hills, CA: Sage.

Dillard, J. P. & Fitzpatrick, M. A. (1985) 'Compliance-gaining in Marital Interaction', *Personality and Social Psychology Bulletin* 11: 419–33.

Falbo, T. (1977) 'Multidimensional Scaling of Power Strategies', *Journal of Personality and Social Psychology* 35:537–47.

Gordon, D. & Ervin-Tripp, S. (1984) 'The Structure of Children's Requests', in R. L. Schiefelbusch & J. P. Pickar (eds) *The Acquisition of Communicative Competence.* Baltimore, MD: University Park.

Hecht, M. L. (1984) 'Persuasive Efficacy: A Study of the Relationship among Type and Degree of Change, Message Strategies, and Satisfying Communication', *Western Journal of Speech Communication* 48: 373–89.

Hertzog, R. L. & Bradac, J. J. (1984) 'Perceptions of Compliance-gaining Situations: An Extended Analysis', *Communication Research* 11: 363–91.

Klinger, E. (1985) 'Missing Links in Action Theory', in M. Frese & J. Sabini (eds) *Goal Directed Behavior.* Hillsdale, NJ: Erlbaum.

Kipnis, D., Schmidt, S. M. & Wilkinson, J. (1980) 'Intraorganizational Influence Tactics: Explorations in Getting One's Way', *Journal of Applied Psychology* 65: 440–52.

Kruskal, J. B. & Wish, M. (1978) *Multidimensional Scaling.* Beverly Hills, CA: Sage.

Norusis, M. J. (1986) *Advanced Statistics: SPSS/PC+.* Chicago: SPSS.

Reither, F. (1981) 'Thinking and Acting in Complex Situations—A Study of Experts' Behavior', *Simulation and Games* 12: 125–40.

Rule, B. G., Bisanz, G. L. & Kohn, M. (1985) 'Anatomy of a Persuasion Schema: Target, Goals, and Strategies', *Journal of Personality and Social Psychology* 48: 1127–40.

Schank, R. C. & Abelson, R. P. (1977) *Scripts, Plans, Goals, and Understanding.* Hillsdale, NJ: Erlbaum.

Tracy, K. (1984) 'The Effect of Multiple Goals on Conversational Relevance and Topic Shift', *Communication Monographs* 51: 274–87.

COMPLIANCE-GAINING IN MARITAL INTERACTION: POWER BASES, PROCESSES, AND OUTCOMES

Hal Witteman and Mary Anne Fitzpatrick

Couples attempted to gain compliance from their spouses. Specific marital types were determined by using the Relational Dimensions Instrument (Fitzpatrick, 1977). Messages were coded into specific categories of compliance-gaining by the Verbal Interaction Compliance-Gaining Scheme. This scheme references the bases of power speakers use when attempting to gain compliance. The short term outcomes of the interactions were coded as to whether the husband or wife won and whether mutual resolution or no resolution was achieved. Log-linear analysis indicated that the various marital types utilized were found to have different patterns of compliance-gaining communication associated with them.

It has been argued that there is no more essential concept in the social sciences than *power* (Giddens, 1984; Russell, 1938). The concept of power has been particularly important in understanding the dynamics of various interpersonal relationships (Olson & Cromwell, 1975). Although few question the conceptual importance of power in social relationships, confusion has reigned about how to define and to measure it. Some argue that power is best conceived of as a static resource (Blau, 1964); others suggest defining power in terms of interaction outcomes (Pollard & Mitchell, 1972); still others focus on the interaction process (Ericson & Rogers, 1973). In this study, we examine the ability of individuals in ongoing relationships to influence the behavior of partners through their message choices. This influence process is often studied under the rubric of compliance-gaining.

Much research has centered on how individuals attempt to gain compliance (e.g., Clark, 1979; Cody, McLaughlin & Jordan, 1980; Miller,

Boster, Roloff & Seibold, 1977; Wiseman & Schenck-Hamlin, 1981) or to get others to do what they want (Wheeless, Barraclough & Stewart, 1983). Since individuals who live together under conditions of mutual interdependence must continuously adjust their behaviors to one another, attempts to gain compliance are undoubtedly frequent.

COMPLIANCE-GAINING IN MARITAL INTERACTION

Most prior research on compliance-gaining has relied on the self reports of individuals (see Wheeless et al., 1983 for a review). Both deductive (Cody, McLaughlin & Schneider, 1981; Fitzpatrick & Winke, 1977; Marwell & Schmitt, 1967; Miller et al., 1977) and inductive (Clark, 1979; Falbo, 1977) approaches to compliance-gaining have employed self report data. One purpose of this study was to develop a verbal interaction coding scheme for identifying what individuals in intimate ongoing relationships say in compliance-gaining situations.

The coding of compliance-gaining interaction can be greatly aided by carefully attending to existing conceptual schemes for classifying strategies or tactics. Of particular use is a recent review (Wheeless et al., 1983) of eight major compliance-gaining schemes. This review isolated the underlying similarities in the strategies described by the various authors. In the compliance-gaining literature, message types can be categorized into

Source: The Article is taken from *Communication Monographs* [53: 130–143, 1986]. Reprinted by permission of the Speech Communication Association, 5105 Backlick Rd., Annandale, VA 22003.

one of three broad classes of influence based on the different bases of power people have at their disposal.

First, messages can induce compliance because of the expectancies or consequences associated with interactants' behaviors. *Activity* and *Power* messages fall into this category. Activity messages stress the negative or positive outcomes an individual can expect by engaging in specific behaviors while Power messages emphasize the consequences of compliance or noncompliance. Second, messages can induce compliance because of the interactants' conception of the relationship and the requirements entailed by belonging to it. *Us, Direct,* and *Search* categories represent such messages. Third, messages can induce compliance because of the values or obligations held by interactants. *Me, You,* and *External* categories are based on how an interactant sees or values the self, the other, or things external to the relationship. Table 1 summarizes the eight categories of the Verbal Interaction Compliance-Gaining Scheme (VICS) and the exemplars used in coding each category.

This approach uses a sieve coding scheme because not all messages serve a persuasive function. A hierarchical coding scheme that first separates messages functioning to elicit compliance from other messages is employed. The first level of the VICS scheme codes messages as: Compliance, Refutation, Discount, Agreement, and Other.[1]

To study compliance-gaining message behaviors in marital interaction, we adopted a typological approach. The utility of typologies for studying close relationships has been argued extensively by Fitzpatrick and her colleagues (Fitzpatrick, 1977; 1984; Fitzpatrick & Indvik, 1982; Fitzpatrick & Badzinski, 1985). The typological approach assumes that different interaction styles are employed in different types of relationships (Fitzpatrick, 1983).

The polythetic typological scheme used in this study is based on three underlying conceptual dimensions: *Autonomy/Interdependence* stresses the connectedness of relational participants physically, temporally, and psychologically; *Conventional/Nonconventional Ideology* taps the beliefs,

standards, and values that participants hold concerning their relationships; and *Conflict Engagement/Conflict Avoidance* represents both the willingness of participants to engage in conflict and the degree of assertiveness between partners.

Based on these conceptual dimensions, three types of individual relational definitions have emerged: traditionals, separates, and independents. Traditionals hold conventional values about the relationship. These values emphasize stability as opposed to spontaneity. Traditionals exhibit interdependence, both physically and psychologically, and tend not to avoid conflict. Separates hold ambivalent views on the nature of relationships, report having the least interdependence, and avoid open marital conflict. Independents hold fairly nonconventional relational values and maintain some interdependence, yet not with respect to some of the physical and temporal aspects of their lives. Also, Independents report some assertiveness and tend to engage in conflict.

Couple types can be defined by combining the relational definitions of husbands and wives. Couples' rather than individuals' self reports and communication behaviors are compared and analyzed because the former are a more meaningful analytic unit. Prior research (Fitzpatrick, 1976, 1977, 1981, 1983; Fitzpatrick & Best, 1979; Fitzpatrick, Fallis & Vance, 1982; Fitzpatrick & Indvik, 1982; Fitzpatrick, Vance & Witteman, 1984; Sillars, Pike, Jones & Redmon, 1983) has shown that couple types can be discriminated on a number of self report and behavioral dimensions.

Despite extensive information concerning different perceptions and behaviors exhibited by various couple types, a consideration of power is conspicuously missing from the approach. Power is primarily tapped on the assertiveness factor of the RDI, which asks for an individual's assessment of how often he or she tries to persuade the spouse to do something. Because of minimal variability, assertiveness is the only factor of the RDI which has not consistently discriminated among couples. All individuals have stated that they are not very assertive towards their spouses.

Individuals in close relationships are often reluctant to discuss the role of power in their own

TABLE 1
Verbal Interaction Compliance-Gaining Scheme (VICS)

Referencing Expectancies/Consequents

I. ACTIVITY: Force to comply comes from the nature of the specific activity, the importance of the activity, or from the outcome of the activity.
  a. Positivity/Importance of Own Activity or Compromise.
  b. Negativity/Unimportance of Own Activity or Compromise.
  c. Positivity/Importance of Other's Activity or Compromise.
  d. Negativity/Unimportance of Other's Activity or Compromise.

II. POWER: Focus is on the exertion of control in the relationship. Control may be manifested in attempts to constrain behavior (both verbal and physical) and internal states or processes of either participant.
  a. Exclamations/Cursing.
  b. Constraining Other. Other's behavior is constrained either by actor or other.
  c. Constraining Self. Actor's behavior is constrained either by self or by other.

Invocation of Identification/Relationship

III. US: Force to comply comes from the relationship between the interactants.
  a. Identity. The focus is on the relationship's more stable characteristics.
  b. Internal. The focus is on the *needs* of the relationship.
  c. Feelings Between Spouses—Positive.
  d. Feelings Between Spouses—Negative.
  e. Names.

IV. DIRECT: Nonevaluative statement or question expressing past, current, or future activity or activities (excluding behavioral regularities of Me, You, or Us).
  a. Statement of Situation. *Direct* thought units that do not act as *Requests*.
  b. Direct Request for Compliance.

V. SEARCH: Information search in question form. Questions are evaluatively neutral.
  a. Relational/Self/Other Information.
  b. External Information.

Appeals to Values/Obligations

VI. ME: Force to comply comes from within the actor.
  a. Positive Self Casting. The focus is on the actor as a "good" person.
  b. Negative Self Casting. The focus is on the actor as a "bad" person.
  c. Identity. The focus is on the actor's stable characteristics.
  d. Internal. The focus is on the actor's transient characteristics.

VII. YOU: Force to comply comes from within the other.
  a. Positive Altercasting. The focus is on the target as a "good" person.
  b. Negative Altercasting. The focus is on the target as a "bad" person.
  c. Identity. The focus is on the target's stable characteristics.
  d. Internal. The focus is on the target's transient characteristics.

VIII. EXTERNAL: Focus to comply comes from a specific (enabling or disabling) agent(s) outside of the participants or their relationship.
  a. Time.
  b. Cultural/Moral/Social Norms.
  c. Third Parties.

marriages (Huston, 1983). In both self reports of ideological orientations to appropriate male and female behavior (Fitzpatrick & Indvik, 1982) and in typical interaction patterns for resolving conflict in their marriages (Williamson, 1983), indirect evidence has suggested that the bases of power and the techniques of influence differ for the various couple types. Furthermore, in studies of compliance-gaining tactics used by married couples, Kipnis, Castell, Gergen, and Mauch (1976) have found differences in reports of various types of husbands and wives about the likelihood they would use certain persuasive strategies.

THEORETICAL PREDICTIONS: POWER BASES, PROCESSES, AND OUTCOMES

To examine how various couple types seek compliance from one another in interaction, hypotheses for the couple type interactions at both levels of the coding scheme hierarchy will be generated. Research relevant to the first level of the coding scheme has indicated that Separates report avoiding conflict (Fitzpatrick, 1977). Separates have been shown behaviorally to avoid extreme control moves (Best, 1979; Williamson, 1983) and discussion of sensitive conflict topics (Sillars et. al., 1983). Thus, it seems reasonable to assume that Separates avoid unpleasant interactions and assertiveness in their marriages. Consequently:

H₁: *Separates will use fewer compliance messages than any other couple type.*

Independents tend not to avoid conflict (Fitzpatrick, 1977) and display more competitively symmetrical communication transactions (refusing control moves of the other) regardless of the importance of the issue under discussion (Best, 1979; Williamson, 1983). Independents are thus less likely to comply to persuasive attempts made by their partner. Thus:

H₂: *Independents will use more refutation and discount messages than any other couple type.*

The second level of the coding scheme focuses on the frequency of use of specific compliance-gaining messages by various couple types. Traditionals are concerned with relational stability and are expressive with their spouses (Fitzpatrick, 1977). Based on their self reports, Traditionals are the most well-adjusted and have less intense and fewer conflicts than other couple types (Fitzpatrick & Best, 1979). In interaction, Traditionals quickly concede control to the spouse in conversations about unimportant issues, but not when the issue is perceived to be important (Best, 1979). Traditionals rely on intense control moves only in serious conflict discussions (Williamson, 1983). The Traditionals' communication style is flexible, and while these couples are likely to seek compliance, they are not likely to employ messages that would disrupt the stability of the relationship, threaten the other, or raise doubts about the spouse's values. Since Power messages are quite threatening, when referencing expectancies or consequences as a means to gain compliance from their spouse, Traditionals would be more likely to use the *Activity* than *Power* messages.

Traditional couples know how the other is likely to perceive the relationship and what values each holds (Fitzpatrick, 1984). For this reason, Traditionals should avoid the message categories most likely to raise doubts about the other's beliefs. In referencing the identification between partners or the relationship between them, Traditionals will thus be less likely to use *Us* strategies. In discussing values and obligations, Traditionals will similarly be unlikely to use the *Me* or *You* messages. The value orientations of Traditional couples are not only shared, but also are relatively stable and predictable. Given the nature of their values and the presumption of understanding with which Traditionals typically operate, we expect they would rely heavily on *Direct* messages. When Traditionals wish to invoke the relationship as a basis of power, a Direct message allows the major premise to be unspoken. Traditionals have little need to reinforce verbally the shared and stable value orientations each hold. Consequently:

H₃: *Traditionals will use less Power, Us, Me, You, and more Activity and Direct messages than other couple types.*

Separates report they avoid conflict (Fitzpatrick, 1977), experience less satisfaction with the relationship (Fitzpatrick & Best, 1979), and are the least accurate in predicting one another (Fitzpatrick, 1984). Separates use fewer competitively symmetrical transactions (Best, 1979), give in to the other's relational control attempts regardless of topic saliency (Williamson, 1983), and are more likely to deny verbally the existence of conflict than other couple types (Sillars et al., 1983).

The Separates' style can be characterized as one of avoidance. Since Separates avoid extended discussions with the spouse on any issue, they will rely on those strategies that require minimal discussion time when seeking compliance: *Power* in the expectancy class and *External* in the obligation class. Power entails little discussion because it involves a strong demand for compliance. External messages require little discussion because they symbolically remove the issue from the hands of the spouse.

By the same reasoning, Separates will be unlikely to use Search messages that may involve the Separate in extended discussion. Furthermore, because of their emotional divorcement, Separates are unlikely to use relationship/identification messages. They particularly are unlikely to use *Us,* which implies a direct identification with the relationship. Thus:

H₄: *Separates will use less Us, Direct, and Search and more Power and External messages than other couple types.*

Independents favor change over stability, tend not to avoid conflict (Fitzpatrick, 1977), and employ more competitive symmetrical communication (Best, 1979) in conflict discussions regardless of topic saliency (Williamson, 1983). Independents are expected to engage actively in compliance-gaining communication. This engagement style is structured around intense messages, such as *Power* messages in the expectancy/ consequence class.

The powerful identification of Independents with one another should lead to greater reliance on messages that invoke the relationship as a means of influence. While Traditionals are likely to leave unspoken the major relational premise of their compliance-gaining attempts, Independents are renegotiating their relational roles continuously. Since Independents "agree to disagree," they are likely to employ messages that appeal to the state of the relationship, that seek out information about the relationship and the other, and that request compliance from the other: the *Us, Search,* and *Direct* messages found in the relationships influence class. Given their ideological

commitment to freedom, however, Independents are expected *not* to employ appeals based on values or obligations. Therefore:

H₅: *Independents will use less Me, You, and External and more Power, Us, Direct, and Search messages than other couple types.*

Separate/Traditionals are the most ideologically conservative of the couple types in terms of appropriate family values (Fitzpatrick & Indvik, 1982) and report a level of marital satisfaction as high as the Traditionals (Fitzpatrick & Best, 1979). No specific predictions can be made concerning the degree to which Separate/ Traditionals use the expectancy/consequences messages. In the relationship/identification class, Separate/Traditionals are likely to use more *Us* and less *Search* strategies because they are concerned and have opinions about the relationship, but to avoid asking the opinions of the spouse (Fitzpatrick et al., 1984). These couples are likely to reference values when seeking compliance since both spouses maintain similar orientation toward important family values. Although Separate/Traditionals openly discuss their opinions and thoughts with one another, they do not presume to understand one another (Fitzpatrick et al., 1984). In attempting to gain compliance, Separate/Traditionals are then more likely to use *Me* and *You* messages rather than *External* ones when referencing values/obligations. Thus:

H₆: *Separate/Traditionals will use less Search and more Me, You, and Us messages than other couple types.*

Little is known about other Mixed types, so no specific hypotheses are generated concerning their compliance-gaining behavior.

METHOD

Sample

Couples randomly drawn from lists of married students living in university housing and a small number of couples who had participated in Marriage Encounter Weekends participated in this study. The total sample included 51 couples. One couple was later dropped because of a recording equipment malfunction. The mean length of marriage was 7.8 years (range, < 1 year to 33 years). Mean age of husbands was 31.7 (range, 22 to 57 years), and of wives 30.4 (range, 21 to 55 years). The average number of children was two. Combined annual income ranged from less than $5,000 to over $25,000. The distribution of frequencies in this sample of the three Pure types, the Separate/Traditionals, and the Mixed types does not differ significantly (χ^2, 4 df = 7.16, p > .05) from those found in a major random sample of couple types (Fitzpatrick & Indvik, 1982). A complete description of the sample and procedures used in this experiment can be found in Vance (1981).

Laboratory Procedure and Coding of Data

After a 10 minute conversation, couples were asked to carry out two role plays, each requiring 15 minutes. The role play situations were chosen to represent areas of conflict that occur in most marriages at some time. One role play was concerned with sharing time together and the other was concerned with the manner of bringing new friends into the relationship.[2] Before each role play began, interviewers helped make the role plays conform as much as possible to the overall structure of the couple's relationship and interaction style. Each person was asked who in the marriage was more likely to want to spend time with the other or who was more likely to wish to bring new friends into the relationship. Roles for husband and wife were assigned on the basis of these rather extensive probes (Gottman, 1979, pp. 138–140). After the coaching session, couples were brought into a simulated living room and instructed to try to gain compliance from the other spouse for the course of action they had chosen. Compliance-gaining conversations were videotaped and subsequently transcribed.

Initial analyses of the conversations revealed that spouses often employed more than one strategy within a speaking turn and even within

a sentence. Consequently, we opted for the psychological thought unit, rather than the sentence or speaking turn, as the basic unit of compliance-gaining. Results from various types of discourse studies (cued recalls, free recall, reading time and recall, and priming) reveal the existence of cognitive processing schemas focused on the understanding and processing of psychological thought units (van Dijk & Kintsch, 1983). Psychological thought units are the most basic level at which verbal compliance-gaining messages are produced and processed.

The coding scheme was developed in a hierarchial manner.[3] The first step in developing the VICS was to unitize the data. Unitizing reliability for the thought units was .95 (Guetzkow, 1950).[4] The second step involved coding the thought units into one of five main categories. Cohen's kappas (1960) were: Comply (.74), Refute (.69), Discount (.65), Agree (.80), and Other (.73). The third step involved the coding of the Compliance category into eight specific compliance-gaining message types. We added the message type Compromise at this point because verbal offers of compromise were prevalent in this data set.[5] The overall Cohen's kappa was .79 and figures ranged from a high of .91 for the Search category to a low of .62 for the Us category.

As a final developmental step, we partially validated the scheme by comparing the frequency of use of these strategies with the outcome of the exchanges between partners. Previous research has indicated that an important dimension of compliance-gaining situations is that of long term versus short term consequences (Miller et al., 1977). We focused on the short term outcome of marital compliance gaining with the expectation that the VICS scheme will be differentially related to the various outcomes of the role play. In these experimental role plays, it is possible that: The husband wins; the wife wins; both mutually resolve the situation; or that no resolution takes place. Agreement for coding the role play outcomes was .87.

Couple types were generated from the individual scores on the Relational Dimensions Instrument (Fitzpatrick & Indvik, 1982). The means of each subscale for each respondent were input into a linear typal analysis program (Overall & Klett, 1972). In this sample, there were 13 Traditionals, 10 Separates, six Independents, five Separate/Traditionals, and 17 Mixed types. For the particular clustering of the couples in this study see Vance (1981).

Data Analysis

As a manipulation check, couples' perceptions of the two major role plays were compared. Findings indicated that couples perceived both role plays as being moderately natural, comfortable, important, and similar to real life situations. The correlated *t*-tests using a conservative alpha level (.01) indicated that there were no differences between role plays on: naturalness, comfortableness, importance, and similarity. The role plays were therefore combined for the subsequent analyses.

The average frequency counts for each communication category were analyzed using log-linear analysis (Bishop, Feinberg & Holland, 1975; Kennedy, 1983). Since we were interested in seeing if couple types use different patterns of communication, we focused on models involving couple types. All of these models contain sex, couple type, and communication category main effects. All models also contain a sex by couple type interaction because this interaction is automatically fixed by sampling plan (see Swafford, 1980). Beyond this interaction, the models of interest contain: just the communication category main effect; the sex by communication category interaction; the couple type by communication category interaction; and both the sex by communication and couple type by communication category interactions.

A number of criteria were used to select the best fitting model. The first was based on the probability level of the model. The appropriate level of probability for the best fitting model ranges from anything over .05, as implied by Brown (1983) and Kennedy (1983), to between .10 to .35 (Knoke & Burke, 1980). We used the latter more conservative standard to achieve a

---

STATISTICAL SUMMARY 1

Log-linear analysis is a statistical technique for testing whether three or more variables are associated or related to each other. It is used with variables that have categories (e.g., ethnicity might have African American, white American, Mexican American; gender includes male and female; and income might have high, medium, and low), and shows you if the category of each variable tends to occur more frequently together (e.g., African American, female, low income). Log-linear analysis is sensitive to the variables included, and different results will be found if one includes or excludes a certain variable.

Witteman and Fitzpatrick used log-linear analysis to see if couple type, sex, type of communication, and outcomes or effects were related to each other. The first analysis (Level 1) showed that couple type was, in fact, related to the type of communication (Compliance, Refutation, Discount, Agreement, Other messages) between couples, although not all of the hypotheses were supported. Independents used more Refutation and Discount messages.

The second analysis (Level 2) showed that couple type was also related to the specific type of comments made (see I–VIII in Table 1). The findings provided some support for Hypotheses 3 to 6, although not all of the findings were consistent. Traditional couples used proportionally fewer Me, You, and Power messages, and more Activity and Direct messages. Separates used less Search, Us, and Direct, and more External messages. Independents used fewer External messages and more Search messages. Separates and Independents both used more Power messages than Traditionals.

The final log-linear analysis took into account the actual outcome of the interaction. Here, results showed that the strongest relationships were between sex and type of communication, and between type of communication and the outcome. Couple type did not play a role in determining the outcome. Winners used more Activity, Direct, and Search strategies than losers, and husbands used proportionally more "Us" messages than wives. Compliance was gained by people who showed the positive and/or negative aspects of the activity, and who used questions and nonevaluative statements to gain information or ask for compliance.

moderately robust and yet parsimonious model to explain the data. If no model fell within this range, the model with a level of probability above and closest to .35 was selected. This again ensured that the more parsimonious model was selected. In addition, only the model that added a significant component chi-square (G^2) was accepted as the best fitting model.

Once the best fitting model had been selected, the respective Freeman-Tukey deviates for the best fitting model were examined. The deviates for this model were tested for significance at the $p < .001$ significance level (Bishop et al., 1975). The pattern of Freeman-Tukey deviates was examined to determine if the hypotheses were statistically supported. As a validation for the coding scheme, we tested a number of models based on outcome type using log-linear analysis. The best fitting model was chosen with the same criteria employed for hypothesis testing.

RESULTS
Couple Types at Level One of VICS

Log-linear analysis (Table 2) indicates that the model containing the category by couple type interaction is a better-fitting model than one including only the communication categories. Examination of the Freeman-Tukey deviates (Table 3) indicates that Hypothesis 1, which predicts Separates will use fewer compliance-gaining messages than other couple types, is not supported by the data. Hypothesis 2, which predicts that Independents will use more Refutation and Discount messages than other couple types, is supported. The greater frequency of use of these strategies by Independents suggests that Independent couples debate one another relatively intensely.

TABLE 2
Log-Linear Analysis of Couple Types at Level One of VICS

Model*	df	Likelihood Ratio χ^2	ρ	df	G^2	p
ST × C	36	58.65	.01			
ST × SC	32	51.65	.02	4	7.00	>.05
ST × TC	20	17.79	.60	12	33.86	<.01
ST × SC × TC	16	10.72	.82	4	7.07	>.05

*S = sex, T = couple type, and C = communication categories (Comply, Refute, Discount, Agree, and Other).

TABLE 3
Proportions of Messages Used at Level One of VICS by Couple Type[a]

Message	Traditional	Separate	Couple Type Independent	Separate/Traditional	Mixed
Comply	.18(+)*	.20(+)*	.19(−)*	.22	.21
Refute	.16(−)*	.22(+)*	.29(+)*	.13(−)*	.20
Discount	.13(−)*	.24(+)*	.35(+)*	.12(−)*	.17(−)*
Agree	.18	.17(−)*	.16(−)*	.27(+)*	.23(+)*
Other	.16(−)*	.17(−)*	.22(+)*	.26(+)*	.19(−)*

[a]The proportions sum to one across the rows of the table. These indicate differences among the couple types in their usage of messages. An asterisk signifies the Freeman-Tukey deviates associated with the frequency in each cell is $p < .001$. Positive or negative signs in parentheses indicate whether the observed value is more or less, respectively, than that expected by chance.

Couple Types at Level Two of VICS

Log-linear analysis (Table 4) indicates the model that includes the category by couple type interaction is a better-fitting model than one only including the communication categories. The Freeman-Tukey deviates (Table 5) for this model reveal general support for the hypotheses. Specifically, Hypothesis 3 predicted that Traditionals would use relatively fewer Me, You, Us, and Power and more Activity and Direct messages than other couple types. Except for Us messages,

results confirm this hypothesis. Hypothesis 4 predicted that Separates would use less Search, Us, and Direct and more Power and External messages than other couple types. The results confirm this hypothesis. Hypothesis 5 predicted that Independents would use fewer Me, You, and External and more Search, Us, Direct, and Power messages than other couple types. The findings partially confirm this hypothesis. Independents do use fewer Me and External and more Power and Search messages. Conversely, however, Independents are significantly less likely to employ

TABLE 4
Log-Linear Analysis of Couple Types at Level Two of the VICS

Model*	df	Likelihood Ratio χ^2	ρ	df	G^2	p
ST × C	72	101.12	.01			
ST × SC	64	79.13	.09	8	21.99	<.05
ST × TC	40	46.89	.21	24	32.24	>.05
ST × SC × TC	32	26.73	.73	8	20.16	<.05

*S = sex, C = communication categories, and T = couple type.

TABLE 5
Proportions of Messages Used at Level Two of VICS by Couple Type[a]

Message	Couple Type				
	Traditional	Separate	Independent	Separate/Traditional	Mixed
Expectancies					
Activity	.26(+)*	.19(−)*	.16(−)*	.16(−)*	.22(+)*
Power	.15(−)*	.25(+)*	.24(+)*	.11(−)*	.26(+)*
Relationship					
Us	.17	.16(−)*	.14(−)*	.33(+)*	.21
Direct	.20(+)	.19(−)*	.18(−)*	.21(−)*	.23(+)*
Search	.20(+)*	.17(−)*	.24(+)*	.18(−)*	.22(+)*
Values					
Me	.14(−)*	.20	.19(−)*	.29(+)*	.18(−)*
You	.14(−)*	.22(+)*	.20(+)*	.29(+)*	.15(−)*
External	.17(−)*	.26(+)*	.17(−)*	.22	.18(−)*

[a]The proportions sum to one across the rows of the table. These indicate differences among the couple types in their usage of the compliance-gaining messages. An asterisk signifies the Freeman-Tukey deviates associated with the frequency in each cell is $p <$ .001. Positive or negative signs in parentheses indicate whether the observed value is more or less, respectively, than that expected by chance.

Us and Direct messages as references to the relationship when seeking compliance and are more likely to reference values and obligations by using You messages. Finally, Hypothesis 6 predicted that Separate/Traditionals use fewer Search and more Me, You, and Us messages than other couple types. Results confirm this hypothesis and further indicate that Separate/Traditionals use fewer Activity and Power messages than other couple types. Finally, the Mixed types were found to reference both expectancies and the relationship, but not values, when attempting to achieve compliance.

VICS Validation

Log-linear analysis (Table 6) indicates that the model containing the sex by communication category and the outcome by communication category interactions is the best-fitting model. Examination of the Freeman-Tukey deviates (Table 7) indicates that the coding scheme does discriminate outcome types by the use of compliance messages by husbands and wives.

TABLE 6
Log-Linear Analysis of Outcome Type at Level Two of VICS

Model*	df	Likelihood Ratio χ^2	p	df	G^2	p
SO × C	56	90.65	.00			
SO × SC	48	67.00	.04	8	23.65	<.05
SO × OC	32	49.87	.02	16	17.13	>.05
SO × SC × OC	24	22.93	.52	8	26.94	<.05

*S = sex, C = communication categories, and O = outcome type.

TABLE 7
Proportions of Messages Used at Level Two of VICS by Outcome Type[a]

	Outcome Type							
	Wife Wins		Husband Wins		Mutual Resolution		No Resolution	
Messages	Wife	Husband	Wife	Husband	Wife	Husband	Wife	Husband
Expectancies								
Activity	.22(+)*	.19(+)*	.16(−)*	.32(+)*	.34(+)*	.26(+)*	.28(−)*	.23(−)*
Power	.20	.12(−)*	.24(+)*	.29	.17(−)*	.17(−)*	.39(+)*	.42(+)*
Relationship								
Us	.11(−)*	.16	.57(+)*	.37(+)*	.11(−)*	.16(−)*	.21(−)*	.32(+)*
Direct	.24(+)*	.16(−)*	.12(−)*	.34(+)*	.30(+)*	.24(+)*	.35	.27(−)*
Search	.22(+)*	.15(−)*	.20(−)*	.33(+)*	.26(+)*	.23	.32(−)*	.30
Value								
Me	.20	.22(+)*	.23(+)*	.23(−)*	.22(−)*	.25(+)*	.36(+)*	.31(+)*
You	.20	.19(+)*	.12(−)*	.30	.20(−)*	.16(−)*	.47(+)*	.35(+)*
External	.17(−)*	.21(+)*	.20	.39(+)*	.20(−)*	.14(−)*	.43(+)*	.27(−)*
Compromise	.21(+)*	.19(+)*	.24(+)*	.24(−)*	.29(+)*	.31(+)*	.27(−)*	.26(−)*

[a]The proportions sum to one across the rows of the table for husband or wife proportions. These indicate differences among outcome types by husbands and wives in the usage of the compliance-gaining messages. An asterisk signifies the Freeman-Tukey deviates associated with the frequency in each cell is $p < .001$. Positive or negative signs in parentheses indicate the observed value is more or less, respectively, than that expected by chance.

When one looks at who won regardless of sex, winners tended to use relatively more Activity strategies in the expectancies influence class and more Direct and Search strategies in the relationship/identification influence class. In addition, husbands who win use relatively more Us messages. Thus, appealing to the positive or negative nature of the activity and seeking information to use for future compliance attempts are associated with actually gaining compliance. Those who ultimately give in completely to the compliance-gaining attempts of the spouse, regardless of sex, use relatively fewer Direct and Search and relatively more Me and Compromise messages. Males who give in use relatively more message types that appeal to values and obligations. Females who give in use more Power and Us messages. Thus, messages in all three influence classes can be used to discriminate those who gain compliance from those who surrender to compliance attempts.

Individuals who are involved in a mutual resolution of the role play use more Compromise messages and fewer Power, Us, You, and External messages. Finally, couples involved in a compliance-gaining outcome where no resolution is achieved use more Power, Me, and You messages, and relatively fewer Compromise messages. Thus, it appears our coding scheme can validly discriminate among outcomes in persuasive situations.

DISCUSSION

Three general conclusions emerge from this study. First, couple types as defined by the Relational Dimensions Instrument rely on different power bases when attempting to gain compliance from their spouses. For instance, Traditionals reference expectancies in their attempts to gain compliance. Given the shared conventional value orientation of these couples and their fairly high levels of openness, Traditionals can discuss the expected positive and negative outcomes of a given course of action. This shared value orientation, however, does not result in the Traditionals using any message category in the values/

obligations class. Rather, Traditional couples use the relationship as a basis of power.

Separates avoid using identification or relationally based messages when seeking compliance from their spouses and tend to focus on the negative consequences of noncompliance. The messages of the Separates are blatant attempts to constrain the behavior, and in some cases even the internal states of their spouses. The emergent picture of this relational type is a richer, more multifaceted one than the sketches drawn in previous research. Separates are not without affect in their interactions, but instead have a guerrilla-like communication style that demands acquiescence from the spouse without verbally staying to fight the whole battle.

The Independents are the only couple type that use all three bases of power when seeking spousal compliance, albeit a restricted range of message types within each class. Contrary to our predictions, the Independents do appeal to obligations and values by referencing the values of the other. Overall, Independents employ a wider variety of power bases in their messages than do other couple types.

The compliance-gaining style of the Separate/Traditionals stresses values and obligations; expectancies and consequences are not referenced; and opinions about the relationship are provided, yet not sought. Other Mixed types use compliance-gaining styles where values and obligations are not discussed, relying instead on references to the consequences of noncompliance and to the characteristics of their relationships. This difference occurs because the couples have, by definition, varying orientations toward salient relational values.

The second general conclusion emerging from this research is that the use of different compliance-gaining messages leads to different interaction outcomes. Curiously, the compliance-gaining literature rarely focuses on the conditions leading to successful and unsuccessful compliancegaining. In searching for the conditions under which communicators are likely to choose certain strategies, researchers have lost sight of the basic question of the effectiveness of these strategies.

This study provides some beginning answers to the latter question.

We construe this concern with outcomes broadly and would like to see variables other than the interaction specific ones of win, lose, or mutually resolve incorporated in future research. A broader concern for the effects of compliance (noncompliance) on the communicator, the relationship, and the utilization of other forms of persuasion (Kipnis et al., 1976) is needed. In many theoretical discussions, power is defined as the actual, not the potential achievement of ends. Current research does not reflect the richness of our theoretical perspectives on the nature and use of power in intimate relationships.

The third general conclusion to be drawn from this study concerns the utility of the self report schemes of various compliance-gaining message types. These schemes have isolated major possible verbal avenues individuals can travel to achieve compliance. These schemes thus begin to define the potential range of persuasive strategies at the disposal of the communicator and offer a useful starting point for developing a verbal coding scheme. Note, however, that the most frequently utilized compliance-gaining message type across this sample of husbands and wives (Dillard & Fitzpatrick, 1984) is the simple direct request. Furthermore, this relatively straightforward message led to either a mutually satisfying outcome or victory in the role play by the communicator who used it. The frequent use of direct requests of a spouse for compliance and their general effectiveness as a compliance-gaining strategy suggest that our theories of persuasion may be more complex and byzantine than those implicit theories implied by the actual repertoire of messages used by communicators.

NOTES

1. In this coding scheme, the main category of Compliance can be thought of as any verbal compliance-gaining message not in agreement with what the other has said (the category of Agreement), that does not negate the other's Compliance message in the immediately previous speaking turn (category of Refutation), that does not negate the other's Refutation

message in the immediately previous speaking turn (category of Discount), and that is not coded Other. Simply put, refutations are best represented by messages indicating "I don't want to comply," "I disagree," or "No" in response to a message in the other's previous speaking turn. Discounts are best represented by messages indicating "You can comply," or "I disagree," in response to the other's Refutation messages. Finally, Agreement is best indicated by messages indicating "I agree," or "I accept," to the other's request for compliance, to the other's negation of one's own request, or to the other's negation of one's own negation of the other's request. Other was a necessary category because of the number of uninterpretable mumbles and fillers such as "You know," and "Ah."

2. The role plays are the same ones used by Gottman (1979), and are available from the first author.

3. We wish to thank Corbin Hunter and Beth Tenney whose assistance in coding the data helped make this study possible.

4. Rules for unitizing the interaction were adapted from Stiles's (1978) directions for coding thought units. Stiles's rules had to be modified since they are based on coding structured question-answer interviews, not on free-wheeling interaction containing grunts, false starts, incomplete sentences, and run-on sentences.

5. At this time, the authors noted that messages related to negotiating the outcome of the role play occurred with such frequency that it was necessary to include such negotiations in the second-level coding scheme. Compromise messages are those that focus on a mutually satisfying activity or activities that could be carried out. Included here are any messages focusing on the form of the activity or activities to be performed, any scheduling of the activities, and any definition of the conditions under which the activity or activities would be carried out.

REFERENCES

Best, P. (1979). Communication control patterns in relational types. Unpublished masters thesis, University of Wisconsin-Milwaukee.

Bishop, Y. M., Feinberg, S. E., & Holland, P. W. (1975). *Discrete multivariate analysis.* Cambridge, MA: MIT Press.

Blau, P. (1964). *Exchange and power in social life.* New York: John Wiley.

Brown, M. B. (1983). Frequency tables. In W. J. Dixon (Ed.), *BMDP statistical software* (pp. 143–206). Berkeley, CA: Regents of California.

Clark, R. A. (1979). The impact of self-interest and desired liking on selection of persuasive strategies. *Communication Monographs, 46,* 257–273.

Cody, M. J., McLaughlin, M. L., & Jordan, W. J. (1980). A multidimensional scaling of three sets of compliance-gaining strategies. *Communication Quarterly, 28,* 34–46.

Cody, M. J., McLaughlin, M. L., & Schneider, M. J. (1981). The impact of intimacy and relational consequences on the selection of interpersonal persuasion tactics: A reanalysis. *Communication Monographs, 29,* 91–106.

Cohen, J. (1960). A coefficient of agreement for nominal scales. *Educational and Psychological Measurement, 20,* 37–46.

Dillard, J. P., & Fitzpatrick, M. A. (1984). The short and long term outcomes of compliance gaining in marital interaction. Paper presented at the annual meeting of the International Communication Association, San Francisco.

Ericson, P. M., & Rogers, E. L. (1973). New procedures for analyzing relational communication. *Family Process, 12,* 245–267.

Falbo, T. A. (1977). A multidimensional scaling of power strategies. *Journal of Personality and Social Psychology, 35,* 537–547.

Fitzpatrick, M. A. (1976). A typological approach to communication in relationships. Unpublished doctoral dissertation, Temple University.

Fitzpatrick, M. A. (1977). A typological approach to communication relationships. In B. D. Ruben (Ed.), *Communication yearbook 1* (pp. 263–275). New Brunswick, NJ: Transaction.

Fitzpatrick, M. A. (1981). Directions for interpersonal communication research. In G. I. Friedrich (Ed.), *Education in the 80's: Speech communication* (pp. 73–81). National Education Association: Washington, D.C.

Fitzpatrick, M. A. (1983). Predicting couples' communication from couples' self-reports. In R. N. Bostrom & B. H. Westley (Eds.), *Communication yearbook 7* (pp. 49–82). Beverly Hills, CA: Sage Publishers.

Fitzpatrick, M. A. (1984). A typological approach to marital interaction: Recent theory and research. In L. Berkowitz (Ed.), *Advances in experimental social psychology* (Vol. 18, pp. 2–47). New York: Academic Press.

Fitzpatrick, M. A., & Badzinski, D. (1985). All in the family: Communication in kin relationships. In M. Knapp & G. R. Miller (Eds.), *Handbook of interpersonal communication* (pp. 687–736). Beverly Hills, CA: Sage Publishers.

Fitzpatrick, M. A., & Best, P. (1979). Dyadic adjustment in traditional, independent, and separate relationships: A validation study. *Communication Monographs, 46,* 167–178.

Fitzpatrick, M. A., Fallis, S., & Vance, L. (1982). Multifunctional coding of conflict resolution strategies in marital dyads. *Family Relations, 37,* 611–670.

Fitzpatrick, M. A., & Indvik, J. (1982). The instrumental and expressive domains of marital communication. *Human Communication Research, 8,* 195–213.

Fitzpatrick, M. A., Vance, L. E., & Witteman, H. (1984). Interpersonal communication in the casual interaction of marital partners. *Journal of Language and Social Psychology, 3,* 81–95.

Fitzpatrick, M. A., & Winke, J. (1979). You always hurt the one you love: Strategies and tactics in interpersonal conflict. *Communication Quarterly, 27,* 3–11.

Giddens, A. (1984). *The constitution of society.* Berkeley, CA: University of California Press.

Gottman, J. M. (1979). *Martial interaction.* New York: Academic Press.

Guetzkow, H. (1950). Unitizing and categorizing problems in coding qualitative data. *Journal of Clinical Psychology, 6,* 47–58.

Huston, T. L. (1983). Power. In H. H. Kelley, E. Berscheid, A. Christensen, J.H. Harvey, T. J. Huston, G. Levinger, E. McClintock, L. A., Peplau & D. R. Peterson, *Close relationships* (pp. 169–219). New York: Freeman.

Kennedy, J. J. (1983). *Analyzing qualitative data.* New York: Praeger.

Kipnis, D., Castell, P., Gergen, M., & Mauch, D. (1976). Metamorphic effects of power. *Journal of Applied Psychology, 61,* 127–135.

Knoke, D., & Burke, P. J., (1980). *Log-linear models.* Beverly Hills, CA: Sage Publishers.

Marwell, G., & Schmitt, D. R. (1967). Dimensions of compliance-gaining behaviors: An empirical analysis. *Sociometry, 30,* 350–364.

Miller, G., Boster, F., Roloff, M., & Seibold, D. (1977). Compliance-gaining message strategies: A typology and some findings concerning effects of situational differences. *Communication Monographs, 44,* 37–51.

Olson, D. H., & Cromwell, R. E. (1975). Power in families. In R. E. Cromwell & D. H. Olson (Eds.), *Power in families* (pp. 3–14). New York: John Wiley & Sons.

Overall, J. E., & Klett, C. J. (1972). *Applied multivariate analysis.* New York: McGraw-Hill.

Pollard, W. E., & Mitchell, T. R. (1972). Decision theory analysis of social power. *Psychological Bulletin, 78,* 433–446.

Russell, B. (1938). *Power: A new social analysis.* New York: W. W. Norton.

Sillars, A. L., Pike, G. H., Jones, T. S., & Redman, K. (1983). Communication and conflict in marriage. In R. N. Bostrom & B. H. Westley (Eds.), *Communication yearbook 7* (pp. 414–431). Beverly Hills, CA: Sage Publishers.

Stiles, W. B. (1978). *Manual for a taxonomy of verbal response modes.* Chapel Hill, NC: Institute for Research in Social Science.

Swafford, M. (1980). Three parametric techniques for contingency table analysis: A non-technical commentary. *American Sociological Review, 45,* 664–690.

van Dijk, T. A., & Kintsch, W. (1983). *Strategies of discourse comprehension.* New York: Academic Press.

Vance, L. E. (1981). Dimensions of autonomy-interdependence reflected in casual marital interactions. Unpublished masters thesis, University of Wisconsin-Madison.

Wheeless, L. R., Barraclough, R., & Stewart, R. (1983). Compliance gaining and power in persuasion. In R. N. Bostrom & B. H. Westley (Eds.), *Communication yearbook 7* (pp. 105–145). Beverly Hills, CA: Sage Publishers.

Williamson, R. (1983). Relational control and communication in marital types. Unpublished doctoral dissertation, University of Wisconsin-Madison.

Wiseman, R., & Schenck-Hamlin, W. J. (1981). A multidimensional scaling validation of an intuitively derived set of compliance-gaining strategies. *Communication Monographs, 48,* 251–270.

CHAPTER 6 ⊙

Interpersonal Politics and Conversational Management

INTRODUCTION

Sometimes in relationships there are attempts to strategically cope with issues. In doing so, we often play politics in our relationships. There are many ways to do that, such as in the first article by Petronio and Martin where they examine consequences of revealing private information.

Another outcome of strategic communication is the reaction to embarrassment. When people are embarrassed, they use face-saving techniques. Metts and Cupach investigate the ways that people respond to embarrassing predicaments, elaborating and synthesizing the literature to date on embarrassment. Of course, one way that people might try to get out of an embarrassing situation is to lie. Miller, Mongeau, and Sleight examine both impersonal and personal relationships to determine whether lying and its outcomes differ between the two.

In the article by Petronio, we find a theoretical proposal on the way privacy regulation is enacted communicatively between marital couples.

As a part of politics, we find that conversational management is often used by individuals in their interactions with others. The next three readings examine the ways in which conversation functions strategically. Daly, Vangelisti, and Daughton's article on conversational sensitivity takes a global approach to these issues. They examine the nature of conversational sensitivity and explore the communication characteristics of people who are high and low in conversational sensitivity. Craig, Tracy, and Spisak examine how politeness is displayed in conversation. They explain a variety of ways that requests are made and the types of politeness strategies people use in an attempt to have their requests fulfilled. Finally, Alberts examines a very specific type of conversational act, the complaint sequence. She explores how satisfied and dissatisfied couples differ in their conversational complaint behavior. Thus, each of these articles examines, at different levels, how individuals engage in conversational interaction.

Finally, comforting is studied by Samter and Burleson in their article that explains what effective comforting is in relationships and which people are likely to comfort others.

RAMIFICATIONS OF REVEALING PRIVATE INFORMATION: A GENDER GAP

Sandra Petronio and Judith N. Martin
University of Minnesota

The study examined the frequency with which men (N = 126) and women (N = 126) anticipated positive and negative ramifications to disclosure of information in four topic areas: Parental, achievement, sexual, and global. The findings indicate that men predicted more negative ramifications for all topics than women, while women predicted more positive ramifications than men. In terms of topic, men predicted more negative ramifications than women when they were disclosing information about achievement. Overall, it was found that respondents expected more positive than negative ramifications. However, when topic was considered, respondents predicted negative ramifications most frequently for the sexual topic and least frequently for the achievement topic. Implications were discussed in terms of boundary regulation and achievement orientation for men and women.

Why do men and women differ in their disclosive behavior? Research long has supported the notion that women tend to disclose more frequently than men (e.g., Highlen & Gillis, 1978; Jourard, 1971). Yet, the rationale for this apparent gender difference has received little attention other than to attribute the reason broadly to socialization. The argument states that women are socialized to be open, empathic, and revealing, whereas, men are taught to be more concealing, less expressive, and unemotional. Implicit in this explanation is the assumption that men and women use the same criteria for disclosure, but that men tend to exercise a higher threshold and to reveal less about themselves than do women.

An alternative proposal may be that men and women are socialized in a very specific way. That is, men and women are taught to use different criteria in deciding whether to disclose private information. For women, it may be that they are taught differential criteria, which are met more easily than those used by men. Petronio, Martin, and Littlefield (1984) present an example; they found that women primarily use receiver characteristics as a prerequisite condition for disclosure, which once met, facilitates frequent openness. Thus, men and women seem to be regulating the floor of private information through the use of different criteria, which gives impetus for examining gender differences for other salient factors used to judge willingness to disclose.

In order to enhance the premise that men and women use differential criteria, basic assumptions about the nature of disclosive behavior must be clarified. Altman (1975) and Derlega and Chaikin (1977) propose a scheme to study disclosure that is useful in extending this premise through utilizing the concepts of privacy and interpersonal boundary regulation. These authors suggest that individuals implement an ''interpersonal boundary process by which a person or group regulates interaction with others'' (Altman, 1975, p. 6). ''Adjustment in self-disclosure outputs and inputs is an example of boundary regulation and the extent of control we maintain over this exchange of information contributes to the amount of privacy we have in a social relationship'' (Derlega & Chaikin, 1977, p. 103).

Source: The article is taken from the *Journal of Clinical Psychology* [42: 499–506, 1986]. Reprinted with permission of Clinical Psychology Publishing Co. Inc., 4 Conant Square, Brandon, VT 05733.

FIGURE 1   Model of interpersonal boundary regulation process as it occurs in self-disclosure.

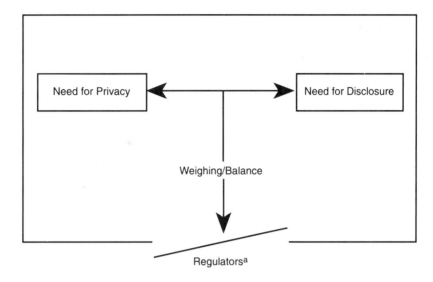

a *Prerequisite Conditions*
Anticipated Ramifications

In this framework, revealing private information about the self is regulated by criteria that the individual implements. As Rawlins (1983) suggests in his discussion of openness, when there is a need to be open, there is a simultaneous need to be self-protective. The dual process of protecting one's privacy and needing to be open calls for mediating mechanisms that help to manage the privacy boundaries. Figure 1 illustrates this conceptualization of boundary regulation.

In a preliminary study conducted by Petronio and Littlefield (1982), two boundary regulators were found: The first regulator was prerequisite conditions of disclosure, while a follow-up study showed that men and women based their decision to disclose on different conditions (Petronio et al., 1984), and the second regulator found was anticipated ramifications of disclosure. The focus of this study was to investigate whether there are gender differences when anticipated ramifications are used as criteria to regulate privacy boundaries and, therefore, to disclose information about the self.

Anticipated Ramifications

Because disclosure is intentional, individuals necessarily take into account the outcomes of revealing private information before they disclose. Barrell and Jourard (1976), in their study on honesty, liking, and disclosure, point out that "the variable found to differentiate reluctance from willingness to disclose to a liked person was the way we imagined how the results of our disclosing would affect the relationship. . . . The crucial variable which apparently determined whether or not we are willing to disclose to someone whom we like appears to be how we imagine the consequences of the disclosure" (p. 191). Rawlins (1983) suggests that this occurs because "the individual's tolerance of vulnerability is at stake. Disclosing personal information makes the self susceptible to hurt by others. This being so, self's willingness to unveil personal matters will depend upon whether the resulting vulnerability is perceived to be tolerable" (p. 7). Thus, individuals make judgments about potential ramifications that may result from their disclosure. When an individual anticipates ramifications, he/she is weighing the need to disclose against the need to protect private information about the self. In this way, anticipated ramifications function as one type of boundary regulator mechanism that balances the opposing needs to be open and closed. Whether the balance tips toward disclosure is contingent upon expecting positive or negative ramifications.

For example, Burke, Weir, and Harrison (1976) reported from their study on marital disclosure that "wives and husbands who specified only positive personal or interpersonal benefits from disclosure tended to communicate more frequently, whereas husbands and wives who specified only the barriers to disclosure tended to disclose significantly less" (p. 539). Thus, in order to weigh wanting to disclose against reluctance to disclose, we anticipate positive or negative outcomes and judge whether it is worth revealing private information to others. The criterion, anticipating ramifications, is one way to balance or regulate the interpersonal boundaries that we use to maintain control over privacy about the self.

In line with the previous research, this study hypothesizes that men and women differ in their use of anticipated ramifications used as boundary regulators. However, Derlega and Chaikin (1977) speculate that interpreting the difference in boundary adjustments between men and women may be dependent upon the topic of disclosure. Therefore, this research asks, in addition, whether the predictions made by men and women vary for different topics of disclosure.

Research Questions

1. Do men and women differ in predicting the frequency of positive and negative anticipated ramifications?
2. Do men's and women's predictions of positive and negative ramifications vary for different topics?
3. Do individuals differ overall in predicting the frequency of positive and negative ramifications?
4. Do predictions of positive and negative ramifications vary overall for different topics?

METHOD

Subjects and Procedures

A questionnaire was administered to 252 student respondents (126 males and 126 females).[1] A sample of students enrolled in a basic course in speech communication at a midwestern university were used in the study. The survey consisted of four parts, each of which represented a different topic on which the individual would disclose: (a) private information disclosed about parental problems (parental); (b) private information revealed about aspirations and achievements (achievement); (c) private information about sexual activities (sexual); and (d) private information revealed in general without a specific topic designated (global).[2]

For each topic, respondents were asked the degree to which they would predict negative and positive ramifications of disclosure on a 4–point scale: 4 = always true; 3 = frequently true; 2 = occasionally true; 1 = never true. The negative ramifications included: (a) predicting that one would feel vulnerable; (b) feeling uncomfortable; (c) predicting an exposed weakness; (d) predicting that revealing information would lead to rejection by the receiver. The positive ramifications included: (a) predicting clarification of information about the self; (b) predicting increased intimacy; (c) predicting increased level of trust; (d) predicting increased satisfaction; (e) predicting increased feelings of acceptance by a target person. Thus, each respondent predicted the ramifications, both positive and negative, for each topical area mentioned above.

The questionnaire items were developed on the basis of a pilot study conducted by Petronio and Littlefield (1982). Two hundred and fifteen randomly selected respondents, enrolled at a midwestern university, were asked to give their own definitions of self-disclosure through the use of an open-ended questionnaire. The goal of this

T A B L E 1 **Reliability Coefficients of Positive** **and Negative Ramifications**		
Topic	Ramification	Cronbach's alpha
Global	Positive	.69
	Negative	.71
Parental	Positive	.84
	Negative	.76
Achievement	Positive	.86
	Negative	.78
Sexual	Positive	.82
	Negative	.74

study was to understand the way in which individuals subjectively conceptualize the notion of self-disclosure.

The reliability of the items that represented anticipated ramifications of disclosure was tested for positive and negative outcomes in the four topical areas by Cronbach's alpha, as shown in Table 1.

STATISTICAL SUMMARY 1

Reliability indicates how accurately and consistently a concept has been measured. If a measure is highly reliable then you can be confident that the scores are very accurate, and the items or indicators are either consistent with each other or consistent over time. In this study the reliabilities ranged from moderate (.69) to moderately high (.86). Thus, all the measures were fairly accurate and consistent.

Scales were built to represent positive and negative ramifications for disclosure. Scores on the resulting eight scales (two ramifications × four topics) were computed by adding each person's response to the item and dividing by the total number of items for each of the eight scales (i.e., global negative; global positive; parental positive and negative; achievement positive and negative; sexual positive and negative).

Analysis

A three-factor repeated measures univariate analysis of variance was performed using SPSS MANOVA. The first factor represented Ramifications (positive-negative); the second factor represented Topic (global, parental, achievement, sexual); the third factor represented Gender (male-female). A repeated measures design was used because each respondent predicted the frequency of occurrence for two ramifications and for all four topics.[3]

STATISTICAL SUMMARY 2

Next, an analysis of variance (ANOVA) was computed. Analysis of variance is a technique for seeing if three or more groups differ from each other. For example, if you have three discussion groups, you may want to know which one talks the most.

The analysis of variance in this study was conducted to see if the three independent variables (four topics, positive and negative ramifications, male and female gender) affected the dependent variable (frequency of occurrence). These tests showed that ramifications and topic had a combined effect. Achievement was the least threatening topic and had the fewest negative ramifications. Further, sexual and global topics resulted in more positive than negative ramifications. Ramifications also combined with gender. Overall, men predicted more negative ramifications from disclosure, and this was particularly noticeable when disclosing about things they would like to achieve.

RESULTS

Gender, Topic, and Ramifications represented the independent variables, and predicting the frequency of occurrence represented the dependent variable. Two main effects, Topic and Ramifications, were found to be significant. The test for Ramifications indicated a significant difference

TABLE 2
Mean Scores on Predicting Frequency: Ramifications, Topic, Gender

Ramifications	Global	Parental	Topic achievement	Sexual	All topics
Negative					
Male & female	2.12	2.01	1.79	2.32	2.06
Male	2.12	2.05	1.89	2.35	2.10
Female	2.12	1.98	1.69	2.30	2.02
Positive					
Male & female	2.77	2.54	2.46	2.76	2.63
Male	2.72	2.49	2.43	2.72	2.59
Female	2.82	2.58	2.49	2.81	2.66

Note.—Maximum score = 4 (Always true).
Minimum score = 1 (Never true).

in predicting the frequency of occurrence for positive and negative ramifications, $F(1, 234) = 296.16$, $p < .00005$. The test for Topic indicated a significant difference in predicting frequency of occurrence for different topics, $multF(1, 234) = 62.99$, $p < .00005$. Two significant disordinal interactions were found: One between Ramifications × Topic and another between Ramifications × Gender. Table 2 presents the mean scores of Topic, Ramifications, Gender to show how the significant interactions of Topic × Ramifications and Ramifications × Gender may be decomposed.[4]

Ramifications × Topic

A significant interaction was found between predicting ramifications and topic, $multF(3, 232) = 12.69$, $p < .00005$. A follow-up test for simple effects (Winer, 1971) was conducted and used a family error rate set at $p < .04$. The interaction effect appears with the achievement, sexual, and global topics. Compared to all topics, achievement was perceived to be the least threatening and produced the least frequently predicted negative ramifications overall. For the sexual topic,

respondents reported positive ramifications more frequently than negative ramifications, and for the global topic, they reported positive ramifications more frequently than negative ramifications. It is notable that the global and sexual topics were perceived as equally likely to have positive ramifications.

Ramifications × Gender

A significant interaction also was found between predicted ramifications of disclosure and gender, $F(1, 234) = 6.43$, $p < .012$. A follow-up test for simple effects also was conducted and used a family error rate set at $p < .04$. The test showed that, overall, men predicted more negative ramifications of disclosure than did women, and women predicted more positive ramifications than did men. Only one comparison, which analyzed the Ramifications × Gender interaction, was significant: Men tended to predict more negative ramifications when they were disclosing about things they would like to achieve than did women.

DISCUSSION

For the first research question, the results showed that men predicted more negative ramifications for all topics than did women. That is, men predicated a greater occurrence of vulnerability, feelings of being uncomfortable, exposed weakness, and the possibility that revealed information would lead to rejection. These expectations may result from the way men are taught to maintain boundary controls over private information. The literature suggests that from the earliest ages, men are taught to maintain control over their feelings (Forisha, 1978). Implicit in that lesson is the message that loss of control is equated with negative outcomes, whereas, having control equals positive results. Disclosing, by definition, requires the opening up of boundaries to private information about the self, a risk-taking experience that assumes giving up control over a part of the self. If men are taught to maintain stringent boundaries and to expect negative outcomes when those boundaries are not maintained, then it stands to reason that men will disclose less frequently.

As for women, the findings in this study indicate that they predict more positive ramifications than do men. In many studies, women were found to disclose more intimate-private information about themselves than did men (Chelune, 1976; Gitter & Black, 1976; Rubin, Hill, Peplau, & Dunkel-Schetter, 1980). Women have been encouraged to be expressive and have been rewarded for doing so: "expressive behavior of women occurs because they continue to expect reinforcement and approval for such behavior" (Derlega & Chaikin, 1976, p. 377). If this reward system is reinforced continually by society, it stands to reason that women would perceive more positive outcomes from disclosing. The boundaries around private information are regulated based on predicted rewards. Thus, the controls that seem necessary for men seem inconsistent with the way women define their private boundaries and the goals of disclosure.

With regard to topic, this research showed that men anticipated more negative ramifications when disclosing about things they would like to achieve than did women. This finding was interpreted through the use of achievement motivation literature. One proposal made about gender differences in the achievement research indicates that men and women may differ in their orientation toward achievement (Battistich, Thompson, Mann, & Perlmutter, 1982). As Veroff (1977) suggests, men tend to emphasize a social achievement orientation, while women tend to emphasize autonomous achievement. Autonomous achievement is defined as a person's ability "to accomplish an activity by one's own choice and effort. . . . This type of motivation focuses entirely on the self as the regulator of striving" (Veroff, 1977, p. 287). Veroff (1977) cites several studies that support the proposal that women are more autonomous in their achievement motivation than men. For example, a study by Langsam (1973) is presented, wherein it was found that "men were less interested in autonomy than women when there was no peer present. A man's autonomy was evident only when a peer was judging him" (p. 287).

Social achievement is defined as incorporating a competitive orientation and social comparison, whereby

> doing best at an activity is a commonly used measure on which to compare people. This motivation is easily and consistently engendered in males in our society and is what induces such remarkably high concern in men about failure at a deep level. In the projective assessment of motivation in the Detroit survey we found that men have a much higher level of this deep fear than women (Veroff, McClelland, & Ruhland, 1975). Furthermore, such a competitive orientation drives men to seek unrealistically high social comparison for their achievement (Veroff, 1977, p. 289).

Hence, men use a social achievement orientation wherein comparisons with other people serve as the basis for judging success. This places evaluation of achievement into a public arena for men. Given that public evaluation is critical to men as an indicator of success, disclosing about their desired achievement may be risky. Therefore, men may tend to predict negative ramifications because they are sensitive to public scrutiny when they disclose about their achievements and aspirations.

On the other hand, females depend on autonomous achievement that is not necessarily linked to public assessment. The prediction of negative ramifications may be lessened because making achievement desires public is not a prerequisite for acknowledging success.

The third and fourth research questions concerned the relationship between topic and ramifications for people in general. Question three asked whether individuals differ in predicting the frequency of positive and negative ramifications. The findings indicate that more positive than negative ramifications were predicted. Thus, generally positive outcomes were perceived to result when one is disclosing private information. Individuals in this population appeared to feel that being open, on the whole, is going to produce more benefits with minimum threats to one's privacy.

However, it is necessary to look further at the results obtained for the fourth research question, which asked whether predictions of positive and negative ramifications vary for different topics? The results indicate that topic has an impact on the predictions of positive and negative ramifications. Respondents most frequently predicted positive ramifications for the global topic. This category is nonspecific, in that no topic actually is defined. The assumption is that when asked to predict outcomes for disclosure without specifying a topic, individuals tend to gravitate toward a norm, as evidenced by a similar prediction for all topics. The fact that individuals were equally likely to predict positive ramifications for the sexual topic as they were for the global topic suggests that individuals may be using the most intimate of topics as an indicator to predict positive outcomes for revealing private information about the self.

In the prediction of negative ramifications, a differential comparison base is used. Individuals judged that negative outcomes would result most frequently from revealing private information about sexual issues and least frequently from disclosing information about achievement.

Topic clearly has an impact on the prediction of negative and positive ramifications. For prediction of positive outcomes, a topic-free (Wheelness & Grotz, 1976) measure would yield information indicative of highly intimate topics, whereas, one would be cautioned not to assume that such a measure would be an accurate predictor with regard to negative ramification of disclosure.

Conceptualizing the act of disclosure in terms of a boundary regulation process appears to be a useful framework for understanding gender differences. Men and women differ in their disclosure behavior in part because they use differential criteria to judge whether to reveal private information. Future research is needed to identify other boundary regulators to understand more clearly why gender differences occur in disclosure.

REFERENCES

Altman, I. (1975). *The environment and social behavior: Privacy, personal space, territory, crowding.* Monterey, CA.: Brooks/Cole.

Barrell, J., & Jourard, S. (1976). Being honest with persons we like. *Journal of Individual Psychology, 32,* 185–193.

Battistich, V., Thompson, E., Mann, I., & Perlmutter, L. (1982). Gender differences in autonomous and social achievement orientations. *Journal of Personality, 50,* 98–114.

Burke, R., Weir, T., & Harrison, D. (1976). Disclosure of problems and tensions experienced by marital partners. *Psychological Reports, 38,* 531–542.

Chelune, G. (1976). Reactions to male and female disclosure at two levels. *Journal of Personality and Social Psychology, 34,* 1000–1003.

Derlega, V., & Chaikin, A. (1976). Norms affecting self-disclosure in men and women. *Journal of Counseling and Clinical Psychology, 44,* 376–380.

Derlega, V., & Chaikin, A. (1977). Privacy and self-disclosure in social relationships. *Journal of Social Issues, 33,* 102–115.

Forisha, B. (1978). *Sex roles and personal awareness.* Morristown, NJ: General Learning Press.

Gitter, A., & Black, H. (1976). Is self-disclosure self-revealing? *Journal of Counseling Psychology, 23,* 327–332.

Highlen, P. S., & Gillis, S. F. (1978). Effects of situational factors, sex, and attitude on affective self-disclosure and anxiety. *Journal of Counseling Psychology, 25,* 270–276.

Jourard, S. (1971). *The transparent self.* New York: Van Nostrand.

Langsam, I. (1973). The effect of sex and social setting in help-seeking behavior in a problem-solving situation. Doctoral dissertation, University of Michigan. *Dissertation Abstracts International, 34,* 5313A, (University Microfilms No. 74–3668).

Lombardo, J., & Berzonsky, M. (1979). Sex differences in self-disclosure during an interview. *Journal of Social Psychology, 107,* 281–281.

Morgan, B. (1976). Intimacy of disclosure topics and self-differences in self-disclosure. *Sex Roles, 2,* 161–166.

Petronio, S., & Littlefield, R. (1982). *Perceived definition of disclosure: A pilot study.* Unpublished raw data.

Petronio, S., Martin, J., & Littlefield, R. (1984). Prerequisite conditions for self-disclosing: A gender issue. *Communication Monographs, 51,* 268–273.

Rawlins, W. (1983). Openness as problematic in ongoing relationships: Two conversational dilemmas. *Communication Monographs, 50,* 1–13.

Rubin, Z., Hill, C., Peplau, L., & Dunkel-Schetter, C. (1980). Self-disclosure in dating couples: Sex roles and the ethic of openness. *Journal of Marriage and the Family, 42,* 305–317.

Veroff, J. (1977). Process vs. Impact in men's and women's achievement motivation. *Psychology of Women Quarterly, 1,* 283–293.

Veroff, J., McClelland, L., & Ruhland, D. (1975). Varieties of achievement motivation. In M. Mednick, S. Tangri, & L. Hoffman (Eds.), *Women and achievement: Social and motivational analyses.* New York: John Wiley.

Wheelness, L., & Grotz, J. (1976). Conceptualization and measurement of reported self-disclosure. *Human Communication Research, 2,* 338–346.

Winer, B. (1971). *Statistical principles in experimental design.* New York: McGraw Hill.

NOTES

1. Four respondents were deleted randomly to balance the cells for analysis.

2. The four topics (global, parental, achievement and sexual) were chosen after a review of the literature and represent varying degrees of "privateness" of information (e.g., Lombardo & Berzonsky, 1979; Morgan, 1976).

3. See Winer (1971, pp. 539–559) for a detailed explanation of a three-factor experiment with repeated measures (case 1).

4. Personal communication with Professor Lahiff, Department of Applied Statistics, University of Minnesota, Minneapolis.

SITUATIONAL INFLUENCE ON THE USE OF REMEDIAL STRATEGIES IN EMBARRASSING PREDICAMENTS

Sandra Metts and William R. Cupach

The present study investigated how the use of remedial strategies for coping with embarrassment is affected by various types of embarrassing predicaments. Respondents completed surveys in which they described a significant embarrassing event, what they did to reduce their felt embarrassment, and what other social actors present did to reduce the respondent's embarrassment. Log-linear analysis of frequency distributions indicated that for embarrassed persons, excesses were more likely to be used in mistake situations and less likely in recipient situations, justification was more likely in a faux pas situation, humor and remediation were more likely in accident situations, and aggression was used exclusively in recipient situations.

Source: The article is taken from *Communication Monographs* [56: 151–162, 1989]. (c) Speech Communication Association, 5105 Backlick Rd., Annandale, VA 22003. Reprinted by permission.

Embarrassment is a frequent and uncomfortable consequence of social interaction. It "occurs when there is some public violation of a taken-for-granted rule which is part of the actor's repertoire" (Semin & Manstead, 1982, p. 368). If the rule is not known to the violator, embarrassment is still likely to result if the reactions of others present inform the violator that some transgression has occurred. In short, embarrassment is a particular kind of social predicament characterized by an inconsistency between the manner in which a person actually behaves and the manner in which he/she would have liked to behave (Edelmann, 1985, p. 200). Furthermore, although embarrassment may be felt most keenly by the transgressor, observers too experience awkwardness to the extent that they empathize with the transgressor's discomfort (Miller, 1987; Semin & Manstead, 1981), and to the extent that their own role enactment has been disrupted by the transgression (Goffman, 1967).

While research has significantly enhanced our understanding of the causes and manifestations of embarrassment (e.g., Archibald & Cohen, 1971; Brown & Garland, 1971; Edelmann & Hampson, 1979, 1981; Garland & Brown, 1972; Modigliani, 1971; Sattler, 1965), little empirical work has examined the communicative strategies that embarrassed persons and other participants use to cope with embarrassing events (e.g., Cupach, Metts, & Hazleton, 1986; Petronio, 1984). In addition, although various typologies of embarrassing situations have been proposed (e.g., Buss, 1980; Gross & Stone, 1964; Modigliani, 1968; Sattler, 1965; Weinberg, 1968), little effort has been devoted to determining the association between situational characteristics and the use of remedial strategies. The purpose of the current investigation is twofold: (1) to determine the relative frequency of types of strategies used by embarrassed persons and others to manage embarrassing predicaments, and (2) to determine the extent to which strategies vary as a function of the type of situation causing the embarrassment.

STRATEGIES FOR COPING WITH EMBARRASSMENT

Typologies of remedial strategies derive principally from the literature on "facework" (Goffman, 1956, 1967, 1971; Modigliani, 1971) and on predicaments (also known as fractured social interaction, breaches, failure events; Cody & McLaughlin, 1985; Schlenker, 1980; Schonback, 1980; Tedeschi & Riess, 1981).

Scholarship has traditionally focused on four classes of remedial strategies: apologies, accounts, avoidance, and humor. Apologies are statements which acknowledge blameworthiness and seek atonement for an inappropriate or untoward act (Goffman, 1971; Schlenker, 1980; Schlenker & Darby, 1981; Tedeschi & Riess, 1981). Accounts are attempts to restore a discredited identity by explaining an untoward act (Buttny, 1985; Schlenker, 1980; Scott & Lyman, 1968; Semin & Manstead, 1983; Tedeschi & Riess, 1981). An account may take the form of an excuse (statements which minimize the actor's responsibility for an act) or a justification (statements which minimize the pejorative consequences of an act). Avoidance refers to a variety of tactics which enable an offending actor to avoid explaining untoward behavior. Tactics commonly associated with avoidance include, for example, mystification (Scott & Lyman, 1968; Tedeschi & Riess, 1981), refusal to provide an account or denial that an untoward event has occurred (Schonback, 1980), avoiding or changing embarrassing conversational topics (Goffman, 1967), silence (McLaughlin, Cody, & O'Hair, 1983), and physically retreating from the situation. Humor enables an offending actor to cope with embarrassment through implicit acknowledgment of blameworthiness while at the same time releasing situational tension (Edelmann, 1985; Emerson, 1970; Fink & Walker, 1977).

In a study of respondent-generated remedial strategies, Cupach, Metts, and Hazleton (1986) found two additional strategies: description and remediation. Description involves simple statements which acknowledge the presence of an embarrassing predicament without attempting to explain or apologize for its occurrence. Remediation includes direct and immediate attempts to correct or "fix" a failed episode (e.g., wiping up spilled gravy).

THE ROLE OF OTHERS IN EMBARRASSING PREDICAMENTS

The role of other actors in embarrassing predicaments is largely unexplored. Consistent with Goffman's (1967) observation that the maintenance of one's own face is dependent upon the willing cooperation of others in the interaction, it is unlikely that a rational communicator would intentionally contribute to the loss of another's face. Indeed, the "remedial interchange" is an important ritual designed to restore social order as unobtrusively as possible when face loss has occurred (Goffman, 1967). Although social actors do, on occasion, call for accounts to explain untoward behavior (Scott & Lyman, 1968), they are less likely to do so in embarrassing predicaments since the transgression is unintentional. In fact, observers may empathize with the embarrassed person's "feelings of conspicuousness, nervousness, tension and embarrassment" (Semin & Manstead, 1981, p. 255; also see Miller, 1987).

To the degree that empathy influences observer behavior, we might expect observers to initiate remedial strategies which reconfirm the embarrassed person's loss of projected identity, acknowledge the unintentionality of the embarrassing act, and reduce the conspicuousness of the embarrassed person. When the embarrassed actor has already provided an initial remedial strategy, we might expect observers to assist by "playing along" (Edelmann, 1985, p. 208) and accepting a proffered explanation or facilitating its acceptance by other observers.

The experience of embarrassment arises from a number of different types of situations. For example, Knapp, Stafford, and Daly (1986) studied the occurrence of "regrettable" messages, some of which are likely to produce embarrassment for the speaker. However, embarrassing predicaments constitute a broader domain than regret-

table messages to the extent that the events producing embarrassment need not be verbal and need not be created by the person who feels embarrassed (e.g., Goffman, 1967).

Several researchers have identified the types of circumstances that specifically precipitate an embarrassing predicament. The early research by Gross and Stone (1964) focused on two general types of situations: loss of social identity (inability to perform one's role), and loss of personal poise (inability to control one's body and nearby props). Buss (1980), summarizing and extending previous work by Sattler (1965), identified five types of events that commonly lead to embarrassment: (1) impropriety (e.g., improper dress, dirty talk), (2) lack of competence (e.g., failure of social graces), (3) conspicuousness (e.g., being singled out for attention by others), (4) breach of privacy (e.g., invasion of personal space or undesired leakage of emotion), and (5) overpraise (e.g., receiving more acclaim than is desired).

Weinberg (1968) derived four types of "basic forms of embarrassment" by crossing two dimensions that are fundamental to social actors' interpretation of a disrupted routine: the intended or unintended nature of the offending act, and the correct or incorrect definition of the situation. These four basic forms include (1) faux pas (intentional behavior that is defined post facto as inappropriate to the social situation), (2) accidents (unintended acts occurring in correctly defined situations), (3) mistakes (unintended acts occurring in incorrectly defined situations), and (4) duties (intended acts occurring in correctly defined situations but causing embarrassment because one's internal audience experiences embarrassment).

Indirect evidence exists that the selection of remedial strategies is influenced by the type of situation causing the embarrassment. Cupach et al. (1986) conducted two studies of remedial strategies for coping with embarrassing predicaments. In the first study, respondents rated the effectiveness and appropriateness of strategies supplied by the researchers in a loss of poise and an improper identity situation. In the second study, respondents generated their own strategies for the same two situations and rated them on perceived appropriateness and effectiveness.

Results from both studies suggest that certain strategies (e.g., apologies and remediation) are preferred across situations. Results from study two also indicated that accounts are not likely to be used in either situation, while humor and escape are more likely to be used in a loss of poise situation and description is more likely to be used in a loss of identity situation. The authors concluded that "social actors select and expect certain patterns of remedial behaviours in certain situations" (p. 197).

RESEARCH QUESTIONS

Although several typologies of remedial strategies exist in the literature, no systematic attempt has been made to integrate these typologies and test them against respondent-generated embarrassing predicaments. In addition, no attempt has been made to determine whether such typologies are adequate to describe the strategies that observers use in managing embarrassing predicaments. Finally, although the findings reported by Cupach et al. (1986) indicate probable associations between strategy use and situation, methodological limitations necessitate additional research. Cupach et al. (1986) used only two stimulus situations (both of which were hypothetical) and assessed only strategies used by the embarrassed person. Other types of situations and strategies used by observers have not been explored. In order to address these concerns, we pose four research questions:

1. Are certain remedial strategies more likely to be used by embarrassed persons to manage predicaments than other remedial strategies?
2. To what extent are remedial strategies used by embarrassed persons more likely to be present in certain types of situations than in other types?

3. Are certain remedial strategies more likely to be used by observers to manage predicaments than other remedial strategies?
4. To what extent are remedial strategies used by others more likely to be present in certain types of situations than in other types?

METHOD

Respondents

Respondents were students enrolled in a large introductory course in interpersonal communication at Illinois State University which fulfills part of the university's core curriculum requirements. Questionnaires were completed during regularly scheduled class time. Participation was voluntary and respondents were assured of anonymity. Twelve respondents returned the questionnaire blank or indicated that they could not recall a significant embarrassing event. A total of 49 males and 71 females returned completed surveys ($N = 120$).

Questionnaire

Respondents were asked to think of a specific incident in which they were significantly embarrassed. Each person described the situation and the surrounding circumstances. Respondents were also asked to explain why they found the described situation embarrassing. They then rated the degree of embarrassment felt before trying to correct the situation by marking a seven-point semantic differential scale. Mean level of perceived embarrassment was 5.3 for the total sample.

Next, respondents were asked to describe as specifically as possible what they said or did to try to reduce their embarrassment. In parallel fashion, respondents were asked what, if anything, the other person(s) present said or did to try to reduce the respondent's embarrassment.

TABLE 1	
Types of Embarrassing Situations	
Situation	Description
Faux Pas	Acts that are intentionally performed but which prove to be inappropriate when the correct interpretation of the situation becomes clear. Example: Wearing informal attire to a formal function.
Mistake	Intentional acts that would be appropriate to the situation but are not because they are incorrectly or incompletely executed. Example: A customer is attempting to purchase items at a department store but is using an expired credit card and has no checks with her to complete the transaction.
Accident	Unintentional acts which are inappropriate to the situation. Example: Falling, tripping, spilling, tearing one's clothes, etc.
Recipient	Predicaments which arise for the embarrassed person because of the behavior of others. In these situations, the embarrassed person is made to feel conspicuous by the unexpected positive or negative attention of others or the unexpected intrusion of the other person into the embarrassed person's personal or private activity. Example: Being criticized in class, receiving excessive praise in public, or having one's parents appear unexpectedly while one is only "partially clothed" in the living room with one's boyfriend.

Coding

Responses to the open-ended questions were coded for the three variables of interest: type of situation, embarrassed person's remedial strategies, and other persons' remedial strategies. In order to assess the adequacy of preliminary typologies, initial coding was done by the authors working together with half of the questionnaires.

For type of situation, a modification of Weinberg's (1968) typology was used. Since no instances of "duties" appeared, it was dropped from the coding. In addition, several instances of embarrassment caused by the actions of other people (rather than some action of the embarrassed person) necessitated the creation of a category called "recipient." This category was used to indicate embarrassment resulting from an unexpected intrusion of another person or unexpected attention (positive or negative) from another person. Both of these cause the embarrassed person to feel conspicuous despite having done nothing that is socially inappropriate (see Buss, 1980). A complete description of situation types and examples is presented in Table 1.

For the embarrassed person's remedial strategy, the extended typology presented by

Cupach et al. (1986) was used. During initial coding, two additional categories emerged: "aggression" and "avoidance." Aggression represented acts of physical or verbal hostility in response to embarrassment. The avoidance category was similar to Cupach et al.'s description category but somewhat broader, and was therefore used in its place. Avoidance represented not only instances of stating the "fact" that caused one to be embarrassed (i.e., description), but also instances of continued role performance *as though remedial work were not necessary.* A complete description of the embarrassed person's remedial strategies and examples are presented in Table 2.

Since no typology of other persons' strategies exists in the literature, coding began with the same typology used for the embarrassed person's strategies. Two additional categories emerged during coding: support and empathy. Empathy represented instances of other persons assuring the embarrassed person that his/her situation was not unique. Support represented messages of continued positive regard for the embarrassed person

T A B L E 2	
Remedial Strategies Used by Embarrassed Persons	

Strategy	Description
Simple Apology	Cliché statements of regret and requests for pardon. Examples: "I'm sorry," "Please excuse me," "Please forgive me."
Excuse	Acknowledgment of an untoward act but minimizaton of one's responsibility for its occurrence. Example: [Almost forgetting a lunch date with a friend and arriving late] "I've had so much on my mind with exams and papers."
Justification	Acknowledgment of responsibility for an untoward act but minimization of the offensiveness of the act. Example: [Necking in the driveway with a high school boyfriend and mother opens the car door] "Mom, this is not what it seems."
Humor	Laughter and jokework. Examples: "I just laughed it off." [After falling down the stairs into the center of the guests at a party while wearing high heels and a full skirt] "Hi, I just thought I'd drop in."
Remediation	Proactive attempts to correct or repair damage done by the untoward behavior. Example: All instances of cleaning up spills, collecting dropped packages, and reconstituting oneself after a fall.
Escape	Physically retreating from the scene after an untoward act has occurred. Example: In grade school during a game of touch tag, a boy accidentally pulls the embarrassed person's pants down; she runs off the playground and into the school.
Avoidance	A protective strategy employed after the untoward act has occurred. The embarrassed person continues to enact his/her role, without addressing the act or his/her blameworthiness. Example: [After spilling beer on his pants at a party] "I just smiled and acted like it didn't bother me."
Aggression	Physically or verbally attacking another person present such that embarrassment appears to be justified anger. Example: After being forced from the locker room wearing only a towel, the embarrassed person attacks the perpetrators and returns the deed.

in spite of his/her predicament. A complete description of other persons' remedial strategies and examples is presented in Table 3.

After coding categories were established, the researchers independently coded the remaining half of the questionnaires. Thirty-five percent of the respondent descriptions contained multiple remedial strategies used by the embarrassed person, and 23 percent of the descriptions contained multiple strategies used by observers. Each strategy was coded and constituted the unit of analysis. Inter-coder consistency was assessed on 25 questionnaires randomly selected from this group. Unitizing reliability was determined via Guetzkow's U ($U = .028$ for the embarrassed person's strategies, $U = .019$ for other persons' strategies). Categorizing reliability was calculated using the formula for Scott's pi. Pi values were 1.0 for situation (100% coder agreement), .94 for the embarrassed person's strategies (95% agreement), and .88 for other persons' strategies (90% agreement).

TABLE 3
Remedial Strategies Used by Other Persons

Strategy	Description
Simple Apology	Expressions of regret offered by observers who feel responsible for the embarrassment of another. Example: "I'm sorry" offered by a person who bumped a drink tray, causing the respondent's embarrassing incident.
Excuse	Acknowledgment of an untoward act but minimization of the embarrassed person's responsibility for its occurrence. Example: [When an embarrassed person fell while sweeping a floor at work, her boss offered] "The broom handle is rotten."
Justification	Acknowledgment of responsibility for an untoward act but minimization of the offensiveness of the act. Example: [When an embarrassed person spilled gum and candy while restocking at a checkout counter, a coworker said] "There's nothing to be upset about, it's just gum, not glassware."
Humor	Laughing along with the embarrassed person or doing jokework. Example: [The manager of a fast food restaurant is sprayed with strawberry milkshake because the embarrassed person did not put a lid on the blender but says] "It's okay, I look good in pink."
Remediation	Helping to clean up messes, spills, dropped packages, repairing faulty mufflers.
Avoidance	A passive strategy by which participants simply act as though no infraction has occurred. Examples: [An embarrassed person tripped in church after receiving communion] "my family just slid down and let me in the pew as if nothing had happened." When an embarrassed person gets confused while ordering dinner in a fancy restaurant, a friend introduces a new topic of conversation.
Empathy	Assurance to the embarrassed person that his/her predicament and/or behavior is not unique and that it happens to others. Empathy serves to de-individuate the embarrassed person. Example: [When an embarrassed person finds that he has been sitting in the wrong class for ten minutes, a classmate says] "the same thing happened to me last semester."
Support	Verbal and nonverbal assurances of continued positive regard for the embarrassed person. When the embarrassed person tripped in church, her mother patted her on the leg when she returned to her seat.

STATISTICAL SUMMARY 1

Reliability is a measure of how accurate and consistent the scores are. If a measure is highly reliable then you can be confident that the scores are very accurate, and that the items or indicators are either consistent with each other or consistent over time. This study was concerned with two types of reliability or accuracy of measurement. First, unitizing reliability measured the coders' agreement on what was an embarrassing situation. These were adequate. Second, categorizing reliability measured coders' agreement about the type of embarrassing situation. These reliabilities were high, indicating considerable accuracy and consistency.

Data Analysis

Two hierarchical log-linear analyses were performed, one for the embarrassed person's strategies by situation and one for other persons' strategies by situation. In both cases, significant first-order effects would indicate that some strategies are used more frequently than others, and significant second-order effects would indicate that strategy use varies as a function of situation. In addition, standardized z-values corresponding to parameter estimates allow the presence of interactions between specific strategies and specific situations to be identified.

STATISTICAL SUMMARY 2

Three log-linear analyses were computed. Log-linear analysis is used to see if three or more variables are related to each other. It is used with variables that have categories (e.g., ethnicity might have African American, white American, Mexican American; gender includes male and female; and income might have high, medium, and low), and shows you which categories of which variables tend to occur more frequently together (e.g., African American with female and middle income). The first analysis in this study showed that some strategies were used more frequently than others regardless of the situation. Avoidance was used more often and aggression was used less often.

The second log-linear analysis indicated that people used different embarrassment strategies in different situations (see Table 2 for a list of the situations). Excuses were more likely to be used when a mistake was made and less likely to be used when someone else caused the embarrassment (recipient situation). Justification was more likely to be used when a faux pas occurred, humor and remediation when an accident occurred, and aggression when someone else caused the embarrassment.

The third log-linear analysis focused on perceptions of other people and their embarrassment strategy use. People reported that others used more support or less remediation. Results also showed that respondents felt other people used fewer strategies than they did.

The fourth log-linear analysis showed that other people's strategy use was not perceived to change depending on the situation. This finding may have been due to inadequacies in the research design (small sample size).

RESULTS

Respondents described a total of 111 embarrassing predicaments that could be coded. Nine descriptions (approximately 7%) were anomalous or too vague to be coded for type of situation and were placed in an "other" category. Faux pas were infrequent relative to other predicaments (13%), but mistakes (32%), accidents (28%), and recipient predicaments (27%) appeared with approximately equal frequency.

The first research question asked whether certain strategies were more likely to be used, regardless of situation, than other strategies. Respondents reported a total of 168 remedial strategies used to reduce their own embarrassment. Of these, ten were associated with uncodable situations. The remaining 158 strategies and 102 situations were submitted to hierarchical log-linear analysis with backward elimination of effects.

Results indicated a significant effect for strategy (partial X^2 [7] = 34.50, p = .000, n = 158). Standardized z-values indicated that avoidance was used significantly more often than would be expected by chance, and that aggression was used significantly less often than would be expected by chance. The reported frequencies for remediation, humor, excuse, escape, apology, and justification did not differ significantly (see Table 4).

The second research question concerned possible influences of type of situation on remedial strategies. Results of the log-linear analysis indicated a significant interaction between strategy and situation (X^2 LR[21] = 52.02, p = .0002; Pearson X^2 [21] = 55.45, p = .0002). Thus, the type of remedial strategy used by an embarrassed person varies with the type of situation in which the embarrassment occurs.

Examination of z-values associated with parameter estimates indicated six significant cells: (1) excuses were more likely to be used in mistake situations than in other situations, but (2) were less likely to be used in recipient situations (in which someone else caused the embarrassment); (3) justification was more likely to be used in faux pas situations than in other situations; (4) humor and (5) remediation were more likely to be used in accident situations than other situations; and (6) aggression was more likely to be used in recipient situations than in other situations (see Table 5).

TABLE 4
Frequencies and Proportions of Remedial Strategies Used by Embarrassed Persons

Strategy	Frequency	Proportion
Simple Apology	17	.11
Excuse	20	.13
Justification	10	.06
Humor	23	.15
Remediation	27	.17
Escape	18	.11
Avoidance	37	.23+
Aggression	6	.04 -
TOTAL	158	1.00

Note. + or − denotes deviation from expected proportion, $p < .05$.

TABLE 5
Conditional Proportions of Embarrassed Person's Remedial Strategies by Situation

Strategy	Faux Pas	Mistake	Accident	Recipient
Simple Apology	.29	.41	.18	.12
Excuse	.15	.60+	.15	.10 -
Justification	.40+	.30	.10	.20
Humor	.04	.26	.48+	.22
Remediation	.04	.26	.48+	.22
Escape	.17	.33	.33	.17
Avoidance	.08	.27	.22	.43
Aggression	.00	.00	.00	1.00+
	($n = 18$)	($n = 51$)	($n = 45$)	($n = 42$)

Note. + or − denotes deviation from expected proportion, $p < .05$.

The third research question asked whether certain strategies were more likely to be used by observers, regardless of situation, than other strategies. Respondents reported a total of 108 strategies that they perceived other persons used to help them reduce their embarrassment. Of these, 12 were associated with uncodable situations. The remaining 96 strategies and 102 situations were submitted to hierarchical log-linear analysis with backward elimination of effects.

Results indicated a significant effect for strategy (partial X^2 [6] = 31.10, $p = .000$, $n = 96$). Standardized z-values indicated that support was used significantly more often than would be expected by chance and that remediation was used significantly less often than would be expected by chance. Empathy and humor were used relatively often but did not reach significance. In comparison to the frequency profile found for strategies used by the embarrassed

TABLE 6
Frequencies and Proportions of Remedial Strategies Used by Observers

Strategy	Frequency	Proportion
Excuse	7	.07
Justification	9	.09
Humor	15	.16
Remediation	5	.05 ⁻
Avoidance	11	.12
Empathy	18	.19
Support	31	.32⁺
TOTAL	96	1.00

Note: Because only one instance of simple apology was reported for other persons, it was not included in the analysis.
+ or − denotes deviation from expected proportion, $p < .05$.

TABLE 7
Conditional Proportions of Other Persons' Remedial Strategies by Situation

Strategy	Faux Pas	Mistake	Accident	Recipient
Excuse	.14	.00	.43	.43
Justification	.22	.11	.44	.22
Humor	.07	.27	.40	.27
Remediation	.00	.40	.60	.00
Avoidance	.00	.09	.27	.64
Empathy	.17	.44	.28	.11
Support	.13	.35	.29	.23
	($n = 11$)	($n = 27$)	($n = 33$)	($n = 25$)

Note: Because only one instance of simple apology was reported for other persons, it was not included in the analysis.
+ or − denotes deviation from expected proportion, $p < .05$.

person, the profile of strategies used by other persons is less varied. Apart from support, empathy, humor and avoidance, no other strategy constituted more than ten percent of the strategies reported (see Table 6).

The final research question concerned possible influences of type of situation on remedial strategies used by observers. Results of the log-linear analysis indicated that the two-way interaction was nonsignificant ($X^2_{LR}[18] = 26.14$, $p = .10$; Pearson X^2 [18] $= 22.37$, $p = .216$). Thus, strategies used by other persons to reduce embarrassment do not appear to be strongly related to the type of situation in which the embarrassment occurs (see Table 7). However, it should be noted that the small sample size may have reduced the power to find a small or medium-sized effect. Power for detecting a medium-sized effect is estimated to be less than .40 and power to detect a small effect is less than .20. Therefore, future research should test this question with a larger sample.

DISCUSSION

Out data indicate that both embarrassed actors and others use a finite set of strategies for helping embarrassed persons cope with embarrassing predicaments. Despite the fact that the strategies used by embarrassed persons and other persons exhibit considerable overlap, some strategies are unique to one group or the other. Specifically, aggression and escape are exclusive to embarrassed persons. Empathy and support, on the other hand, are exclusive to other persons, and make up 50 percent of all strategies used by others to help reduce the actor's embarrassment.

Strategies for managing embarrassment are not utilized with equal frequency. Embarrassed persons engage in avoidance more frequently, and aggression less frequently, than other strategies. Observers, on the other hand, manifest support more than other strategies and provide remediation less often than other strategies. We suspect that these remedial strategies accomplish goals specific to actor/observer roles. Avoidance on the part of embarrassed persons may allow them to restore interactional equilibrium quickly, and to demonstrate poise in the face of adversity, thereby demonstrating a form of social competence. At the same time, support offered by other persons may assist the embarrassed actor in overcoming feelings of chagrin through awareness that no offense was taken and negative attributions were not made.

The Role of Situation in Strategy Use

The type of embarrassing situation is clearly useful in understanding the likelihood of embarrassed persons using various remedial strategies. As our findings indicate, excuses are more likely to be used by an embarrassed actor in mistake situations, but less likely to be used in recipient situations. By definition, mistakes are unintentional acts. Because excuses minimize responsibility, they are a logical choice for actors to use in circumstances in which a mistake has caused embarrassment. By contrast, to excuse oneself in

a recipient situation would seem superfluous since one's lack of responsibility should be apparent to other bystanders.

An embarrassed actor is inclined to use a justification in response to committing a faux pas. The act constituting the faux pas is intentional and it is therefore difficult for an actor to deny responsibility for the event, even though he or she "did not mean it." Once the act has been recognized by the offended parties, an attempt to minimize the severity of the offense is appropriate. The embarrassed person uses a justification to downplay the pejorative implication of the faux pas for others.

Humor is a particularly appropriate strategy in response to an accident. These situations do not usually involve inconvenience or damage to another person. The typical scene presented by our respondents centered on falling, slipping, dropping items, and so forth. Since only the embarrassed person's face has been diminished, laughing or joking about the event does not compound an affront or offense, as it might in situations of mistakes or faux pas. Humor in accident situations allows actors to compensate for a loss of social competence with a subsequent display of social competence. In discussing laughter and jokework as two forms of humor, Edelmann (1985) notes that "both can be used to reduce tension inherent in the situation, while a joke can have the added advantage of turning a potential loss of social approval into a gain in social approval" (p. 209).

The use of remediation in accidents is also especially appropriate. Accidents frequently involve physical disruption and loss of poise. Remediation constitutes acknowledgement that an untoward act has been committed, as well as indicating a willingness to restore social order by "correcting" or "fixing" that which has gone awry.

Aggression is used exclusively in recipient situations. This is to be expected since the cause of one's embarrassment in these situations is another social actor who, presumably, can be sanctioned in an attempt to restore social order. In this sense, aggression seems to be a reaction to the other person who is committing a face threatening act rather than a response to the ensuing embarrassment per se. Perhaps the ''fight'' response is also an attempt to keep similar intentional offenses from being perpetrated in the future.

Unlike the strategies discussed above, apology, escape, and avoidance appear to be general strategies whose likelihood of use is not constrained by the type of embarrassing predicament. In the case of apology, it is likely that it serves an augmentation function for other strategies. As Cupach and colleagues (1986) reported, apologies frequently co-occur with other remedial strategies. Avoidance is also used frequently across situations. This strategy allows the passive resumption of social activity without exacerbating embarrassment by calling undue attention to the failure event. While escape is perhaps the ultimate form of avoidance, it is used infrequently, probably due to its ineffectiveness. Aside from the fact that escape precludes the possibility of actively repairing the disrupted social equilibrium, it is sometimes not feasible. Many respondents described a situation from which they could not very logically escape, e.g., classrooms, at work, giving a speech, playing in a ballgame, etc. When escape was used, respondents typically described a situation occurring when they were children and presumably less aware of more sophisticated strategies.

Future Directions

We believe the data presented here support the contention that situational variables are important in understanding remedial behavior in embarrassing predicaments. There are a number of ways in which the findings here can be extended. First, numerous other situational variables undoubtedly influence remedial action (e.g., see Cody & McLaughlin, 1985). We chose a global, componential approach to conceptualizing types of embarrassing situations. An alternative would be to assess the salient dimensions upon which

actors perceive situations. (For a comparison of componential and dimensional approaches to situation, see Furnham & Argyle, 1981.) For example, severity of the predicament and the nature of the relationship between offended and offending parties would seem particularly relevant to embarrassing situations. Moreover, exploring the interface between personality variables (e.g., communicative competence, self-monitoring, embarrassability) and situational features will give us a more complete picture of the nature of remedial action.

Finally, it is apparent that both actors and observers often utilize multiple strategies to reduce an actor's embarrassment. In fact, 35 percent of our respondents reported combinations of two, three, or four remedial strategies to deal with their embarrassing situations, and 23 percent of respondents reported multiple strategies for other persons. Although we did not assess the various strategy combinations, it is apparent that extricating oneself from an embarrassing predicament is often a complicated process. It is unclear from our limited sample how some strategies embellish, augment, or modify other strategies when used collectively. Future investigations will need to take a more sophisticated look at remedial action by examining the effects of sequences or clusters of behaviors.

REFERENCES

Archibald, P.W., & Cohen, R. L. (1971). Self-presentation, embarrassment, and facework as a function of self-evaluation, conditions of self-presentation, and feedback from others. *Journal of Personality and Social Psychology, 20*, 287–297.

Blumstein, P.W., Carssow, K.G., Hall, J., Hawkins, B., Hoffman, R., Ishem, E., Maurer, C. P., Spens. D., Taylor, J., & Zimmerman, D.L. (1974). The honoring of accounts. *American Sociological Review, 39*, 551–566.

Brown, B.R., & Garland, H. (1971). The effects of incompetency, audience acquaintanceship, and anticipated evaluative feedback on face-saving behavior. *Journal of Experimental Social Psychology, 7*, 490–502.

Buss, A.H., (1980). *Self-consciousness and social anxiety.* San Francisco, CA: W.H. Freeman.

Buttny, R. (1985). Accounts as a reconstruction of an event's context. *Communication Monographs, 52*, 57–77.

Cody, M.J., & McLaughlin, M.L. (1985). Models for the sequential construction of accounting episodes: Situational and interactional constraints on message selection and evaluation. In R.L. Street, Jr., and J.N. Cappella (Eds.), *Sequence and pattern in communicative behavior* (pp. 50–69). Baltimore, MD: Edward Arnold.

Cupach, W.R., Metts, S., & Hazleton, V. (1986). Coping with embarrassing predicaments: Remedial strategies and their perceived utility. *Journal of Language and Social Psychology, 5,* 181–200.

Darby, B.W., & Schlenker, B.R. (1982). Children's reactions to apologies. *Journal of Personality and Social Psychology, 43,* 742–753.

Edelmann, R.J. (1982). The effect of embarrassed reactions upon others. *Australian Journal of Psychology, 34,* 359–367.

Edelmann, R.J. (1985). Social embarrassment: An analysis of the process. *Journal of Social and Personal Relationships, 2,* 195–213.

Edelmann, R.J., & Hampson, S. E. (1979). Changes in non-verbal behavior during embarrassment. *British Journal of Social and Clinical Psychology, 18,* 385–390.

Edelmann, R.J., & Hampson, S.E. (1981). The recognition of embarrassment. *Personality and Social Psychology Bulletin, 7,* 109–116.

Emerson, J.P. (1970). Behavior in private places: Sustaining definitions of reality in gynecological examinations. In H.P Dreitzel (Ed.), *Recent sociology (No. 2, Patterns of communicative behavior)* (pp. 74–97). New York: Macmillan.

Fink, E.L., & Walker, B.A. (1977). Humorous responses to embarrassment. *Psychological Reports, 40,* 475–485.

Furnham, A., & Argyle, M. (Eds.). (1981). *The psychology of social situations: Selected readings.* Oxford: Pergamon Press.

Garland, H., & Brown, B.R. (1972). Face-saving as affected by subject's sex, audience's sex and audience expertise. *Sociometry, 35,* 280–289.

Goffman, E. (1956). Embarrassment and social organization. *American Journal of Sociology, 62,* 264–271.

Goffman, E. (1967). *Interaction ritual: Essays on face-to-face behavior.* New York: Pantheon Books.

Goffman, E. (1971). *Relations in public.* New York: Basic Books.

Gross, F., & Stone, G.P. (1964). Embarrassment and the analysis of role requirements. *American Journal of Sociology, 70,* 1–15.

Knapp, M.L., Stafford, L., & Daly, J.A. (1986). Regrettable messages: Things people wish they hadn't said. *Journal of Communication, 36*(4), 40–58.

McLaughlin, M.L., Cody, M.J., & O'Hair, H.D. (1983). The management of failure events: Some contextual determinants of accounting behavior. *Human Communication Research, 9,* 208–224.

McLaughlin, M.L., Cody, M.J., & Rosenstein, N.E. (1983). Account sequences in conversations between strangers. *Communication Monographs, 50,* 102–125.

Mehrabian, A. (1967). Substitute for apology: Manipulation of cognitions to reduce negative attitude toward self. *Psychological Reports, 20,* 687–692.

Miller, R.S. (1987). Empathic embarrassment: Situational and personal determinants of reactions to the embarrassment of another. *Journal of Personality and Social Psychology, 53,* 1061–1069.

Modigliani, A. (1968). Embarrassment and embarrassability. *Sociometry, 31,* 313–326.

Modigliani, A. (1971). Embarrassment, facework, and eye contact: Testing a theory of embarrassment. *Journal of Personality and Social Psychology, 17,* 15–24.

Petronio, S. (1984). Communication strategies to reduce embarrassment: Differences between men and women. *Western Journal of Speech Communication, 48,* 28–38.

Sattler, J.M. (1965). A theoretical, developmental, and clinical investigation of embarrassment. *Genetic Psychology Monographs, 71,* 19–59.

Schlenker, B.R. (1980). *Impression management: The self-concept, social identity, and interpersonal relations.* Monterey, CA: Brooks/Cole Publishing.

Schlenker, B.R., & Darby, B.W. (1981). The use of apologies in social predicaments. *Social Psychology Quarterly, 44,* 271–278.

Schonbach, P. (1980). A category system for account phases. *European Journal of Social Psychology, 10,* 195–200.

Scott, M.B., & Lyman, S.M. (1968). Accounts. *American Sociological Review, 33,* 46–62.

Semin, G.R., & Manstead, A.S.R. (1981). The beholder beheld: A study of social emotionality. *European Journal of Social Psychology, 11,* 253–265.

Semin, G.R., & Manstead, A.S.R. (1982). The social implications of embarrassment displays and restitution behavior. *European Journal of Social Psychology, 12,* 367–377.

Semin, G.R., & Manstead, A.S.R. (1983). *The accountability of conduct: A social psychological analysis.* London: Academic Press.

Tedeschi, J., & Riess, M. (1981). Verbal strategies in impression management. In C. Antaki (Ed.), *The psychology of ordinary explanations of social behavior* (pp. 271–309). New York: Academic Press.

Weinberg, M.S. (1968). Embarrassment: Its variable and invariable aspects. *Social Forces, 46,* 382–388.

FUDGING WITH FRIENDS AND LYING TO LOVERS:
DECEPTIVE COMMUNICATION IN PERSONAL RELATIONSHIPS

Gerald R. Miller, Paul A. Mongeau & Carra Sleight

Although a considerable body of recent research has addressed the problem of deceptive communication, few studies have examined deceptive communication in personal relationships. We argue that the occurrence, substance, and outcomes of deceptive communication are markedly influenced by the nature of the communicators' relationship. To redeem this claim, we examine how several differences between impersonal and personal relationships may influence deceptive exchanges, and consider some of the implications of the distinctions for future research dealing with deceptive communication in personal relationships.

The past fifteen years have witnessed a burgeoning literature on deceptive communication. The most comprehensive review to date (Zuckerman et al., 1981) lists 217 references, the lion's share conducted during the 1970s. More modest overviews have also appeared (Knapp & Comadena, 1979), as well as reviews dealing with such limited topics as modality effects in the detection of deception (De Paulo et al., 1980), verbal and nonverbal behaviours influencing assessment of the credibility of trial witnesses (Miller & Burgoon, 1982), and cognitive and social processes affecting the physiological detection of deception (Waid & Orne, 1981). Three meta-analyses focusing on the deception literature have been reported (Kalbfleisch, 1985, unpub.; Kraut, 1980; Zuckerman et al., 1981). Certainly, it does not

seem unduly deceptive to assert that investigation of factors influencing the processes and outcomes of deceptive communication has attracted a wide following. Along with a lively scientific curiosity, numerous social and political events have stimulated the current concern with deceit. Knapp & Comadena see it this way:

> [During the late 60s and early 70s] we were exposed to a staggering number of lies by public officials about Vietnam and Watergate. . . . During this same period, the subject of openness and honesty became a focus for renewed self-examination and experimentation in daily social activities and personal relationships. In both public and private domains, then, we began to feel that there was a growing imbalance in the truth/deception ratio; deception was perceived to be dangerously overrepresented and the peaceful coexistence of the two approaches was threatened. But perhaps the overriding influence was that these events only served to remind us that this society was built and is maintained on the assumption that others will generally tell us what they believe to be truth. (1979, p. 271)

Though few, if any, would dispute Knapp & Comadena's emphasis on both the public and the private contexts of deception, little of the presently available research fits comfortably in the latter domain. The strategies and procedures used to study deceptive communication are more clearly linked to the marketplace than to the fireplace; the research results seem more germane to stockholders than to handholders; the entire investigational enterprise is largely geared to the boardroom, not the bedroom. In short, prior research on deceptive communication has centred on momentary impersonal encounters (indeed, even non-encounters) between strangers or

Source: The article is taken from the *Journal of Social and Personal Relationships* [3: 495–512, 1986]. (c) Sage Publications Ltd, 6 Bonhill St., London EC24A 4PU, UK. Reprinted by permission of Sage Publications Ltd.

casual acquaintances rather than ongoing personal relationships between friends and lovers.

If it could be argued cogently that the impersonal relational context of prior deception research poses no serious difficulties in generalizing the findings to ongoing personal relationships, the dearth of studies dealing with such established relationships would be less troublesome. But convincing arguments supporting this position are hard to come by; quite the contrary, it seems patently obvious that both the substance and the outcomes of deceptive transactions are markedly influenced by the nature of the communicators' relationships. To redeem this claim, we examine several important differences between brief encounters and casual relationships, on the one hand, and personal relationships, on the other, emphasizing how these differences may influence deceptive exchanges and noting some of their implications for future research on deceptive communication in personal relationships. Before embarking on our primary task, however, some definitional attention to the term 'deceptive communication' should be helpful.

DECEPTIVE COMMUNICATION: A DEFINITION

The term 'deceptive communication' is itself deceptively simple; numerous writers have devoted attention to its definition, as well as the definition of allied terms such as 'deception' and 'lying' (e.g., Bok, 1978; Eck, 1970; Ekman, 1985; Hopper & Bell, 1984; Knapp & Comadena, 1979; Ludwig, 1965; Miller, 1983). The definition guiding our discussion is taken from Miller (1983, pp. 92–3): *'Deceptive communication refers to message distortion resulting from deliberate falsification or omission of information by a communicator with the intent of stimulating in another, or others, a belief that the communicator himself or herself does not believe'*.

Several implications of this definition merit brief scrutiny. To commence, it should be underscored that the presence of terms such as 'message distortion' and 'information' takes the occurrence of symbolic exchange as a given. This defining characteristic helps distinguish 'deceptive communication', as we conceive of it, from the closely related terms 'deception' and 'lying' mentioned above. More specifically, an exhaustive inventory of activities that might qualify as instances of *deception* could include, as Hopper & Bell (1984) have noted, such verbal activities as purposeful ambiguity and implication cues and such nonverbal strategies as context-sensitive implication. [Hopper and Bell (1984, p. 289) go so far as to point out circumstances when the *truth* can be used to deceive: 'Consider the con-artist, the counter-spy, and the philanderer who may craft each utterance to be as truthful as possible'.] And at the other end of the continuum, if one were to conceive of *lying* in the ordinary sense only of uttering untrue verbal statements (Hopper & Bell, 1984), it could be taken as a species of the genus, *deceptive communication*. In short, we conceive of 'deceptive communication' as somewhat narrower than 'deception' and somewhat broader than 'lying'.

Though it is often troublesome to divine, *intent* is a common ingredient of almost all definitions of 'deceptive communication' found in the literature. Two closely related considerations mandate the inclusion of this defining characteristic. First, since most behavioural narratives and accounts are, of necessity, truncated, there is a sense in which almost all communication is deceptive. When a spouse is queried by her or his mate about 'the day's activities', it is understood that the spouse is neither capable of reciting, nor required to recite every single thing that occurred in the space of eight or ten hours. Only when it is perceived that information has been falsified or omitted with the conscious intent of engendering false beliefs is the spectre of deceptive communication likely to intrude on the conversation.

In addition to the limits of communicative time and space, imperfections of human memory virtually ensure inaccuracies or omissions in accounts of past behaviour. When such distortions are perceived as honest errors, questions about deceptive communication are deemed irrelevant. Thus, the statement, 'My spouse is terrible about remembering the things we did on our honeymoon' implies doubts about the *accuracy* of accounts but not about the *motives* of the communicator.

To be sure, disagreements about the presence or absence of deceptive intent sometimes poison the relational waters, particularly in personal relationships. When recounting the day's happenings, our hypothetical spouse may suffer an honest lapse of memory and fail to mention that an attractive co-worker was part of the luncheon group. If the mate has reason to believe the co-worker went to lunch with the group, he or she may infer or attribute deceptive intent because of the omission. Indeed, if the mate suspects a relationship between the spouse and the co-worker, he or she may inquire whether the co-worker was at lunch even though there is no specific evidence to suggest it. Having been cued about the omission, a subsequent denial by the spouse would qualify as an instance of deceptive communication, rather than an honest memory lapse. Questions about relational and individual factors predisposing partners to leap to or to discount attributions of deceit are fair game for researchers interested in deceptive interpersonal transactions, but the fact that disagreements about intent often occur does not argue against its importance as a defining characteristic of deceptive communication.

Finally, a broad implication of our definition is that we conceive of deceptive communication as arising from actual or anticipated dialogue in ongoing relationships. Stated differently, the mere fact that someone neglects to mention something to a relational partner is not itself sufficient to establish an instance of deceptive communication. Granted, some students of personal relationships argue for the value of full and complete disclosure by relational partners, but regardless of the merits of this position, inclusion of this criterion would result in an unrealistically broad and ambiguous definition of deceptive communication. Instead, we restrict deceptive communication to two broad relational situations: situations in which a comment or a query

motivates intentional message distortion by a relational partner and situations in which an *anticipated* query motivates the partner to conjure a deceptive message. Thus, if our hypothetical spouse anticipates that the partner will ask questions about the day's luncheon companions, he or she may attempt to 'steal the partner's thunder' by reciting a list of diners that excludes the attractive co-worker. Reliance on this strategy stems from the assumption that volunteering distorted information may assuage the partner's suspicions, thus reducing the likelihood of subsequent dialogue centering on the area of concealment.

Obviously, any definition of such a complex and ubiquitous phenomenon as deceptive communication is bound to be fraught with some ambiguity. Nevertheless, the definition we have sketched limits the domain of personal symbolic exchange falling within the confines of deceit. It remains, then, to consider differences in impersonal and personal relationships that are likely to influence the occurrence, substance, and outcomes of deceptive communication.

IMPERSONAL VERSUS PERSONAL RELATIONSHIPS: THREE IMPORTANT DIFFERENCES

Duration of Relational History

It is almost a definitional truism to assert that personal relationships are characterized by their extensive histories. Indictments of marital strangers and insensitive friends notwithstanding, most people feel they 'know' their relational intimates, with this feeling being founded on the knowledge that they have spent considerable time and energy interacting with these intimates. Rightly or wrongly, most people probably also believe that while P.T. Barnum may be able to fool them some of the time, their friends and lovers are unlikely to succeed in this objective, primarily because the latters' flights into deceit will deviate from their usual communicative flight patterns.

Contrast this personal relational situation with the circumstances of a typical study dealing with deceptive communication. In most cases, some persons are first induced to lie and/or to tell the truth about something—e.g., to misrepresent their feelings when viewing pictures of disfigured burn victims (Ekman & Friesen, 1974; Hocking et al., 1979) or to concoct a strategy that explains their success in an ambiguous task where they have been implicated in cheating (Bauchner et al., 1977; Bauchner et al., 1980; Exline et al., 1970). Though such studies occasionally include a live presentational condition (e.g., Bauchner et al., 1977), a more common procedure involves recording truthful and deceptive messages on videotapes and later preparing audiotapes and written transcripts from the tapes if these modes of presentation are to be used in the study.

Once message stimuli are prepared, another group of persons is assembled to act as deception detectors. Seldom are the detectors acquainted with the deceivers, and unless the study includes a live condition, the deceivers and detectors have no face-to-face contact. Detectors observe a series of truthful and untruthful messages, making veracity judgements after each message. In a few studies (e.g. Hocking, 1976, unpub.; Hocking et al., 1979), they also provide subjective estimates of confidence in each of their judgements.

The most strikingly consistent finding of these studies is that people are generally not very accurate at detecting deception. Most studies involve 50 percent truthful and 50 percent untruthful messages; thus, totally unschooled guesses should produce about 50 percent accuracy. Actual accuracy ranges from about 45 percent to 60 percent (Knapp & Comadena, 1979; Kraut, 1980; Miller & Burgoon, 1982). Considering the widely shared conventional wisdom about the way liars behave and people's general tendency to believe they can spot a liar when they encounter one, such levels of accuracy leave little cause for optimism. The picture is further clouded by the fact that detectors express considerable confidence in their judgements even though they are not very accurate (Hocking, 1976, unpub.; Littlepage & Pineault, 1979).

Undoubtedly, numerous factors contribute to these lack-lustre performances by deception detectors. One persistent issue concerns the extent to which research participants are motivated to scrutinize carefully the nonverbal and verbal behaviours of potential deceivers. Although detectors are often exhorted to attend closely or are told that success in detecting deception is evidence of intelligence or social skill, there are seldom any dire outcomes associated with failure to detect deceit. Certainly, when contemplating a substantial expenditure such as buying a used car or weighing the merits of making a profound relational commitment such as marriage, fateful consequences accompany the decision and the person is strongly motivated to test the other party's honesty.

Of particular import here is the likelihood that lack of familiarity with the potential deceiver's typical, truthful communicative behaviours contributes heavily to judgemental errors. When asked to make veracity judgements about a stranger, detectors are forced to rely on their stereotypical notions of how liars behave; in the language of Miller & Steinberg (1975), they are forced to employ noninterpersonal rather than interpersonal information. Granted, evidence indicates that some cues generally believed to signal deception frequently are present when people are lying (Miller & Burgoon, 1982; Zuckerman et al., 1981). Nevertheless these same behavioural cues may be triggered by sources of arousal other than awareness that one is attempting to deceive. With strangers, then, the trick is to make the correct attribution, to infer correctly that a particular behavioural display results from awareness of intent to deceive, rather than arousal-producing factors associated with the person him/herself—e.g., communication apprehension or manifest anxiety—or other stressful features associated with the situation—e.g., testifying in court about an extremely traumatic experience such as rape. That such alternative sources of arousal can produce substantial error is supported by findings of large individual differences in ability to deceive

(Hocking et al., 1979; Kraut, 1980). When communicating with strangers, some people are clearly 'good' liars—almost all of their messages, both truthful and deceitful, are judged as truthful. Conversely, others are 'poor' truthtellers—both their truthful messages and their lies are usually judged as untruthful. Though we are unaware of any systematic content analyses of the messages of these two groups, casual perusal of the Hocking et al. tapes reveals that the good liars seldom manifest many of the nonverbal and verbal behaviours stereotypically linked with lying while the poor truthtellers present such behaviours consistently.

The previous circumstances vary markedly from the state-of-affairs in personal relationships. Since partners in close relationships have the benefit of an extensive history, they do not have to rely on cultural and sociological generalizations about the behaviour of liars. Instead, partners' relational history allows for the collection of idiosyncratic information about the partner's typical symbolic activity. This collection of observations can be used to form a 'behavioural baseline', a kind of template of truthful behaviours; which, in turn, provides a basis for evaluating behaviours suspected of being deceptive. To borrow again from the argot of Miller & Steinberg (1975), parties in personal relations have access to psychological, idiosyncratic information. Any deviation from the baseline, although it can be caused by many factors, may be attributed to the partner's deceptive intent.

The existence of behavioural baselines implies that strangers and relational intimates use different cognitive processes in detecting deception. Specifically, strangers, lacking idiosyncratic information about the person's typical communicative style, may be forced to rely on the logical structure and/or the consistency of the communicator's story or 'line'. Lacking baseline data, strangers are bombarded with a wide variety of verbal, nonverbal, and paraverbal cues with limited means of interpreting the relevance of these cues to truth and deception. Relational partners, on the other hand, can not only evaluate the logical structure and/or the consistency of the 'line' being presented, but have the added capacity to use their behavioural baseline in order to focus on deviations from normal symbolic activity.

A model depicting the development of behavioural baselines is presented in Figure 1. In this model, relational history and extent of interaction are thought to be highly, but not perfectly correlated. Both relational history and the extent of interaction are presumed to influence the amount of idiographic information participants possess about their relational partners—again, the correlation is expected to be strong, but not perfect. In short, both duration of relational history and extent of interaction between partners are thought to have an effect on the type and amount of in-

FIGURE 1   The process of developing a behavioral baseline of idiographic knowledge.

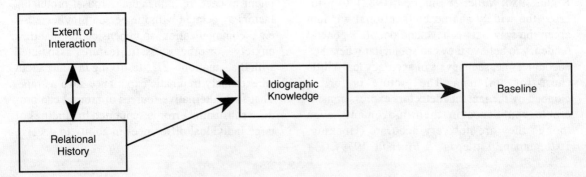

formation held by relational partners. The amount and type of information held by partners are posited to have an effect on the amount and type of information in the behavioural baseline.

To illustrate, when strangers meet, the extent of interaction as well as the the relational history are, by definition, zero. Thus, there is no idiographic knowledge shared between 'partners'. Since there is no shared idiographic knowledge, the behavioural baselines are empty, or perhaps more accurately, filled with impersonal normative information. Since there is no shared idiographic knowledge regarding the other person, strangers must rely largely on the logical structure of the story line being presented to make truth-deception attributions. Strangers may also use culturally normative information that is thought to indicate deception—e.g.; lack of eye contact, shuffling feet, etc.; however, previous deception experiments have indicated the limited value of this information.

As a relationship develops, the amount of information about the partner increases. Put another way, general information in the baseline is replaced with information specific to the partner's behaviour. In Miller & Steinberg's (1975) terms, cultural and sociological information are partially replaced and supplemented with psychological information. In the case of relational partners, then, when the veracity of one partner is suspect, there exists a 'store' of baseline information on the suspected partner's normal behaviour. This baseline information can be used as a comparison point for evaluating the veracity of present behaviour. In addition, the data in the baseline will probably contain past deceptive as well as past truthful behaviours, for there are many occasions where one relational partner has the opportunity to observe the other partner deceiving others—e.g., telling the boss's wife that a distasteful meal was delicious or telling a potential buyer that a used car has 'only' 49,000 miles on it. Thus, when deception is suspected in an ongoing relationship, the suspecting partner has a store of truthful and deceptive behaviour to be used in evaluating behaviour—e.g., 'You acted this way when you lied to me about your

secretary,' or 'You never play with your hair when you tell the truth'. This store of truthful and deceptive behaviour gives the relational partner a great advantage when it comes to detecting deception when compared to the detection ability of strangers.

Limited evidence supporting the existence of such behavioural baselines comes from a pilot study conducted by the authors (Miller et al., 1984, unpub.). In this study, relationally involved couples were asked to indicate, among other things, which cues given off by their relational partners triggered suspicions of deceit. In most cases, respondents indicated that a *change* in some verbal, nonverbal, or paraverbal cue triggered doubt. Specifically, respondents indicated that changes in eye contact, message length, and hand or foot movements often engendered suspicions of deceit. The report of the change in the behaviours of the relational partner as a clue to deceptive intent indicates that behavioural baselines of (allegedly) truthful behaviours are collected throughout the course of the relationship. Apparently, relational partners do consciously attempt to compare present symbolic behaviours, suspected of being deceptive, with past symbolic activities, presumed to be truthful.

From the same study comes limited evidence that the process of detecting deception by strangers does indeed differ from the process of detecting deception by relational intimates. Respondents reported that when trying to detect deceit by intimates, they concentrate primarily on the person's verbal and nonverbal behaviours; when trying to assess the veracity of strangers, they focus carefully on the story or 'line' being presented, listening attentively for inconsistencies and using probing queries. This difference suggests that when the potential deceiver is a partner in a personal relationship, the detector has the benefit of a behavioural baseline. This baseline is unavailable for strangers, forcing detectors to concentrate more heavily on the consistency or believability of the story line. Put another way, relational intimates concentrate on the baseline while strangers concentrate on the story line. Although the existence of behavioural baselines does not solve all the difficulties of identifying deceit, it suggests that relational intimates should be better than strangers at detecting deception, at least under the passive observational conditions used in most prior deception studies.

This suggestion has received at least limited support. In an as yet uncompleted study, Bauchner (cited in Miller et al., 1981) had each deceiver's spouse, a friend, and a stranger observe the deceiver through a one-way mirror. Deceivers engaged in both self-feeling deception and deception about matters of fact. Though there were no differences in detection accuracy for factual information, partial analyses for data obtained with twelve deceivers revealed that friends were significantly more accurate then either spouses or strangers at detecting self-feeling deception. Moreover, friends were 74 percent accurate, a better detection rate than has been observed in studies using strangers in the deceiver and detector roles. Though no confident explanation can be offered for the detection superiority of friends over spouses, perhaps marital partners often develop avoidance mechanisms to 'shut out' the possibility that their mates may be deceiving them. Indeed, McCornack & Parks (1986) have recently so argued to explain their finding that confidence in the ability to detect an intimate's deceit is negatively associated with actual detective success.

In a more extensive study aimed at assessing the relative detection accuracy of friends versus relational intimates, Comadena (1982) assigned intimates the roles of both deceivers and detectors, while friends took only the detector role. Deceivers engaged in both self-feeling and factual deception in responding to a standard set of interview questions posed by detectors. Thus, the opportunity existed for limited interaction, but interviewers could not deviate from the protocol questions to probe responses of deceivers.

Primary analyses provided an indication that familiarity—which we argued earlier is a crucial component of relational history—affected detection accuracy ($p = 0.07$, eta $= 0.22$, power $= 0.50$). Moreover, most of the difference was due to female intimates, who were more accurate in detecting deception than were their male counterparts, but the accuracy of male and female friends did not differ. In a subsequent supplementary analysis, intimates were asked to observe the interviews passively and to make veracity judgements. In this passive observation, intimates were more accurate in detecting emotional than factual deception, a prediction made but not confirmed in the primary analyses. Comadena suggests that intimates saw something the second time that tipped them off to the emotional deception. As amplified in our next section, an alternative explanation is that being removed from the active role of interviewing permitted intimates to focus attention solely on the message behaviours of their partners.

Our purpose is not to explore painstakingly the implications of differences in relational history, but rather to emphasize that the more extensive histories of personal relationships have important implications for research dealing with deceptive communication. Having stressed this point, we turn to our second important difference between impersonal and personal relationships.

Extent of Interaction Opportunities

Personal relationships encourage relatively high levels of interaction; indeed, it is hard to imagine situations where parties to such relationships would lack the opportunity to explore, probe, and question the messages communicated by their partners. Conversely, impersonal relationships and isolated encounters often inhibit the chances for interaction. In every election, voters attempt to assess the veracity of the various political candidates. They make judgements without the benefit of any face-to-face interaction; at best, they may be privy to questions raised by reporters and other interrogators or to exchanges between the candidates themselves should 'Great Debates' come to pass. As people engage in daily marketplace transactions with relative strangers, interaction sometimes occurs, but the extent to which it is possible is frequently limited. Furthermore, to return to a previous theme, lack of a relational history makes it difficult to assess the results of probes and questions aimed at testing veracity.

Suppose, however, that a spouse suspects infidelity, but the mate steadfastly professes innocence. The question of fidelity may become a topic of repeated conversations; barring an angry walkout by the accused, a suspicious spouse can query his or her mate interminably. Both the relative privacy and the amount of time together afforded by personal relationships enhance interaction opportunities.

At first glance, the chance to interact extensively with a suspected liar appears to increase the chances of detecting deceit. Cues indicating skepticism about the veracity of messages could trigger nonverbal and paralinguistic behaviours that provide valid indicators of deception, responses that deviate from the relational partner's typical symbolizing. Probes and questions might trap the prevaricator in contradictions and inconsistencies. In short, dialogue might be expected to enhance deception detection.

Upon closer examination, however, there are at least two reasons why interaction could conceivably make deception detection more difficult. When passively observing the communicative activities of a suspected deceiver, observers can attend totally to the cues presented by the deceiver. By contrast, when interacting, their attention must also be directed at encoding appropriate messages of their own. This dual sender-receiver role increases the cognitive demands of the task and fosters information overload. Recall that relational intimates and friends did not differ in detection accuracy during the interview phase of Comadena's (1982) study, but that intimates were more accurate at detecting self-feeling deception than they were at detecting factual deception when they passively observed the deceptive messages of their partners.

Dialogue between detectors and suspected deceivers might also detract from accurate judgements of veracity if it caused truthful communicators to emit cues thought to provide valid indicators of deceit. Suppose, for instance, that our hypothetical mate is actually innocent of any philandering, but the aggrieved spouse continues to express suspicion and to question the partner accusingly. These cues of suspicion and distrust are themselves likely to trigger heightened arousal that, in turn, produces deviations from typical communicative behaviour interpreted as evidence of intent to deceive. Stated differently, protestations of doubt and disbelief directed at a truthful communicator may themselves elicit the nonverbal and verbal behaviours commonly associated with lying.

Though not conducted with parties to a personal relationship, a recent study by Stiff & Miller (1986) investigated this possibility. In its initial phase, naive participants were paired with a confederate to undertake an ambiguous task requiring them to estimate the number of dots on a series of cards (Bauchner et al., 1977; Bauchner et al., 1980; Exline et al., 1970). They were told that the dyad with the best score would receive a cash award. Midway through the trials, the experimenter left the room, ostensibly to take an important telephone call. During 50 percent of these absences, the confederate implicated the naive participant in cheating by looking in a folder left by the experimenter that supposedly contained the answers. During the rest of the absences, the naive participant was not implicated in cheating.

After the trials were completed, the experimenter told all participants they had improved dramatically in the latter portion of the trials and requested to interview them about the strategy used by their dyad. Naive participants were told both members of the dyad would be interviewed, but the naive participant was always selected to be interviewed first. None of the implicated participants confessed to cheating but instead concocted strategies to explain their success; hence they communicated deceptively with the experimenter. The non-implicated participants also sought to explain their success, and since they had not been involved in cheating, they communicated truthfully, albeit in some cases, uncertainly.

One-half of the truthful and one-half of the untruthful participants were asked four positive interrogating probes by the experimenter. These probes contained phrases suggesting the experimenter was accepting their accounts—e.g.,

'Come to think of it that seems quite plausible', and 'Now that you've given a good explanation for your success'. The remaining truthful and untruthful participants responded to a series of four negative interrogating probes containing phrases suggesting that the experimenter doubted their stories—e.g., 'Come to think of it, that doesn't seem very plausible', and 'Frankly, I'm a little skeptical about your explanation'.

Stiff & Miller predicted that regardless of whether the participants were telling the truth or lying, positive probes would produce behaviours that were more likely to be perceived as signals of veracity whereas negative probes would create the opposite effect. In other words, it was posited that supportive comments would culminate in a truthful bias, while skeptical probes would result in a lying bias.

Before the tapes were shown to detectors, the evaluative phrases were edited from the probes so as to ensure that detectors' judgements would not be influenced by the content of the probes. Though the detection results were clear cut, they were exactly opposite to expectations. In all conditions, responses to positive probes were more likely to be judged deceptive and responses to negative probes were more likely to be judged truthful. Though the outcomes were puzzling, the researchers speculated that impression management theory (Tedeschi & Lindskold, 1976) might offer an explanation; i.e., communicators who were subjected to negative probes may have subsequently exerted more effort to present themselves in a positive manner.

Fortunately, Stiff & Miller's misguided hypothesizing does not detract from the thrust of the argument presented here. Clearly, some interactive characteristics influence subsequent judgements of veracity, even when 'interaction' is highly constrained. Since personal relationships are characterized by more frequent opportunities to interact in more numerous ways over a wide spectrum of topics, issues regarding deceptive communication in such relationships should be approached differently than transitory deceptive exchanges between relative strangers. We shall be content with this caveat and turn next to the third important difference between impersonal and personal relationships that has implications for the study of deceptive communication.

Concern for Relational Outcomes

In many impersonal situations involving deception, prevaricators have little concern for the relational implications of their deceptive behaviour. If a door-to-door salesperson misrepresents a product or a contract, the seller's primary concern centers on the customer's acceptance of the deceptive message so the deal can be closed. Should the customer later discover the seller's duplicity, his or her resultant negative attitudes towards the salesperson are usually of little moment to the latter. Indeed, in some particularly odious transactions, such as handkerchief drops and other confidence operations, the perpetrators are callously unconcerned with the mark's feelings about them so long as they reap a profit from the transaction.

In contrast, personal relationships are characterized by the partners' concern for relational outcomes. To be trapped in a lie not only thwarts the immediate objective of the deceit, it also casts a pall over the relationship itself. Being lied to by a stranger is often economically or professionally punishing, but being lied to by a close friend or a romantic partner is personally devastating. As a result, the relationship between the exploiter and the exploited is usually drastically altered.

There are, of course, exceptions to this generalization. Not all falsehoods stem from Machiavellian motives of self-interest; some are proffered with altruistic intent. In the case of such 'white lies', parties to personal relationships might be more predisposed to stray from the truth than participants in transitory, casual, impersonal relationships. But if detection is likely to poison the relational waters, friends and lovers will undoubtedly weigh the consequences of deceit more carefully.

Since maintenance of personal relationships is important, however, it might also be expected that many falsehoods that do occur seek to protect and to preserve the relationship itself. A momentary indiscretion may be denied or concealed because of its potential for placing the relationship in jeopardy. Thus, while it is possible that less deception occurs in personal relationships, the difference may be one of kind rather than amount. Moreover, one rather cynical view of close relationships holds that they are particularly fertile fields for deceptive communication. This view is illustrated by the following plaintive compliant uttered by Normie, a character in the American sitcom 'Cheers': 'It's no fun lying to your wife when the trust has gone out of the relationship'. In other words, the very relational danger and intrigue associated with duplicity in personal relationships maximizes deceptive temptation. Although this pessimistic assessment undoubtedly applies to some personal relationships, we question its general validity. We readily admit, however, that our scepticism is grounded primarily in faith rather than data, for we are unaware of research investigating the ways that concern for relational outcomes affects deceptive practices in personal relationships.

Since deceit has profound consequences for personal relationships, parties to such relationships are likely to operate from a strong *truth bias* in their communicative exchanges; i.e., they will probably assume veracity on their partners' parts unless presented with considerable conflicting evidence. In our pilot study mentioned earlier (Miller et al., 1984, unpub.), respondents reported that relatively little deception occurred in their relationships, even though they also endorsed the belief that some deception is necessary to keep the relationship on an even keel. Moreover, McCornack & Parks (1986) found, not surprisingly, that when intimates attribute general truthfulness to their partners, they are less successful at detecting deception by the partner when it does occur. Findings such as these, while only scratching the surface of the problem, suggest that intimates' concern for relational maintenance and growth may lead them to assess the consequences of deception detection quite differently when the target of deceit switches from a stranger to a close friend or romantic partner.

A FINAL THOUGHT

We have identified several important differences between impersonal and personal relationships thought to influence the occurrence, substance, and outcomes of deceptive communication. Hopefully, the implications of these distinctions will help to guide future research dealing with deceptive communication in personal relationships, both in the laboratory and in natural settings. Such investigations will be difficult to engineer, particularly since in natural environs it is usually impossible to ascertain when deceptive transactions are occurring. Given the societal pervasiveness of deceptive communication, however, the exploratory game appears to be worth the candle: though fudging with friends and lying to lovers is an ageless activity, our understanding of these deceptive pursuits still leaves much to be desired.

REFERENCES

Bauchner, J.E., Brandt, D.R. & Miller, G.R. (1977). 'The truth/deception attribution: Effects of varying levels of information availability'. In B.D. Ruben (ed.), *Communication Yearbook 1*. Transaction Books: New Brunswick, NJ.

Bauchner, J.E., Kaplan, E.P. & Miller, G.R. (1980). 'Detecting deception: The relationship of available information to judgmental accuracy in initial encounters'. *Human Communication Research* (6), 251–64.

Bok, S. (1978). *Lying: Moral Choice in Private and Public Life*. Pantheon Books: New York.

Comadena, M.E. (1982). 'Accuracy in detecting deception: Intimate and friendship relationships'. In M. Burgoon (ed.), *Communication Yearbook 6*. Sage Publications: Beverly Hills, CA.

DePaulo, B.M., Zuckerman, M. & Rosenthal, R. (1980). 'Modality effects in the detection of deception'. In L. Wheeler (ed.), *Review of Personality and Social Psychology*. Sage Publications: Beverly Hills, CA.

Eck, M. (1970). *Lies and Truth*. Collier-Macmillan: London.

Ekman, P. (1985). *Telling Lies: Clues to Deceit in the Marketplace, Politics, and Marriage*. W.W. Norton: New York.

Ekman, P. & Friesen, W.V. (1974). 'Detecting deception from the body or face'. *Journal of Personality and Social Psychology* (29), 288–98.

Exline, R.V., Thibaut, J., Hickey, C.B. & Gumpert, P. (1970). 'Visual interaction in relation to Machiavellianism and an unethical act'. In R. Christie & F. Geis (eds), *Studies in Machiavellianism*. Academic Press: New York.

Hocking, J.E. (1976). 'Detecting deceptive communication from verbal, visual, and paralinguistic cues: An exploratory study'. Unpublished PhD dissertation, Michigan State University, East Lansing, MI.

Hocking, J.E., Bauchner, J.E., Kaminski, E.P. & Miller, G.R. (1979). 'Detecting deceptive communication from verbal, visual, and paralinguistic cues'. *Human Communication Research* (6), 33–46.

Hopper, R. & Bell, R.A. (1984). 'Broadening the deception construct'. *Quarterly Journal of Speech* (70), 288–302.

Kalbfleisch, P.J. (1985). 'Accuracy in deception detection: A quantitative review'. Unpublished PhD dissertation, Michigan State University, East Lansing, MI.

Knapp, M.L. & Comandena, M.E. (1979). 'Telling it like it isn't: A review of theory and research on deceptive communication'. *Human Communication Research* (5), 270–85.

Kraut, R.E. (1978). 'Verbal and nonverbal cues in the perception of lying'. *Journal of Personality and Social Psychology* (36), 380–91.

Kraut, R.E. (1980). 'Humans as lie detectors: Some second thoughts'. *Journal of Communication* (30), 209–16.

Littlepage, G.E. & Pineault, M.A. (1979). 'Detection of deceptive factual statements from the body and the face'. *Personality and Social Psychology Bulletin* (5), 325–8.

Ludwig, A.M. (1965). *The Importance of Lying*. Charles C. Thomas: Springfield, IL.

McCornack, S.A. & Parks, M.R. (1986). 'Deception detection and relationship development: The other side of trust'. In M.L. McLaughlin (ed.), *Communications Yearbook 9*. Sage: Beverly Hills.

Miller, G.R. (1983). 'Telling it like it isn't and not telling it like it is: Some thoughts on deceptive communication.' In J. Sisco (ed.), *The Jensen Lectures: Contemporary Communication Studies*. USF Press: Tampa, FL.

Miller, G.R. & Burgoon, J.K. (1982). 'Factors affecting assessments of witness credibility'. In N.L. Kerr & R.M. Bray (eds), *The Psychology of the Courtroom*. Academic Press: New York.

Miller, G.R. & Steinberg, M. (1975). *Between People: A New Analysis of Interpersonal Communication*. Science Research Associates: Chicago, IL.

Miller, G.R., Bauchner, J.E., Hocking, J.E., Fontes, N.E., Kaminski, E.P. & Brandt, D.R. (1981). ''. . . And nothing but the truth'': How well can observers detect deceptive testimony?'' In B.D. Sales (ed.), *Perspectives in Law and Psychology, Volume II: The Trial Process*. Plenum: New York.

Miller, G.R., Mongeau, P.A. & Sleight, C. (1984). 'Fudging with friends and lying to lovers: Deceptive communication in interpersonal relationships'. Paper presented at the Second International Conference on Personal Relationships, July, Madison, WI.

Stiff, J.B. & Miller, G.R. (1986). '' ' Come to think of it . . .''. Interrogative probes, deceptive communication, and deception detection'. *Human Communication Research* (12), 339–57.

Tedeschi J.T. & Lindskold, S. (1976) *Social Psychology: Interdependence, Interaction, and Influence*. Wiley: New York.

Waid, W.M. & Orne, M.T. (1981). 'Cognitive, social, and personality processes in the physiological detection of deception'. In L. Berkowitz (ed.), *Advances in Experimental Social Psychology, Vo. XIV*. Academic Press: New York.

Zuckerman, M., DePaulo, B.M. & Rosenthal, R. (1981) 'Verbal and nonverbal communication of deception'. In L. Berkowitz (ed.), *Advances in Experimental Social Psychology, Vol. XIV*. Academic Press: New York.

COMMUNICATION BOUNDARY MANAGEMENT:
A THEORETICAL MODEL OF MANAGING DISCLOSURE
OF PRIVATE INFORMATION BETWEEN MARITAL COUPLES

Sandra Petronio

This article presents a theoretical approach that may be used to understand the way individuals regulate disclosure of private information. The communication boundary management perspective, while more generally applicable, in this presentation focuses on the way marital couples manage talking about private matters with each other. This theoretical perspective presents a boundary coordination process representing couples' management of communication boundaries in balancing a need for disclosure with the need for privacy. The theory identifies the prerequisite conditions for disclosure and the message strategies a disclosing spouse may use to tell private information, as well as the strategic messages of marital partner may use to reply. In addition, a proposal for the way the disclosing spouse and receiving partner manage the coordination of their communication boundaries is presented.

In our relationships we often are faced with paradoxical demands requiring us to manage dialectical needs for intimacy and autonomy when we wish to disclose private information. These demands occur in parent-child relationships, friendships, relationships with our supervisors, and most obviously, with our spouses. This article presents another puzzle piece in an ongoing research program that examines the way people regulate disclosure of private information.

The basic thesis of this research program assumes that revealing private information is risky because there is a potential vulnerability when revealing aspects of the self. Receiving private information from another may also result in the need for protecting oneself. In order to manage both disclosing and receiving private information, individuals erect a metaphoric boundary to reduce the possibility of losing face and as a means of protection. Also, people use a set of rules or criteria to control the boundary and regulate the flow of private information to and from others.

Thus far, this program of research has investigated the way individuals separately manage their communication boundaries by examining conditions prerequisite to revealing private information (Petronio, 1990a; Petronio & Chayer, 1988; Petronio & Martin, 1986; Petronio, Martin & Littlefield, 1984). Also, research has investigated boundary reconstruction after invasion of privacy has occurred (Petronio, 1990b; Petronio & Braithwaite, 1987; Petronio & Harriman, 1990; Petronio, Olson & Dollar, 1988). These studies have been conducted in several contexts including families, groups, organizations, relational partners, and between parents and children.

The theory presented in this article extends the scope of previous research; it focuses on a proposal for the way two communication boundaries may coordinate when one person wishes to tell private information that another has not requested. This scenario represents only one possible way in which an individual's communication boundary may interact with another's. For example, one might also solicit private information. The boundary coordination for soliciting

Source: The article is taken from *Communication Theory* [1:311–335, 1991] © 1991 Guilford Publications Inc, 72 Spring Street, New York, NY 10012. Reprinted by permission.

private information may be different from that found for unsolicited disclosure. While both conditions are important, the theoretical discussion presented in this article is limited to a disclosure condition that is punctuated by an individual giving unsolicited private information.[1]

This theoretical proposal also limits the contexts in which the discussion about boundary coordination is presented. While the principles outlined in this article may be applicable to many different arenas, interaction between marital couples is selected as a case in point. The decision to use marital couples is based on the desire to present a context in which there is high salience regarding disclosure of private information. Marital couples are expected to tell each other private thoughts and feelings to increase openness. At the same time, they are expected to maintain a sense of their own identity by protecting themselves through controlling the flow of private information to each other (Berardo, 1974).

Regulating the disclosure of private information has been identified by some as a more productive route to a successful marriage than practicing complete openness. For example, Levinger and Seen (1967) suggest that selectivity in communicating private information contributes more to marital harmony than telling everything. Bienvenu's (1970) findings suggest that selective communication in marital interactions is often preferable to complete and unrestricted disclosure about private issues, and Cozby (1973) notes that ''discretion may be important in preventing boredom from occurring in interpersonal relationships'' (p. 88). Thus, discretion is instrumental in developing a satisfactory interpersonal bond not only because it leaves room for surprises but also because it protects vulnerabilities. These findings indicate that persons in significant relationships, such as marital couples, appear to benefit from exercising selectivity through managing disclosure of private information with each other. The notions of discretion and selectivity of disclosure may be important to a variety of relationships. However, marital relationships most clearly illustrate the dynamics involved in regulating private information within a specific context.

A couple's successful boundary management of private information may contribute to the quality of their marital relationship. Management is critical because it is the process through which the partners balance giving up autonomy by disclosing and increasing intimacy by sharing private information.

FRAMING THE THEORY: COMMUNICATION BOUNDARY MANAGEMENT

The theoretical perspective articulated in this article functions on two interrelated levels—macro and micro. On a macro level, the theory applies a systems approach in the form of a boundary management process. This level provides the overarching structure and identifies the general parameters within which marital couples regulate revealing and reacting to private information. On a micro level (which constitutes the majority of the essay), the strategic nature of this communication boundary management perspective is examined. For this discussion, the beginning of the process is punctuated by a spouse's unsolicited disclosure of private information. This process is represented by interactive episodes where the needs of one spouse establish expectations to be fulfilled by the other spouse. The extent to which the expectations are met may affect the marital relationship.

An explanation of the activities involved at the micro level is necessarily more specific. The interactive patterns found between the disclosing spouse and receiving partner at this level are more strategic. Miell and Duck (1986) and Chelune (1976) point out that, especially in significant relationships, disclosure is more strategic than previous literature has suggested. As Bochner (1983) notes, in general, expressiveness and disclosure highlight ''a strategic predicament created by a need to balance pressures of self-revelation against pressures of self-restraint'' (pp. 608–609). The strategic nature of the interaction becomes more of a theme when the disclosure is unsolicited by the spouse. As Miell and Duck (1986) point out, individuals in relationships are more strategic about their communicative interactions, especially when unexpected information is encountered.

Thus, the macro level provides a systems framework where communicative boundaries are regulated when private information is disclosed. The micro level provides an analysis of the strategic nature of the interactive process punctuated by a spouse's unsolicited decision to disclose private information to a marital partner. When the decision is made by a spouse to disclose, a sequence of events follow. The micro level of analysis is used to assess those events and to present a series of strategic decision-making options marital couples may use when communicating about and reacting to private information. The goal of the macro level is to provide a framework while the goal of the micro level is to suggest a possible set of patterns and to identify the variables salient for consideration in managing private information between marital partners.

MACRO LEVEL COMMUNICATION BOUNDARY MANAGEMENT

When individuals wish to reveal private information, there is a need to regulate the way they communicate in order to control potential risk to the self. To do so, people erect a protective boundary that is used to manage the flow of private information from self to other (Altman, 1975; Altman, Vinsel & Brown, 1981). A boundary is also erected by the recipient to protect himself or herself. Since receiving disclosive information is also risky, the boundary is needed to regulate the potential vulnerability to the self as well. These boundaries represent the other perimeter of a communicative system for each individual.

These communication boundaries are regulated strategically according to decision criteria individuals use to judge expectations for interaction (Petronio & Martin, 1986). The boundaries may be loosely or tightly controlled depending upon the degree of risk associated with the privacy of the information (Minuchin, 1974). Thus, the more private the information, the more perceived risk from the disclosed information and the more the partners feel a need to control their respective boundaries (Johnson,

1974). When boundaries are tightly controlled, access to information about the person is limited, autonomy is achieved, and vulnerability is at a minimum.

When there is a need for one partner to reveal private information, the disclosing spouse and the receiving partner negotiate the way in which their boundaries intersect. As one system opens up, the needs of the disclosing spouse set up expectations for a response from the receiving partner. Thus, revealing private information has a direct effect on the way the partner manages his or her own communication boundary. The receiving spouse's boundaries are often regulated in response to the expectations communicated by the discloser of private information.

Thus, on the macro level, this theoretical model suggests that there is a coordination of boundaries where the marital partners maintain separate yet connected communicative systems that are used to protect vulnerabilities when there is a need to disclose private information. In so doing, the marital couple works to balance their personal autonomy and relational intimacy. Because the system structure of the macro level is not detailed enough to give this theoretical perspective sufficient explanatory power it is necessary to provide a micro-level analysis.

The following three assumptions underpinning the theoretical proposal highlight the interrelationship between the macro and micro levels: (1) marital partners erect boundaries to control autonomy and vulnerability when disclosing and receiving private information. The boundary is more tightly managed with private information than with other types that are less risky to the individual; (2) because disclosing private information and receiving disclosive information is risky and may cause potential vulnerability, the marital partners regulate their communication boundaries strategically to minimize risks; (3) as the partners' individual boundary systems intersect, decision rules are used to determine when, with whom, and how much private information is disclosed as well as how to respond to the disclosure to balance personal autonomy with relational intimacy. Figure 1 illustrates the overall framework for the macro level.

Having identified the general parameters of the communication boundary management perspective, the remainder of the article focuses on the micro level of analysis where a sequence of events is triggered by one spouse disclosing unsolicited private information to his or her marital partner.

MICRO LEVEL OVERVIEW

The theoretical perspective of communication boundary management is transactional. While the macro level represents a systems view, the micro level attempts to identify how patterns might evolve from certain kinds of transactional exchanges. The transactional patterns are marked by a demand-response sequence. When a spouse discloses private information that is unsolicited by the partner and opens up his or her communication boundary, there is an implied demand for a response that will satisfy certain expectations. The needs of the disclosing spouse set up expectations for the type of response that will most likely be fulfilling to him or her.

But, the response from the receiving spouse may or may not fit with the desired expectations.

FIGURE 1   Macro-level communication boundary management.

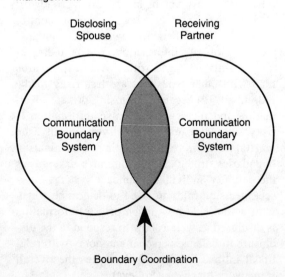

Boundary Coordination

The extent to which the reactions of the spouse accommodate this demand represents the level of boundary coordination achieved. Over time, the patterns of coordination may lead to increasing or decreasing relational quality and happiness.

The underlying notion suggested here is that of need complementarity. As Duck (1988) points out, complementarity develops with the relationship. Marital couples are more inclined to fulfill the needs of their partner in a complementary way (Berg & Clark, 1986). Carson (1979) suggests a general description of need complementarity. Complementarity exists when a need of one person is fulfilled by another and where that fulfillment produces satisfaction for person A, a corresponding level of satisfaction for person B, and overall satisfaction for the relationship. Thus, when there is a degree of fit between what one person needs and another is able to provide, there is an overall outcome that is positive for the relationship. This is a similar thesis to the one Rogers-Millar and Millar (1979) propose in their work on dominance and the one often used in understanding role relationships between marital couples (Lewis & Spanier, 1979).

Thus, managing the demand-response relationship produces a perceived outcome that results from coordinating respective boundaries. The negotiated outcome for the marital relationship represents an attempt to manage the demands of one spouse with the available responses from the marital partner. The process of management between a demand from the disclosing spouse communicating a set of expectations and a response by the receiving partner follows an episodic route in which the intersection of the couple's communication boundaries is coordinated.

Strategic Process of Boundary Management

In order more clearly to identify the episodic sequence that follows the demand-response coordination of communication boundaries between the marital partners, a discussion of the individual boundary management processes for the disclosing spouse and the receiving marital partner is first presented. In the discussion thereafter, the coordination process of the intersecting boundaries is proposed.

Generally, the boundary management process for the disclosing spouse is regulated by taking into account at least five variables: (1) need to tell, (2) predicted outcomes, (3) riskiness of telling this information to the partner, (4) privacy level of the information, and (5) his or her degree of emotional control. The consideration of these variables determines the message strategy selected to communicate the disclosive demand message. Boundary management for the receiving partner generally includes (1) evaluating expectations; (2) attributional searches; and (3) determining a message response.

Boundary coordination represents the extent to which there is a fit between the demand (expectations) made by the disclosing spouse and the reactions of the receiving partner. The interrelationship between the demands and responses may lead to four different degrees of fit or coordination: (1) satisfactory fit; (2) overcompensatory fit; (3) deficient fit; (4) equivocal fit.

Over time, the degree of coordination may result in positive or negative outcomes for the couple. For instance, over the course of a relationship, when there is a satisfactory fit between the disclosure messages and the responses given by the receiving partner, this pattern of boundary coordination may yield a benefit for the marital relationship. If there is overcompensatory fit, the response may exceed the expectations of the disclosive message for the interaction. The pattern that develops from this type of boundary coordination may be negative for the relationship. Deficient fit may produce a negative pattern for the relationship as well. When there is equivocal fit, if the response message accommodates the disclosure expectations the outcome may be positive. But, since fit is equivocal, there may also be times where the coordination results in a misfit between the disclosure expectation and the message response. Over time, if a pattern emerges, the outcome for the relationship may be more negative. In order to understand boundary coordination, it is useful to examine the disclosing

spouse's and receiving partner's boundary management separately, then assess how these boundaries intersect.

DISCLOSING SPOUSE'S BOUNDARY MANAGEMENT

When a spouse wishes to disclose private information, he or she must take many issues into consideration. One primary concern is the demand message used to convey the private information. The demand message includes three different aspects: (1) the expectations communicated about a response to the demand message; (2) the strategy used to communicate the message, using either an explicit or implicit message type; (3) the content of the message (in this case, it is the information communicating private thoughts and feelings).[2]

The demand message is critical to the boundary coordination process between the disclosing spouse and the receiving marital partner. The judgments made by the receiving spouse concerning his or her options for response are largely triggered by the expectations communicated through the content and message strategy. Thus, interpreting the meaning of the disclosure may depend upon the way the demand message is communicated by the spouse and understood by the marital partner.

Expectations Communicated in the Disclosive Demand Message

Demand messages entail an implied expectation of a response from the partner. The disclosing spouse's expectations for the type of response are influenced by the function or purpose of the disclosure. Derlega and Grzelak (1979) suggest at least five reasons for revealing private information: (1) expression; (2) self-clarification; (3) social validation; (4) relationship development; and (5) social control (Derlega & Grzelak, 1979, p. 154). For each type of disclosure, there is a corresponding expectation communicated that influences the choice of response.

When a marital partner discloses private information for the purpose of expression, he or she wants to talk about a feeling or thought. For example, the disclosing spouse may feel sad about a friend and need the partner to listen. Such a message implies the expectation for an active listener and perhaps a supportive statement in return from the spouse. When the reason for disclosure is self-clarification, the expectation communicated is for acknowledgment of the spouse's position. For example, the disclosing spouse may reveal strong feelings about an issue. The implied message is that the partner should indicate that he or she understands the point made by the spouse. When the reason for disclosing is social validation, the spouse may wish to receive confirmation about his or her self-esteem. The expectation from the partner is for feedback ratifying the worth of the spouse. If the reason for disclosing private information is relationship development, the partner may be expected to reciprocate with private information in return. Finally, when the purpose for disclosure is to gain social control over the partner, the demand implied in the message may be for compliance by the spouse.

Hence, the purpose of the disclosive message affects the type of response expected from the receiving partner. But these expectations are understood within the context of the strategies the disclosing spouse uses to communicate the private information. The disclosive demand message is therefore a combination of the expectations the disclosing spouse has, given the reasons for revealing private information, and the strategy used to communicate the disclosure. The demand message strategy is a means by which the disclosing spouse regulates or manages his or her own communication boundary.

Disclosive Demand Message Strategies: Explicit or Implicit

Demands concerning private information are communicated through explicit and implicit message strategies. The use of one or the other has implications for the way both sender and receiver coordinate their respective communication boundaries. For the purposes of this article, these terms reflect a simplified interpretation of the voluminous literature by scholars of speech act theory (e.g., Jacobs & Jackson, 1983; Sanford & Roach, 1987; Tracy, Craig, Smith & Spisak, 1984) and compliance-gaining researchers (e.g., Baxter, 1984; Boster & Stiff, 1984; Cody & McLaughlin, 1980; Cody, McLaughlin & Schneider, 1981; Cody, Woelfel & Jordan, 1983; Wiseman & Schenck-Hamlin, 1981) as well as the discussion on explicit and implicit metacommunication presented by Baxter and Wilmot (1984), Wilmot (1980), and Parks and Logan (1988).

Explicit Message Strategy: High Certainty Demand Characteristics

With an explicit message strategy, an imperative force is communicated (Sanford & Roach, 1987) that shapes the responses to the disclosive demand message and has implications for the boundary management process. The demands are stated without disguise, in a direct and unencumbered way. These are, thus, high certainty demand messages; the intentions of the demand are obvious, and the content is clearly articulated. Politeness is sacrificed for clarity (Lakoff, 1975). A spouse may say, for example, "Dear, stop correcting my stories; it really bugs me. They're my stories, and I will tell them the way I want." Within this explicit message system, demand strategies such as commands and statements calling for immediate action are used. The level of uncertainty is often lower because the partner issuing the demand concerning private information communicates expectations for a specific response from the marital partner in a straightforward manner. Consequently, for the recipient, managing the communication boundary to protect vulnerability may be more difficult.

With high clarity message strategies, the autonomy granted the recipient is lower (Baxter, 1984; Sanford & Roach, 1987). The partner is expected to provide a response and, because of the demand style, is limited in his or her control of the communication boundary. With a direct demand, there appears to be more pressure for compliance (Clark, 1979); the marital partner imposes an obligation that the spouse is expected to acknowledge. Thus, with an explicit message strategy, clarity of the demand is high, uncertainty is lower, and politeness is often abandoned. This strategy often places the receiving spouse in a more threatening position (Brown & Levinson, 1978). Autonomy for the receiving spouse is also lower, reducing the types of overt responses he or she has available to fulfill the demand where private information is concerned.

Implicit Message Strategy: Low Certainty Demand Characteristics

With the implicit message strategy, the disclosive demands are stated within conversations that "frame" the expectations or assumptions. The marital partner's purpose for issuing the demand is less clear than with an explicit strategy. These are low certainty demand messages. The ambiguity functions to afford the receiving spouse more control over opening or closing his or her communication boundary. By using this message strategy the disclosing spouse gives the receiving marital partner more autonomy in responding to the demands. Disclosing spouses who couch their demands in hints, prompts, and prerequests afford their partners the choice of more varied responses. For example, the receiving spouse is able to feign ignorance concerning the expectations implied in the demand or interpret the meaning of the information in a way that is more positive to himself or herself than perhaps intended. For example, in a discussion about the couple's relationship, the disclosing spouse may say: "Sometimes I understand things and other times I just don't." The partner is free to probe for a clarification or simply acknowledge the statement depending on the extent to which he or she wishes to pursue the information.

The equivocal communication discussed by Bavelas, Black, Chovil, and Mullett (1990) is one type of example of an implied message strategy. Using an equivocal type of communication is less direct and may provide a shield that protects the communication boundaries for both the disclosing spouse and the partner responding. The spouse communicating the disclosive demand message is intentionally ambiguous, and this choice of message type serves a specific function within the interaction sequence.

Bavelas et al. (1990) give the following example; if someone says, "How do you like my hairdo?" The equivocal response is, "Hey, that's a real change" (p. 34). The ambiguity of the message strategy gives the spouse the option of intentionally sending mixed messages concerning the reason for revealing and expectations for a response.

The uncertainty may stimulate more interaction (Berger & Calabrese, 1975); however, this may be mediated by a partner calculating the positive or negative outcome of seeking clarification (Sunnafrank, 1986). The receiving partner may decide he or she is satisfied with being unclear about the information communicated. The partner may perceive the issue as threatening and be content with an ambiguous message. Thus, using an implicit message strategy tends to be low in clarity. The partner receiving the message is more careful to assess the possible meanings so as to protect his or her own boundary and avert damage to the relationship.

Given the ramifications of the choice of message strategy and the risk of disclosure of private information for the individuals involved, as well as the relationship, marital partners use certain prerequisite conditions in order to select one or the other type of disclosive demand message strategy.

Strategy Choice: Prerequisite Conditions

The decision criteria for choosing implicit or explicit message strategies in close relationships are not clearly identified in the literature (Baxter, 1984; Brown & Levinson, 1978). The use of an implicit or explicit message strategy may depend upon the emotional control the partners exercise (Bercheid, 1983), predicted outcomes of the exchange (Sunnafrank, 1986), the need for disclosure, and the degree to which the information is considered private. These considerations represent additional boundary management concerns for the disclosing spouse.

Because disclosure of private information is risky, it may arouse emotions (Chelune, 1979; Stiles, 1987). The extent to which the disclosing spouse controls his or her emotions may influence the choice of explicit or implicit messages to disclose private information. The marital partner who has difficulty controlling his or her feelings while engaged in a disclosive interaction may suspend considerations of face saving for the spouse, choosing a direct demand message found in explicit message strategies. On the other hand, marital partners who exercise more emotional control may strategically choose a more indirect approach, giving the receiving spouse more autonomy to respond by using implicit message strategies.

Using an implicit or explicit message system may also depend upon the predicted ramifications for disclosing. In order to manage privacy and protect himself or herself from potential vulnerability, the marital partner may anticipate outcomes resulting from disclosure (Petronio, Martin & Littlefield, 1984). The disclosing spouse judges the extent to which there might be positive or negative ramifications (Petronio & Martin, 1986).

When the disclosing partner perceives a negative outcome, for example, he or she may select an implicit message strategy because the ambiguity of the message affords some protection from possible adverse effects of the disclosed information. If the private information is revealed in an ambiguous way, the disclosing spouse has more latitude to shift the meaning and avoid or minimize the predicted negative outcome. The disclosing spouse may say that he or she was only kidding or that the partner misunderstood the meaning of the message.

A spouse who perceives a positive impact from disclosing private information may tend to use a more direct form of message demand. Since the partner does not predict a negative outcome, he or she may candidly communicate private information. The receiving spouse concurrently judges the extent to which his or her response requires opening up the communication boundary protecting privacy.

Marital couples may differ in their need or desire to exchange private information (Stiles, 1987). The need to tell private information is assumed in this model, but the immediacy varies. For example, certain stressful events instigate a sense of pressure to discuss the experience quickly (Stiles, 1987). A tension builds that the experience of disclosing helps ease by giving meaning to the events, such as when those living in San Francisco experienced the (November 1989) earthquake, when a person is diagnosed as having a disease, or when a person is having relationship problems.

Partners who have a greater desire to reveal private feelings, thoughts, and experiences may tend to use an explicit message strategy. In addition, this greater need carries a stronger sense of self-interest (Clark, 1979) that may affect the way the message is communicated. When the need to disclose is high, therefore, the individual may be more concerned about himself or herself than the partner. But the partner may react similarly and respond using direct message strategies. Conversely, when need to disclose is low, the partner may be more able to concern himself or herself with the feelings of the spouse. Hence, there may be a tendency to use an implicit message strategy when the need to disclose is less intense thereby allowing for more ambiguity and facesaving and giving the receiving partner more control over his or her own communication boundary.

The extent to which information is considered private also has an impact on the choice to use implicit or explicit messages. Informational privacy (Burgoon, 1986) may be thought of as information about the self to which no one else has the right to access (Schoemen, 1984). Westin (1970), in a further refinement, states that ''[p]rivacy is the claim of individuals, groups or institutions to determine for themselves when, how, and to what extent information about them is communicated to others'' (p. 7). The individual claims the right to control the disclosure of personal information that is salient to himself or herself (Johnson, 1974). This class of information represents risky personal issues for which an individual feels he or she has the right to keep hidden or make public by telling someone.

The levels of informational privacy range from very private to slightly private (Petronio, 1986). The level of informational privacy is often contingent on the perceived degree of risk involved in disclosing the information (e.g., very private information is high risk; slightly private information is lower risk). The level of informational privacy influences the decision to use implicit or explicit message strategies. More private information may lead to a greater likelihood of using an implicit message strategy. Less private information, on the other hand, may lead to a greater likelihood of using an explicit message strategy.

Thus, explicit messages may be implemented when there is less emotional control, a prediction of positive outcomes, greater need for disclosure, and when the person wishes to disclose less private information with lower perceived risk to the self. The implicit message strategies are used when there is more emotional control, a prediction of negative outcomes, lesser desire for disclosure, and when the person wishes to reveal high risk private information.

The style of communicating the disclosed private information clearly has an impact on the receiving partner's strategic choices for responding. But, there are expectations also implied in the message that influence the recipient and the overall assessment of a fit between the demand and corresponding response. The intersection of communication boundaries between the marital partners is affected by the extent to which the disclosing partner's expectations are met by the receiving spouse.

RECEIVING PARTNER'S BOUNDARY MANAGEMENT

The process of reacting to the disclosive demand messages represents the way in which the receiving partner manages her or his own communication boundary as a recipient of private information. In order to provide a response to the demand message, the partner may engage in the

following three processes: (1) evaluation of expectations; (2) attributional search; and (3) determination of a message response strategy. Overall, the history of interaction and patterns that have developed in the relationship are important factors that influence these processes. It should be noted that consideration of these processes by the receiving partner may appear to follow a linear progression in this discussion, but the dynamic nature of interaction may lead to the enactment of these processes in any number of sequences. Hence, the receiving partner evaluates the incoming disclosure using information available to interpret the message and judge how he or she wishes to respond.

Evaluating Expectations

To evaluate the expectations for responses to private information, the receiving marital partner is influenced by at least two interrelated factors, (1) the sense of responsibility for action and (2) the degree of autonomy perceived in responding.

Responsibility

When receiving a disclosure demand message, there are two issues that influence a sense of responsibility to answer that demand for action (Rawlins, 1983). First, the disclosing spouse is presumed to have a legitimate right to ask for a response (McLaughlin, Cody & Robey, 1980). Legitimacy may often stem from the commitment implied in the definition of a marriage as well as the bond resulting from intimacy. Thus, the legitimate right of the disclosing spouse to make a demand establishes a baseline sense of responsibility for the partner to respond. The model therefore assumes that (1) the disclosing spouse has a right to expect a response because of the marital relationship; (2) the partner has at least a minimal obligation to respond in some fashion (Roloff, Janiszewski, McGrath, Burns & Manrai, 1988).

The second issue influencing feelings of responsibility is the communicated expectations for a response. The message affects the receiving partner's sense of obligation because it plays on an "egocentric bias" (Ross & Sicoly, 1979; Thompson & Kelley, 1981) found in marriage and close relationships. Research suggests that partners tend to overattribute responsibility for events to themselves (Ross & Sicoly, 1979; Thompson & Kelley, 1981). Thus, when receiving a message indicating an expectation to act, this type of message increases the existing sensitivity to feel responsible.

However, the extent to which the message affects the level of perceived responsibility may be mitigated by the degree of clarity with which the expectation is communicated. Thus, there may be times when a partner receives private information that clearly identifies an expectation for an action. This message has high degree of certainty, and the receiving partner may feel a stronger sense of responsibility to meet the demand. On the other hand, if a message is ambiguous in nature, thus carrying a low degree of certainty about the expectations, the sense of responsibility for action may decrease accordingly. Of course, the obligation felt by the partner depends on a multitude of factors, but the message strategy may have a significant impact on how much responsibility is expected in that exchange.

With each message strategy, therefore, the level of baseline responsibility may vary depending upon the degree of certainty the receiving partner feels concerning the expectations to respond. If, for example, a husband says that he needs his wife to understand his position, the clarity of that message may carry a sense of responsibility to meet his demand. The demand message clearly states the expected conditions of a response. In so doing, the degree of responsibility communicated in the message may influence the receiving partner's feelings of autonomy in responding and the feeling of control over his or her own communication boundaries.

With the use of implicit message strategies, the partner may perceive more flexibility to respond with a greater number of options in meeting the demand. The receiving partner may feel a greater ability to regulate his or her communication boundary and manage a response.

The sense of responsibility to respond may be lower when the disclosing spouse uses implicit message strategies. The feelings of autonomy may increase because the partner does not perceive a strong obligation to answer the demand. Again, this outcome may be influenced by the patterns developed in the relationship. But the response may, in part, depend upon the message strategy.

The receiving partner may have varying degrees of responsibility and obligations, but, in order to respond in some fashion, he or she must assess the motivation for sending the disclosure message. Thus, the receiving partner may make attributional searches to determine the expected response to the disclosive demand message. Attributional searches represent the process of seeking information to determine reasons for the disclosive messages communicated by the spouse. The extensiveness of the attributional search is dependent, in part, upon the level of clarity and certainty found in the message strategy. Thus, when the disclosing partner uses implicit message strategies, the level of ambiguity may be high regarding the expectations for a response. The receiving partner may, therefore, rely more heavily on attributional searches for information to select a response. When the disclosing partner uses explicit message strategies, the level of ambiguity is lower. In this case, there is less reliance on attributional searches for information in order to determine an acceptable response.

Attributional Searches

The disclosing spouse who has a need to talk about his or her private feelings and experiences is imposing a demand calling for a response by the receiving partner. In order to judge an acceptable response, the receiving partner attributes motivation or reasons why the spouse is communicating private information. Recent research has shown that attributional searches evaluating motivations tend to be triggered when an event or message is unexpected (Thompson & Snyder, 1986).

When a person receives private information that is unsolicited, the information is communicated unexpectedly (Gilbert, 1977). In this case, the receiving spouse will likely try to identify the purpose for the information and the expectations for a response. Baucom (1987) argues that "attributions in marriage are most likely to occur when a spouse's behavior or a marital event is unpredictable, novel, negative or perceived as particularly important to oneself or one's marriage" (Thompson & Snyder, 1986, p. 132). The need for attributional searches may, however, vary with the degree of message certainty. Thus, for implicit message strategies, attributional searches may tend to occur with more frequency than where explicit message strategies have been used to communicate disclosive demand messages.

In order to make attributions for assessing the spouse's motivations and expectation in communicating disclosive information, the receiving partner may take at least five sources into account: (1) relational memory that is used to employ known information and scripts (Abelson, 1976; Douglas, 1983); (2) the content of the message; (3) the context in which the disclosure of private information is made; (4) the environment in which disclosure occurs; and (5) the nonverbal cues.

An example of the way these factors are used in conjunction with one another is seen in the following scenario: Suppose a wife discloses private information to her husband about problems she is having with her boss. For the husband to judge the significance of this information and provide a response, he assesses her motivation by (1) taking into account past interaction patterns (she has never complained about work before); (2) attending to the content (she remarks that she always seems to feel tired lately whenever she talks about her work); (3) attending to the context (the husband knows that the boss has been giving his wife a difficult time at work); (4) noting the environment (the disclosure occurs in their own home, away from other people, indicating that she feels uncomfortable about these events); and (5) reading the nonverbal cues (the husband interprets his wife's stooped posture, reduction of gestures, and lack of eye contact to mean she is defeated by the events at work). When taken as a whole, the husband may assess this information and conclude that the motivation for disclosing to him is to communicate a need for support and help with her problem.

Thus, the receiving spouse assesses the reasons for the disclosure to determine the response options he or she may use to meet the demand. From the attributional search the partner determines the reason for sending the private information and assesses the expectations for a response.

There are cases where the attributional search identifies a need for additional information to determine a response that the partner feels appropriately meets the demand. For example, a husband might ask his wife why she is telling him her feelings about her mother. Generally, these are times when the disclosing spouse tends to use low certainty message demand strategies. Often probes are used to access information needed to judge a response. Probes are typically questions asked by the receiving partner to clarify the message demand being communicated as suggested in the above example. The probes form a bridge between assessing the expectation for a response and a decision about the actual response strategy.

As with the disclosive demand message strategies, the receiving partner may respond with direct or indirect response messages. These responses may also range from low to high certainty in reaction to the expectations communicated by the disclosing spouse.

Response Strategies: Direct and Indirect Message Responses

While a wide range of behavioral options could be used, in this discussion the strategies presented are limited to response *messages*. As with the demand messages, the general categories of response messages may be direct or indirect. But, the ambiguity or clarity of the message response reflects the extent to which the receiving spouse is able and/or chooses to meet the demands of the disclosing partner. The degree to which the disclosing spouse's demands are met ultimately has implications for the marital relationship.

High Certainty Responses: Direct Message Strategies

Direct strategies represent the communication of high certainty responses where the partner believes he or she is sure of the expectations communicated by the spouse and perceives he or she has adequately fulfilled the obligation of these demands. The receiving partner, therefore, sends direct messages in which he or she perceives the demands of the disclosing spouse are clearly being met. The responses are issued in a straightforward manner giving less attention to politeness, are less equivocal, and give more attention to providing information that answers the demand.

When the receiving partner uses a direct response message, he or she is reasonably certain of having assessed the demands accurately. The receiving partner is confident that he or she has used past relational information appropriately and evaluated the context, informational content, and environmental and nonverbal cues correctly. The use of this type of response strategy may also signal confidence and trust in the relationship. The willingness to risk possible vulnerability by responding in a direct manner (with the ever-present potential for mistaking the intent of the demand) might reflect the degree of trust perceived by the receiving partner. Thus, the communication boundaries are more loosely controlled when the partner uses direct response strategy and his or her autonomy is minimized.

Low Certainty Responses: Indirect Message Strategies

Indirect strategies, such as changing the topic, metaphors, association clues, understatements, or rhetorical questions represent the communication of low certainty responses. The receiving partner sends messages that ambiguously meet the demands from the disclosing spouse when using this approach. The receiving partner may use these strategies to answer the demand because he or she is not confident of having understood the demand accurately, may have a low success rate with past responses, or is not willing to risk vulnerability because the trust level is too low in the relationship. Consequently, the receiving partner may use a more purposively ambiguous response because he or she does not predict a positive outcome for himself or herself in meeting the demand.

This functional use of ambiguity gives the receiving partner a way to meet the responsibility of responding without compromising his or her own position. Thus, the communication boundary may be more tightly controlled in this condition, thereby minimizing possible vulnerability for the partner.

BOUNDARY COORDINATION: INTEGRATION OF DEMAND AND RESPONSE

The demand-response boundary management process may be assessed by examining the fit or coordination between the disclosive demand message and the receiving partner's message response. Over time, as expectations are met or violated, the patterns of interaction that develop may benefit or negatively affect the marital relationship. Coordination of boundary management may be represented in a variety of ways, but the focus of this discussion is the fit between message strategies and the implicit expectations communicated in the message.

As suggested earlier, boundary coordination may result in at least four types of fit: (1) satisfactory, (2) overcompensatory, (3) deficient, or (4) equivocal. The type of fit reflects the degree of need complementarity achieved in the interaction. As Table 1 illustrates, these degrees of fit are contingent upon the integration of message strategies from the disclosing spouse and the receiving marital partner. The interaction sequences discussed below represent the way in which the communication boundaries of the marital partners are coordinated as the boundary lines intersect during disclosure of private information.

T A B L E 1		
Micro-Level Boundary Coordination		

Disclosive demand message	Response Message	
	Direct [high certainty response]	Indirect [low certainty response]
Explicit [high certainty response]	Satisfactory fit	Deficient fit
Implicit [low certainty response]	Overcompensatory fit	Equivocal fit

High Certainty Demand, High Certainty Response

In the first type of boundary coordination sequence, the disclosing spouse uses explicit message strategies and the receiving partner uses direct response messages. The expectations are clear for the receiving partner, and the partner chooses to meet the demand in a straightforward manner. The outcome for this type of sequence is a satisfactory fit between the disclosive demand message and the response by the marital partner.

For example, Steve says to Sue: "I think our kids have been doing pretty well in school lately, don't you?" Sue responds by saying: "Yes, they seem to have overcome the trauma of moving." There is an explicit message about the expectations for a reply. Sue meets those expectations, and the interaction sequence is satisfactorily coordinated leading to adequate fit between the disclosive demand message and receiving partner's response.

This type of interaction pattern generally leads to positive feeling in the relationship because the communicative expectations of one spouse are being met by the other spouse. This type of coordination regarding disclosure of private information is potentially beneficial for the marital relationship.

High Certainty Demand, Low Certainty Response

In the next type of boundary coordination sequence, there is a high certainty demand message and a low certainty response. As in the first sequence, the disclosing spouse uses an explicit

message strategy that clearly communicates the expectations for response to the demand. The receiving partner, however, reacts by using an indirect strategy that represents a low certainty response. Thus, whether the receiving partner has met the expectations is not clear to the disclosing spouse. As a result, there is a different fit between the demand message and the response by the partner. Because of the ambiguity of the response, the spouse is likely to feel that his or her expectations have not been met, and there is, therefore, a perceived deficient fit.

This type of coordination may be perceived as beneficial for the receiving partner because he or she may not have been ready to cope with the revealed information. Yet, the disclosing spouse may be unhappy with the response because it did not meet the expectations set up in the demand message. He or she may indicate those feelings to the partner and diminish the feelings of benefit for the receiving partner.

If this outcome occurs frequently, it may contribute to feelings of relational discontent that have potential for a negative influence on the marriage. This type of demand-response relationship may lead to further demands by the disclosing spouse in an attempt to have his or her expectations fulfilled because the first attempt had been frustrated. An example is useful to illustrate this type of boundary coordination.

Mary (the wife) says to Jim (the husband) as they are getting ready for bed: "Sometimes I feel that we just aren't as romantic as we use to be. Maybe we have too many things to do; we don't have candlelit dinners any more and you don't send me flowers just for the heck of it. You are so different from the way you used to be." Jim replies: "I don't know; it is hard to figure out sometimes."

In this exchange, Jim's response ambiguously answers the demand message, and, hence, this reaction represents a deficient fit regarding boundary coordination. Mary communicates an explicit message about her feelings concerning the relationship with a corresponding set of expectations for a specific type of response from Jim. Jim chooses to reply by using an indirect message strategy thereby tightly controlling his own communication boundary and not explicitly meeting Mary's expectations for a response.

On a short-term basis, this type of boundary coordination may result in disappointment for Mary. To cope with the exchange she may escalate the demand for a response. If Jim satisfactorily meets Mary's expectations, these interaction sequences may not be problematic for their relationship. However, if this type of interaction becomes a long-term pattern occurring when one or the other partner communicates an explicit demand message, continuous deficient fit may be detrimental to the relationship.

With this type of boundary interaction, whenever the receiving partner uses responses such as polite indirectness, interruptions, tangential responses, or impervious responses, there is a potential deficient fit between the message demand and the response message, and need complementarity has not been achieved.

Low Certainty Demand, High Certainty Response

For this type of boundary coordination, there is a low certainty demand message and a high certainty response. The disclosing spouse uses an implicit message strategy that ambiguously communicates expectations to the receiving partner. Although the spouse wishes to disclose private information, he or she more tightly controls the communication boundary by sending implicit demand messages.

After the receiving partner assesses the disclosive message and corresponding expectations for a response, the partner decides on his or her reply.

The certainty of the message communicates the belief that he or she has accurately assessed the appropriateness of the response. This boundary coordination results in overcompensatory fit because the disclosing spouse communicates a message that has low certainty while the receiving partner overinterprets the needs of the spouse. The receiving partner sends a high certainty message in response. The receiving partner overloads the disclosing spouse with information in his or her reply, thus exceeding the expectations. The outcome may be problematic for the disclosing spouse and/or the receiving partner. As with the deficient fit coordination sequence, if overcompensation becomes a frequent pattern it may lead to difficulties for the marital relationship.

For example, a wife (Carol) and her husband (Alex) have the following exchange. Alex says: "How was your day, Carol? I called but I guess that you were busy. I found out that my mother is ill." Carol says in reply: "I suppose that you are angry now because I wasn't around when you called. How was I suppose to know that your mother is sick?"

The receiving partner seems clear about the expectations for a specific type of response to the implicitly communicated disclosive message. The husband is sending out a test balloon framing the statement in an implicit way, but the wife provides an excessive, overcompensating response. The receiving partner may feel guilty because she was not available when her husband called and copes by accusing her husband of being angry. This response goes beyond the expectations communicated in the demand message.

A second example of this type of coordination is presented in the following scenario. Jason (the husband) using a low certainty demand message to disclose, says: "I got a strange note today." Helen (the wife) replies: "Who was it from? I bet it was that woman you met the other day who seemed so infatuated with you. You better be careful with your response; you may lead her on."

As these examples suggest, this boundary coordination sequence may be more evident when the receiving spouse engages in escalation as a form of response. In each case there is overcompensatory fit that is problematic for the wife, the husband, and the relationship, because the response overestimates the expectations of the disclosing spouse. The disclosing spouse selects a more ambiguous message strategy to communicate private thoughts or feelings. When the receiving partner reacts by overstating the issues, the disclosing spouse is forced to cope with the direct statements of the receiving partner's actions. For each example, the disclosing spouse may not have been ready to deal with the information. Thus, the disclosing spouses may have been put into a position of addressing the partners' responses when they might have preferred to leave the issues in a more ambiguous state. As a function of the need complementarity of the exchange in making the issues more explicit, both the husband and the wife in each example must cope with the receiving partner's response.

Low Certainty Demand, Low Certainty Response

With this type of boundary coordination sequence, the disclosing spouse communicates private information using implicit message strategies that represent a low certainty demand. The receiving partner, in turn, uses indirect messages strategies to respond. The clarity of both the demand and the response is low. There is ambiguity about the expectations for a response and the extent to which the demand has been met. The outcome for the disclosing spouse in this sequence is represented by equivocal fit. Thus, the fit might be satisfactory because the disclosing spouse wishes to keep the expectations uncertain and a reply of ambiguity matches the expectations for a response. Or, if the receiving partner's choice of response does not meet the expectations communicated in the disclosive demand message this may lead to a deficient fit from the perspective of the disclosing spouse.

Examples for each type of fit outcome may be helpful. Consider first the satisfactory fit scenario when there is a low certainty demand and low certainty response. In using an implicit message

strategy of previewing a problem, John and Amy have the following exchange. John (the husband) says to Amy (the wife): "I have been feeling tired lately; it's possible I have had too much on my mind." Amy replies by saying: "I have to get some work done I brought home tonight; you don't mind, do ya?"

Within the context of their relationship, this statement is a hint that John has been having a difficult time at work but is not ready to talk in depth about the problems. He does not wish to be explicit about the issue and wants Amy to understand implicitly that there is a problem, but he indicates that he does not want to deal with this issue right now. His statement is used, however, to prepare her for the information, thereby "previewing" the topic beforehand. Amy's response satisfactorily meets the demand of the disclosive message and fulfills her husband's expectations. This demand-response coordination may contribute to their relationship because the needs of one spouse are being fulfilled by the other spouse successfully.

There is deficient fit if the receiving partner does not accurately interpret the demands of the exchange. Sometimes, when a spouse uses an implicit message strategy and is not clear about the expectations for a response, it is because he or she wants to be probed for the information. When communicating private thoughts, especially if they concern the other person or have a potential for affecting the relationship, a spouse may not want to use explicit messages because he or she would be taking on a higher level of responsibility for identifying the problem.

Thus, if the disclosing spouse uses a message strategy that only hints at the issue (not being clear about the expectations), the receiving partner may determine a need for questioning the disclosing spouse about his or her meaning to clarify the statements communicated. If shifting the responsibility is the intent of the message, and the receiving partner ignores the expectations of the disclosing spouse, this may lead to deficient fit between the disclosive demand message and the response of the marital partner.

For example, Mary and Jim are discussing Christmas vacation and Mary says to Jim: "I don't think that we should go away for Christmas this year, the timing isn't right." Jim responds by saying: "Oh, O.K." Mary wants to discuss why the timing isn't right, but she wants Jim to probe for the reason; he obviously does not do so, leaving Mary with the responsibility of continuing the discussion. Thus, there is a deficient fit between the response and the demand message that may lead to frustration and possibly conflict. This type of demand-response boundary coordination sequence over time may have a negative effect on the quality of the marital relationship.

As these examples have shown, expectations are discerned from the context of the relationship, the relational history, and the intention of the disclosing spouse for revealing private information. The demands reflect the needs of the disclosing spouse. The receiving partner must determine the expectations in order to respond to the demand appropriately. The receiving partner fulfills the expectations of the disclosing spouse to a greater or lesser extent. The degree to which these expectations are met over time may contribute to the overall benefit of the marital relationship.

CONCLUSION

The communication boundary management perspective suggests an extensive program of research. This theoretic proposal identifies numerous issues that are in need of empirical testing. These include both assumptions on which this theory is based and hypothesized relationships among concepts. In hope of stirring interest, several areas of research are identified in this discussion. Limited by space, however, not all possibilities can be discussed nor can the points raised be elaborated. Thus, only a sampling of areas is presented.

There are at least five potential research areas generated by this theory: (1) macro assumptions; (2) micro assumptions; (3) the disclosing spouse; (4) the receiving partner; and (5) boundary coordination. Research issues in each areas will be discussed briefly.

Macro Assumptions

The macro assumptions in this theory suggest, first, that the recipient is a critical factor in the disclosure equation. The receiver of unsolicited disclosure has been largely ignored, with the exception of Gilbert's (1977) work. We know very little about how recipients respond to disclosure and learn to cope with information that they did not request. This theory proposes ways in which the receiver might respond to unsolicited disclosure of private information. Much research is needed to understand the role of the recipient better.

A second issue relates to the use of rules. The concept of communicative rules is not new, but this theory proposes that we regulate openness and closedness by implementing rules or criteria. We know a little about the rules that people might use, but this theory challenges us to determine, in a more extensive fashion, which rules are used and how they are employed to manage our privacy boundaries and what sanctions are involved when they are violated.

A third global issue concerns the extent to which the level of privacy is important. We know intuitively that information varies in privacy, but this theory suggests the need for more extensive investigations into the impact of the privacy of information on our need for boundary control.

A fourth concern suggested by this theory focuses on the broader use of a boundary metaphor. Altman (1975) and his colleagues pioneered this approach with regard to privacy. The communication boundary management perspective extends Altman's original proposal by suggesting a process for boundary coordination, applying the concept more specifically to informational privacy, and examining expectations that reflect our boundary regulation rules. This discussion applies the boundary metaphor to coordination of marital couples, but this same proposal might also work to explain how co-workers, supervisors and subordinates, and parents and children negotiate their privacy boundaries. This perspective might provide a way to examine dyadic interaction regarding private information in a number of different situations.

Micro Assumptions

The micro assumptions that this theory identifies open several issues for investigation. For example, one can test whether the meanings disclosure has for the recipient depend on the way a message is communicated. The communication boundary management perspective assumes that the way messages are sent communicates expectations about a response and influences the meaning ascribed to the message by the receiver. In addition, the theory proposes that the expectations disclosers have regarding their messages influence the message strategies they select to communicate private information. While there is some research available that suggests the existence of these relationships within the context of disclosure, these assumptions need direct empirical testing.

Disclosing Spouse

The proposals made regarding the person disclosing private information are numerous and in need of empirical testing. For example, how useful are hints, prerequests, or prompts as ways to forecast upcoming disclosure? Do these strategies prepare the recipient for the subsequent private information? To what extent does this type of functional ambiguity serve an important purpose in disclosure interactions?

The theory further proposes that emotional control, degree of private information, need for disclosure, and predicted ramifications are used to determine a disclosure message strategy that communicates expectations for a response. Research is needed to establish whether these elements are, in fact, utilized. From this, it is hypothesized that explicit disclosure messages are implemented when there is less emotional control, a prediction of positive outcomes, and greater need for disclosure, and when a person wishes to disclose less private information with lower perceived risk to the self. Conversely, implicit message strategies are used when there is more emotional control, a prediction of negative outcomes, and less desire for disclosure, and

when the person wishes to reveal high risk private information. These hypotheses as well are in need of research.

Receiving Partner

In examining the receiving partner, the theory assumes that three elements influence the way a respondent reacts to a disclosive message: (1) evaluation of expectations, (2) need for attributional searches, and (3) making a determination about an appropriate response. The extent to which these elements function in the ways identified by the theory is an empirical question. Also, examination of whether a sense of responsibility to respond to a disclosive message by a receiving party does, in fact, influence the way a person responds should be conducted. Investigations also are needed to test whether message clarity mitigates this sense of responsibility. Further, research is needed on whether low certainty messages about expectations tend to lead to a higher need for attributional searches as suggested by the theory.

The communication boundary management perspective proposes that respondents use direct and indirect response message strategies. An examination of these message types with regard to private information is necessary. What kinds of message content are there and do these message types range on a continuum or are they discrete categories?

Boundary Coordination

In considering the final phase of this theory where the issues raised converge into boundary coordination, five questions representing the different types of boundary fit found between disclosure message and response message call for empirical investigation. First, does a high certainty disclosure message met by a high certainty response lead to feelings of satisfactory fit between the boundaries of the marital partners? Second, does a high certainty disclosure message met by a low certainty response lead to deficient fit between the privacy boundaries of the marital partners? Third, does a low certainty disclosure message met by a high certainty response lead to overcompensatory fit between the privacy boundaries of the marital partners? Fourth, does a low certainty disclosure message met by a low certainty response lead to satisfactory fit if the desires of the spouses are to keep the messages uncertain? Or, fifth, does a low certainty disclosure message met by a low certainty response lead to a deficient fit between the boundaries if one spouse wishes the other to take more responsibility for the information?

As suggested by this discussion, these issues and relationships proposed by the theory of communication boundary management require a broad program of empirical research, some of which is currently under way. Privacy has become an important topic in the last decade and promises to be more salient in the decades to come. Understanding the dynamics of managing informational privacy is becoming acknowledged as a key to relationships of all types. This is especially true in those cultures, such as the United States, that emphasize individualism, because managing and coordinating private information contributes to a sense of autonomy and independence. While communication is the vehicle by which we are social, management of privacy is the mechanism that balances individual identity with social interaction.

NOTES

1. For this article, private information refers to "the individual's phenomenological experience, to which no one else has direct access" (Tedeschi, 1986, p. 5) or right to access. The concept of informational privacy concerns the perceived right to control information about the self. (For a fuller discussion see Baumeister, 1986; Burgoon, 1982; Schoeman, 1984.)

2. The content of the messages contributes to determining the expectations for a response. In addition, the content of the message communicating private information appears to have a higher probability of representing problems, issues of concern, difficult situations, and events that were embarrassing or made individuals feel uncomfortable. These reflect issues that have a level of risk if disclosed to others (Petronio, 1986).

REFERENCES

Altman, I. (1975). *The environment and social behavior: Privacy, personal space, territory and crowding.* Monterey, CA: Brooks/Cole.

Altman, I., Vinsel, A., & Brown, B. (1981). Dialectic conceptions in social psychology: An application to social penetration and privacy regulation. *Advances in Experimental Social Psychology, 14,* 108–159.

Abelson, R. (1976). Scripts processing in attitude formation and decision making. In J. Carroll & J. Payne (Eds.), *Cognition and social behavior,* Hillsdale, NJ: Erlbaum.

Baucom, D. (1987). Attributions in distressed relations: How can we explain them? In S. Duck & D. Perlman (Eds.), *Heterosexual relations, marriage and divorce.* London: Sage.

Baumeister, R. (Ed.). (1986). *Public self and private self.* New York: Springer-Verlag.

Bavelas, J., Black, A., Chovil, N., & Mullett, J. (1990). *Equivocal communication.* Newbury Park, CA: Sage.

Baxter, L. (1984). An investigation of compliance-gaining as politeness. *Human Communication Research, 10,* 427–456.

Baxter, L., & Wilmot, W. (1984). "Secret tests": Social strategies for acquiring information about the state of the relationship. *Human Communication Research, 11,* 171–201.

Berardo, F. M. (1974). Family invisibility and family privacy. In S. Margulis (Ed.), *Privacy.* Stony Brook, NY: Environmental Design Research Association.

Bercheid, E. (1983). Emotion. In H. Kelley, E. Bercheid, A. Christensen, J. Harvey, T. Huston, G. Levinger, E. McClintock, L. Peplau, & Peterson, D. (Eds.), *Close relationships* (pp. 110–168). New York: Freeman.

Berg, J., & Clark, M. (1986). Differences in social exchange between intimate and other relationships: Gradually evolving or quickly apparent? In V. Derlega & B. Winstead (Eds.), *Friendship and social interaction* (pp. 101–124). New York: Springer-Verlag.

Berger, C., & Calabrese, R. (1975). Some explorations in initial interaction and beyond: Toward a developmental theory of interpersonal communication. *Human Communication Research, 1,* 99–112.

Bienvenu, M. (1970). Measurement of marital communication. *Family Coordinator, 19,* 26–31.

Bochner, A. (1983). The functions of human communication in interpersonal bonding. In C. Arnold & J. Bowers (Eds.), *Handbook of rhetorical and communication theory* (pp. 544–621). Boston: Allyn and Bacon.

Boster, F., & Stiff, J. (1984). Compliance-gaining message selection behavior. *Human Communication Research, 10,* 539–556.

Brown, P., & Levinson, S. (1978). Universals in language usage: Politeness phenomena. In E. N. Goody (Ed.), *Questions and politeness: Strategies in social interaction.* New York: Cambridge University Press.

Burgoon, J. (1982). Privacy and communication. In M. Burgoon (Ed.), *Communication yearbook 6* (pp. 206–249). Beverly Hills, CA: Sage.

Carson, R. (1979). Personality exchange in developing relationships. In R. Burgess & T. Huston (Eds.) *Social exchange in developing relationships* (pp. 247–266). New York: Academic Press.

Chelune, G. (1976). A multidimensional look at sex and target differences in disclosure. *Psychological Reports, 39,* 259–263.

Chelune, G. (1979). Measuring openness in interpersonal communication. In G. J. Chelune (Ed.), *Self-disclosure: Origins, patterns and implications of openness in interpersonal relationships* (pp. 1–27). San Francisco, CA: Jossey-Bass.

Clark, R. (1979). The impact of self interest and desire for liking on the selection of communication strategies. *Communication Monographs, 46,* 257–273.

Cody, M., & McLaughlin, M. (1980). Perceptions of compliance-gaining situations: A dimensional analysis. *Communication Monographs, 47,* 132–148.

Cody, M., McLaughlin, M., & Schneider, M. (1981). The impact of relational consequences and intimacy on the selection of interpersonal persuasion tactics: A reanalysis. *Communication Quarterly, 29,* 91–106.

Cody, M., Woelfel, M., & Jordan, W. (1983). Dimensions of compliance-gaining situations. *Human Communication Research, 9,* 99–113.

Cozby, P. (1973). Self-disclosure: A literature review. *Psychological Bulletin, 79,* 73–91.

Dance, F., & Larson, C. (1976). *Functions of human communication: A theoretical approach.* New York: Holt, Rinehart, Winston.

Derlega, V., & Grzelak, J. (1979). Appropriateness of self-disclosure. In G. J. Chelune (Ed.), *Self-disclosure: Origins, patterns and implications of openness in interpersonal relationships* (pp. 151–176). San Francisco, CA: Jossey-Bass.

Douglas, W. (1983). Scripts and self-monitoring: When does being a high self-monitor really make a difference? *Human Communication Research, 10,* 81–96.

Duck, S. (1988). *Relating to others,* Milton Keynes, England: Open University Press.

Gilbert, S. (1977). Effects of unanticipated self-disclosure on recipients of varying levels of self-esteem: A research note. *Human Communication Research, 3,* 368–371.

Jacobs, S., & Jackson, S. (1983). Strategy and structure in conversational influence attempts. *Communication Monographs, 50,* 285–304.

Johnson, C. (1974). Privacy as personal control. In S. T. Margulis (Ed.), *Privacy.* Stony Brook, NY: Environmental Design Research Association.

Lakoff, R. (1975). *Language and woman's place.* New York: Harper and Row.

Levinger, G., & Senn, D. (1967). Disclosure of feelings in marriage. *Merrill-Palmer Quarterly, 13,* 237–249.

Lewis, R., & Spanier, G. (1979). Theorizing about the quality and stability of marriage. In W. Burr, R. Hill, F. I. Nye, & I. Reiss (Eds.), *Contemporary theories about the family* (Vol. 1 pp. 268–294). New York: Free Press.

McLaughlin, M., Cody, M., & Robey, C. (1980). Situational influences on the selection of strategies to resist compliance-gaining attempts. *Human Communications Research, 7,* 14–36.

Miell, D., & Duck, S. (1986). Strategies in developing friendships. In V. Derlega & B. Winstead (Eds.), *Friendship and social interaction* (pp. 129–141). New York: Springer-Verlag.

Minuchin, S. (1974). *Families and family therapy.* Cambridge, MA: Harvard University Press.

Parks, M., & Logan, C. (1988). *Verbal metacommunication, taboo topics and dyadic involvement in opposite-sex relationships.* Paper presented at the International Communication Association Convention, New Orleans, LA.

Petronio, S. (1986). *Understanding private information.* Unpublished manuscript, University of Minnesota, Minneapolis.

Petronio, S. (1990a). The use of a communication boundary perspective to contextualize embarrassment research. In J. Anderson (Ed.), *Communication yearbook 13* (pp. 365–373). Newbury Park, CA: Sage.

Petronio, S. (1990b). *The recipient of unsolicited disclosure: A study of pregnant women and their partners.* Paper presented at the Speech Communication Association Convention, Chicago, IL.

Petronio, S. & Braithwaite, D. (1987). I'd rather not say: The role of personal privacy in small groups. In M. Mayer & N. Dollar (Eds.), *Issues in group communication* (pp. 67–79). Scottsdale, AZ: Prospect Press.

Petronio, S., & Chayer, J. (1988). *Communicating privacy norms in a corporation: A case study.* Paper presented at the International Communication Association, New Orleans, LA.

Petronio, S., & Harriman, S. (1990). *Parental privacy invasion: The use of deceptive and direct strategies and the influence on the parent-child relationship.* Paper presented at the Speech Communication Association Convention, Chicago, IL.

Petronio, S., & Martin, J. (1986). Ramifications of revealing private information: A gender gap. *Journal of Clinical Psychology, 42,* 499–506.

Petronio, S., Martin, J., & Littlefield, R. (1984). Prerequisite conditions for self-disclosure: A gender issue. *Communication Monographs, 51,* 268–273.

Petronio, S., Olson, C., & Dollar, N. (1989). Privacy issues in relational embarrassment: Impact on relational quality and communication satisfaction. *Communication Research Reports, 6,* 21–27.

Rawlins, W. (1983). Individual responsibility in relational communication. In M. Mander (Ed.), *Communication in transition.* New York: Praeger.

Rogers-Millar, L. E., & Millar, F. (1979). Domineeringness and dominance: A transactional view. *Human Communication Research 5*, 238–246.

Roloff, M., Janiszewski, C., McGrath, M., Burns, C., & Manrai, L. (1988). Acquiring resources from intimates: When obligation substitutes for persuasion. *Human Communication Research, 14*, 364–396.

Ross, M., & Sicoly, F. (1979). Egocentric biases in availability and attribution. *Journal of Personality and Social Psychology, 37*, 322–336.

Sanford, D., & Roach, J. (1987). *Imperative force in request forms: The demanding vs. pleading dimension of directives.* Paper presented at the International Communication Association Convention, Montreal, Canada.

Schoeman, F. (Ed.). (1984). *Philosophical dimensions of privacy: An anthology.* Cambridge: Cambridge University Press.

Stiles, W. (1987). "I have to talk to somebody": A fever model of disclosure. In V. Derlega & J. Berg (Eds.), *Self-disclosure. Theory, research and therapy.* New York: Plenum.

Sunnafrank, M. (1986). Predicted outcome value during initial interactions: A reformulation of uncertainty reduction theory. *Human Communication Research, 13*, 3–33.

Tedeschi, J. (1986). Private and public experiences and the self. In R. Baumeister (Ed.), *Public self and private self.* New York: Springer-Verlag.

Thompson, S., & Kelley, H. (1981). Judgments of responsibility for activities in close relationships. *Journal of Personality and Social Psychology, 41*, 469–477.

Thompson, J., & Snyder, D. (1986). Attribution theory in intimate relationships: A methodological review. *American Journal of Family Therapy, 14*, 123–138.

Tracy, K., Craig, R., Smith, M., & Spisak, F. (1984). The discourse of requests: Assessment of a compliance-gaining approach. *Human Communication Research, 10*, 513–538.

Westin, A. (1970). *Privacy and freedom.* New York: Atheneum.

Wilmot, W. (1980). Metacommunication: A re-examination and extension. In D. Nimmo (Ed.), *Communication yearbook 4.* (pp. 61–69). New Brunswick, NJ: Transaction Books.

Wiseman, R., & Schenck-Hamlin, W. (1981). A multidimensional scaling validation of an inductively-derived set of compliance-gaining strategies. *Communication Monographs, 48*, 251–270.

THE NATURE AND CORRELATES OF CONVERSATIONAL SENSITIVITY

John A. Daly
Anita L. Vangelisti
Suzanne M. Daughton
University of Texas at Austin

People differ in their sensitivity to what happens during conversations: Some individuals enjoy listening to social exchanges, pick up hidden meanings in conversations, can generate optimal ways of saying things in interactions, and are generally "savvy" about the different sorts of power and affinity relationships exhibited in conversations. In this article we explore the nature and correlates of conversational sensitivity. People high in sensitivity make more high-level inferences when listening to social exchanges, unitize conversation in smaller chunks, emphasize conversation characteristics in their memories of interactions, and make more self-referents about conversations than less sensitive individuals. In addition, conversational sensitivity is positively related to self-monitoring, private self-consciousness, perceptiveness, self-esteem, assertiveness, empathy, and social skills. It is inversely related to communication apprehension, receiver apprehension, and social anxiety.

Source: The article is taken from *Human Communication Research* [14: 167–202]. © International Communication Association, 8140 Burnet Rd., Austin, TX 78766. Reprinted by permission of Sage Publications, Inc. and ICA.

In a final study, conversational sensitivity is construed not as an individual difference but as situational response: In some settings under some conditions, people become more sensitive to what happens in conversation.

Go into any meeting, observe any conversation, discuss previous conversations with others, and you will probably find that people seem to differ in their sensitivity to what occurs in interactions. Some people seem very "savvy" about social interaction: they sense what is "really" being said in conversations, who is truly in charge, who likes whom, and so on. They find conversations both stimulating and memorable. Given the centrality of social interaction to them, they are often quite sophisticated about what happens in social exchanges. At the other extreme are people far less sensitive about phenomena involved in conversations. They take conversations at face value, seldom wondering about the underlying assumptions, relationships, and meaning implicit in every social exchange. Our goal in the research described in this article is to describe empirically the nature and correlates of this construct, which we choose to label "conversational sensitivity."

Conceptually, the idea of conversational sensitivity can be couched within J. J. Gibson's (1966, 1979) broader theoretic framework of social affordances. Gibson argues that the perceptual systems of different species have evolved so that information of particular relevance to survival is "picked up" from the environment. Affordances involve conjunctions between the properties of the organism and the environment within which that organism resides. Thus, for the dolphin, the ability to detect high-frequency sonic sounds is an essential property given its environment. For humans, who reside in a conversation-centered world, spontaneous communication is a major social affordance (Buck, 1984), involving the production as well as the reception and interpretation of such messages.

People differ in the degree to which they have optimized their utilization of various affordances. For instance, in the case of social perceptions, the difference between a skilled and a naive perceiver lies in the fact that the former can extract more information from stimuli, detecting features and higher-order structures to which the naive perceiver is not sensitive (Gibson, 1969). Similarly, the degree to which people have developed a sensitivity to social interaction varies. The conversational sensitivity construct attempts to tap these differences. In broad terms, conversational sensitivity is the propensity of people to attend to and interpret what occurs during conversations. Greater sensitivity, in other words, represents more optimal use of an important aspect of the social affordance of communication.

While numerous strands of communication scholarship center on the production of conversations, including many that emphasize differences among people in producing social discourse (e.g., communication competence, communication apprehension), far fewer investigations examine differences in the ways people attend to social interaction. The research that is available, however, clearly indicates that people differ in their attainment of various forms of such sensitivity. Most of this work falls into two clusters: (1) the recognition and interpretation of both nonverbal and verbal messages and (2) personality traits that include an aspect of sensitivity in their formulation.

Research on nonverbal decoding abilities focuses on personality correlates of nonverbal sensitivity (e.g., Hall, 1978; Isenhart, 1980), the direct assessment of such sensitivity (Buck, 1976, 1983; Rosenthal, Hall, DiMatteo, Rogers, & Archer, 1979), and people's accuracy in decoding different aspects of a person's behaviors (e.g., Archer & Akert, 1977; Sabatelli, Buck, & Dreyer, 1982). Similarly, work on listening skills (e.g., Petrie & Carrel, 1976), as well as on personality correlates that affect listening comprehension (e.g., Beatty & Payne, 1984), indicate that people vary in both their willingness and ability to listen effectively in social interaction. While research on nonverbal decoding skills and listening in actual social conversation is limited, the literatures clearly suggest that people reliably differ in their sensitivity to social interaction.

Allusions to conversational sensitivity are implicit in a number of socially centered personality constructs, notably self-monitoring, empathy, and rhetorical sensitivity. Falling under the rubric of social intelligence (Walker & Foley, 1973) or social acuity (Funder & Harris, 1986), these personality characteristics have sensitivity to conversational behavior as implicit themes. When contrasted with low *self-monitors,* high self-monitors are well attuned to their social environment. They have better developed cognitive schemes for others (Snyder & Cantor, 1980) as well as for what occurs in conversations (Douglas, 1984). This enhanced sensitivity results in a greater adaptability by high self-monitors both to other interactants and to the social demands of the situation. *Empathic skills* demand, as a precursor, something akin to conversational sensitivity. Taking the role of another requires attention to what is said and what is meant in an interaction as well as an understanding of the potentially different interpretations people have of any social act (Davis, 1983; Johnson, Cheek, & Smither, 1983). One major characteristic of *rhetorical sensitivity* (Hart & Burks, 1972; Hart, Carlson, & Eadie, 1980) is interaction consciousness (Goffman, 1967) or the tendency of speakers to adapt to the situation and other people. To do so effectively demands something akin to conversational sensitivity since judgments about what is socially appropriate require sensitivity to what has gone on in the conversation.

Most directly relevant to the sensitivity construct is *interaction involvement* (Cegala, 1981, 1984; Cegala, Savage, Brunner, & Conrad, 1982). Composed of three dimensions (perceptiveness, attentiveness, and responsiveness), the research comparing high and low involved individuals has found that highly involved people remember more from conversations, have more positive feelings about social interactions, are more effective at managing conversations, and make fewer body-focused gestures than less involved people. Conceptually, conversational sensitivity and interaction involvement, especially the perceptiveness dimension of interaction involvement, should be related. However, interaction involvement is so broadly construed that the specific components that make people differentially perceptive in conversations are not clearly delineated.

Two general conclusions can be drawn from the related literatures. First, people differ in how sensitive they are to what goes on in social interactions; some people are more nonverbally sensitive, more active in their listening, and more predisposed to focus on conversations than others (e.g., those high in self-monitoring, empathy, rhetorical sensitivity, and interaction-involvement). Second, while extant literature clearly hints at the nature of conversational sensitivity, there is no clear, empirically grounded definition of the construct. It may include a tendency to enjoy listening to social interaction; it may be a knack for picking up hidden meanings in what people say; it may be a proclivity for remembering what is uttered in conversations. While all of these are obvious candidates for inclusion in a definition of conversational sensitivity, are there other components? Answering this question was one focus of the studies that follow. We sought to enumerate empirically the major elements of conversational sensitivity. After describing these elements, we sought to tie sensitivity to memory for social interaction, the ways people organize their impressions of conversations, and a number of other variables that play significant roles in social interaction. Finally, we propose that conversational sensitivity can also be conceived of as a reaction or response to a variety of contextual characteristics.

STUDY I

For the first study, a group of graduate students in communication (n = 21) were given a general description of conversational sensitivity and asked to generate items to include in a measure of the characteristic. The group generated more than 150 items that, when pruned for redundancies and obviously inappropriate items, left 73 items. In total, 149 undergraduate students then responded on five-step scales (bounded by strongly agree and strongly disagree) to the 73 items. Their responses were factor analyzed. Given the preliminary nature of the items and the small sample size, results of this factor analysis were used to refine the item pool. These results led to the deletion of some items, construction of additional items potentially tapping dimensions hinted at by the factor analysis, and development of other items representing dimensions that seemed appropriate to the construct but were not tapped by the original item pool. A total of 443 undergraduate students then completed the revised, 58-item questionnaire and their responses were factor analyzed (principal components with an orthogonal rotation). The optimal solution appeared to be a seven factor one. The seven factors included: (1) Detecting Meanings, (2) Conversational Memory, (3) Conversational Alternatives, (4) Conversational Imagination, (5) Conversation Enjoyment, (6) Interpretation, and (7) Perceiving Affinity. After settling on the dimensional structure, some additional items were written for factors that had very few items and an eighth dimension was created to tap subjects' sensitivity about power relationships in social interactions. The specific items tapping each of the eight factors are presented in Table 1. The factor loadings from the main factor analyses are also presented in the table.

A major purpose of this project was to delineate the structure of conversational sensitivity. The first investigation, based on responses to a wide variety of items tapping potential dimensions of sensitivity, reveals that the major components of sensitivity include: (1) perceptiveness in finding deeper and often multiple meanings in what others say; (2) a capacity to remember, better than most, what is uttered; (3) a sense of conversational tact—being able to come up with alternatives in conversations that are particularly well suited to a given situation; (4) a proclivity to imagine conversations; (5) a strong liking for listening to conversations, even when not participating; (6) an ease in conversational word play

(e.g., punning, paraphrasing); (7) a sense of who likes whom in conversational settings; and (8) a skill in determining power or control relationships in conversations. While there may be additional components imaginable, the eight identified here very likely represent much of what is central to conversational sensitivity.

In the studies described in this article, sensitivity was treated as a unidimensional construct although there appeared to be underlying factors. This was done for a number of reasons: First, the question raised about conversational sensitivity focused on the general construct rather than its more specific components. In the studies that follow, we wanted to link sensitivity, in its broadest sense, to a number of communication-related behaviors and personal characteristics. Second, it can be argued that a composite index is appropriately used when the relationship of that measure to the dependent variable(s) under examination is typically stronger than the relationships of the underlying factors to the same variable(s) (Snyder & Gangestad, 1986). The results of the studies reported here indicated that this was the predominant pattern. Moreover, in most cases, the patterns of correlation using the different subscales were such that their direction seldom varied from the direction of the composite measure. Third, provided that the composite index is sufficiently reliable, collapsing across dimensions is a commonly used procedure in personality research both in communication (e.g., Cegala, 1984; McCroskey, 1984) and psychology (e.g., Fletcher, Danilovics, Fernandez, Peterson, & Reeder, 1986). When all the items composing the sensitivity measure are taken together as a single composite, the internal consistency estimates (*alpha*) are always above .80. That magnitude of reliability is reasonable for the investigations reported in this article.

It is important to note that our primary aim was not to develop a highly reliable, multifactor instrument tapping the sensitivity construct. Instead, we sought to explicate empirically the general construct. We do not argue that the operationalization of sensitivity used in the

TABLE 1
Items In Final Sensitivity Measure

1. (10)　I often find myself detecting the purposes or goals of what people are saying in conversations. (1; .49; .42)

2. (12)　Many times, I pick up from conversations little bits of information that people don't mean to disclose. (1; .48; .18; .54; .44)

3. (25)　I can often understand why someone said something even though others don't see that intent. (1; .60; .19; .45; .38)

4. (35)　In conversations I seem to be able to often predict what another person is going to say even before he or she says it. (1; .60; .20; .48; .42)

5. (40)　I often hear things in what people are saying that others don't seem to even notice. (1; .61; .22; .60; .57)

6. (43)　I often find hidden meanings in what people are saying in conversations. (1; .65; .23; .79; .53)

7. (52)　I often notice double meanings in conversation. (1; .59; .29; .56; .50)

8. (33)　I often have a sense that I can forecast where people are going in conversations. (1; .53; .27)

9. (18)　I think I remember conversations I participate in more than the average person. (2; .63; .28; .68; .45)

10. (21)　I'm terrible at recalling conversations I have had in the past. (2; .75; .26; .70; .46)

11. (38)　If you gave me a few moments I could probably easily recall a conversation I had a few days ago. (2; .76; .16; .71; .55)

12. (41)　I have a good memory for conversations. (2; .89; .14; .98; .50)

13. (44)　I can often remember specific words or phrases that were said in past conversations. (2; .55; .25; .55; .52)

14. (2)　I have the ability to say the right thing at the right time. (3; .55; .21; .58; .44)

15. (23)　If people ask me how to say something I can come up with a number of different ways of saying it. (3; .46; .24; .68; .40)

16. (34)　I am very good at coming up with neat ways of saying things in conversations. (3; .76; .16; .69; .41)

17. (46)　I am good at wording the same thought in different ways. (3; .89; .14; .77; .43)

18. (56)　In virtually any situation I can think of tactful ways to say something. (3; .60; .17; .62; .40)

19. (19)　I like to think up imaginary conversations in my head. (4; .75; .13; .82; .38)

---

studies reported here is the optimal assessment for tapping the construct. Rather, the measure is a first attempt—one that can serve as a sufficiently reliable indicator of the construct to demonstrate its existence and importance. Future scholarship on the topic may broaden and refine the construct by devising highly reliable measures of the different factors and by exploring their individual correlates. With these caveats in mind, we do, where appropriate, summarize the relationships of the various dimensions to the different variables examined. These relationships hint at possible additional questions.

The studies that follow focus on three major concerns: personality correlates of conversational sensitivity (Study II and Study III), behavioral indicators of the construct (Studies IV and V), and the nature of sensitivity as a response to various contextual characteristics (Study VI). Taken together, the investigations clarify the nature of the construct, as well as its role in some important communication processes.

STUDY II

This study examines a number of personality correlates of conversational sensitivity. The rationale for conducting the study is twofold. First, we wanted to examine the relationship between sensitivity and a variety of personality variables that have, in the past, been related to important communication outcomes. By examining these correlations, we gain a sense of how sensitivity relates to other important communication variables. For instance, a good deal of scholarly work in communication has explored the correlates of

20. (51)   I often make up conversations in my mind. (4; .74; .24; .94; .43)
21.   Compared to most people, I don't spend much time inventing "make-believe" conversations. (.59; .39)
22. (13)   I would enjoy being a fly on the wall listening in on other people's conversations. (5; .52; .19; .72; .18)
23. (28)   Conversations are fascinating to listen to. (5; .68; .28; .63; .23)
24. (36)   I really enjoy overhearing conversations. (5; .54; .19; .86; .27)
25.   I'm less interested in listening to others' conversations than most people. (.58; .29)
26. (17)   I'm usually the last person in a conversation to catch hidden meanings in puns and riddles. (6; .53; .15; .55; .32)
27. (49)   I often have difficulty paraphrasing what another person said in a conversation. (6; .44; .29; .72; .30)
28. (57)   I'm not very good at detecting irony or sarcasm in conversations. (6; .61; .20; .63; .28)
29. (16)   Often, in conversations, I can tell whether the people involved in the conversation like or dislike one another. (7; .53; .25; .74; .37)
30. (45)   I can tell in conversations whether people are on good terms with one another. (7; .34; .32; .90; .35)
31. (48)   I can often tell how long people have known each other just by listening to their conversation. (7; .39; .20)
32.   I'm not very good at figuring out who likes whom in social conversations. (.43; .25)
33.   I can often tell when someone is trying to get the upper hand in a conversation. (.69; .29)
34.   I'm often able to figure out who's in charge in conversation. (.84; .37)
35.   Most of the time, I'm able to identify the dominant person in a conversation. (.78; .35)
36.   In group interactions, I'm not good at determining who the leader is in the conversation.

Note: The number in parentheses at the beginning of each item is the number of the item as it appeared in the original factor analysis. The first three numbers at the end of the item represent the factor the item is associated with, the loading of the item on that factor, and the highest secondary loading the item has, respectively. The fourth value is the primary loading of the item in a factor analysis of the measure in Study II. The final value is the item-total correlation using the sample in Study II. Items 21, 25, 32, 33, 34, and 35 were created after the first major factor analysis. The two values following each of these items are the primary loadings from Study II and the item-total correlation from Study II. Item 36 was not used in either investigation.

communication apprehension (e.g., Daly & McCroskey, 1984). Are apprehensive individuals more sensitive to what happens in conversations? Competing hypotheses seem plausible. One might argue that apprehensive individuals are more sensitive to what happens in social exchanges because they participate less in the ongoing talk—they are, instead, quiet observers. On the other hand, one could suggest that apprehensive individuals, given their tendency to avoid participating in conversations, would, if from nothing more than a lack of familiarity, be less sensitive to what happens during interaction. Second, it is important to determine if the sensitivity construct is redundant with previously established personality dimensions relevant to communication. If correlations among sensitivity and other variables are high, then we are not introducing a distinct construct, but are instead simply rediscovering, under a different label, an already established construct. Duplicative constructs are not particularly useful and before any further work was completed it seemed important to ensure the relative independence of sensitivity from other constructs. If we discover that sensitivity is relatively independent, then the patterns of association will provide preliminary evidence of the construct's convergent and discriminant validity. There are, in other words, some variables sensitivity ought to correlate with and others it should not.

We entered the investigation with some expectations, the most general of which was that sensitivity ought to correlate positively with various personality traits associated with greater, and more positive, experiences in communication as well as with measures tapping social acuity, "the ability and inclination to perceive the psychological state of others" (Funder & Harris, 1986, p. 530). For instance, conversational sensitivity should correlate positively with *self-monitoring*. The self-monitoring construct implicitly contains aspects of conversational sensitivity and taps a person's social acuity. Individuals who are highly sensitive to conversations ought to be more adept at determining when and how they should behave in social situations. Similarly, *communication apprehension* (McCroskey & Beatty, 1986) and *social anxiety* (Fenigstein, Scheier, & Buss, 1975) should be inversely related to sensitivity. To the extent that highly apprehensive people avoid social interactions, their experiences in social exchanges should be relatively few, and this decreased experiential base should result in lower sensitivity to conversations. In addition, people who are less sensitive to social exchanges are also less likely to receive the various rewards that can accompany social interaction. The lack of such rewards certainly should not reduce anxiety, and may even increase it. Conversationally sensitive individuals, who have a strong tendency to enjoy listening to conversations, should not score high on a measure of *receiver apprehension,* which taps people's tendencies to dislike and avoid receiving messages (Wheeless, 1975). Instead, there should be an inverse relationship. Finally, *empathy,* or the ability to see another's point of view, is inherently a social exercise as well as a mark of social acuity. As such, there should be a positive relationship between empathy and conversational sensitivity.

In addition to assessing the relationship among conversational sensitivity and a variety of communication-related traits, we wanted to ensure that responses to the sensitivity instrument were not systematically biased by a tendency to respond in a socially desirable way. To test this subjects completed a measure of social desirability.

Methods

In total, 230 undergraduate students enrolled in introductory communication courses participated in this project. Each received a packet containing a variety of personality measures. The order of the measures was random. Measures included the sensitivity scale (see Table 1); McCroskey's (McCroskey & Beatty, 1986) Personal Report of Communication Apprehension (which has subcomponents assessing communication apprehension in the public speaking, meeting, small group, and conversation settings); Davis's (1983) four-factor empathy scale that includes measures of perspective-taking, empathy, fantasy, and distress; the revised UCLA Loneliness scale (Russell, Peplau, & Cutrona, 1980); Snyder's self-monitoring measure (Snyder, 1974, 1979), which was also considered, in this study, as a three-factor measure tapping dimensions of acting, extroversion, and other-directedness (Briggs, Cheek, & Buss, 1980); Lorr and More's (1980) four-factor measure of assertiveness, which includes dimensions of defense of rights, directiveness, independence, and social assertiveness; Rosenberg's (1965) measure of self-esteem; Wheeless's (1975) receiver apprehension measure; Hart et al.'s (1980) measure of rhetorical sensitivity composed of three subscales measuring what they labeled noble selves, rhetorical reflectors, and rhetorical sensitives; Fenigstein et al.'s (1975) measures of public and private self-consciousness as well as their instrument assessing social anxiety; and Crowne and Marlowe's (1964) measure of social approval seeking.

Results

Reliabilities

Table 3 summarizes the *alpha* reliabilities associated with the measures. Reliabilities ranged from a high of .93 for the communication apprehension measure to a low of .53 for the rhetorical reflector dimension of the rhetorical sensitivity scale.

The sensitivity measure was factor analyzed and an eight dimension, orthogonal solution was chosen as optimal. The primary loadings from the analysis are shown in Table 1. By and large, the loadings were as expected. In every case, the strongest loading for an item fell on the expected factor. In addition, item-total correlations of each item with the total measure were calculated. They are also reported in Table 2.

TABLE 2
Factor Analysis and Item-Total Correlations of Sensitivity Measure in Personality Correlates Study

Item	r with total	I	II	III	IV	V	VI	VII	VIII
2	.44		.54						
3	.38		.45						
4	.42		.48						
5	.57		.60						
6	.53		.79						
7	.50		.56						
9	.45	.68							
10	.46	.70							
11	.55	.71							
12	.50	.98							
13	.52	.55							
14	.44			.58					
15	.40			.68					
16	.41			.69					
17	.43			.77					
18	.40			.62					
19	.38						.82		
20	.43						.94		
21	.39						.59		
22	.18				.72				
23	.23				.63				
24	.27				.86				
25	.29				.58				
26	.32								.55
27	.30								.72
28	.28								63
29	.37							.74	
30	.35							.90	
32	.25							.43	
33	.29					.69			
34	.37					.84			
35	.35					.78			

Note: In this investigation, items 1, 8, 31, and 36 (see Table 1) were not used. They did not load well on their expected dimensions.

TABLE 3
Summary of Correlational Analyses

Measure	*alpha* reliability	r with sensitivity
Sensitivity	.82	
PRCA	.93	−.35[c]
Conversaton	.85	−.28[c]
Group	.87	−.42[c]
Meeting	.90	−.34[c]
Speaking	.81	−.05
Self-Monitoring	.64	.19[b]
Extroversion	.65	.27[b]
Acting	.58	.33[b]
Other-Directed	.63	−.01
Rhetorical Sensitivity		
Noble Self	.82	.28[c]
Rhetorical Reflector	.53	−.04
Rhetorical Sensitivity	.84	−.24[c]
Receiver Apprehension	.83	−.22[c]
Social Approval Seeking	.82	.01
Self-Consciousness		
Social Anxiety	.69	−.21[c]
Private Self-Consciousness	.80	.24[c]
Public Self-Consciousness	.83	.07
Loneliness	.89	−.07
Self-Esteem	.83	.20[b]
Assertiveness	.87	
Defense of Rights	.76	.27[c]
Directiveness	.85	.39[c]
Social Assertiveness	.86	.22[c]
Independence	.68	.29[c]
Empathy		
Empathy	.75	.18[b]
Fantasy	.77	.21[c]
Perspective-Taking	.71	.12[a]
Distress	.81	.22[c]

a. $p < .05$.   b. $p < .01$.   c. $p < .001$.

STATISTICAL SUMMARY 1

Study II

Reliability indicates how accurately and consistently a concept has been measured. If a measure is highly reliable then you can be confident that the scores are very accurate, and that the items or indicators are either consistent with each other or consistent over time. Table 3 lists the reliabilities that were found in this study. They ranged from a low of .58, which was fair, to a high of .93, which was quite good. Reliabilities above .70 are moderate and above .80 are moderately high. A lower reliability means that errors have been made in measuring the concepts and the scores will not be very accurate nor consistent.

Correlational Analysis

For reasons of both space and interest, only the correlations with the total sensitivity measure are presented in Table 3.[1] By and large, the magnitudes and directions of the correlations were as anticipated. First, none of the personality measures had sizable (in terms of magnitude) associations with the sensitivity construct. This is important since some of the measures, notably the receiver apprehension instrument and the various empathy measures, might, at first glance, be expected to tap the sensitivity construct. Second, the statistically significant correlations were, in most cases, quite interpretable. People with greater sensitivity ought to be more experienced with conversation. To the degree that social anxiety, receiver apprehension, and communication apprehension tap experience, inverse correlations between these personality dimensions and sensitivity would be anticipated. That was found. An interesting pattern emerged in the correlations among sensitivity and the different aspects of communication apprehension. Since sensitivity is conversation focused, no meaningful relationship with public speaking anxiety should be expected. But the other three dimensions (meeting, group, and conversation) should correlate significantly with sensitivity. That was what was found. Definitionally, sensitivity and empathy ought to be related, and they were: The correlations were both positive and significant. In addition, greater sensitivity was associated with more private self-consciousness, greater self-esteem, and more assertiveness. The self-esteem relationship is particularly interesting. The sensitivity construct could be seen as tapping something akin to conversation-focused self-esteem. Individuals who respond positively to the sensitivity measure may be reflecting a general positive self-regard for their conversational skills.

STATISTICAL SUMMARY 2

Correlations are used to see if two concepts are related to each other. A positive correlation means that as the score on one concept increases, the score on the second concept increases as well. A negative correlation means that as the score on one concept increases, the score on the second concept decreases. The closer the correlation is to either +1.00 or −1.00, the more similar the two concepts are.

Daly et al. showed that their sensitivity measure was not highly related to the other personality measures. However, when a relationship did exist, it was between sensitivity and a similar concept. This means that it probably measured something that was not measured by the other personality measures.

Conversational sensitivity was unrelated to public self-consciousness, other-directedness (as measured in the self-monitoring measure), loneliness, and social approval-seeking. This last cor-

relation, between approval seeking and sensitivity, is especially important. The measure tapping approval-seeking is often used to assess the social desirability of a self-report instrument. Finding no correlation suggests that, at least in terms of personality dispositions, the sensitivity measure is not confounded by respondents' generalized tendencies to seek social approval. The correlations with the rhetorical sensitivity measure raise some questions.[2] There was a positive relationship between sensitivity and the "noble self" dimension and an inverse relationship between sensitivity and the dimension called "rhetorical sensitivity." An examination of the scoring routine used for the measure presents a possible explanation. Scoring high on the rhetorical sensitivity dimension means that one answers items on the questionnaire with midrange responses (e.g., frequently true, sometimes true, infrequently true) and avoids extreme responses (e.g., almost always true, almost never true). Underlying this scoring scheme is the assumption that individuals who are very sure of their feelings about communication are not "rhetorically sensitive." It might be argued that people who have the savvy and concern for conversation that is represented by high scores on the sensitivity measure might respond with extremes to many of the rhetorical sensitivity items. People less sure about their feelings about social interaction (i.e., high "rhetorical sensitives") may be less conversationally centered and thus would score lower on the sensitivity measure. In addition, the rhetorical sensitivity measure is focused primarily on the construction of messages. Conversational sensitivity, on the other hand, has as its primary focus the reception of messages. It is quite possible for people to be highly sensitive to conversations yet be less than entirely articulate in producing their own messages.

STUDY III

In the preceding study, good convergent and discriminant validities in terms of communication-related personality variables were found. Sensitivity had low correlations with other personality indices and, in general, had statistically meaningful associations with only those variables one would expect it to. A hypothesis arose at this point about the relationship between conversational sensitivity and general social skills: The greater one's conversational sensitivity, the better one's social skills ought to be. The development of sensitivity should, in all likelihood, co-occur with the development of social skills as much of social skill acquisition is probably tied to involvement in, and sensitivity to, what happens in conversations—the most social of activities. In this study we sought to examine, in a preliminary way, the relationship between conversational sensitivity and social skills.

Methods

A total of 73 undergraduate students enrolled in basic communication courses completed the 36-item conversational sensitivity measure and a recently reported measure of social skills (Riggio, 1986). Riggio's social skills inventory taps seven dimensions of basic social skills: emotional expressivity, emotional sensitivity, emotional control, social expressivity, social sensitivity, social control, and social manipulation. Taken as a composite, the scale purportedly measures an individual's basic level of social skills.

Results

Reliabilities

The seven dimensions of the social skills index were all sufficiently reliable for further analysis (emotional expressivity: .67; emotional sensitivity: .79; emotional control: .77; social expressivity: .87; social sensitivity: .84; social control: .89; social manipulation: .71; total score: .85). The reliability of the sensitivity measure was .87.

STATISTICAL SUMMARY 3

Study III

The reliabilities in this study ranged from fair (.67) to good (.89). Sensitivity was found to be related to social skills, although these relationships were small to moderate.

Correlations

Conversational sensitivity was positively and significantly related to emotional expressivity ($r = .25$, $p < .02$), emotional sensitivity ($r = .47$, $p < .001$), and social control ($r = .21$, $p < .04$). Overall, the total score for social skills was positively and significantly associated with conversational sensitivity ($r = .39$, $p < .001$).

These results suggest a positive relationship among conversational sensitivity and a variety of social skills. The strongest correlation was between conversational sensitivity and what Riggio (1986) labels emotional sensitivity. A close reading of the description of emotional sensitivity suggests that of all the social skills dimensions, this is the one most related to the reception of social stimuli. Many of the other dimensions emphasize the opposite issue—production of socially skillful messages and behaviors. These, if they correlate at all with conversational sensitivity, have much smaller associations.[3]

STUDY IV

The previous two studies demonstrated that conversational sensitivity has some convergent validity—it correlates with other related personality variables in the manner expected. What remains is to demonstrate the construct's predictive validity: Is it associated with actual behavioral differences important in social interaction?

One of the most likely behavioral correlates of conversational sensitivity is the remembrances people take away from interactions. Since sensitivity emphasizes people's receptivity to conversation, memory measures represent a likely behavioral indicator of the construct. In other words, we would anticipate that high and low sensitive individuals would differ in the ways they remember conversations. Given their stronger focus on conversation and their reported tendency to find multiple meanings in most utterances, highly sensitive people should draw more inferences from interactions than their counterparts, low in sensitivity. Less sensitive individuals, if asked about what occurred in a conversation, ought to emphasize more surface features of the text since they report not making as many inferences about what goes on in conversations, whether it has to do with meanings, relationships, or words. In addition, highly sensitive people should be more accurate in what they remember about conversations than low sensitive individuals. Given the greater centrality of social interaction to highly sensitive individuals, they should also find stronger personal relevance in conversations than those low in sensitivity. In essence, the cognitive scheme of highly sensitive individuals for conversations should be deeper and more personal. This should be reflected in the ways they remember social interaction.

Methods

Subjects

Undergraduate students enrolled in a large introductory communication course completed the sensitivity measure at the start of the semester. From the group, 19 individuals who scored one standard deviation above the mean and 17 who scored one standard deviation below the mean were asked to participate in an extra-credit project on communication five to six weeks after completing the instrument.

Procedures

Subjects participated in the project in small groups composed of both high and low sensitive individuals. Each group viewed short portions of two movies first released more than fifteen years ago. Two movies were used to avoid confounding due to such things as familiarity or involvement. For instance, had only one movie been used, results would be limited to that movie. With two, assuming that there are little or no differences in results between the two movies, conclusions can be more general. The two movies, *In the Heat of the Night* and *Who's Afraid of Virginia Woolf* were selected for three reasons. First, both were primarily "conversational movies": physical action was minimal. Second, each contained sequences where conversation moved quickly from, in the case of *In the Heat of the Night*, openness and self-disclosure to acrimony and, in

Who's Afraid of Virginia Woolf, pleasantness to anger. Third, neither movie was familiar to undergraduates (only four subjects said they had seen either movie). After watching each excerpt, subjects summarized what they had seen. The specific instructions were as follows:

> Now that you've seen the short excerpt we would like you to write down all your impressions, memories, and thoughts about the excerpt and especially about the conversations you saw in the excerpt. You might write down things like what was said, why it was said, how it was said, what the people really meant by what they said, and so on. Be analytic, if you want, but understand that there are no right or wrong answers.

The order in which subjects saw the two movie excerpts was random. After completing the memory task for the first excerpt subjects were shown the excerpt from the second movie.

The written summaries were coded into idea units (Stafford & Daly, 1984). Two raters completed this task with initial agreement exceeding 95%. When there were disagreements, the two raters discussed the issue until agreement was reached.

To test the hypotheses of this study, six coding categories were created and each idea unit was coded for whether it fit each category. The six categories were as follows:

1. Text: Idea units in this category were straightforward reports of what occurred in the excerpt (e.g., "Husband comes out of bathroom when the guests are going to arrive.").
2. Inference: Plausible inferences from the film excerpts making up this category. Included were general impressions, judgments of relationships, and such (e.g., "Perhaps, however, they are both unhappy deep down because it is apparent they both need alcohol to be around each other.").
3. Self-Referents: This category included descriptions of the personal relevance of the excerpts (e.g., "I felt uncomfortable simply because I hate when people use foul language to argue.").

4. Conversation: Idea units in this category were ones that were inferences tied directly to the conversations (e.g., "Their conversation seemed to slip into a form they must have used when they were in love.").
5. Errors: Clear errors in descriptions of what happened in the film excerpts fell into this category.
6. Quotations: Idea units in this category were direct quotations from the film excerpts (e.g., "When the white man asked how lonely, the black fellow said 'No lonelier than you.' ").

While an idea unit could be coded only into one of the first two categories it could, plausibly, be placed into more than one of the final four. Two raters completed this coding task. Across categories their level of agreement (adjusted for chance agreements [Krippendorff, 1980] ranged from a low of 79% [for errors] to a high of 100% [for quotes and self-referents]). Because of the potential for differences among subjects in the number of idea units generated, all values used in the analysis were computed as proportions of the total number of idea units generated by a subject for a film excerpt.

Results

Preliminary Analyses

Because two different movie excerpts were used it was critical to determine whether there were differences due to the movie or an interaction between movie and subject condition. A series of seven two-way analysis of variances were calculated where one factor was the level of subject conversational sensitivity (high/low) and the other was the movie excerpt (considered as a repeated factor). There were no statistically significant main effects due to movie excerpt or significant interactions attributable to movie excerpt by subject condition for any of the dependent measures save the proportion of direct quotations. For quotations, there was a significant main effect ($p < .003$) due to movie excerpt. A

significantly larger proportion of quotations were generated when subjects described the movie *In the Heat of the Night* (M = .05) than when they described *Who's Afraid of Virginia Woolf* (M = .01). This, however, was the only significant effect. There were no meaningful effects for the total number of idea units produced, for the number of inferences, the number of text ideas, the number of errors, the number of self-referents, or the number of conversation inferences. Overall, the conclusion is that the movie excerpt itself had a very limited impact on the inferences made by subjects. Since the differences due to movie were negligible, the responses to the two films were averaged.

STATISTICAL SUMMARY 4

Preliminary Analyses

Study IV: Seven analyses of variance (ANOVA) were computed. Analysis of variance (ANOVA) is a technique for seeing if three or more groups differ from each other. For example, if you have three groups, you may want to know which one talks the most. The analyses in this study indicated that the conversational sensitivity was not related to the movie excerpts, and the movies had little effect on any of the dependent variables (i.e., total number of ideas and the six coding categories). This allowed Daly et al. to combine the scores from the two movies.

Main Analyses

The primary analyses were conducted in a series of steps. The first was a comparison of high and low sensitive individuals on the total number of idea units they produced. The question here was whether there was a difference in the sheer number of idea units produced as a function of sensitivity. A simple t-test between the two subject groups yielded a nonsignificant value ($t(34) = .97$, ns). The average number of idea units produced by subjects was 20.67 (sd = 6.72) with a range from 8 to 34.

TABLE 4
Summary of Analyses for Sensitivity and Inferences

Variable	Low		High		t-value	p
Text	.36	(.21)	.22	(.17)	2.23	.02
Inference	.63	(.21)	.75	(.16)	1.80	.04
Error	.03	(.04)	.01	(.02)	2.13	.02
Self	.02	(.04)	.07	(.13)	1.69	.05
Conversation	.13	(.11)	.22	(.12)	2.37	.01

Notes: Values are means and, in parentheses, standard deviations. Statistical power estimates (Cohen, 1977) for small, medium, and large effects were, respectively, .15, .43, and .76.

The second step was a one-way multivariate analysis of variance with the six proportion scores serving as dependent variables and subject condition (high versus low sensitivity) as the independent variable. The analysis yielded a significant overall effect ($F(6,29) = 2.77$, p $<$ .03). A series of t-tests were then calculated to identify the specific variables affected by subject condition. Since directional predictions were made, one-tailed significance levels were used. Five of the six dependent variables had significant t-values associated with them. Only the proportion of quotes was nonsignificant ($t(34) = -.42$, ns). As anticipated, high sensitive subjects offered proportionally fewer text units and made proportionately fewer errors than low sensitive subjects. On the other hand, highly sensitive subjects made proportionately more inferences, more self-referents, and more conversational inferences than their counterparts, low in sensitivity. Table 4 summarizes the relevant numerical information.[4]

People who describe themselves as especially sensitive to conversations focus more on the structure and nature of conversations than do less sensitive individuals. Less sensitive individuals take conversations at face value, reporting mostly on what is actually uttered. Compared to highly sensitive individuals, they apparently fail to integrate deeply what they observe into their memories. Highly sensitive people relate the

STATISTICAL SUMMARY 5

Main Analyses

A t-test was used to compare the number of ideas produced by people with different sensitivity scores. T-tests tell you if there is a difference between two groups. For example, you might want to see if one group (e.g., males) had more eye contact than a second group (e.g., females). The t-tests in Daly et al. indicated that the same number of ideas were produced by high and low sensitive people.

Next, multivariate analyses of variance (MANOVA) were computed. This is an analysis which allows you to test if two or more groups differ from each other on two or more dependent or outcome variables. For example, if you have three groups, you may want to know which one talks the most and establishes the closest distance. Multivariate analysis of variance (MANOVA) allowed Daly et al. to show that the sensitivity of the viewer influenced the six coding categories. T-tests were then used to compare people who are either high or low in their sensitivity. Those high in sensitivity wrote fewer text units and made fewer errors. They also made more inferences, more self-referents, and more conversational inferences. These findings were consistent with expectations.

information in the conversations to themselves and draw more inferences about what, conversationally, is occurring in the interactions than less sensitive individuals. These findings fit well with the sensitivity construct. Conversationally sensitive people should see more alternative meanings in conversations, thus drawing more inferences about what occurs. Cognitively, given their interest in conversations, they ought to have better developed representational schema for storing information about the nature of the conversations they observe. And, since social interaction is, theoretically, more central to their lives, they ought to link whatever they see in a conversation to themselves. All of these expectations were confirmed.

STUDY V

The results of Study IV provide initial evidence for the predictive validity of conversational sensitivity. More high-level inferences, an emphasis on conversation characteristics, and a tendency to relate conversations to self, mark the recall of highly sensitive individuals. Sensitivity affects what people take away from social interactions. Due to the nature of the data collected, however, it is not possible to determine whether sensitivity affects the ways people perceive social interactions, the ways they recall conversations, or indeed both. An obvious next step is to devise a way to separate these potential outcomes. One way of assessing perceptual differences between high and low sensitive individuals is to conceive of listeners as parsing, or unitizing, incoming stimuli into meaningful chunks of information. Newtson (1976) proposed a procedure for tapping this unitizing process (see Dickman, 1963). Whenever subjects in his experiment felt that a "meaningful event" had occurred in videotapes they were observing, they pressed a button, in essence breaking the observed actions into units. Cohen and Ebbeson (1979), using this procedure, found that when people focus on specific behaviors they use a greater number of units than when they attempt to form general impressions of actors depicted in a videotape. Goodman (1980)

noted that the more people focus on a particular aspect of a behavioral enactment, the more units they perceive in that aspect. When told to focus on emotions, subjects parse on the basis of the emotional expressions shown by actors; but when told to focus on meaningful actions, they chunk according to the pattern of instrumental actions by the actors in a videotape. Previous research thus suggests that greater focusing yields more perceived units on those items related to the focus. In the case of conversational sensitivity, highly sensitive individuals should be more focused on social interactions than their less sensitive counterparts. To the degree that this is true, high sensitive people ought to unitize displays that were conversational in nature more finely than low sensitive individuals.

Methods

In total, 37 undergraduate students enrolled in communication courses participated in this project. They were selected from a larger group because their scores on the sensitivity measure were at the extremes of the group (i.e., top and bottom quartiles). There were 19 students in the low sensitive group (M = 109.21, sd = 10.94) and 18 were in the high sensitive group (M = 139.33, sd = 7.10). The difference between the groups in sensitivity scores was significant ($t(35)$ = 9.88, $p < .0001$).

Subjects came to a room containing small listening booths. After sitting down at booths, subjects listened and watched taped portions of two films that included substantial amounts of social conversation. The two taped excerpts were the same as those used in Study IV. One was from *Who's Afraid of Virginia Woolf;* the other was from *In the Heat of the Night.* We chose these excerpts for two reasons. First, they are conversationally quite rich. Second, by using the same materials we were able to see if the effects observed in Study IV were a function of the choice of dependent variables. Subjects were told:

> When people observe or even participate in an interaction they often find themselves breaking the exchange into units. That is, they don't

always see an exchange as one continuous event but rather as a series of somewhat discrete units. Some people see many different units in a conversation; others see very few. There are no correct answers to this activity. We want you to watch each of the tapes and when you see a new unit happening we want you to tap your finger on the board. By tapping you are indicating that, in your mind, a new unit, however you may define it, has begun.

A two-track tape recorder stored the tapes subjects made along with the conversation they were observing. The order of presentation of the tapes was random.

Results

Preliminary analyses revealed that the sensitivity measure, as a whole, was highly reliable (*alpha* = .94). The coding of the unitizing behaviors was also reliable. When two coders separately coded each tape, their average agreement was greater than 90%.

STATISTICAL SUMMARY 6

Study V

In this study the measure of sensitivity was highly reliable (i.e., accurate). The coding also appeared to be accurate. However, no statistically significant differences were observed when t-tests were used to compare the responses of people high on sensitivity from those who were low.

The unitizing patterns of subjects for each tape were intercorrelated. The correlation was .60 ($p < .001$). While this value was statistically significant, it was not high enough to justify combining the two unitizing activities. Consequently, separate analyses were conducted for each film excerpt. For the *Virginia Woolf* excerpt, the difference between high and low sensitive subjects was not statistically significant, although the means were in the expected direction with high sensitive subjects reporting more units

($M = 15.35$, sd = 4.37) than low sensitive subjects ($M = 13.58$, sd = 5.71). For the excerpt from *In the Heat of the Night,* the difference between high ($M = 11.65$, sd = 5.63) and low ($M = 8.63$, sd = 5.83) sensitive subjects approached significance ($t(34) = 1.57$, $p < .06$). In short, there was a clear trend for highly sensitive subjects to perceive more units than their counterparts low in sensitivity.[5] A separate analysis was done to determine whether there were differences in where high and low sensitive subjects saw breaks. The units were coded into three categories: units set at the start of turns, units set within turns, and units set by major changes in nonverbal patterns. In these analyses the relative proportion of units falling in each category served as the dependent variables. There were no significant effects due to sensitivity.[6]

STUDY VI

Up to this point, conversational sensitivity has been conceptualized as an individual difference: People are assumed to differ reliably in the degree to which they are sensitive and aware of what happens in social interaction. In this vein, a variety of personality and behavioral correlates have been noted. Personality correlates, such as self-monitoring, communication apprehension, and empathy, have been found along with memory and perceptual differences.

An alternative, and equally plausible, perspective views sensitivity as a situational response tied, in part, to the purposes of the interaction and the contextual characteristics of the exchange. Some sorts of interactions may cause people to be far more sensitive to what is happening, conversationally, than others. For instance, discussing a familiar topic in a comfortable setting with little expectancy that the conversation will have any import is likely to arouse far less conversational sensitivity than an exchange with potentially great impact. Quite a bit of research suggests this is a reasonable approach. For instance, the greater one's perceived dependency on another, the more one pays attention to the conversation of the other (Berschied, Graziano, Monson, & Dermer, 1976), the greater one's feeling of being subordinate to another, the more attune one is to the other's behaviors (Snodgrass, 1985), and the better one's mood, the more one will attend to the positive aspects of conversation (Forgas, Bower, & Krantz, 1984). Moreover, expectations of future interactions (Knight & Vallacher, 1981) and one's goals in an interaction (Hamilton, Katz, & Leirer, 1980; Stafford & Daly, 1984) affect how sensitively one approaches the conversation. In short, various situational contingencies surrounding an interaction can make people more or less sensitive to social exchanges. Under what conditions are people especially sensitive to conversations? Study VI probed this question.

Methods

In total, 38 undergraduates received three packets of materials. The first two packets focused on the situational characteristics of conversational sensitivity. In one packet they were asked to remember a recent conversation where they had been particularly sensitive to what occurred. In the other packet they were asked to recollect an exchange where they had been less than entirely sensitive. The order in which subjects completed the two packets was random. At the beginning of each packet subjects read a paragraph describing the situation they were to remember. The paragraph for the high sensitive condition was:

> In this exercise we want you to think of a conversation you recently had when you felt that you were especially perceptive, sensitive, and aware of what was happening in the interaction. We want you to remember a time when you really enjoyed listening to what people were saying, when you were especially attuned to the relationships among people involved in the conversation (e.g., who liked whom, who was in charge), when you were able to "hear" hidden meanings in what people were saying, when you found the conversation memorable, and when you could see, ahead of time, where people were going with what they were saying.

The paragraph for the low sensitive situation was as follows:

> In this exercise we want you to think of a conversation you recently had when you felt you were not particularly concerned or worried about what was happening in the interaction. We want you to remember a time when you really didn't care, one way or the other, about listening to the conversation, when you weren't concerned with the relationships among the interactants (e.g., who liked whom, who was in charge), when you took what was said at face value (not looking for hidden or deeper meanings), when you found little or nothing memorable in the conversation, and when you didn't spend time thinking of what might be coming up in the conversation.

A questionnaire containing items describing a number of potential characteristics of the situation followed each paragraph. After completing the questionnaire for one of the situations, subjects moved to the second packet, read the paragraph describing the other situation they were to remember, and then again completed the questionnaire. Responses to the two questionnaires served as the dependent variables. Finally, subjects completed the third packet containing the 36-item conversational sensitivity measure.

The questionnaire used with each paragraph contained items tapping various aspects of a situation that might enhance a person's sensitivity to social interaction. Items were based upon available literature (e.g., Cody & McLaughlin, 1985) as well as systematic interviews with people who described what made them more or less sensitive in conversations. After data were collected, items were combined to form clusters tapping different aspects of situations. Those clusters are described below.

Results

In addition to answering the questionnaires, subjects responded, in each condition, to the statement "Thinking of that conversation, how aware, interested, sensitive and involved were you?" using a nine-step scale bounded by the labels ''very much'' and ''very little.'' A t-test for correlated samples between the two conditions indicated that in the high sensitive condition (M = 1.61, sd = 1.07) subjects reported they were significantly ($t(35) = 21.06$, $p < .00001$) more interested, sensitive, and involved in the conversation than they were in the low sensitive condition (M = 7.25, sd = 1.40).

STATISTICAL SUMMARY 7

Study VI

A t-test was used to compare responses in the two situations (i.e., high and low sensitive situations). The situations differed from each other: In the high sensitive situation, people reported being more interested, sensitive, and involved. This showed that Daly et al. had actually created two different situations.

Next, a series of t-tests were computed to compare the two situations on the dependent variables. These tests suggested that people were more sensitive when conversations dealt with more personal topics, violated expectations, and were formal, interesting, involving, and unpredictable. People were more sensitive if they entered a conversation in a positive mood and had a specific purpose in mind (e.g., creating a positive impression on the other person). Familiarity with the topic, type of relationship, and tension did not affect the amount of sensitivity.

Twelve clusters were generated from the questionnaire. Clusters were created when more than one item referenced the same dimension of the situation. The statistical results are presented in Table 5 where the items composing the clusters, average reliability indices, means, and standard deviations are reported.

Briefly, the results suggest that greater conversational sensitivity, as a response to situational characteristics, happens when conversations focus on personal, nonsuperficial topics ($t(35) = 7.22$, $p < .0001$), violate expectations ($t(34) = 4.25$, $p < .0001$), are formal ($t(36) = 2.48$, $p < .02$), interesting and involving ($t(36) = 14.55$, $p < .0001$) but unpredictable ($t(36) = 1.76$, $p < .08$), and involve people one likes ($t(36) = 4.01$, $p < .0001$). People are more sensitive when they enter conversations in a positive mood ($t(36) = 1.89$, $p < .06$) with distinct purposes in mind ($t(36) = 6.44$, $p < .0001$), and are concerned with creating a positive impression of themselves ($t(37) = 5.70$, $p < .0001$). On the other hand, familiarity with the topic ($t(36) = 1.17$, ns), acquaintanceship with the other interactants ($t(37) = 1.15$, ns), and the amount of tension in the exchange ($t(34) = 1.59$, ns) were unrelated to the degree of sensitivity a person felt. A series of additional analyses were completed in which the 36-item sensitivity measure was used as covariate. The results described above were not substantially different when conversational sensitivity, as a dispositional characteristic, was controlled.

CONCLUSIONS

The studies described in this article were conducted to discover the nature and correlates of conversational sensitivity. The first study, composed of three separate data collections, suggested that sensitivity includes an ability to detect meanings in what others say, a good memory for conversations, an ability to generate a variety of alternative ways of saying something in a social exchange, an interest in listening to conversations, skill at detecting affinity and power relationships in conversations, and an appreciation for the nuances for what is said in social interaction.

The convergent and discriminant validities of the construct were examined in the second and third investigations. Inverse and significant correlations were found among conversational sensitivity and social anxiety, receiver apprehension, and communication apprehension. Positive and significant associations were found among sensitivity and empathy, private self-consciousness, assertiveness, self-monitoring, and self-esteem. Where significant correlations were found, their

TABLE 5
Means, Standard Deviations, and Alpha Levels
for Situational Dimensions
of Conversatonal Sensitivity

Dimension	alpha	Low		High	
Expectation. ("The conversation was very different from most of the conversations I have." "During the conversation something happened that wasn't expected." "What was said was no different than what is said in most conversations." "The other person(s) said something I didn't expect.")	.65	9.26	(3.29)	12.29	(2.75)
Predictability. ("I knew, before the conversation, what the other(s) believed and felt about the topics we discussed." "Even before the conversation started, I knew what was expected: what I should say and what the other would say." "The course of the conversation (i.e., the way it went) was very predictable.")	.83	7.32	(3.06)	8.68	(3.08)
Mood. ("I felt tired and run-down before the conversation began." "I was feeling "up" (in a good mood) before the conversation began.")	.50	6.63	(1.85)	7.32	(2.17)
Topic Familiarity. ("The topic we discussed was unfamiliar to me before the conversation." "The topic of the conversation was one I knew little about." "I felt I knew a lot about the topic that was being discussed." "The other people in the conversation knew a lot about what we were talking about.")	.71	14.61	(3.00)	15.39	(3.12)
Acquaintance. ("The people involved in the conversation were people I see and talk with everyday." "I knew the other(s) in the conversation well." "I felt I would never see the people involved in the conversation again.")	.71	5.95	(2.44)	5.29	(2.95)
Tension. ("The conversation was more tense than most." "The conversation was unfriendly." "The conversation was calm." "The conversation was a friendly one." "There was a good deal of conflict in the conversation.")	.85	19.46	(3.47)	17.69	(5.66)
Purpose. ("I entered the conversation with many questions in mind." "In the conversation I had a special purpose or goal that I was trying to accomplish." "I entered the conversation with a purpose in mind." "The outcomes of the conversation were going to affect me directly.")	.69	15.68	(2.64)	11.00	(3.77)
Formality. ("The conversation was a very informal one." "The conversation was more formal than most.")	.42	3.54	(1.41)	4.51	(2.01)
Personal. ("The topic being discussed was a very personal one." "The talk was 'superficial'." "The conversation was an emotional one.")	.76	10.72	(3.40)	5.44	(2.66)
Affinity. ("I didn't like the other person(s)." "The others involved in the conversation were people I really cared for." "I liked the people in the conversation." "I did not trust the other person." "The other person(s) was very similar to me.")	.78	11.51	(4.06)	9.00	(3.18)
Impression-Leaving. ("I was really trying to make a good impression in this conversation." "I wanted people to think well of me in this exchange." "I wanted the other person(s) to think I cared about what was said." "In the conversation I felt a good deal of pressure to say 'the right thing'.")	.72	13.63	(3.07)	10.18	(3.26)
Involvement. ("I found the conversation of special interest." "I was very involved in the conversation." "The conversation was boring." "The conversation was dull and boring.")	.68	14.57	(2.87)	5.68	(1.77)

magnitude was not sizable, indicating that conversational sensitivity, while conceptually related to a variety of other constructs, is not equivalent to them. The third study addressed the very specific question as to whether or not conversational sensitivity was related to self-reported basic social skills as measured by Riggio's (1986) social skills inventory. Sensitivity was positively and significantly correlated with emotional expressivity, emotional sensitivity, social control, and the composite measure of social skills.

Behavioral correlates of conversational sensitivity were examined in the next two studies. In the fourth investigation, highly sensitive individuals' memories of conversations were hypothesized to differ from those of less sensitive individuals. An analysis of subjects' accounts of their "impressions, memories, and thoughts" concerning two movie excerpts revealed that individuals high in conversational sensitivity made proportionately more inferences, self-referents, and conversation-related inferences than their low sensitive counterparts. Those low in sensitivity, on the other hand, made proportionately more direct references to the text and more errors in those references. In the fifth study, subjects unitized conversations from two film excerpts. Since conversationally sensitive individuals ought to be more highly attuned to what happens during an interaction, we hypothesized that these individuals would unitize the conversation into a greater number (smaller) chunks than would those low in sensitivity. The data supported this notion.

Finally, in the sixth study, conversational sensitivity was reconceptualized as a response to a number of contextual variables. Sensitivity is aroused in situations where conversations focus on personal topics, violate expectations, and are unpredictable, formal, interesting, and involving. In situations where sensitivity is aroused, people are in a positive mood, enter with particular purposes, and are concerned with impression management.

Conceptually, the idea of conversational sensitivity can be considered in terms of the framework presented by Dworkin and Goldfinger (1985) on social affordances. In accordance with Gibson's (1966) notions, they propose that people differ in their processing biases, paying attention to, anticipating, and remembering different affordances of a situation. They demonstrate, for instance, that there may be a general processing bias for social situations and that sociability affects this processing bias. Some people anticipate, focus on, and remember more of the sociability affordances of a situation than others. Individuals high in conversational sensitivity should, likewise, emphasize the affordances tied to social interaction more than others. This greater attention to conversational affordances data may, in the long run, affect the ways highly sensitive individuals organize information about conversation.

In examining the available literature related to conversational sensitivity, it became apparent that the most relevant existing construct in communication research was Cegala's notion of interaction involvement. While sensitivity was conceived independently of Cegala's construct, an examination of the involvement measure raises the concern of duplication. To test whether the same general construct was being tapped, 67 undergraduate students completed the 36-item sensitivity measure and the 18-item interaction involvement instrument (Cegala, 1984). The overall correlation ($r = .28$, $p < .02$), while statistically significant, was not of the magnitude to suggest isomorphism. Among the subscales of the interaction involvement instrument, only the perceptiveness dimension had a significant correlation ($r = .55$, $p < .001$) with sensitivity. The distinction between the perceptiveness dimension of interaction involvement and sensitivity may lie in two areas. First, conversational sensitivity includes dimensions unrelated to the perceptiveness construct (e.g., conversational enjoyment had no correlation with perceptiveness [$r = .00$, ns]). Second, perceptiveness has a subtle emphasis on self-awareness (e.g., "I am keenly aware of how others perceive me during my conversations") that is missing in the sensitivity construct. In short, the two constructs, while related, tap different components of people's beliefs about their interaction behavior.[7]

Another question that arises when considering the construct of conversational sensitivity is whether or not any sex differences are associated with the construct. Previous research with constructs related to sensitivity is mixed on the issue of sex differences. On the one hand, Hall (1978), in a meta-analysis of nonverbal decoding studies, found females more sensitive than males. On the other hand, Bronfenbrenner, Harding, and Gallwey (1958) and Maccoby and Jackin (1974) found little evidence for sex differences (see Hoffman, 1977). In the current studies, where information on respondent's sex was available, there were no differences between males and females on either the overall measure or on the various factors (an exception was that females (M = 15.46, sd = 3.13) were significantly higher ($t(71)$ = 3.92, p < .05) on listening than males (M = 12.47, sd = 3.27). One explanation for the very few gender differences may be that sex and status have been confounded in research where sex has been a significant predictor of variables akin to sensitivity (Snodgrass, 1985).

Up to this point some of the components and correlates of self-reported conversational sensitivity have been identified. When sensitivity is considered an individual difference, much remains to be done. A major question left unanswered in the studies described in this article is the veridicality of the self-reports. That is, are people who say they are sensitive actually that way? In some ways, our behavioral studies (Studies IV and V) suggest a match between report and actual behavior. Indeed, it is impressive that a general self-report measure correlates, with some regularity, and in the anticipated directions, with a variety of perceptual and memory indicators. But more needs to be done. There is a long history in psychology of work exploring the accuracy of people's judgment of others (e.g., Bronfenbrenner et al., 1958), which continues today (e.g., Snodgrass, 1985). However, when the focus of attention moves from person perception to conversation or interaction perception, there is far less work. We know relatively little of even the categories people use in organizing their knowledge of conversation (see Forgas,

1979; Forgas & Bond, 1985; Wish, Deutsch, & Kaplan, 1976).

Future research will also have to be concerned with the consequences of conversational sensitivity. Are people who are particularly sensitive to conversational stimuli actually more effective in social interactions? The central emphasis of the sensitivity construct is on people's *receptive* skills, not their *production* skills. There may, however, be some carryover: More sensitive people may also be more effective conversationalists. At the same time, conversational sensitivity may be a double-edged sword. On the one hand, highly sensitive people may leave a conversation with a wealth of information and impressions that others are ignorant about. But, on the other hand, in some situations they may spend far too much time focusing on, interpreting, and remembering the most mundane of conversations. They may, in short, overanalyze what happens. It may well be that in most situations, people who would score high on measures of conversational sensitivity are no more sensitive than anyone else. Instead, they may have the capacity to "turn on" their sensitivity when it is demanded or especially needed and "turn off" their sensitivity at other times. In addition, the studies that have been completed focus solely on passive reception of conversations. In both the fourth and fifth investigations subjects watched conversations. Would there be a different pattern of results were subjects actively participating in an exchange?

Finally, how conversational sensitivity develops represents an interesting avenue for future research. We would anticipate that the more varied communication experiences an individual has, the more conversationally sensitive he or she should be. Participating in a wide variety of social encounters should provide people with experiences that broaden their categories for interaction behavior, making them in turn both more sensitive to interaction and more complex in their construals of social exchanges (Daly, Bell, Glenn, & Lawrence, 1985). In addition, the development of critical skills that emphasize approaches to social interaction from a variety of perspectives should, in all likelihood, enhance sensitivity. Research on the development of role-taking skills is obviously relevant here (Applegate, 1982).

Some comments should be made about approaching conversational sensitivity as a response to aspects of a situation. In the final study this sort of conversational sensitivity was affected, at least in terms of self-reports, by a number of contextual characteristics such as formality, predictability, and topic salience. Future work needs to further examine this conceptualization of sensitivity. First, a good measure of situational sensitivity is required. Obviously, self-report measures can be devised. But are there other, more behavioral, manifestations of sensitivity that serve as indications of people's attentiveness to social interaction? Second, attention should be paid to the components of situations that induce sensitivity. In the study described in this article, situational characteristics were drawn, in an ad hoc fashion, from interviews and previous research. What is required, though, is a systematic analysis of those circumstances that arouse sensitivity. Everyone has experienced, at times, feelings that they should be especially sensitive in a conversation. What happens in interactions to make people feel this way? What keys people to know they should be sensitive? Is it the others involved in the exchange, the potential consequences, something that is said in a certain way? Moreover, do people who vary in dispositional conversational sensitivity react differently when contextual factors hint at the necessity for situational sensitivity? Are highly sensitive people more successful at detecting situational cues prescribing sensitivity than their less sensitive counterparts?

The program of study described in this article started with the observation that people seem to differ in how sensitive they are to what happens in social exchanges. We found that sensitivity has at least eight components, that it correlates in meaningful ways with a number of communication-related personality characteristics, and is related to the ways people process and recall social interactions. Moreover, sensitivity need not be conceived of solely as an individual difference; it can also be viewed as one response people have to certain characteristics of conversational settings.

NOTES

1. Significant correlations ($p < .05$) were found between the individual factors of the sensitivity measure and a number of the personality measures implemented in this study. Detecting meaning was associated with both the noble self (.21) and the rhetorical sensitivity (−.16) dimensions of the rhetorical sensitivity measure; with fantasy (−.22) and distress (.13) dimensions of the empathy measure; with the overall PRCA (−.18) and its subdimensions of group (−.27), meeting (−.19), and conversation (−.14) apprehension; with the directiveness (.27), defense of rights (.26), and independence (.24) dimensions of the assertiveness scale; with the overall self-monitoring scale (−.17) as well as its subdimensions of extroversion (−.19) and acting (−.27); and with both public (.12) and private (.26) self-consciousness. Conversational memory was related to all three of the dimensions of rhetorical sensitivity (noble self: .20; rhetorical sensitivity: −.14; rhetorical reflector: −.16); the empathy (−.24) and distress (.12) subscales of the empathy instrument; the overall PRCA (−.26) as well as the group (−.26), meeting (−.27), and conversations (−.14) subscales; the directiveness (.17) and independence (.24) scales of the assertiveness measure; all three of the self-monitoring subscales (extroversion: −.12; other-directedness: .19; acting: −.16); and the public (.11) and private (.14) self-consciousness measures. Conversational alternatives was correlated with the noble self (.16) and rhetorical sensitivity (−.11) dimensions of the rhetorical sensitivity measure; the empathy (−.15) and distress (.26) dimensions of the empathy measure; the overall PRCA scale (−.33) as well as its subdimensions of group (−.32), meeting (−.30), conversation (−.24), and speaking (−.17) apprehension; the directiveness (.38), social assertiveness (.31), defense of rights (.28), and independence (.26) subdimensions of the assertiveness scale; the loneliness measure (−.15); the self-esteem measure (.25); the overall self-monitoring scale (−.27) and its subdimensions of extroversion (−.34) and acting (−.32); the receiver apprehension scale (−.26); and the social anxiety dimension (−.35) of the self-consciousness measure. Conversational imagination was tied to the fantasy dimension (−.26) of the empathy scale; the acting dimension (−.11) of the self-monitoring measure; and private self-consciousness (.11). Conversation enjoyment was associated with both the noble self (.12) and the rhetorical sensitivity (−.14) dimensions of the rhetorical sensitivity measure and the speaking (.15) subdimension of the PRCA. Interpretation was related to the distress (.26) dimension of the empathy measure; the overall PRCA (−.23) and its subdimensions of group (−.17), meeting

(−.13), conversation (−.22), and speaking (−.21) apprehension; the directiveness (.23), social assertiveness (.15), and independence (.22) subdimensions of the assertiveness measure; the self-esteem (.15) scale; the overall self-monitoring measure (−.14) as well as its subdimensions of extroversion (−.14) and acting (−.21); the receiver apprehension scale (−.28); and the social anxiety (−.12) and private self-consciousness (.13) subdimensions of the self-consciousness measure. Finally, perceiving affinity was correlated with both the noble self (.18) and the rhetorical sensitivity (−.17) subdimensions of the rhetorical sensitivity measure; the perspective-taking (−.13), the empathy (−.12), and the distress (.17) subdimensions of the empathy measure; the overall PRCA (−.14) and its subdimensions of group (−.17) and conversation (−.17) apprehension; the directiveness (.25), social assertiveness (.23), defense of rights (.15), and independence (.20) subdimensions of the assertiveness measure; the loneliness scale (−.13); the self-esteem measure (.22); the extroversion (−.15) dimension of the self-monitoring measure; the receiver apprehension measure (−.13); and the social anxiety (−.15) subdimension of the self-consciousness measure.

2. Hart et al. (1980) suggest that investigators use partial correlations when using their measure. We completed such partials and found no substantial differences from the results described in this study.

3. The individual factors of the sensitivity measure were significantly ($p < .05$) correlated with a number of the subdimensions of the social skills inventory. Detecting meaning was related to emotional sensitivity (.41), emotional control (.23), and social manipulation (.26). Conversational memory and conversational imagination were not correlated with any of the dimensions. Conversational alternatives was associated with emotional control (.23), social control (.39), social sensitivity (−.23), and social manipulation (.25). Conversation enjoyment was related to emotional expressivity (.20), emotional sensitivity (.39), social sensitivity (.37), and emotional control (−.21). Interpretation was associated with social sensitivity (−.31), emotional control (.24) and social control (.25). Perceiving affinity was tied to emotional expressivity (.24) and emotional sensitivity (.60), and perceiving control was correlated with emotional sensitivity (.38).

4. The individual factors of the sensitivity measure were significantly ($p < .05$) correlated with a number of the coding categories. The proportion of text-based idea units was correlated with detecting meaning (−.33), conversational alternatives (−.51), conversational imagination (−.30), and perceiving control (−.28). The inference proportion was correlated with detecting meaning (.29), conversational alternatives (.46), and perceiving control (.27). The proportion of errors was correlated with conversational memory (−.31), conversational alternatives (−.36), conversational imagination (−.60), and perceiving control (−.54). The proportion of self-referents was uncorrelated with any of the subscales. The conversation inferences proportion was correlated with detecting meaning (.29)

and conversational alternatives (.31). The proportion of quotes was related to conversational imagination (.28). It should be remembered, in interpreting these values, that the sample was composed of individuals who scored one standard deviation above or below the mean.

5. When the two unitizing scores were averaged for subjects, the difference between high (M = 13.59, sd = 4.38) and low sensitive (M = 11.0, sd = 5.20) subjects approached significance ($t(34) = 1.54$, $p < .07$).

6. In a separate analysis, the correlations between each of the subscales of the sensitivity measure and the average unitizing index were computed. Only the memory component was correlated significantly ($r = .28$, $p < .05$) with the overall unitizing pattern of subjects. When we examined the correlations of the sensitivity indices with the unitizing scores for each of the film excerpts separately we found somewhat different patterns. For *Who's Afraid of Virginia Woolf* the correlation between the number of units and the "make-up" component of the scale was significant ($r = .27$, $p < .06$); for *In the Heat of the Night* the number of units recorded by subjects was significantly correlated with memory ($r = .33$, $p < .03$) and with liking for conversations ($r = .26$, $p < .07$).

7. It may well be that another component of conversational sensitivity is some degree of self-awareness in social interaction. Sensitivity may include a more refined sense of both how one affects others in conversing and how others respond to the individual's conversation enactments. Additionally, given the significant correlation between the composite sensitivity measure and the perceptiveness dimension of interaction involvement, one might argue that sensitivity represents a refined version of the construct measured by the perceptiveness dimension.

REFERENCES

Applegate, J. L. (1982). The impact of construct system development on communication and impression formation in persuasive contexts. *Communication Monographs, 49*, 277–289.

Archer, D., & Akert, R. M. (1977). Words and everything else: Verbal and nonverbal cues in social interpretation. *Journal of Personality and Social Psychology, 35*, 443–449.

Beatty, M., & Payne, S. (1984). Listening comprehension as a function of cognitive complexity: A research note. *Communication Monographs, 51*, 85–89.

Berschied, E., Graziano, W., Monson, T., & Dermer, M. (1976). Outcome dependency: Attention, attribution, and attraction. *Journal of Personality and Social Psychology, 34*, 978–989.

Bronfenbrenner, U., Harding, J., & Gallwey, M. (1958). The measurement of skill in social perception. In D. C. McClelland, A. L. Baldwin, U. Bronfenbrenner, & F. L. Strodtbeck (Eds.), *Talent and society: New Perspectives in the identification of talent* (pp. 29–111). Princeton, NJ: Van Nostrand.

Briggs, S. R., Cheek, J. M., & Buss, A. H. (1980). An analysis of the self-monitoring scale. *Journal of Personality and Social Psychology, 38,* 679–686.

Buck, R. (1976). A test of nonverbal receiving ability: Preliminary studies. *Human Communication Research, 2,* 162–171.

Buck, R. (1983). Nonverbal receiving ability. In J. M. Wiemann & R. P. Harrison (Eds.), *Nonverbal interaction* (pp. 209–242). Newbury Park, CA: Sage.

Buck, R. (1984). *The communication of emotion.* New York: Guilford.

Cegala, D. J. (1981). Interaction involvement: A cognitive dimension of communication competence. *Communication Education, 30,* 109–121.

Cegala, D. J. (1984). Affective and cognitive manifestations of interaction involvement during unstructured and competitive interactions. *Communication Monographs, 51,* 320–338.

Cegala, D. J., Savage, G. T., Brunner, C. C., & Conrad, A. B. (1982). An elaboration of the meaning of interaction involvement: Toward the development of a theoretical concept. *Communication Monographs, 49,* 229–248.

Cody, M., & McLaughlin, M. (1985). The situation as a construct in interpersonal communication research. In M. L. Knapp & G. R. Miller (Eds.), *Handbook of interpersonal communication* (pp. 263–312). Newbury Park, CA: Sage.

Cohen, J. (1977). *Statistical power analysis for the behavioral sciences.* New York: Academic Press.

Cohen, C. E., & Ebbeson, E. B. (1979). Observational goals and schema activation: A theoretical framework for behavior perception. *Journal of Experimental Social Psychology, 15,* 305–329.

Crowne, D. P., & Marlowe, D. (1964). *The approval motive: Studies in evaluative dependence.* New York: John Wiley.

Daly, J. A., Bell, R., Glenn, P., & Lawrence, S. (1985). Conceptualizing conversational complexity. *Human Communication Research, 12,* 30–53.

Daly, J. A., & McCroskey, J. C. (Eds.). (1984). *Avoiding communication: Shyness, reticence, and communication apprehension.* Newbury Park, CA: Sage.

Davis, M. H. (1983). Measuring individual differences in empathy: Evidence for a multidimensional approach. *Journal of Personality and Social Psychology, 44,* 113–126.

Dickman, H. R. (1963). The perception of behavior units. In R. G. Barker (Ed.), *The stream of behavior.* New York: Appleton-Century-Crofts.

Douglas, W. (1984). Initial interaction scripts: When knowing is believing. *Human Communication Research, 11,* 203–219.

Dworkin, R. H., & Goldfinger, S. H. (1985). Processing bias: Individual differences in the cognition of situations. *Journal of Personality, 53,* 480–501.

Fenigstein, A., Scheier, M., & Buss, A. (1975). Public and private self-consciousness: Assessment and theory. *Journal of Consulting and Clinical Psychology, 43,* 522–527.

Fletcher, G. J. O., Danilovics, P., Fernandez, G., Peterson, D., & Reeder, G. D. (1986). Attributional complexity: An individual differences measure. *Journal of Personality and Social Psychology, 51,* 875–884.

Forgas, J. P. (1979). *Social episodes: The study of interaction routines.* London: Academic Press.

Forgas, J. P., & Bond, M. H. (1985). Cultural influences on the perceptions of interaction episodes. *Personality and Social Psychology Bulletin, 11,* 75–88.

Forgas, J. P., Bower, G. H., & Krantz, S. E. (1984). The influence of mood on perceptions of social interactions. *Journal of Experimental Social Psychology, 20,* 497–513.

Funder, D. C., & Harris, M. J. (1986). On the several facets of personality assessment: The case of social acuity. *Journal of Personality, 54,* 528–550.

Gibson, E. J. (1969). *Principles of perceptual learning and development.* New York: Appleton-Century-Crofts.

Gibson, J. J. (1966). *The senses considered as perceptual systems.* Boston: Houghton Mifflin.

Gibson, J. J. (1979). *The ecological approach to visual perception.* Boston: Houghton Mifflin.

Goffman, E. (1967). *Interaction ritual.* New York: Doubleday.

Goodman, N. R. (1980). *Determinants of the perceptual organization of ongoing action and emotion behavior.* Unpublished doctoral dissertation. University of Connecticut. Summarized in Buck (1984).

Hall, J. A. (1978). Gender effects in decoding nonverbal cues. *Psychological Bulletin, 85,* 845–857.

Hamilton, D., Katz, L., & Leirer, V. (1980). Cognitive representation of personality impressions: Organizational processes in first impression formation. *Journal of Personality and Social Psychology, 39,* 1050–1063.

Hart, R., & Burks, D. (1972). Rhetorical sensitivity and social interaction. *Speech Monographs, 39,* 75–91.

Hart, R., Carlson, R., & Eadie, W. (1980). Attitudes toward communication and the assessment of rhetorical sensitivity. *Communication Monographs, 47,* 1–22.

Hoffman, M. L. (1977). Sex differences in empathy and related behaviors. *Psychological Bulletin, 84,* 712–722.

Isenhart, M. (1980). An investigation of the relationship of sex and sex role to the ability to decode nonverbal cues. *Human Communication Research, 6,* 309–318.

Johnson, J. A., Cheek, J. M., & Smither, R. (1983). The structure of empathy. *Journal of Personality and Social Psychology, 45,* 1299–1312.

Knight, J. A., & Vallacher, R. R. (1981). Interpersonal engagement in social perception: The consequences of getting into the action. *Journal of Personality and Social Psychology, 40,* 990–999.

Krippendorff, K. (1980). *Content analysis.* Newbury Park, CA: Sage.

Lorr, M., & More, W. W. (1980). Four dimensions of assertiveness. *Multivariate Behavioral Research, 15,* 127–138.

Maccoby, E. E., & Jacklin, C. N. (1974). *The psychology of sex differences.* Stanford, CA: Stanford University Press.

McCroskey, J. C., & Beatty, M. J. (1986) Oral communication apprehension. In W. Jones, J. Cheek, & S. Briggs (Eds.), *Shyness: Perspectives on research and treatment* (pp. 279–293). New York: Plenum.

Newtson, D. (1976). Foundations of attribution: The perception of ongoing behavior. In J. H. Harvey, W. J. Ickes, & R. F. Kidd (Eds.), *New directions in attribution research* (Vol. 1, pp. 223–247). Hillsdale, NJ: Lawrence Erlbaum.

Petrie, C. R., & Carrel, S. D. (1976). The relationship of motivation, listening capability, initial information, and verbal organizational ability to lecture comprehension and retention. *Communication Monographs, 43,* 187–194.

Riggio, R. E. (1986). Assessment of basic social skills. *Journal of Personality and Social Psychology, 51,* 649–660.

Rosenberg, M (1965). *Society and the adolescent self-image.* Princeton, NJ: Princeton University Press.

Rosenthal, R., Hall, J. A., DiMatteo, M. R., Rogers, P. L., & Archer, D. (1979). *Sensitivity to nonverbal communication: The PONS test.* Baltimore: Johns Hopkins.

Russell, D., Peplau, L. A., & Cutrona, C. E. (1980). The revised UCLA loneliness scale: Concurrent and discriminant validity evidence. *Journal of Personality and Social Psychology, 39,* 427–480.

Sabatelli, R. M., Buck, R., & Dreyer, A. (1982). Nonverbal communication accuracy in married couples: Relationships with marital complaints. *Journal of Personality and Social Psychology, 43,* 1088–1097.

Snodgrass, S. E. (1985). Women's intuition: The effect of subordinate role on interpersonal sensitivity. *Journal of Personality and Social Psychology, 49,* 146–155.

Snyder, M. (1974). The self-monitoring of expressive behavior. *Journal of Personality and Social Psychology, 30,* 526–537.

Snyder, M. (1979). Self-monitoring processes. In L. Berkowitz (Ed.), *Advances in Experimental Social Psychology* (Vol. 12, pp. 85–128). New York: Academic Press.

Snyder, M., & Cantor, N. (1980). Thinking about ourselves and others: Self-monitoring and social knowledge. *Journal of Personality and Social Psychology, 39,* 220–234.

Snyder, M., & Gangestad, S. (1986). On the nature of self-monitoring: Matters of assessment, matters of validity. *Journal of Personality and Social Psychology, 51,* 125–139.

Stafford, L., & Daly, J. A. (1984). Conversational memory: The effects of recall mode and memory expectancies on remembrances of natural conversations. *Human Communication Research, 10,* 379–402.

Walker, R. E., & Foley, J. M. (1973). Social intelligence: Its history and measurement. *Psychological Reports, 33,* 839–864.

Wheeless, L. R. (1975). An investigation of receiver apprehension and social context dimensions of communication apprehension. *Speech Teacher, 24,* 261–268.

Wish, M., Deutsch, M., & Kaplan S. (1976). Perceived dimensions of interpersonal relations. *Journal of Personality and Social Psychology, 33,* 409–440.

THE DISCOURSE OF REQUESTS:
ASSESSMENT OF A POLITENESS APPROACH

Robert T. Craig
Karen Tracy
Frances Spisak

A corpus of transcribed, oral requests used in a previous study of compliance-gaining strategies (Tracy, Craig, Smith, & Spisak, 1984) is examined interpretively from the perspective of the politeness theory of Brown and Levinson (1978).

Findings include the following: (1) politeness strategies occur in great abundance and variety; (2) superstrategies are mixed in varyingly skillful ways; (3) goals are accomplished through multifunctional discourse; (4) the interpretation of politeness strategies confronts several kinds of indeterminacy; (5) facework strategies that fall outside the scope of the politeness theory, including aggravation and speaker-oriented strat-

Source: The Article is taken from *Human Communication Research* [12: 437–468, 1986]. © International communication Association, 8140 Burnet Rd., Austin, TX 78766. Reprinted by permission of Sage Publications, Inc. and ICA.

egies, are much in evidence. In response to the several theoretical problems that emerge in the course of the analysis, six tenets on which to build a new theory of facework are proposed.

The apparently simple, everyday act of asking a favor, when done effectively, is the product of complex communicative skills. From one point of view, asking a favor can be thought of as an attempt to exert social influence; but getting the hearer to comply with the request is only one among a potentially tangled network of goals and constraints that the skillful speaker is able to manage. Thus a recent study of compliance-gaining strategies in requests concluded that the compliance-gaining analysis, although it was informative, accounted for only a small part of what was most interesting in messages (Tracy, Craig, Smith, & Spisak, 1984). Especially prominent in the discourse were many instances of what Goffman (1967) called ''facework''—tactics designed to protect the speaker or hearer from various kinds of embarrassment that might result from asking or being asked a favor. It was suggested that a study of facework, especially as elaborated by Brown and Levinson (1978) in their theory of politeness, would prove helpful. This research, taking up that suggestion, assesses the utility of a politeness approach to describing the discourse of requests.

Although aspects of Brown and Levinson's (1978) politeness theory have been used in numerous communication studies (e.g., Applegate, 1982; Baxter, 1984; Boyd, 1984; Donohue, Diez, & Stahle, 1983; Fairhurst, Green, & Snavely, 1984; Hiemstra, 1982; Jacobs & Jackson, 1983a, 1983b; Kline, 1981a, 1981b, 1982; McLaughlin, Cody, & O'Hair, 1983; McLaughlin, Cody, & Rosenstein, 1983; Mura, 1983; O'Keefe, 1983; Parkhurst, 1983; Shimanoff, 1977; Tracy, 1983; Tracy et al., 1984), with two exceptions the theory as a whole has not been discussed at much depth.

The first exception is a study by Shimanoff (1977) in which, using a preliminary version of Brown and Levinson's theory, a politeness

coding scheme was developed to assess gender differences. In this study, 19 brief interactions between either a student or faculty member and a female receptionist in a university academic department were analyzed. Shimanoff's (1977) study, though not specifically designed to assess the politeness theory, raises a number of important issues for the theory that we mention later. Her study does not, however, look at discourse across a large enough variety of situations to speak to the central claims Brown and Levinson make.

The second exception, a study by Baxter (1984), is both more ambitious and less successful. Her study attempted to test the politeness theory by means of a self-report, likelihood-of-use analysis of politeness strategies similar to previous studies of compliance-gaining message strategies (e.g., Marwell & Schmitt, 1967; Miller, Boster, Roloff, & Seibold, 1977). Baxter's study did look at politeness use across a number of situations, varied systematically in several regards. Yet, in addition to the general limitations of likelihood-of-use assessments of communicative strategy use (see Tracy et al., 1984), the study is flawed by several problems in its representation and operationalization of the politeness theory.[1]

The strength of Shimanoff's (1977) study is its attention to natural discourse; the strength of Baxter's (1984) is its examination of communication strategies across a range of situations. This study attempts to combine these strengths. The politeness theory is assessed by applying it to actual discourse in a large variety of situations. The analysis draws on two sources of data. The first comprises the 480 transcribed, audio-taped messages that were previously used by Tracy et al. (1984) in a study of compliance-gaining strategies. The messages were produced by 20 speakers (undergraduates at a large midwestern university) who were asked to speak as they actually would to the particular hearer in each of 24 hypothetical request situations. The hypothetical situations vary systematically in three dimensions: (1) familiarity of the hearer (high, low), (2) relative status of hearer (higher, equal, lower), and (3) size of request (large, small), so that for each of the twelve combinations there are two situations. The situations include, for example, asking for an $800 loan from a parent, requesting a stranger to watch one's luggage, asking a friend for a ride to the airport, borrowing a classmate's notes before an exam, and asking a neighbor to watch one's cat over the weekend.[2]

The second source of data consists of approximately 20 hours of audio-taped discussions in which the research team worked on procedures for coding politeness strategies in the requests. We were stimulated to record the coding sessions, in part, by Poole's (1982) proposal that research reports make available information about the process by which coders achieved consensual interpretations of particular items, including background information, assumptions, and reasoning brought to bear. In this case, the coding discussions were incorporated into an interpretive study of the requests.[3]

After providing a summary overview of the politeness theory, we show that the logical structure of the theory makes it difficult to use in ways such as Baxter (1984) and, initially, we attempted to do. We go on to show, however, that the theory can be used, and in being used, challenged by data. The politeness theory illuminates several aspects of the requests, and a politeness approach to the requests illuminates the theory, suggesting ways in which it can be revised and developed.

THE POLITENESS THEORY

Assumptions

Brown and Levinson (1978) offer a pan-cultural theory of politeness designed to explain a large number of remarkably detailed cross-cultural parallelisms in language usage. The theory begins with a set of assumptions that the authors describe as a "tongue-in-cheek" Model Person—a model that bears some resemblance to the rational actor of economic theory.

It is assumed, first, that all persons are concerned about their "face," the self-image they present to others, and that they recognize that other persons have similar face wants. Face is said to have two aspects. The first—negative face—is a person's want to be unimpeded by others: the desire to be free to act as one chooses and not be imposed upon. The second aspect—positive face—is the want to have at least some selected others appreciate and approve of one's self, including one's personality, desires, and wants. Face, then, is "something that is emotionally invested, and that can be lost, maintained or enhanced, and must constantly be attended to in interaction" (Brown & Levinson, 1978, p. 66). The second basic assumption is that, given that one's own face concerns can be sustained only by the actions of others, it is generally in everyone's interest to work to maintain others' face. This will be true except under a restricted set of circumstances in which people are likely to attend to their own face without attending to others'. The third assumption is that people are rational agents. This means that they will choose means to satisfy their goals in maximally efficient ways.

The heart of the politeness theory is the relationships it establishes among: (a) a set of sociological factors that influence the degree of face threat of any communicative act; (b) five general orientations to face-threat, which Brown and Levinson call "superstrategies"; and (c) a description of the ways in which superstrategies could be realized at the level of discourse choices. We now consider each of these aspects of the theory more closely.

Face-Threatening Acts

Many communicative acts inherently threaten the face needs of one or both participants. Requests, threats, compliments, criticisms, and apologies are examples of "face-threatening acts" (FTAs). Each act, however, does not possess a standard amount of face-threat, rather the degree is mitigated or aggravated by three factors (Brown & Levinson, 1987, p. 79). First is the social distance between speaker and hearer: The less socially familiar two people are, the greater the potential face threat of a communicative act between them.

Second is the power or status of the hearer relative to the speaker: The more power a hearer has compared to the speaker, the greater the face threat. Third is the rank or degree of imposition (cost to negative and positive face) intrinsic to a particular act. Although cross-cultural agreement on the ranking of FTAs would not be expected, it is assumed that cultures rank acts in regard to their general degree of imposition. The more imposition an act involves, the more it threatens the face of one or both participants.

Distance, Power, and Rank are assumed to be strongly context-dependent variables, which consequently have to be established uniquely for each communicative act (e.g., the Rank of an act may depend upon the social identities of the speaker and hearer). These three are assumed to mediate all other influences on the seriousness of an FTA. Brown and Levinson (1978, p. 81) provide a formula for combining the three factors to compute an overall index of face threat. Although they do not themselves use the formula quantitatively, they suggest that numerical values could be attached to each factor. The formula simply sums the three factors, assuming no interactions and no differences in importance among them and treating threats to the face of speaker and hearer as equivalent.

Superstrategies and Output Strategies

When contemplating performance of an FTA, speakers may select from among five general strategies, two of which—positive and negative politeness—are realized in a variety of ways in the discourse. We discuss the superstrategies in order of increasing politeness and then look at the output strategies for positive and negative politeness:

1. A speaker may perform the FTA "baldly," making no attempt to acknowledge the hearer's face wants. Thus, for example, a speaker who needed $50 might say, "Lend me $50."
2. A speaker may perform the FTA while attending to the hearer's positive face wants, using what Brown and Levinson

(1978) label a positive politeness strategy. In this case the speaker attempts to convey liking for the hearer and that the hearer's needs and wants are desirable. A speaker using this strategy to gain a $50 loan might say, "Hey, old friend, you're a person I can always count on. Lend me $50, won't you?" As Brown and Levinson (1978, p. 106) note:

The linguistic realizations of positive politeness are in many respects simply representative of the normal linguistic behaviour between intimates, where interest and approval of each other's personality, presuppositions indicating shared wants and shared knowledge, implicit claims to reciprocity of obligations or to reflexivity of wants, etc. are routinely exchanged. Perhaps the only feature that distinguishes positive-politeness redress from normal everyday intimate language behaviour is an element of exaggeration: this serves as a marker of the face-redress aspect of positive-politeness expression, by indicating that even if S can't with total sincerity say "I want your wants," he can at least sincerely indicate "I want your positive face to be satisfied."

3. A speaker may perform the FTA with negative politeness, acknowledging the hearer's negative face wants, the desire to be unimpeded and not imposed upon. An attempt to get a $50 loan using a negative politeness strategy might look like the following: "Excuse me, I hate to ask this of you and I wouldn't normally put you on the spot if I weren't in such dire straits but could you lend me $50 for just a few days? I'd be forever in your debt." Negative politeness, then, is characterized by

self-effacement, formality and restraint, with attention to very restricted aspects of H's [the hearer's] self-image, centering on his want to be unimpeded. Face-threatening acts are redressed with apologies for interfering or transgressing, with linguistic or nonlinguistic deference, with hedges on the illocutionary force of the act, with impersonalizing mechanisms (such as passives) that distances S [speaker] and H [hearer] from the act, and with other softening mechanisms that give the addressee an "out," a face-saving line of escape, permitting him to feel that his response is not coerced (Brown & Levinson, 1978, p. 75).

4. A speaker may "go off-record" in performing the FTA. Here a speaker performs the act but in a vague manner that could be interpreted by the hearer as some other act. So, in this instance, the speaker who actually wanted a $50 loan might casually mention that he or she was having a hard time meeting bills. Because the speaker would hint, never explicitly asking for the loan, the listener would have the option of interpreting the speaker solely as providing financial information.

5. Finally, a speaker may avoid doing the FTA at all. Using this strategy, a speaker who wanted a $50 loan would neither ask for a loan nor hint about being in need of funds. Brown and Levinson's identification of "not saying anything" as a strategy is incongruent with the usual understanding of a communicative strategy—how one attempts to accomplish a goal. Yet it makes sense, if strategy is conceived of as a way to proceed or respond in a situation. Indeed, an option every communicator has is not to talk. Brown and Levinson draw attention to this choice in their identification of avoiding the FTA as a fifth strategy.

The theory hold that speakers contemplating the performance of an FTA will generally choose higher-numbered (more polite) strategies in proportion to the seriousness of the FTA. However, because costs (effort, unclarity, other threats to face) are associated with the use of higher-numbered strategies, speakers will not generally select strategies that are more polite than necessary (Brown & Levinson, 1978, p. 79).

Much of Brown and Levinson's (1978) monograph is devoted to a highly detailed exposition

of linguistic "output strategies" that are available to speakers for implementing the positive and negative politeness superstrategies. Each output strategy is explained in terms of the practical reasoning that links it to the superstrategy, and each is illustrated by examples drawn from several languages. For instance, positive politeness can be realized by the speaker's taking notice of particular aspects of the hearer (e.g., "goodness, you cut your hair"); using in-group identity markers like jargon ("lend us two *bucks* then, wouldja mate?"), and ellipsis ("got any spare cash?"); presupposing knowledge of the hearer's wants or attitudes ("wouldn't you like a drink?"); and giving reasons (thus involving the hearer in the speaker's decision process). The negative politeness strategies are realized, for example, by hedging a request for an action ("I was wondering," "perhaps"); minimizing the imposition (use of words like "just," "a little"); giving deference ("excuse me sir"); apologizing by admitting the impingement ("I'd like to ask you a big favor"), or indicating reluctance ("I hate to impose but"); and going on record as incurring a debt ("I'd be eternally grateful if you would"). Table 1 identifies and gives an example of each of the output strategies.

Speakers exploit the available politeness strategies in sometimes convoluted ways. This accounts for the richness and complexity of politeness phenomena and the corresponding complexity of the politeness theory. For example, "a speaker can use a bald-on-record FTA to claim (by implicature) that he is powerful over H, and does not fear retaliation. This is risky, but if he gets away with it . . . [he] succeeds in actually altering the public definition of his relationship" (Brown & Levinson, 1978, p. 233).

USING THE POLITENESS THEORY

The politeness theory merits the attention of communication scholars for several reasons. First, Brown and Levinson (1978) argue, with massive evidence, that face wants and related politeness strategies are cross-culturally universal, even to

---

T A B L E 1
Output Strategies for Positive and Negative Politeness

Positive Politeness

1. Notice, attend to Hearer (H): "You got a new haircut."
2. Exaggerate interest, approval, sympathy with H: "How horrible that it rained for your party."
3. Intensify interest to H: Exaggerate facts or tell stories in present tense.
4. Use in-group identity markers: "Hey, honey, come here."
5. Seek agreement: Select safe topics on which agreement is expected.
6. Avoid disagreement: "Are you coming tonight?" "Yes, I'll probably stop over but don't count on it."
7. Presuppose, raise, assert common ground: Gossiping before getting down to business, or presupposing knowledge "The A-team was wild last night."
8. Joke: "So you've got nothing to do this week." (said in response to long list of upcoming responsibilities).
9. Assert or presuppose S's knowledge of and concern for H's wants: "I know you'd want to help me out with this if you could, so that's why I'm here."
10. Offer, promise: "Look, I promise to come by and visit you when I come to town."
11. Be optimistic: "You'll stay with the baby, won't you?"
12. Include both S and H in the activity: "Let's put the milk away."
13. Give (or ask for) reasons: "Why don't we go out for pizza?"
14. Assume or assert reciprocity: "You get coffee today. I did it yesterday."
15. Give gifts to H (goods, sympathy, understanding, cooperation).

Negative Politeness

1. Be conventionally indirect: "Can you please pass the salt?"
2. Question, hedge: "I wonder if you could help out?"
3. Be pessimistic: "I don't suppose there is any chance you could help me."
4. Minimize the imposition: "Could I borrow your pencil for just a minute?"
5. Give deference: "I must be stupid. Could you help me fix this?"
6. Apologize: "I hate to ask you this but . . ."
7. Impersonalize S and H: "It's necessary that you do the following things."
8. State the FTA as a general rule: "There's no smoking in this section."
9. Nominalize: "Your poor performance on the exams" versus "you performed poorly."
10. Go on record as incurring a debt, or as not indebting H: "I'd be eternally grateful if you would . . ."

Note: Derived from Brown and Levinson (1978) with constructed examples.

---

the level of parallel "minutiae" in otherwise widely divergent languages. These universal features of language usage are explained in terms of a rational-strategic model of the speaker-hearer that has broad implications for discourse analysis (Jacobs & Jackson, 1983b) and suggests a fresh perspective on the debate about the law and rule theories of communication. Second, the politeness theory offers a particularly fruitful model of a discourse approach to communication, an approach that seeks to draw specific links between linguistic forms and communicative functions. Specifically, it offers an alternative to functional message strategy approaches in which the linguistic realizations of message strategies are not typically of major interest (Tracy et al., 1984). Third, the theory addresses the complexity of motivations and goals that are realized in discourse, and the possible conflicts among them that must be resolved. As an extension of Goffman's (1959, 1967, 1971) important work, it draws our attention especially to goals related to the self-presentations of persons, to which cognitive or task-oriented goals of communication must always be adjusted (Clark & Delia, 1979; Tracy & Moran, 1983).

These general theoretical reasons recommend politeness as an approach to the discourse of requests, but more specific connections are also apparent. Requests are clearly face-threatening acts. An earlier study suggested that politeness strategies play an important role in requests (Tracy et al., 1984). It also happens that the hypothetical situations used in that study vary in three dimensions (familiarity and relative status of hearer, and size of request) that closely match the three sociological variables that determine the amount of face threat according to the politeness theory. Thus the request messages are particularly well suited for a politeness approach.

Indeed, the request messages seemed at first to offer a unique opportunity to test the politeness theory experimentally: If a scheme could be developed for coding or measuring politeness in the request messages, then the hypothesis that politeness is a function of face threat could be tested in a relatively straightforward way. To conduct that test was initially a goal of this research, but the goal was set aside as the difficulty of implementing it as well as its inappropriateness to the theory became evident. The analysis, in the following section, of politeness in the discourse of requests will document some of the difficulties involved in implementing a coding scheme for politeness. In this section, we point out several structural features of the politeness theory that render difficult the sort of experimental interpretation that had been envisioned and propose instead a more feasible and appropriate way to use the theory, which the study of politeness in requests then illustrates.

At least four structural characteristics of the politeness theory inhibit an experimental test of its logic: First, the theory appears to conceptualize politeness (face redress) as a quantity (something measurable in amount or degree) insofar as a continuum can be assumed to underlie the order of the five superstrategies (Baxter, 1984; Shimanoff, 1977). However, no conceptual structure links the lower-level output strategies, via some form of scaling or aggregation, to an underlying continuum of politeness. Could one assume that *all* negative politeness strategies are

more redressive than *any* positive politeness strategy? That the *number* of output strategies in a message is some function of the amount of politeness? That individual output strategies can be *scaled* in some fashion? All of these possibilities may deserve consideration (Shimanoff, 1977, aggregates strategies in several ways), but Brown and Levinson (1978) provide warrant for none of them. The theory makes no claims of being able to predict which output strategies a speaker will select from among those available to realize a given superstrategy.

Second, the output strategies cannot easily be subjected to an analysis like that applied to compliance-gaining message strategies (Tracy et al., 1984) because the output strategies, unlike the compliance-gaining strategies, are not a formal typology; they are not mutually exclusive and exhaustive, but instead are open-ended lists with considerable overlap in meaning among the members of each list and even, to some extent, between lists (Baxter, 1984; Shimanoff, 1977). For example, certain verbal hedges (negative politeness strategy # 2; ''I wonder whether'' or ''I was wondering'') also appear to count as conventional indirectness (negative politeness strategy # 1), as point-of-view distancing (negative politeness strategy # 7), and perhaps even as hedging of opinions (positive politeness strategy # 6). Furthermore, as Shimanoff (1977) notes output strategies are sometimes defined functionally (''intensify interest to hearer'') and other times linguistically (''question, hedge'') without clear attention to the differences implied by each type of definition.

Third, the five superstrategies, although they are a typology and are ordered in terms of degrees of politeness, are not linked to an underlying politeness continuum in a way that would facilitate a quantitative test. One might assume that the superstrategies are mutually exclusive options that speakers choose among according to the amount of face threat. One would expect, on this interpretation, to find a curvilinear statistical relationship between the amount of face threat and the likelihood of use of any particular superstrategy; the superstrategies would occupy overlapping ranges along the continuum of face threat. No such model, however, is warranted by the reasoning of Brown and Levinson (1978).

Fourth, even though an equation is given for computing the amount of face threat as a function of situational parameters (Distance, Power, Rank), the theory does not predict any definite empirical relationship between the situational parameters and the use of politeness strategies. This is because the relations among situation, face threat, and discourse turn out to be very complex (Brown & Levinson, 1978, pp. 233–237). Speakers select strategies in such a way as to exploit the ''logic'' of politeness in order, for example, to portray an imposition as being smaller or the speaker's power over the hearer as being greater than might be expected. Speakers also use politeness strategies for purposes not directly related to face threat, for example, to increase or decrease the closeness of interpersonal relationships. Ironic and playful uses of politeness strategies are also common. One might nevertheless assume that ''on the average'' the amount of politeness in a message can be predicted straightforwardly from the amount of face threat—and to demonstrate such a relationship empirically would indeed be interesting—but the theory, again, provides no clear warrant for the assumption. Like Grice's (1975) conversational maxims, the politeness theory sets forth a model of discourse, much of the value of which resides in the various ways speakers deviate from it for strategic purposes.[4]

The politeness theory does not, then, easily lend itself to experimental or quantitative interpretation. Instead Brown and Levinson (1978) offer a complex interpretive framework, the usefulness of which is made evident by showing how it enables the analyst to make sense of a wide range of examples of language usage that would otherwise be puzzling or understandable only in ad hoc ways. The most obviously appropriate way to test the politeness theory is by applying it to new types of examples. To the extent that the theory sheds light on the examples, it is supported and its evidentiary base broadened; to the extent that puzzles remain or can be eliminated only by

ad hoc interpretations, modifications of the theory—perhaps requiring reinterpretation of the examples that compose its evidentiary base—may be in order.

This study of politeness in the discourse of requests illustrates this process. Conceptual issues that arose in the recorded coding sessions were explored with reference to examples in the data. Several conclusions emerged concerning both the discourse of requests as well as the politeness theory itself.

POLITENESS IN THE DISCOURSE OF REQUESTS

Several tentative generalizations are presented in this section along with illustrative examples from the data. Further theoretical and research implications are also considered where appropriate.

Meaningful Variations

An initial observation is that meaningful variations in the use of politeness strategies are prominent in the requests. Indeed, many of the most noticeable similarities and differences among individuals in how they responded to the request situations can be traced to the use of positive and negative politeness strategies. Consider for instance the messages of four speakers in a situation in which the speaker had to ask an acquaintance, met only once, if he or she could stay in his apartment while the speaker looked for an apartment of his or her own:

Example 1: Hello Jeff, this is Mark. I'm a friend of your, I'm a friend of John Hokey. Yeah, he gave me your, uh, address and phone number because he knew I was going to be coming to St. Louis. In fact I'm moving here. I found a job and what I'm doing right now is, I'm in the process of finding an apartment but, yeah, do you know of any cheap hotels or places that you'd recommend where I could stay while I'm looking for an apartment? Yeah, 'cause do you go to school here? So you're gone most of the day. What do you do—do you spend a lot of time in the library? Well, how 'bout I make a deal with you, or you can think about this a little bit but, uh, maybe I could help you out with the rent on your place, uh, if you'd let me stay there 'till I found another apartment. I'll just be, I'll be spending a lot of time looking for an apartment. Perhaps when I move in, I won't, anything is fine—the couch, the floor, I can bring a sleeping bag if there's no room. I'd really appreciate it 'cause I have, I'm not set enough to, to keep paying for a hotel for all those nights. Yeah, well, why don't you think about it and I'll get back to you later. OK, if you come up with any better ideas just let me know. OK, well, thanks a lot. It's been nice talking to you. Bye bye.

Example 2: Jeff, uh, I was wondering if, uh, I'm moving to St. Louis, I was wondering, uh, I haven't found a place to live yet. By any chance, uh, could I sleep on your floor 'till I find a place?

Example 3: Jeff, I was wondering, would there be any possibility of me staying with you for a few days 'till I get my own place? Uh, I'd really appreciate it if you could let me, uh, move in and stay at your place if you have room. It would really help me out while I'm looking for a place to stay since I don't know anybody in St. Louis.

Example 4: Hi Jeff, I don't know if you remember me or not but, uh, we met at a party of Sandy's. You know Sandy. Yeah, well, she's doing great. You know we've been going out for a couple of years now and yeah, it's been a couple of years. I was talking to her the other day and she mentioned that you had a place up here. Well, I was getting into town and I was wondering if you could give me some information. I don't have a place to stay and where should I look for apartments? I'm totally lost up here. She mentioned that you lived here for a long while and that you really know the town and if anyone knows St. Louis, Sandy said, I should go and talk to you. Also by any chance would it be possible for me to stay here for a day or so? You know, I could look for places to live and come back and hear, and tell you what I found so you could give me an idea of where I could stay because I have no idea. You're the best. You have all the knowledge of the town. It's a big one too and I don't want to make any mistakes and live in the wrong area.

Using the politeness framework we are able to account for many of the similarities and differences among these messages. All of the messages evidence some concern with granting the hearer autonomy and not imposing. This is seen in the use of tentative markers like "by any chance" (Ex. 4), "would there by any possibility" (Ex. 3 and 4), and "I was wondering" (Ex. 2 and 3); and in the attempts to minimize the actual imposition (e.g., sleeping on the floor, Ex. 1 and 2). Example 1 displays some particularly elaborate negative politeness strategies: The speaker signals reluctance to make the request by frequent nonfluencies and a prolonged lead-up, and emphasizes the hearer's right to refuse or come up with alternatives.

Even greater differences among the requests are evident in the use of positive politeness strategies. Example 4 demonstrates the most marked attention to positive politeness; the speaker uses a number of strategies to build friendly interaction and suggest a mutual relationship. By assuming that Jeff, the hearer, is interested in information about their mutual friend, the speaker attends to building common ground. By presuming the hearer would be interested in helping the speaker find the "right place to live" the speaker suggests the two have a relationship of mutual caring. Positive politeness is seen in Example 3 as well, although less markedly. By using phrases like "it would really help me out," and "I appreciate it," the speaker implies that the hearer would be interested in what happened to him, an assumption warranted only in a friendly, cooperative relationship. In Example 1, the speaker establishes common ground through references to a mutual friend and initially formulates the request as an offer ("Well, how 'bout I make a deal with you"), thus asserting a relationship of reciprocity. Example 2, in contrast, displays almost no positive politeness.

The requests thus offer an abundance of politeness phenomena for study. Positive and negative politeness are by far the most frequent superstrategies encountered. Other strategies are rare, but not entirely absent. A message such as

Example 1 might be considered to begin with an off-record strategy, giving the hearer an opportunity to make a voluntary offer before being faced with an on-record request. Speakers even occasionally avoided an FTA entirely, as when, for example, a speaker asking to stay with a friend while she looked for a place to live neglected to mention that she wanted to bring her cat.

Combination of Superstructures

Speakers often do not restrict themselves to a single superstrategy. In particular, complex combinations of positive and negative politeness strategies occur in many of the requests (Shimanoff, 1977).

> *Example 5:* Hey Milly, uh, I got some great news for you. Uh, I'll be moving to Philadelphia to start a new job and, uh, they want me there on, uh, Monday of next week, uh, I don't have a place to live, and, uh, need to take some time to locate at a place. I was wondering, uh, if it would be possible for me to stay with you, uh, at the outside I would guess a couple of weeks, uh, to, uh, give me some time, uh, to find a place. Uh, as you remember I'm a great cat lover and, uh, I'd like to bring my cat with me and I know we'll get along well. It's an awful big favor to ask and I hesitate but what are friends for, would it be possible for me and my cat to stay with you?

Positive politeness is clearly a dominant strategy in Example 5. In this situation, the hearer is a close friend. The speaker uses several devices to emphasize the presupposition that a friendly relationship exists, that the hearer would welcome the speaker's company, that the hearer and speaker have personal knowledge of each other's lives and concern for each other's needs, and so on. Yet emphatic negative politeness is also evident: hedging and indirectness (''I was wondering if it would be possible''); minimization of the imposition (''at the outside I would guess a couple of weeks''); admission of the impingement (''It's an awful big favor to ask''); reluctance to impose (''I hesitate''). As the research team discussed this example, it became apparent that the overall approach of the message is not very well captured by the statement that it includes so many positive politeness strategies and so many negative politeness strategies. In the context of the whole message, much of the negative politeness seems merely pro forma, perhaps even more presumptuous than deferential. Yet some acknowledgment of the hearer's negative face wants is clearly intended. It seems that a message can contain a great deal of *both* positive and negative politeness; yet it seems also that the meaning of individual strategies can be difficult to assess out of context, as when the speaker's ''but what are friends for'' effectively negates the negative politeness that precedes it.

As Brown and Levinson (1978, pp. 235–236) point out, the mixture of superstrategies sometimes produces a hybrid variety in which, for example, a basically positive politeness approach is hedged in order to soften the presumption. In other cases, the mixture of strategies reflects a kind of oscillation between positive and negative politeness that can be accomplished either awkwardly or gracefully. Example 5 might be a hybrid variety or might be of the more awkward sort. Brown and Levinson (1978), most of whose examples are very brief and are intended to illustrate individual output strategies, present few examples of mixed strategies, and none as lengthy or complex as Example 5.

What may be somewhat jarring in Example 5 is the emphatic quality of the positive and negative politeness strategies that are juxtaposed. Example 1 displays a similar awkwardness when the speaker, after pointedly indicating a willingness to stay in a ''cheap hotel,'' introduces a request to stay with the hearer in the presumptuous form of an offer. Example 1, even though, as was noted earlier, it makes use of elaborate negative politeness strategies, does not in general seem particularly respectful of the hearer's negative face wants. Example 4 illustrates a much more finely modulated use of negative politeness markers to mitigate a basically positive-politeness approach. What might explain the occurrence of such differences and their possible effects on the hearer's response or impression of the speaker are questions worthy of further study.

Multifunctionality

Different strategies not only co-occur in the same message but can be realized simultaneously in the same language (Baxter, 1984). This potential for multifunctionality, with its attendant ambiguity, contributes both to the richness of discourse and to possibilities for misunderstanding. It also poses difficulties for the task of identifying politeness strategies in messages.

The nontypological character of the politeness output strategy lists, mentioned earlier, partly results from the multifunctionality of certain linguistic formations. The phrase "do me a favor" provides a particularly vivid illustration of multifunctionality in requests. It seemed obvious to the research team that this phrase performs politeness functions in the request messages. Brown and Levinson (1978, p. 193) suggest that the phrase indicates negative politeness strategy # 6, to apologize (by admitting the impingement). Speakers who refer to their requests, for example, as "a big favor" do seem to be using this strategy. However, observers often distinctly felt (and others sometimes distinctly disagreed) that the phrase *also* functioned as positive politeness, to suggest the existence of a friendly relationship between speaker and hearer such that reciprocal favors might be expected. A younger or lower status person might, for example, be flattered by being asked for a "favor" by someone older or of higher status. Asking a "favor," even a "big favor," seems to suggest a symmetrical, friendly relationship, as in the following examples:

> *Example 6:* Tim, would you mind doing a favor for me? I, I need some things at the store and since you are waiting for Bobby anyway would you mind running down to the store for me and picking up something, picking up a few things?
>
> *Example 7:* Excuse me Marty, wondering if you could do a favor for me? I'm going to be gone, uh, for a little while and I was wondering if you could do me a big favor. I was wondering if you could come over and take care of my cat while I was gone. You know you'd have to come over once a day and, uh, feed him and, uh, I'd be more than happy to pay you for your time.

Example 6 generally takes a positive politeness approach, emphasizing in several ways the presumption that Tim is willing to be cooperative. The phrase "would you mind doing a favor for me?", acknowledges an imposition while suggesting that a "favor" should be granted in this relationship unless the hearer clearly "minds" doing so for some reason. Example 7 generally takes a negative politeness approach; yet the opening sentence with its ellipsis and its reference to a "favor" may suggest a degree of familiarity and a potential for reciprocity in the relationship. This presumption is even more marked in other examples containing formulations such as "listen, I got a favor to ask of you," "you want'a do me a favor?", or "you could do me a favor"—which cast the request as a kind of *opportunity* that is being offered the hearer. "Do me a favor," in short, may well be a kind of apology (potential negative politeness) that is appropriate to friendly symmetrical relationships that are characterized by the reciprocal doing of favors (potential positive politeness).

The multifunctionality of discourse can make politeness strategies difficult to "code," or interpret in actual cases. The examples of strategy usage offered by Brown and Levinson (1978) are of only limited help for this purpose. Brown and Levinson use brief examples, usually single-sentence utterances, to illustrate output strategies, requiring only that the reader see that the discourse *could* reflect the use of a certain strategy, given a congruent context that the reader partly provides. The result is a catalog of strategic possibilities that presumably are available to speakers and hearers. Coding, in contrast, requires the observer to decide whether the discourse *does* in fact include a strategy—a much more difficult decision than whether the strategy *could* be present. What is needed for coding is a scheme of interpretation that shows how a hearer or observer can recognize the intention to use a strategy. The extent to which such a scheme could be constructed in principle is limited, however, by the (unknown) extent to which discourse is genuinely ambiguous, confronting the scientific critic as well as the lay speaker-hearer with irreducible indeterminacies.

Other Sources of Indeterminacy

At least two additional kinds of indeterminacy are encountered by the observer of politeness in the discourse of requests. The first arises from the fact that politeness strategies are often just slightly exaggerated variations of ordinary forms.

Positive politeness in general requires the observer to decide whether what appears to be normal, friendly talk is sufficiently *marked* to constitute the use of a strategy. Positive politeness strategy # 13, to give or ask for reasons, is most clearly marked in a "pushy" request like "Why not lend me your cottage for the weekend?" (Brown & Levinson, 1978, p. 133). But the strategy is actually defined more broadly as one of including the hearer in one's thinking process by giving reasons for the FTA. But does this include *all* acts of giving reasons (which would also overlap with several other strategies) or only those that are in some way marked to indicate inclusion of the hearer in the speaker's reasoning process? How, for example, should one interpret a message such as this?:

> *Example 8:* Excuse me, are you going to be here for a few minutes, 'cause I'm going to go over to the phone over there and make a phone call. I was wondering if you could watch my luggage, I really don't feel like lugging it over there with me. Thanks a lot.

If this message is considered to use positive politeness strategy # 13, then it will be found that nearly *all* requests do so. Speakers usually offer reasons for making requests, presumably because being in a state of need is one of the preconditions for making a valid request (Labov & Fanshel, 1977; Searle, 1969).

Similar problems are encountered with many of the politeness strategies. To mention just briefly a few more examples: Negative politeness strategy # 1—conventional indirectness—requires the observer to decide whether an indirectly phrased request is *conventionally* indirect, thus used to convey a sense of not burdening the hearer with unnecessary indirectness or whether the speaker is in fact using the hedges, impersonalization markers, and the like as negative politeness strategies. A speaker who utters a demonstrative such as "this" or "here" might be using positive politeness strategy # 7, a point-of-view shift that presupposes common ground with the hearer; similarly, the choice of "that" or "there" might be negative politeness strategy # 7, impersonalization. The observer must decide whether a given use of one of these common words is sufficiently marked to constitute the use of a strategy (see "here," Ex. 9; "that," Ex. 10). Equally as difficult are the several positive politeness strategies that invoke presupposition: Because *all* utterances presuppose shared, taken-for-granted information, the observer must decide whether a given presupposition is sufficiently marked to count as strategic. The research team found such decisions extremely difficult to make in many cases. In examining the audio-taped discussion of our attempts to develop coding rules, there were numerous disagreements about whether presupposition was being used "strategically."

Study of the audio-taped discussions revealed a second source of indeterminacy, briefly alluded to by Shimanoff (1977): Judgments about a message's politeness were extremely context-dependent. The research team attempted for a time to rate the overall amount or degree of positive and negative politeness in each request on a nine-point scale anchored at 1 = "minimal," 5 = "average," and 9 = "emphatic." Raters often found it difficult, in judging the politeness of a request, to avoid confounding politeness with the closely related concept of appropriateness. Disagreements between raters often turned on whether one could "bracket out" the particular situation in making a judgment. A message might, for example, include several negative politeness markers yet still strike the rater as being rather low in negative politeness *for that situation;* whereas a message including similar markers in another situation might strike the same rater as taking a rather exaggerated negative politeness approach. The issue here is not whether raters can learn to ignore the situation and focus on markers in the message; the issue is whether the markers mean the same thing or have the same politeness implications in different contexts. If politeness judgments are inherently confounded with appropriateness judgments, then statements about the "amount" of politeness that is appropriate in situations varying, for example, in face threat, become difficult to interpret; for the "scale" for measuring politeness is then different in each situation, making cross-situational comparisons highly problematic.

Raters disagreed, for example, in their judgments of the following messages:

Example 9: Hi Molly, how's it going for you? I was wondering, I just got a new job here and I'm in a bind and, uh, I'd like, wanted to know if I could stay at your place until I find a place of my own.

Example 10: Hi Patti, you know, I'm going away this summer and, uhm, I'm going to need someone, uhm, to take care of my plants and feed my cat and stuff while I'm gone. If you're going to be around for the summer would you do that for me?

Some raters initially considered Example 9 to be low in both positive and negative politeness because so little is actually said, especially in view of the magnitude of the imposition. Other raters argued that the very brevity of the message suggests a friendly, cooperative relationship in which little needs to be said to justify asking a favor; such a straightforward request would be quite inappropriate between strangers. Depending upon how one imagines unknown contextual features, either interpretation can be persuasive. The brevity of the message stood out for some raters, but not for others, as a marked positive-politeness strategy that largely accounted for its tone. And even after having taken part in the discussion just described, raters differed in their judgments of Example 10, some feeling that the brevity of the message contributed to a global tone of positive politeness in the given context, whereas others were more impressed by the relative lack of overt politeness markers.

The difficulty of rating politeness independently of appropriateness suggests that a distinction should be made between politeness as a system of *message strategies* and politeness as a *social judgment*. Politeness strategies can be identified in messages, albeit often with some difficulty, with limited use of context. Politeness judgments, on the other hand, are highly context-dependent, perhaps highly variable social-cognitive phenomena. Politeness judgments, although influenced by politeness strategies, are far from wholly determined by them. We would expect to find wide variation in the politeness ratings of messages by untrained judges.[5] The variance of politeness judgments might turn out to be an interesting phenomenon to study in its own right: What impact does variation in discourse strategy use have on politeness judgments? What discourse strategies influence politeness judgments the most? What impact do characteristics of the judges have on politeness judgments? What situational factors influence the evaluation of a message's politeness? What are the effects of shifting emphasis among elements of context? How exactly are judgments of politeness related to judgments of appropriateness and effectiveness?

Aggravation and Speaker-Oriented Facework

A final observation is that speakers, in making requests, often make use of facework strategies that cannot be accounted for within the existing framework of the politeness theory.

Politeness strategies are conceived to be oriented primarily to the face wants of the hearer. As Brown and Levinson (1978, p. 65) explain:

> Given that face consists in a set of wants satisfiable only by the actions (including expressions of wants) of others, it will in general be to the mutual interest of two [Model Persons] to maintain each other's face. So [the speaker] will want to maintain [the hearer's] face, unless he can get [the hearer] to maintain [the speaker's] without recompense, by coersion, trickery, etc.

This statement must be qualified by at least two conditions. One is that speakers, in choosing strategies,

> take into consideration the relative weightings of (at least) three wants: (a) the want to communicate the content of the FTA, . . . (b) the want to be efficient or urgent, and (c) the want to maintain [the hearer's] face to any degree. (Brown & Levinson, 1978, p. 73)

It follows from the earlier quotation that (c) is largely a function of the degree to which the relationship between the speaker and hearer is cooperative. In a competitive or hostile relationship, speakers would not in general weigh (c) very heavily. Indeed (a point that Brown and Levinson occasionally acknowledge but do not much emphasize or elaborate) a hostile speaker, not hoping to receive any face support from the hearer, might well be motivated to attack and aggravate the hearer's face wants rather than merely ignore them.

The second qualifying condition is that people are not merely passive recipients of others' face supports, nor do they depend entirely upon reciprocity as a means of soliciting satisfaction of their face wants. Speakers in fact use any number of strategies to mitigate threats to their own face, including strategies of self-presentation and self-defense that may or may not also involve either supporting or attacking the hearer's face.

Brown and Levinson (1978) do not systematically analyze strategies of face attack (aggravation of FTA) or speaker-oriented facework (self-presentation and self-defense). Both sorts of strategies fall outside the scope of the politeness theory strictly construed; yet they impinge on the theory in ways that threaten its coherence.

Aggravation is easily thought of as occurring toward the pole opposite mitigation (politeness) on a continuum of discourse strategies (Applegate, 1982; Kline, 1981a, 1981b, 1982; Labov & Fanshel, 1977). Thus at first glance it would seem a simple matter to take account of aggravation by adding a sixth superstrategy, less polite than the bald-on-record strategy, to the politeness theory. What further changes would then be required to preserve the theoretical logic is a question

beyond the scope of this study. We can, however, illustrate a problem resulting from the *failure* to treat aggravation strategies systematically.

Consider an example discussed by Brown and Levinson (1978, p. 88): "Look, sonny, it might not be advisable to just go pushing your little fingers into this little pie." This is analyzed only as an attempt to exploit the additive relationship among the three factors affecting face threat, so as to enhance the speaker's implied power by minimizing social distance ("sonny") and the rank of the imposition ("little," "just"). What is ignored is the heavy irony of those same, incongruous markers of intimacy and minimization in the context of what is essentially a threat. To say that the speaker is emphasizing his or her own power by emphasizing social closeness of the hearer and the smallness of the imposition is to miss what is to us an obvious possible intent of the utterance, which is to belittle the hearer, not merely to perform an FTA but to do so rather sneeringly. In order to analyze such an example coherently, the politeness theory would have to be expanded to encompass discourse strategies for aggravating rather than mitigating FTAs.

Its failure to account for speaker-oriented face-work also threatens the coherence of the politeness theory. The formula for computing the seriousness of a threat to face (Brown & Levinson, 1978 p. 81) makes no distinction between threats to the speaker's and hearer's face; yet the selection of output strategies, including the selection of strategies outside the framework of positive and negative politeness, would seem to depend in part on whose face is threatened by the act and in what ways. Brown and Levinson (1978, pp. 70–73) acknowledge that some FTAs (thanks, excuses, promises, apologies, etc.) primarily threaten the speaker's face, and that "redressive action may be addressed to any potential aspect of the face threat, not necessarily just to the most relevant one" (p. 296). This suggests that it would be helpful to provide a more systematic treatment of speaker-oriented strategies.

Perhaps it will ultimately be possible to subsume the politeness theory along with aggravation and speaker-oriented strategies within a more general theory of facework. Not yet being ready to attempt the job, we can only note some examples in the request data of facework strategies that are not easily couched in the existing politeness framework.

Actually, one would expect to find very little aggravation and only a moderate amount of speaker-oriented facework in the request messages. None of the hypothetical situations is described in a way that would suggest a hostile or noncooperative relationship, and it seems unlikely that many speakers would spontaneously project such a relationship in a favor-asking situation. And as for speaker-oriented facework, it is clear that the act of making a request, a direct impingement on the hearer's freedom, primarily threatens the hearer's negative face, not the speaker's face. Yet the act of making a request also potentially calls into question the responsibility, competence, independence, and so on, of the requester, so some speaker-oriented facework would be expected.

It is not, then, surprising that only a few of the requests can be interpreted as including any marked aggravation of the FTA. Most of these examples occur in just 3 of the 24 hypothetical situations and take the form of more-or-less explicit suggestions that the hearer has an obligation to comply with the request or is in some other way not entirely free to refuse. In the situation of a student asking a professor for extra help, several speakers implied an obligation by hinting that their poor performance in the class was at least in part the professor's fault (''your lectures are not getting through to me''; ''the material is just not clear to me''; ''I'm really have a bad time in this class of yours''; ''I should be doing better than I am''). In the situation of a parent asking a daughter who is planning to go to a party to babysit instead, several speakers presumed compliance by displacing the daughter's plans to the past tense (''you were planning''), and at least two phrased the request in ways that could be interpreted in context as an indirect command (''I'm going to ask you''; ''I really need you to babysit''). In one request, the obligation to comply was made explicit (''it's only fair that you make a sacrifice one night''); other speakers

alluded to the long-suffering parental role, implying a debt on the part of the child. In the situation of a boss asking a newly hired secretary to do extensive overtime work, one speaker referred to an obligation (''as a new worker we would expect a little extra out of you''), and another issued what seems to be a thinly veiled threat (''if you don't think you can do it I might hafta find someone else''). If this is a threat it is unique in our data; all other examples of aggravation (including, perhaps, ''what are friends for'' in Example 5) involved reference to an obligation to comply, a strategy that, though it does aggravate rather than mitigate the impingement on the hearer's freedom, does so in a way that presupposes a basically cooperative speaker-hearer relationship. Many of these formulations could be interpreted as being just particularly emphatic positive politeness strategies were it not for the slightly hostile or coercive edge that they tend to have in context.

Speaker-oriented facework is more common in the requests but presents some difficulties of analysis. Just as positive politeness strategies are often only slightly exaggerated variations of typical, friendly discourse, speaker-oriented facework strategies are often difficult to distinguish from normal social behavior. Speakers, for example, who adorn their requests with the usual, appropriate politeness markers could be said to be *presenting themselves* as competent members of society—which they undoubtedly are. *All* social behavior is self-presentation in this general sense, but speaker-oriented facework strategies, extending the logic of the politeness theory, must have a more specific function: the strategic *manipulation* of normal forms so as to mitigate some threat to the speaker's positive or negative face.

The multifunctionality of discourse often renders speaker-oriented strategies ambiguous. In many of the request messages, for example, speakers are at pains to portray themselves as responsible, competent, self-reliant individuals who do not ordinarily ask other people to do what the speakers could do for themselves. This sort of move often can be interpreted as a negative politeness strategy, one of implying, perhaps, that the hearer's preserve of freedom would be breached only out of genuine necessity. Sometimes it can also be interpreted as a persuasive strategy, such as minimizing the risk involved in making a loan. *In addition,* such a move might be designed to mitigate threats to the speaker's face that inhere in any expression of need or helplessness, and *also,* possibly, to raise the stakes by implying that a refusal of the request would amount to an attack on the speaker's self-image.

Hence the most that can be claimed in many cases is that speakers *might* be using speaker-oriented facework strategies when they: imply their essential normality by acknowledging the unusualness of a request (''I realize this is pretty out of line''; ''I know this sounds really crazy''; ''crazy as it is''); imply their essential morality by acknowledging personal fault (''I've been really stupid''; ''I realize it's my own fault''; ''I'm probably at fault''); make excuses (''I have, uh, for one reason or another''; ''I've been ill for the last few weeks''); imply that their state of need is a matter of temporary bad luck (''damned if you wouldn't know . . . nothing has been going right today''); mention their own efforts prior to the request (''I have like half the down payment saved''; ''you know I've been trying to save money''); emphasize their reliability (''you know me, you know, I'll be sure and get them cleaned for you''; ''you know me, I'm reliable and all that''); or assert their competence (requesting a job transfer: ''I think I've done an excellent job for you''; ''you know, I probably am the best qualified for the job'').

The case for a speaker-oriented strategy is strengthened by pointing to markers that in context are more difficult to interpret in other ways. For instance, the formulation ''I'm not set enough to, to keep paying for a hotel'' (Example 1) would be an inefficient way to express the need for a place to stay unless it were also intended to avoid an implication of absolute poverty (''keep paying'') or that the speaker's lack of money is a permanent condition (''set enough'').

Speaker-oriented strategies are particularly obvious when they are otherwise dysfunctional. A speaker asking a roommate for tutoring (''Pat, how do you manage to do so well in that stupid French class''; ''How's it going in French? Wow, I wish I was doing that lucky''), or to borrow another student's lecture notes (''if you don't I'm likely to fail that stupid class''), can hardly hope to flatter the hearer by derogating the object of the hearer's more successful efforts (''stupid class'') or implying that success is merely a matter of luck. These are clearly attempts to mitigate threats to speaker self-image, even at the price of alienating the hearer. Similarly, the speaker who, when asking to borrow a camera, appends the disclaimer, ''if it is a good camera, if it is I don't really want to be responsible for it,'' is apparently more interested in avoiding a possible debt (threat to speaker's negative face) than in offering any assurance than the hearer's camera will be well cared for.

Thus the discourse of requests makes use of aggravating and speaker-oriented facework strategies as well as the hearer-oriented, redressive strategies that are the central focus of the politeness theory. Efforts to catalog such strategies and incorporate them into an expanded theory of face-work that would preserve the essential logic of the politeness theory might, it seems to us, prove very well spent.

CONCLUSION

A previous study, having shown that speakers asking favors use only a few different compliance-gaining strategies (primarily appeals to altruism and promises of compensation) concluded with the observation that much of the variety and interest of the discourse of requests may be found in the ways speakers pursue a multiplicity of goals in addition to that of gaining compliance (Tracy et al., 1984). This study expands that observation by examining more closely the use of politeness and other facework strategies in requests. Applying the politeness theory of Brown and Levinson (1978), we have seen that positive and negative politeness strategies appear in the messages in great abundance and variety; that speakers use mixtures of different strategies with varying degrees of skill; that speakers often accomplish more than one purpose by means of a single linguistic formulation (multifunctionality); that politeness strategies are often ambiguous and are problematically related to politeness judgments; and that, in addition to politeness strategies more narrowly construed, speakers use a variety of strategies to accomplish other kinds of facework, including aggravation of threats to the hearer's face, and mitigation of threats to the speaker's face. The situational and individual factors that influence the use of these strategies, and the interactional consequences of using them, are subjects now in need of research.

In the course of using the politeness theory to study requests, we have also learned a great deal about the politeness theory itself. Brown and Levinson (1978) have given us a powerful and highly suggestive theory of discourse that poses important issues for communication research. In finding ways to exploit the resources of this theory, we must, however, take due account of its logical structure and the complexity of the concepts that it introduces. Our initial efforts to develop a coding scheme and a quantitative test of the theory were set aside in view of the barriers that emerged. Instead, those efforts became incorporated as data within a larger interpretive study of the requests. That this study not only applied but challenged the politeness theory is evidenced by the numerous empirical and conceptual problems raised, pointing the way to theoretical advances.

What is needed, we believe, is a new theory of facework that would extend and correct the Brown and Levinson framework. On the basis of this research, we propose six tenets that should be taken as starting points for developing such a theory:

1. *In selecting facework strategies, speakers distinguish between threats to their own face and threats to that of the hearer.* Brown and Levinson (1978, pp. 72–73) identify speaker and hearer face as two distinct face wants in the opening section of their monograph; yet, when it comes to assessing the face-threat of an act, the two are added together as if it made no difference whose face was threatened. Our analysis of the requests suggests that speakers, when their own face is threatened, use different strategies—making excuses for their apparent failings or boasting about their competence, for instance—that are not captured by Brown and Levinson's superstrategies. Because many speech acts raise potential threats for both parties, an assessment of face threat should consider both speaker and hearer face distinctly, rather than add them together or dichotomize acts into ones that threaten speaker or hearer.

2. *In selecting facework strategies, speakers distinguish between threats to positive face and threats to negative face.* Facework strategies depend on the type of face threatened, not just the overall amount of face threat; and it is quite common for a situation to raise significant threats to both positive and negative face. Positive and negative face are distinct needs, both of which may be very important in the same relationship. Bochner (1982, 1984) argues that intimates have strong needs for both connectedness (positive face) and autonomy (negative face). Our request messages indicated that people often give significant attention to both positive and negative face in the same message. An adequate theory, then, should consider both the positive and negative face threats that an act would entail for both the speaker and the hearer.

3. *Facework strategies reflect the tension between cooperation and antagonism in social relationships.* Brown and Levinson assume that, with a few exceptions, social situations are cooperative, and it is in everyone's best interest to support each other's face. In

contrast, we propose that all situations involve some degree of tension between cooperation and antagonism. Few relationships are completely antagonistic, yet even the most cooperative act may have hostile undertones. It is common for a compliment to imply a criticism or a description of a state of affairs to convey a negative evaluation. Speakers are concerned about their own face. Because one way to support one's own face is to derogate another's, messages are often a complicated tangle of support and attack. Besides calling into question Brown and Levinson's work, this tenet has implications for all research based on Grice's (1975) Cooperative Principle. We question the validity of any study that assumes cooperation is the overriding or only goal of social interaction. If we are to account for the aggravated strategies often used to perform face-threatening acts, an adequate theory of facework must start with a more complex understanding of social life.

4. *Facework strategies reflect the rights and obligations of particular social relationships.* Brown and Levinson (1978) claim that three factors determine the amount of face threat of an act: Power, Distance, and Rank. Their discussion of these factors is particularly ambiguous. The three factors are considered to be independent and meaningful across a variety of situations (pp. 81–83), yet each factor is acknowledged to be highly context-dependent (pp. 83–84). If in fact, as our analysis also suggests, the assessment of an act's face threat is highly context-dependent, then the claim that face threat is determined by three abstract factors is at best misleading. It leads us away from the careful scrutiny of social situations as face threats are assessed.

For instance, if we assume that the Power and Distance relations between student and professor are roughly similar to those between boss and secretary, a noncontextual view of Rank leads to a prediction that the same act would hold equal face threat in the two relationships. Yet if we consider the face-threat involved in asking that student or that secretary to type a 30-page report, the prediction is not plausible. For the secretary, given the obligations of the role, the face threat (other things being equal) would obviously be much smaller. Hence an adequate theory of facework must come to terms with the ways in which role rights and obligations as well as other contextual factors influence perceptions of face threat.

5. *Facework strategies and social judgments of politeness and facework appropriateness are distinct constructs.* An adequate theory of facework must distinguish between message strategies and situated social judgments of whether a message "is polite." Certainly, it is reasonable to expect a relationship between the two. But our analysis of the request messages indicates that that relationship is likely to be more complicated than, for example, a simple correlation such that perceptions of politeness increase as the number of output strategies in a message increases. Earlier we suggested several research questions that might be pursued in an effort to clarify the relationship.

6. *A scheme of facework strategies should: (a) separate strategies oriented to speaker face from those oriented to hearer face; (b) distinguish strategies geared to positive face from those geared to negative face; (c) include antagonistic (aggravating) as well as cooperative (mitigating) moves; (d) be typological in form; and (e) describe*

strategies at both a functional level of analysis and at the level of linguistic outputs. Brown and Levinson's catalog of politeness strategies is a major contribution, one that a new theory of facework should systematically revise and extend. Requirements (a) through (c) that a new scheme of facework strategies should satisfy are warranted, respectively, by tenets (1) through (3) above. The call for (d) a typological (mutually exclusive and exhaustive) scheme is warranted by a desire for conceptual coherence as well as suitability for quantitative studies. And the same reasons partly warrant (e) an effort to include both functional and discourse-level strategies in systematic relation. Without the detailed discourse realizations of strategies, functional message strategies become relatively empty abstractions. It is important to know, for instance, how ''establish common ground'' or ''downplay hearer's accomplishments'' can actually be accomplished in language. Brown and Levinson have demonstrated that such discourse realizations are neither trivial nor random, that the ''minutia'' of language usage are important objects for study. On the other hand, without strategies that are identified at a functional level, there is no way to sort the linguistic minutia into meaningful categories (Shimanoff, 1977) or to examine rigorously the broader relationships between social factors and strategy selection.

Taken as a whole, the six tenets present the task of constructing a new theory of facework as a daunting prospect, but we believe a theory consistent with these principles is possible. A research program that might culminate in such a theory would examine messages across a range of situations that varied in type and degree of face threat, and would analyze global judgments of

''politeness,'' ''appropriateness,'' and so on, in light of the functional and discourse-level strategies evidenced.

NOTES

1. Baxter (1984, p. 449) erroneously lists speaker gender as one of ''four factors advanced in the theory to explain one's motivation to enact politeness,'' and also provides an inaccurate list of superstrategies for performing face-threatening acts, erroneously attributing to Brown and Levinson a superstrategy less polite than bald-on-record performance of face-threatening acts (see the following discussion of superstrategies). Lack of space prohibits a detailed discussion of Baxter (1984). Some of the questions that such a discussion might raise include the following: whether the experimenter's list of message strategies validly represents the theoretical politeness strategies; whether the practical reasoning process that theoretically underlies the selection of strategies is reflected in the self-reported likelihood-of-use measure; and whether a relationship between the likelihood-of-use estimates and the particular experimental manipulation of face threat would be expected. The most fundamental problem of Baxter (1984), as will become clear in the following discussion of using the politeness theory, results from a failure to recognize that the Brown and Levinson theory does not logically permit the prediction of message strategy selection.

2. The complete, verbatim list of role play situations is available as Table 1 in Tracy et al. (1984, pp. 520–522). Note 1 (p. 535) of the same article discusses some of the limitations of this kind of data. The discourse produced in role play situations may, of course, vary somewhat from what people actually say when confronted with similar situations in everyday life.

3. Several specific examples and points of analysis that were drawn from the coding session tapes are so identified in this article. In a broader perspective, the selection of issues and examples for analysis was done following a thorough review of the tapes. We have not yet attempted any more systematic analysis of these very interesting tapes.

4. Of course, the politeness ''logic'' must have psychological reality or speakers would not be able to exploit it. Hence it ought to be possible to apply it experimentally as, for example, Tracy (1982, 1983, 1984) has applied Grice's (1975) maxim of relevance. In pointing out that the Brown and Levinson theory does not logically permit the prediction of message strategies, we do not imply that prediction would not be a good thing, only that this theory is not intended for doing it. Nor do we imply that the theory should remain forever inviolate. Quantitative work has contributions to make to the study of politeness phenomena, and we see no reason why such an

interesting theory should not be adapted for whatever uses can be made of it. It is, however, important to recognize the difference, to take due account of the logic of the theory and the existing evidence that supports it.

5. Reliability could, we assume, be attained by raters with sufficient training; but it might be attainable only by sacrificing what Poole and Folger (1981) call "representational validity." The resulting scientific construct of "politeness," that is, might have only an indeterminate relationship to the ordinary judgments of politeness that were the original object of investigation. Correlations, for example, between the "politeness" construct and the face threat of a situation would not necessarily reveal a relationship between face threat and social judgments of politeness. This is, of course, an empirical issue.

REFERENCES

Applegate, J. (1982). *Construct system development and identity-management skills in persuasive contexts.* Paper presented at the meeting of the Western Speech Communication Association.

Baxter, L. A. (1984). An investigation of compliance-gaining as politeness. *Human Communication Research, 10,* 427–456.

Bochner, A. P. (1982). On the efficacy of openness in close relationships. In M. Burgoon (Ed.), *Communication yearbook 5* (pp. 109–124). New Brunswick, NJ: Transaction Books.

Bochner, A. P. (1984). Functions of communication in interpersonal bonding. In C. Arnold & J. W. Bowers (Eds.), *Handbook of rhetorical and communication theory* (pp. 544–621). Boston, MA: Allyn & Bacon.

Boyd, R. E. (1984). *The impact of televised interviewing on questioning and politeness strategies.* Paper presented at the convention of the Speech Communication Association, Chicago, IL.

Brown, P., & Levinson, S. (1978). Universals in language usage: Politeness phenomena. In E. Goody (Ed.), *Questions and politeness: Strategies in social interaction* (pp. 56–289). Cambridge: Cambridge University Press.

Clark, R. A., & Delia, J. G. (1979). Topoi and rhetorical competence. *Quarterly Journal of Speech, 65,* 187–206.

Cody, M. J., McLaughlin, M. L., & Schneider, M. J. (1981). The impact of intimacy and relational consequences on the selection of interpersonal persuasive strategies: A reanalysis. *Communication Quarterly, 28,* 91–106.

Donohue, W. A., Diez, M. E., & Stahle, R. B. (1983). New directions in negotiation research. In R. N. Bostrom (Ed.), *Communication yearbook 7* (pp. 249–277). Beverly Hills, CA: Sage.

Fairhurst, G. T., Green, S. G., & Snavely, B. K. (1984). Face support in controlling poor performance. *Human Communication Research, 11,* 272–295.

Goffman, E. (1959). *The presentation of self in everyday life.* Garden City, NY: Doubleday Anchor Books.

Goffman, E. (1967). *Interaction ritual: Essays on face-to-face behavior.* Garden City, NY: Doubleday Anchor Books.

Goffman, E. (1971). *Relations in public.* New York: Harper & Row.

Grice, H. P. (1975). Logic and conversation. In P. Cole & J. L. Morgan (Eds.), *Syntax and semantics. Vol. 3: Speech Acts* (pp. 41–58). New York: Academic Press.

Hiemstra, G. (1982). Teleconferencing, concern for face, and organizational culture. In M. Burgoon (Ed.), *Communication yearbook 6* (pp. 874–904). Beverly Hills, CA: Sage.

Jacobs, S., & Jackson, S. (1983a). Strategy and structure in conversational influence attempts. *Communication Monographs, 50,* 285–304.

Jacobs, S., & Jackson, S. (1983b). Speech act structure in conversation: Rational aspects of pragmatic coherence. In R. T. Craig & K. Tracy (Eds.), *Conversational coherence: Form, structure, and strategy* (pp. 47–66). Beverly Hills, CA: Sage.

Kline, S. L. (1981a). *Construct system development and face support in persuasive messages: Two empirical investigations.* Paper presented to the annual meeting of the International Communication Association, Minneapolis, MN.

Kline, S. L. (1981b). *Construct system development, empathetic motivation, and the accomplishment of face-support in persuasive messages.* Paper presented to the annual meeting of the Speech Communication Association, Anaheim, CA.

Kline, S. L. (1982). *The effect of instructional set on the provision of face-support by persons differing in construct system development.* Paper presented to the annual meeting of the Speech Communication Association, Louisville, KY.

Labov, W., & Fanshel, D. (1977). *Therapeutic discourse: Psychotherapy as conversation.* New York: Academic Press.

Marwell, G., & Schmitt, D. R. (1967). Dimensions of compliance-gaining behavior: An empirical analysis. *Sociometry, 39,* 350–364.

McLaughlin, M. L., Cody, M. J., & O'Hair, H. D. (1983). The management of failure events: Some contextual determinants of accounting behavior. *Human Communication Research, 9,* 208–224.

McLaughlin, M. L., Cody, M. J., & Rosenstein, N. E. (1983). Account sequences in conversations between strangers. *Communication Monographs, 50,* 102–125.

Miller, G. R., Boster, F., Roloff, M. E., & Seibold, D. R. (1977). Compliance-gaining message strategies: A typology and some findings concerning effects of situational differences. *Communication Monographs, 44,* 37–51.

Mura, S. S. (1983). Licensing violations: Legitimate violations of Grice's conversational principle. In R. T. Craig & K. Tracy (Eds.), *Conversational coherence: Form, structure, and strategy* (pp. 101–115). Beverly Hills, CA: Sage.

O'Keefe, B. J. (1983). *Consequences of differences in interactional goals for interpersonal strategies and interpersonal impressions.* Paper presented to the Conference on Social Cognition and Interpersonal Behavior, University of Kansas.

Parkhurst, J. T. (1983). *Children's requests in social situations.* Paper presented to the Speech Communication Association, Washington DC.

Poole, M. S. (1982). Notes on observational methods. Paper presented to the Speech Communication Association, Louisville, KY.

Poole, M. S., & Folger, J. P. (1981). A method for establishing the representational validity of interaction coding systems. *Human Communication Research, 8,* 26–42.

Searle, J. (1969). *Speech acts: An essay in the philosophy of language.* New York: Cambridge University Press.

Shimanoff, S. B. (1977). Investigating politeness. In E. O. Keenan & T. L. Bennet (Eds.), *Discourse across time and space* (pp. 213–241). Los Angeles: University of Southern California.

Tracy, K. (1982). On getting the point: Distinguishing "issues" from "events," an aspect of conversational coherence. In M. Burgoon (Ed.), *Communication yearbook 5.* New Brunswick, NJ: Transaction Books.

Tracy, K. (1983). The issue-event distinction: A rule of conversation and its scope condition. *Human Communication Research, 9,* 320–324.

Tracy, K. (1984). Staying on topic: An explication of conversational relevance. *Discourse Processes, 7,* 447–464.

Tracy, K., Craig, R. T., Smith, M., & Spisak, F. (1984). The discourse of requests: Assessment of a compliance-gaining approach. *Human Communication Research, 10,* 513–538.

Tracy, K., & Moran, J. P. (1983). Conversation relevance in multiple-goal settings. In R. T. Craig & K. Tracy (Eds.), *Conversational coherence: Form, structure, and strategy* (pp. 116–135). Beverly Hills, CA: Sage.

AN ANALYSIS OF COUPLES' CONVERSATIONAL COMPLAINTS

Jess K. Alberts

This study sought to examine the connections between couples' complaint behavior and their feelings about their relationships. Associations among complaint type, complaint response type, complaint affect, and relational adjustment were analyzed. Results indicated that adjusted couples were significantly more likely to manifest behavioral complaints, positive affect, and agreement responses. Maladjusted couples were significantly more likely to engage in personal characteristic complaints, negative affect, and countercomplaint responses. No other associations were found. It was also determined that adjusted and maladjusted couples did not differ significantly with regard to the number of complaints made.

Communication scholars, psychologists, and sociologists, among others, have attempted to determine why some marital relationships are successful while others are not. In attempting to determine this, a number of these scholars have discovered that verbal interaction between husbands and wives can account for much of the variance in marital success or failure (Burgess, 1981; Fitzpatrick, 1983; Gottman, 1979). More specifically, studies by Locke, Sabagh, and Thomas (1957) and Navran (1967) indicate that marital satisfaction and "good" communication are correlated at .80. Consequently, a number of studies have attempted to describe how satisfied and dissatisfied (or adjusted versus maladjusted) couples communicate and manage conflict (Fitzpatrick, 1983; Gottman, 1979; Thomas, 1977) in order to determine more precisely the communication strategies associated with marital adjustment.

Source: The article is taken from *Communication Monographs* [55: 184–197, 1988]. Reprinted by permission of the Speech Communication Association, 5105 Backlick Rd., Annandale, VA 22003.

Reported here are the results of a study which was conducted in order to extend our knowledge of couples' marital adjustment and their communication behavior. Specifically, this study examined couples' conversational complaint behavior; it sought to determine how variables such as complaint type, complaint affect, and complaint response are associated with couples' subjective feelings about their relationships. Complaint behavior was chosen as the area of examination because complaints are pervasive, problematic and likely to be connected to a couple's relational satisfaction or adjustment.

An analysis of couples' complaint interactions is best conducted in the context of the research on remedial work and account episodes. Remedial work is defined by Goffman (1971, p. 109) as interaction which transforms "what could be seen as offensive into what can be seen as acceptable." Accounting sequences are one conversational strategy used to enact such remedial work. The account sequence consists of four parts: the failure event, reproach, account, and evaluation (of the account) (Schonbach, 1980, p. 195). Failure events are defined by Schonbach (p. 195) as "deviant acts committed or obligations omitted," and the account is the "statement made . . . to explain (the) unanticipated or untoward behavior" (Scott & Lyman, 1968, p. 46).

Complaint episodes, which consist of a complaint and complaint response, are attempts to perform remedial work during conversational interaction. A complaint is defined by the *Oxford English Dictionary* (1971, p. 722) as "an outcry against or because of injury; representation of a wrong suffered; utterance of a grievance." Both Doelger (1984, p. 15) and Paulson (1982, p. 4) define complaints as statements of dissatisfaction with the actions (or lack of action) of another. The essential nature of a complaint is best captured by Edmondson's (1981) corollary "H did P, P bad for S" (where H = hearer and S = speaker). A complaint, then, is a call for remedial work; it functions as a reproach in response to some failure event. In order to enact the necessary remedial work, the complaint recipient must provide some type of explanation of his/her behavior during the complaint response, which

functions as an account. Thus, complaint interactions are one type of account episode.

While extensive research has been conducted on account behavior (Blumstein et al., 1974; Cody & McLaughlin, 1985; McLaughlin et al., 1983a, 1983b; Morris, 1985; Remler, 1978; Schonbach, 1980; Scott & Lyman, 1968), most of it has focused predominantly on the account rather than the reproach (McLaughlin et al., 1983b is one notable exception). Also, relatively little research has concentrated upon complaint interactions as a type of accounting sequence. However, research on both accounts and complaints indicates that remedial work of this nature is important in intimate relationships.

Morris (1985) explains that many accounting episodes occur in response to disagreements about rules and that rules (and discussions of such) become substantive issues when dispreferred outcomes are experienced. He adds that experiencing dispreferred outcomes is most likely when participants' rules are substantially different, the participants are highly interdependent, and the interaction is highly consequential, a set of circumstances likely to occur in romantic relationships. Cody and McLaughlin (1985, p. 50) write that "in long-term interpersonal relationships . . . persons are often reproached for behavior which appears to violate the requirements of a role (for example, lover, child, subordinate) vís a vís some focal counter-role (lover, parent, superior)." For these reasons, accounting episodes are likely to occur frequently in intimate relationships such as marriage.

Several studies on complaints reveal that complaining behavior, as well as being pervasive, is problematic for many married couples. On the basis of two studies (Cunningham, Stanbull, & Kelley, 1973; Tiggle, Peters, & Kelley, 1977, cited in Kelley, 1979), Kelley developed a fifteen category typology of problems couples believed that they faced. The first three categories were primarily instances of conflict about conflict behavior. The third of those categories consisted of influence attempts and nagging (or complaining[1]). As early as 1938, a study by Lewis

Terman showed that unhappy couples were distinguished from happy ones by the extent to which they reported their partner's being argumentative, critical, nagging, etc. (Kelley, 1979, p. 154). Thus, complaining may be a central and difficult aspect of marital relationships.

Research focusing upon couples' relational satisfaction and/or their complaint interactions indicates that relational satisfaction and complaining behavior are associated. Cousins and Vincent (1983) examined aversive and supportive behavior following spousal complaints involving non-marital issues. They discovered that negative responses tended to inhibit further complaining while, unexpectedly, positive responses had no affect on further complaining. The researchers suggested that a decrease in aversive responses rather than an increase in supportive responses would improve marital complaint interactions. However, this study measured only verbal activity; increased verbal output is not a guarantee of a successful complaint interaction.

Gottman (1979) and Thomas (1977) examined couples and their conflict and complaining behavior. Gottman performed a detailed sequential analysis of the videotaped conversations of twenty-eight couples, half of whom were drawn from a clinical sample and half of whom were not. Gottman concluded that the most dysfunctional complaint interaction, and the one most frequently enacted by unhappily married couples, was cross-complaining, a complaint-countercomplaint sequence. Gottman also examined audiotapes of a group of distressed couples previously studied by Raush et al. (1974) and determined that a similar pattern was obtained in this study—discordant couples manifested cross-complaining (Gottman, 1970, pp. 129–130).

In a series of studies conducted both in the laboratory and in couples' homes, Thomas analyzed couples' conflict interactions and decision-making. He discovered that the two most frequent complaint sequences for dissatisfied married couples were complaint-countercomplaint and complaint-disagreement.

Other studies have examined complaints as a conversational phenomenon (Coulthard, 1977;

Doelger, 1984; Edmondson, 1981; Turner, 1970). These analyses suggested that complaints are likely to engender disagreeing, justification, or apology responses. All of this research tended to focus almost exclusively upon the complaint response; it did not address other aspects of the complaint interaction.

The research on accounts, complaints, and couples' relational satisfaction suggests that remedial work is important to romantic relationships, occurs frequently, and often creates problems. Furthermore, studies such as those by Gottman, Raush and Thomas indicate that relational satisfaction may be connected to a couple's conflict and complaint interactions. What none of these studies explained was what it is people complain about; nor do they provide information about the range of responses complaint recipients use. As well, those studies which focused on marital complaints examined only the behavior of distressed couples; little information was provided about how non-distressed couples interact. Thus, much is still unknown about couples' complaint interactions and their feelings about their relationships.

While a variety of research on accounting episodes has been conducted, little of that research has examined such episodes in the context of close relationships. Much of it has analyzed interactions between strangers (McLaughlin et al., 1983b), examined subjects' perceptions of unknown others' behavior (Blumstein et al., 1974), or was based on recall data of episodes with a variety of intimate and non-intimate partners (McLaughlin et al., 1983a). Research on couples' complaint behavior, therefore, can contribute not only to greater understanding of communication strategies and relational adjustment but also to increased understanding of accounting behavior in close relationships.

Prior research on repair and complaint episodes has focused on the account/response portion of these interactions. As Cody and McLaughlin (1985, p. 52) point out, only recently has the focus shifted to the constraints, both interactional and situational, on the kinds of moves participants are likely to make during accounting behavior. This is even more true of the complaints research. Thus far, studies on complaining have examined the complaint response exclusively. These studies have not considered what contextual factors, aside from relational adjustment, could be influencing the choices that interactants make during a complaint episode.

Cody and McLaughlin (1985, p. 52) propose that in accounting episodes two factors, which they call the aggravation-mitigation continuum (Labov & Fanshel, 1977) and perception of the situation, influence the type of account a participant makes. They suggest that moves which are more 'mitigating' tend to elicit like moves while moves which are relatively 'aggravating' tend to engender aggravating moves (Cody & McLaughlin, 1985, p. 52). For example, McLaughlin et al. (1983a) found that one of the best predictors of an interactant's choice of remedial strategy was the way in which that person was reproached; they also found that more mitigating accounts tended to lead to more mitigating evaluations of those accounts.

It follows, then, that during complaint interactions, the 'aggravation' level of the complaint could also affect the response type selected by the complaint recipient. In fact, I would suggest that during couples' complaint episodes it is the type of complaint and the affect with which that complaint is offered which influence the response a complaint recipient is likely to choose. It is not clear how relational adjustment might interact with these two factors. A couple's relational adjustment could influence the complaint type and/or affect as well as the complaint response, as has been suggested. Or it is possible that it is merely complaint type and/or affect which actually contribute.

However, it has not been established previously what types of complaints are offered nor how these complaints tend to be delivered. Therefore, before a study could be conducted to analyze the relative contribution of these factors, a preliminary study had to be performed in order to develop a typology of complaint types and affect. As well, although a category system of accounts has been established and a number of complaint responses suggested by a variety of sources, no definitive typology of complaint responses had been delineated. Consequently, a preliminary study was performed in order to determine appropriate categories for describing complaint type and response type, as well as affect.

A Taxonomy of Couples' Complaint Behavior

In a preliminary study (Alberts, 1987), 52 heterosexual couples were interviewed concerning their complaint interactions with each other. Each member of the couple provided an example of a complaint given to and one received from the relational partner. Additional information concerning intent, location, and timing of the interaction, preceding and succeeding events, and beliefs about desirable complaint behavior was collected (see Appendix A).

The collected data were used to provide a descriptive taxonomy of couples' complaint and response types. Based on a content analysis, it was determined that appropriate categories for couples' complaint types were: behavioral, performance, personal characteristic, personal appearance, and complaining. The complaint responses collected in the study were placed in five categories: agree, justify, denial, countercomplaint and pass. These response categories roughly correspond to the accounts categories delineated in McLaughlin et al. (1983a): concessions, excuses, justifications, refusals, and silence. The complaints taxonomy combined excuses and justifications[2] and added the category of countercomplaints.

A behavioral complaint was a complaint made about actions done or not done. For example, a man complained ''Why haven't I had a cooked meal all week?'' A performance complaint, on the other hand, had to do with how an action was performed (not whether or not it was done), such as ''You're driving too fast.'' A personal characteristic complaint concerned the whole person, his/her personality, attitudes, emotional nature or belief system. One man said to his partner,

"You're a snob." Personal appearance complaints involved comments about the partner's looks, such as "You have a fat butt and better lose weight." Finally, there were complaints about complaining, for example, "You're always complaining," or "Quit whining."

The complaint responses fell into five categories as well. The largest number of responses were justifications/excuses. For example, when one man received the complaint he did not talk enough, he replied "The other people talk so much I never had a chance to say a word." Denial responses included statements which refused to acknowledge the legitimacy of the complaints, disagreed with the complainer, or which refused the requested change. A husband who received the complaint he never listened replied, "I do too." Agreement responses were statements which either explicitly agreed that the complaint was legitimate or that change was necessary, or which provided implicit agreement through an apology. Countercomplaints involved responses which answered the complaint with a complaint. One female complained her husband was "too wizzy," and "turned the corner too fast," to which he replied "I'd rather be wizzy than pokey like you." Also included in the response typology was the pass. A pass occurred whenever the recipient ignored the complaint or failed to respond verbally.

The preliminary study indicated that behavioral complaints were by far the most frequently occurring complaint type (accounting for 72% of the complaints); these complaints were met most frequently with justification responses. Personal characteristic complaints tended to occur second most frequently (17%) and were most often answered with denials. The study also revealed that men and women did not differ significantly in their reported complaint types, response types, nor in the responses they gave to particular types of complaints. In addition, the data, unexpectedly, suggested that satisfied and dissatisfied couples did not differ in their reports of their complaint behavior. However, because these results were based on a small subsample (19 of the

52 couples)[3] and couples' *reports* of their behavior, a study of couples' actual conversational behavior needed to be conducted.

METHOD

Participants

Forty heterosexual couples engaged in the taped interactions examined in this study. All of the couples had been either married or living together for a minimum of 6 months; twenty-three (53%) of the couples were married and seventeen (47%) were living together. The individuals ranged from 19 to 71 years old. A diversity of socioeconomic and educational backgrounds was represented. Three of the individuals had only an elementary school education, and 12 held college degrees. Two of the 12 were pursuing graduate degrees, and 1 had attained a master's degree. The sample included a blue collar worker, bank teller, department store clerk, several housewives, a bank president, a religious education director, and a variety of others. The sample was acquired through solicitation of volunteers. Undergraduate students recommended couples (friends, parents, other relatives), and a snowball technique was employed. That is, couples who were initially contacted for participation in the study recommended other couples as potential participants. Though the initial participants were suggested by undergraduate students, no couples composed only of undergraduate students were used, and only four subjects in the pool were undergraduate students.

As the sample was formed, couples were selected whose relational adjustment scores represented a range that could be divided into the subgroups of adjusted and maladjusted. Twenty couples were chosen who fell into each category based on Spanier's Dyadic Adjustment Scale (1976). For this study, because it was designed to study normal couples and not clinical ones, it was decided to place all couples in the category of maladjusted in which one member had a score of 100 or less. The adjusted couples had a mean

DAS score of 242.5 while the maladjusted couples had a mean score of 195.5. The obtained alpha reliability estimate for the Dyadic Adjustment Scale was .90. A *t*-test was conducted on the DAS scores for the two groups; the two groups were significantly different, $t(38) = 7.49$, $p < .001$.

Procedures

Participants were informed that the experimenter was interested in learning how couples discuss issues on which they disagree. First, each member of the couple filled out Spanier's (1976) Dyadic Adjustment Scale privately. Once the DAS was completed, each member was given a modified version of Strodtbeck's Revealed Differences Form (1951). The Revealed Differences Form was modified by updating some of the scenarios and adding a few additional scenes. In addition to the twenty items on the Revealed Differences Form, each member of the couple was asked to write a scene which described a problem area or area of disagreement in their relationship.

After the participants completed the forms, the investigator circled all items on the Revealed Differences Form on which the couple disagreed. The couple was then instructed to discuss these items while a tape recorder recorded the interaction. The couples were encouraged to strive for agreement, but, if that was not possible, they were allowed to "agree to disagree." They also were asked to discuss the item they each had written. The couple was encouraged to talk for between thirty minutes and an hour.

Coding of Complaint Type, Complaint Affect, and Response Type

The 40 tapes yielded 19 hours and 43 minutes of interaction. The length of the tapes ranged from 15 minutes to 1 hour. Of the approximately 20 hours of tape, 47% (9 hours, 16 minutes) was produced by adjusted couples and 53% (10 hours, 27 minutes) was produced by maladjusted couples.

Once the data were collected, each tape was transcribed. These transcriptions were typed in script form and attempted to capture both overlapping speech and laughter as well as the actual words spoken.

After the tapes were transcribed, 25% (10) of the tapes were coded to establish coding reliability. First, three coders listened to each tape as they read through the transcript. Three additional passes were then made through the transcripts while the tapes were playing; at each pass, a different variable was coded: presence of complaints and responses, category of complaints and responses, and complaint affect.

The first task required the coders to read through each of the transcripts while listening to the tapes and to indicate which utterances contained complaints and responses. Once agreement among the three coders was reached as to which utterances were complaints and responses, the coders once again read through the transcripts and listened to the tapes; this time, however, the coders marked each complaint and response with the appropriate category label. Surprisingly, only behavioral and personal characteristic complaints were located on the transcripts; however, responses were located which fell into all of the response categories.

The third pass through the transcripts involved coding the complaints for affect. Complaint affect was coded as positive, neutral, or negative, a standard categorization for affect (Krokoff, Gottman, & Roy, 1986, p. 12).[4] To aid in coding for affect, the coders used four semantic differential scales which provided an operational definition for positive, negative, and neutral affect. The four scales measured kindness/cruelty, positivity/negativity, softness/hardness, and humor/seriousness.

For the three coding tasks, simple agreement among the coders was 88% for presence of complaints and responses, 93% for category placement, and 83% for affect. Cohen's Kappa reliability index for the three were .69, .71, and 64.[5] Differences were resolved through discussion. The remainder of the data were coded by the researcher.

TABLE 1 **Complaint Type, Affect, and Complaint Response for Adjusted and Maladjusted Couples**							
			Response Type				
Marital adjustment	Complaint type	Affect	Agree	Deny	Justify	Countercomplain	Pass
Adjusted	Behavioral	Positive	6	5	4	3	3
		Neutral	17	6	24	5	8
		Negative	9	10	6	0	1
	Personal Characteristic	Positive	3	1	1	0	3
		Neutral	3	1	5	0	4
		Negative	1	3	1	0	2
Maladjusted	Behavioral	Positive	4	1	5	1	2
		Neutral	10	16	20	16	12
		Negative	7	15	14	8	8
	Personal Characteristic	Positive	2	1	2	1	4
		Neutral	5	8	7	4	8
		Negative	6	10	5	9	4

STATISTICAL SUMMARY 1

Reliability indicates the accuracy and consistency of coding. If a coding system is used in a reliable fashion, you can be confident that the scores are very accurate, and that the items or indicators are either consistent with each other or consistent over time. Here the coding was moderately accurate and consistent (i.e., .64 to .71).

Finally, the transcripts were placed into the proper category for relationship status, 20 in the adjusted and 20 in the maladjusted, based on the couples' Dyadic Adjustment Scores.

RESULTS

Once the data were coded they were placed into a contingency table for analysis (see Table 1). After the data were tabled, the cells were weighted by 0.5 to compensate for the empty cells, and the data were subjected to log linear analysis.[6]

A log linear analysis was conducted on the tabled data in order to establish the relationships among the four variables (A = marital adjustment, B = complaint type, C = complaint affect, D = response type). Initially, the likelihood-ratio chi-square values were generated in order to determine the hierarchy of effects to be entered into the log linear model (see Table 2). An examination of the residual and component chi-square comparisons resulted in the selection of Model Seven.

The most parsimonious model, then, included A, B, C, D, and the A X B, A X C, and A X D interactions. In order to test the associations among the four variables, specific-effects parameters were tested with a z statistic. This was a two-tailed test, so a z statistic of 1.96 or greater was needed to achieve significance. However, because of the repeated z tests being conducted on the data and the associated probability of an increase in Type I error, each z test was performed at an enhanced numerical level of significance. Consequently, an experimentwise z statistic of 2.12 was needed to achieve significance.

TABLE 2
Likelihood-Ratio Chi-Square Values

Model	Marginals	Residual		Component		
		L^2	df	L^2	df	p
1	A	219.07	58			
2	A B	169.15	57	49.92	1	0.01
3	A B C	93.71	55	75.98	2	0.01
4	A B C D	80.21	51	13.5	4	0.01
5	AB C D	73.32	50	6.89	1	0.01
6	AB AC D	61.48	48	11.84	2	0.01
7	AB AC AD	45.21	44	16.27	4	0.01
8	AB AC AD BC	40.92	42	4.29	2	0.10
9	AB AC AD BC BD	34.75	38	6.17	4	0.25
10	AB AC AD BC BD CD	22.32	30	12.43	8	0.10
11	ABC AD BD CD	22.28	28	0.04	2	0.50
12	ABC ABD C	19.63	24	2.65	4	0.50
13	ABC ABD ACD	6.88	16	12.75	8	0.10
14	ABC ABD ACD BCD	3.26	8	3.62	8	0.50
15	ABCD	0	0	3.62	8	0.50

L^2 = maximum likelihood-ratio chi-square

Having established there was an association between marital type and complaint type, $z = 2.13$; between marital type and affect, $z = 2.27$; and between marital type and response type, $z = 2.48$, the lambda effects were examined to determine which levels of marital type were associated with which levels of complaint type, affect, and response type (see Tables 3, 4, and 5). The analysis revealed that there was a significant association between relationship type and complaint type, $L^2(1) = 6.89$, $p < .01$. As Table 3 reveals, when compared to satisfied couples, dissatisfied couples' complaint interactions were composed of significantly more personal characteristic complaints. Conversely, the satisfied couples' complaints were composed of significantly more behavioral complaints.

There was also a significant association between marital type and affect, $L^2(2) = 11.84$, $p < .01$. The data indicate that satisfied couples' complaints did tend to be delivered more frequently with positive affect while dissatisfied couples' complaints were more frequently delivered with negative affect. However, there was no difference between the couples in terms of neutral affect.

The final significant association found was between relationship type and response type, $L^2(4) = 16.27$, $p < .01$. Prior research had indicated that dissatisfied couples engaged in countercomplaint and disagreement (or denial) responses (Gottman, 1979; Thomas, 1977), but no research had suggested what responses satisfied couples used. As Table 5 reveals, the data from the study confirm Gottman and Thomas' contention that dissatisfied couples' complaints tended to be responded to more often with countercomplaints; however, it does not confirm Thomas' claim that dissatisfied couples are more likely to use denial responses. These data also revealed that adjusted

TABLE 3
Specific Effects for Marital Type and Complaint Type

	Marital Type		
	Adjusted	Maladjusted	
Complaint type	λ	λ	z test
Behavioral	.152	−.152	2.133*
Personal Characteristics	−.152	.152	−2.133*

*$p < .05$ (experimentwise)

TABLE 4
Specific Effects for Marital Type and Affect

	Marital Type		
	Adjusted	Maladjusted	
Affect	λ	λ	z test
Positive	.260	−.260	2.274*
Neutral	−.002	.002	−0.019
Negative	−.258	.258	−2.536*

*$p < .05$ (experimentwise)

TABLE 5
Specific Effects for Marital Type and Response Type

	Marital Type		
	Adjusted	Maladjusted	
Response type	λ	λ	z test
Agree	.325	−.325	2.447*
Deny	−.003	.003	−0.024
Justify	.136	−.136	1.070
Countercomplain	−.406	.406	−2.219*
Pass	−.041	.041	−0.289

*$p < .05$ (experimentwise)

couples' complaints were significantly more often answered with agreement responses than were maladjusted couples'.

No other significant associations were found. The data indicated that neither complaint type and response type, $L^2(4) = 6.17$, $p < .25$, nor affect and response type, $L^2(8) = 12.43$, $p < .10$, nor complaint type and complaint affect, $L^2(4) = 4.29$, $p < .25$, were significantly associated.

STATISTICAL SUMMARY 2

Log-linear analysis was used by Alberts to determine the relationships among four variables: marital adjustment, complaint type, complaint affect, and response type. Log-linear analysis tests whether three or more variables are associated or related to each other. It is used with variables that have categories (e.g., ethnicity might have African American, white American, Mexican American; gender includes male and female; and income might have high, medium, and low), and shows you if the category of each variable tends to occur more frequently together (e.g., African American, female, middle income).

The log-linear analysis revealed relationships between marital adjustment and complaint type, marital adjustment and complaint affect, and between marital adjustment and response type. This analysis revealed that poorly adjusted couples were more likely to complain about personal characteristics and use negative affect in their complaints, while well-adjusted couples complained about specific behavior and used positive affect more frequently. Poorly adjusted couples also tended to respond to each other's complaints with complaints of their own, while among well-adjusted couples, complaints were more likely to lead to agreement.

Aside from discovering the differences in actual complaint behavior, another question which needed to be answered was whether adjusted and maladjusted couples differed in the number of complaints in which they engaged. It could have been that it was not so much how the couples complained as it was the number of complaints which affected their feelings about their relationship. It was discovered that adjusted couples did engage in fewer complaints than did maladjusted (135 vs. 215), but this difference was not significant, $t(38) = 1.52$, $p < .20$.

STATISTICAL SUMMARY 3

Finally, t-tests were computed to compare well-adjusted and poorly-adjusted couples. T-tests tell you if there is a difference between two groups. For example, you might want to see if one group (e.g., males) had more eye contact than a second group (e.g., females). The t-test in this study revealed that well-adjusted and poorly-adjusted couples did not differ in the number of complaints they made.

DISCUSSION

This study was designed to examine the relationship between couples' complaint behavior and their feelings about their relationships. It had been claimed that distressed and non-distressed couples interacted differently during complaint exchanges. If this were true, what aspects of the complaint interaction differed between the two couple types? Earlier research on complaints had focused almost exclusively upon how relationship type influenced complaint response type. However, research on account episodes suggested that other variables, such as reproach (or complaint) type, could influence accounting behavior. Therefore, the study examined whether interactional variables such as complaint type and complaint affect could be influencing the type of response an interactant chose, apart from his or her feelings about the partner.

It was determined that adjusted and maladjusted couples differed in their complaint behavior. Furthermore, it was found that they differed not only in the type of responses they used during complaint interactions but also in the type of complaints made and the type of affect they used when offering those complaints. It was shown that adjusted couples tended to offer more behavioral complaints, used more positive affect, and responded more often with agreement responses. Maladjusted couples, on the other hand, offered more personal characteristic complaints, used negative affect more often, and more often responded with countercomplaints. These findings suggested a more complex view of what occurs during a complaint interaction.

Because the couples differed along all three dependent variables, it was necessary to discover if those variables were associated with each other as well as with relationship adjustment. McLaughlin and Cody's (1983a) study, for example, indicated that type of reproach was the best predictor of an interactant's choice of remedial account. Thus, it was anticipated that complaint type or complaint affect would play an influencing role in the types of complaint response that interactants chose. However, in the present study this was not the case. It was revealed that it is relationship type which has the strongest influence on the type of response a participant is likely to offer to a given complaint. It could be that in such intimate relationships as romance and marriage one's feelings about one's partner color one's communication behavior more strongly than that partner's immediate behavior.

This further suggests that if a couple wishes to alter their complaint behavior, it will require effort on the part of both participants to make that change. Merely having the complainer make more behavioral complaints will not necessarily result in more positive affect nor in more agreement responses. Instead, each participant would need to make changes in his or her complaint behavior.

The implications of this study seem clear: Couples' feelings bout their relationship are connected to their complaint behavior. What is not clear is whether the differences in complaint behavior preceded or followed the couples' feelings about their partners. Other research (Kelley et al., 1985; Markman, 1979; 1981) indicates that negative communication precedes relational dissatisfaction; however, it is quite likely that couples'

relational definitions and their communication behavior mutually influence one another. Thus, it is probable that if couples do make changes in their complaint behavior, their feelings about the relationship will be influenced.

The results of this study provide a more comprehensive view of couples' conversational complaint behavior than has previous research. Complaint research to date has focused primarily upon response types without considering other variables that might characterize couples' complaint behavior. As well, prior research focused on distressed couples' behavior without delineating how it is that non-distressed couples perform complaint interactions. It is not enough to know what distressed couples do; if dysfunctional couples wish to change, they need a model of effective complaint behavior.

It is now with somewhat greater confidence that researchers may state that complaint behavior is connected to couples' feelings about their relationships. However, there are several aspects of this research which should be pursued. First, an analysis similar to this one could profitably be conducted on couples who offered a wider range of relationship adjustment, particularly in the lower range. A study with a normal and a "clinical" population might not only be of interest but might offer additional insight into what is "dysfunctional."

As well, in future research on complaints, it would be more productive to use the response categories suggested by the accounts research. In the present study, excuses and justifications were combined into one category on the basis that both were attempts to relieve the complaint recipient of negative typification because of the complainable. (A second motive was to minimize the presence of small cell frequencies.) However, accounts research indicates excuses and justifications can function in different ways and have different consequences. Consequently, it would be advisable in future studies to place excuses and justifications into separate categories. In addition, by using similar categories, the findings from accounts and complaints research can be more fully integrated.

Finally, a most important study to pursue would be one that provides an in-depth analysis of the structure of couples' complaint interaction. This project did not allow such a comprehensive study, yet such an analysis could reveal much about how couples differ in the structure of their interactions as well as what types of complaint structures lead to quick or "successful" resolutions. In addition, this research could reveal more about how complaint behavior is sequenced.

This and other research indicates that a couple's feelings about their relationship are, in fact, related to how they engage in conflict communication. As well, this study reveals it is not the presence or absence of such communication that makes a difference, it is how that communication in enacted. Therefore, through studying *how* it is that satisfied and dissatisfied couples perform complaint and other conflict communication, it is possible to contribute to a developing theory of both marital relationships and conflict communication.

NOTES

1. Nagging is defined as finding fault or complaining in a persistent manner. (*Random House College Dictionary*, 1972, p. 883).

2. Justifications and excuses were combined into one category because both response types attempt to maintain the face of the complaint recipient. As well, separating the categories would lead to introducing yet another level into the contingency table and would increase the number of small cell frequencies. Combining the categories minimized the problems associated with the presence of numerous small cell frequencies and the resultant difficulties in attaining sufficient statistical power.

3. In the preliminary study there were few highly adjusted or maladjusted couples. For the most part, the couples tended to be moderately adjusted; the mean DAS for the couples was 223. Couples who fell one standard deviation above and one standard deviation below the mean were selected to represent adjusted and maladjusted couples. Ten couples had scores one standard deviation above and 9 couples had scores one standard deviation below the mean, so a subsample of 19 was used for this analysis.

4. Affect was categorized based on a hierarchy of vocal cues. Positive cues included caring, warmth, tenderness, empathy, cheerfulness, affection, happiness, laughter and concern. Negative cues included tension, whining, fury, coldness, impatience, blame, sarcasm, and anger. Neutral affect was assigned when vocal cues carried no discernable affect.

5. Cohen's Kappa reliability index assesses interobserver agreement beyond that which would be expected by chance alone. It is a conservative index which is usually lower than the standard reliability index of agreements divided by agreements plus disagreements.

6. The presence of void cells does not preclude log-linear analysis if the cells are a result of sampling artifacts (that is, are sampling zeroes as opposed to structural zeroes), as is true in these data. To proceed mathematically a small numerical quantity, usually .5, is added to each cell count to facilitate the computation of chi-square statistics (Kennedy, 1983, pp. 225–226).

REFERENCES

Alberts, J. (1987, February). *A descriptive taxonomy of couples' conversational complaints.* Paper presented at the annual meeting of the Western Speech Communication Association, Salt Lake City, UT.

Blumstein, P. W., Carson, K. G., Hall, J., Hawkins, B., Hoffman, R., Ishem, E., Maurer, C. P., Spens, D., Taylor, J., & Zimmerman, D. L. (1974). The honoring of accounts. *American Sociological Review, 39,* 551–566.

Burgess, E. W. (1953). *Courtship, engagement and marriage.* Philadelphia: J. B. Lippincott.

Cody, M. J., & McLaughlin, M. L. (1985). Models for the sequential construction of accounting episodes: Situational and interactional constraints on message selection and evaluation. In R. L. Street & J. N. Capella (Eds.), *Sequence and pattern in communicative behaviour* (pp. 50–69). London: Edward Arnold.

Cody, M. J., Woelfel, M. L., & Jordan, W. J. (1983). Dimensions of compliance-gaining situations. *Human Communication Research, 9,* 99–113.

Coulthard, M. (1977). *An introduction to discourse analysis.* New York: Longman.

Cousins, P. C., & Vincent, J. P. (1983). Supportive and aversive behavior following spousal complaints. *Journal of Marriage and the Family, 45,* 678–681.

Doelger, J. (1984). *A descriptive analysis of complaints and their use in conversation.* Unpublished master's thesis. University of Nebraska, Lincoln, NE.

Edmondson, W. J. (1981). On saying you're sorry. In F. Coulmas (Ed.), *Conversational routine: Explorations in standardized communication situations and prepatterened speech* (pp. 273–288). New York: Moulton Publishers.

Fitzpatrick, M. A. (1983). Predicting couples' communication from couples' self-reports. In R. N. Bostrom (Ed.), *Communication Yearbook 7* (pp. 49–82). Beverly Hills: Sage.

Goffman, E. (1971). *Relations in public: Microstudies of the public order.* New York: Basic Books.

Gottman, J. M. (1979). *Marital interaction.* New York: Academic Press.

Kelley, H. H. (1979). *Personal relationships: Their structure and processes.* New York: Wiley & Sons.

Kelly, C., Huston, T. L., & Cate, R. M. (1985). Premarital relationship correlates of the erosion of satisfaction in marriage. *Journal of Marriage and the Family, 47,* 167–178.

Kennedy, J. J. (1983). *Analyzing qualitative data.* New York: Praeger.

Krokoff, L., Gottman, J. M., & Roy, A. K. (1986). *The blue-collar couple: A re-evaluation.* Unpublished manuscript.

Labov, W., & Fanshel, D. (1977). *Therapeutic discourse.* New York: Academic Press.

Locke, H. J., Sabagh, G., & Thomas, M. M. (1967). Interfaith marriages. *Social problems, 4,* 319–333.

Markman, H. L. (1979). Application of a behavioral model of marriage in predicting satisfaction of couples planning marriage. *Journal of Consulting and Clinical Psychology, 47,* 743–749.

Markman, H. L. (1981). Prediction of marital distress: A five-year follow-up. *Journal of Consulting and Clinical Psychology, 49,* 760–762.

McLaughlin, M. L., Cody, M. J., & O'Hair, H. D. (1983a). The management of failure events: Some contextual determinants of accounting behavior. *Human Communication Research, 9,* 208–224.

McLaughlin, M. L., Cody, M. J., & Rosenstein, N. E. (1983b). Account sequences in conversations between strangers. *Communication Monographs, 50,* 102–125.

Morris, G. H. (1985). The remedial episode as a negotiation of rules. In R. L. Street & J. N. Capella (Eds.), *Sequence and pattern in comunicative behaviour* (pp. 70–84). London: Edward Arnold.

Navran, L. (1967). Communication and adjustment in marriage. *Family Processes, 6,* 173–184.

Oxford English Dictionary. (1971). New York: Oxford University Press.

Paulson, C. J. (1982). Confirmation and the complaining process. Unpublished doctoral dissertation, University of Denver, Denver, CO.

Random House College Dictionary. (1972). New York: Rand MacNally.

Rausch, H. L., Barry, W. A., Hertel, R. K., & Swain, M. A. (1974). *Communication, conflict, and marriage.* San Francisco: Josey Bass.

Remler, J. E. (1978). Some repairs on the notion of repairs. *Chicago Linguistic Society, Papers from the Ninth Regional Meeting, 14,* 391–402.

Schonback, P. (1980). A category system for account phases. *European Journal of Social Psychology, 10,* 195–200.

Scott, M. N., & Lyman, S. M. (1968). Accounts. *American Sociological Review, 33,* 46–62.

Spanier, G. B. (1976). Measuring dyadic adjustment: New scales for assessing the quality of marriage and similar dyads. *Journal of Marriage and the Family, 38,* 15–28.

Strodtbeck, F. L. (1951). Husband-wife interaction over revealed differences. *American Sociological Review, 17,* 468–473.

Thomas, E. J. (1977). *Marital communication and decision making: Analysis, assessment, and change.* London: Collier Macmillan.

Turner, R. (1970). Words, utterances, and activities. In J. Douglas (Ed.), *Understanding everyday life* (pp. 169–187). Chicago: Aldine.

APPENDIX A

Complaints Interview Schedule

Couple # _____

Hi. I am conducting interviews on complaint behavior between men and women in romance relationships. I would like to interview each of you separately. I appreciate your volunteering to help me out.

All of us give and receive complaints. We can complain about ourselves, complain directly to other people, and complain about events or people who are not present. Little is known about how people make complaints directly to other people nor how people respond to such complaints in romance relationships. I'm trying to learn more about this behavior.

  I. First, I'd like to ask you some demographic information.
   1. Male _____   Female _____
   2. How long have the two of you been romantic partners? 6 mos.–1 yr. _____
      1–5 years _____ 6–10 yrs. _____
      11–15 years _____
   3. Are you married or living together?
   4. How old are you?

 II. Now I'd like to ask you about a complaint you have made.
   1. Please try to recall the exact wording of a complaint you have made to your partner.
   2. How did your partner respond?
   3. Please try to repeat as exactly as possible what your partner said.
   4. When did this complaint occur?
      Where were your?
      What were you doing?
   5. What was said or done just before this complaint was made?
   6. What was said or done after your partner responded to the complaint?
   7. Why did you make the complaint? What did you hope to accomplish?
      Did you? Why/why not?

III. Now I'd like to ask you about a complaint you have received.
1. Please try to recall the exact wording of the complaint you have received from your partner.
2. How did you respond?
3. Please try to repeat as exactly as possible what you said.
4. When did the complaint occur?
   Where were you?
   What were you doing?
5. What was said or done just before the complaint was made?
6. What was said or done after you responded as you did?
7. Why did you respond as you did? What did you hope to accomplish?
   Did you? Why/why not?

IV. Now I'd like to ask you some general questions about complaints.
1. What do you normally complain about to your partner?
2. What does your partner normally complain about to you?
3. When do complaints between the two of you usually occur?
4. What type of complaints do you find hardest to deal with?
5. Have you ever felt your partner was complaining to you but s/he was not?
   Could you give me an example?
   Why did you think it was a complaint?
6. Have you made a complaint to your partner but s/he did not realize it?
   Could you give me an example?
7. What type of responses do you think are effective? Ineffective?
8. What do you think is the best way to complain?
   The worst way?
9. Ideally, how would you like for your partner to respond to your complaints?

COGNITIVE AND MOTIVATIONAL INFLUENCES ON SPONTANEOUS COMFORTING BEHAVIOR

Wendy Samter
Brant R. Burleson

Most previous research concerned with comforting communication skills has studied comforting by having subjects respond to hypothetical situations. A major goal of the present study was to examine the relation of several cognitive and motivational variables to the comforting behaviors displayed by persons in a "real world" situation. Subjects (73 female college students) interacted with a female confederate who appeared to be emotionally distressed about having been left by her boyfriend. These interactions were covertly videotaped and content analyzed. Measures of interpersonal construct differentiation, emotional empathy, communication apprehension, and locus of control orientation were also obtained. As expected, interpersonal construct differentiation was positively related to qualitative features of the comforting behaviors exhibited by subjects. Also as expected, highly apprehensive subjects tended to avoid interacting with the distressed confederate and engaged in relatively little comforting behavior. Emotional empathy and locus of control orientation were unrelated to the comforting behaviors of subjects. These results are discussed in terms of a general model of comforting behavior.

Source: The article is taken from *Human Communication Research* [11:231–260, 1984]. (c) International Communication Association, 8140 Burnet Rd., Austin, TX 78766. Reprinted by permission of Sage Publications, Inc. and ICA.

In recent years communication scholars have focused increasing attention on the message strategies that persons employ in the pursuit of various everyday social goals. Reflecting the discipline's historical concern with rhetorical communication, many studies have examined the use of strategies intended to persuade, regulate, or gain compliance (e.g., Applegate, 1982; Cody, McLaughlin, & Jordan, 1980; Miller, Boster, Roloff, & Seibold, 1977; Wiseman & Schenk-Hamlin, 1981). Other, more affect-centered communication strategies have also received attention (e.g., Baxter, 1982; Cody, 1982). In particular, the strategies used to provide comfort to emotionally distressed others have recently been the focus of several empirical studies (e.g., Applegate, 1980a; Burleson, 1982a; Ritter, 1979).

Comforting strategies can be conceptualized as those messages having the intended function of alleviating or lessening the emotional distress arising from a variety of everyday hurts and disappointments (Burleson, 1984a). Viewed as the management of everyday disappointments and hurts, comforting communication represents a theoretically and pragmatically interesting form of behavior. Theoretically, comforting may be viewed as a type of functional communication skill and as a form of prosocial behavior. Functional or strategic communicative competencies are those communicative skills directed at the accomplishment of certain social objectives (Allen & Brown, 1976; Clark & Delia, 1979). Typical functional skills include informing others, persuading others, controlling others, and instructing others. Prosocial or altruistic behavior refers to those actions carried out with the primary intention of benefitting another without the expectation of receiving rewards from external sources (Macaulay & Berkowitz, 1970; Mussen & Eisenberg-Berg, 1977). Frequently studied forms of prosocial behavior include helping, sharing, cooperating, rescuing, donating, and sympathizing (see the review of Rushton, 1980).

Because comforting has a clear social objective (i.e., improving the affective state of a distressed other) and is usually enacted with the primary intention of benefitting another, it may be usefully viewed as a type of prosocial functional communication.[1] Conceptualizing comforting as a type of functional communication permits, as will be seen, an analysis of the specific skills enabling persons to engage in sensitive comforting. On the other hand, viewing comforting as a type of prosocial behavior brings into relief the special motivational status of comforting viz. other types of functional communication. As argued below, consideration of the prosocial motivation underlying comforting permits an analysis of the factors influencing the actual performance of comforting acts in concrete contexts. Although comforting thus shares important commonalities with other prosocial behaviors and other functional communication skills, recent research has found only limited empirical coherence among different forms of prosocial behavior (e.g., Payne, 1980; Underwood & Moore, 1982) and different forms of functional communication skill (e.g., Burleson & Delia, 1983). These findings suggest that a detailed understanding of comforting cannot be achieved solely through the study of related forms of behavior; rather, comforting itself must become an object of investigation.

Pragmatically, the study of comforting is warranted by research results indicating that the manner in which speakers comfort distressed others has significant consequences for both the producer and recipient of comforting messages. Many studies (e.g., Dlugokinski & Firestone, 1973; Rubin, 1972) have found that among groups of children, individual differences in both functional communication skills and prosocial activities are positively related to social acceptance and peer popularity. More specifically, Burleson (1985) found that among 6 different measures of communication skill, comforting skill best differentiated between groups of popular and unpopular children. These findings are especially important as longitudinal studies (e.g., Cowen, Pederson, Babigian, Izzo, & Trost, 1973; Roff, Sells, & Golden, 1972) have found that unpopular and unaccepted children are much more susceptible later in life to a host of psychological and social adjustment problems. Among adults,

Burleson and Samter (1984) found that persons employing more "sophisticated" comforting strategies were perceived by naive social actors as behaving more sensitively, responsively, and sympathetically toward a distressed other. Finally, research conducted within the framework of peer social support (e.g., Heller & Lakey, 1984; Heller & Swindle, 1983), as well as research in psychotherapeutic contexts (e.g., Aspy, 1975; Traux & Caukhuff, 1967), indicates that distressed persons receiving sensitive comfort experience fewer long-term emotional and psychosomatic problems. Research on the outcomes of comforting thus suggests the need for developing models of the individual-difference variables underlying the production of sensitive comforting behavior.

Most research on individual differences in comforting skill has been conducted from the constructivist theoretical perspective, a view that emphasizes the contributions of social perception skills to the formulation of effective, sensitively adapted messages (see the general discussion of Delia, O'Keefe, & O'Keefe, 1982). According to the constructivist view all social perception processes occur through the application of the cognitive structures termed "interpersonal constructs" (Delia, 1976). Bipolar in nature, interpersonal constructs are the basic dimensions through which persons interpret, evaluate, and anticipate the thoughts and behaviors of others. Thus, persons with more differentiated (i.e., quantitatively larger) and abstract (i.e., psychologically centered) systems of interpersonal constructs are better able to infer the relevant features of a listener's characteristics and perspective and adapt to these characteristics and perspective in the process of formulating a message. In support of this general thesis, individual differences in construct differentiation and abstractness have been found moderately related to individual differences in persuasive, regulative, referential, and comforting communication skill (see the reviews of Delia & O'Keefe, 1979; Delia et al., 1982; and O'Keefe & Sypher, 1981).

Methods for the study of comforting messages were developed by Applegate (1978), who constructed a 9-level hierarchical coding system that

scores comforting strategies for the extent to which they either deny, implicitly recognize, or explicitly articulate, elaborate, and legitimize the feelings and perspective of a distressed other. Considerable evidence supports the validity of this approach to coding comforting strategies. For example, Burleson and Samter (1984) presented subjects with 36 preformulated comforting strategies varying in sophistication according to Applegate's hierarchy. The subjects were instructed to rate each strategy in terms of overall quality. Subjects' mean ratings and rankings of the preformulated strategies were found to correspond exactly with the ordering of the strategies defined by Applegate's hierarchical coding system. A subsequent study (Burleson & Samter, in press) found that several individual-difference variables explained very little variance in subjects' orderings of preformulated comforting messages, a result suggesting that there is a high degree of consensus among naive actors about the properties of "good" comforting strategies. Other evidence supporting the validity of this hierarchical approach to coding comforting messages is summarized by Burleson (1984a).

In the typical constructivist study of comforting communication, subjects have been asked to respond (either orally or in writing) to several hypothetical situations involving emotionally distressed others. For example, mothers have been asked to state what they would say to comfort a child who was upset about being excluded from a classmate's party (Applegate, Burke, Burleson, Delia, & Kline, in press; Applegate & Delia, 1980), children have been asked to report what they would say to comfort a friend who had been frightened by a scary movie on television (Burleson, 1982a, 1982b, 1984b), and college students have been asked what they might say to a roommate who was depressed about not receiving a scholarship (Applegate, 1978; Borden, 1979; Burleson, 1983). In all of these studies messages elicited in response to the hypothetical situations have been scored within versions of the hierarchical coding system developed by Applegate (1978). The results of these studies are impressively consistent: In 10 of 11 studies significant positive relations have been observed between the sensitivity of employed comforting strategies and independent assessments of interpersonal construct differentiation and/or abstractness (see the review of Burleson, 1984a).

Although the consistency of these results is impressive, there are at least two features of existing constructivist research on comforting that are possible sources of concern. First, all of these studies have obtained comforting strategies by having subjects respond to hypothetical situations. The use of hypothetical situations in studies of message behavior has a number of clear methodological advantages (e.g., standardization, use of multiple situations to enhance reliability, ease of data collection). In addition, there is some evidence indicating that comforting strategies elicited in response to hypothetical situations correspond with those actually used by persons in "real world" situations (Applegate, 1980b). Thus far, however, there is no direct evidence indicating that individual differences in interpersonal construct system development are predictive of aspects of the comforting strategies employed by persons in real world situations. Consequently, one goal of the present study was to assess the relation between interpersonal construct system development and the sensitivity of comforting strategies spontaneously employed by persons in a natural context.

A second problem with existing constructivist research on comforting lies in the fact that nearly all of these studies have examined differences in comforting skill only in terms of construct system development. Although constructivist researchers have readily admitted that other cognitive and motivational processes probably influence the use of highly sensitive comforting strategies, only two studies (Borden, 1979; Burleson, 1983) have included assessments of other potential correlates of comforting behavior. Indeed, it would be argued that constructivist research has too often focused on how one independent variable (construct system development) affects varied forms of communicative behavior and has too infrequently focused on how other variables may contribute to skill in specific forms of communication. Clearly, detailed models of specific forms of communicative behavior are needed in addition to more general analyses of communicative functioning.

Burleson (1984a; also see Burleson & Samter, 1983) recently proposed a general model of the determinants of comforting behavior. Drawing on models of both functional communication skills and prosocial behavior Burleson's model proposes that there are two general classes of variables affecting comforting behavior: those that influence the competence to provide sensitive comfort and those that affect the motivation to engage in comforting acts. Competence-determinants pertain to the type of knowledge underlying a speaker's ability to produce sensitive comforting strategies. Four types of knowledge are identified: listener knowledge (knowledge of the characteristics and perspective of the listener), topic knowledge (general knowledge of emotional dynamics and defense mechanisms), rhetorical knowledge (knowledge of how to express information and sequence arguments and appeals), and metacommunicative knowledge (knowledge of the communicative process itself). As the interpersonal construct system constitutes a central mechanism through which speakers acquire information about listeners, Burleson argues that construct system differentiation and abstractness represent important indices of the competence or ability to provide comfort to distressed others.

Possession of the ability to provide sensitive comfort does not, of course, ensure that this competence will be exercised. If sensitive comforting is to occur a speaker must also be motivated to engage in comforting acts. Burleson's model distinguishes between two classes of variables presumed to affect the motivation to engage in comforting acts: those affecting the desire to reduce another's distress and those affecting the willingness to undertake acts of comforting. Desire refers to a speaker's wanting to reduce another's distress whereas willingness pertains to the extent to which a speaker accepts and becomes involved with the task of reducing the other's distress. Desire and willingness must both be present if comforting is to occur.

A variety of personality and situational variables conceptually related to either the desire or the willingness to engage in comforting have been found to influence behavioral indices of comforting behavior. For example, Feinberg (1977) and Grodman (1979) both found that a personality trait termed ''prosocial orientation'' (created by summing the factor-weighted scores of several personality measures such as Machiavellianism, values orientation, and acceptance of social responsibility) predicted the amount of comforting directed toward a distressed experimental confederate. Moreover, these researchers observed that certain situational variables (e.g., the confederate's need for help, the perceived cost of helping) also influenced the amount of comforting behavior directed at the confederate. Other research (Applegate, 1980a; Burleson, 1982a, 1983; Ritter, 1979; see the review of Burleson, 1984a) further indicates that certain situational and personality variables influence the desire and/or willingness to provide comfort.

Among the possible variables underlying the desire to provide comfort, one of the more important is ''emotional empathy.'' Defined as the spontaneous tendency to feel what another feels (Mehrabian & Epstein, 1972), emotional empathy has been hypothesized to underlie a wide array of prosocial behaviors (Feshback, 1978; Hoffman, 1981). Because emotionally empathic individuals are more likely to experience distress themselves on viewing another's distress, they should develop a stronger desire to reduce the despondent states of others. Following this line of reasoning Burleson (1983) found that emotional empathy was positively related to the sensitivity of comforting strategies elicited in response to hypothetical situations. The present study assesses the effect of an emotionally empathic disposition on comforting behavior exhibited in a real world situation.

Many personality traits may influence the willingness to provide comfort. For example, the extensive literature concerned with ''communication apprehension'' indicates that some individuals consistently avoid communicative interactions with others (see the reviews of McCroskey, 1977, 1982). Persons with relatively high levels of communication apprehension may

thus be less willing to become involved with and provide comfort to an emotionally distressed other. It is also possible that a person's locus of control orientation (Rotter, 1966) affects his or her willingness to provide comfort. Individuals with a high external locus of control may believe that they could not have a meaningful effect on another's emotional distress, and thus would be less likely to engage in comforting acts. In contrast, persons with a high internal locus of control may be more willing to engage in acts of comforting because of the belief in their general capacity to influence events. Previous research focused on other prosocial behaviors has found that high internals are more likely to provide help than high externals (Fincham & Barling, 1978; Midlarsky, 1971). Thus, one objective of the present study was to assess the effects of communication apprehension and locus of control on comforting behavior exhibited in a natural context.

In sum, the present study had two major goals. First, we attempted to extend existing constructivist research on comforting by assessing the relation between interpersonal construct system development and comforting behavior in a natural context. Second, we wished to assess the impact of variables assumed to underlie the desire and willingness to engage in comforting on behavior exhibited in a natural context. Following the tenets of Burleson's (1984a) model, we expected that individual differences in construct system development would primarily influence the quality or sensitivity of observed comforting efforts. In contrast, we expected that the motivational indices (i.e., emotional empathy, communication apprehension, locus of control) would primarily affect the quantity of exhibited comforting behavior. More specifically, it was hypothesized that within the context of a natural comforting episode interpersonal construct differentiation would be positively related to the proportion of comforting appeals employed, the proportion of relatively sophisticated comforting appeals employed, the proportion of relevant questions asked, and an index reflecting the use of both comforting strategies and relevant information-seeking attempts. It was expected that emotional empathy, a presumed determinant of the desire to provide comfort, would be positively associated with the total number of comforting strategies produced, the total number of advisory comments made, and the number of distress-reducing strategies employed (an index created by summing the number of comforting strategies and the number of advisory statements). Finally, it was expected that two presumed determinants of the willingness to provide comfort, locus of control orientation and communication apprehension, would be significantly related to the number of comforting strategies produced; internal locus of control orientation should be positively associated with this variable, whereas communication apprehension should be negatively associated. Furthermore, it was expected that communication apprehension would be negatively associated with the total amount of talk produced during the course of the interactional episode.

METHOD

Subjects

Participants in the study were 73 female college students enrolled in basic communication courses at a large midwestern university. All participants received class extra-credit points for involvement in the study. With an N = 73 and p = .05, statistical power was .74 for medium effect sizes (r = .30) and in excess of .99 for large effect sizes (r = .50).

General Procedures

The basic design of the study was modeled on procedures and materials developed by Feinberg (1977) and Grodman (1979). Subjects were recruited during regularly scheduled class periods. Those volunteering for participation in the study were told to report to an initial experimental session scheduled during a weekday evening. During this initial session subjects completed questionnaires designed to assess several cogni-

tive and motivational variables. After completing the questionnaires subjects were asked to sign up for an additional experimental session to be held several weeks later. During the second experimental session subjects individually interacted with another female college student (in actuality, an experimental confederate) who appeared to be quite distressed about having been dropped by her long-term boyfriend the prior evening. These interactions were covertly observed and videotaped by an experimenter (additional details regarding these interactions are reported below). The interactions were subsequently transcribed and content analyzed.

Assessments of Cognitive and Motivational Variables

During the initial experimental session all subjects completed four randomly ordered questionnaires, designed to provide assessments of interpersonal construct differentiation, emotional empathy, communication apprehension, and locus of control orientation. Details regarding the nature and scoring of these questionnaires are reported below.

Interpersonal Construct Differentiation

Subjects were asked to complete a modified version of Crockett's (1965) Role Category Questionnaire (RCQ) in which they provide separate written descriptions of a liked and disliked peer. Following procedures outlined by Crockett, Press, Delia, and Kenny (1974), each description was coded for the number of interpersonal constructs it contained. To form an index of construct differentiation the number of constructs scored in each description was then summed. Two independent coders each scored approximately 20% (N = 15) of the protocols; interrater reliability, as assessed by Pearson correlation, was .98. The extensive evidence supporting the reliability and validity of RCQ measurements of cognitive complexity is summarized by O'Keefe and Sypher (1981).

STATISTICAL SUMMARY 1

Reliability is a measure of how accurate the scores are. If a measure is highly reliable, then you can be confident that the scores are very accurate. Reliability was estimated for construct differentiation by correlating the scores of the two raters. The correlation was very high (.98), meaning that the raters agreed which people produced more constructs. This correlation did not necessarily mean, however, that they agreed on how many constructs were present. Reliability for the empathy measure was moderately high (.77).

Emotional Empathy

Viewed as the tendency to feel what another feels, emotional empathy was assessed through Mehrabian and Epstein's (1972) Emotional Empathy Questionnaire (EEQ). The EEQ is composed of 33–point Likert items tapping aspects of empathy such as susceptibility to emotional contagion, emotional responsiveness, appreciation of others' feelings, and sympathetic orientation. Although the 33 items composing this scale load on several distinct factors, virtually all previous research employing the EEQ has used the total empathy score in conducting analyses; this practice was followed in the present study. Cronbach's alpha for the total 33 item questionnaire was .77. Mehrabian and Epstein report a split-half reliability of .84 for the EEQ; in the current investigation, split-half reliability was .71. Evidence supporting the construct and criterion related validity of the EEQ is summarized by Mehrabian and Epstein (1972) and by Burleson (1983).

Communication Apprehension

Levels of interpersonal communication apprehension were assessed through Burgoon's (1976) Unwillingness to Communicate Scale (UCS). The UCS was chosen over other measures of communication apprehension because its items reflect an exclusive concern with communication

in interpersonal (rather than public) settings. Burgoon reports that the 20 items composing the UCS load on two distinct factors: 10 items load on an approach/avoidance factor (gauging the extent to which persons avoid interacting with others in interpersonal settings), and 10 items load on a reward factor (gauging the extent to which persons find interpersonal communication rewarding). In the present study a principal components factor analysis (with Varimax rotation) of the UCS items yielded a two factor solution similar to that reported by Burgoon. However, only 9 items loaded appreciably on the approach/avoidance factor and only 7 items loaded appreciably on the reward factor; only those items with significant loadings were retained in subsequent analyses. In the current investigation reliabilities (alpha coefficients) were .85 for the 9-item approach/avoidance factor and .55 for the 7-item reward factor. Evidence supporting the validity of the UCS is summarized by Burgoon.

STATISTICAL SUMMARY 2

The Unwillingness to Communicate Scale was factor analyzed. Factor analysis is a method for grouping variables together into a smaller number of categories. If you have a large number of variables, you may want to see if two or more of them actually combine or work together. Here, the analysis suggested two groupings. One grouping, called approach/avoid, was fairly reliable (.85), while the other, reward, did not demonstrate adequate reliability (.55).

Reliability for the locus of control measure was reported from previous studies.

Locus of Control

Subjects' locus of control orientation was measured by Rotter's (1966) Internal/External Locus of Control Questionnaire (I/E Scale). The I/E Scale is composed of 29 forced-choice items, including 6 fillers intended to make the purpose of the test more ambiguous. The 23 "true" items deal with an individual's general beliefs about reinforcement in the world; that is, the items tap expectations about the sources of control over events in the environment. Rotter (1966) reports an average internal consistency of .71 for the 23 scored items and an average test-retest reliability of .76. The considerable evidence supporting the validity of the I/E Scale is summarized by Rotter.

Comforting Interactions

On arriving for the second experimental session, subjects were paired with and introduced to one of six experimental confederates. The subject and confederate were left alone for a few minutes during which the pair engaged in small talk (e.g., majors in school, the weather, classes). The experimenter then reentered the room and explained that the pair would be asked to read several literary passages, form an impression of the protagonist in each passage, and then write that impression. After answering any questions the experimenter left the room and returned to an observation deck concealed behind a one-way mirror. The second of the literary excerpts comprising the "Passages Test" (adapted from Feinberg, 1977) described the actions of an unfaithful husband. The content of this passage provided a natural context for the confederate to introduce the topic of her boyfriend problem. After ensuring that the subject had completed her response to the first passage and had read the target second passage, the confederate stated that she was having hard time concentrating on the task because the second passage reminded her of what had happened the previous evening. The confederate then related that her long-term boyfriend had told her that he wished to end their dating relationship, but that no detailed explanation of this desire had been given. The confederate generally followed a prepared script throughout the interaction (adapted from Feinberg, 1977), emphasizing that she was quite upset, confused, and depressed about the boyfriend situation (for a detailed description of these procedures see Samter, 1983). The interaction proceeded naturally until the subject suggested returning to the "Passages" task or the topic of conversation moved completely away from the breakup situation (at which point the experimenter reentered the room). A variety of situational factors known to influence comforting behavior (e.g., the other's need for help, the cost of helping, similarity to the distressed other) were controlled to ensure the maximum likelihood of comforting.

Interactions ranged in length from 1 minute to over 20 minutes, and averaged 8 minutes. After the interactional episode had ended the experimenter reentered the room, dismissed the confederate under a pretense, had the subject complete a postexperimental questionnaire, and then interviewed and debriefed the subject. The postexperimental questionnaire and the interview contained items designed to assess the subject's perceptions of the confederate and the experimental situation.

Content Analysis of the Interactions

Verbatim transcripts of the 73 interactions were prepared and content analyzed. The coding scheme developed for the present study was partially adapted from the work of Feinberg (1977), Grodman (1979), and Burleson (1982a). The conversational turn was used as the basic unit of analysis. After unitization, each subject utterance was coded into 1 of 6 content categories including: "acknowledgment," "information-seeking," "disclosure," "advice," and "comfort." The sixth content category, labeled "other," was reserved for those utterances that did not meet the definitional requirements of the preceding categories. With the exception of the other category, each of the general content categories was divided into hierarchically ordered subcategories.

Within the general acknowledgment category (turns in which subjects sought simply to acknowledge the confederate's prior utterance) there were 3 subcategories hierarchicalized according to the affective tone of the subject's acknowledgment. Thus, turns scored at level 1 represented a negative affective tone, turns scored at level 2 represented a neutral tone, and turns scored at level 3 were positive in affective tone and demonstrated the subject's emotional involvement with the confederate.

A turn in which the subject sought knowledge concerning a particular fact, circumstance, or feeing was defined as information-seeking. Within this general category were 3 subcategories hierarchicalized according to the extent to which the sought information focused on the feelings, attitudes, or other psychological states of those involved in the breakup situation. Turns scored at level 1 requested information topically unrelated to the confederate's problem. Questions seeking information about either the actions of those involved in the situation or objective features of the relationship were scored at level 2, and questions seeking information about the feelings, attitudes, or other psychological states of the confederate were scored at level 3.

The third content category, disclosure, was defined as a turn in which the subject revealed information, experiences, and/or feelings of her own or of a known other's past; 3 ordered subcategories were defined. Turns scored at level 1 represented disclosure that was topically unrelated to the breakup situation. Turns scored at level 2 disclosed information topically related to the breakup situation, but did not directly link or explicitly apply the disclosed information, experiences, or feelings to the confederate's situation. Turns scored at level 3 not only disclosed information topically related to the breakup situation, but also linked or explicitly applied the information, experiences, or feelings to the confederate's immediate problem.

A turn in which the subject made a recommendation for the confederate's future conduct was defined as advice. Within this general advice category a distinction was drawn between those recommendations that focused on specific lines of behavior in which the confederate should engage (level 1), and those recommendations that referred to the emotional and/or psychological states of the confederate (level 2).

The fifth content category, comfort, encompassed turns in which the subject empathized with the confederate, provided an explanation for another's actions, offered sincere sympathy and support, or suggested a broader perspective from which the confederate could view the breakup situation. Within the general comfort category there were 3 major divisions reflecting the extent to which the subject acknowledged, elaborated, and legitimized the feelings and perspective of the distressed other. These divisions included denial of individual perspectivity (major level 1), implicit recognition of individual perspectivity (major level 2), and explicit recognition and elaboration of individual perspectivity (major level 3). Each major division was further divided into 3 hierarchically ordered subcategories, thus resulting in a 9 category hierarchy for the coding of comforting utterances. Originally developed by Applegate (1978) and revised by Burleson (1982a), the validity of this hierarchy has been supported by several studies that have found a subject's level of comforting strategy use appropriately associated with social-cognitive, demographic, personality, and communicative indices (see the review of Burleson, 1984a).

In sum, the present coding scheme contained 6 general content categories and 21 subcategories. Table 1 presents a complete overview of the coding system (for a detailed description of the coding system, see Samter, 1983). In cases where one turn contained several statements, each with varied emphases, it remained the interpretive decision of the coder to determine the primary theme or focus of the utterances as they functioned together within the turn. In cases where one conversational turn contained two or more levels of a given content category, the higher level was recorded (additional coding rules are described by Samter, 1983). Coding reliability was assessed by having two independent coders score all subject utterances in 15 transcripts (20% of the protocols). The two coders achieved perfect unitizing reliability (1.0). Exact agreement (# of agreements/# of aggreements + # of disagreements) over the 21 category content-analytic system was 82%.

TABLE 1
Content Analytic System for Coding Subject's Behavior

Acknowledgments (Utterances that serve to indicate that the other's statement has been heard)

Avoidance acknowledgments: Utterances that attempt to break off interaction with the confederate.

> Confed: I just am so shocked. I don't know what to do.
> Subject: I don't know either. [Said curtly, with subject then returning immediately to the task]

Simple acknowledgments: Utterances that only indicate the confederate's prior statement has been heard.

> Confed: It's just so weird.
> Subject: Mm-hmm.

Responsive acknowledgements: Utterances that indicate the confederate's prior statement has been heard and is emotionally supported.

> Confed: He just said he didn't want to see me anymore.
> Subject: Really! Oh my gosh!

Information-Seeking (Utterances designed to gain knowledge about a particular fact, circumstance, or feeling)

Topically unrelated information: Utterances in which the requested knowledge has no relevance to the breakup situation.

> "Do you know Brian Egan? He went to La Salle High School, too."

Topically related demographic/behavioral information: Utterances through which the subject seeks knowledge concerning the demographic or behavioral features of the situation or those involved.

> "What year is he in?"

Topically related psychological information: Utterances through which the subject seeks knowledge concerning the psychological states of those involved in the breakup situation.

> "Do you still like him?"

Disclosure (Utterances through which the subject reveals information, experiences, or feelings of her own or a known other's past)

Topically unrelated disclosure: Utterances in which the subject's disclosure has no relevance to the breakup situation.

> "I like the little exercises we do in communication class."

Topically related, nonapplied disclosure: Utterances in which the subject's disclosure is topically related but not explicitly applied to the confederate's immediate problem.

> "My boyfriend got a job in Columbus. We're supposed to get married in a couple of years. But I don't think we'll last that long."

Topically related, applied disclosure: Utterances in which the subject's disclosure is topically related and explicitly applied to the confederate's immediate problem.

> "The very same thing just happened to a friend of mine. She'd been going out with her boyfriend for about a year too. Bad news for both of you!"

Advice (Utterances through which the subject makes a recommendation for the confederate's future conduct)

Line of behavior advice: Utterances in which the subject advocates a specific course of action.

> "Go talk to him. Demand your rights!"

Emotional/psychological advice: Utterances in which the subject suggests methods of coping that center on emotional or psychological states.

> "Give yourself some time and space to think about it for awhile."

Comfort (Utterances through which a subject demonstrates sincere sympathy or support, provides an explanation for another's actions, or suggests a broader perspective from which the confederate can view the situation.)

Speaker condemns the feelings of the other.

> "It's really stupid to feel so bad. You're an adult now and should realize that these things happen."

Speaker challenges the legitimacy of the other's feelings.

> "No guy is worth getting so worked up about."

Speaker ignores the other's feelings.

> "I'd just forget about him and find somebody else."

Speaker attempts to divert the other's attention from the distressful situation and the feelings arising from that context.

"He's gonna realize he can't live without you and you guys will get back together."

Speaker acknowledges the other's feelings, but does not attempt to help the other understand why those feelings are being experienced or how to cope with them.

"I'm really sorry to hear that. That's too bad."

Speaker provides a nonfeeling centered explanation of the situation to reduce the other's distressed emotional state.

"Sometimes guys don't say much. But maybe he just needs some time to himself, you know? Maybe he just needs some space."

Speaker explicitly recognizes and acknowledges the other's feelings but does not provide an elaborated explanation of these feelings.

"Boy, I know this must be really hard to cope with. It hurts so much when you really like somebody."

Speaker provides an elaborated acknowledgment and explanation of the other's feelings.

"Gosh, I really know it hurts now. The same thing happened to me and I really understand how rotten it makes you feel. But believe me, in a few months, you'll be over it. Time's the most important thing."

Speaker helps the other to gain a perspective on her own feelings and attempts to help the other see these feelings in relation to a broader context or the feelings of others in the situation.

"You're so young. I know that's not what you want to hear, cause you're feeling a lot of hurt and rejection right now. And that's OK. But you have so much time ahead of you. There'll be lots of other guys and, you know, you're gonna find someone who treats you right."

<u>Other</u> (Utterances that do not meet the definitional requirements of the preceding categories)

"Are these tests all that we do? Cause I saw a TV screen and I wonder if we write this and then we see like a little action play of this or something. To see if we're right. I don't know."

Dependent Measures

Frequencies and proportions were calculated for all general categories and subcategories. In addition, several theoretically motivated indices were constructed by summing across certain subcategories.

A noted above, it was expected that interpersonal construct differentiation would be a significant predictor of comforting competence or skill. The following dependent measures were regarded as indices of the quality of the comforting behavior exhibited by subjects: (1) the proportion of comforting units; (2) the proportion of advanced comforting units (i.e., those that either implicitly or explicitly acknowledged and legitimized the perspective of the distressed confederate); (3) the proportion of relevant information-seeking units (i.e., the proportion of units

requesting information about the breakup situation); and (4) the proportion of problem focused communication (an index created by summing the number of comforting units with the number of relevant information-seeking units and dividing this sum by the total units scored). The proportion of comforting units was regarded as a particularly important index of comforting competence as this measure reflects the relative extent to which a subject defined the situation as one specifically calling for the alleviation of the confederate's distress (as opposed to pursuing alternative interactional goals). The proportion of advanced comforting units index reflects the extent to which the subject employed relatively sophisticated communicative strategies in the effort to reduce the other's distress. The proportion of relevant information-seeking units was regarded as an important index of comforting competence on the assumption that it was vitally important for the subject to acquire a detailed understanding of the distressed other's view of the situation. The problem focused communication index reflects the relative extent to which subjects both sought information about the situation and actively attempted to manage the confederate's affective distress.

It was expected that the three personality measures (i.e., emotional empathy, communication apprehension, and locus of control) would be significant predictors of the motivation (desire and/or willingness) to provide comfort. In general, level of motivation to provide comfort can be inferred from the amount or quantity of comforting behavior exhibited. Thus, the following dependent measures were regarded as especially significant indicants of the motivation to provide comfort: (1) the total number of utterance units, and (2) the number of topically relevant units (an index created by summing the frequencies for subcategories reflecting a direct concern with the breakup situation; i.e., information seeking levels 2 and 3, disclosure levels 2 and 3, and all advice and comforting units). In addition, it was expected that the motivational variables would be inversely related to the number and proportion of uninvolving communication units (indices created by summing the frequencies for subcategories reflecting a focus on topics other than the breakup situation; i.e., information seeking level 1, disclosure level 1, and other). More specifically, it was anticipated that communication apprehension would be inversely related to the frequency of units scored in each major content category (on the assumption that high apprehensives should be less inclined to engage in any form of communication with the confederate). In addition, it was anticipated that emotional empathy would be positively related to an index termed "distress-reducing communication" (created by summing the number of advice and comforting units); because more emotionally empathic individuals presumably have a greater desire to reduce the other's distress, they should engage in a greater number of behaviors relevant to this goal.

RESULTS

Manipulation Checks and Analyses of Confederate Effects

Several questions posed either on the postexperimental questionnaire or by the experimenter during the postexperimental interview were utilized to assess the extent to which subjects (a) actually perceived the confederate as emotionally distressed, (b) believed it was appropriate to converse with the confederate, and (c) were suspicious of the experimental circumstances. Of the subjects surveyed, 89% described the confederate as having a negative or depressed affect state, 8% described the confederate in neutral affective terms, and only 3% perceived the confederate as having a positive emotional state. Additional information gleaned from the postexperimental questionnaire and the postexperimental interview indicated that the majority of subjects believed it was fully appropriate to converse with the confederate. Finally, although 41% of the subjects reported some degree of global suspicion about the experimental circumstances, only 10% reported harboring any specific suspicion about the behavior of the confederate. Moreover, even those subjects suspicious about the behavior of the confederate indicated that they tried to help the confederate rather than risk exacerbating her situation by ignoring a potentially real problem. None of the subjects deduced the actual nature of the experimental situation. In sum, the manipulation checks indicated that the vast majority of subjects perceived the confederate as experiencing real emotional distress, considered it appropriate to converse with the confederate, and generally were not suspicious of the confederate's behavior. Indeed, on being told the true nature of the experimental manipulation, many subjects commented on how thoroughly they had been taken in by the situation.

Because logistical reasons made it necessary to employ six different confederates, the effect of confederate on subjects' behaviors was assessed. A series of one-way ANOVAs was conducted on each of the 22 dependent variables with confederate serving as the independent variable. Only one significant F-ratio was detected in these analyses, well within what would be expected on the basis of chance given the number of F-tests performed. Moreover, a follow-up Neuman-Keuls test on this single significant effect failed to locate a specific confederate as the source of variation. Thus, it appears that subject behavior did not substantially vary as a function of confederate.

Relations Between Cognitive and Motivational Factors and Comforting Behavior[2]

Table 2 reports the zero-order correlations between the independent and dependent variables included in the study. Viewed as a determinant of the competence to provide sensitive comfort, interpersonal construct differentiation was expected to be significantly associated with the following dependent measures: proportion of relevant information-seeking units, proportion of comforting units, proportion of advanced comforting units, and proportion of problem focused communication. Construct differentiation was positively associated with each of these dependent measures at a significant level, with correlations ranging from .21 to .36 (see Table 2). Construct differentiation was also significantly associated with the following additional dependent measures: number of comforting units ($r = .22$), number of advanced comforting units

($r = .22$), proportion of acknowledgments ($r = -.21$), proportion of information seeking ($r = .22$), and proportion of other units ($r = -.21$).

Although the significant correlations between cognitive complexity and the proportions of relevant information seeking, comforting strategies, advanced comforting strategies, and problem-focused communication confirm the hypotheses pertaining to the relation between cognitive complexity and the competence to engage in sensitive comforting, the magnitudes of these significant correlations are not particularly large. Moreover,

TABLE 2
Correlations Between Comforting Determinants and Comforting Behaviors

Dependent variables	Independent Variables				
	Cognitive complexity	Emotional empathy	Comm Ap avoidance	Comm Ap reward	Internal locus of control
Total Units	.06	.05	−.26*	.11	.03
Number of Acknowledgment Units	−.14	.06	−.20	−.14	.00
Number of Information-Seeking Units	.17	−.03	−.29*	.17	.01
Number of Relevant Information-Seeking Units	.19	−.04	−.25*	.16	−.03
Number of Disclosure Units	.02	−.04	−.17	.18	−.01
Number of Advice Units	.03	.13	−.19	.15	.03
Number of Comforting Units	.22*	.15	−.26*	.19	−.02
Number of Advanced Comforting Units	.22*	.15	−.24*	.20	−.01
Number of Other Units	−.15	.10	.03	−.17	.29*
Proportion of Acknowledgments	−.21*	.00	.25*	−.26*	.04
Proportion of Information Seeking	.22*	−.08	−.12	.11	−.06
Proportion of Relevant Information Seeking	.21*	−.06	−.03	.13	−.09
Proportion of Disclosure	−.10	−.09	−.09	.18	−.05
Proportion of Advice	−.02	.15	−.17	.11	−.03
Proportion of Comforting	.33*	.10	−.16	.16	−.05
Proportion of Advanced Comforting	.33*	.09	−.14	.13	−.07
Proportion of Other	−.21*	.07	.03	−.21*	.21*
Number of Topic-Relevant Units	.17	.08	−.30*	.27*	−.06
Number of Distress-Reducing Units	.20	.16	−.26*	.20	−.01
Problem Focused Communication	.36*	.05	−.14	.19	−.08
Number of Uninvolving Communication Units	−.05	−.08	−.01	−.08	.14
Proportion of Uninvolving Communication	−.19	−.10	.28*	−.10	.05

Note: N = 73. *Indicates rs with $p < .05$.

it might be argued that the relations between cognitive complexity and comforting competence observed here might actually be due to the operation of some other variable or set of variables—such as the motivational variables included in the present study. In order to test this possibility, the influence of emotional empathy, locus of control, and the two aspects of communication apprehension was partialled out from the relations between cognitive complexity and the four indices of comforting competence. The zero-order correlations between cognitive complexity and the proportions of relevant information

seeking, comforting strategies, advanced strategies, and problem-focused communication were .21, .33, .33, and .36, respectively (all ps < .05). The fourth-order partial correlations between these variables were .20, .30, .31, and .34, respectively. As can be seen, controlling for the four motivational variables had little effect on the magnitudes of the correlations between cognitive complexity and the four indices of comforting competence; only the relation between cognitive complexity and proportion of relevant information seeking fell below conventional levels of statistical significance (p < .10) when controlling for the four motivational variables. The results of the partial correlational analysis thus indicate that the relationship between cognitive complexity and the competence to provide sensitive comfort is not confounded by underlying motivational orientations.[3] These results are fully consistent with the model of comforting behavior presented above as motivational variables were not expected to affect the ability to comfort others sensitively, but only the application of this ability in concrete contexts.

As a presumed determinant of the willingness to provide comfort, the approach/avoidance aspect of communication apprehension was expected to be negatively associated with all quantitative indices of communicative behavior (i.e., with all frequency counts). This hypothesis was generally confirmed: The approach/avoidance factor of communication apprehension was negatively associated at significant levels with the total number of units scored ($r = -.26$), and with frequencies in most of the general content categories (see Table 2). In addition, the avoidance aspect of communication apprehension was negatively associated with the number of topic-relevant units ($r = -.30$) and the number of distress-reducing units ($r = -.26$), but was positively associated with the proportion of acknowledgments ($r = .25$) and the proportion of uninvolving communication ($r = .28$).

A somewhat curious pattern of results emerged with respect to the reward aspect of communication apprehension. This aspect of communication apprehension was significantly associated with the following dependent measures: proportion of acknowledgements ($r = -.26$), proportion of other units ($r = -.21$), number of topically relevant units ($r = .27$), and number of distress-reducing units ($r = .20$). Thus, those who reported finding communication with friends and family unrewarding generally employed more topic-relevant and distress-reducing units, and employed a smaller proportion of simple acknowledgments and other units. Possible reasons for this rather surprising set of findings are discussed below.

Emotional empathy was not significantly associated with any dependent measure. Internal locus of control was significantly associated only with the number and proportion of units scored in the other category ($rs = .29$ and $.21$, respectively). Thus, the hypotheses pertaining to these motivational determinants were not confirmed.

DISCUSSION

The results of this study suggest two broad generalizations and raise a number of interesting questions. The first generalization is that interpersonal construct differentiation, a presumed determinant of the competence to engage in sensitive comforting, is consistently associated with measures tapping the quality of comforting behavior displayed in natural situations. Highly differentiated subjects employed a greater number of comforting strategies, a greater number of sophisticated comforting strategies, and asked more relevant questions about the distressed other's view of the breakup situation. In addition, highly differentiated subjects devoted proportionately more time to the activities of comforting and seeking relevant information. Moreover, differentiated subjects spent proportionately less time talking about matters unrelated to the break up situation and made relatively fewer simple acknowledgments of the distressed other's utterances. This pattern of results suggests that subjects with relatively differentiated systems of interpersonal constructs spontaneously defined the situation as one calling for the alleviation of the confederate's distress, and further pursued this objective through the use of sophisticated comforting strategies and the asking of relevant questions.

The present study represents one of the first attempts to apply constructivist theory and methods to data acquired in a relatively natural situation (in contrast to data elicited by hypothetical situations). Thus, the observation of significant relations between interpersonal construct system development and comforting behavior in this study represents an important extension of the constructivist program. Individual differences in interpersonal construct system development do have a clear impact on the type of communicative behaviors enacted by persons in real world situations. Although the magnitudes of the relations between construct system development and communicative behavior observed in the present study (generally .21 to .36) are somewhat weaker than those observed when hypothetical situations have been used (rs generally ranging from .40 to .60), this is only to be expected given the relatively uncontrolled research design employed in the present study. Moreover, it is important to note that controlling for the four motivational variables assessed in this study (emotional empathy, locus of control, the avoidance aspect of communication apprehension, and the reward aspect of communication apprehension) did not appreciably affect the magnitudes of the associations between construct differentiation and indices of the ability to provide sensitive comfort. This latter finding is significant in suggesting the robustness of the relation between construct differentiation and comforting behavior in a natural context. Taken in conjunction with recent research indicating that individual differences in construct system development predict aspects of real world persuasive behavior (Applegate, 1982; O'Keefe, 1983), the present study provides strong support for the constructivist analysis of the role of social perception in functional communication.

The second major generalization to be drawn from the present results is that the self-reported tendency to avoid interpersonal interaction manifests itself quantitatively in quasi-natural comforting episodes. That is, individuals high in the avoidance aspect of communication apprehension generally had shorter interactions with confederates, and produced fewer units in most of the content categories. Consistent with the hypotheses advanced above, then, persons generally likely to avoid communicating with others are less willing to interact with and provide comfort to a distressed other.

Interestingly, the avoidance aspect of communication apprehension was generally associated negatively only with dependent measures indexing the quantity of interaction and was generally unrelated to dependent measures indexing the quality of interaction (i.e., the proportional indices). The only exceptions to this general pattern were the positive associations between the avoidance factor and the proportion of acknowledgment units and the proportion of uninvolving communication. Simple acknowledgments of another's utterances (e.g., ''yeah,'' ''mmm,'' ''uh-uh'') are often a means of avoiding content-relevant interaction. And persons employing a relatively high proportion of uninvolving communication avoid dealing with the other's distress. Thus, these positive associations are fully consistent with expectations for the behavior of highly apprehensive communicators.

Unexpectedly, the reward aspect of communication apprehension was found to be positively associated with several variables assumed to tap quantitative or qualitative features of sensitive comforting (e.g., the number of distress-reducing units). This means that subjects who reported finding communication with family and friends unrewarding engaged in a larger amount of comforting behavior. The reasons for these relations are not entirely clear. Perhaps persons who have had unhappy experiences themselves in communication with intimates are more sympathetic to and understanding of the relational problems faced by others.

Emotional empathy and internal locus of control were generally unrelated to either quantitative or qualitative indices of comforting behavior. The failure of emotional empathy to emerge as a significant predictor of comforting in this study was surprising as this variable had previously been found associated with the sensitivity of strategies used in response to hypothetical situations (Burleson, 1983), and it had been expected that empathy might actually emerge as a stronger predictor of real world comforting behavior. Two factors may account for the failure of empathy to act as a significant predictor. First, in the present study the reliability of the EEQ (.71) was noticeably lower than that reported in previous studies (reliabilities ranging from .81 to .92). Thus, perhaps the empathy construct was not validly tapped due to unreliable measurement. Second, the present study employed only females, and females have been found significantly more empathic than males (see the review of Hoffman, 1977). Thus, perhaps significant relations between empathy and comforting were not observed in the present study due to a truncated range of empathy scores.

Two factors may account for the failure of locus of control to emerge as a significant predictor. First, Rotter's (1966) I/E Scale taps very general beliefs about the control of events in the world; many items pertain to control over large-scale political and social issues. Perhaps an instrument assessing more specific beliefs about control over interpersonal issues would reveal a relation between control orientation and comforting behavior. Second, prior research (e.g., Fincham & Barling, 1978) finding relations between control orientation and prosocial behavior has focused on quite simple forms of behavior (e.g., donating candies to a charity). Although a high internal locus of control may predict the decision to act prosocially in contexts in which the target behavior is relatively simple, this variable may not relate to the performance of much more complicated forms of behavior, such as the management of another's psychological distress.

Although the results of the present investigation significantly extend our knowledge of comforting behavior, several controls were employed that may limit the generality of the study's findings. For example, an exclusively female subject sample was employed in this study. Prior research (e.g., Burleson, 1982a) found that females' comforting skills qualitatively differ from those of males. Thus, it is likely that the behavior of a male or mixed-sex sample would vary from that observed in the present female sample. In addition, many situational factors thought to influence comforting behavior (e.g., similarity of the comforter and distressed other, salience of the other's distress, cost of helping, presence of distracting influences) were controlled in the present study so as to maximize the likelihood of comforting occurring. Paradoxically, some of these

controls may have prevented our hypotheses pertaining to emotional empathy from being confirmed. For example, Batson and his colleagues have found that high empathy results in more helping than low empathy only when the cost of helping is relatively high (Batson, Duncan, Ackerman, Buckley, & Birch, 1981; Toi & Batson, 1982). This suggests that minimization of the cost of helping in the present study may have obscured the effect of an emotionally empathic disposition. Thus, future research should systematically manipulate many of the situational variables controlled in the present study and observe how they combine and interact with cognitive and personality factors in determining displayed levels of comforting skill.

NOTES

1. The issue of whether prosocial behavior must be intended to benefit others to be regarded as truly prosocial (as opposed to benefitting others unintentionally or accidentally) has received extensive discussion in the altruism literature (e.g., Krebs, 1970; Macaulay & Berkowitz, 1970; Staub, 1978). Addressing this issue is further complicated by the fact that it is never possible to know with complete certainty the character of another's intentions. Obviously, we have no solutions to the classic problems involved with the concept of intention. We wish to point out, however, that problems faced by the social scientist in dealing with another's intent (as, for example, in inferring that a given behavior was intended to comfort another) are, in principle, no different than those faced by naive actors in the lifeworld. That is, both social scientists and naive actors must assume that most human behavior is intentional, and both must base their attributions of specific intentions on others' behaviors. Although both the social scientist and the naive actor can be wrong about the intentions they attribute to others, neither can make sense of the social world without relying on the concept of intention.

2. In addition to the correlational analyses reported in this section, a number of multiple regression analyses were conducted to assess whether statistically significant multiple correlations would result. The multiple regression analyses indicated that the inclusion of additional independent variables rarely resulted in statistically significant multiple correlations. Multiple regression analyses including first-order and second-order interaction terms for the independent variables also generally failed to yield statistically significant increases in the explained criterion variance. Because the independent variables

were generally unrelated to one another, multicollinearity cannot be invoked to explain the lack of significant multiple correlations. Rather, it appears that each dependent variable was generally related to only one of the independent variables included in this study. (For a full report of these subsidiary analyses, see Samter, 1983.)

3. The partial correlation analysis reported above supports the more general claims made by O'Keefe and Delia (1982, pp 53–55) about the relation between construct system indices and forms of communicative behavior. O'Keefe and Delia note that some writers have suggested that the correlations between construct system measures and indices of communicative behavior are spurious, resulting from the influence of some third variable underlying both social perception and message production. As O'Keefe and Delia argue, there are several reasons for rejecting this sort of objection, including: (1) The relation between social perception and message production is developmental, so any proposed third variable must also change systematically with age—a requirement met by few plausible third variables; (2) There is some evidence indicating that the interpersonal construct system is directly implicated in the message production process; (3) Many plausible underlying third variables (such as Machiavellianism, rhetorical sensitivity, values orientation, and emotional empathy) have been assessed and found to share very little common variance with measures of construct system and message properties (see the studies cited by O'Keefe & Delia, 1982, pp. 54–55). To the set of disconfirmed third variables listed by O'Keefe and Delia, the present study adds two aspects of communication apprehension and locus of control orientation.

REFERENCES

Allen, R. R., & Brown, K. L. (Eds.). (1976). *Developing communicative competence in children.* Skokie, IL: National Textbook.

Applegate, J. L. (1978). *Four investigations of the relationship between social cognitive development and person-centered regulative and interpersonal communication.* Unpublished doctoral dissertation, University of Illinois at Urbana-Champaign.

Applegate, J. L. (1980a). Person- and position-centered teacher communication in a daycare center: A case study triangulating interview and naturalistic methods. In N. K. Denzin (Ed.), *Studies in symbolic interaction* (Vol. 3, pp. 59–96). Greenwich, CT: JAI Press.

Applegate, J. L. (1980b). Adaptive communication in educational contexts: A study of teacher's communicative strategies. *Communication Education, 29,* 150–170.

Applegate, J. L. (1982). The impact of construct system development on communication and impression formation in persuasive contexts. *Communication Monographs, 49,* 277–289.

Applegate, J. L., Burke, J. A., Burleson, B. R., Delia, J. G., & Kline, S. L. (in press). Reflection-enhancing parental communication. In I. E. Sigel (Ed.), *Parents' constructions of child development.* Hillsdale, NJ: Erlbaum.

Applegate, J. L., & Delia, J. G. (1980). Person-centered speech, psychological development and the contexts of language usage. In R. St. Clair & H. Giles (Eds.), *The social and psychological contexts of language* (pp. 245–282). Hillsdale, NJ: Erlbaum.

Aspy, D. N. (1975). Empathy: Let's get the hell on with it. *Counseling Psychologist, 5,* 10–14.

Batson, C. D., Duncan, B., Ackerman, P., Buckley, T., & Birch, K. (1981). Is empathic emotion a source of altruistic motivation? *Journal of Personality and Social Psychology, 40,* 290–302.

Baxter, L. A. (1982). Strategies for ending relationships: Two studies. *Western Journal of Speech Communication, 46,* 223–241.

Borden, A W. (1979). *An investigation of the relationships among indices of social cognition, motivation, and communicative performance.* Unpublished doctoral dissertation, University of Illinois at Urbana-Champaign.

Burgoon, J. K. (1976). The unwillingness-to-communicate scale: Development and validation. *Communication Monographs, 43,* 60–69.

Burleson, B. R. (1982a). The development of comforting communication skills in childhood and adolescence. *Child Development, 53,* 1578–1588.

Burleson, B. R. (1982b). The affective perspective-taking process: A test of Turiel's role-taking model. In M. Burgoon (Ed.), *Communication Yearbook* (Vol. 6, pp. 473–488). Beverly Hills, CA: Sage.

Burleson, B. R. (1983). Social cognition, empathic motivation, and adults' comforting strategies. *Human Communication Research, 10,* 295–304.

Burleson, B. R. (1984a). Comforting communication. In H. E. Sypher & J. L. Applegate (Eds.), *Communication by children and adults: Social cognitive and strategic processes* (pp. 63–104). Beverly Hills, CA: Sage.

Burleson, B. R. (1984b). Age, social-cognitive development, and the use of comforting strategies. *Communication Monographs, 51,* 140–153.

Burleson, B. R. (1985, April). *Communicative correlates of peer acceptance in childhood.* Paper to be presented at the biennial meeting of the Society for Research in Child Development, Toronto.

Burleson, B. R., & Delia, J. G. (1983, April). *Adaptive communication skills in childhood: A unitary construct?* Paper presented at the biennial meeting of the Society for Research in Child Development, Detroit.

Burleson, B. R., & Samter, W. (1983, September). *Social cognitive and personality influences on prosocial behavior: A model of comforting and an empirical test.* Paper presented at the University of Kansas Conference on Social Cognition and Interpersonal Behavior, Lawrence, KS.

Burleson, B. R., & Samter, W. (1984, April). *Consistencies in theoretical and naive evaluations of comforting messages: Two empirical studies.* Paper presented at the annual convention of the Central States Speech Association, Chicago.

Burleson, B. R., & Samter, W. (in press). Individual differences in the perception of comforting messages: An exploratory investigation. *Central States Speech Journal.*

Clark, R. A., & Delia, J. G. (1979). Topoi and rhetorical competence. *Quarterly Journal of Speech, 65,* 187–206.

Cody, M. J. (1982). A typology of disengagement strategies and an examination of the role intimacy, reactions to inequity, and relational problems play in strategy selection. *Communication Monographs, 49,* 148–170.

Cody, M. J., McLaughlin, M. L., & Jordan, W. J. (1980). A multidimensional scaling of three sets of compliance-gaining strategies. *Communication Quarterly, 28,* 34–46.

Cowen, E. L., Pederson, P., Babigian, J., Izzo, L. D., & Trost, M. A. (1973). Long-term follow-up of early detected vulnerable children. *Journal of Consulting and Clinical Psychology, 41,* 438–446.

Crockett, W. H. (1965). Cognitive complexity and impression formation. In B. A. Maher (Ed.), *Progress in experimental personality research* (Vol. 2, pp. 47–90). New York: Academic.

Crockett, W. H., Press, A. N., Delia, J. G., & Kenney, C. J. (1974). *The structural analysis of the organization of written impressions.* Unpublished manuscript, Department of Psychology, University of Kansas.

Delia, J. G. (1976). A constructivist analysis of the concept of credibility. *Quarterly Journal of Speech, 62,* 361–375.

Delia, J. G., & O'Keefe, B. J. (1979). Constructivism: The development of communication. In E. Wartella (Ed.), *Children communicating* (pp. 157–185). Beverly Hills, CA: Sage.

Delia, J. G., O'Keefe, B. J., & O'Keefe, D. J. (1982). The constructivist approach to communication. In F.E.X. Dance (Ed.), *Human communication theory* (pp. 147–191). New York: Harper & Row.

Dlugokinski, E., & Firestone, I. J. (1973). Congruence among four methods of measuring other-centeredness. *Child Development, 44,* 304–308.

Feinberg, H. K. (1977). *Anatomy of a helping situation: Some personality and situational determinants of helping in a conflict situation involving another's psychological distress.* Unpublished doctoral dissertation, University of Massachusetts-Amherst.

Feshback, N. D. (1978). Studies of empathic behavior in children. In B. A. Maher (Ed.), *Progress in experimental personality research* (Vol. 8, pp. 1–47). New York: Academic.

Fincham, F., & Barling, J. (1978). Locus of control and generosity in learning disabled, normal achieving, and gifted children. *Child Development, 49,* 530–533.

Grodman, S. M. (1979). *The role of personality and situational variables in responding to and helping an individual in psychological distress.* Unpublished doctoral dissertation, University of Massachusetts-Amherst.

Heller, K., & Lakey, B. (1984). Perceived support and social interaction among friends and confidants. In T. G. Sarason & B. R. Sarason (Eds.), *Social support: Theory, research, and application.* The Hague: Martinus Nihoff.

Heller, K., & Swindle, R. W. (1983). Social networks, perceived social support, and coping with stress. In R. D. Felner, L. A. Jason, J. Montisugu, & S. Farber (Eds.), *Preventive psychology: Theory, research, and practice in community intervention* (pp. 87–103). New York: Pergamon Press.

Hoffman, M. L. (1977). Sex differences in empathy and related behaviors. *Psychological Bulletin, 84,* 712–722.

Hoffman, M. L. (1981). The development of empathy. In J. P. Rushton & R. M. Sorrentino (Eds.), *Altruism and helping behavior: Social, personality, and developmental perspectives* (pp. 41–63). Hillsdale, NJ: Erlbaum.

Krebs, D. L. (1970). Altruism—An examination of the concept and a review of the literature. *Psychological Bulletin, 73,* 258–303.

Macaulay, J., & Berkowitz, L. (Eds.). (1970). *Altruism and helping behavior.* New York: Academic.

McCroskey, J. C. (1977). Oral communication apprehension: A summary of recent theory and research. *Human Communication Research, 4,* 78–96.

McCroskey, J. C. (1982). Oral communication apprehension: A reconceptualization. In M. Burgoon (Ed.), *Communication Yearbook* (Vol 6, pp. 136–170). Beverly Hills, CA: Sage.

Mehrabian, A., & Epstein, N. (1972). A measure of emotional empathy. *Journal of Personality, 40,* 525–543.

Midlarksy, E. (1971). Aiding under stress: The effects of competence, dependency, visibility, and fatalism. *Journal of Personality, 39,* 132–149.

Mussen, P., & Eisenberg-Berg, N. (1977). *Roots of caring, sharing, and helping: The development of prosocial behavior in children.* San Francisco: W. H. Freeman.

O'Keefe, B. J. (1983, September). *Consequences of differences in interactional goals for interpersonal strategies and interpersonal impressions.* Paper presented at the University of Kansas Conference on Social Cognition and Interpersonal Behavior, Lawrence, KS.

O'Keefe, B. J., & Delia, J. G. (1982). Impression formation and message production. In M. E. Roloff & C. R. Berger (Eds.), *Social cognition and communication* (pp. 33–72). Beverly Hills, CA: Sage.

O'Keefe, D. J., & Sypher, H. E. (1981). Cognitive complexity measures and the relationship of cognitive complexity to communication: A critical review. *Human Communication Research, 8,* 72–92.

Payne, F. D. (1980). Children's prosocial conduct in structured situations and as viewed by others: Consistency, convergence and relationships with person variables. *Child Development, 51,* 1252–1259.

Ritter, E. M. (1979). Social perspective-taking ability, cognitive complexity, and listener-adapted communication in early and late adolescence. *Communication Monographs, 46,* 40–51.

Roff, M., Sells, S. B., & Golden, M. W. (1972). *Social adjustment and personality development in children.* Minneapolis: University of Minnesota Press.

Rotter, J. B. (1966). Generalized expectancies for internal versus external control of reinforcement. *Psychological Monographs, 80,* (Whole No. 609).

Rubin, K. H. (1972). Relationship between egocentric communication and popularity among peers. *Developmental Psychology, 7,* 364.

Rushton, J. P. (1980). *Altruism, socialization, and society.* Englewood Cliffs, NJ: Prentice-Hall.

Samter, W. (1983). *Effects of cognitive and motivational variables on comforting behavior in a quasi-natural situation.* Unpublished masters thesis, Purdue University, West Lafayette, IN.

Staub, E. (1978). *Positive social behavior and morality, Vol. 1: Social and personal influences.* New York: Academic.

Toi, M., & Batson, C. D. (1982). More evidence that empathy is a source of altruistic motivation. *Journal of Personality and Social Psychology, 43,* 281–292.

Truax, C. B., & Carkhuff, R. R. (1967). *Toward effective counseling and psychotherapy: Training and practice.* Chicago: Aldine.

Underwood, B., & Moore, B. S. (1982). The generality of altruism in children. In N. Eisenberg (Ed.), *The development of prosocial behavior* (pp. 25–52). New York: Academic.

Wiseman, R. L., & Schenk-Hamlin, W. (1981). A multidimensional scaling validation of an inductively derived set of compliance-gaining strategies. *Communication Monographs, 48,* 251–270.

SECTION IV

Developmental Processes

CHAPTER 7

Interpersonal Bonding

INTRODUCTION

The readings in this chapter examine communication and relationships from a developmental perspective. That is, they examine how communication changes as relationships develop and/or how communication influences relationships at different stages of development. For example, in the first article, Burgoon and Hale report the results of three studies designed to measure the themes underlying relational messages. Their study examines messages from a variety of different types of relationships: acquaintances, work associates, and parents and their children.

Knapp, Ellis, and Williams analyze how people's perceptions of their communication behavior are influenced by the type of relationship in which they are communicating. The study evaluates the communication behaviors of people engaged in relationships with romantic partners, best friends, friends, pals, colleagues, and acquaintances. Baxter and Bullis provide an analysis of the turning points couples see as influencing the development of their romantic relationships. The authors examine the behaviors and communication that influence increases and decreases in commitment on the part of individuals involved in these relationships.

Finally, Marston, Hecht, and Robers present a study of the communication patterns of romantic partners engaged in different types of love relationships. Each of the studies in this chapter, then, addresses how communication is affected by the type of relationship between the people involved.

VALIDATION AND MEASUREMENT OF THE FUNDAMENTAL THEMES OF RELATIONAL COMMUNICATION

Judee K. Burgoon and Jerold L. Hale

A recently advanced schema for relational communication proposes as many as 12 fundamental and distinctive themes underlying relational message exchange. Reported here are the results of three measurement studies using exploratory oblique and orthogonal factor analyses and confirmatory factor analysis. These offer empirical validation for seven to 10 of the themes. Additionally, results from seven experiments using the relational communication measure provide reliability estimates and predictive validity data. The final recommended measurement instrument is a 30-item scale incorporating eight independent themes or clusters of themes.

Source: The article is taken from *Communication Monographs* [54: 19–41, 1987]. Reprinted by permission of the Speech Communication Association, 5105 Backlick Rd., Annandale, VA 22003.

318

In a theoretical analysis of the fundamental topoi of relational communication, Burgoon and Hale (1984) proposed 12 conceptually distinct but interrelated message themes that are central to defining interpersonal relationships. The schema is grounded in a synthesis of theory and research from such diverse areas as classifications of biological displays, psychological analyses of the dimensions of meaning and person perception, sociological studies of the dimensions of group interaction, and communication analyses of relationship development and definition. The proposed 12 continua along which relational partners are presumed to exchange interpersonal messages and to define their relationship are: (1) dominance–submission, (2) emotional arousal, (3) composure–noncomposure, (4) similarity–dissimilarity, (5) formality–informality, (6) task vs. social orientation, (7) intimacy, and the subcomponents of intimacy, (8) depth (or familiarity), (9) affection (attraction and liking), (10) inclusion–exclusion, (11) trust, and (12) intensity of involvement.

Although much of the literature supporting the schema came from empirical investigations—for instance, factor analytic and content analytic studies of the dimensions of emotional expressions, credibility, and relationship descriptors—it is important that the final proposed set of dimensions itself be subjected to empirical verification. Reported here are the results of three studies designed to validate the schema and produce a reliable measurement instrument. Additionally, reliability and validity data from seven studies employing the relational communication instrument are presented.

STUDY 1

This multipurpose study had five goals: (1) to assess the interrelatedness of the 12 topoi, (2) to create a reliable and valid measurement instrument for self-report and observational use in interactional studies of relational communication, (3) to determine the ability of the different message themes to discriminate different interaction conditions, (4) to test a model of violations of expectations, and (5) to examine the relationship between communication reticence and nonverbal and relational communication. Of primary interest here are the first three goals. The experimental manipulations designed for those purposes, however, permitted evaluation of the extent to which the relational topoi reported by participants and observers corresponded to the actual manipulated changes in the interactional circumstances and thus supply the first validity data from the relational communication measure.

Instrument Development

The relational communication scale was developed by examining all the measurement instruments used in a wide range of prior research and culling from them concepts and wording applicable to relational communication. New items were then created for nonrepresented topoi so that there were at least two items per theme. To inhibit response bias, attempts were made to create both positively and negatively worded items. Graduate students from a seminar in relational communication then contributed additional items representative of ''statements'' relational partners could make to one another. The resultant pool of 32 items was cast in Likert format with a range of one (strongly agree) to seven (strongly disagree).

Two versions were produced, one for use by respondents and one for use by observers. Respondents were instructed to indicate what types of messages, verbal and nonverbal, they thought the other person had communicated to them during the interaction, e.g., ''He/she was interested in talking to me.'' Observers were asked to watch one participant and to rate what messages, verbal and nonverbal, they thought the target person had communicated to his or her partner. Wording was modified accordingly, e.g., ''He/she was interested in talking to the other person.''

Respondents

Respondents were undergraduate students recruited from communication courses at a large Midwestern university, and their friends. Most participated in two dyadic interactions, one with a friend and one with a stranger, for a total of 202 cases. Participation was voluntary and earned course credit.

Procedures

Each respondent reported to the experiment with a friend. Pairs were separated to complete communication reticence scales (Personal Report of Communication Apprehension and the Unwillingness-to-Communicate Scale). Respondents were then instructed that they would be discussing two of four possible topics dealing with social or moral problems and would be expected to arrive at a consensus on a recommended course of action. Respondents discussed one topic with their friend and one with a stranger, with the order of interactions counterbalanced and the four possible topics evenly distributed across dyads.

Out of each pair, one student was designated a ''confederate.'' In a third of the conditions, the confederate was instructed to increase nonverbal immediacy by moving closer, leaning forward, facing the partner directly, increasing eye contact, and maintaining an open posture. In another third, the confederate was instructed to reduce nonverbal immediacy by moving farther away, leaning back, reducing eye contact, and adopting a closed posture and indirect orientation. In both of these conditions, training and practice were provided. In the remaining third, the confederate was instructed to maintain as natural a communication style as possible.

All discussions were videotaped and lasted no more than nine minutes. Following the discussion, respondents completed the 32 relational message scales, plus other measures related to the violations hypotheses. Following both interactions, respondents were debriefed.

Videotapes were rated at a later time by untrained observers who watched either the confederate or naive respondent and rated his or her relational communication toward the dyad partner. Each observer rated two different interactions.

Results

Two types of factor analysis were completed on participants' ratings. The first, a principal components oblique solution with varimax rotation, was undertaken to assess the multidimensionality of relational communication themes. It produced eight factors with eigenvalues greater than 1.0 and at least two items per factor with loadings of .50 or better. The solution accounted for 58% of the variance. Based on an entering assumption of moderate correlation among factors (delta = 0), the eight resulting factors had small or no correlations with one another. Factor VIII had modest correlations with Factors I, VII and VI ($r = .25$, $r = .25$ and $r = .23$, respectively). Factor VII also correlated weakly with Factor III ($r = .22$) and Factor I correlated weakly with Factor VI ($r = .21$). The remaining correlations were less than .20.

STATISTICAL SUMMARY 1

Studies 1 and 2

Factor analysis is a method for grouping variables together into a smaller number of categories. If you have a large number of variables you may want to see if two or more of them actually combine or work together. Burgoon and Hale used factor analysis to see if there was any commonality or groupings among the items. The initial analyses revealed eight factors (similarity/receptivity/inclusion, dominance, task vs. social orientation, nonimmediacy (distance), honesty, intimacy, arousal/intensity of involvement, formality). Follow-up analysis suggested these may be reduced to four ultimate factors or groups of items: dominance, nonimmediacy, intimacy, and arousal/intensity of involvement/inclusion.

The factor structure and item means and standard deviations appear in Table 1. Although factors are labeled using only one end of the message continuum, it should be stressed that

TABLE 1
Oblique Factor Structure, Means, and Standard Deviations: 32-Item Measure

Factors and items	Mean[1]	Standard deviation	Factor Loadings							
			I	II	III	IV	V	VI	VII	VIII
I. SIMILARITY/RECEPTIVITY/INCLUSION										
He/she was different than me.	4.12	1.91	−.67	.12	.13	.18	.16	.39	.07	−.22
He/she tried to establish good relations (rapport).	2.37	1.48	.56	.13	−.48	−.32	−.13	−.28	−.39	.49
He/she emphasized agreement between us.	3.07	1.74	.54	−.17	−.30	−.19	−.21	−.11	−.01	.41
He/she was willing to listen to me.	1.84	1.23	.49	−.14	−.26	−.18	−.46	−.17	−.37	.24
He/she wanted the discussion to be casual.	2.85	1.70	.39	−.04	−.24	−.25	−.18	−.25	−.37	.29
II. DOMINANCE										
He/she attempted to persuade me.	4.70	1.81	−.20	.71	−.02	−.07	.14	−.14	.16	.01
He/she was competitive.	4.51	1.82	.04	.66	−.05	.20	.11	−.01	−.13	−.23
He/she tried to win my approval.	3.92	1.64	.09	.64	−.14	−.23	−.02	−.15	−.02	.01
He/she wanted to dominate the conversation.	4.97	1.86	.04	.61	.10	.30	.05	.33	−.09	.01
He/she communicated aggressiveness.	4.43	1.87	−.05	.58	−.11	−.18	−.04	−.10	−.35	.06
III. TASK VS. SOCIAL ORIENTATION										
He/she was sincere.	2.15	1.44	.21	−.06	−.64	−.19	−.20	−.26	−.06	.40
He/she was very work-oriented.	3.71	1.61	.01	.32	−.60	.13	.03	.03	−.07	−.23
He/she wanted to appear reasonable.	2.13	1.27	.32	.11	−.58	−.10	.21	−.06	−.36	.14
He/she was more interested in a social conversation than the task at hand.	5.09	1.99	.46	.05	.56	.05	.31	−.05	.06	.07
He/she felt hostile toward the other person.	6.17	1.27	−.28	.20	.47	−.22	.33	.34	.35	−.37
IV. NONIMMEDIACY (DISTANCE)										
He/she was very unemotional.	4.68	1.74	−.21	−.02	−.09	.70	.10	.14	.14	−.15
He/she created a sense of distance between us.	5.50	1.77	−.24	.00	.15	.55	.06	.16	.42	−.40
He/she seemed to have higher status than me.	5.73	1.35	.05	.24	.16	.45	.40	.23	.30	−.39
V. HONESTY										
He/she was not honest in communicating with me.	5.78	1.81	−.11	−.17	.08	.06	.73	−.05	.24	−.05

(Continued)

Table 1—*Continued*

Factors and items	Mean[1]	Standard deviation	Factor Loadings							
			I	II	III	IV	V	VI	VII	VIII
VI. INTIMACY (DEPTH, AFFECTION, TRUST, INCLUSION)										
He/she didn't care if I liked him/her.	4.85	1.75	−.10	.10	.01	.01	.00	.77	.10	−.27
He/she wanted me to trust him/her.	2.79	1.39	.32	.27	−.21	−.22	−.05	−.66	−.28	.24
He/she expressed attraction toward me.	4.03	1.76	.28	.34	−.08	−.16	.23	−.65	−.35	.13
He/she seemed to desire further communication with me.	3.36	1.91	.38	.22	−.16	−.22	−.13	−.63	−.29	.32
He/she made the conversation seem intimate.	3.94	1.97	.23	.16	−.21	−.25	.24	−.51	−.43	.28
He/she considered us equals.	2.31	1.53	.30	−.23	−.18	−.12	−.54	−.55	−.12	.26
He/she felt very relaxed talking with me.	2.50	1.73	.48	.21	−.12	−.27	−.23	−.52	−.49	.30
VII. AROUSAL/INTENSITY OF INVOLVEMENT										
He/she acted bored by the conversation.	5.13	1.75	.01	−.05	.26	.24	.17	.34	.69	−.16
He/she made the conversation seem superficial.	4.85	1.83	−.21	−.07	.13	.13	.20	.15	.60	−.32
He/she was frustrated with the other person.	5.70	1.64	−.29	.26	.27	−.36	.19	.23	.56	−.37
VIII. FORMALITY										
He/she made the interaction very formal.	5.30	1.80	−.19	.04	.04	.12	.06	.16	.25	−.79
He/she was willing to self-disclose personal thoughts to me.	2.91	1.88	.21	.10	−.12	−.14	−.07	−.33	−.13	.67
He/she was unresponsive to my ideas.	5.68	1.47	−.15	.29	.42	.21	.02	−.02	.38	−.44
Cumulative percent of variance accounted for by each factor			22%	33%	39%	43%	47%	51%	55%	58%

1. Based on a scale from 1 (strongly agree) to 7 (strongly disagree)

each of these dimensions does, in fact, represent a continuum—e.g., dominant to submissive—rather than a category. The majority of the theorized topoi emerged in predicted configurations. As anticipated, *Dominance* is a highly independent theme (Factor II) composed of such elements as competitiveness, aggressiveness, ingratiation, and persuasive intent as well as dominance per se. Also as anticipated, several subthemes come together to form the broad theme of *Intimacy (Depth, Affection, Trust)* (Factor VI). Messages related to trust, liking, attraction, depth, and equality all loaded on this factor. Somewhat correlated with this factor is the *Similarity/Receptivity (Inclusion)* theme (Factor I). Its relatedness to the intimacy factor is probably due to the affiliative implications of its component messages, which entail emphasizing agreement, lack of difference, rapport, and willingness to listen (at the similar/receptive end of the message continuum). The label "receptivity" has been introduced because it seems to be a more apt descriptor than its equivalent concept of inclusion.

Another relatively independent dimension is *Task vs. Social Orientation* (Factor III). Messages at the task end of the continuum include being work-oriented, sincere, nonhostile, reasonable, and not being more interested in the social situation than the task. This cooperative angle to the work end of the continuum may have been induced partly by the nature of the experimental task. To show a greater social orientation might have been seen as negative behavior signaling a flippant attitude toward the experiment.

The *Formality* theme (Factor VIII) is somewhat less independent. Like the similarity and intimacy message clusters, it, too, has inclusion implications. An informal demeanor corresponds to being responsive and disclosive. These elements, which also signal involvement, account for the modest correlation with Factor VII.

The unexpected pattern in the factor analysis is the emergence of two separate factors related to involvement and immediacy. The first (Factor IV) has been labeled *Nonimmediacy (Distance)* because it is primarily concerned with creating a sense of distance emotionally, socially, and psychologically. The second (Factor VII) has been labeled *Involvement/Arousal* because of the activation connotations of the frustration item. However, it should be noted that the distance item has a strong secondary loading on this factor, indicating that the two factors are indeed related.

One other anomaly is the emergence of *Honesty* (Factor V) as a separate factor. The item with the highest loading on this factor had been expected to load with intimacy but failed to do so and failed to show a relationship with any other factor. Instead, the item, "He/she considered us equals," loaded strongly on this factor (but had its primary loading on the intimacy factor).

Finally, *Composure* failed to emerge as a separate factor. However, items tapping it appear on three different factors that conceptually could relate to being relaxed and at ease: similarity, intimacy, and involvement/arousal. Thus, it may still be a distinguishable theme that is more interrelated with the other relational communication themes than most.

To produce a reliable and efficient measurement instrument, orthogonal factor analyses with varimax rotation were conducted. The goal was to identify the minimum number of independent message clusters needed to represent the range of relational communication themes. Because interpersonal communication research frequently entails the use of multiple dependent measures, it is useful for statistical purposes to reduce a set of correlated dimensions to a small number of uncorrelated ones.

Criteria for selecting a factor solution were as follows: (1) all factors had to have eigenvalues of 1.0 or better; (2) the Scree test had to indicate reasonable incremental improvement in variance accounted for by the addition of a given factor; (3) all retained factors had to contain at least three items with primary loadings of .50 or better and secondary loadings below .30 for those items; (4) all items retained had to have a primary loading of .50 or better; and (5) among solutions meeting the first three criteria, the one accounting for the most variance was to be selected.

An initial rotated solution produced four factors. Items with low communalities and low primary loadings were dropped from subsequent analyses. The final and best solution retained 20 items in four factors and accounted for 51% of the variance.

The dimensions and items that were retained were:

I: *Intimacy* (didn't care if I liked him/her, expressed attraction toward me, wanted me to trust him/her, seemed to desire further communication with me, felt very relaxed talking to me, made our conversation seem intimate, considered us equals);

II: *Involvement/Arousal/Inclusion* (felt hostile toward me, was frustrated with me, was sincere, tried to establish good relations between us, was unresponsive to my ideas, wanted to appear reasonable);

III: *Dominance* (was competitive, attempted to persuade me, tried to win my approval, communicated aggressiveness, wanted to dominate the conversation);

IV: *Nonimmediacy* (was very unemotional, created a sense of distance between us).

Coefficient alpha reliabilities computed on these four dimensions produced the following: $r = .81$ for intimacy, $r = .72$ for involvement/arousal/inclusion, $r = .69$ for dominance, and $r = .46$ for nonimmediacy. The somewhat low reliabilities for the latter two dimensions presaged a need to increase the number of items measuring each.

STATISTICAL SUMMARY 2

Reliability tells you how accurately and consistently you have measured something. If a measure is highly reliable then you can be confident that the scores are very accurate, and that the items or indicators that are part of the measure are consistent with each other or consistent over time. Some of the measures in this study were not very accurate or consistent.

To determine the ability of the relational message themes to distinguish different interaction conditions, analyses of variance were completed on the three immediacy conditions for each of the four orthogonal message clusters. It was expected that as the violator's nonverbal immediacy increased, respondents would perceive the violator's relational communication to show (1) increased intimacy, (2) increased inclusiveness and responsiveness (or decreased negative arousal), and (3) decreased detachment (i.e., increased immediacy). We further speculated that both increases and decreases in nonverbal immediacy

would be perceived as more dominant than would observing the normative interaction pattern. Finally, we expected that violations would cause victims to alter their own relational communication and that observers would be able to detect such differences, if the relational measure were valid.

The immediacy violations results, part of which are reported in Hale and Burgoon (1984) and the remainder of which will be reported in more detail elsewhere, produced the following significant findings, all consistent with predictions: (1) as the violator's nonverbal behavior became more immediate, respondents rated the violator as more intimate, $F(2,38) = 3.50, p < .05$; (2) as the violator's manipulated immediacy increased, respondents rated the violator as less detached, $F(2,38) = 4.38, p < .01$; (3) violations in either direction (becoming more or less immediate) were perceived by respondents as more dominant than maintaining the normative pattern, $F(2,38) = 3.91, p < .05$; (4) observers rated respondents as more intimate in the close than the norm and far conditions, $F(2/38) = 4.18, p < .05$; (5) observers rated respondents as most involved, inclusive, and nonaroused in the high immediacy condition and least so in the low immediacy condition, $F(2,38) = 8.35, p < .01$; and (6) respondents were rated as the most dominant in the high immediacy condition, followed by the low immediacy condition, $F(2,38) = 3.86, p < .05$. These results demonstrate that both participants and observers were able to use the relational message scales to reliably discriminate among interaction conditions.

The communication reticence results, which are reported in Burgoon and Koper (1984), showed that strangers rated reticent communicators as more emotionally aroused and uncomposed (UCS-AA $r = .35, p < .05$; UCS-R $r = .36, p < .05$), as more nonimmediate (PRCA $r = .27, p < .05$), as less dominant (PRCA $r = -.40, p < .05$; UCS-AA $r = -.26, p < .10$), and less intimate and similar (PRCA $r = -.30, p < .05$; UCS-AA $r = -.44, p < .01$), while friends rated reticent communicators as more composed and unaroused (UCS-AA $r = -.25$,

$p < .10$) and more intimate and similar (UCS-AA $r = .27$, $p < .10$) but also less immediate (UCS-R $r = .57$, $p < .01$). These results indicate that friends and strangers were able to use the relational communication scales to evaluate differentially the communication of their interaction partners and the scales produced different results across the different dimensions of reticence.

Supplementary Research

Two other experiments using the 32-item version of the relational messages scale were conducted by Burgoon, Buller, Hale, and de Turck (1984) and Buller (1984). In the former, the scales were used by observers to rate the perceived meaning of five different nonverbal immediacy behaviors, distance, gaze, touch, body lean, and smiling, as they were varied by two interactants appearing on videotape. Reliabilities for the scales were .86 for intimacy, .79 for nonimmediacy, .76 for involvement/arousal/inclusion, and .60 for dominance. All four sets of message scales significantly differentiated between high and low amounts of nonverbal immediacy on two or more of the dependent variables.

In his dissertation testing the effects of vocalic cues in a persuasive interaction, Buller (1984) used a 24-item abbreviated version of the scale in follow-up interviews with 177 respondents who rated one of 10 interviewers who had just completed a telephone interview with them. Coefficient alpha reliabilities for the four subscales were: .70 for intimacy, .74 for nonimmediacy, .71 for involvement/arousal, and .76 for dominance. All four dimensions: (1) significantly differentiated a hostile voice condition from pleasant and neutral voice conditions, (2) correlated with three or more dimensions of credibility, and (3) correlated with one or more personality attributes of the respondents.

Discussion

The findings from the first study provided empirical support for the multidimensionality of the relational communication construct and the specific topoi proposed by Burgoon and Hale (1984). The

obtained measurement dimensions largely conformed to the conceptual ones, demonstrating that dyadic interactants do distinguish multiple themes in the relational communication of their partners. Moreover, the experimental findings and those from the supplementary investigations supported the internal reliability and predictive validity of the measurement instrument that was created.

There were, however, some shortcomings. That some proposed dimensions failed to emerge or to emerge as distinct entities raised the possibility that the pool of scale items was too small to permit their emergence or that the nature of the particular communication context constrained some facets of relational communication (e.g., formality), thereby influencing their position in the factor structure. Second, in retrospect, the 32 items that were generated did not seem to reflect adequately the full range of positively and negatively valenced relational message themes. This may have limited the breadth of the individual subscales and may have affected the factoring such that only positively worded items loaded on a particular factor. It was therefore deemed necessary to increase the number and mix of positively and negatively worded scale items and to replicate use of the scales in less constrained contexts. Additionally, it was important to verify the stability of the topoi dimensions with a new sample. Hence, the second study was undertaken.

STUDY 2

Respondents

Respondents ($N = 300$) were undergraduates enrolled in communication courses at a large Midwestern university, who participated voluntarily.

Procedure

Respondents were asked to recall the last dyadic conversation they had participated in that lasted at least 15 minutes. They were asked to record the nature of their relationship with the interactant—e.g., parent, friend, acquaintance, work associate, supervisor—and to complete relational message scales on their partner's communication *during that interchange*. The instructions specifically asked respondents to indicate what types of messages, verbal and nonverbal, they thought the other person had communicated to them during the interaction.

Relational Messages Measure

The previous measure was expanded to 68 items. A primary goal in creating the new items was to represent each theme by both positively and negatively worded items. This would permit determination of whether a message's actual content or its degree of positivity was controlling its factoring; it would give some themes a better opportunity to emerge as separate dimensions, and it would increase the pool of available items to be used in constructing a measurement instrument. A second goal arose out of an earlier conceptual question about the unidimensionality of some message continua, such as task–social orientation and dominance–equality–submission.

Such dimensions may actually be two dimensions, not one; i.e., one may judge the degree to which someone is or is not task oriented and make a separate judgment about his or her sociability. Similarly, the concept of equality may not be the same as the absence of dominance or submission. Accordingly, new items were introduced to allow for this possibility. In all, the new scale contained the original 32 items plus 32 items reflecting their polar opposites and four new items.

Results

As in Study 1, the data were analyzed through oblique and principal components factor analyses with varimax rotation. The oblique analysis produced nine factors containing three or more items with primary loadings of .50 or better and accounting for 59% of the variance. The factor structure, displayed in Table 2, brings into sharper focus the factors that appeared in Study One.

TABLE 2
Oblique Factor Structure, Means, and Standard Deviations: 68-Item Measure

Factors and items	Mean	Standard deviation	I	II	III	IV	V	VI	VII	VIII	IX
I. RECEPTIVITY/INCLUSION/TRUST											
He/she tried to establish good relations (rapport) between us.	1.96	1.20	−.67	.02	−.19	.14	.18	−.32	−.27	.31	.47
He/she wanted to appear reasonable.	2.29	1.28	−.65	−.01	−.09	−.23	−.05	−.22	−.17	.15	.22
He/she was unresponsive to my ideas.	5.81	1.26	.64	.09	.46	.14	−.31	.30	.40	−.33	−.28
He/she was willing to listen to me.	1.78	1.12	−.63	.08	−.39	−.09	.15	−.24	−.28	.33	.42
He/she was open to my ideas.	2.30	1.37	−.63	−.24	−.46	−.04	.33	−.35	−.32	.30	.29
He/she was cooperative.	2.25	1.38	−.61	−.29	−.32	−.02	.22	−.37	−.27	.34	.22
He/she emphasized agreement between us.	2.78	1.51	−.60	.01	−.21	−.06	.31	−.22	−.06	.23	.27
He/she wanted me to trust him/her.	1.82	1.07	−.56	.20	−.04	−.21	.13	−.14	−.30	.40	.55
He/she was interested in talking with me.	1.63	.99	−.52	−.07	−.24	−.26	.38	−.34	−.46	.34	.50
He/she was sincere.	1.85	1.05	−.50	−.03	−.11	−.24	.11	−.17	−.45	.33	.39
He/she communicated coldness rather than warmth.	6.25	1.17	.50	.13	.34	.29	−.21	.43	.44	−.29	−.36

Factors and items	Mean	Standard deviation	I	II	III	IV	V	VI	VII	VIII	IX
He/she expressed anger toward me.	6.07	1.38	.49	.34	.17	−.18	−.38	.44	.46	−.38	−.11
He/she was not willing to listen to me.	6.11	1.46	.45	.25	.32	.19	−.15	.29	.40	−.22	−.25
He/she tried to show he/she was similar to me.	3.26	1.86	−.45	.07	−.11	.04	.38	−.13	.20	.14	.18
II. PERSUASION/INGRATIATION											
He/she didn't try to win my favor.	4.11	1.77	−.02	−.73	−.07	−.04	.05	.10	−.16	.06	−.15
He/she didn't attempt to influence me.	4.15	1.79	−.07	−.71	−.09	.09	−.03	−.17	.14	.01	.02
He/she attempted to persuade me.	3.87	1.76	.03	.71	.35	−.16	−.10	.10	.04	−.08	.09
He/she tried to win my approval.	3.36	1.59	−.16	.54	.31	−.07	−.12	.10	.19	−.18	.19
III. DOMINANCE/SIMILARITY											
He/she wanted to dominate the conversation.	5.06	1.72	.23	.39	.74	−.12	−.09	.14	.14	−.04	−.18
He/she tried to control the interaction.	4.74	1.74	.16	.34	.71	−.14	−.23	.19	.12	.01	−.10
He/she was competitive.	4.53	1.81	.13	.26	.57	.05	.05	.16	.20	−.28	−.07
He/she seemed to have higher status than me.	5.77	1.48	.20	.01	.52	.23	−.26	.06	.02	−.31	.01
He/she didn't treat me as an equal.	6.16	1.35	.40	.12	.51	.19	−.27	.17	.26	−.43	−.02
He/she communicated aggressiveness.	4.83	1.76	.20	.27	.47	−.25	−.08	.16	.22	−.32	−.15
He/she was very work-oriented.	4.50	1.88	−.23	−.12	.42	.10	−.35	.18	.01	−.06	−.11
He/she avoided dominating the conversation.	3.55	1.67	−.18	−.03	−.40	.27	.06	−.13	.22	.05	.11
He/she was different than me.	4.23	1.81	.27	.14	.35	.12	−.32	.12	.04	−.13	−.23
He/she was very passive.	4.86	1.69	−.08	.03	−.27	.21	.21	.19	.18	.08	−.11
IV. AROUSAL/INTENSITY OF INVOLVEMENT											
He/she was intensely involved in our conversation.	2.32	1.28	−.30	.11	.00	−.69	.14	−.08	−.28	.11	.25
He/she was not very emotional around me.	3.98	1.78	.03	.19	.12	−.60	−.12	.06	.18	.09	.26
He/she was very unemotional.	5.24	1.61	.18	.04	.04	.55	.13	.33	−.04	−.24	−.24
He/she was bored by our conversation.	6.25	1.14	.34	.05	.19	.47	−.22	.38	.32	−.11	−.14
He/she tried to move the conversation to a deeper level.	3.61	1.77	−.06	.29	−.09	−.38	.08	.02	−.19	.18	.37

(Continued)

Table 2—*Continued*

Factors and items	Mean	Standard deviation	I	II	III	IV	V	VI	VII	VIII	IX
V. TASK VS. SOCIAL ORIENTATION											
He/she was more interested in a social conversation than the task at hand.	3.93	2.09	.01	−.03	−.06	.07	.67	−.17	−.04	.07	−.04
He/she was more interested in working on the task at hand than having a social conversation.	5.00	2.02	.08	.13	.26	.02	−.65	.35	.30	−.11	.00
He/she was very socially oriented.	2.69	1.53	−.40	−.24	−.02	−.13	.55	−.33	−.10	.11	.13
VI. FORMALITY											
He/she made the interaction very formal.	6.23	1.26	.08	.08	.15	.11	−.08	.75	.16	−.18	−.04
He/she wanted the discussion to be informal.	6.19	1.24	.14	.07	.06	.10	−.24	.70	.15	−.10	−.12
He/she tried to make the interaction informal.	2.09	1.39	−.17	−.08	.06	.06	.26	−.60	−.06	.28	.22
He/she wanted the discussion to be casual.	2.15	1.42	−.24	−.10	−.15	.22	.21	−.53	−.16	.09	.05
He/she was frustrated with me.	5.67	1.67	.46	.33	.23	−.18	−.33	.47	.47	−.47	−.07
He/she emphasized disagreement between us.	5.37	1.79	.30	.37	−.01	−.23	−.25	.44	.37	−.36	.00
He/she seemed to have lower status than me.	5.82	1.52	.25	−.07	.17	.16	−.10	.33	.18	−.32	.02
VII. NONIMMEDIACY (DISTANCE)											
He/she indicated no desire for further conversation with me.	6.13	1.48	.14	.01	.07	.16	−.24	.28	.59	−.18	−.25
He/she felt very tense talking with me.	5.97	1.64	.33	.11	.07	−.03	−.27	.22	.55	−.45	.05
He/she created a sense of distance between us.	6.11	1.25	.46	.11	.29	.15	−.25	.44	.55	−.42	−.14
He/she felt hostile toward me.	6.21	1.24	.48	.26	.17	−.12	−.24	.44	.54	−.46	−.21
He/she made the conversation seem superficial.	5.74	1.39	.19	.07	.33	.32	−.01	.20	.49	−.33	−.25
He/she made our conversation seem distant.	6.12	1.17	.41	−.01	.33	.36	−.28	.33	.49	−.08	−.20
He/she was willing to appear unreasonable.	5.28	1.88	.33	.21	.16	−.13	−.13	.33	.48	−.15	−.17
He/she showed no hostility toward me.	2.07	1.67	−.28	−.21	.01	.17	.19	−.28	−.41	.38	.25
VIII. COMPOSURE											
He/she was comfortable interacting with me.	1.62	1.13	−.27	.01	−.04	.05	.41	−.39	−.24	.68	.29
He/she felt very relaxed talking with me.	1.71	1.19	−.38	−.18	−.09	−.05	.46	−.27	−.37	.66	.25
He/she was unwilling to self-disclose personal information and feelings to me.	4.94	2.30	.01	.07	.07	.06	.12	.07	.01	−.56	−.12

Factors and items	Mean	Standard deviation	I	II	III	IV	V	VI	VII	VIII	IX
He/she considered us equals.	2.10	1.36	−.48	.07	−.40	−.25	.36	−.16	−.21	.54	.04
He/she was honest in communicating.	1.71	1.05	−.51	−.13	−.29	−.26	.10	−.28	−.47	.52	.31
He/she was not honest in communication.	6.02	1.62	.36	.01	.13	.20	.02	.29	.31	−.36	−.18
He/she appeared insincere.	5.97	1.66	.21	.02	−.08	.18	−.15	.24	.27	−.29	−.13
IX. INTIMACY (AFFECTION, DEPTH, INCLUSION, TRUST)											
He/she was not attracted to me.	5.41	1.66	.07	−.07	.08	.15	.07	.15	.14	−.08	−.73
He/she expressed attraction toward me.	2.67	1.56	−.21	.07	−.04	−.12	.03	−.05	.08	.08	.73
He/she didn't care if I liked him/her.	6.05	1.27	.38	−.16	.25	.10	.06	.17	.31	−.22	−.59
He/she made our conversations seem intimate.	2.84	1.76	−.29	.10	−.11	−.40	.15	.04	−.18	.27	.58
He/she seemed to care if I liked him/her.	2.25	1.50	−.22	.21	−.22	.04	.11	−.22	−.03	.34	.57
He/she seemed to like me.	1.73	1.04	−.52	−.05	−.13	−.24	.26	−.21	−.39	.33	.55
He/she created a sense of closeness between us.	2.18	1.39	−.53	−.01	−.20	−.28	.21	−.29	−.40	.41	.54
He/she seemed to desire further communication with me.	2.11	1.38	−.38	.06	−.06	−.29	.31	−.17	−.49	.14	.53
He/she was willing to self-disclose personal thoughts to me.	1.94	1.27	−.29	−.03	−.07	−.41	.14	−.20	−.25	.32	.49
He/she didn't care if I trusted him/her.	6.11	1.36	.22	−.08	.27	.20	.08	.31	.37	−.19	−.39
Cumulative percent of variance accounted for by each factor			22%	35%	41%	46%	49%	52%	55%	57%	59%

The first, *Receptivity/Inclusion/Trust,* replicates and amplifies a factor found in the previous study. It combines the intimacy components of inclusion and trust. Because of its emphasis on rapport, openness and sincerity, it again carries a strong connotation of receptivity. It also contains some aspects of similarity, as occurred in Study 1, but similarity does not load exclusively on this factor.

The second and third factors, *Persuasion/Ingratiation* and *Dominance/Similarity,* reveal that the previous dominance dimension is actually composed of two facets, one that includes more socially acceptable and favor-seeking behavior and one that includes more direct control of another. The remaining similarity items fit on the dominance dimension, with expressions of dissimilarity corresponding to the exercise of control.

The fourth dimension, *Arousal/Intensity of Involvement,* duplicates and expands one by the same name in the first study. It includes the level of emotional activation and degree of involvement or boredom that is expressed. Thus, these two activity dimensions continue to be seen as related.

The fifth and sixth dimensions, *Task vs. Social Orientation* and *Formality,* also repeat ones by the same names in the previous study but now narrow the dimensions down exclusively to work versus social orientation and degree of formality or casualness that the partner introduces into the interaction.

The seventh factor, *Nonimmediacy,* like its predecessor entails the degree of distancing, psychologically and socially, that the partner generates. Distance carries with it some degree of negative affect, but it is clear that the degree of immediacy can be separated in the respondent's mind from the amount of attraction and liking that is fostered.

The eighth factor, *Composure,* is also new and is one proposed in the original schema. Its elements of comfort, relaxation, disclosiveness, and equality indicate that one can communicate a level of poise that is separate from one's involvement and arousal.

The final factor, *Intimacy,* brings together most of the proposed subcomponents of intimacy, namely, attraction, liking, depth, trust, and inclusion. Its distinction from the first factor is that it is more centered on the liking theme, but the two do overlap.

The orthogonal solution again produced as the best solution four factors accounting for 58% of the variance (when reduced to the 28 items maintaining primary loadings of at least .50). The four factors were as follows:

I: *Arousal/Composure/Formality/Task Orientation* (combining most of the same elements appearing on those factors in the oblique solution);

II: *Intimacy/Similarity* (combining the inclusion and intimacy factors from the oblique solution);

III: *Nonimmediacy* (essentially the same as in the oblique solution but with some of the involvement items);

IV: *Dominance* (combining dominance and persuasion/ingratiation).

These factors can be seen to preserve most of the hypothesized themes but to cluster them in four interrelated groupings. The first factor captures the sense of activity and activation, positive or negative, that is present in a partner's communication, with formality and task orientation conveying less activity and animation. The second cluster reveals the relatedness of similarity themes to the communication of liking, trust, receptivity, and familiarity. The third factor again underscores the distinction that is made between closeness or distance as a signal of attraction and liking and closeness or distance as a signal of engagement and involvement. The fourth factor reaffirms the independence of the dominance theme.

Supplementary Research

Two experiments employed the 68-item version of the relational messages scale. Burgoon, Manusov, Mineo, and Hale (1985) tested the effects of eye contact violations on hiring, credibility, attraction, and perceived relational communication of a job applicant. The reliabilities they obtained for the four orthogonal factors were: .74 for arousal/composure/formality, .86 for intimacy/similarity, .83 for nonimmediacy, and .76 for dominance. High degrees of gaze were found to communicate increased composure and informality, increased intimacy and similarity, and increased immediacy compared to gaze aversion. In a modified replication of that experiment, Manusov (1984) obtained reliabilities of .70 for arousal/composure/formality, .77 for intimacy/similarity, .78 for nonimmediacy, and .68 for dominance. Her tests of hypotheses produced significant effects for only two of the relational communication dimensions: (1) more "rewarding" interviewees were seen as communicating more composure, less formality, and less negative arousal; and (2) interviewees using high amounts of eye contact were seen as expressing more immediacy than those engaging in gaze aversion.

Discussion

The present round of results was encouraging. It demonstrated stability in the use of the scales when applied to new contexts; it showed them to attain respectable (though not optimally desirable) levels of reliability, and it reinforced the predictive validity of the scales. Before final conclusions were drawn, however, about the theoretical dimensions of relational communication and the viability of the measurement instrument that had been created, one further study was undertaken. Its aims were to improve the reliability of the scales further, to refine the wording, to design a more manageable instrument in terms of length, and to discern the independent dimensions obtainable from the revised instrument. The third scale revision and analysis were completed as part of a larger experiment, which itself provided yet another test of the predictive validity of the instrument.

STUDY 3

Relational Messages Scale

The 68-item scale was modified in two ways. Because the previous versions of the scale had only included negative forms of arousal such as hostility and frustration, some new items intended to measure positive forms of arousal were added. In addition to creating a more balanced instrument, it was thought that their inclusion might alter the factoring. Second, to reduce the pool of items to a more efficient and reliable set of subscales, those items that had failed to load consistently on any factors and that had low communalities were eliminated. This resulted in a temporary pool of 60 items that was to be further reduced through factor analysis and reliability analysis.

Respondents

Respondents were 145 undergraduate communication students at a large Southwestern university whose participation earned class credit.

Procedure

The experiment in which the revised measurement instrument was used was a modified replication of Burgoon et al. (1985) and Manusov (1984). Respondents served as interviewers in a simulated interview with confederate interviewees who were assigned one of two levels of reward and who manipulated one of three levels of gaze (see Burgoon, Coker & Coker, in press, for more detail).

Upon completion of the interview, respondents were asked to evaluate the interviewer and indicate their willingness to hire him or her. As part of that evaluation, respondents completed the 60-item relational messages measure. Once again, the six different experimental conditions ensured that the relational messages scale would be responded to under a variety of conditions, thereby permitting assessment of the discriminability of the subscales.

Results

The 60 items were initially subjected to oblique factor analysis. Although it was recognized that the small sample size made such an analysis less stable and potentially misleading, it was considered a necessary first step in reducing the pool of items to half by eliminating those with weak loadings or communalities. It also had the potential of further demonstrating the stability of the previously obtained factor structures with a new sample.

A number of oblique solutions were interpretable and met minimal criteria. The best solution appeared to be 10 factors that accounted for 57% of the variance. The factors preserved essentially the same factor structure as that obtained in the previous studies, with the addition of an equality factor (see Table 3). Despite the relatively small sample size, the factor structure showed good stability as factors were added or deleted. The addition of new factors caused new message themes or clusters to emerge rather than significantly altering the preexisting factors. Reliabilities for the 10 obtained subscales were also generally good (when retaining those items with primary loadings of .50 or better). The alpha coefficients for the 10 factors were: .88 for involvement, .58 for social distance, .74 for formality, .83 for composure, .58 for attraction, .75 for dominance, .52 for equality, .42 for task orientation, .85 for depth/similarity, and .76 for trust/receptivity. The relatively good reliabilities for many of these dimensions argue for their utility as subscales in measuring certain facets of relational communication.

TABLE 3
Oblique Factor Structure, Means, and Standard Deviations: 60-Item Measure

Factors and items	Mean	Standard deviation	I	II	III	IV	V	VI	VII	VIII	IX	X
I. INVOLVEMENT												
He/she was detached during the conversation.*	4.87	1.64	−.56	.07	.35	.32	.45	.30	−.29	.14	−.26	−.31
He/she was interested in talking.*	4.59	1.40	.58	.12	−.33	−.31	−.20	−.33	.19	−.12	.39	.47
He/she showed enthusiasm while talking.*	4.34	1.64	.65	.10	−.30	−.39	−.19	−.33	−.03	−.09	.44	.21
He/she seemed to find the conversation stimulating.*	3.81	1.35	.59	.11	−.25	−.30	−.45	−.22	.27	−.29	.45	.32
He/she was very reserved with me.*	3.68	1.66	−.67	.00	.12	.28	.12	.06	−.31	.06	−.33	−.12
He/she communicated coldness rather than warmth.*	4.77	1.60	−.68	.01	.21	.48	.31	.24	−.22	.18	−.37	−.23
He/she created a sense of distance between us.*	4.53	1.61	−.59	.00	.27	.44	.45	.21	−.26	.19	−.48	−.09
He/she acted bored by our conversation.*	4.89	1.53	−.73	.11	.09	.35	.26	.15	−.05	.18	−.27	−.22
He/she was intensely involved in our conversation.	4.24	1.49	.52	.16	.02	−.40	−.23	−.36	.17	−.08	.39	.20
He/she communicated aggressiveness.	2.76	1.46	.40	.24	.20	−.14	.20	−.37	−.19	−.28	.33	.01
He/she didn't like me.	5.13	1.32	−.42	.30	−.02	.32	.35	.12	−.35	.01	−.24	−.26
He/she was assertive with me.	3.80	1.49	.53	.11	.01	−.19	.18	−.32	.22	.04	.33	.14
He/she was unwilling to share personal information/ feelings with me.	4.33	1.63	−.37	−.19	−.07	−.17	.35	−.02	.07	.07	−.11	−.14
II. SOCIAL DISTANCE												
He/she was very emotional around me.*	2.03	1.32	.06	.67	.01	.13	−.04	−.15	.06	−.11	.09	−.06
He/she made the differences between us evident.*	2.68	1.53	−.13	.70	−.03	.21	.01	−.09	−.21	.04	−.10	−.13
He/she seemed to have higher status than me.*	2.57	1.32	.11	.38	.32	−.09	.07	−.21	−.31	.29	.16	−.06

Factors and items	Mean	Standard deviation	I	II	III	IV	V	VI	VII	VIII	IX	X
He/she made our conversation seem intimate.*	2.27	1.35	.25	.51	−.12	−.15	−.15	−.17	.03	.19	.38	−.05
He/she was more interested in a social conversation than the task at hand.*	4.24	1.49	−.17	.41	−.20	.28	.02	−.13	−.14	−.33	−.06	−.32
III. FORMALITY												
He/she made the interaction very formal.*	3.99	1.68	−.20	−.06	.62	.22	.31	−.07	−.21	.14	.00	.24
He/she wanted the discussion to be casual.*	3.28	1.47	.18	.03	−.81	−.22	−.13	−.07	.26	−.16	.18	.21
He/she wanted the discussion to be informal.*	3.79	1.61	−.06	.05	−.80	−.13	−.05	.02	.03	−.05	.18	.05
IV. COMPOSURE												
He/she was comfortable interacting with me.*	2.74	1.34	.48	−.19	−.37	−.67	−.06	−.19	.28	−.24	.24	.32
He/she felt very tense talking with me.*	3.10	1.70	−.36	.17	.22	.69	.04	−.00	−.41	.17	−.18	−.09
He/she was calm and poised with me.*	2.56	1.24	.17	.05	−.03	−.77	−.09	.03	.24	.03	.22	.24
He/she felt very relaxed talking with me.*	2.97	1.48	.30	−.09	−.28	−.83	−.02	−.15	.25	−.22	.37	.35
He/she seemed nervous in my presence.*	2.92	1.51	−.15	.17	.21	.70	.16	.14	−.10	.20	−.04	−.00
V. ATTRACTION												
He/she created a sense of closeness between us.*	4.48	1.34	.35	.29	−.24	−.41	−.47	−.05	.07	.14	.32	.14
He/she did not want us to develop a deeper relationship.*	3.75	1.45	−.13	.05	.15	.16	.73	.01	−.14	.18	−.24	−.14
He/she was not attracted to me.*	4.21	1.28	−.21	−.14	.11	.07	.60	.19	.04	−.02	−.14	−.10
VI. DOMINANCE												
He/she attempted to persuade me.	4.84	1.79	.15	.19	.10	−.07	.03	−.74	.08	−.08	.12	.08
He/she tried to gain my approval.*	4.65	1.57	.35	−.04	.02	−.20	−.06	−.49	.05	−.22	.44	.51
He/she did not attempt to influence me.*	4.36	1.72	−.22	−.12	.10	.03	.15	.72	−.10	.10	−.06	−.20

(Continued)

Table 3—*Continued*

Factors and items	Mean	Standard deviation	I	II	III	IV	V	VI	VII	VIII	IX	X
He/she tried to establish rapport between us.*	3.88	1.60	.52	.17	−.29	−.06	.03	−.50	.28	−.04	.41	.27
He/she did not try to win my favor.*	4.21	1.62	−.22	.13	.06	.28	.11	.57	−.24	.23	−.43	−.08
He/she tried to control the interaction.	5.19	1.36	−.09	.17	−.06	−.01	−.07	−.60	−.26	.09	.18	−.21
He/she had the upper hand in the conversation.	5.55	1.43	.11	.11	.00	−.05	.02	−.51	−.06	.17	.28	−.30
VII. EQUALITY												
He/she considered us equals.*	4.51	1.45	−.06	.02	−.24	−.16	.14	−.12	.63	−.06	.23	.05
He/she did not treat me as an equal.*	5.40	1.45	−.15	.21	.15	.29	.23	.05	−.67	.12	−.02	.11
He/she wanted to cooperate with me.*	5.61	1.24	.30	−.02	−.00	−.22	−.05	.02	.61	−.11	−.08	.39
VIII. TASK ORIENTATION												
He/she wanted to stick to the main purpose of the interaction.*	5.36	1.45	−.08	−.09	.16	.08	.20	.18	−.05	.54	−.01	.16
He/she was unresponsive to my ideas.*	3.21	1.33	−.32	.11	−.02	.40	−.00	−.03	−.18	.52	−.35	−.37
He/she was open to my ideas.*	3.05	1.06	.13	−.04	−.15	−.35	.00	.16	.20	−.49	.30	.49
IX. DEPTH/SIMILARITY												
He/she made me feel we had a lot in common.*	3.76	1.50	.46	.24	−.28	−.29	−.40	−.20	.45	−.03	.53	.16
He/she made me feel he/she was similar to me.*	3.94	1.53	.31	.26	−.36	−.29	−.29	−.24	.42	−.17	.55	.19
He/she was very socially oriented.*	3.97	1.58	.53	.02	−.31	−.28	−.28	−.22	.33	−.28	.58	.18
He/she tried to move the conversation to a deeper level.*	2.75	1.42	.29	.21	−.08	−.16	−.00	−.29	−.13	−.09	.75	.01
He/she acted like we were good friends.*	3.37	1.58	.41	.18	−.32	−.47	−.20	−.15	.34	−.06	.63	.08
He/she seemed to desire further communication with me.*	3.54	1.51	.42	.20	−.14	−.31	−.27	−.25	.23	−.05	.68	.29
He/she seemed to care if I liked him/her.*	4.16	1.45	.33	.09	−.31	−.22	−.30	−.30	.23	−.00	.59	.25

Factors and items	Mean	Standard deviation	I	II	III	IV	V	VI	VII	VIII	IX	X
He/she was willing to open up his/her private thoughts.	3.43	1.63	.41	.39	−.29	−.18	−.21	−.13	.15	−.27	.50	.21
He/she made the conversation seem superficial.			−.38	.23	.26	.32	.36	.12	−.24	.05	−.47	−.16
He/she didn't care if I liked him/her.	4.34	1.59	−.37	.25	.11	.12	.38	.16	−.05	.27	−.53	−.28
X. TRUST/RECEPTIVITY												
He/she wanted to appear reasonable.*	5.68	.99	.04	−.16	.03	−.35	.16	.02	.29	−.05	.31	.52
He/she was sincere.*	5.79	1.01	.38	−.16	−.41	−.25	.06	−.19	.10	.07	.19	.57
He/she wanted me to trust him/her.*	4.80	1.37	.23	−.04	−.07	−.08	−.23	−.24	.16	−.10	.23	.60
He/she was willing to listen to me.*	5.70	1.10	.20	−.17	−.13	−.41	−.10	.06	.19	−.15	.19	.66
He/she seemed irritated with me.*	6.01	1.24	−.44	.23	.22	.33	−.04	−.02	−.33	.34	−.16	−.46
He/she was honest in communicating with me.*	5.85	1.10	.34	−.11	−.26	−.36	−.02	−.05	.10	−.05	.13	.62
He/she indicated no desire for further conversation with me.	4.38	1.67	−.34	−.11	.20	.36	.27	.17	−.22	.36	−.20	−.48
He/she wanted to dominate the conversation.	5.70	1.46	−.10	.44	.08	.02	−.06	−.27	−.25	−.14	.15	−.47
Cumulative percent of variance accounted for by each factor			24%	31%	36%	40%	43%	46%	49%	52%	54%	57%

*These items have primary loadings of .50 or better

The original goal of the third wave of research, however, was to reduce an instrument to a smaller pool of items and to determine what independent dimensions could be used for measurement purposes. Accordingly, based on an examination of the loadings and communalities of the three most viable factor solutions, the pool of 60 items was reduced to 30. These 30 were then subjected to orthogonal factor analysis, confirmatory factor analysis, and reliability analysis. The resulting dimensions were used in the experimental tests of hypotheses.

The orthogonal factor analyses with varimax rotation produced as the best solution seven independent factors. These same factors were then subjected to ordinary least squares confirmatory factor analysis (Hunter & Cohen, 1969) to verify their internal consistency and parallelism. The data fit the seven factor relational message solution well. Four items that were either not internally consistent with their factor and/or not parallel with other factors in the model were dropped from their respective four factors, resulting in a 26-item pool. The final, seven-factor solution produced factors that were internally consistent and parallel with other factors in the model. The deviations between expected and obtained item and factor correlations were well within sampling error. The final factor structure and inter-factor correlations appear in Table 4.

T A B L E 4
Confirmatory Factor Analysis: Seven-Factor Solution, 26-Item Version

Factors and items	I	II	III	IV	V	VI	VII
I. IMMEDIACY/AFFECTION							
He/she did not want a deeper relationship between us.	.42	.31	.30	.21	−.30	−.01	.22
He/she was intensely involved in our conversation.	.59	.50	.43	.40	−.13	.31	.32
He/she found the conversation stimulating.	.73	.64	.53	.38	−.39	.32	.35
He/she communicated coldness rather than warmth.	.74	.51	.58	.50	−.36	.27	.38
He/she created a sense of distance between us.	.77	.66	.45	.45	−.40	.21	.36
He/she acted bored by our conversation.	.66	.40	.45	.40	−.20	.18	.20
II. SIMILARITY/DEPTH							
He/she made me feel he/she was similar to me.	.58	.58	.42	.37	−.51	.26	.44
He/she tried to move the conversation to a deeper level.	.36	.58	.19	.15	−.06	.23	−.10
He/she acted like we were good friends.	.54	.74	.36	.47	−.42	.16	.42
He/she seemed to desire further communication with me.	.62	.82	.45	.33	−.16	.27	.25
III. RECEPTIVITY/TRUST							
He/she was sincere.	.35	.29	.68	.29	−.25	.15	.27
He/she was interested in talking with me.	.66	.57	.55	.38	−.36	.35	.28
He/she was willing to listen to me.	.42	.25	.71	.38	−.16	.05	.28
He/she was open to my ideas.	.34	.24	.52	.36	−.18	−.13	.31
He/she was honest in communicating with me.	.41	.27	.66	.37	−.21	.05	.33
IV. COMPOSURE							
He/she felt very tense talking to me.	.42	.31	.33	.68	−.39	.07	.54
He/she was calm and poised with me.	.39	.33	.41	.67	−.17	.00	.31
He/she felt very relaxed talking with me.	.51	.52	.64	.84	−.40	.17	.42
He/she seemed nervous in my presence.	.37	.22	.24	.65	−.32	.06	.29
V. FORMALITY							
He/she made the interaction very formal.	−.28	−.20	−.08	−.27	.68	.06	−.20
He/she wanted the discussion to be casual.	−.33	−.37	−.42	−.34	.68	−.12	−.38
VI. DOMINANCE							
He/she attempted to persuade me.	.16	.21	.03	.08	.04	.72	.07
He/she didn't attempt to influence me.	.32	.26	.19	.07	−.09	.72	.12
VII. EQUALITY							
He/she considered us equals.	.12	.28	.20	.20	−.22	.10	.38
He/she didn't treat me as an equal.	.31	.17	.11	.35	−.29	.02	.75

STATISTICAL SUMMARY 3

Study 3

Finally, a confirmatory factor analysis was used to test the eight- and four-factor models. Confirmatory factor analysis allows you to identify the most effective groupings of items and the items which are working most effectively. This analysis revealed seven factors: similarity/depth, receptivity/trust, immediacy/affection, dominance, equality, composure, and formality. The measures of these, however, were not all reliable.

The 26-item measure yielded the following coefficient alpha reliabilities: .81 for immediacy/affection, .77 for similarity/depth, .76 for receptivity/trust, .80 for composure, .61 for formality, .66 for dominance, and .52 for equality.

These seven dimensions—*similarity/depth, receptivity/trust, immediacy/affection, dominance, equality, composure,* and *formality*—represent a refinement over the four-factor orthogonal solutions produced previously and can be regarded as a more precise depiction of the distinctive message themes or clusters of themes recognized by interactants. The reliabilities for the seven subscales support their internal consistency conceptually and demonstrate that they can be used as reliable measures of the various themes. However, for future measurement purposes, some additions to the current set of items may be warranted. Items measuring task versus social orientation were removed from the current instrument when the pool was reduced from 60 to 30 because they had low communalities. For measurement purposes, if this facet of relational communication is considered pertinent, items from the current 60-item version or the previous 68-item version should be added. Additionally, the dimensions of formality, dominance, and equality will yield higher reliabilities if some previously used items are restored to the scale. The reduction to a 30- and then a 26-item version caused the number of items comprising each of

these scales to be reduced below optimum. The recommended eight dimensions (including task orientation) and the pool of possible items appear in Table 5 along with their reliability estimates across the studies conducted to date.

Finally, the results from the experiment itself added further evidence of the predictive utility of the instrument. Variations in eye contact, reward level, and/or gender of the interviewers resulted in different perceptions of the relational communication of immediacy/affection, $F(1,133) = 5.54$, $p < .05$ for reward; $F(2,133) = 3.17$, $p < .05$ for gaze, trust/receptivity, $F(2,133) = 2.54$, $p = .08$ for gaze by gender, similarity/depth, $F(2,133) = 2.53$, $p = .08$ for gaze, and dominance, $F(2,133) = 4.06$, $p < .05$ for gaze by reward by gender. Male and female confederates were also perceived to send different relational messages along the themes of formality, dominance, and immediacy/affection, multivariate $F(5,129) = 3.32$, $p < .01$.

STATISTICAL SUMMARY 4

Next, F-tests were used to see if there was a difference between two groups. For example, you might want to see if one group (e.g., males) had more eye contact than a second group (e.g., females). These tests showed that many factors were influenced by eye gaze, reward level, or gender.

DISCUSSION

The three measurement studies reported here were designed to demonstrate the validity of the conceptualization of relational communication advanced by Burgoon and Hale (1984) and to develop a valid and reliable instrument measuring the themes of relational messages. The results from these studies, along with supplementary data from several experiments utilizing the scales, strongly demonstrate that interpersonal exchanges may express a wide array of relational

T A B L E 5
Dimensions and Internal Reliabilities for Eight Dimensions of Relational Message Themes

Dimensions	Reliability in third study	Comparable Reliabilities in Previous Studies				
		B & K	B, B, H & D	Buller	Manusov	B, M, M & H
I. IMMEDIACY/AFFECTION (INTIMACY I) (intensely involved in our conversation) (did not want deeper relationship) (not attracted to me) (seemed to find conversation stimulating) (communicated coldness rather than warmth) (created sense of distance between us) (acted bored by our conversation) (interested in talking to me) (showed enthusiasm while talking to me)	.81	.46	.79	.74	.78	.83
II. SIMILARITY/DEPTH (INTIMACY II) (made me feel similar) (tried to move conversation to deeper level) (acted like good friends) (desired further communication) (seemed to care if I liked him/her)	.77	.81	.86	.70	.77	.86
III. RECEPTIVITY/TRUST (INTIMACY III) (sincere) (interested in talking) (wanted me to trust) (willing to listen) (open to my ideas) (honest in communicating with me)	.76					

Dimensions	Reliability in third study	Comparable Reliabilities in Previous Studies				
		B & K	B, B, H & D	Buller	Manusov	B, M, M & H
IV. COMPOSURE (felt very tense talking with me) (calm and poised) (very relaxed talking with me) (nervous in my presence) (comfortable interacting with me)	.80					
		.72	.76	.71	.70	.74
V. FORMALITY (made interaction formal) (wanted discussion casual) (wanted discussion informal)	.74					
VI. DOMINANCE (attempted to persuade me) (did not attempt to influence me) (tried to control the interaction) (tried to gain my approval) (didn't try to win my favor) (had the upper hand in the conversation)	.66					
		.69	.60	.76	.68	.76
VII. EQUALITY (considered us equals) (did not treat me as an equal) (wanted to cooperate)	.52					
VIII. TASK ORIENTATION (wanted to stick to main purpose) (was more interested in social conversation than task at hand) (was very work-oriented) (more interested in working on task at hand than having social conversation)	.42					

message themes. Interactants are able to discriminate from seven to ten distinctive dimensions along which interactional partners are seen to impart messages. Moreover, these dimensions are not mere potentials that may seldom be realized in real interactions. Variations in the actual communication behavior of dyadic participants produce different relational interpretations by partners on multiple dimensions. For example, gaze aversion conveys different meanings than frequent gaze along all of these message themes: intimacy/similarity, immediacy, involvement, arousal/composure/formality, and dominance.

The final orthogonal factor analyses provide a clearer understanding of the interrelatedness and separateness of various themes. Although immediacy and affection emerge as separate dimensions in oblique solutions, they come together when independence of factors is forced. This is consistent with Mehrabian's original theorizing about immediacy behaviors conveying liking or disliking, and is consistent with Burgoon and Hale's subordination of these themes under the larger theme of intimacy. The combining of receptivity with trust demonstrates, as hypothesized, that these intimacy-related themes are intertwined and that greater inclusiveness usually goes hand in hand with a sense of trust. The coupling of similarity with depth similarly suggests, consistent with much theorizing about the attraction process, that greater similarity promotes a greater sense of familiarity and willingness to move a relationship to a deeper, more intimate level.

The emergence of composure and formality as independent factors also confirms the Burgoon and Hale expectation that these would be regarded as relatively separate themes. This does not mean that these themes will always or even typically be perceived as unrelated to other themes. In fact, the composure and formality themes are likely to form composites with other topoi when circumstances dictate a relaxed, informal, and nonaroused communication style. However, it is important to realize that when composites such as arousal/composure/formality/

task orientation are used, they are just that—composites of several distinctive and recognizable themes.

Throughout the series of studies, dominance has consistently emerged as an independent theme, as predicted. However, in the second oblique analysis it split into separate subcomponents, one related to persuasiveness/ingratiation and one to more overt aggressiveness, control, and lack of equality or similarity. In the final wave, with new items added to the measurement instrument, a separate equality factor finally appeared. This would seem to answer the earlier question of whether equality is seen as the midpoint of the dominance-submission scale or not. Apparently, the concept of equality is perceived as different from dominance and control and may entail some implicit notions about mutual respect.

The other question of whether task–social orientation forms a single dimension cannot be unequivocally answered at this stage, because the items measuring it do not consistently hold together across these three studies. In the first two studies, the social and task items loaded together in the oblique solutions but separated in the orthogonal solutions and failed to obtain sufficiently high loadings to merit labeling on those factors. In the third study, the items separated onto two different factors even in the oblique solution and again failed to appear in the final orthogonal solution because of low communalities. It is possible that the problem lies with the wording of items, but it seems more likely that task and social orientation do not form the conceptual poles of a continuum. Despite the tradition of dichotomizing leaders and group discussants into task versus socio-emotional contributors, these do not have to be mutually exclusive categories. A person who is very task oriented may still demonstrate sociable tendencies. Consequently, in assessing a person's relational communication, different criteria may be applied to the judgment of task involvement as compared to social orientation. In the future, it may therefore be advisable to seek better measurement of an ''all-business,'' task-focused communication style and to treat the sociability of an individual as part of the affiliative (inclusive) theme.

If task involvement is restored to the pool of relational communication factors, then the evidence to date suggests that there are at least eight nonindependent clusters of message themes: dominance, equality, immediacy/affection, receptivity/trust, similarity/depth, composure, formality and task orientation. It is important to stress that the nature of the interaction and the relationship among interactants may alter the factor structure at times, causing more or fewer of these dimensions to emerge as relatively independent. For example, a highly intimate interaction among friends who rate each other may cause all the intimacy factors to collapse into a single, global measure of intimacy. Conversely, under circumstances where high degrees of hostility can be induced or observed, emotional arousal, conversational involvement, and composure may separate into two or three separate components. Although the current studies ran the gamut from personal and informal conversations to formal interviews; from interactions with strangers or friends to recalled interactions with parents, acquaintances, and other conversational partners; and from participant reports to observer ratings, the relational communication scales need to be used with additional populations and in new contexts to establish further the stability of the various message themes. Research in progress with an adult population seeking interview training should provide further useful validation of the relational theme factors.

For the present, the measurement instrument that has evolved has shown strong predictive validity and good reliability. The various versions of the measurement instrument used in experiments to date have differentiated: (1) nonverbally immediate from nonverbally nonimmediate behavior, (2) high from low levels of gaze, (3) pleasant from hostile voices, (4) high from low reward communicators, and (5) male from female communicators. They have also correlated with (6) dimensions of credibility and (7) dimensions of personality. The scales thus

appear to have strong utility and could be used productively in a wide range of interpersonal and organizational contexts. Participants or observers could use them, for example, to assess the relational import of transactions between employer and employee, interviewer and interviewee, parent and child, husband and wife, or union and management representatives. With some adaptation, the scales might be used by audiences to judge the self-presentational communication of politicians, media broadcasters, and other public figures. They could also be used as manipulation checks on the presumed meaning of various nonverbal behaviors, linguistic choices, or verbal strategies. Or they could be used to verify the extent to which actors and observers make the same attributions about communication events. While the specific measurement instrument can benefit from further refinement, it should be evident that relational communication scales hold great promise for uncovering the symbolic relational meanings that are embedded in all communication interchanges.

REFERENCES

Buller, D. B. (1984). *The effects of vocalics and nonverbal sensitivity in a persuasive interaction: A replication and extension.* Unpublished doctoral dissertation, Department of Communication, Michigan State University.

Burgoon, J. K., Buller, D. B., Hale, J. L., & deTurck, M. A. (1984). Relational messages associated with nonverbal behaviors. *Human Communication Research, 10,* 351–378.

Burgoon, J. K., Coker, D., & Coker, R. (in press). Communicative effects of gaze behavior: A test of two contrasting explanations. *Human Communication Research.*

Burgoon, J. K., & Hale, J. L. (1984). The fundamental topoi of relational communication. *Communication Monographs, 51,* 193–214.

Burgoon, J. K., & Koper, R. J. (1984). Nonverbal and relational communication associated with reticence. *Human Communication Research, 10,* 601–626.

Burgoon, J. K., Manusov, V., Mineo, P., & Hale, J. L. (1985). Effects of eye gaze on hiring, credibility, attraction and relational message interpretation. *Journal of Nonverbal Behavior, 9,* 133–146.

Hale, J. L., & Burgoon, J. K. (1984). Models of reactions to changes in nonverbal immediacy. *Journal of Nonverbal Behavior, 8,* 287–314.

Hunter, J. E., & Cohen, S. H. (1969). PACKAGE: A system of computer routines for the analysis of correlational data. *Educational and Psychological Measurement, 29,* 697–700.

Manusov, V. L. (1984). *Nonverbal violations of expectations theory: A test with gaze behavior.* Unpublished master's thesis, Department of Communication, Michigan State University.

PERCEPTIONS OF COMMUNICATION BEHAVIOR ASSOCIATED WITH RELATIONSHIP TERMS

Mark L. Knapp, Donald G. Ellis and Barbara A. Williams

Individuals use a variety of terms to designate the nature of their relationships with others, e.g., friend, lover, pal, etc. Although expectations for certain types of communicative behavior surely accompany the use of these terms, it was not clear what their communicative referents were. The first phase of this study obtained intimacy-scaled ratings from 100 subjects to 62 relationship terms. Then more than 1,000 subjects ranging in age from 12 to 90 from eight locations across the United States responded to the six relationship words selected (lover, best friend, friend, pal, colleague, acquaintance) in terms of associated communicative behavior. The three factors central to these responses (personalness, synchrony, difficulty) were then used to analyze the relationship terms varied according to the gender, age, and marital status of the subject and the composition of a relationship to a specific other by gender. Among other findings: All age groups perceived increases in both personalized and synchronized communication as the terms rated became more intimate. Difficult communication was perceived as a part of both intimate and non-intimate relationships. Personalized communication was associated more with female and male–female relationships than with male relationships. Younger respondents (below age 22) perceived more personalized and synchronized communication in all relationships than did those over age 41.

Our daily affairs are conducted in a reality largely shaped by language. The way we choose to label something often provides us with expectations and perceptual orientations which we deem appropriate to the label. Thus, the labels we use to describe our relationships with others (lover, friend, pal, etc.) may play a central role in the way these relationships develop.

In fact, some of the problems in achieving specific and personal relationship definitions may be directly linked to ambiguities associated with the referents of commonly used relationship terms.[1] To qualify for the label, "lover," for instance, some require sexual intercourse; for others, affection may take other forms and commitment to the relationship may be the key behavioral requirement. John A. Lee identified at least six different styles of loving—any one of which may be used as the referent for the label, "lover."[2] Friendships are also subject to multiple referents.[3] Some think one's lover and best friend can be the same person[4] while others see less overlap in these two types of relationships. Josephine Klein noted a frequent "confusion" between the terms friend, neighbor and relative.[5] Myron Brenton observed, "some people called them

Source: The article is taken from *Communication Monographs* [47: 262–278, 1980]. Reprinted by permission of the Speech Communication Association, 5105 Backlick Rd., Annandale, VA 22003.

[friendships] 'close' though from my personal perspective I saw them as superficial."[6] Suzanne B. Kurth distinguished between friendly relations (associated with more formal role requirements) and friendships which "clearly establish the voluntary nature of our interaction, recognize the uniqueness of the relationship, develop a high level of intimacy, and . . . [involve us] . . . in a network of obligations."[7] Murray S. Davis points out that ex-intimates often use the term "friend" as a euphemism for a relationship more closely associated with acquaintances. And, if these ex-intimates agree to become "strangers," Davis argues, it may be more like becoming enemies.[8] Paul H. Wright summarizes some of these problems associated with multiple referents for relationship terms:

> Subjective definitions of friendship tend to be variable and untrustworthy. Initially, interviewees ordinarily identify as friends anyone whom they know more than casually and do not dislike. . . . Friendship is a relationship with extremely broad and ambiguous boundaries.[9]

In contrast to those who note the variety of referents which may be associated with relationship terms are those who seek underlying commonalities. Some of these efforts have been limited to a single type of relationship or intimacy stage—e.g., friendship.[10] Other studies, using factor analysis, have attempted to uncover common dimensions for a wide variety of relationship types. Gerald Marwell and Jerald Hage elicited ratings of 100 types of relationships (e.g., husband–wife, landlord–tenant, etc.) on scales which identified characteristics of interaction such as frequency, effort, commitment, etc.[11] Intimacy was the most significant dimension along which these relationships varied, but two other factors which the authors called visibility and regulation of behavior were also noted. Triandis et al. also used 100 role relationships and had subjects from the United States and Greece rate them according to 120 behaviors such as disagree with, kiss, show concern for, etc.[12] Four factors common to both cultures were identified: intimacy (e.g., kiss, love, pet, etc.); dominance (e.g., apologize, look down upon, feel superior to,

etc.); affect (e.g., compliment, help, hate, reward, etc.); and hostility (e.g., lie to, quarrel with, cheat, laugh at, etc.). Wish et al. asked people to make judgments about 45 different types of relationships.[13] These subjects tended to view interpersonal relationships along four main dimensions according to the researchers' multidimensional scaling analysis: cooperative–friendly vs. competitive–hostile; equal vs. unequal; intense vs. superficial; and socioemotional–informal vs. task oriented–formal. All of these studies address three common aspects: (1) a certain psychological–social distance or closeness between the partners; (2) a certain degree of perceived subordination, equality or superordination between the partners; and (3) a certain type of behavioral style between the partners which may vary along several axes—formality and cooperation representing two of them. Despite the utility of this general information about various relationship types, the manner in which specific communication behavior manifests itself has been largely ignored, de-emphasized or hidden within more abstract terminology.

Altman and Taylor, and Knapp, however, proposed eight broad dimensions of communicative behavior which are thought to vary with perceived changes in intimacy.[14] Perceived changes in communicative behavior along these eight dimensions are also thought to precipitate altered perceptions of intimacy. Although these dimensions were originally conceptualized as a means of describing overt communicative behavior, they also provide a viable framework within which to elicit perceptions of actual communicative behavior. Communicative behavior represented by the dimensions which comprise this theoretical framework is thought to generally increase with increasing intimacy. It should not, however, be construed as an unchanging linear progresson—i.e., as intimacy increases, the breadth, depth, uniqueness, spontaneity, etc. of communication will increase correspondingly. The theory does predict gradual increases in uniqueness, depth, breadth, flexibility, smoothness, efficiency, and overt evaluations as intimacy increases, but many configurations of communicative behavior are possible. For instance, self-disclosure, which is typically associated with the depth of communication, may increase along the continuum to a point where pain, anger and conflict work to inhibit increased self-disclosure. Yet these people feel they have an intimate relationship—and measures on other dimensions support their perception. Further, there may be some lovers who will exhibit lower levels of some types of communication than good friends do. Berger et al. found that lovers were judged significantly less understanding and reinforcing than close friends.[15] Perhaps all the dimensions follow a curvilinear path with the peak of communicative behavior for any given dimension occurring prior to the time when the relationship stabilizes. With perceived deterioration of intimacy, we may again see some or all of the eight dimensions peaking if the participants want to restore the closeness of the jeopardized relationship.

This framework recognizes that most relationships are composed of coexisting forces which seem in opposition to one another. Warmth behaviors are mixed with cold. Intimacy is not conceptualized as a continually increasing amount of any type of behavior. We will likely see some public behaviors, some awkwardness, some rigidity, some stylizedness, some difficulty and some hesitancy in intimate relations. For most relationships a degree of instability is part of the definition of stability. As the insightful social analyst Georg Simmel said nearly a century ago:

> Intimate relations, whose formal medium is physical and psychological nearness, lose the attractiveness, even the content of their intimacy as soon as the close relationship does not also contain, simultaneously and alternatively, distances and intermissions.[16]

Within this perspective, the following dimensions of communicative behavior provided the theoretical framework of our study.

Uniqueness of Interaction.　As relationships reach toward greater intimacy, communication may manifest a more "personalistic focus"[17] or adaptation to the specific other. It is a gradual movement away from an impersonal, stylized communication used with many others; the person is gradually being "appreciated as a unique self rather than simply a particular instance of a general class."[18] Simmel put it this way:

> In probably each relation, there is a mixture of ingredients that its participants contribute to it alone and to no other, and of other ingredients that are not characteristic of it exclusively, but in the same or similar fashion are shared by its members with other persons as well. The peculiar color of intimacy exists if the ingredients of the first type, or more briefly, if the "internal" side of the relation, is felt to be essential; if its whole affective structure is based on what each of the two participants gives or shows only to the one other person and to nobody else.[19]

Parks found that perceived uniqueness was associated with both perceived closeness of the relationship and the stage of the relationship.[20] Extending this concept to actual communicative behavior suggests that there will be a more idiosyncratic system for more intimate relationships.

Depth of Interaction.　Sometimes we tend to reveal more of ourselves to another as we gain more knowledge of that person. There is an increasing accessibility to the other or what Kurth called deeper levels of involvement.[21] One of the two most important criteria for identifying close friends in Marion Crawford's survey of 306 married couples was, "Someone I can talk to about personal or financial matters and know that it will be kept confidential."[22] Paul C. Cozby's review of the self-disclosure literature also tends to support the association of self-revelation or disclosure and relationship development.[23] Parks' research also found that depth of communication was associated with perceived closeness and stage of relationship.

Breadth of Interaction.　Less intimate pairs may be more restricted than intimates in the number of topics discussed, the amount of detail brought out within each topic area and the general amount of interaction. Studies by Altman and Haythorn, and Frankfurt both indicated an increasing number of topics discussed as relationships developed.[24] Dalmas A. Taylor's thirteen-week observation of previously unacquainted male roommates also revealed an increase in breadth of exchange over time.[25] Again, Parks noted that perceived closeness of the relationship was also associated with breadth of communication.

Difficulty of Interaction.   Early relationship stages seem to have a high potential for interaction problems, inaccuracies and general communicative inefficiency. Thus, we might expect less difficulty as relationships become closer, but some relationships labeled as intimate are also difficult to maintain. Wright says the difficulty of friendship maintenance is a characteristic of friendships independent of friendship strength—i.e., strong friendships are sometimes the most difficult to maintain.[26]

Flexibility of Interaction.   Communication in relationships developing toward greater intimacy may also reflect more options in the way a given idea or feeling is presented. Interactants at early stages of intimacy appear to be more dependent on standardized approaches involving fewer channels.

Spontaneity of Interaction.   Intimates may be less inclined toward hesitancy and caution in their exchanges. The listener is expected to grant a certain ''latitude of understanding'' which allows the speaker some freedom and relaxation which may not exist with newer acquaintances. Parity of exchanges for intimates may be more relaxed. George J. Keiser and Irwin Altman, using role-playing techniques with college actresses, found that ''good friends''—especially when talking about non-intimate topics—manifested nonverbal patterns more indicative of relaxation and high immediacy than did acquaintances.[27]

Smoothness of Interaction.   As knowledge of the other person increases, we should be better able to predict responses. This, in turn, suggests the possibility for greater synchronization of interaction associated with more intimacy. Stanley Feldstein and Joan Welkowitz reviewed research related to conversational congruence.[28] Congruence describes the occurrence, within the span of one or more conversations, of similar intensity, frequency or durational values for the participants on one or more of the parameters that characterize temporal patterning. This review offers support for two findings related to the smoothness dimension: (1) the extent to which the conversational participants become congruent depends, in part, on their perceived enjoyment of the contacts they have with their partners; and (2) temporal congruence was found to be positively related to observer's ratings of warmth, genuineness and empathy of the participants. Other research related to smoothness of interaction has been conducted under headings such as synchrony,[29] symmetry,[30] and pattern matching.[31] Howard Giles and P. F. Powesland observe that people will sometimes accommodate their speech style to another person to enhance perceptions of similarity and increase attraction.[32] This convergence of styles is sometimes associated with perceptions of more rapport and understanding by the interactants.

Evaluation of Interaction.   The closer the relationship, the greater the likelihood that the participants will freely give and receive positive and negative feedback. Both criticism and praise may be more common to intimate relationships. Shirley J. Gilbert and Gale C. Whiteneck found positive statements were disclosed significantly earlier than negative statements at nonintimate and moderately intimate levels of closeness. Negative statements occurred significantly earlier for intimate relationships.[33] Making overt judgments about the other person (positive or negative) has the potential for impacting strongly on the relationship—a tendency we may generally reserve for those relationships to which we have stronger commitments. It has been observed that during periods of high conflict, relationships have, simultaneously, the most to gain and the most to lose.

It was the purpose of this study to examine the extent to which statements about specific communicative behavior reflecting these eight dimensions were associated with words used to identify relationships at various states of intimacy. Although exceptions would be expected, we pre- dicted that a general tendency for perceptions of uniqueness, depth, breadth, efficiency, flexibility, smoothness, spontaneity and overt evaluations would increase as relationships move from less intimacy to more intimacy. Less intimate relationships, then, would be generally characterized by more stylized, public, narrow, difficult, rigid, awkward, hesitant communication and suspended evaluations of the other's behavior.

		TABLE 1						
		Intimacy Scaled Relationship Terms						
Rank	Term	Mean	S.D.		Rank	Term	Mean	S.D.
1.	Husband	1.38	1.0710		32.	Aunt	4.10	1.4035
2.	Wife	1.44	1.1487		33.	Companion	4.20	1.6392
*3.	Lover	1.50	1.1146		34.	Chum	4.24	1.3862
4.	Fiance(e)	1.51	1.0100		35.	Uncle	4.25	1.7660
5.	Mate	1.53	1.1587		36.	Dependent	4.26	2.0082
6.	Intimate	1.54	1.2425		37.	Roommate	4.39	1.7517
7.	Spouse	1.56	1.4236		38.	Date	4.51	1.5922
8.	Beloved	1.93	1.3200		39.	Paramour	4.70	1.8007
9.	Mother	2.29	1.2333		40.	Partner	4.71	1.6410
10.	Boy/Girlfriend	2.31	1.1608		41.	Cousin	4.78	1.5478
11.	Sweetheart	2.31	1.4333		42.	Playmate	4.79	1.6593
12.	Honey	2.38	1.3542		*43.	Pal	4.88	1.7424
13.	Son	2.42	1.3271		44.	Comrade	4.89	1.6630
14.	Betrothed	2.43	1.9241		45.	Sidekick	4.98	1.8694
*15.	Best Friend	2.48	1.0869		46.	Kinsman	5.00	1.7056
16.	Daughter	2.48	1.2511		47.	Consort	5.05	1.8000
17.	Sister	2.57	1.2573		48.	Admirer	5.09	1.8152
18.	Dear	2.60	1.2144		49.	Cohort	5.27	1.7515
19.	Mistress	2.61	1.7227		50.	Idol	5.72	2.2069
20.	Father	2.64	1.6050		51.	Schoolmate	5.82	1.5465
21.	Steady	2.76	1.4711		52.	Crony	5.82	1.7944
22.	Brother	2.86	1.4841		53.	Accomplice	5.85	2.3241
23.	Close Friend	3.05	1.2008		54.	Escort	5.88	1.6470
24.	Beau	3.12	1.8273		*55.	Colleague	5.89	1.6871
25.	Confidant	3.39	1.7747		56.	Associate	6.06	2.0292
26.	Grandparent	3.52	1.6544		57.	Fellow	6.10	1.9306
27.	Flame	3.74	1.8347		58.	Aide	6.22	1.8067
28.	Buddy	3.77	1.3016		59.	Co-worker	6.26	1.7328
*29.	Friend	3.83	1.1639		60.	Neighbor	6.33	1.6333
30.	Adorer	3.99	2.0226		*61.	Acquaintance	6.96	1.7345
31.	Suitor	4.06	1.7628		62.	Employer	7.00	1.7638

*Terms selected for use in this study.

METHOD

Selecting Relationship Terms

We collected 62 relationship terms from various sources. The list of terms generally described people rather than relationship states (e.g., spouse rather than marriage; fiance(e) instead of engaged) or task-specific role relationships (e.g., guard–prisoner; teacher–student; etc.). These terms were rated by 100 subjects on a nine-point intimacy scale (1 = intimate; 9 = nonintimate). Table 1 presents the results of these ratings. Several criteria were used to select the terms eventually used for the study. First we sought terms which represented fairly equidistant points along the intimacy continuum. We avoided the selection of kinship terms (e.g., mother, cousin, uncle, etc) and age-specific terms (e.g., playmate). Thus, the terms selected for use in this study included: lover (1.50); best friend (2.48); friend (3.83); pal (4.88); colleague (5.89);[34] and acquaintance (6.96).

Selecting Statements About Communicative Behavior

The primary theoretical framework from which this study arose was outlined by Altman and Taylor, and Knapp. Hence, we developed statements about communicative behavior which seemed consistent with the eight broad dimensions put forth by these authors. In addition, one statement about the frequency of interaction was included. These statements, then, comprised the thirty items on the questionnaire administered to subjects. Figure 1 lists the statements and the general dimensions which they seemed to represent. The general dimensions were not listed on the questionnaire subjects received, and the items from each dimension were interspersed with items from other dimensions.

Sample

A person's age might make a difference in how he or she perceived the communicative behaviors associated with various relationship terms. Several authors suggest that we perceive our rela-

tionships with others differently at different life stages.[35] Marilyn Rands and George Levinger obtained ratings for expected behavior between today's 22-year-olds.[36] College students rated current expectations for relationshps while senior citizens rated behavior of 50 years ago. Among other differences between these two groups, today's pairs were expected to be more expressive, do more together, reveal more positive and negative feelings toward each other and have more physical contact. Responses from the older subjects suggested a less active role for women in male–female relationships of 50 years ago. The activities central to certain life periods or life crises seem to be influential in producing differences in relationship perceptions. Therefore, we gathered data from nine separate age categories: 12–16; 17–21; 22–27; 28–33; 34–40; 41–45; 46–52; 53–64; and above 65. Although some arbitrary grouping was inevitable, we tried to keep the categories broadly within the theoretical framework of adult development stages explicated by the aforementioned researchers. There were approximately 113 subjects in each age category—about 19 each responding to each of the six relationship terms. The total sample was 1,114.

We did not systematically seek a given distribution of males and females for each age category, but subjects were asked to identify their own gender and the gender of the person they mentally anchored to each relationship term. Several studies suggest different expectations and behavior for males and females in various relationships. Lawrence Weiss and Marjorie Fiske Lowenthal say that males emphasize sharing activities and interests more than do females, whereas females emphasize the importance of warm supportiveness.[37] Alan Booth suggests that female friends do things more spontaneously than male friends.[38] Sidney M. Jourard observed that female friends disclosed more intimate details about their lives than male friends did.[39] Paul H. Wright summed up his own research and that of others on gender differences in friendship by saying that there do seem to be differences in male friendships and female friendships, but they are not great.[40] He infers from the differences that

---

Figure 1
ITEMS ABOUT SPECIFIC COMMUNICATIVE BEHAVIOR

General
1. We talk to each other frequently.

Uniqueness of Interaction
*2. We talk to each other in much the same way we talk to a lot of other people.
3. We use words which have "special meanings" to just the two of us.
4. We can tell when one another is upset or frustrated without being told.
5. We seem to know what each other means to say—even when the words don't quite do the job.

Depth of Interaction
6. We share secrets with each other.
7. We talk to each other about important feelings we have.
*8. We don't really know much about each other.
9. We tell each other personal things about ourselves—things we don't tell most people.
10. We are open with each other.

Breadth of Interaction
11. We discuss a wide variety of topics.
*12. Our conversations are limited to some specific topics.

Difficulty of Interaction
*13. We have communication breakdowns.
*14. We have trouble understanding each other.
15. We do a good job of accurately communicating with each other.
16. If asked, we could probably repeat back what the other says in most conversations.
*17. It is difficult for us to know when the other person is being serious or sarcastic.
18. We are attentive to each other's comments.

Flexibility of Interaction
19. We communicate our pleasure and displeasure with each other in many different ways.
20. We can communicate the same idea with facial expressions or gestures instead of words.

Smoothness of Interaction
*21. We find it hard to talk to each other.
*22. Our conversations are strained and awkward.
23. Our conversational styles seem well coordinated with each other.
24. Conversationally, we are a lot alike.
25. Due to mutual cooperation, our conversations are generally effortless and smooth flowing.

Spontaneity of Interaction
*26. We choose our words carefully to avoid misunderstandings.
27. We are not hesitant or cautious about what we say to each other.
28. Our conversations are spontaneous, informal and relaxed.

Evaluation in Interaction
*29. We avoid openly giving praise and criticism of each other.
30. We tell each other when we like or do not like the way the other has behaved.

---

*These items represent reversals from expected behavior with increasing intimacy.

women's friendships emphasize personalism, self-disclosure and supportiveness; men's are more likely to emphasize external interests and mutually involving activities. Crawford's research also found a number of differences between male and female respondents on questions of friendship. We expected differences in our sample as well.

A person's marital status may also affect the way subjects perceive communication behavior at various levels of intimacy. Although subjects could select one of seven categories of marital status, these seven generally represented: married (married, remarried) and not married (never married; separated; divorced; widowed; and not married but living with someone).[41]

Data Collection

Subjects responded to each of the 30 statements about communicative behavior on a seven-point scale ranging from "strongly agree" (1) to "strongly disagree" (7) that the behavior is associated with the relationship term being analyzed. Subjects were also asked to complete the questionnaire while thinking of "a specific person you know who most closely represents the term at the top of the page." Each subject was asked to complete only two forms (two terms) to avoid problems associated with fatigue. We also avoided giving any subject two relationship terms with adjacent intimacy ratings—e.g., lover and best friend or best friend and friend, etc. Questionnaire order was randomized.

Data were collected from numerous individuals and intact groups. Groups included employees of commercial organizations, church groups, high school and college students; individual respondents were the relatives and others known to students who were asked to administer the questionnaire as part of a class assignment. In addition, the assistance of several colleagues provided us with a wide geographical sample of urban, suburban and rural respondents in California, Georgia, Indiana, Illinois, Oklahoma, Michigan, New Mexico and West Virginia.[42]

Data Analysis

First, the data were factor analyzed using the SPSS subprogram FACTOR. The terms were submitted to a principal factoring method with orthogonal rotation. Each factor had a minimum eigenvalue of 1.0 before being included in the rotation. An item was considered part of a factor if it had a primary loading of .60 with no secondary loading greater than .40.

STATISTICAL SUMMARY 1

Factor analysis is a method for grouping variables together into a smaller number of categories. If you have a large number of variables, you may want to see if two or more of them actually combine or work together. Here, the authors wanted to see which of the thirty statements went with each other. This analysis showed that the thirty statements could be grouped into three factors or general categories: personalized, synchronized, and difficult communication.

Then a $2 \times 2 \times 5$ factorial design with three between subject variables (sex of subject × sex of relationship × relationship type) was analyzed with a multivariate analysis of variance.[43] The dependent measures for this analysis and all others were the factors which emerged from the factor analysis of the instrument. Since we asked our respondents to describe actual relationships, we were not surprised to find relatively few "lover" relationships involving members of the same gender. Because of the disproportionately small number of respondents in this category, it was eliminated for those analyses. Next, the age and marital status variables were separately combined with relationship type. This resulted in one 6×9 MANOVA (six types of relationships × nine age categories) and one 6×7 MANOVA (six types of relationships × seven marital status categories). Subsequent MANOVA analyses were performed by reducing the number of age categories to three (22 and below; 23–40; and 41 and above); and the marital status categories to two (married and never married). The age changes were made when the original analyses revealed that the only significant differences were between the 17–21 age group and two age groups over 45. The expected discriminations between several age categories throughout the lifespan did not materialize. In addition, the seven marital categories were greatly unbalanced since 946 of the 1,015 subjects were in one of two categories—married or never married. With minor exceptions, these category reductions did not change the overall results, so the data tables reflect the subsequent analyses. Factor III (difficulty) was not included in these subsequent analyses since the original MANOVA indicated virtually no influence of this factor on age or marital status.

STATISTICAL SUMMARY 2

Next, multivariate analyses of variance were calculated. A multivariate analysis of variance (MANOVA) tells us if groups differ on two or more variables. In all of the analyses the dependent variables (or effects) were the three types of communication.

In the first MANOVA, the groups, or independent variables, were the type of relationships engaged in by males and females with males and females. This showed that relationships between males and females were seen as the most personal. In addition, males in intimate relationships with other males saw greater synchrony in their communication.

In the second MANOVA, the groups, or independent variables, were the type of relationships engaged in by younger and older people. This analysis showed that younger people saw their relationships as more personal and synchronous, particularly if the relationship was intimate.

In the final MANOVA, the groups, or independent variables, were the type of relationships engaged in by married or single people. Married people were more extreme in their ratings. They rated less intimate relationships as less personal than those who had never been married, and rated more intimate relationships as more personal than those who had never been married.

RESULTS

Factor Analysis

The results of the factor analysis appear in Table 2. Three factors emerged which accounted for 47.5% of the variance. Factor I was labeled *personalized communication* and is closely related to an intimacy or disclosure construct. The factor is related to how close the interactants feel toward one another and the "special" nature of their communication. Factor II describes the extent to which the communication is coordinated and smooth-flowing so it was called *synchronized communication*. Factor III seemed to encompass what some people refer to as "barriers" to communication—reflecting a strained and awkward character. Thus, we felt this factor described *difficult communication*. The factor structure for Factors I and II were stable across the six relationship types. Alpha reliabilities were: Factor I, .83; Factor II, .79; Factor III, .77.

Item no.	Factor I (personalized)	Factor II (synchronized)	Factor III (difficult)
9.	.74*	.23	.18
6.	.72*	.31	.18
20.	.61*	.37	.06
30.	−.70*	−.13	−.01
19.	.68*	.17	−.04
4.	.60*	.28	.15
3.	.67*	.17	.00
7.	.66*	.33	.22
15.	−.24	−.60*	−.24
28.	.30	.66*	.24
25.	.27	.73*	.21
24.	.17	.66*	.00
18.	−.19	−.64*	−.17
23.	.31	.65*	.17
14.	.01	−.23	−.62*
21.	.07	.09	.68*
17.	−.09	−.10	−.73*
22.	.14	.31	.64*

TABLE 2
Results of Factor Analysis

MANOVA Analyses

The first analysis combined the sex of the subject (subsex) with the sex of the other person in the relationship (relsex) and the relationship type (reltype). Table 3 reports the results of these analyses. There was a multivariate main effect for subject sex and relationship type on Factors I and II. The data indicate that male subjects were less personal and less synchronized in their relationship perceptions than were female subjects. Moreover, the relationship types, as predicted, were less personal as they moved from lover to acquaintance. But the nonintimate relationships were more discrepant from one another than the intimate relationships were. The same was true for Factor II on relationship types. The univariate F for relationship sex suggests that when responding to relationships with females, subjects tend to perceive more personalized communication.

The interactions, however, temper the main effects. The two-way interaction for subject sex and relationship sex suggests that males rating relationships with females see these relationships as more personal. And females rating male relationships also respond more personally. The triple interaction indicates that synchrony increases as males rate increasingly intimate male relationships. The same was true for the females.

The next analysis involved age by relationship type. The results for relationship type showed progressively less personalized and synchronous communication patterns from lover through acquaintance. On both Factors I and II, the

TABLE 3
Summary of Multivariate and Univariate Tests for Subsex, Relsex and Reltype

	Factor I	Factor II	df	Wilk's lambda
Main Effects				
Subsex	15.95*	11.46*	1/906	.97*
Relsex	6.92*	1.14	1/906	.99
Reltype	77.15*	33.41*	4/906	.73*
Two-Way Interaction				
Subsex × Relsex	15.8*	.14	1/906	.97*
Subsex × Reltype	1.87	1.36	4/906	.98
Reltype × Relsex	1.20	1.92	4/906	.99
Three-Way Interaction				
Subsex × Relsex × Reltype	1.74	2.47*	4/906	.98*

*$p < .05$.

TABLE 4
Summary of Multivariate and Univariate Tests for Age by Relationship Type

	Factor I	Factor II	df	Wilk's lambda
Main Effects				
Age	7.89*	3.87*	2/1096	.98*
Reltype	87.45*	27.25*	5/1096	.68*
Interaction				
Age × Reltype	1.99*	2.31*	10/1096	.95*

*$p < .05$.

	Factor I	Factor II	df	Wilk's lambda
T A B L E 5				
Summary of Multivariate and Univariate Tests for Marital Status by Relationship Type				
Main Effects				
Marital Status	5.5*	1.9	1/934	.99**
Reltype	76.80*	24.70*	5/934	.68*
Interaction				
Msts × Reltype	4.50*	1.90	5/934	.96*

*p < .05.
**p < .06.

youngest respondents (aged 22 and below) differed significantly from the oldest (41 and above). The youngest subjects perceived relationships as more personal and more synchronous. The two variables interacted, however, on both factors. The youngest subjects perceived more personalness and synchrony as relationships increased in intimacy than did the older age group.

The final analysis matched marital status with relationship type on the two major factors. There was a main effect for relationship type on both Factors I and II. Of course, the communication was perceived as less personal and less synchronous as relationship types decreased in intimacy. The main effect for marital status on the personalness dimension indicates that never married individuals perceived communication more personally (x = 24.6) than did married subjects (x = 25.7). The interaction effect, however, suggests that the married subjects perceived communication more personally for the more intimate relationship types. The personalness of the communication for married subjects was greater than that of the never married for the lover and best friend relationship types. There was a decrease in personalness for the other relationship types.

DISCUSSION

Comparison of Theoretical Predictions and Factor Analytic Results

This study was designed to examine the extent to which statements representing eight broad dimensions of communication were associated with words we commonly use to identify relationships of varying degrees of intimacy. These statements, based on the theoretical framework set forth by Altman and Taylor and by Knapp, were found to represent three factors which we labeled:

(1) *personalized communication;* (2) *synchronized communication;* and (3) *difficult communication.* Personalized communication is most closely aligned with the concept of depth as outlined in the theory—i.e., the exchange of more private meanings, feelings and information. For the respondents in this study, some aspects of the dimensions of uniqueness, flexibility and providing overt evaluations of the other's behavior were also aligned with the depth dimension. The synchrony factor, as might be expected, was primarily identified with the theoretical dimension focusing on smoothness of interaction. Some statements representing spontaneity and the lack of communicative difficulty were also associated with the synchrony factor in this study. The difficulty factor was represented by the difficulty dimension outlined in the theory—as well as the antithesis of interaction smoothness—awkwardness of interaction. There were two statements related to the breadth of interaction and one about the frequency of talk which did not load on any factor. Thus, at least seven of the eight dimensions originally drawn from social penetration theory were active in the perceptions of the subjects in this study. The dimensions of communication which predicted changes in the depth, smoothness and difficulty of interaction with perceived changes in intimacy seem to have a centrality around which the other dimensions cluster.

This conclusion is, of course, limited by the number and type of statements used to illustrate each dimension in this study.

When we compare our results which focused specifically on communicative behavior with those factor–analytic studies which examined many facets of relationships, some interesting similarities emerge. For instance, all of the studies reviewed earlier uncovered an intimacy or closeness factor which is comparable to our personalized communication dimension. While our synchrony dimension refers to interactional synchrony, it may reflect broader psychological orientations which other studies have called subordination, equality and superordination. Certainly one's success in achieving synchrony with another is contingent on appropriate resolution of such matters. Finally, all the previous studies discussed various behavioral orientations such as coordination and formality which, although less clear than the other two comparisons, may be infused in our difficulty factor.

Since subjects in this study generally perceived relationships to manifest more personalized and more synchronized communication as the descriptive terms became more intimate, there is a possibility that we tapped a relationship ideology common to this culture—namely, the expectation that intimacy is associated with all things good. This "utopia syndrome" is a common source of relationship problems when the painful discrepancy between what "is" and what "should be" comes into focus for the participants. It is conceivable that these *perceptions* of communicative behavior affected by cultural stereotypes or socially desirable ideals are not closely linked to *actual* communicative behavior. Logically, one would predict otherwise, however. Even though unrealistic images of communication in relationship development may comprise part of our results, some offsetting perceptions were uncovered. For instance, one of the statements associated with personalized communication, "we tell each other when we like or do not like the way the other has behaved," received a strong negative correlation. This suggests a knowledge that indiscriminately "telling

it like it is" does not go hand in hand with intimacy. Similarly, the increasing perceptions of communication synchrony with increasing intimacy were accompanied by responses which acknowledged that synchrony may not bring attentiveness and accuracy with it. And the existence of a difficulty factor which did not decrease with intimacy also argues for some realistic grounding in the subjects' perceptions.

Personalized Communication

Since this study examined perceptions of intimacy terms, it is not surprising that the factor which accounted for the most variance (33.4%) is closely related to the intimacy construct. Broadly, this factor deals with accessibility, openness and self-disclosure. The term *intimacy* is derived from Latin words meaning "to make known" and "innermost." The act of personalizing messages for the subjects in this study included: (1) telling another person things we don't tell most people—feelings, secrets, personal things—but not indiscriminately giving opinions of their behavior; (2) relying on a greater variety of channels for sending and receiving messages—including subtle nonverbal channels which may be considered a more specialized or personal domain; and (3) cultivating and using messages which are more personal to the interacting pair only.

All age groups perceived personalized communication to decline as the term used to describe the relationship became less intimate. The differences, however, between the more intimate terms (lover, best friend, and friend) were less distinct than were those separating the less intimate terms (pal, colleague, and acquaintance). This seems to support the findings reported earlier regarding the frequent ambiguity of referents and confusions uncovered when people were asked to describe friends and lovers. It appears that the subjects in this study perceived differences between the personalized communicative behavior of friends, best friends and lovers, but that these differences were less clear than were the differences for those relationships which had less intimacy. Two of these terms used the same word (friend and best friend) which may have contributed to the finding, but we may also be noting a tendency for people to perceive behavioral differences in personalized communication for more intimate relationships as simply progressing by smaller gradations.

We found some interesting gender differences relevant to perceptions of personalized communication. Females tended to be generally associated with more personalized communication. In general, subjects perceived relationships with females in a more personal way. William Ickes and Richard D. Barnes[44] provide some behavioral support for this finding. Further, this seems reasonably in line with the findings from many studies of self-disclosure reviewed by Cozby which generally show women to be more willing to disclose information about themselves than men are. In fact, some men seem to be suspicious of and more hesitant to strike up a relationship with men willing to freely discuss personal information.[45] We also found that our subjects' perceptions of any male/female relationship (males rating females or females rating males) involved more personalized communication than same gender pairs—even though males seem to be generally less personal in their relationship perceptions. This finding tends to provide support for two common observations of sex role stereotypes in this culture. Women, it is argued, have traditionally been taught to value and display more warmth and affection in a greater variety of situations than men.[46] Rands and Levinger found that female/female pairs were expected to engage in more self-disclosure, other-enhancement, and physical contact than were male/male pairs. This is consistent with the generally less personal perceptions of the males in this study. The fact that both men and women perceived male/female relationships as a relationship with more personalized communication seems closely related to the observation that platonic relationships between men and women in this culture are infrequent and that the most common relationship is

a romantic one. Janet S. Chafetz states the position when she says:

> Most Americans suspect that platonic relationships between a male and a female are something other than they appear. . . . Both male and female sex role stereotypes encourage individuals to define members of the opposite gender in broadly sexual terms. Females are taught to view males primarily as potential mates or husbands.[47]

There were not as many differences between age groups as we expected. It appears that the differences worth noting are between those who are 22 or younger and those who are 41 or older. The youngest age period seems to hold a particular salience for personalized and synchronized communication in various relationships. This age group tended to see relationships in a more personalized and synchronized fashion—especially as the type of relationship became more intimate. We can only speculate that the younger group is just beginning to fully explore and experience the intricacies of many types of relationships. They may also be influenced by cultural myths regarding idealized aspects of relationships. The decade of the 40s may bring with it a heightened realism about the extent to which relationships can manifest personalness and synchrony—a perception which may contribute to lower ratings than those assigned by the younger group. For some, perhaps many, of the subjects over 65 there may be an increasingly depersonalized aura associated with many relationships. They may have fewer things of a private nature to share; declining physical ability may make reliance on a variety of communication channels difficult; and, as information sources and experiences are cut off, the person may increasingly rely on more generalized, stereotypical bases for messages.[48]

The finding for marital status and relationship type was interesting, since, all things considered, the never married group perceived more personalness in their communication. Perhaps the married subjects take personalness for granted. Their typical daily interaction involves an intimate relationship, but this relationship may be more concerned with efficiency and coordination. On the other hand, the data do not indicate that the married subjects perceive significantly more synchrony. But the married subjects perceived communicaton to be more personal with lovers and best friends whereas the never married were more personal with friends. We may see here the impact of the unique marital relationship. Someone who is not married may be more personal with a greater variety of people. The never married are more personal with acquaintances, colleagues, etc. These people probably have more relationships and greater breadth of interaction. However, there is no substitute for relationship history when judging the personalness of communication. For this reason, the more personal communication is perceived between married lovers. Although this finding is not startling, it does illustrate how relationship terms and their attendant perceptions of communication vary as a function of one of the most significant relationships in our society—marriage.

Synchronized Communication

Other studies have found heightened verbal and nonverbal synchrony between intimate pairs like mothers and their babies and courting males and females.[49] Albert E. Scheflen suggested that "sharing" (synchrony) promotes a feeling of closeness, involvement or rapport.[50] For the participants in this study, the mutual accommodation or synchrony manifested itself as: conversations which are smooth-flowing, effortless, spontaneous, relaxed, informal and well-coordinated. This factor accounted for 8.2% of the variance. This synchrony, which is developed by the joint efforts of the two interactants, also seems to contribute to interactant perceptions of greater conversational similarity. Conversational similarity and synchrony, however, did not seem to automatically involve perceptions of accurate communication or even attentiveness for our subjects.

This seems to be in contrast to Adam Kendon who said, "To *move* with another is to show that one is 'with' him in one's attentions and expectancies,"[51] and William S. Condon who hypothesized that interactional synchrony provided constant feedback from listener to speaker regarding the former's level of attention and interest.[52] These observations which associate attentiveness with synchrony may be accurate on some occasions, but it does not seem unreasonable to assume heightened synchrony between two long time intimates, for example, without corresponding perceptions of attentiveness.

Again, all age groups perceived synchronous communication to increase as the relationship term became more intimate. Joseph J. McDowall failed to find significantly greater behavioral synchrony among long-term friends than among acquaintances in a group discussion.[53] It could be argued that groups might discourage more particularized behaviors involved in dyadic synchrony. As we noted earlier for Factor 1, the differences between the more intimate terms were less distinct than were those separating the less intimate terms. In sum, then, the two factors which most clearly distinguish relationship terms across the spectrum of intimacy are personalized communication and synchronized communication—but the distinctions along these two factors seem to be clearer for less intimate relationships than for more intimate ones. Rands and Levinger obtained similar results. Rated characteristics of good friends were consistently closer to close friends than casual friends. Berger et al. also noted that dimensions used to evaluate interpersonal attraction in relationship development tended to lose distinctiveness as the relationship evaluated became more intimate.

Generally, males report less synchronous communication in relationships than do females, but, with increasing intimacy, males rate other males higher on synchrony. This was also true of females. The more intimate the female–female relationship, the greater the chance that it was rated synchronous. It seems, therefore, that same gender relationships are perceived to be more synchronous—especially when they are more intimate. This is in contrast to the earlier finding that same gender relationships were perceived lower on personalized communication. But perception of increased synchrony for more intimate relationships seems to be consistent with other research on similarity and effective communication.[54]

Difficult Communication

This factor, as we noted earlier, is probably describing a range of perceived "barriers" to effective communication. On the surface, it appears to be the polar opposite of synchronized communication. It seems, however, to refer to a more general strain, difficulty and awkwardness of interaction. There may be many sources of such problems other than a perceived lack of conversational coordination. Furthermore, the difficulty involved does not necessarily mean greater inaccuracy in communication.

This factor did not systematically vary across relationship types. The reason may be that intimate and nonintimate relationships alike have difficulties and these difficulties may be equally hard to manage—but for different reasons. Some might even argue that closer or more intimate relationships would manifest greater difficulty in relationship maintenance. The more one learns about another, the better the chances that he or she will find something which conflicts with his or her own interests, needs or goals. Thus, close relationships may be free of some of the difficulties and awkwardness found at earlier relationship stages, but they are not free of other difficulties. Age, gender and marital status differences did not occur on this factor which accounted for the least variance (5.9%).

NOTES

1. Teru L. Morton, James F. Alexander and Irwin Altman, "Communication and Relationship Definition," in *Explorations in Interpersonal Communication*, ed. Gerald R. Miller (Beverly Hills: Sage, 1976), pp. 105–125.

2. "Styles of Loving," *Psychology Today*, 8 (1974), 43–51.

3. Gerald M. Phillips and Nancy J. Metzger, *Intimate Communication* (Boston: Allyn & Bacon, 1976).

4. Elizabeth J. Kaiser, "An Exploratory Analysis of Women's Communication Behavior, Adjustment and Role Definition Following Divorce," Diss. Purdue 1978.

5. *Samples from English Cultures* (London: Routledge & Kegan Paul, 1965).

6. *Friendship* (New York: Stein & Day, 1974), p. 18.

7. "Friendships and Friendly Relations," in *Social Relationships*, ed. George J. McCall (Chicago: Aldine, 1970), p. 169.

8. *Intimate Relations* (New York: The Free Press, 1973).

9. "Toward a Theory of Friendship Based on a Conception of Self," *Human Communication Research* 4 (1978), 199.

10. Aristotle, *Nichomachean Ethics*, trans. Martin Ostwald (Indianapolis: Bobbs-Merrill, 1962); Bernard I. Murstein and Leah T. Spitz, "Aristotle and Friendship: A Factor-Analytic Study," *Interpersonal Development*, 4 (1973–1974), 21–34; and John M. Reisman and Susan I. Shorr, "Friendship Claims and Expectations Among Children and Adults," *Child Development*, 49 (1978), 913–916.

11. "The Organization of Role Relationships: A Systematic Description," *American Sociological Review*, 35 (1970), 884–900.

12. Harry C. Triandis, Vasso Vassiliou and Maria Nassiakou, "Three Cross-Cultural Studies of Subjective Culture," *Journal of Personality and Social Psychology*, Monograph Supplement, 8 (1968), No. 4, Part 2, 1–42.

13. Myron Wish, Morton Deutsch and Susan J. Kaplan, "Perceived Dimensions of Interpersonal Relations," *Journal of Personality and Social Psychology*, 33 (1976), 409–421.

14. Irwin Altman and Dalmas A. Taylor, *Social Penetration* (New York: Holt, Rinehart & Winston, 1973); Mark L. Knapp, *Social Intercourse: From Greeting to Goodbye* (Boston: Allyn & Bacon, 1978).

15. Charles R. Berger, Marylin D. Weber, Mary Ellen Munley and James T. Dixon, "Interpersonal Relationship Levels and Interpersonal Attraction," in *Communication Yearbook I*, ed. Brent D. Ruben (New Brunswick, N.J.: Transaction Books, 1977), pp. 245–261.

16. Kurt H. Wolff (trans. and ed.), *The Sociology of Georg Simmel* (New York: Free Press, 1950), p. 126.

17. Wright, p. 199.

18. Gerald D. Suttles, "Friendship as a Social Institution," *Social Relationships*, p. 100.

19. P. 315.

20. Malcolm R. Parks, "Communication and Relational Change Processes: Conceptualization and Findings," Diss. Michigan State 1976.

21. Pp. 136–170.

22. ''What is a Friend?'' *New Society,* 42 (1977).

23. ''Self-Disclosure: A Literature Review,'' *Psychological Bulletin,* 79 (1973), 73–91.

24. Irwin Altman and William W. Haythorn, ''Interpersonal Exchange in Isolation,'' *Sociometry,* 23 (1965), 411–426; Leslie P. Frankfurt, ''The Role of Some Individual and Interpersonal Factors in the Acquaintance Process,'' Diss. American University 1965.

25. ''Some Aspects of the Development of Interpersonal Relationships: Social Penetration Processes,'' *Journal of Social Psychology,* 75 (1968), 79–90.

26. P. 205.

27. ''Relationship of Nonverbal Behavior to the Social Penetration Process,'' *Human Communication Research,* 2 (1976), 147–161.

28. ''A Chronography of Conversation: In Defense of an Objective Approach,'' in *Nonverbal Behavior in Communication,* ed. Aron W. Siegman and Stanley Feldstein (Hillsdale, N.J.: Lawrence Erlbaum, 1978), pp. 329–378. Also see Stanley Feldstein, ''Temporal Patterns of Dialogue: Basic Research and Reconsiderations,'' in *Studies in Dyadic Communication,* ed. Aron W. Siegman and Benjamin Pope (New York: Pergamon Press, 1972), pp. 91–113.

29. James T. Webb, ''Interview Synchrony: An Investigation of Two Speech Rate Measures,'' in *Studies in Dyadic Communication,* pp. 115–133.

30. Leo Meltzer, William N. Morris and Donald P. Hayes, ''Interruption Outcomes and Vocal Amplitude: Explorations in Social Psychophysics,'' *Journal of Personality and Social Psychology,* 18 (1971), 392–402.

31. Louis Cassotta, Stanley Feldstein and Joseph Jaffe, *The Stability and Modifiability of Individual Vocal Characteristics in Stress and Nonstress Interviews,* Research Bulletin Number 2 (New York: William Alanson White Institute, 1967).

32. *Speech Style and Social Evaluation* (New York: Academic Press, 1975).

33. ''Toward a Multidimensional Approach to the Study of Self-Disclosure,'' *Human Communication Research,* 1 (1976), 347–355.

34. The term ''colleague'' seems to reflect more variability along the intimacy continuum than the other terms selected. A colleague may be a lover, best friend, friend, pal or acquaintance. Since the term did not show unusual variability among the respondents, it appears that people will generally select a friendly, but relatively nonintimate person when asked to anchor the term colleague.

35. Brenton; Robert L. Gould, *Transformations* (New York: Simon & Schuster, 1978); Daniel J. Levinson, *The Season's of a Man's Life* (New York: Alfred Knopf, 1978); Robert R. Sears and S. Shirley Feldman, *The Seven Ages of Man* (Los Altos, Calif.: Wm. Kaufmann, 1964); and Gail Sheehy, *Passages* (New York: E. P. Dutton, 1974).

36. ''Implicit Theories of Relationship: An Intergenerational Study,'' *Journal of Personality and Social Psychology,* 37 (1979), 645–661.

37. ''Life-Course Perspectives on Friendship,'' in *Four Stages of Life,* ed. Marjorie F. Lowenthanl, Majda Thurnher, David Chiriboga et al. (San Francisco: Jossey-Bass, 1975), pp. 48–61.

38. ''Sex and Social Participation,'' *American Sociological Review,* 37 (1972), 183–192.

39. *Self-Disclosure: An Experimental Analysis of the Transparent Self* (New York: Wiley, 1971).

40. ''Men's Friendships, Women's Friendships and the Alleged Inferiority of the Latter,'' Unpublished manuscript, University of North Dakota, 1979.

41. Our inexperience in designing materials appropriate for multiple age categories was evident when the majority of a high school class checked ''Not married but living with someone.'' With later samples from the younger age groups we explained this did not mean living with one's parents. Another 89-year-old respondent living in a facility for older women checked both ''Never Married'' and ''Not married but living with someone.''

42. We are especially grateful for the assistance of John Daly, Paul Feingold, Michael Scott, Gary Shulman, Deborah Weider-Hatfield, Mary Ann and Tim Wingard and John Wiemann.

43. Donald F. Morrison, *Multivariate Statistical Methods* (New York: McGraw-Hill, 1976).

44. ''The Role of Sex and Self-Monitoring in Unstructured Dyadic Interactions,'' *Journal of Personality and Social Psychology,* 35 (1977), 315–330.

45. Vello Sermat and Michael Smyth, ''Content Analysis of Verbal Communication in the Development of a Relationship: Conditions Influencing Self-Disclosure,'' *Journal of Personality and Social Psychology,* 26 (1973), 332–346.

46. Janet S. Chafetz, *Masculine/Feminine or Human? An Overview of the Sociology of Sex Roles* (Itasca, Illinois: F. E. Peacock, 1974).

47. P. 163.

48. Knapp, pp. 233–252.

49. Margaret Bullowa, ''When Infant and Adult Communicate How Do They Synchronize Their Behaviors?'' in *Organization of Behavior in Face-to-Face Interaction,* ed. Adam Kendon, Richard M. Harris and Mary R. Key (Chicago: Aldine, 1975), pp. 95–129; and William S. Condon and Louis W. Sander, ''Neonate Movement is Synchronized with Adult Speech: Interactional Participation and Language Acquisition,'' *Science,* 183 (January 11, 1974), 99–101; Condon's research on courtship behavior is cited by Davis in Flora Davis, *Inside Intuition* (New York: McGraw-Hill, 1971), p. 103.

50. ''The Significance of Posture in Communication Systems,'' *Psychiatry,* 27 (1964), 316–331.

51. "Movement Coordination in Social Interaction: Some Examples Described," *Acta Psychologica,* 32 (1970), 124.

52. "Multiple Response to Sound in Dysfunctional Children," *Journal of Autism and Childhood Schizophrenia,* 5 (1975), 37–56.

53. "Interactional Synchrony: A Reappraisal," *Journal of Personality and Social Psychology,* 36 (1978), 963–975.

54. Donn Byrne, *The Attraction Paradigm* (New York: Academic Press, 1971); Paul C. Feingold, "Toward a Paradigm of Effective Communication: An Empirical Study of Perceived Communicative Effectiveness," Diss. Purdue 1976.

TURNING POINTS IN DEVELOPING ROMANTIC RELATIONSHIPS

Leslie A. Baxter
Connie Bullis

The 80 partners from 40 romantic relationships were independently interviewed using the RIT procedure with regard to the turning points of their respective relationships; 26 types of turning points were found, which reduced to 14 supra-types. These supra-types differed in their association with relational commitment, with some events strongly positive, some strongly negative, and others relatively modest in reported change in commitment. About half of the turning points involved explicit metacommunication between the relationship parties, but the likelihood of relationship talk varied by turning point type. About half of the 759 identified turning points were agreed upon by relationship partners, but agreement differed depending on turning point type. Neither partner agreement nor the presence of explicit metacommunication was related to the respondent's current satisfaction with the relationship. However, the proportion of total turning points that were negative correlated negatively with current satisfaction. Two turning point events, Exclusivity and Disengagement, individually differentiated more from less satisfied relationship parties.

Source: The article is taken from *Communication Research* [12: 469–493, 1986]. © International Communication Association, 8140 Burnet Rd., Austin, TX 78766. Reprinted by permission of Sage Publications, Inc. and ICA.

Almost 25 years ago, Bolton (1961) argued the centrality of the "turning point" as a unit of analysis in understanding developmental processes in romantic relationships. However, to date only a handful of studies have examined relational turning points, and a basic descriptive profile is still lacking of what events are associated with relational change. As Hinde (1981) has observed, a descriptive base is crucially important if the study of relationships is to advance. The purpose of this study is to provide such a descriptive base for relational turning points.

The turning point is a unit of analysis that potentially affords a rich understanding of relationship processes. Conceptualized as any event or occurrence that is associated with change in a relationship, the turning point is central to a process view of relationships. Turning points are the substance of change. Yet despite an increased focus by relationship researchers on process issues of growth and decay (see Duck & Perlman, 1985), the field cannot yet answer such fundamental questions as "What events are related to a positive or negative change in relationships?"

Other features of turning points also hold heuristic value. Do relationships progress in a series of small, incremental, and positive shifts in commitment, as the positively sloped line envisioned by Altman and Taylor (1973) would suggest? In contrast, perhaps relationships progress through a series of discrete events each of which results in a major escalation in commitment, as the staircase metaphor advanced by Knapp (1984) would suggest. As yet a third alternative conception of relationship progress, relationships may develop dialectically with both positive and negative changes occurring as the parties construct their joint history (Altman, Vinsel, & Brown, 1981). Examination of the intensity, valence, and sequencing of turning points offers the promise of insight into the basic nature of relationship dynamics.

Last, studying relationship dynamics through the turning point unit of analysis affords communications researchers a useful lens by which to examine communication and meaning in relationship development. Turning points, by definition, afford insight into events and actions that are steeped in metacommunicative or relational meaning. A description of what phenomena comprise turning points may shed important insight into people's implicit theories of relationships (Davis & Todd, 1982; Rands & Levinger, 1979; Wilmot & Baxter, 1984). In addition to insights about implicit metacommunication, turning point analysis allows opportunity to examine instances when explicit metacommunication, or direct relationship talk, is enacted. In contrast to the common folk myth, which regards relationship talk as both pervasive and significant (Katriel & Philipsen, 1981), work in explicit metacommunication suggests that relationship talk is both infrequent (Wilmot, 1980) and unrelated to couple adjustment (Gottman, Markman, & Notarious, 1977). This apparent inconsistency between folk myth and research findings may be the result of a highly selective role performed by relationship talk. Relationship talk may be central to some turning points and not others. The turning point unit of analysis potentially allows researchers to sort out occasions in which relationship talk is a salient feature of relationship development.

In short, the turning point is a conceptually rich tool by which to understand relationship processes, a tool that has been underutilized to date by researchers. This study seeks to extend our understanding of relationship development through the examination of five research questions, detailed below.

Although the turning point has not been frequently studied, a handful of investigations have been undertaken. However, these studies are collectively limited in several ways. Several studies have employed the turning point unit of analysis, but typically the use was directed toward acquisition of information other than the content of turning points per se. The studies summarized by Huston, Surra, Fitzgerald and Cate (1981), for example, have focused exclusively on the rates of change in relationship progress, typically producing multiple trajectories to reflect rapid versus slow progress. Although these studies make an important contribution in demonstrating the range in rates of progress, they fail to examine the specific phenomena themselves that are related to these changes.

Several studies have considered turning point phenomena but are overly reductionistic in their analyses. Two studies (Lloyd & Cate, 1984; Surra, 1984) categorized respondent reasons for turning points into four basic categories: (1) dyadic, that is, reasons rooted in the interaction between the parties; (2) individual, that is, reasons rooted in the parties' personal belief systems; (3) network that is, reasons attributed to interactions with third parties; and (4) circumstantial, that is, reasons that suggest that the parties had no control over the event. Reasons for turning points may not be equivalent to the turning point events themselves, but apart from this conceptual issue, the four-category coding scheme lacks sufficient richness. The ''dyadic'' category, for example, subsumes everything from ''having a fight,'' to ''having sex,'' to ''getting engaged.'' A finer-grained analysis seems warranted.

Some research has been overly reductionistic by concentrating on units of analysis larger than the turning point. Braiker and Kelley (1979), for example, focused on the relationship stage or period, identifying the themes of love, conflict, maintenance (i.e., openness), and ambivalence. However, relationship stages or periods may consist of multiple turning point events that merit a finer-grained analysis. The theme of love, for example, may involve the turning point events of "first kiss," "first sex," and "expression of 'I love you'" all embedded in the Serious Dating stage.

If some studies have erred on the side of insufficient detail, others have erred on the side of noncomprehensiveness. Several studies have examined isolated types of events without embedding these types into a holistic view of turning points characteristic of romantic relationship histories. Planalp and Honeycutt (1985), for instance, have investigated the subset of events that increase uncertainty in relationships. To the extent that uncertainty is negatively regarded (Berger & Calabrese, 1975), these events are likely candidates to emerge as negative turning points in relationships. Similarly, the work in expressed reasons for relationship disengagement (Baxter, in press; Cody, 1982) poses likely candidates to emerge as negative turning points. Work on the single events of "expressing 'I love you'" (Nydick & Cornelius, 1984) and "first physical affection" (Wilmot & Baxter, 1984) suggest these two events as likely candidates to emerge as positive turning points in relationship histories. All of these studies provide detailed looks at isolated event types, but none is comprehensive in determining how these events fit in the broader portrait of turning points in relationship progress.

In sum, extant work is either too reductionist or lacking in comprehensiveness, resulting in the absence of a complete profile of the phenomena that comprise relationship turning points. Thus, our first research question:

RQ1: *What phenomena comprise relationship turning points in the perceptions of romantic relationship partners?*

The second research question examines the role that metacommunication or relationship talk plays in a relationship's turning points. The question has inherent appeal from a communications perspective, yet it has been investigated in only one of the studies that have dealt with turning points. Braiker and Kelley (1979) observed the

theme of maintenance in their respondent accounts of courtship stages. Unfortunately, the operationalization of maintenance employed in the researchers' work was muddied; items referenced self-disclosure, relationship talk, and proactive behavior to make the relationship work, all of which may be conceptually distinct from one another. Thus, it is difficult to know how to interpret the Braiker and Kelley (1979) finding that maintenance activity increases over the courtship stage. This finding may be the result of increased personal self-disclosure alone, increased relationship talk alone, increased proactive work and effort alone, or any combination of the above. Extant work in relationship talk suggests that relationship parties are cautious in its use. Although Baxter and Wilmot (1984) found direct talk about the relationship in people's repertoire of strategies by which to discern the state of the relationship, the strategy was far outweighed by many more indirect "secret tests." The prevalence of indirectness may be accounted for by people's beliefs about the consequences of direct relationship talk. Baxter and Wilmot (1985) found that direct talk about the state of the relationship was the most frequently reported "taboo topic" among developing romantic couples, which the partners attributed to the fragility of developing relationships and the resultant risk entailed in going "on record" with relationship talk. Given its apparent risk, relationship talk may be used quite selectively in relationship development, occurring only for certain types of turning points. The role of direct relationship talk in developing relationships is examined in the study's second research question:

RQ2: *Do turning point types differ in their likelihood of involving relationship talk between the partners?*

Although a relationship is a jointly realized social entity, each relationship party holds his or her own perceptions of that construction process. Indeed, a substantial research history supports the claim that the two parties to a relationship occupy separate phenomenological worlds (see

Sillars & Scott, 1983). Although substantial research has examined the issue of perceptual congruence between relationship partners in a variety of attitude domains (see Sillars & Scott, 1983), additional work is needed on the basic building block of a relationship, that is, the turning point. On the one hand, one might argue that turning points constitute the relationship's history, thereby suggesting a high correlation in partner perceptions. Extant work on turning points has found a remarkably high correlation (.80) between partner's month-by-month relationship commitment levels (Huston et al., 1981). However, partners could agree about their basic levels of affective involvement and still disagree about the events associated with those changes. The research on spouse monitoring of day-to-day events in their marriage suggests substantial discrepancy in the perceptions of the marital partners (Christensen & Nies, 1980; Jacobson & Moore, 1981). The third research question examines partner agreement about turning points:

RQ3: *To what extent do relationship partners agree in their identification of turning point types?*

Despite Bolton's (1961) suggestion that turning points may range from trivial to dramatic in their effects on relationships, extant work has not examined the issue of differential turning point intensities. The studies summarized by Huston et al. (1981) have come closest to this question by examining differential *rates of change* in the likelihood of marriage. However, rate of change as a measure confounds the intensity of change in relationship commitment with change in time. Further, as mentioned above, turning point types were not systematically analyzed in the Huston et al. (1981) research. The issue of intensity is important, for it will shed insight into whether relationship dynamics proceed by modest increments or larger bursts. Thus, the fourth question under investigation in this study is:

RQ4: *Do turning points vary in their perceived intensity?*

In addition to the consideration of perceived intensity of turning points, it seems useful to consider the possibility of delayed, cumulative, or long-term effects of turning points through assessment of the current relationship status. Relationship satisfaction, and its companions of dyadic relationship quality, adjustment, and success, are without doubt the single most frequently studied aspect of close relationships (Lewis & Spanier, 1979). Despite the plethora of variables that researchers have correlated with relationship satisfaction (see Spanier & Lewis, 1980), no comprehensive study exists that considers the association of current satisfaction with a relationship's turning point history. The effects of isolated events (e.g., the birth of a first child) have been considered, but it is useful to embed the effects of isolated turning point phenomena within the larger framework of the relationship's total history of change. Given the centrality of the turning point as a unit of change in relationships, it seems only reasonable to expect that some association might be present with current relationship satisfaction.

Several features about a relationship's turning point history merit particular attention with regard to current relationship satisfaction. First, it seems useful to investigate the overall relationship between satisfaction and the proportion of negative turning points. Despite the common folk myth that crisis brings a couple closer, it seems reasonable to expect satisfaction to correlate negatively with the proportion of a relationship's turning points that are negative.

The degree to which the partners agree on their relationship's turning points also merits examination with regard to satisfaction. Sillars and Scott (1983) have advanced the guarded conclusion that some association between perceptual congruence and adjustment (satisfaction) appears evident in the research literature but that there are many exceptions, particularly when perceptual congruence is unnecessary for compatible interaction between the partners. Sillars and Scott (1983) urge researchers to begin sorting out the instances when congruence is and is not likely to correlate with adjustment. This study examines the association between current relationship satisfaction and the proportion of a partner's identified turning points that were present in the other's account.

As mentioned above, openness in communication is often viewed as the *sine qua non* of relationship quality or satisfaction. However, recent thinking has challenged this commonly held belief (Bochner, 1982; Parks, 1982). Similar to the mixed findings on perceptual congruence and satisfaction, it strikes us as important to sort out what kinds of communication are and are not related to satisfaction. This study examines the possible relationship between satisfaction and the proportion of turning points that involve relationship talk.

The final facet of a relationship's turning point history relevant to satisfaction is whether the presence or absence of a given turning point type is related to current satisfaction. There may be certain events from which parties find it difficult to recover. For example, events such as physical separation that are often devastating to relationships (Wilmot, Carbaugh, & Baxter, 1985) may negatively correlate with current relational satisfaction. Similarly, there may be turning points whose function is so important to the bonding of the couple that their absence per se is linked with reduced satisfaction.

The discussion in terms of current relationship satisfaction can be summarized in this final research question:

> **RQ5:** *To what extent does turning point type, partner agreement on the identification of turning points, relationship talk surrounding turning points, and the proportion of negative turning points correlate with current relationship satisfaction?*

METHODS

Sample of Respondents

The sample was composed of the romantic partners from 40 romantic relationships, producing a final N of 80 respondents. The researchers employed several methods in acquiring the sample of couples. First, a story about the research project was placed in the weekly college newspaper. Second, volunteers were solicited from the lower-division classes of the researchers. Third, the majority of the sample came from using "network sampling" (Granovetter, 1976) with the student interviewing team that collected the data for the study. Team members were asked to generate the names of all the romantic pairs in their social network, and interviewers were then randomly assigned in pairs to romantic couples unknown to them personally. Upon completion of their interviews, these romantic couples were asked to identify other couples in their respective social networks who might be interested in participating. No couple was included in the sample unless its history as a romantic relationship exceeded an arbitrary length of 6 months. The average duration of relationships included in the study was 22.1 months. All respondents were taken from the student population of a private college, the vast majority of whom were 18–22 years of age.

Measures

Turning point data were acquired using the Retrospective Interview Technique (RIT), a frequently employed methodology in the study of turning points (Huston et al., 1981). The RIT asks each individual respondent to identify all of the turning points in his or her relationship since time of first meeting, plotting these points on a graph whose abscissa axis represents monthly intervals from time of first meeting until the time of the interview and whose ordinate axis reflects some index of relationship commitment, most commonly the estimated likelihood of marriage from 0% to 100% (Huston et al., 1981). At each identified turning point, the interviewer probes for additional information about that particular point. In asking subjects to keep weekly graphs as well as retrospective graphs, Miell (1984) found that people were remarkably accurate in their recall of turning point phenomena, thus lending some validity to the technique.

The interview schedule that accompanied the graphing procedure was adapted from Lloyd

(1983). After an introduction that explained the study's purpose and assured confidentiality, respondents were initially asked to construct the graph's abscissa and ordinate axes. First, the respondent was asked to recall the first time that the two partners met; these data were placed on the abscissa of the graph and monthly intervals were marked from that point until the time of the interview. Second, respondents were asked to construct the ordinate axis of the graph by indicating what "100% commitment," "50% commitment," and "0% commitment" meant for a relationship. The ordinate axis was marked off in intervals of 10% and keywords generated by the respondent were written beside the 0%, 50%, and 100% markers to serve as reminders. Although Lloyd (1983) used the "likelihood of marriage" from 0–100%, we opted instead for the more general term "100% commitment" based on our feeling that marriage may not be fully meaningful to our sample of college romances. In fact, we found that our respondents overwhelmingly defined "100% commitment" as a serious and exclusive relationship that was projected to continue into the foreseeable future but need not end in marriage.

Next, respondents proceeded to fill in the graph's turning points. Respondents were first asked to plot the relationship's commitment level at the point of first meeting and to plot the current level of relationship commitment to provide markers by which to calibrate the plotting of turning points in between these two endpoints. Respondents were then asked to go back to the first time the relationship partners met and to "plot in all of the times when there were changes in the joint commitment level that you can recall." After each point had been plotted, interviewers probed with questions designed to solicit information on the following: the event associated with the commitment change; whether the event was anticipated in advance of its occurrence; whether the event was intentionally created by one or both of the parties and, if so, to whom the event initiation was attributed and why; whether the turning point involved relationship talk; and last, anything else surrounding the turning point that the respondent felt important to mention in helping the interviewer understand what was going on at this turning point. After completing these probes, the interviewer asked the respondent to connect the prior point with the most recently plotted point and to explain the nature of the connecting line. The point connection information was used to check the incrementalism of commitment change. This cycle was repeated as the interviewer and the respondent worked their way chronologically along the graph's abscissa axis. After all turning points were identified, the interviewer asked the respondent to take "a minute or two to look over the graph and think about [the] discussion of the relationship." Respondents were allowed to make any alterations they thought appropriate at this time.

Current relationship satisfaction was assessed using Norton's (1983) six-item quality index. Although described as a measure to assess marital satisfaction, it draws heavily from the Dyadic Adjustment Scale (Spanier, 1976) designed for any close romantic relationship.

Procedures

Interviewers were trained in the RIT procedure for three 2-hour sessions. They were then assigned to work in pairs, each interview pair responsible for interviewing a specified number of couples from among those they were randomly assigned after controlling for interviewer familiarity with potential couple participants. Interviewers contacted couple partners to determine if they would be interested in participating in the study. In order to prevent the couple partners from contaminating one another's data, the two partners were interviewed at the same time but in separate locations by the two interviewers. Interviews took approximately 1½–2 hours each. Following the completion of a given couple's interviews, interviewers turned in to the researchers the RIT graphs, respondents' satisfaction measures, and written versions of the taped interviews.

Data Analysis

The researchers inductively derived a set of 26 turning point types from the interview data (see Results section) and independently coded a 20% sample of interviews, reaching an absolute agreement of .79 on the identification of turning point types (Cohen's, 1960, kappa = .78, p < .000). Deeming this an adequate level of reliability, each researcher coded turning point types for half of the remaining interviews.

STATISTICAL SUMMARY 1

Reliability is a measure of accuracy. If a measure is highly reliable then you can be confident that the scores are very accurate. Kappa is a statistic for determining how reliable or accurate two coders are. While coding in this study was moderately reliable, the satisfaction scale was quite reliable.

The researchers developed a three-category coding of partner agreement in the identification of turning points: (1) agree; (2) disagree; (3) agree on point identification but disagree on the point's valence. An independent coding of a 20% sample of interviews produced an absolute agreement of .83 in coding partner agreement (kappa = .66, p < .000), and the researchers equally divided the coding of the remaining interviews. A three-category code was derived for the role of communication in the turning points: (1) not mentioned at all; (2) mention of content-level communication only; and (3) mention of relationship talk. The absolute agreement between the researchers across a 20% sample of interviews was .79 (kappa = .61, p < .000), allowing each researcher to code independently half of the remaining interviews.

The internal reliability of the current satisfaction scale using Cronbach's alpha was .88. A respondent's satisfaction score was the sum across all six of the satisfaction items. Satisfaction correlated r = .80 (p < .000) with current relationship commitment, lending credence to the

measure's validity for nonmarital romantic relationships.

Change in commitment level was derived directly from respondent graphs: commitment at current turning point minus commitment at immediately prior turning point. Positive turning points were those with a commitment difference score greater than zero; negative turning points were those with difference scores less than zero.

RESULTS

Research Question #1 inquired about the phenomena that comprise turning points in romantic relationships. The interview data revealed a rich array of events that were associated with change in relationship commitment. A total of 759 turning points were identified, with a mean of 9.5 events per respondent account and a range of 3–20 events. The researchers inductively derived 26 different types of events whose frequency distribution is reported in Table 1. Because 26 categories were too cumbersome for data analysis purposes, the texts of respondent interviews were examined in order to derive groupings of turning point types that were talked about in similar ways. The resulting 14 supra-types are summarized in Table 1.

The supra-type of "Get-to-Know Time" was the most frequently mentioned by respondents, consisting of three turning point events that facilitate the parties getting to know one another. "First Meeting" refers to the first time the two relationship parties ever met. "Activity Time" captures the time early in the relationship when the parties spent time together enacting various activities, such as studying together. Based on respondent accounts, it was apparent that this time was valued for its quantity, not necessarily the quality of the activity. "First Date" refers to the first time the respondent regarded the two of them going on a boy-girl date.

The supra-type of "Quality Time" also consists of three turning point types, all of which are special occasions for the pair to appreciate one another and their relationship for its own sake. "Quality Time" captures the time the relationship parties spent together as a couple just

TABLE 1
Distribution of Turning Point Types

Supra-types and subtypes	Frequency (N = 759)	%
I. Get-to-Know Time	144	19.0
A. First Meeting	80	10.5
B. Activity Time	46	6.1
C. First Date	18	2.4
II. Quality Time	117	15.4
A. Quality Time	85	11.2
B. Meet the Family	17	2.2
C. Getting Away Time	15	2.0
III. Physical Separation	76	10.0
IV. External Competition	70	9.2
A. New Rival	39	5.1
B. Competing Demands	16	2.1
C. Old Rival	15	2.0
V. Reunion	57	7.5
VI. Passion	48	6.3
A. First Sex	23	3.0
B. First Kiss	10	1.3
C. "I love you"	9	1.2
D. Whirlwind Phenomenon	6	.8
VII. Disengagement	46	6.1
VIII. Positive Psychic Change	42	5.5
IX. Exclusivity	34	4.5
A. Joint Exclusivity Decision	23	3.0
B. Dropping All Rivals	11	1.4
X. Negative Psychic Change	29	3.8
XI. Making Up	25	3.3
XII. Serious Commitment	24	3.2
A. Living Together	13	1.7
B. Marital Plans	11	1.4
XIII. Sacrifice	23	3.0
A. Crisis Help	14	1.8
B. Favors or Gifts	9	3.2
XIV. Other	24	3.2

enjoying each other's presence and their relationship without the necessary presence of some activity to be enacted and not necessarily for a large quantity of time. The event of "Meeting the Family" afforded the relationship parties an opportunity to focus on their coupleness in the presence of family members. "Getting Away Time" refers to occasions when the parties broke the routine of school and work and went away to be together.

"Physical Separation" is the only turning point event in the supra-type of the same label. This event refers to separation generated by vacations, school breaks, and overseas trips rather than separations that result from a disengagement or break-up of the relationship. The fact that the sample was drawn from a college population contributes to the relatively high quantity of physical separations experienced by the romantic couples.

The supra-type of "External Competition" consists of three turning event types. "New Rival" refers to the appearance of a third-party rival for the affection of one of the parties. In contrast, "Old Rival" refers to the reemergence of an old boyfriend or girlfriend. "Competing Demands" captures nonromantic competition for the parties' time and attention, typically school, work, or sports. Because respondents often suspected the presence of a romantic rival in such circumstances, however, this event type is logically grouped with the two romantically based competing demands.

"Reunion" is a single-event supra-type that refers to reunion after Physical Separation. The disparity in the frequency of this event and the frequency of the Physical Separation event underscores the fact that not all reunions constituted turning points. Further, some physical separations did not affect commitment but the reunion event did have an impact on the parties' commitment. Thus, there is no necessary one-to-one correspondence between Physical Separation and Reunion events in these data.

The supra-type of "Passion" refers to four events that involve physical/emotional affection between the parties. "First Kiss" and "First Sex" were important marker events for these respondents in affecting or signaling relationship commitment. Similarly, the expression of "I love you" constituted an important turning point. The "Whirlwind Phenomenon" refers to the proverbial love-at-first-sight experience.

"Disengagement" is a single-event supra-type that refers to any deescalation in the relationship, including total break-up or dissolution. "Making Up" refers to events in which the parties repaired their relationship after its disengagement or break-up. As was the case with the events of Physical Separation and Reunion, the "Disengagement" and "Making Up" events bear no necessary one-to-one correspondence in the data. For some respondents, the disengagement was eventful but the make-up was not; for others the disengagement was relatively uneventful but the making up was significant.

The single-event supra-types of "Positive Psychic Change" and "Negative Psychic Change" refer to intrapsychic changes of attitude for the respondent. Unlike other turning points, these two lack perceived external events as catalysts to change that respondents could recall.

"Exclusivity" is a supra-type that consists of two turning point events. The "Joint Exclusivity Decision" refers to a joint decision by the relationship parties to be romantically involved with only each other. "Dropping All Rivals" refers to default exclusivity by breaking romantic involvement with all others except the partner.

The supra-type of "Serious Commitment" involves two turning point events. "Living Together" refers to the parties' decision to move in together as a couple. "Marital Plans" refers to the joint decision to marry, typically the event of getting engaged.

"Sacrifice" is a supra-type that consists of two turning point events. "Crisis Help" refers to assistance provided by the other party when the respondent was experiencing some personal problem. "Favors or Gifts" refers to a sacrifice made by the other party or by the respondent in the form of gifts or favors.

Overall, 3.2% of the turning point events could not be classified into 1 of the above 25 types or 13 supra-types. These "Other" events captured a miscellany of experiences, none of which occurred with sufficient frequency to warrant the addition of another turning point type category.

The second research question probed the role of explicit metacommunication in turning point events. The three-category coding scheme described above was dichotomized by collapsing the first two categories into a single category of "No Relationship Talk." Overall, 55.1% of the turning point events involved relationship talk. However, relationship talk was not equally likely for all types of turning point events. Table 2 presents the proportions of each type of turning point that entailed relationship talk. A chi-square test indicated that differences were significant beyond the p = .0000 level ($\chi^2 = 117.07$, df = 12; $C^2 = .17$). Get-to-Know Time, Physical Separation, and Sacrifice were least likely to involve relationship talk. In contrast, the turning point types of Exclusivity, Making Up, Disengagement, Serious Commitment, and Passion were most likely to involve talk about the relationship.

STATISTICAL SUMMARY 2

Chi square is a statistical test that tells you if two variables are related to each other. It is used with variables that have categories (e.g., ethnicity might have African American, white American, Mexican American; and income might have high, medium, and low) and shows you if one category of one variable (e.g., African American) tends to occur more frequently with a category of a second variable (e.g., middle income). In this study a chi-square test was used to see if relationship talk was related to the type of turning point. A relationship did exist, with the turning points of Get-to-Know Time, Physical Separation, and Sacrifice less likely to involve talk about the relationship, and Exclusivity, Making Up, Disengagement, Serious Commitment, and Passion as more likely to involve relationship talk.

A chi-square test also showed that the partners in a relationship differed on what they considered to be turning points, but that this was not affected by gender.

The third research question inquired about partner agreement in the identification of turning point events. For purposes of analysis, the three-category coding scheme described above was reduced to two categories by collapsing the general disagreement category with the valence disagreement category. Overall, 54.5% of all turning points were agreed upon by relationship partners. Table 3 summarizes the proportions of each turning point supra-type about which relationship partners agreed. A chi-square test indicated a significant departure from chance at beyond the $p = .0001$ level ($\chi^2 = 39.16$, df $= 12$; $C^2 = .05$). Partner agreement in identifying turning points was notably low with External Competition, Positive Psychic Change, Sacrifice, and Quality Time. Partner agreement was especially evident for Reunion, Exclusivity, Serious Commitment, and Get-to-Know Time. In order to determine whether systematic gender differences were at play in the 45% discrepant cases, a chi-square test was performed on the frequency of supra-types reported by males and females. No systematic gender difference was found ($\chi^2 = 9.86$, 12 df,

TABLE 2
Turning Point Types That Involved Relationship Talk

Turning point type	%
Get-to-Know Time	19.8
Quality Time	59.4
Physical Separation	37.3
External Competition	59.0
Reunion	50.0
Passion	76.7
Disengagement	79.1
Positive Psychic Change	65.2
Exclusivity	90.9
Negative Psychic Change	61.9
Making Up	86.4
Serious Commitment	77.3
Sacrifice	20.0
Overall	55.1

TABLE 3
Turning Point Types About Which Partners Agreed

Turning point type	%
Get-to-Know Time	68.8
Quality Time	45.3
Physical Separation	53.9
External Competition	42.0
Reunion	63.2
Passion	50.0
Disengagement	56.5
Positive Psychic Change	38.1
Exclusivity	67.6
Negative Psychic Change	48.3
Making Up	56.0
Serious Commitment	75.0
Sacrifice	30.4
Overall	54.5

TABLE 4
Means and Standard Deviations for Change in Relationship Commitment Level by Turning Point Types

Turning point type	Mean change commitment	Standard deviation
Get-to-Know Time	+21.13	17.50
Quality Time	+15.18	13.07
Physical Separation	− 0.30	22.69
External Competition	−13.44	23.83
Reunion	+10.72	21.28
Passion	+20.35	17.56
Disengagement	−23.28	26.74
Positive Psychic Change	+18.98	20.00
Exclusivity	+19.21	21.91
Negative Psychic Change	− 9.00	13.96
Making Up	+21.60	28.85
Serious Commitment	+23.26	24.78
Sacrifice	+17.61	14.70
Other	− 1.04	22.36

p = .63; power estimated at beyond .99 for a medium effect size at alpha = .05; Cohen, 1969).

The fourth research question asked if turning point types varied in their intensity. A one-way ANOVA was conducted on the 13 supra-types (excluding ''Other'') with reported change in commitment level serving as the dependent variable. The means and standard deviations are reported in Table 4. The main effect on turning point type was significant at beyond the .001 level (F = 27.45, df = 12, 650; eta^2 = .34).[1] The turning point types are composed of three major negative change events—Disengagement, External Competition, and Negative Psychic Change—none of which differs from the other two but all of which differ from the positive change events based on subsequent Scheffé tests. The most positive events are Serious Commitment, Making Up, Get-to-Know Time, Passion, Exclusivity, and Positive Psychic Change, none of which differs from the other five events based on subsequent Scheffé tests.

STATISTICAL SUMMARY 3

Analysis of variance (ANOVA) is a technique for seeing if three or more groups differ from each other. For example, if you have three groups, you may want to know which one talks the most. Here, Baxter and Bullis used ANOVA to show that the turning points differed from each other in their intensity.

The fifth research question explored a variety of possible associations between turning points and current relationship satisfaction; with N = 80 and a two-tailed alpha of .05, the correlation statistic employed in these analyses had an estimated power of .78 for a medium effect size (Cohen, 1969). An insignificant correlation was found between a respondent's current satisfaction with the relationship and the proportion of his or her identified turning points with which the partner agreed (r = .08; p = .25). The pattern of association of satisfaction with partner agreement in the identification of turning points remained insignificant when positive turning points were examined separately from negative turning points (r values of .06 and .19, respectively). Current relationship satisfaction was not significantly correlated with the proportion of turning point events that involved relationship talk (r = .09, p = .22). The absence of a relationship between explicit metacommunication and satisfaction held when negative turning points and positive turning points were analyzed separately (r values of .10 and .04, respectively). Current satisfaction with the relationship correlated significantly with the proportion of a respondent's identified turning points that were negative (r = −.39, p < .000).

STATISTICAL SUMMARY 4

Correlations are used to see if two or more variables are related to each other. A high correlation shows that two variables are very much related to each other. A zero correlation may mean that they are independent of each other or unrelated. A positive correlation means that as the scores of one variable increase, the scores on the second variable increase as well. Thus, if someone scores high on one variable (e.g., talkativeness) they are likely also to score high on the other variable (e.g., number of friends).

Here, relational satisfaction was not related to agreement with one's partner about turning points or to the amount of relational talk, but was related to the relative number of negative turning points.

In order to discern which turning point events were associated with current satisfaction level, a series of t-tests was performed that compared satisfaction level between respondent accounts in which a given turning point type was present versus absent. Significant differences emerged for the Exclusivity turning point event (t = 2.39, df = 78, p = .019; r^2_{pb} = .07) with satisfaction greater for those respondents who identified this

turning point in their relationship. The presence of the Disengagement event produced less satisfaction for respondents than was the case for respondents whose relationships lacked a Disengagement event (t = 2.57, df = 78, p = .012; r^2_{pb} = .08). The presence or absence of the remainder of the turning point types was not significantly related to satisfaction (power of the t-test estimated at .60 for two-tailed alpha = .05 and medium effect size; Cohen, 1969).

STATISTICAL SUMMARY 5

T-tests were used to compare the effects of each turning point on satisfaction. T-tests tell you if there is a difference between two groups. Here, the groups were those relationships with a certain turning point and those without the turning point. For example, the authors wanted to know if there was greater satisfaction with relationships that had experienced physical separation than with those in which there had never been a physical separation. Greater satisfaction was experienced when Exclusivity was present and/or when Disengagement was not present.

DISCUSSION

This research has explored Bolton's (1961) turning point as a lens through which to examine relationship change. Researchers should profit from the discoveries that the set of turning points is finite yet diverse enough to capture richly relational change and that participants are able to identify those turning points that they consider meaningful in their relational histories. In contrast to the image of relationship development as a process of creeping incrementalism with indistinguishable points of change, these findings provide tentative support for a view of relationship growth as a series of discrete events that are accompanied by positive or negative explosions of relational commitment. However, respondents provided their relational histories retrospectively, and the possibility exists that creeping incrementalism may nonetheless capture relationship change as it is experienced at the time; cognitive reframing into discrete events may simply be a memory artifact. Such events are self-contained "packages" of salient and concrete actions, perhaps easier to recall than nondistinct incremental changes. The possibility exists also that the RIT procedure biased the data in favor of discrete turning point events. However, the interviewers observed informally that their respondents had little difficulty in recalling turning point events. Such events may be salient to relationship parties because they provide useful "story lines" about which the parties can reminisce or present their relationship to others. Future work needs to monitor relationship development longitudinally to address the issue of how change actually is experienced at the time in relationships as opposed to how such change is recalled after the fact.

Because this study dealt with perceived changes in commitment associated with turning point phenomena, it is impossible to determine causality. Conceptually, however, it would appear useful to distinguish capstone or marker turning points from causal events. In some instances, an internalized change in commitment may produce a turning point. Such a turning point serves to formalize or mark the felt change in commitment, constituting a capstone event. The declaration of exclusive commitment, for example, is likely to serve as such a capstone event in going "on record" about the parties' already changed feelings about one another. Other turning point events may serve a more direct causal function, producing change in felt commitment. Sacrifice events, for example, were always reported as turning points that produced a change in commitment. The display of sacrifice by the other party on one's behalf resulted in increased commitment toward the other. The distinction between capstone and causal turning points is somewhat artificial, however, for reciprocal causality between event and commitment is likely for both types of turning point events. Capstone events may formalize an internalized affective change in commitment, but once such events have occurred, they likely serve as causal forces in propelling further commitment. Similarly,

some causal turning points probably involve a prior internalized affect change in one of the parties. Sacrifice, for instance, probably involves some prior affective change in the other to motivate the sacrificial act.

The turning point framework was helpful in probing instances of direct relationship talk. Overall, 55% of the turning points involved relationship talk, a figure that may seem high given that extant work reports the infrequency of explicit metacommunication. This discrepancy is tempered by the realization that turning points themselves occur relatively infrequently; the typical relationship party reported about one turning point every two months or so.

The fact that relationship talk was not equally distributed across turning point types supports the selective use of explicit relationship talk in romantic couples. Some of the events associated with direct metacommunication, especially Exclusivity, Making Up, and Serious Commitment, appear to be events that, by definition, would be difficult to accomplish in the absence of relationship talk. Our Passion category may tap a set of events that is critical to defining the relationship, is accomplished mutually, and provides meaningful events ripe for explicit relationship talk. The fact that Disengagement was strongly associated with relational talk fails to support prior work in relationship break-up that has found indirectness a pervasive strategy (see Baxter, 1985). However, these relationships were still intact, in contrast to the dissolved relationships that have been studied in extant disengagement work. Perhaps relationship talk prevents disengagement events from turning into complete dissolutions.

Other turning point events are noteworthy because of the absence of relationship talk. Get-to-Know Time may tap an initial stage when the relationship is particularly vulnerable and thus direct relationship talk is avoided for fear of destroying the relationship (Baxter & Wilmot, 1985). Similarly, Physical Separation is associated with relational vulnerability and may also be avoided in direct metacommunication. In short, the presence or absence of relationship talk may depend on the specific type of turning point event.

An association between explicit metacommunication and overall relational satisfaction was not evident in this study, consistent with the conclusion drawn by critics of the talk-as-elixir folk myth. It may be that relationship talk is related to satisfaction but in a complex way not tapped in the relatively crude presence-absence distinction employed in this study. Explicit metacommunication might differ in quantity, content, context, strategies, and outcomes depending on the specific turning point. The relationship between metacommunication and overall satisfaction may be mediated by these intervening contingencies.

Partner agreement in reported turning points was about 55%. This figure is comparable to that noted by other researchers in assessing partner agreement in monitoring day-to-day behavior (Christensen & Nies, 1980; Jacobson & Moore, 1981). Further, this behavioral monitoring research has reported the greatest partner agreement with objective behaviors as opposed to behaviors which involve subjectivity by the observer (Christensen & Nies, 1980; Jacobson & Moore, 1981). A comparable pattern was found in this study for partner agreement in reported turning points; agreement was higher for events that appear to be most objectively verifiable and lower for subjectively experienced events. The types of turning points most characterized by low partner agreement appear to be highly individualized as experienced and interpreted by relational partners. For example, the experience of Positive Psychic Change is by definition an internal psychological phenomenon. Quality Time and Sacrifice may also occur predominantly in one individual's interpretation. When one partner experiences External Competition, she or he may withhold the experience from the other (Baxter & Wilmot, 1985), thereby creating a unilateral and subjectively realized turning point. In contrast, those events most characterized by partner agreement (Reunion, Exclusivity, Serious Commitment, and Get-to-Know Time) are events that are more easily externally verifiable.

If accounts of turning points are regarded as objective records of relational histories, the relatively low partner agreement found in this study fails to meet minimum standards of measurement reliability between partner observers. However, if partner reports of the events in their relationship are regarded as important in their own right, rather than as reliable observations about objective events, it becomes moot to cast partner agreement in terms of measurement reliability. Instead, a focus on the phenomenology of relationship partners makes differences in partner reports a theoretically interesting issue. The relatively low agreement between partners suggests that relationship parties indeed coexist in separate phenomenological relationship worlds. However, these differences do not neatly fit into "his" and "her" social realities, for no systematic gender differences were observed for the types of reported turning points.

Partners who experienced more agreement were not found to be more satisfied with their relationships. This suggests that perceptual consensus may not be necessary for overall relationship success, a conclusion consistent with the argument by Sillars and Scott (1983) discussed above. As those researchers noted, the compatibility of the partners' disparate perceptions may be a more predictive indicator of relationship success. That is, partners may successfully function in their relationship despite different cognitive constructions of their history so long as those constructions do not obstruct one another.

Further explorations of agreement need to use diverse measurement methods. For example, in this study, agreement occurred only when both partners' independent accounts of their relationship included the same event. Different measurement methods such as joint interviews or having partners verify one another's accounts should be employed as well.

Turning points were shown to differ in their associated levels of commitment change. Although some turning point events were clearly very positive or very negative in impact, other events, such as Physical Separation, were relatively unclear in their impact. It is likely that events such as Physical Separation are either positive or negative, depending on how the parties manage the event (Wilmot et al., 1985). In general, the turning points highest in reported commitment change (in either a positive or negative direction) were also those turning points likely to be highest in partner agreement and likely to involve relationship talk. This finding suggests that partners share a partially common phenomenological reality, perhaps enhanced through relationship talk, on those turning point events regarded as most significant to the relationship. Alternatively, events that are discussed and agreed upon may simply be accorded more importance retrospectively.

Given that the proportion of events that were negative correlated inversely with overall relational satisfaction, turning points may function in a cumulative manner to affect current relational satisfaction. Alternatively, more satisfied relationship parties may simply fail to recall many negative events for their relationship. Only 2 of the 13 supra-types were individually related to current satisfaction with the relationship: Disengagement and Exclusivity. This finding suggests that there may be some specific events whose presence or absence during relationship development may differentiate between more and less satisfied partners, regardless of the total proportion of negative (and positive) events in a relational history.

The specific turning point types that emerged in this study provide some confirmatory insights into people's implicit relationship theories. The early event type of Get-to-Know Time contrasted with the later event of Quality Time suggests that quantity may be an important indicator of an early romance whereas the quality criterion becomes more important to a closer romantic relationship. Hays (1984) has observed a similar transformation from quantity to quality criteria in the development of same-sex friendships. The Sacrifice event suggests the salience of demonstrable caring on the other's behalf as an important indicator of romantic involvement. Displays of physical affection (the Passion event) appear important in transforming a platonic opposite-sex relationship into a full-blown romantic relationship type, a finding consistent with prior work (Wilmot & Baxter, 1984). The turning point events of External Competition and Exclusivity point to the salience of loyalty and fidelity to people's implicit theories of romantic relationships, qualities that have emerged in extant work as well (Baxter, in press; Davis & Todd, 1982; Wilmot & Baxter, 1984).

In summary, the turning point should provide a fruitful construct for relationship research. Participants retrospectively cast their relationship development as a series of positive and negative turning points. Turning point analysis is valuable as an approach to explicit metacommunication, partner congruence of perspectives, overall satisfaction, and relational commitment levels. Future research should examine possible differences in turning point accounts for relationships that experience different trajectories of growth (Huston et al., 1981). Work in relationship cultures should consider the role that turning points play in maintaining the relationship through consideration of reminiscing interaction. Because turning points constitute useful story lines, with self-contained "chunks" of a relationship's history, their role in the public presentation of the relationship by its parties should be considered as well.

NOTE

1. Bartlett's test of homogeneity of variance was $F = 6.01$, $p < .001$, indicating that the various turning point supra-types had different variances. However, Keppel (1973) observes that analysis of variance is sufficiently robust to perform with variances even more divergent than those found here. Nonetheless, the nonparametric Kruskal-Wallis one-way analysis of variance test was performed on supra-type differences in change in commitment, with $H = 261.45$, $p < .000$. The pattern of mean ranks replicated the pattern found with the ANOVA findings. That is, Disengagement, External Competition, and Negative Psychic change composed the least positive events, and the six most positive events were as reported in the text of the article.

REFERENCES

Altman, I., & Taylor, D. (1973). *Social penetration: The development of interpersonal relationships.* New York: Holt, Rinehart & Winston.

Altman, I., Vinsel, A., & Brown, B. (1981). Dialectic conceptions in social psychology: An application to social penetration and privacy regulation. In L. Berkowitz (Ed.), *Advances in experimental social psychology* (Vol. 14). New York: Academic Press.

Baxter, L. (1985). Accomplishing relationship disengagement. In S. Duck & D. Perlman (Eds.), *Understanding personal relationships: An interdisciplinary approach.* London: Sage.

———. (in press). Gender differences in the heterosexual relationship rules embedded in break-up accounts. *Journal of Social and Personal Relationships.*

Baxter, L., & Wilmot, W. (1984). "Secret tests": Social strategies for acquiring information about the state of the relationship. *Human Communication Research, 11,* 171–201.

———. (1985). Taboo topics in close relationships. *Journal of Social and Personal Relationships, 2,* 253–269.

Berger, C. R., & Calabrese, R. (1975). Some explorations in initial interaction and beyond: Toward a developmental theory of interpersonal communication. *Human Communication Research, 1,* 99–112.

Bochner, A. P. (1982). On the efficacy of openness in close relationships. In M. Burgoon (Ed.), *Communication yearbook 6.* New Brunswick, NJ: Transaction Books.

Bolton, C. D. (1961). Mate selection as the development of a relationship. *Marriage and Family Living, 23,* 234–240.

Braiker, H. B., & Kelley, H. H. (1979). Conflict in the development of close relationships. In R. L. Burgess & T. L. Huston (Eds.), *Social exchange in developing relationships.* New York: Academic Press.

Christensen, A., & Nies, D. C. (1980). The spouse observation checklist: Empirical analysis and critique. *American Journal of Family Therapy, 8,* 69–79.

Cody, M. (1982). A typology of disengagement strategies and an examination of the role intimacy, reactions to inequity and relational problems play in strategy selection. *Communication Monographs, 49,* 148–170.

Cohen, J. (1960). A coefficient of agreement for nominal scales. *Educational and Psychological Measurement, 20,* 37–48.

———. (1969). *Statistical power analysis for the behavioral sciences.* New York: Academic Press.

Davis, K. E., & Todd, M. J. (1982). Friendship and love relationships. In K. E. Davis & T. Mitchell (Eds.), *Advances in descriptive psychology* (Vol. 2). Greenwich, CT: JAI Press.

Duck, S., & Perlman, D. (1985). *Understanding personal relationships: An interdisciplinary approach.* London: Sage.

Gottman, J., Markman, H., & Notarious, C. (1977). The topography of marital conflict. *Journal of Marriage and the Family, 39,* 461–478.

Granovetter, M. S. (1976). Network sampling: Some first steps. *American Journal of Sociology, 81,* 1287–1303.

Hays, R. (1984). The development and maintenance of friendship. *Journal of Social and Personal Relationships, 1,* 75–98.

Hinde, R. A. (1981). The bases of a science of interpersonal relationships. In S. Duck & R. Gilmour (Eds.), *Personal relationships 1: Studying personal relationships.* New York: Academic Press.

Huston, T. L., Surra, C., Fitzgerald, N. M., & Cate, R. (1981). From courtship to marriage: Mate selection as an interpersonal process. In S. Duck & R. Gilmour (Eds.), *Personal relationships 2: Developing personal relationships.* New York: Academic Press.

Jacobson, N. S., & Moore, D. (1981). Spouses as observers of the events in their relationship. *Journal of Consulting and Clinical Psychology, 49,* 269–277.

Katriel, T., & Philipsen, G. (1981). "What we need is communication": "Communication" as a cultural category in some American speech. *Communication Monographs, 48,* 301–317.

Keppel, G. (1973). *Design and analysis.* Englewood Cliffs, NJ: Prentice-Hall.

Knapp, M. (1984). *Interpersonal communication and human relationships.* Boston: Allyn and Bacon.

Lewis, R. A., & Spanier, G. B. (1979). Theorizing about the quality and stability of marriage. In W. Burr et al. (Eds.), *Contemporary theories about the family* (Vol. 1). New York: Macmillan.

Lloyd, S. (1983). *A typological description of premarital relationship dissolution.* Unpublished doctoral thesis, Oregon State University.

Lloyd, S., & Cate, R. (1984). *Attributions associated with significant turning points in premarital relationship development and dissolution.* Paper presented at the Second International Conference on Personal Relationships, Madison WI.

Miell, D. (1984). *Strategies in information exchange in developing relationships: Evidence for a unique relational context.* Paper presented at the Second International Conference on Personal Relationships, Madison WI.

Norton, R. (1983). Measuring marital quality: A critical look at the dependent variable. *Journal of Marriage and the Family, 45,* 141–151.

Nydick, A., & Cornelius, R. (1984). *What we talk about when we talk about love.* Paper presented at the Second International Conference on Personal Relationships, Madison WI.

Parks, M. R. (1982). Ideology in interpersonal communication: Off the couch and into the world. In M. Burgoon (Ed.), *Communication yearbook 6.* New Brunswick, NJ: Transaction Books.

Planalp, S., & Honeycutt, J. (1985). Events that increase uncertainty in personal relationships. *Human Communication Research, 11,* 593–604.

Rands, M., & Levinger, G. (1979). Implicit theories of relationships: An intergenerational study. *Journal of Personality and Social Psychology, 37,* 645–661.

Sillars, A., & Scott, M. (1983). Interpersonal perception between intimates: An integrative review. *Human Communication Research, 10,* 153–176.

Spanier, G. B. (1976). Measuring dyadic adjustment: New scales for assessing the quality of marriage and similar dyads. *Journal of Marriage and the Family, 38,* 15–28.

Spanier, G. B., & Lewis, R. A. (1980). Marital quality: A review of research in the seventies. *Journal of Marriage and the Family, 42,* 825–839.

Surra, C. (1984). *Attributions about changes in commitment: Variations by courtship style.* Paper presented at the Second International Conference on Personal Relationships, Madison WI.

Wilmot, W. (1980). Metacommunication: A re-examination and extension. In D. Nimmo (Ed.), *Communication yearbook 4.* New Brunswick, NJ: Transaction Books.

Wilmot, W., & Baxter, L. (1984). *Defining relationships: The interplay of cognitive schemata and communication.* Paper presented at the Western Speech Communication Association Annual Convention, Seattle WA.

Wilmot, W., Carbaugh, D., & Baxter, L. (1985). Communication strategies used to terminate romantic relationships. *Western Journal of Speech Communication, 49,* 204–216.

'TRUE LOVE WAYS': THE SUBJECTIVE EXPERIENCE AND COMMUNICATION OF ROMANTIC LOVE

Peter J. Marston
Michael L. Hecht
Tia Robers

Whereas previous research into romantic love has focused upon the traits of love objects, beliefs about love and/or types of loving relationships, these two studies examine the subjective experience of love and the manners in which love is communicated. In Study I seventy-six respondents participated in face-to-face interviews. Responses were content and cluster analysed. Cluster analysis revealed six 'ways of romantic love': Collaborative Love, Active Love, Secure Love, Intuitive Love, Committed Love and Traditional Romantic Love. In Study II 185 respondents completed a questionnaire version of the Study I interview. Respondents then employed the six love clusters in self-coding their responses, providing representational validity for the previous cluster analysis. Further, a confirming cluster analysis—using a subset of the Study II data—provided construct validity for four of the six love clusters. A fifth cluster split into two new clusters. These studies support two general conclusions. First, love may be experienced in a variety of different ways: in terms of relational constructs, physiological responses, behavioural actions and/or non-verbal perceptions. Second, there is strong coherence in lovers' experience of love and in their reports of how love is communicated.

Of all human emotions, romantic love is perhaps the most mysterious and the most personal. 'Falling in love' is often described as an irrational experience—but one with an almost magical emancipatory capacity to transcend the very limitations of one's human existence. The transcendent and subjective nature of romantic love seems to defy verbal expression, let alone rational explanation. While there are those who

Source: The article is taken from the *Journal of Social and Personal Relationships* [4: 387–407, 1987]. © Sage Publications Ltd., 6 Bonhill St., London EC24A 4PU, UK. Reprinted by permission of Sage Publications Ltd.

will say that romantic love is necessarily naive and idealistic, there are also those, confident for the moment, who will say that for one who has loved, no explanation is necessary, and that for one who has never loved, no explanation is possible. However, if the nature and functions of romantic love are to be understood by researchers, then some explanation must be attempted.

The importance of love, romantic and otherwise, has been articulated by scholars from a variety of fields. Arnold (1960) classifies love as a primary emotion—one which is inherent to human experience. In De Rivera's (1977) structural theory of emotion, love is one of four basic 'movements' in human relationships, and as such, is a central component of the human system of emotions. An even higher status is accorded love in Montagu's (1970) description of human development. Montagu maintains that the need for love is the most important of all human needs, and that love is the primary directional force in human development.

Although romantic love has been a prominent, even ubiquitous theme in literature and the popular arts, until recently there has been relatively little empirical or theoretical work on the subject. Prior to the rise of the social sciences, the scholarly study of love was restricted to the efforts of philosophers and theoretical psychologists. Writers from Plato (1969) to Fromm (1956) have addressed the issues of romantic love from an idealistic, normative perspective, speculating on the nature of a 'higher' love. The works of such writers, though insightful, are not empirically grounded and therefore may not reflect accurately the nature of romantic love *as it exists* in human relationships. Indeed, both Plato and Fromm articulate their conceptions of romantic love as alternatives to prevailing social practices.

Recently, however, romantic love has become a reputable area for social scientific inquiry (Hendrick et al., 1984). To date, social scientific research concerning romantic love has employed analyses which are typically either correlational or dimensional.

Many scholars have sought to correlate emotions such as love with underlying cognitive processes (e.g., Seligman et al., 1980) and physiological responses (e.g., Clynes, 1978; Pribram, 1980). While cognitivists seek to examine emotions in terms of mental processes, emphasizing the logical and rational elements, physiologists focus upon the electrochemical and bodily responses associated with emotional states. Although the findings of this research are useful in relating romantic love to the larger frameworks of cognitivism and behaviourism, such explanations do not reveal the various ways in which love is experienced, but rather the manifestations of love within a particular paradigm of human nature. Such analyses tend to ignore the complex character of romantic love. As De Vito (1980:498) observes, love is 'an activity of the whole person, in which body and mind and emotions are all actively involved'. Any analysis which attempts to locate and define love within a single realm of experience is likely to give us a vision of romantic love which is, at best, incomplete. Indeed, the very fact that researchers find empirical evidence for both cognitive *and* physiological bases of love belies the ambitions of any unilateral analysis.

Interactionists such as Schachter & Singer (1962) attempt to integrate cognitive and physiological conceptions of emotion. Yet, to date, such research has excluded consideration of behavioural elements (e.g., communication and physical intimacy). Other interactionists (e.g., Kemper, 1978) focus heavily on communication and social interaction, but ignore physiology and cognition. The need remains, therefore, for a holistic examination of love—one which seeks to integrate the cognitive, physiological and behavioural aspects of this complex emotion.

Researchers have also sought to correlate romantic love with a variety of psychological and personality constructs. In this type of study, romantic love is used as an independent variable, measured against other variables such as shyness (Morolodo, 1982), hypnotic susceptibility

(Mathes, 1982), self-preoccupation (Johnston & Jeremko, 1979) and cognitive orientation (Seligman et al., 1980). Although such studies are valuable in developing relationships between love and other constructs, they demonstrate little concern with the subjective experience of love.

The most notable dimensional analyses of romantic love are those of Rubin (1970, 1973) and Lee (1973). Both Rubin and Lee attempt to describe romantic love in a qualitative sense by establishing dimensions of love and then validating these dimensions empirically. Rubin (1970) begins deductively, hypothesizing three international attitudes associated with love objects: affiliative and dependent need, predisposition to help, and exclusiveness and absorption. He later designates these as: attachment, caring and intimacy (Rubin, 1973). Using these attitudes as dimensional components of loving, Rubin (1970) develops a measure of romantic love which he validates against couples' perceptions of their relationship and their likelihood of marriage.

Although Rubin finds significant correlations between his measure and the perceptions of the tested couples, there are certain limitations to his analysis. First, as a deductively derived system, Rubin's dimensions may not be exhaustive (Wiseman & Schenck-Hamlin, 1981). Given his methodology, there is no empirical basis to reject the possibility that other components of love have been overlooked, even after validating all or part of his measure. Second, Rubin restricts his analysis to *attitude* towards love objects. As noted above, love is a complex emotional experience involving not only attitudes but also behaviours and physiological, somatic responses which may not be mediated by propositional constructs such as those suggested by Rubin. Third, Rubin (1970: 266) defines romantic love as 'love between unmarried opposite-sex peers, of the sort which could possibly lead to marriage', and accordingly validates his measure with a sample of dating (unmarried, non-engaged) couples. The bifurcation of romantic love and marriage is problematic, especially given our sociocultural identification of these two experiences.

Whereas Rubin examines attitudes towards love objects, Lee focuses his analysis on the behavioural referents associated with love. He begins inductively, categorizing over 4000 literary and philosophical statements concerning love behaviours. Lee (1973) arrives at three behavioural dimensions: Eros (eroticism), Ludus (playfulness) and Storge (friendship). These dimensions exist separately or in combination, resulting in a typology of nine styles or 'colours' of loving. Through interviews with 112 men and women, Lee empirically confirms eight of the nine styles.

The contributions of Rubin and Lee are clearly significant and useful: each has provided a coherent theory of romantic love as it is manifested within a major realm of human experience (i.e., attitudes towards love objects and behavioural styles of loving). Accordingly, it is not our intention to refute or replace their dimensional typologies. However, these researchers have largely ignored the holistic subjective experience of love which is the central focus of the present analysis.

Two more recent studies have sought to examine subjective perceptions of romantic love. Prentice et al. (1983) analyse the attitudes of American university students towards behaviours which students themselves perceive to be romantic. Three categories of behaviours were significantly correlated with romantic love: traditional romance (e.g., saying 'I love you'), sexual behaviour, and routine activities (e.g., jogging together). In his study of interpretive themes in relational communication, Owen (1984) considers a variety of relationships: married couples, romantic dating couples, relatives, live-in friends and other friends. Although the nature of romantic love is not examined as an independent construct, this study does reveal the interpretive themes employed by married and dating couples to make sense of their relational episodes. Married couples are likely to see their relationships as unique, fragile and based upon mutual consideration, whereas dating couples are more likely to view their relationships as based upon commitment. Although these two studies do not examine the subjective experience of love in its entirety, they are significant in that they focus directly upon the perceptions of lovers.

Our contention that romantic love is a complex emotion which cannot be reduced to any single realm of human experience is predicated upon a phenomenological understanding of human emotions. As such, it will be useful to explicate briefly the underlying theoretical assumptions of such a position (see Sartre, 1957, 1977). First, love is a mode of *being:* a fundamental orientation of the individual to the other, to the world and, indeed, to the self (Sartre, 1957:60). Thus love involves the individual in all aspects of his or her being: thought (attitudes, beliefs, cognition), action (behaviours) and feelings (physiological, somatic responses). Although it is possible to differentiate such realms of experience analytically, they are not truly separable in the actual stream of human experience. Indeed, as Sartre maintains, it is the active and complex interaction of these shifting realms of experience which endows emotions with a magical, spontaneous, captivating and ephemeral quality (Sartre, 1977). Second, the existence of love precedes its essence. As Sartre observes: 'there is . . . no love other than one which manifests itself in a person's being in love' (1957:32). Accordingly, the appropriate starting point for the study of love *as it exists* is the subjective experience of lovers. Third, as a complex emotional experience, love is characterized by polyvalent perceptions which may appear in any number of combinations within a given lover's experience. Thus, although we cannot reduce romantic love to any single definition, we can understand love as the *variety* of ways in which love is experienced.

The central ambition of the present study is to determine these polyvalent perceptions as they are manifest in the subjective experiences of lovers. Whereas previous research into romantic love has focused upon the traits of love objects, beliefs and attitudes about love, and/or types of loving relationships, the subjective experience of love (the thoughts, actions and feelings associated with love) remains to be examined in a systematic manner. Further, we seek to understand the manners in which love is communicated, for

it is our belief that communication is the fundamental action which both expresses and determines the subjective experience of romantic love. Although previous studies concerning love have largely ignored the role of communication and its impact on loving relationships, the importance of communication in determining and altering relationships is paramount, as Knapp (1978:8) suggests: 'Communication may be affected by the existing relationship, but it will also structure the nature of any future relationship'. We have chosen to limit our analysis to reciprocated, heterosexual romantic love. This limitation is necessary in keeping our analysis manageable within the formal constraints of a journal article. However, this limitation is a logical one, in that unrequited and/or homosexual manifestations of love are likely to involve substantially different experiences. We approach this study inductively, seeking our primary data from lovers themselves, in hopes of developing a more complete and integrated understanding of romantic love.

STUDY I

The data for Study I were obtained through face-to-face interviews with 76 respondents selected by the interviewers. Respondents were chosen by two criteria: that the interviewer and respondent had an interpersonal relationship, and that the interviewer considered the respondent to be perceptive about emotions and interpersonal relationships. Although these criteria entailed some bias in the resulting sample, it was hoped that respondents selected in this manner would provide more detailed and intimate responses than would respondents selected in a more random fashion.

The sample consisted of equal numbers of men and women. Ages ranged from 21 to 54, with 52 percent of the sample over 30 years old. Respondents were single [$n=15$], married [$n=48$], divorced [$n=9$] of cohabiting [$n=4$]. The sample included both partners of 19 love dyads (50 percent of the total sample). Respondents' income ranged from $10,000 to $110,000 per year. Educational background varied considerably, with 60 percent of the sample having college degrees.

Interviewers were trained to follow an interview schedule and use follow-up questions to obtain full and complete responses. Because of variance in the interview conditions, interviewers recorded the responses as close to verbatim as the situation permitted. This minimized the effects of interviewer interpretation regarding the data.

Interviews were typically held in the respondent's residence and lasted between twenty and thirty minutes. Each respondent was given a brief oral description of the study's intent. They were informed that they were participating in a study of human emotions and the communication of these emotions. When both partners of a love dyad were present, the respondents were separated and interviewed separately so they could not discuss the questions until the interviews had been completed.

The interview schedule consisted of two sections. The first section included four questions designed to elicit the respondent's own experiential definition of love. Respondents were asked to focus their attention upon an actual love relationship—a heterosexual, romantic, reciprocated love—either in the present or the recent past. They were then asked four questions: (1) What is the feeling of love? (2) What physiological factors or changes are associated with love? (3) If this love has/had a 'colour', what would it be? (4) If you could say a rhythm expresses/expressed this love, what would it be? Questions were asked in sequence, with responses following each separate question. In this manner, respondents were unlikely to anticipate subsequent questions. Question 1 was the central question in this section, with the other questions designed to prompt a more complete consideration of the respondent's love experience. While question 2 asked for descriptions of physiological responses associated with love, questions 3 and 4 sought to circumvent the logical, rational, left-brained type of response likely to be elicited by question 1. It was hoped that these latter questions concerning love's 'colour' and 'rhythm' would tap into the unreflective, intuitive aspects of love. Although other such 'intangibles' (e.g., shape, texture, weight) could have been employed, we believe colour and rhythm to be promising starting points for this sort of analysis. Colour was selected because of its frequent appearance in literary and poetic references to love (e.g., 'Love is blue', 'My love is like a red, red rose'). The use of rhythm, on the other hand, is suggested by Clynes (1978) who notes that many emotions are characterized by a rhythmic component, but who has not yet examined romantic love. Respondents were not required to answer all questions, and indeed most respondents reported that they could not answer one or more of the latter questions or that it was unnecessary to do so.

The second section of the interview schedule concerned the communication of love. Respondents were asked to describe how they communicated love to their partner (sending love), and how their partner communicated love to them (receiving love).

Results

Responses from the interviews were analysed in three stages. First, categories were constructed from content analysis. Second, the categories were used to code the interviews. Third, the category frequencies were cluster analysed.

In the content analysis of interview responses, separate analyses were conducted for each of the six questions included in the interview schedule. The answers to each question were copied on to index cards. If an answer included more than one discrete thought, these thoughts were placed on separate cards. In this manner, a response could produce more than one card, and most did. Two of the researchers individually sorted the cards into the smallest number of discrete categories. The individual category systems were then combined, with the third researcher serving as the arbiter. Through this procedure, four category systems were produced. Colour and rhythm responses were grouped based on identical match and were non-controversial. However, the fact that many respondents could not articulate colours and rhythms makes these categories somewhat problematic.

In the second stage, the category systems were used to code the interviews. Answers to each question were examined for instances of the categories and one answer could be assigned to multiple category coding. For example, a verbal definition which read 'Love is wanting to be with the other person, and makes me feel sure of myself and healthy', would be coded in three categories—togetherness, confident and healthy. Two of the researchers were trained on the category systems and reached 90 percent agreement during practice sessions. Disagreements were discussed and resolved. Coders then individually analysed answers to four of the six questions (general definition, physiological responses, sending love and receiving love). Inter-rater reliability was assessed using formulae provided by

Holsti (1969) and were 0.65, 0.80, 0.82 and 0.78 respectively. These were deemed adequate, particularly given the subjective nature of the data. The category labels, frequencies and percentages are reported in Tables 1–4.

STATISTICAL SUMMARY 1

Study 1

Reliability shows how accurate and consistent your measures are. If a measure is highly reliable then you can be confident that the scores are very accurate, and that the items or indicators are either consistent with each other or consistent over time. Here reliability showed that the coders were fairly accurate and consistent.

T A B L E 1
Definitional Categories[a]

Category	Description	Frequency (percentage)[b]
Intensifier	Feel other emotions more intensely	58 (76)
Warm fuzzies	Peaceful, caring, satisfying	46 (61)
Doing together	Wide range of activities done with other	24 (31)
Togetherness	Connectedness, want to be with other, sharing friendship	21 (28)
Healthy	Healthy feeling, more open to people, feeling of completeness	19 (25)
Confident	Self-assurance, feeling sure	18 (24)
Negative	Variety of negative emotions (e.g., anxiety)	13 (17)
Think about other	Concern for other, anticipating being with other	12 (16)
Commitment	Long-term or future commitment	12 (16)
Secure	Stable, safe, secure	11 (14)
Needs me	Somebody relies on me, needs me	7 (9)
Autonomy	Independence, freedom	4 (5)

Notes: [a]Categories derived from answers to the question: What is the feeling of love? (Reliability of coding=0.65)
[b]Percentages reflect the proportion of all *respondents* coded in a given category. Since a single respondent could be coded into multiple categories, percentages sum over 100 percent.

TABLE 2
Physiological Categories[a]

Category	Description	Frequency (percentage)[b]
Energy	More energy, intensified feelings	24 (31)
Beautiful	Beautiful, healthy, mature, intelligent	13 (17)
Warmth	Warm, safe, secure	11 (14)
Nervous	Butterflies, knot in stomach	7 (9)
Feel strong	Stronger	4 (5)
Appetite loss	Can't eat	4 (5)

Notes: [a]Categories derived from answers to the question: What physiological factors or changes are associated with love (Reliability of coding=0.80)
[b]Percentages reflect the proportion of all *respondents* coded in a given category. Since respondents were not required to answer this question (and indeed, many respondents did not), percentages sum less than 100 percent.

TABLE 3
Sending Categories[a]

Category	Description	Frequency (percentage)[b]
Told her/him	Face-to-face and telephone conversation saying 'I love you'	57 (75)
Doing things	Doing special or traditional things for other	37 (49)
Support	Understanding, attentive	33 (43)
Physical	Touch	32 (42)
Being together	Just being with other	24 (31)
Negotiate	Talk things out, co-operate	10 (13)
Future commitment	Plan or discuss future, commit to other forever	8 (11)
Written	Notes, letters, cards	8 (11)
Sexual	Sex with other	8 (11)
Non-verbal	Smiles, dress, relaxed look	8 (11)
Eye contact	Look in eyes, looking at other	7 (9)

Notes: [a]Categories derived from answers to the question: How do/did you communicate your love to your partner? (Reliability of coding=0.82)
[b]Percentages reflect the proportion of all *respondents* coded in a given category. Since a single respondent could be coded into multiple categories, percentages sum over 100 percent.

In the final stage, cluster analysis was used to reduce and combine the data across interview questions. This procedure produced holistic combinations of definitional and communicative perceptions of love. SAS subroutine VARCLUS was utilized with the oblique principal component option (Ray, 1982). A disjoint method was used to place each respondent in one and only one cluster (non-overlapping clusters). VARCLUS starts with a single cluster and continues to interactively split the weaker cluster until further splitting would produce a cluster which explains very little variance. These procedures were chosen for three reasons. First, they allow a large set of variables to be replaced by a smaller set of clusters with little loss of information. Second,

Category	Description	Frequency (percentage)[b]
TABLE 4		
Receiving Categories[a]		
Other told me	Partner says 'I love you'	53 (70)
Touch	Physical or sexual contact	33 (43)
Supportive	Responds to me, reciprocates, lets me be myself	30 (39)
Do for me	Actions done for me	28 (37)
Togetherness	Meshing, harmony, shows need for me	21 (28)
Communicating emotion	Tells me what s/he is feeling	21 (28)
Eye contact	Look in eyes, way s/he looks at me	14 (18)
Future commitment	Plans or discusses future, commits to me forever	10 (13)
Facial expression	Smiles, look on face	5 (7)
Vocalics	Sound of other's voice	3 (4)
Topics	Reveals or talks about intimate topics	2 (3)

Notes: [a]Categories derived from the question: How does/did your partner communicate her/his love to you? (Reliability of coding=0.78)
[b]Percentages reflect the proportion of all *respondents* coded in a given category. Since a single respondent could be coded into multiple categories, percentages sum over 100 percent.

results obtained through these procedures are typically easier to interpret than those produced by other clustering and factoring methods. Third, these procedures produce correlated or interrelated clusters. Thus, while respondents are placed in only one cluster (to facilitate cluster interpretation), the correlations between clusters suggest that respondents may have secondary or even tertiary associations. The final clusters, therefore, are not mutually exclusive, but rather reflect the polyvalence of love experiences.

STATISTICAL SUMMARY 2

Cluster analysis was used to group the descriptions into the ways of loving. Like factor analysis, cluster analysis is used for grouping variables together into a smaller number of categories. If you have a large number of variables, you may want to see if two or more of them actually combine or work together. The six clusters found in this study were: collaborative love, active love, secure love, intuitive love, committed love, and traditional romantic love.

Determining the number of clusters to examine is a controversial process. Ordinary significance tests are not valid and other procedures are of questionable utility (Ray, 1982; Everitt, 1979, 1980). We decided, therefore, to use three decision rules. First, we tried to maximize the number of interpretable clusters. Second, we sought to minimize the correlations between clusters. Third, we decided that no cluster should have fewer than five members. Based on these criteria, a six-cluster solution was selected for interpretation. The cluster names and the main categories within each are reported in the first column of Table 5.

The success of the clustering procedures may be seen in a variety of ways. First, results show uniformly high correlations between the categories and their own cluster. Second, there are small ratios of the squared correlation between the categories and the next closest cluster and the squared correlation between the categories and their own cluster. Ultimately, however, success must be judged by the heuristic value of the clusters. Although the clusters could be applied to styles of loving or types of lovers, they are primarily intended to represent the ways in which

TABLE 5
Study I and Study II Cluster Loadings

	Study I clusters and factor loadings[a]	Study II confirming factor loadings[b]	Study II other factor loadings[c]
Cluster 1: Collaborative Love			
Definition:	Intensifier (0.21)		Secure (0.20)
Physiology:	Energy (0.41)	Energy (0.19)	
Sending:	Negotiate (0.42)	Support (0.71)	
	Support (0.21)		
Receiving:	Supportive (0.53)	Supportive (0.69)	
Colour:	Red (0.22)		
Rhythm:	Zig-Zag (0.26)		
Cluster 2: Active Love			
Definition:	Doing together (0.56)	Doing together (0.39)	Confident (0.60)
Physiology:	Strong (0.74)		Nervous (0.39)
Sending:			
Receiving:	Comm. emotion (0.23)		
Colour:			Pink (0.24)
Rhythm:	Erratic (0.61)	Erratic (0.47)	
	Faster (0.47)		
Cluster 3: Secure Love (received no substantial support in confirmatory cluster analysis)			
Definition:			
Physiology:			
Sending:			
Receiving:	Topics (0.73)		
	Do for me (0.25)		
Colour:	Blue (0.24)		
Rhythm:	Circle (0.72)		
Cluster 4: Intuitive Love			
Definition:			Intensifier (0.27)
			Negative (0.21)
Physiology:	Warmth (0.28)	Warmth (0.06)	
	Nervous (0.21)		
	Appetite loss (0.21)		
Sending:	Eye contact (0.56)	Eye contact (0.32)	
	Non-verbal (0.39)	Non-verbal (0.37)	
Receiving:	Eye contact (0.34)	Eye contact (0.43)	Facial expression (0.19)
			Vocalics (0.19)
Colour:			
Rhythm:			
Cluster 5: Committed Love			
Definition:			Togetherness (0.42)
Physiology:	Being together (0.71)	Being together (0.47)	Physical (0.56)
Sending:	Future commitment (0.63)		
Receiving:	Future commitment (0.38)		Touch (0.55)
Colour:	Yellow (0.31)		
Rhythm:			

	Study I clusters and factor loadings[a]	Study II confirming factor loadings[b]	Study II other factor loadings[c]
Cluster 6: Traditional Romantic Love (This cluster appeared to split into two relatively distinct clusters in the confirmatory factor analysis)			
Expressive Love			
Definition:			
Physiology:	Beautiful (0.49)		
Sending:	Doing things (0.38)	Doing things (0.32)	Negotiate (0.38) Told him/her (0.38)
Receiving:	Other told me (0.54)	Other told me (0.38)	Do for me (0.43) Comm. emotion (0.34)
Colour:			
Rhythm:	Wave (0.21)		
Traditional Romantic Love			
Definition:			Togetherness (0.27) Healthy (0.21)
Physiology:	Beautiful (0.49)	Beautiful (0.52)	
Sending:	Doing things (0.38)		
Receiving:	Other told me (0.54)		Future commitment (0.32)
Colour:			
Rhythm:	Wave (0.21)		

Notes: [a]Only Study I factor loading over 0.20 is presented in this table.
[b]All confirming Study II factor loadings are presented.
[c]Only non-confirming Study II factor loadings over 0.20 are presented.

love is experienced. The term 'way' is admittedly an ambiguous one; but, as our data suggest, it is an ambiguity which is inherent to the study of romantic love. For some lovers, romantic love is a way of thinking; for others, it is a way of feeling, or a way of behaving towards one's partner, or even a way of being treated by one's partner. Indeed, for most lovers, it is a combination of these various 'ways'.

The first cluster describes *Collaborative Love,* which is characterized by feelings of increased energy and intensified emotional response. Lovers associated with this cluster report that they communicate their love by being supportive of their partners and that their partners reciprocate in this regard. They also report that this mutual supportiveness contributes to their feelings of increased energy. The second cluster, *Active Love,* is indicated by feelings of strength. This love is experienced through doing things together and is communicated by discussion of emotions. The third cluster describes *Secure Love.* Lovers associated with this cluster defined love in terms of security and report that love is communicated when their partner talks about intimate topics and does things for them. *Intuitive Love* constitutes the fourth cluster. This love is experienced (warmth, nervousness, loss of appetite) and communicated non-verbally. The fifth cluster is *Committed Love,* which is communicated by being together and talking about future commitment. The final cluster is *Traditional Romantic Love.* This love is indicated by feeling beautiful and confident. Lovers associated with this cluster rely on their partner to profess their love verbally by saying 'I love you' and express their love by doing things for the other person. This cluster is labelled traditional romantic love because it seems to reflect a traditional, idealized notion of love.

STUDY II

The purpose of the second study was to establish both representational and construct validity of the six love clusters revealed in Study I. First, given the phenomenological assumptions of our inquiry, we thought it important to establish the representational validity of the six love clusters (i.e., whether or not these clusters are phenomenologically salient to *lovers*). In the first study we asked lovers for qualitative descriptions of love and then imposed our own content and statistical analyses in interpreting that data. In the second study, however, we sought to demonstrate the salience of our interpretation by asking lovers to employ our clusters in describing their own love experiences. Second, in order to establish the construct validity of the six love clusters, we replicated both the coding and clustering procedures employed in Study I on a subset of the Study II data.

The data for Study II were obtained through written responses to a questionnaire. Respondents were selected from two very different groups: participants at a singles seminar and college students. All respondents were either currently involved in a reciprocated, heterosexual love relationship or had been involved in such a relationship in the past.

Three samples were employed in this study. The first consisted of individuals attending a singles seminar sponsored by a community group in the south-western United States ($n=29$). This sample was predominantly female (72 percent); had an average family income of $23,460; and represented a wide range of ages (21–62) and educational backgrounds. None of these respondents was currently in love, and therefore all were asked to recall a past love relationship. The second and third samples consisted of undergraduates in an introductory-level communication course at a large south-western university. These respondents included communication, business, architecture and nursing majors in relatively equal numbers. On the basis of an initial self-report item, respondents were placed in one of two samples: those currently in love (Students/Present Love; $n=94$) and those with a past love relationship (Students/Past Love $n=62$). Students who had never been in love were eliminated from the study. Of the Students/Present Love sample, 78 percent were female; of the Students/Past Love sample, 52 percent were female. The student samples had average family incomes of approximately $44,000 and demonstrated an average age of 20.5 years. The relationships that were the focus of the students' responses ranged in length from 1 to 44 months, with an average relational length of 22.8 months.

As noted above, the singles group and the two student samples differed in several respects. The singles group was older, had a lower family income and had a greater variety of educational experience. Further, these three samples differed notably from the sample employed in Study I and, accordingly, provide a suitable test for the phenomenological salience of the six love clusters described above.

The procedures employed in all three samples were identical. A short questionnaire was distributed, asking for demographic information as well as responses to the six love questions employed in Study I. After the questionnaires were completed, the results of Study I were presented to each sample, providing detailed descriptions of the six love clusters. Respondents then coded themselves into one or more of the love clusters. Since these clusters were not conceptualized as mutually exclusive, respondents could employ one or more clusters in their self-coding. Further, respondents were informed that some love experiences may not fit any of the clusters and, therefore, that they were not required to employ the cluster system if they believed it inadequate to describe their experiences. If respondents could successfully use the six love meanings to describe their love experiences, then representational validity would be established.

In order to demonstrate the construct validity of the six love clusters, the responses to the six love questions from the Students/Present Love group were subjected to a replication of the analysis employed in Study I. This subset of the

Study II data was selected for two reasons. First, we believed that combining the Singles and Students groups would result in a sample that would more likely reveal the variance between students and 'singles' than a more natural variance in love experiences. Second, we believed that individuals currently in love would provide the most reliable phenomenological data. Combining even the two Students groups would have provided a sample heavy in 'past' lovers.

The responses to the six love questions from the Students/Present Love group were coded by two independent raters using the categories derived in Study I (see Table 1). Both raters were naive to the respondents' self-coding into the six love clusters. Inter-rater reliabilities for the coding of four of these six love questions were 0.72 (general definition), 0.79 (physiological responses), 0.80 (sending love) and 0.80 (receiving love). These reliability figures were slightly higher than those obtained in Study I. As in the earlier study, the 'colours' and rhythms of love were grouped based upon identical match and were non-controversial.

Results

The respondents' self-coding was generally successful in establishing the phenomonological salience of the six love clusters: overall, 92 percent of the respondents placed themselves in one or more of the clusters (Singles: 96 percent, Students/Present Love: 92 percent; Students/Past Love: 89 percent). Among the Singles group, 23 percent of the respondents employed only one cluster, while 46 percent employed two clusters and 27 percent employed three or more clusters. Among the Students/Present Love group, 30 percent employed only one cluster, 51 percent employed two or more clusters and 10 percent employed three or more clusters. Finally, among the Students/Past Love group, 40 percent employed one cluster, 35 percent employed two clusters and 13 percent employed three or more clusters. These findings provide support for the representational validity of the six love clusters.

As noted above, the coded responses to the original six love questions were cluster analysed (using the same procedures as Study I) in order to establish the construct validity of the six love clusters. Again, a six-cluster solution was selected for interpretation. The second and third columns in Table 5 present a comparison of the results of the Study I and Study II cluster analyses. The latter analysis provides support for four of the six original love clusters (Collaborative Love, Active Love, Intuitive Love, Committed Love), while a fifth cluster appears to have split in the confirming cluster analysis (Traditional Romantic Love).

The *Collaborative Love* cluster received strong support from the Study II data. Supportiveness as a model of sending and receiving love loaded highly in both studies, as did the physiological response of increased energy. However, whereas the original cluster included negotiation as the primary mode of sending love, this result was not replicated in the confirming cluster. Further, the confirming cluster introduced security as a new loaded factor.

The *Active Love* cluster also received support in the Study II analysis. Both the original and confirming clusters included joint activities and an erratic rhythm as two of the highest loading factors. The major differences between the original and confirming clusters were: (1) the confirming cluster did not include the physiological response of increased strength or a 'faster' rhythm; and (2) the confirming cluster introduced confidence, nervousness and the colour pink as new loaded factors. It is important to note, however, that two of these distinguishing categories occurred in very low frequencies in Study II, namely confidence [n=1] and increased strength [n=0].

The *Intuitive Love* cluster appeared in both analyses and, further, in both the original and confirming clusters the following factors received the highest loadings: eye contact and non-verbal communication as modes of sending love and, again, eye contact as a mode of receiving love.

The physiological response of warmth also appeared in both clusters, although with a considerably lower loading. The confirming analysis, however, introduced four new factors to the cluster, each of which is consistent with the general character of the original cluster: intensified emotional response, negative emotions, as well as facial expression and vocalics as modes of receiving love.

The *Committed Love* cluster received only partial support in the confirming analysis. Being together, as a mode of sending love, is a central factor in both the original and the confirming clusters. However, in Study II the namesake factor, future commitment, did not load. Due to the relatively low frequency with which future commitment was reported by the student respondents in Study II as a mode of sending love [$n=1$] and receiving love [$n=2$], we are led to conclude that future commitment may play a less significant role in the love experiences of younger (i.e., college-aged) lovers. Further, the confirming cluster introduced three new factors: physical contact as a mode of both sending and receiving love and togetherness as a mode of receiving love. Each of these new factors suggest that, for younger lovers, physical and relational closeness may fulfill needs that, as lovers and love relationships mature, may be fulfilled by an act or feeling of commitment.

Another of the original clusters, *Traditional Romantic Love*, appeared to split into two relatively distinct clusters in the confirming analysis. The first of these new clusters (which we designate as *Expressive Love*) is characterized by the modes of communicating love that were associated with the Traditional Romantic Love cluster in Study I: namely, doing things for the other and telling the other as modes of sending love, and being told by the other as a mode of receiving love. Further, the new cluster also introduced two other, similar factors: communicating emotion and having things done by the other as modes of receiving love. Finally, the confirming cluster also loaded negotiation as a mode of sending love—a loading that is consistent with the communication emphasis of the cluster.

The second new cluster retains the most salient characteristics of a traditional, idealized conception of romantic love, and, for this reason, also retains the name of the original cluster, *Traditional Romantic Love*. This cluster is characterized by the physiological response of feeling beautiful that was associated with the Traditional Romantic Love cluster in Study I. Further, this new cluster loaded another similar factor (a healthy feeling) and two other factors that are consistent with a traditional conception of romantic love (togetherness and, as a mode of receiving love, future commitment).

The remaining original cluster, *Secure Love*, received no substantial support in the confirming cluster analysis.

Discussion

These two studies provide three different types of information concerning the subjective experience and communication of romantic love. First, the coding categories used in the content analysis of the interviews in Study I demonstrate the wide range of experiences and modes of communication which lovers associate with love. Second, the cluster analysis of these categories reveals six identifiable, polyvalent 'ways of romantic love'. Third, the frequencies reported in the self-coding of respondents in Study II indicate the various combinations in which these 'ways of romantic love' appear in the subjective experiences of lovers. In this section we will examine the implications of each set of findings and suggest avenues for further research.

An examination of the categories derived in Study I (see Tables 1–4) reveals three important conclusions concerning the nature of love as it is experienced by lovers. First, the categories suggest that the subjective experience of love may be conceptualized in a variety of different manners, each reflecting a different realm of experience. As we anticipated, lovers defined love in terms of propositional relational constructs (such as commitment and security), physiological responses (such as intensified emotional experience and feelings of warmth and nervousness) and behavioural actions (such as doing things with and/or for the other). Although the questions concerning the 'colours' and 'rhythms' of love were not entirely successful in tapping the intuitive aspects of love (as demonstrated by the generally weaker frequencies of responses), non-verbal perceptions were reported as an important means of communicating love (for example, through eye contact and 'ways of looking').

Second, any given lover may conceptualize love by employing elements of any or all of the four manners described above (relational constructs, physiological responses, behavioural actions and non-verbal perceptions). This finding is of key importance. Whereas Rubin suggests that love is conceptualized only in terms of relational constructs (attachment, caring and intimacy), the present study finds this not to be the case. Many lovers employed *no* relational constructs in their definition of love, but rather used only physiological responses or behavioural actions. This indicates that love need not be conceived in strictly relational terms, even when love is reciprocated.

Third, not only is there no single manner of conceptualizing love, there is also no predominant manner. Responses were widely distributed across categories, suggesting a strong pluralism of conceptions.

The sending and receiving categories provide additional information concerning the manners in which people communicate love. While responses to the sending and receiving questions exhibited a great deal of convergence, there was a notable divergence in the use of supportiveness, a response common to both sets of categories. Support is seen as expressing love through understanding and acceptance, but is received as an indication of love through reciprocation and responsiveness. If lovers look for reciprocity and responsiveness as a sign of supportiveness (and therefore, love), but attempt to communicate support through other forms (such as acceptance), misunderstandings and misinterpretations are a clear possibility. Again, further research is necessary in examining the causes and effects of this apparent divergence.

While the coding categories indicate a great diversity in love experiences, the cluster analysis demonstrates a strong coherence in lovers' perceptions of love and in their reports of how love is communicated. Further, there seems to be some overlap between the clusters obtained in the present studies and constructs reported in previous research concerning the subjective experience of romantic love. While the Collaborative and Secure Love clusters are unique to this study, the three categories derived by Prentice et al. (1983) seem somewhat comparable to three of the present clusters. Both studies report traditional romantic love, and the routine activity category of Prentice et al. parallels the Active Love cluster derived in the current study. The sexual behaviour category reported by Prentice et al. may be a subset of Intuitive Love as described above. In addition, the Committed Love cluster reflects the central theme associated with dating couples in Owen's (1984) study of relational interpretation. Further, the Expressive Love cluster obtained in Study II reflects the communication emphasis reported in Sternberg & Grajek's (1984) correlational study of love measures. What is significant, however, is the degree to which the current cluster system integrates and extends the findings of previous research.

The results of lovers' self-coding in Study II demonstrate the phenomenological salience of the love clusters and suggest three additional implications. First, these results indicate that the six 'ways of romantic love' are indeed polyvalent, appearing both individually and in various combinations. Across all three samples, Collaborative Love ($n=18$), Traditional Romantic Love, ($n=13$) and Intuitive Love ($n=11$) were the most common single clusters used by respondents to describe their love experiences. Frequent combinations included: Collaborative/Active ($n=22$), Collaborative/Traditional Romantic ($n=20$), Collaborative/Intuitive ($n=18$), Active/Intuitive ($n=18$), Collaborative/Committed ($n=15$) and Active/Traditional ($n=14$). Although a majority of respondents employed either one or two clusters in the self-coding ($n=114$), the use of three or more was not infrequent ($n=55$).

Second, there are notable differences between the self-coding of current and past love relationships. Whereas current lovers employed the Committed Love cluster in 34 percent of their self-codings, past lovers employed this cluster less frequently (19 percent). A similar divergence is apparent in the use of Collaborative/Active Love combinations, which were employed more frequently by past lovers (13 percent) than by current lovers (4 percent). Although these differences may simply be the results of relational hindsight, further research may provide more detailed explanations.

Third, the self-coding results indicate that very few respondents employed the Secure Love cluster in describing their love experiences and, further, that those respondents who used this cluster employed it in conjunction with either the Intuitive Love or Committed Love clusters. Since this cluster also failed to appear in the confirming cluster analysis, it is likely that this cluster is not phenomenologically salient. Accordingly, it is tentatively removed from the system.

These studies have two further general implications for future research into the nature of romantic relationships and the communication of love. First, the question should be addressed: How do the different 'ways of love' fit together in loveships? For example, Collaborative Love seems to require a reciprocal love for a successful relationship, due to the unique means of communicating love associated with this cluster. The same reciprocity seems necessary for Intuitive Love. However, Traditional Romantic Love may fit successfully with Committed Love.

A second implication concerns the degree of consistency and flexibility in lovers' perceptions of love and their communication of love. Two questions surround this issue: To what extent do lovers maintain consistent experiences of love across a relationship or a series of relationships? and To what extent do lovers' experiences of love evolve or change through a series of relationships or through the development of a single relationship?

REFERENCES

Arnold, M. B. (1960) *Emotion and Personality.* New York: Columbia University Press.

Clynes, M. (1978) *Sentics: The Touch of Emotions.* Garden City, NY: Anchor Books.

De Rivera, J. (1977) *A Structural Theory of the Emotions.* New York: International Universities Press.

De Vito, J. A. (1980) *The Interpersonal Communication Book.* New York: Harper & Row.

Everitt, B. (1979) 'Unresolved Problems in Cluster Analysis', *Biometrics 35:* 169–81.

———. (1980) *Cluster Analysis,* 2nd ed. London: Heinemann Educational.

Fromm, E. (1956) *The Art of Loving.* New York: Harper & Row.

Hendrick, C., Hendrick, S., Foote, F. H. & Slapion-Foote, M. J. (1984) 'Do Men and Women Love Differently?' *Journal of Social and Personal Relationships* 1: 177–95.

Holsti, O. R. (1969) *Content Analysis for the Social Sciences and Humanities.* Reading, MA: Addison-Wesley.

Johnston, T. L. & Jeremko, M. E. (1979) 'Correlational Analysis of Suggestibility, Self-preoccupation, Styles of Loving, and Sensation-seeking', *Psychological Reports* 45:23–6.

Kemper, T. D. (1978) *A Social Interactional Theory of Emotions.* New York: Wiley.

Knapp, M. L. (1978) *Social Intercourse: From Greeting to Goodbye.* Boston, MA: Allyn Bacon.

Lee, J. L. (1973) *Colours of Love: An Exploration of the Ways of Loving.* Toronto: New Press.

Mathes, E. W. (1982) 'Mystical Experiences, Romantic Love and Hypnotic Susceptibility', *Psychological Reports* 50: 701–2.

Montagu, A. (1970) *The Direction of Human Development.* New York: Hawthorn Books.

Morolodo, G. (1982) 'Shyness and Love in College Campus Relationships', *Perceptual and Motor Skills* 55: 819–24.

Owen, W. F. (1984) 'Interpretive Themes in Relational Communication', *Quarterly Journal of Speech* 70: 274–87.

Plato (1969) 'The Symposium', in *Plato: The Collected Dialogues* (trans. M. Joyce). Princeton, NJ: Princeton University Press.

Prentice, D. S., Briggs, N. E., & Bradley, D. W. (1983) 'Romantic Attitudes of American University Students', *Psychological Reports* 53: 815–22.

Pribram, K. H. (1980) 'The Biology of Emotion', in R. Plutchik & H. Kellerman (eds.) *Emotion: Theory Research and Experience.* Vol. 1. New York: Academic Press.

Ray, A. E. (ed.) (1982) *SAS Users Guide: Statistics.* Cary, NC: SAS Institute.

Rubin, Z. (1970). 'Measurement of Romantic Love', *Journal of Personality and Social Psychology* 16: 256–73.

———. (1973) *Liking and Loving: An Invitation to Social Psychology.* New York: Holt, Rinehart & Winston.

Sartre, J. P. (1957) *Existentialism and Human Emotions.* New York: Philosophical Library.

———. (1977) *Essays in Existentialism.* Secaucus, NJ: Citadel Press.

Schachter, S. & Singer, J. (1962) 'Cognitive, Social, and Physiological Determinants of Emotional State', *Psychological Review* 69: 379–99.

Seligman, C., Fazio, R. H. & Zanna, M. P. (1980) 'Effects of Salience of Extrinsic Rewards on Liking and Loving', *Journal of Personality and Social Psychology* 38: 453–60.

Sternberg, R. J. & Grajek, S. (1984) 'The Nature of Love', *Journal of Personality and Social Psychology* 47: 312–29.

Wiseman, R. L. & Schenck-Hamlin, W. (1981) 'A Multidimensional Scaling Validation of an Inductively-Derived Set of Compliance-Gaining Strategies', *Communication Monographs* 48: 251–70.

CHAPTER 8

Interpersonal Competence

INTRODUCTION

This chapter consists of readings which focus on interpersonal competence. Competence refers to effective and appropriate communication. The articles in this chapter attempt to explain how communicators achieve success through communication that is appropriate to the situation and the relationship.

The Wiemann article represents one of the earliest approaches to this topic. Wiemann describes the competent communicator as one who leaves an impression, and his study shows that the ability to manage the flow of the interaction is one of the keys to effectiveness. The Hecht study proposes satisfaction as a criterion of effectiveness, reviews different ways of conceptualizing satisfaction, and proposes a definition. The paper argues that there are similarities among a variety of conceptual definitions and develops its approach out of this overlap.

The Spitzberg and Canary paper utilizes a model of relational competence, arguing that competence must be viewed in the context of the relationship—what is effective for people separately *and* together. The article reports that lonely people perceive themselves and others as less competent. The Andersen and Andersen paper examines six theoretical explanations of intimacy, explaining and evaluating each. This paper is included here since the development of intimacy is one of the keys to competence in relationships.

The final paper is written by Stiff et al. and tests a model of empathic communication. The ability to empathize with others is another skill that competent communicators have. This paper helps us understand how empathy leads to comforting behavior. Thus, each of these papers examines how people communicate competently. The papers at the beginning of the chapter deal with competence more broadly, while those at the end focus on more specific types of competence.

EXPLICATION AND TEST OF A MODEL OF COMMUNICATIVE COMPETENCE

John M. Wiemann
Rutgers University

This research investigated the concept of communicative competence. A definition and a five-component model of communicative competence is proposed. Interaction management, empathy, affiliation/support, behavioral flexibility, and social relaxation are identified as components of competence, with interaction management playing a central role. In an experiment designed to partially test the model, 239 Ss were assigned to evaluate a confederate's role-played communicative competence in one of four interaction

Source: The article is taken from *Human Communication Research* [3: 195–213, 1977]. (c) International Communication Association, 8140 Burnet Rd., Austin, TX 78766. Reprinted by permission of Sage Publications, Inc. and ICA.

management treatment conditions. Results indicated a strong, positive, linear relationship between interaction management and communicative competence. Positive correlations between competence and other components of the model were observed. The competent communicator is thus described as empathic, affiliative and supportive, and relaxed while interacting; he is capable of adapting his behavior as the situation within an encounter changes and as he moves from encounter to encounter. The manner in which the interaction is managed contributes, in part at least, to his fellow interactants' perceptions of his competence.

It must be the nature of man to first examine those things which are exotic in his environment. Only later, after the exotic has been dealt with, does he take note of the "normal" conditions of his day-to-day life. Such seems to be the case, at least, in the study of man's communication behavior. In spite of the pervasiveness of everyday face-to-face interaction, it has received comparatively less study than most other rhetorical situations. While communication scholars have at their disposal a wealth of research on, for example, effective persuasion or interviewing, there is very little dealing with effective or "good" conversational behavior.

Though research may fail us in this regard, "common sense" does not. It is a fact of our everyday experience that there are some people with whom we would rather converse than others. While most of us can easily identify these "desirable" conversational partners, it is probably more difficult to specify why they are more desirable. The implication is that certain sets of behaviors are more desirable than others in any given specific situation. Further, it is problematic for the interactant to determine which behaviors afford him the best chance of bringing off an encounter in such a way that all participants will evaluate it positively.

PURPOSE AND RATIONALE

The purpose of this study was to explore the substructure of everyday social conversation which allows for judgments of competent conversation behavior in the context of initial interactions.

While many people might label the behavior discussed here as "ordinary" social grace, behavioral scientists have dealt with this phenomenon under the rubrics *social skill, interpersonal effectiveness, interpersonal competence,* and *communicative competence.*[1] Because the primary concern here is with communicative behavior, the term "communicative competence" (CC) is used. A little reflection will lead one to believe that such behavior is anything but ordinary.

The importance of communicative competence in everyday conversation lies in the role that such conversation plays in the development of the social identity of the members of any society. While a conversational encounter can serve many functions, its primary function is the establishment and maintenance of self and social identities of the participants (Goffman, 1959, 1967; McCall & Simmons, 1966). The competent communicator, therefore, is in a better position to present and to have accepted his own definition of himself and others. To the extent that identities are the product of negotiation among participants in an encounter, communicative competence must be viewed as a *dyadic* concept. It is not *necessarily* competent to force one's self/situation definition on others. Such force, while possible, generally does not take into account the needs of other participants. Thus, *effectiveness* in an intrapersonal sense—that is, the accomplishment of an individual's goals—may be incompetent in an interpersonal sense if such effectiveness precludes the possibility of others accomplishing their own goals. Since the competent communicator arrives at a self/situation definition through a process of interpersonal negotiation, the definition reached may not be exactly the same as the definition either participant had in mind when the encounter began. But, if the participants are competent, they should be able to arrive at a definition that is the ''best possible'' for both.

Consequently, even the highly Machiavellian communicator can be judged as competent if he is able to maintain social relationships *over time* that are mutually satisfactory for all concerned. This dyadic notion of CC has seldom been made explicit in past writing on the subject, but does seem to be part of the underlying reasoning of previous approaches to competence.

Approaches to the Study of Competence

The concept of competence in face-to-face interaction has been influenced by three main schools of thought which can be characterized as: (1) the human relations or T-group approach (Argyris, 1962, 1965; Holland & Baird, 1968; Bochner & Kelly, 1974), (2) the social skill approach (Argyle & Kendon, 1967; Argyle, 1969), and (3) the self-presentation approach (Goffman, 1959, 1961, 1963, 1967; Weinstein, 1966; Rodnick & Wood, 1973).

While each of these approaches differs from the others in some ways, their similarities are more striking than their differences—differences more of emphasis than of kind. All three approaches characterize competence in terms of ''effectiveness.'' For example, Bochner and Kelly (1974) define competence as ''a person's ability to interact effectively with other people'' (288). Taking a social skill approach, Habermas (1970) states that ''communicative competence means the mastery of an ideal speech situation'' (p. 138). Argyle (1969), using the terms *social competence* and *social skill* synonymously, suggests that the concept carries ''the assumption that some people are better at dealing with social situations in general than others are'' (p. 330). Each approach is briefly discussed below, with emphasis on its contribution to the understanding of competent communication behavior, and with an eye to constructing a model of CC.

The Self-Presentation Approach

In his seminal work dealing with self-presentation, Goffman (1959) describes man as an actor who must play various roles (in both the theatrical sense and the social psychological-role theory sense) to various audiences (i.e., those co-present in any face-to-face encounter). Goffman's work, in particular, leads to the conclusion that competence is a dyadic construct. He views encounters as ''situational constraints'' on an interactant's communicative behavior. It is the person's *duty* to play an appropriate role at any given time, for it is through each person's role enactment that particular situations are defined, thus creating and reinforcing social reality.

The competent communicator, in Goffman's sense, is one who is aware of the sacred quality of encounters as demonstrated by (1) his presentation of appropriate faces and lines (that is, social identities his fellow participants can support without jeopardizing their own faces and lines) and (2) his support of the faces and lines presented by others. Additionally, the competent person is adept at helping others ''save face''—for example, helping to maintain the other's identity when it is threatened by a *faux pas* (Goffman, 1967; see also Garfinkel, 1972).

Synder (1974) concludes that these self-presentation skills are differentially distributed through the population. That is, some people are better at self-presentation than others and thus are more effective in social situations.

The T-Group Approach

Bochner and Kelly (1974), expanding previous work by Argyris (1962, 1965), propose three criteria against which CC can be judged: ''(1) ability to formulate and achieve objectives; (2) ability to collaborate effectively with others, i.e., to be interdependent; and (3) ability to adapt appropriately to situational or environmental variations'' (288). Five skills which would allow a person to meet these criteria are: (1) empathy; (2) descriptiveness, i.e., the manner in which feedback is given and received; (3) owning feelings and thoughts, i.e., the assumption of responsibility for one's feelings and thoughts; (4) self-disclosure; and (5) behavioral flexibility, i.e., the ability to recognize the behavioral choices open in a given situation and the capacity to relate in new ways given the present combination of participants, situation, and the history of the relationship (Bochner & Kelly, 1974).

The Social Skill Approach

In a more explicit model than either of the other approaches, Argyle (1969), suggests that social behavior can be studied in much the same way that motor skills are studied. He defines ''skill'' as an ''organised, coordinated activity in relation to an object or a situation, which involves a whole chain of sensory, central, and motor mechanisms. One of its main characteristics is that the performance, or stream of action, is *continuously under the control of the sensory input''* (p. 180, emphasis added). The specific dimensions of CC discussed by Argyle are: (1) extroversion and affiliation, (2) dominance-submission, (3) poise-social anxiety, (4) rewardingness, (5) interaction skills, (6) perceptual sensitivity, and (7) role-taking ability.

A Model of Communicative Competence

Based on these three approaches to communicative competence, a tentative identification of its behavioral dimensions can be undertaken. To this point, I have dealt with previous attempts to define competence that have in common the equating of competence with ''effective'' communication. All, however, suffer from imprecision and/or the confounding of communicative and noncommunicative (e.g., personality traits) elements.

Based on literature dealing with face-to-face conversational encounters, a definitional model of communicative competence composed of the following five dimensions was developed: (1) affiliation/support, (2) social relaxation, (3) empathy, (4) behavioral flexibility, and (5) interaction management skills.

In general, this model suggests that the competent interactant is other-oriented to the extent that he is open (available) to receive messages from others, does not provoke anxiety in others by exhibiting anxiety himself, is empathic, has a large enough behavioral repertoire to allow him to meet the demands of changing situations, and, finally, is supportive of the faces and lines his fellow interactants present. The competent person's interaction management skills allow him to realize (present) this other-orientation. Competence, however, does not mean that the interactant is completely selfless, i.e., completely other-oriented. In spite of this other-orientation, he is successful in accomplishing his own goals in any given interaction. This notion of mutual satisfaction with the self/situation definition leaves open the possibility that one interactant may be able to persuade the other to accept a specific definition—such persuasion is well within the bounds of competent communication *if* the outcome is functional for the long-term maintenance of the social relationship.

To illustrate this point, consider the stereotypic used car salesman—the person often held up as the example of high Machiavellianism. In his relationships with customers, our salesman may or may not be considered competent, depending on the measures of sales competence used. If ''cars sold'' is the measure, then the means to that end make little difference. But, if ''repeat customers'' or ''new customers referred by old customers'' are used as measures, then the means by which sales are made become important because relationships with customers *over time* become important. The point is that, regardless of the measure of competence used, cars are sold; the manner in which the salesman is evaluated, however, will determine whether or not he is considered competent at this profession.

The same case can be made for communicative behavior in the social sphere. A person can always have his way in a relationship and be judged effective only if the end (i.e., having his way) is considered of primary importance. But if the maintenance of the relationship is paramount (or if it is considered the ''end'' in and of itself), then the manner in which relational decisions are made is critical. The competent communicator is the person who can have his way in the relationship while maintaining a mutually acceptable definition of that relationship.

This notion of competence becomes especially meaningful when the temporal aspects of relationships are considered. If a relationship is to be (or has been) in existence for some period of time, then individual acts generally become less significant than the aggregate of relationally oriented acts (Altman & Taylor, 1973). The person who is considered "effective" by the "I had my way" criterion is really incompetent if the relationship is terminated because the other party in it could not live with a self-definition of "loser." In many cases, a person is considered pathological if his communicative behavior across situations is of the "I must get my way" variety.

From this description, communicative competence can be defined as (*the ability of an interactant to choose among available communicative behaviors in order that he may successfully accomplish his own interpersonal goals during an encounter while maintaining the face and line of his fellow interactants within the constraints of the situation*).

Each of the dimensions of CC can be defined according to discreet, molecular behaviors (as opposed to configurations of behaviors), all readily observable in face-to-face encounters by "normal," (i.e., untrained) interactants. Following is a list of the behavioral cues[2] of each of the dimensions of the model:

Affiliation/Support:

1. Eye behavior (Argyle, 1969; Exline, 1971; Mehrabian & Ksionzky, 1972; Wiemann, 1974).
2. The alternation and co-occurrence of specific speech choices which mark the status and affiliative relationships of the interactants, e.g., honorifics— "Professor," "Your Honor"—pet names, or multiple names as markers of

a relationship (Brown & Gilman, 1960; Ervin-Tripp, 1964, 1972; Wiener & Mehrabian, 1968; Argyle, 1969).
3. Head nods (Mehrabian, 1972).
4. Duration of speaking time and number of statements per minute (Mehrabian, 1972).
5. Pleasantness of facial expression— smiling (Mehrabian, 1972; Rosenfeld, 1972).
6. Statements indicating "owning" of one's perceptions about another (Bochner & Kelly, 1974).
7. Physical proximity chosen during interaction (Argyle & Dean, 1965; Hall, 1966).

Social Relaxation:

1. General postural relaxation cues, including rocking movements, leg and foot movements, and body lean (Mehrabian, 1971, 1972; Mehrabian & Ksionzky, 1972).
2. Rate of speech (Argyle, 1969).
3. Speech disturbances, hesitations, and nonfluencies (Kasl & Mahl, 1965).
4. Object manipulations (Mehrabian & Ksionzky, 1972).

Empathy:

1. Reciprocity of affect displays, e.g., smiling and other immediacy cues (Argyle & Dean, 1965; Mehrabian, 1972).
2. Verbal responses indicating understanding of and feeling for the other's situation, e.g., "I know how you feel."
3. Perceived active listening as indicated by head nods and verbal listener responses or reinforcers (Dittman, 1972; Wiemann & Knapp, 1975).

Behavioral Flexibility:

The adaptations one makes within a situation and from situation to situation, including:

1. Verbal immediacy cues (Wiener & Mehrabian, 1968).
2. The alternation and co-occurrence of specific speech choices which mark the status and affiliative relationships of interactants (Brown & Gilman, 1960; Ervin-Trip, 1964, 1972; Argyle, 1969; Robinson, 1972).

Interaction Management:

Argyle (1969) lists two general interaction management skills that are critical to competence: (1) "the ability to establish and sustain a smooth and easy pattern of interaction" (pp. 327–328) and (2) the ability to maintain control of the interaction without dominating—"responding in accordance with an internal plan, rather than simply reacting to the other's behavior" (p. 328).

The first of these skills is dependent on the rule-governed nature of face-to-face encounters. It is the adherence or nonadherence to these culturally sanctioned rules which behaviorally define this dimension of communicative competence. Of the many rules applicable to face-to-face encounters, those most pertinent to communicative competence are:

1. Interruptions of the speaker are not permitted (Goffman, 1967; Duncan, 1973; Speier, 1973; Wiemann & Knapp, 1975).
2. One person talks at a time (Duncan, 1973; Speier, 1973; Sacks et al., 1974; Wiemann & Knapp, 1975).
3. Speaker turns must interchange (Speier, 1973; Sacks et al., 1974; however, this rule is subject to different interpretations, cf. Schegloff, 1972; Scheidel, 1974).

4. Frequent and lengthy pauses should be avoided (Jaffee & Feldstein, 1970).
5. An interactant must be perceived as devoting full attention to the encounter (Goffman, 1967).

The second of the above-mentioned interaction management skills—responding according to plan—can be described behaviorally as the topic control exercised by an interactant.

The behavioral cues associated with each of the five proposed dimensions of competence are summarized in Table 1.[3]

Before proceeding, a note about the importance of interaction management is in order. Interaction management is concerned with the "procedural" aspects that structure and maintain an interaction. These include initiation and termination of the encounter, the allocation of speaking turns, and control of topics discussed. Skillful interaction management is defined as the ability to handle these procedural matters in a manner that is mutually satisfactory to all participants. There is more evidence relating interaction management skills to communicative competence than is available for any of the previously discussed components of the model. It is the mastery of these skills which permits a person to implement (or conform to) the interaction rules of his culture. Speier (1972) states this position strongly:

> Competence in using conversational procedures in social interaction not only displays adequate social membership among participants in the culture, but more deeply, it *provides a procedural basis for the ongoing organization of that culture* when members confront and deal with one another daily. (p. 398, emphasis in original)

Based on the available evidence, it seems that interaction management is the *sine qua non* of competence.

Some consideration of the "quantity" of competent behaviors is also in order. As presented to

TABLE 1
Summary of Behavioral Cues Associated with Communicative Competence

Cue	Component of Competence				
	Interaction management	Empathy	Affiliation/ support	Social relaxation	Behavior flexibility
eye behavior	X		X		
speech choices marking relationships			X		X
head nods	X		X		
speech rate/speaking time			X	X	
smiling			X		
"owning" of one's behavior			X		
proximity			X		
relaxation cues (e.g., leaning)				X	
speech disturbances				X	
object manipulations				X	
reciprocity of affect displays		X	X		
verbal immediacy		X			X
perceived active listening (indicated by reinforcers, etc.)		X	X		
speaker interruptions	X				
"smooth" interchanges	X				
gesticulations	X				
self-manipulations	X			X	
pauses	X				
topic control	X				

this point, the CC model implies that "more is better." Both intuition and empirical evidence (though inconclusive) argue against this position. Intuitively, the interactant who is too smooth, too practiced, is suspect. His "commitment" to his message seems out of proportion to the spontaneity common to conversational encounters (cf. Hart & Burks, 1972, for a discussion of "appropriate commitment" in social interaction). Additionally, evidence reported by Exline (1971), Mehrabian (1972), Wiemann (1974), and others indicates that a moderate amount of any given behavior is more highly valued by interactants than either extremely high or low amounts. Consequently, it seems that there is an inverted parabolic relationship between the performance of behaviors indicative of CC and judgments of actual competence.

Hypotheses

Because of its apparent centrality to communicative competence, interaction management skill was the independent variable used to partially test the model. Subjects' evaluations of the competence of a person was the dependent variable of primary interest. Subjects viewing an encounter (as third-party observers) made judgments of the competence of a person in an ongoing interaction. Since the model indicates that a "moderate" or "medium" level of exhibited management skill is *optimal*—too little or too much management will be dysfunctional—Hypothesis 1 can be stated:

H₁: *The level of interaction management skill displayed by an interactant is nonlinearly related to observers' perceptions of that interactant's communicative competence. Specifically, it is an inverted parabolic relationship.*

If the model is valid, the other four components of CC should be correlated with the level of interaction management, and all components should be related to a general measure of communicative competence as is interaction management. In any given situation, a person evaluated as highly competent, because of the management skills displayed, should also be judged high on affiliation/support, empathy, behavioral flexibility, and social relaxation.

Stated differently, the components of the model *do not appear to be independent;* each component defines—partially, at least—relatively the same domain of experience (i.e., communicative competence). For example, some behaviors that convey empathy can also serve to manage the interaction. These components are distinguishable from each other to the extent that *not all* empathic behavior, for example, serves as interaction management.

Thus, it was further hypothesized that:

H₂: *An interactant's interaction management skill as perceived by observers is positively and linearly related to perceptions of that interactant's:
(a) behavioral flexibility, (b) empathy,
(c) affiliativeness/supportiveness, and,
(d) social relaxation.*

A corollary of this hypotheses is that the relationship of these four dependent variables with perceived competence can also be described as an inverted parabola.

METHOD AND PROCEDURE
Operational Definitions

Interaction management was operationalized in terms of the behaviors which implement the interaction rules listed earlier. Two behaviors were manipulated in this study: (1) conversational turn-taking synchronization, and (2) topic control. *Conversational turn-taking synchronization* is the ability to smoothly intermesh each participant's speaking turn, thus avoiding simultaneous turns due either to interruptions or both participants beginning a turn at the same time. *Topic control* is the extent to which each individual contributes to deciding what is to be talked about at any given time during the interaction. From one person's perspective, topic control can be conceived as a continuum anchored by a completely directive interview on one end and a completely nondirective interview on the other.

For the purposes of this research, *highly competent interaction management* was defined as smooth synchronization of speaking turns as evidenced by no attempts at simultaneous turns, no pauses in the conversation of three seconds or longer (based on data presented by Goldman-Eisler, 1968), and bilateral topic control. Interruptions, pauses of three seconds or more, and unilateral topic changes were defined as *interaction management errors.*

Three levels of interaction management were thus defined:

Management Level	Type of Error			
	Interruptions	Pauses	Topic Changes	Total
High	0	0	0	0
Medium	3	2	1	6
Low	6	4	2	12

The interaction management errors used in this research are primarily nonverbal. While some interaction management functions can be performed verbally, they usually are not. Verbal comments on the ongoing interaction are seldom made (Ekman & Friesen, 1969), and when they are, such comments are perceived as being very strong, forceful, or out of place.

Communicative competence, affiliation/support, empathy, social relaxation, and *behavioral flexibility* were operationalized in terms of the measuring instrument designed specifically for this research.

Treatment Stimuli

Four levels of interaction management were employed: high management (Hi), medium management (Me), low management (Lo), and "rude" (Ru) or very low management. The level of management skill was manipulated during a videotaped, role-played initial interaction.

Two female confederates role-played a situation in which they were asked to "get to know each other." Topic development in the role play compared favorably with topic development observed by Berger (1972) in natural initial interactions.

Interaction management errors were programmed into the role play such that one confederate—the "on camera" confederate—would vary her management behavior across the different treatment conditions, but the content of her verbalizations would remain virtually unchanged. The verbal and vocal nonverbal behaviors of the "off-camera" confederate were held constant across the four conditions.[4]

Errors were programmed at the following rate for each treatment: Hi, no management errors; Me, 1.5 errors per minute, six errors total; Lo, 3.0 errors per minute, 12 errors total. The rude condition was not programmed. Rather, the on-camera confederate was asked to "be rude" to her fellow interactant. A subsequent count of errors revealed 5.0 errors per minute—13 interruptions, 5 pauses, and 2 topic changes.

Verbal and nonverbal cues, other than interaction management cues, were not controlled. Following Wiener and Mehrabian's (1968) proposition that messages are isomorphic with experience, it was felt such behaviors as gaze direction, body orientation, etc., would take care of themselves. That is, increase of management errors (being "rude" or "insensitive") would reflect on all other components of behavior.[5]

Subjects

Students in a basic speech communication course were randomly assigned to treatment conditions: fifty-nine *S*s were in each of the Hi, Lo, and Ru treatments; 62 *S*s were in the Me treatment.

Instrument Development

When a review of several published instruments designed to measure communicative competence or some aspect of competence indicated that a brief but comprehensive, reliable, and valid instrument did not exist, such an instrument was constructed for this research. Separate subscales were written for general communicative competence, affiliation/support, social relaxation, behavioral flexibility, and empathy. A subscale was also included to measure the success of the interaction management manipulation.

Initially, 57 Likert-type items were written and pretested; those showing the greatest between-treatment discrimination were retained. In a *post hoc* analysis of the revised instrument, its reliability was estimated at .96 using Cronbach's *alpha* (Lord & Novick, 1968). Using Friedman's (1968) Estimation of the Magnitude of Experimental Effect, statistical power was calculated to be .74, indicating more than adequate protection against Type II error.

STATISTICAL SUMMARY 1

Reliability indicates how accurate and consistent a measure is. If a measure is highly reliable, then you can be confident that the scores are very accurate and consistent. Here, the reliability was .96, indicating a great deal of accuracy and consistency.

Power indicates how effective your research methods are as a whole. The higher the power, up to 1.00, the more likely you are to be able to accurately describe what really occurs in your study. The power in this study was moderately high, meaning that Wiemann had a good chance of finding out what was really going on in his study.

<table>
<tr><td></td></tr>
</table>

STATISTICAL SUMMARY 2

Hypothesis 1

An inverted parabolic relationship is represented by the broken line (— — —) in Figure 1. Wiemann predicted that, in general, people would find interactions that contained fewer errors to be more competent. However, if there were no errors at all, Wiemann predicted that people would rate this less positively than if there were a few small errors.

To test this hypothesis, an analysis of variance was conducted which showed that the four experimental conditions (high, medium, low interaction management, and rude) were different from each other. Analysis of variance is a technique for seeing if three or more groups differ from each other. For example, if you have three groups, you may want to know which one talks the most.

Next, a Scheffe procedure was used to compare each condition to the other. Scheffe tests tell you if there is a difference between two groups. For example, you might want to see if one group (e.g., males) had more eye contact than a second group (e.g., females). The hypothesis predicted that the correct order of competence ratings should be rude, low, high, medium. However, Wiemann found that the correct ordering was rude, low, medium, and high. This ordering was also examined using a linearity test which showed that the conditions were ordered sequentially from rude to high.

RESULTS[6]

Hypothesis 1

The first hypothesis, which predicted an inverted parabolic relationship between the level of interaction management and observers' perceptions of communicative competence, was not supported.

To test this hypothesis, a one-way analysis of variance was computed on subjects' evaluations on the Competence subscale. The statistically significant F-ratio (76.154; df = 3/235; p < .001) indicated that the level of interaction management displayed by the confederate did indeed affect subjects' perceptions of that confederate's communicative competence. Additionally, a *post hoc* analysis of the differences among means, using the Scheffe Procedure, demonstrated that the four treatment means differed significantly (see Table 2). A test for deviations from linearity (Winer, 1971) showed that perceived communicative competence is a positive linear function of interaction management (F = 0.342; df = 2/235). The predicted and observed relationships are displayed in Figure 1.

Two rival hypotheses to H_1 should be considered. The first of these takes the form of the traditional null hypothesis: perceptions of communicative competence are independent of displayed interaction management. The second is an alternative research hypothesis: perceived communicative competence is positively and linearly related to displayed interaction management. These data strongly support this second rival hypothesis. The smoother the management of the interaction, the more competent the communicator was perceived to be.

TABLE 2
One-Way Analysis of Variance and Scheffe Procedure for Competence

Source	df	MS	F	P
Between Treatments	3	1121.9061	76.154	< .001
Within Treatments	235	15.9139		
Scheffe Procedure:				
Treatment	Hi	Me	Lo	Ru
Mean*	25.4407$_a$	21.5000$_b$	18.5593$_c$	14.7458$_d$

*The larger the mean the higher the rating. Means with common subscripts do not differ significantly from each other (p = .05).

FIGURE 1   Observed and predicted competence-interaction management relationship.

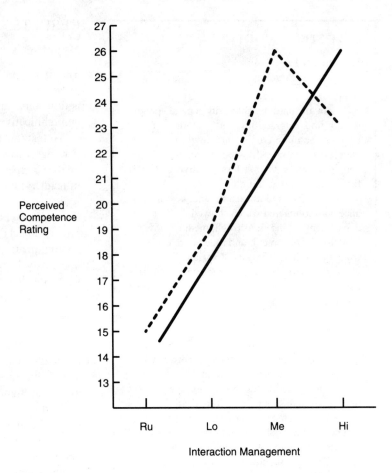

Perceived Competence Rating

Interaction Management

Observed Relationship = ━━━   *Predicted Relationship =* ▬ ▬

STATISTICAL SUMMARY 3

Hypothesis 2

Next, a factor analysis was conducted using all of the items other than those measuring interaction management. Factor analysis provides a way of statistically testing to see if items can be placed in groups. Wiemann expected the items to group into four clusters, one each for behavioral flexibility, empathy, affiliativeness/supportiveness, and social relaxation. Instead, the results indicated that there was a single, overall factor he called general competence.

Wiemann used the original hypothesized four clusters in his remaining data analyses. Again, tests of linearity were conducted for each of these four variables. These showed that the variables were related to interaction management in a sequential, straight-line pattern from high to low. Finally, each of the four variables was found to have significant correlations with interaction management. This meant that as each of the four variables increased, interaction management did as well. The more flexible someone was, the better they were at interaction management.

Hypothesis 2

The second hypothesis predicted a positive linear relationship between perceptions of interaction management and perceptions of: (a) behavioral flexibility, (b) empathy, (c) affiliativeness/supportiveness, and (d) social relaxation. Each of the four parts of H_2 was supported.

The hypothesized relationships were assessed by correlating the Management subscale with the subscales of each of the other variables within each of the four treatments and then for all treatments combined (Table 3). Additionally, a principal factors analysis with iteration followed by an oblique rotation and retaining eigenvalues of 1.0 or greater was performed on data for all treatments combined (Table 4). Since factor analysis yielded what amounts to a single-factor solution and the data generally conformed to the same pattern, the results for all variables are discussed together.

As can be seen in Table 3, interaction management correlates at statistically significant levels with behavioral flexibility, affiliation/support, empathy, and social relaxation in all treatments, with one exception. This exception is social relaxation in the Me treatment.

The changes in the ratings of the dependent variables as displayed interaction management changes are presented graphically in Figure 2. Deviations from linearity were tested for each variable; no statistically significant deviations were found (see Table 5).

The factor analysis yielded a four-factor solution, with the first factor accounting for 82.8 percent of the variance. These factors do not conform with the proposed components of the communicative competence model; rather, they indicate that the subjects do not differentiate among general competence, affiliation/support, empathy, and behavioral flexibility. Items measuring social relaxation loaded on Factors II, III and IV (but not on Factor I). These factors can be characterized as: Factor I, general communicative competence (82.8%); Factor II, social relaxation (10.3%); and Factors III and IV (3.7% and 3.2%, respectively), which seem to be variants of social relaxation. When the factor correlations are considered, however, it seems it would be most useful not to distinguish among factors, that is, to treat this as a one-factor solution.

The factor analysis lends further support for H_2 with the exception of the social relaxation relationship.

TABLE 3
Pearson Correlation Coefficients: Interaction Management with Dependent Variables by Treatments and Across Treatments

Dependent variable	Treatment				
	Hi	Me	Lo	Ru	All
	Interaction Management				
Flexibility	.47**	.51**	.60**	.57**	.73**
Affiliation	.67**	.53**	.48**	.68**	.78**
Empathy	.62**	.52**	.50**	.57**	.74**
Relaxation	.65**	.08	.34*	.21*	.51**
n	59	62	59	59	239

*p < .05; **p = .001

TABLE 4
Oblique Factor Pattern Loadings for Dependent Variables

Factor I. (82.8% of the variance)

1. S finds it easy to get along with others. (C)**	−.55
2. S can adapt to changing situations. (BF)	−.57
3. S treats people as individuals. (BF)	−.69
5. S is rewarding to talk to. (C)	−.76
6. S can deal with others effectively. (C)	−.74
7. S is a good listener. (A/S)	−.83
8. S's personal relations are cold and distant. (A/S)	−.45
9. S is easy to talk to. (C)	−.70
10. S won't argue with someone just to prove she's right. (E)	−.47
12. S ignores other people's feelings. (E)	−.74
13. S generally knows how others feel. (E)	−.68
14. S lets others know she understands them. (E)	−.72
15. S understands other people. (E)	−.75
17. S listens to what people say to her. (E)	−.81
18. S likes to be close and personal with people. (A/S)	−.58
19. S generally knows what type of behavior is appropriate in any given situation. (BF)	−.59
20. S usually does not make unusual demands on her friends. (C)	−.50
22. S is supportive of others. (A/S)	−.75
24. S can easily put herself in another person's shoes. (E)	−.58
30. S is a likeable person. (A/S)	−.73
31. S is flexible. (BF)	−.66
33. People can go to S with their problems. (A/S)	−.73
34. S generally says the right thing at the right time. (C)	−.74
35. S likes to use her voice and body expressively. (SR)	−.30
36. S is sensitive to others' needs of the moment. (BF)	−.80

Factor II. (10.3%)

16. S is relaxed and comfortable when speaking. (SR)	.83
23. S does not mind meeting strangers. (C)	.50
26. S is generally relaxed when conversing with a new acquaintance. (SR)	.92

Factor III. (3.7%)

29. S enjoys social gatherings where she can meet new people. (SR)***	.37

Factor IV. (3.2%)

29. S enjoys social gatherings where she can meet new people. (SR)***	.33
32. S is not afraid to speak with people in authority. (SR)	.50

Factor Correlations

	II	III	IV
I	−.50	−.26	−.06
II		.33	.26
III			.08

N = 239; Nvar = 30; Eigenvalue = 1.0; Delta = 0.0

*Items which constitute the manipulation check (i.e., the Interaction Management subscale—numbers 4, 11, 21, 25, 27, and 28) were omitted from this analysis.

**The letter in parentheses indicates the subscale of which the item is part: C = Competence; E = Empathy; A/S = Affiliation and Support; BF = Behavioral Flexibility; and SR = Social Relaxation.

***Item 29 loads weakly on both Factors III and IV

FIGURE 2   Relationship of interaction management to dependent variables.

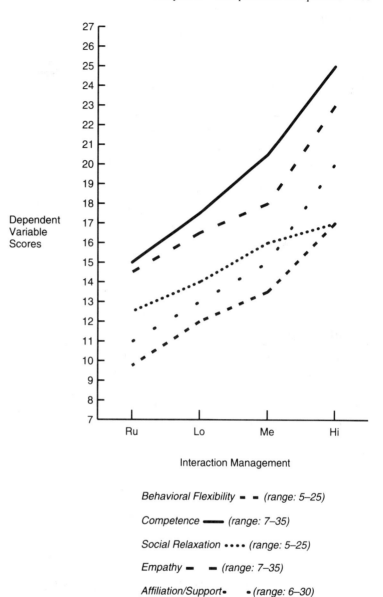

Dependent Variable Scores

Interaction Management

Behavioral Flexibility ▬ ▬ *(range: 5–25)*

Competence ▬▬▬ *(range: 7–35)*

Social Relaxation •••• *(range: 5–25)*

Empathy ▬ ▬ *(range: 7–35)*

Affiliation/Support • • *(range: 6–30)*

TABLE 5
Summary of Deviations from Linearity of Dependent Variables

Variable	$SS_{bet.}$	$SS_{l.r.}$	MS_e	F
Competence	3635.718	3624.843	15.914	0.342
Flexibility	1939.313	1926.723	10.554	0.596
Affiliation	2822.789	2771.119	13.034	1.982
Empathy	2847.601	2748.266	18.210	2.727
Relaxation	868.758	814.733	12.662	2.133

*$p = .05$; $F_{.95}(2, 235) = 3.00$

DISCUSSION

Taken together, the data present a picture of communicative competence which is in general agreement with the model developed here. The agreement can only be characterized as "general" because three facets of the results are at odds with the model. The results (1) did not reflect the predicted inverted parabolic relationship between displayed interaction management and perceptions of communicative competence, (2) revealed a relatively weak (though statistically significant) relationship between social relaxation and interaction management, and (3) yielded a one-factor solution where the model implied a five-factor solution. Each of these facets will be briefly discussed.

The Competence-Management Relationship

Prediction of a nonlinear relationship between interaction management and communicative competence was based primarily on the assumption that too much other-directedness would be dysfunctional. It seemed reasonable that a person displaying "too smooth" a presentation might be seen as trying to appear interested in his audience when, in fact, his interest was really in his message. The appearance of commitment to audience is a facade—an inappropriate claim on the relationship. The prototype of this communicator is the previously mentioned used car salesman who tries to demonstrate interest in his customer's welfare, but is actually interested only in a sale, no matter what must be said or done to achieve his goal.

Why was no nonlinear relationship between interaction management and communicative competence observed in this research? Several explanations are possible. First, the primary assumption—that an overly smooth presentation will be suspect—could be wrong. Perhaps people do not penalize others for being extremely good interactants, since the smoother the management of the interaction, the easier it is for *all* participants to accomplish their objectives.

Second, many of the studies which support the primary assumption tend to be rather artificial. For example, Exline's (1971) research required subjects to *imagine* how they would feel in a particular situation. Mehrabian (1972) also relied on noninteractive situations; his subjects listened to single words or pretended a coat rack was their fellow interactant. In the cases mentioned here, only one component of the interaction was studied at a time, and there was not even a semblance of normal interaction. The generally nonlinear relationships found in these studies could thus be an artifact of the artificially-contrived situations in which the subjects found themselves. The more extreme the treatment, the more unnatural it became, and thus the lower the subjects evaluated it. In the more interactive situation of this study, subjects were able to observe the whole spectrum of behavior. Behavioral extremes of one kind may have been offset by moderation in others, thus affecting the overall perceptions of competence. In spite of the weaknesses of these studies, the nonlinear trends they report are not unlike the commonsense perception that too-practiced a presentation is somehow less valued than a spontaneous one in everyday conversational encounters.

A third possibility for the lack of a nonlinear relationship between management and competence involves the nature of the situation itself. It is possible that in an initial interaction, people are more tolerant of others. They lack information about the other interactant, and consequently, do not judge him too severely. Similarly, in an initial interaction, a person may not spend enough time with the other for his evaluation to crystalize. That is, a nonlinear relationship develops only after some period of time; initially, the smoothness of presentation is acceptable because it is anticipated—everyone is expected to make a good impression, and we do not take offense at even the most practiced attempts. After a time, however, the smoothness is seen as insincerity, phoniness, or shallowness.

Each of these three explanations probably accounts in part for the failure of the nonlinear relationship to emerge in this study—the first to a lesser extent than the latter two. The third explanation, however, seems to be most viable. What these results indicate is that at initial meetings a certain smoothness in presentation is considered communicatively competent; the smoother the initial meeting goes, the more competent the communicator is perceived to be.

The Management-Social Relaxation Relationship

The interaction management-social relaxation relationship is less clear than are the relationships of management with the other components of the model. Only in the Hi treatment condition was social relaxation evaluated in the same way as the other components. In the other treatments, the strength of the relationship either broke down or social relaxation became less salient. The relaxation-competence relationship is similar to the relaxation-management relationship (r's by treatment are: Hi, .81; Me, .15; Lo, .58; Ru, .35; and combined treatments, .63; Hi, Lo, and combined r's are statistically significant at the .001 level; Ru r, at the .003 level; the Me r is not significant). Since the question of primary interest here is one of the appropriateness of including social relaxation in the communicative competence model, this discussion is couched in terms of the competence-relaxation relationship.

Several explanations of this finding present themselves. First, social relaxation may not be a major component of communicative competence. This possibility can be rejected out of hand because of the strong positive correlation between both management and competence and management and social relaxation in the Hi treatment. This treatment was communicative competence in its purest form, the form in which its components should be most easily identifiable. (In fact, Habermas, 1970, argues that competence can only be identified with any certainty in its "ideal" form.)

Another explanation lies in the behaviors used to communicate social relaxation. Such things as body lean and postural shifts may be too subtle to be monitored when there is considerable activity among the other competence components. Thus, the level of social relaxation would be less important or play less of a role in perceptions of communicative competence in any situation except one in which other aspects of the performance were "under control."

This explanation seems to fit these data. In the Hi treatment, social relaxation is clearly evaluated as part of general communicative competence. In the Me treatment—probably the most confusing in terms of what the confederate is doing, i.e., trying but not quite succeeding at being a "good" interactant—relaxation drops out completely. The tie appears again, although relatively weakly, in the Lo and Ru treatments, where clear patterns of behavior are established by the confederates. When all data are considered, however, the relaxation-competence relationship must be considered tentative, at best.

Factor Analysis Results

The results of the factor analysis indicate that subjects saw communicative competence as composed of a single factor (see Table 4). Is this to say that communicative competence should be described as a unitary set of behaviors? For this sample, such a unitary description seems to be in order. Yet, both intuition and empirical data (unfortunately, not these data) argue that different components of communicative competence can and should be differentiated.

The research cited earlier clearly demonstrates that empathy, behavioral flexibility, interaction management, social relaxation, and affiliation/support can be differentiated from each other behaviorally and conceptually. Heuristically, the five-component (or an n-component) model is valuable because it directs us to the types of behaviors which might make a difference in perceptions of competence. The empirical evidence of this one study notwithstanding, the "component" conceptualization of competence should not be abandoned.

While it is often unproductive to let statistical analysis guide one's thinking (cf. Blommers & Lindquist, 1960), the empirical evidence of this study cannot be ignored. These subjects did not distinguish between general competence and specific components (especially behavioral flexibility, empathy, affiliation/support). This could be due to a rating "halo" effect. It seems probable that subjects could not or did not attend to all of the cues available. They made judgments based on the cues to which they attended and then generalized these judgments to include all cues. Another explanation, of course, is that pragmatically, competence is a unitary set of behaviors in that the person who is high on one of the dimensions proposed here will also be high on all of the others.

Communicative Competence: Some Conclusions

In arriving at conclusions, these data leave little room for interpretation; they are sufficiently straightforward that rival interpretations are not parsimonious. Interaction management, affiliation/support, empathy, behavioral flexibility, and social relaxation are interdependent components of communicative competence. It is by definition that competence is the construct that encompasses the five components; it is a more inclusive, abstract construct than interaction management, empathy, or the other components of the model.

In this study the goal of each interactant (the confederates) was to get acquainted with the other. To accomplish this, each was responsible for both giving information about herself and receiving information about the other. Communicative competence was demonstrated when the on-camera confederate facilitated the other's giving of information and reciprocated in kind with her own information. In all but the Hi treatment, this mutuality of exchange was less than ideal, and the subjects evaluated the confederate lower accordingly. (It is interesting to note, in line with the dyadic conceptualization of competence, that each interactant's goal must be met

simultaneously in this type of situation. One interactant must allow the other to give if she is to receive.)

These data also bear out the centrality of interaction management in the communicative competence model. *Even relatively small changes in management behavior resulted in large variations in evaluations of communicative competence.* As interaction management behavior was varied, perceptions of all of the other components of competence and general competence itself varied linearly with it. It remains to be seen whether variations in any of the other components of CC will similarly affect perceptions of interaction management.

These results support the theoretical formulations of competence put forth by Argyle (1969; Argyle & Kendon, 1967) and Bochner and Kelly (1974), as reviewed earlier in this report. Similarly, Goffman's (1959, 1961, 1963, 1967) observations concerning competent self-presentation have withstood this experimental test. The confederate was evaluated as less competent when she did not give complete attention to the interaction, when she showed disrespect of her fellow interactant, and when she did not fully contribute to the maintenance of a smooth and continuous flow of talk. Furthermore, the more negligent she was in these areas, the lower she was evaluated.

In spite of the straightforwardness of the data, the generalizability of this study is limited by two factors: (1) the stimulus situation, and (2) the role the subjects played in the study.

The stimulus situation used here, although pervasive and important, is comparatively unique. Each relationship has only one initial interaction. As has already been suggested, criteria used to evaluate others probably change over time; people may be more tolerant of some types of behavior in initial interactions because they *are* initial interactions. While the basic components of communicative competence as outlined here remain the basis of evaluation, other idiosyncratic components are probably added as the relationship develops. For example, Suttles

(1970) states that one indicator of friendship is development of norms between the friends which often are at odds with general cultural norms concerning polite behavior. It is the implicit agreement to break the cultural norms that is a marker of the friendship. The way idiosyncratic behaviors might modify the basic components of competence is an empirical question.

The second limitation of this study is the role the subjects played—the role of observers. It seems likely that a person's perceptions and evaluations of another interactant are based, in part at least, on the type of communicative relationship the two have at any given time. It would be expected then that a person could perceive another from one perspective when they are interacting with each other and differently when watching the other interact with a third party.

In sum, the competent communicator is one who is other-oriented, while at the same time maintaining the ability to accomplish his own interpersonal goals. This other-orientation is demonstrated by the communicator being empathic, affiliative and supportive, and relaxed while interacting with others. Moreover, the competent communicator is capable of adapting his behavior as the situation within an encounter changes and/or as he moves from encounter to encounter. The way the communicator manages an interaction contributes, in part at least, to his fellow interactants' perceptions of his competence. It is this communicative competence which enables a person, in a very real and practical way, to establish a social identity.

NOTES

1. Communicative competence in the sense used here is not to be confused with linguistic competence. Communicative competence is a performance-based concept (Weinstein, 1966), whereas linguistic competence is a "set of principles" necessary for a person to be a speaker of a language (Dale, 1972). Hymes (1974) argues the necessity for emphasis on the performance aspects of language. Hymes' argument can be extended to all aspects of socially communicative behavior. A knowledge of appropriate behavior is of little use to an interactant if he cannot implement that knowledge when called upon to do so. Therefore, it seems unwise to make the competence-performance distinction for social behavior.

2. These cues can be reliably identified only for middle-class English speakers. The cues for each of the dimensions of competence may vary among cultures, but the salience of the dimensions is probably transcultural.

3. For a complete description of these dimensions see Wiemann (1975).

4. Transcripts used and complete information on the pilot study and instrument development can be found in the author's dissertation (Wiemann, 1975).

5. This assumption of total isomorphism would, of course, be invalid in certain types of interaction, e.g., purposeful deception. However, isomorphism in some channels is always assumed when detection of deception, or leakage cues, is discussed (cf. Mehrabian, 1971, 1972).

6. Before proceeding with the hypothesis testing, the success of the manipulation and the possible effect of subject sex were checked. A one-way analysis of variance for the interaction management subscale produced a significant F-ratio of 72.177 (df = 3/235; p < .001). Using the Scheffe Procedure, it was determined that the Hi treatment was perceived as significantly different from all other treatments, as was the Me treatment. The Lo and Ru treatments were not perceived as statistically different from each other, although the means were in the desired direction. Together these statistics indicated that the manipulation of the independent variable had been successful. In addition, a sex-by-treatment analysis of variance was computed to test the possible effect of sex of subject on judgments of competence. Neither the main effect of sex, nor the sex-by-treatment interaction was statistically significant (F = 0.9744, df = 1/225; and F = 1.7161, df = 3/225 respectively). A complete discussion and the data can be found in Wiemann (1975).

REFERENCES

Altman, I., & Taylor, D. A. *Social penetration.* New York: Holt, Rinehart & Winston, 1973.

Argyle, M. *Social interaction.* Chicago: Aldine Atherton, 1969.

Argyle, M., & Dean, J. Eye contact, distance and affiliation. *Sociometry,* 1965, 28, 289–304.

Argyle, M., & Kendon, A. The experimental analysis of social performance. In L. Berkowitz (Ed.), *Advances in experimental social psychology,* Vol. 3. New York: Academic Press, 1967, 55–98.

Argyris, C. *Interpersonal competence and organizational effectiveness.* Homewood, Ill.: Irwin-Dorsey, 1962.

Argyris, C. Explorations in interpersonal competence—I. *Journal of Applied Behavioral Science,* 1965, 1, 58–83.

Berger, C. R. The acquaintance process revisited: Explorations in initial interaction. Paper presented at the annual convention of the Speech Communication Association, New York, November 1972.

Blommers, P., & Lindquist, E. F. *Elementary statistical methods.* Boston: Houghton Mifflin, 1960.

Bochner, A. P., & Kelly, C. W. Interpersonal competence: Rationale, philosophy, and implementation of a conceptual framework. *Speech Teacher,* 1974, 23, 279–301.

Brown, R., & Gilman, A. The pronouns of power and solidarity. In T. A. Sebeok (Ed.), *Style in language.* Cambridge: MIT Press, 1960, 253–276.

Dale, P. S. *Language development.* Hinsdale, Ill.: Dryden Press, 1972.

Dittman, A. T. Developmental factors in conversation behavior. *Journal of Communication,* 1972, 22, 404–423.

Duncan, S. Toward a grammar for dyadic conversation. *Semiotica,* 1973, 9, 29–46.

Ekman, P., & Friesen, W. V. The repertoire of nonverbal behavior: Categories, origins, usage and coding. *Semiotica,* 1969, 1, 49–98.

Ervin-Tripp, S. An analysis of the interaction of language, topic and listener. *American Anthropologist,* 1964, 66, 86–94.

Ervin-Tripp, S. On sociolinguistic rules: Alternation and co-occurrence. In J. J. Gumperz and D. Hymes (Eds.), *Directions in sociolinguistics.* New York: Holt, Rinehart & Winston, 1972, 213–250.

Exline, R. V. Visual interaction: The glances of power and preference. In J. K. Cole (Ed.), *Nebraska symposium on motivation.* Lincoln: University of Nebraska Press, 1971, 163–206.

Friedman, H. Magnitude of experimental effect and a table for its rapid estimation. *Psychological Bulletin,* 1968, 70, 245–251.

Garfinkel, H. Studies of the routine grounds of everyday activities. In D. Sudnow (Ed.), *Studies in social interaction.* New York: Free Press, 1972, 1–30.

Goffman, E. *The presentation of self in everyday life.* Garden City, N.Y.: Doubleday Anchor, 1959.

Goffman, E. *Encounters.* Indianapolis: Bobbs-Merrill, 1961.

Goffman, E. *Behavior in public places.* New York: Free Press, 1963.

Goffman, E. *Interaction ritual.* Garden City, N.Y.: Anchor, 1967.

Goldman-Eisler, F. *Psycholinguistics.* London: Academic Press, 1968.

Habermas, J. Toward a theory of communicative competence. In H. P. Dreitzel (Ed.), *Recent sociology* (No. 2). New York: Macmillan, 1970, 114–148.

Hall, E. T. *The hidden dimension.* Garden City, N.Y.: Doubleday, 1966.

Hart, R. P., & Burks, D. M. Rhetorical sensitivity and social interaction. *Speech Monographs,* 1972, 39, 75–91.

Holland, J. L., & Baird, L. L. An interpersonal competency scale. *Educational and Psychological Measurement,* 1968, 28, 503–510.

Hymes, D. *Foundations in sociolinguistics.* Philadelphia: University of Pennsylvania Press, 1974.

Jaffe, J., & Feldstein, S. *Rhythms of dialogue.* New York: Academic Press, 1970.

Kasl, S. V., & Mahl, G. F. The relationship of disturbances and hesitations in spontaneous speech to anxiety. *Journal of Personality and Social Psychology,* 1965, 1, 425–433.

Lord, R. M., & Novick, M. R. *Statistical theories of mental test scores.* Reading, Mass.: Addison-Wesley, 1968.

McCall, G. J., & Simmons, J. L. *Identities and interactions.* New York: Free Press, 1966.

Mehrabian, A. Nonverbal betrayal of feeling. *Journal of Experimental Research in Personality,* 1971. 5, 64–73.

Mehrabian, A. *Nonverbal communication.* Chicago: Aldine Atherton, 1972.

Mehrabian, A., & Ksionzky, S. Some determinants of social interaction. *Sociometry,* 1972, 35, 588–609.

Robinson, W. P. *Language and social behaviour.* Baltimore: Penguin, 1972.

Rodnick, R., & Wood, B. The communication strategies of children. *Speech Teacher,* 1973, 22, 114–124.

Rosenfeld, H. M. The experimental analysis of interpersonal influence processes. *Journal of Communication,* 1972, 22, 424–442.

Sacks, H., Schegloff, E. A., & Jefferson, G. A simplest systematics for the organization of turn-taking for conversation. *Language,* 1974, 50, 696–735.

Scheidel, T. M. A systems analysis of two person conversations. Paper presented at the Doctoral Honors Seminar on Modern Systems Theory in Human Communication, University of Utah, 1974.

Schegloff, E. A. Sequencing in conversational openings. In J. J. Gumperz and D. Hymes (Eds.), *Directions in sociolinguistics.* New York: Holt, Rinehart & Winston, 1972, 346–380.

Snyder, M. The self-monitoring of expressive behavior. *Journal of Personality and Social Psychology,* 1974, 30, 526–537.

Speier, M. Some conversational problems for interaction analysis. In D. Sudnow (Ed.), *Studies in social interaction.* New York: Free Press, 1972, 397–427.

Speier, M. *How to observe face-to-face communication: A sociological introduction.* Pacific Palisades, Calif.: Goodyear, 1973.

Suttles, G. D. Friendship as a social institution. In G. J. McCall, M. M. McCall, N. K. Denzin, G. D. Suttles, and S. B. Kurth, *Social relationships.* Chicago: Aldine, 1970, 95–135.

Weinstein, E. A. Toward a theory of interpersonal tactics. In C. W. Backman and P. F. Secord (Eds.), *Problems in social psychology.* New York: McGraw-Hill, 1966, 394–398.

Wiemann, J. M. An experimental study of visual attention in dyads: The effect of four gaze conditions on evaluations of applicants in employment interviews. Paper presented at the annual convention of the Speech Communication Association, Chicago, December 1974.

Wiemann, J. M. An exploration of communicative competence in initial interactions: An experimental study. Unpublished doctoral dissertation, Purdue University, 1975.

Wiemann, J. M., & Knapp, M. L. Turn-taking in conversations, *Journal of Communication,* 1975, 25, 75–92.

Wiener, M., & Mehrabian, A. *Language within language.* New York: Appleton-Century-Croft, 1968.

Winer, B. J. *Statistical principles in experimental design,* 2nd Ed. New York: McGraw-Hill, 1971.

TOWARD A CONCEPTUALIZATION OF COMMUNICATION SATISFACTION

Michael L. Hecht

The study of communication satisfaction is of vital importance to the speech communication field. Although the descriptive investigations characterized by rhetorical analysis, category-based observation, and participant observation provide a useful lexicon with which to discuss communication processes, they do not by themselves examine the outcomes of communication behavior. These outcomes, of which communication satisfaction is but one, provide the basis for a holistic theoretical approach to the field. As Gouran notes, "no working consensus [exists] among small group researchers about the outcomes of interpersonal interaction which are most in need of study."[1] DeLamater[2] and Larson[3] make similar points, noting the necessity of establishing these outcomes in order better to understand the processes involved in human interaction. Not only does the concept of communication satisfaction provide an outcome criterion for assessing process variables and a means for organizing communication strategies, but it also enables the communication researcher to apply communication theory and research to the pursuit of making everyday interaction more fulfilling.

Communication satisfaction, therefore, fulfills three essential functions. First, this variable may be utilized as a criterion for research examining process variables. Second, it may be utilized to organize and evaluate classes of variables, thereby contributing to theory building. And, third, the study of communication satisfaction has direct and straightforward applications to the improvement of communication skills.

The concept of satisfaction is also a recurrent theme in macrotheories of human behavior. Comparable concepts are associated with competing theoretical perspectives: the pleasure/pain principle of hedonism, the validation principle of cognitivism, the reward/cost principle of exchange theory, and the reinforcement principle of Skinnerian behaviorism. Each paradigm logically deduces that an affect becomes associated with or conditioned to the link between the environment and an internal state. From the hedonistic perspective, people seek that which is pleasurable and avoid that which is painful. A successful search for pleasure and/or a successful avoidance of pain produces a satisfaction-type affect. Within the cognitivist paradigm, perception links the past with present behaviors, creating expectations or anticipations which are then construed to be validated or invalidated. Validation is associated with a satisfying affect. From the exchange paradigm, comparison levels of alternatives are created internally and compared with

Source: The article is taken from the *Quarterly Journal of Speech* [64: 47–62, 1978]. Reprinted by permission of the Speech Communication Association, 5105 Backlick Rd., Annandale, VA 22003.

external rewards and costs. If a favorable difference between rewards and costs exceeds these internal comparison levels, then satisfaction results. Finally, from the Skinnerian behaviorist perspective one's history of reinforcement and discriminative stimuli provides the link between the past and the behavior. Reinforcement of the behaviors can then produce a satisfying response. Within each viewpoint, then, satisfaction is one of the core constructs around which the theory is elaborated. To be sure, each theory has a different underlying assumptive base, which results in quite different world views, and consequently they reach different conclusions about causality and relationships. What is crucial to note, however, is the importance which is uniformly attached to a satisfaction-type affect.

Communication satisfaction also contributes to the conceptual basis for a normative approach to the study of communication processes. Within this framework, individuals are seen as assessing communication in terms of expected or anticipated behaviors. Accordingly, deviance from the norm is also a crucial concept. Recent empirical investigations have examined these expectations or discriminations,[4] and beginnings have been made in the investigation of reactions to deviations. Satisfaction is commonly conceived of as the affect associated with the fulfillment or nonfulfillment of normative expectations and therefore contributes to an understanding of communication from within this framework.

Concurrent with this concern for normative aspects of communication behavior has been the development of notions of communication skills competence.[5] The major thrust of this work is the discovery of skills which facilitate effective communication. As an affect commonly associated with effective communication, communication satisfaction should serve as a criterion for evaluating competing notions of communication competence.

In summary, then, satisfaction is an important construct within various competing theoretical viewpoints, is closely associated with a normative approach to the study of communication, and

provides an important criterion for the investigation of communication competence. The role of communication in the creation of satisfaction, however, has been a neglected area. The purpose of the present paper is to review previous conceptualizations of satisfaction in order to facilitate and encourage the investigation of this crucial variable. These conceptualizations are drawn from work in other areas (e.g., organizational satisfaction) due to the dearth of satisfaction research directly related to communication. As general conceptualizations of satisfaction, however, they have straight-forward application to the study of communication satisfaction. After reviewing and analyzing the major conceptualizations of satisfaction, a revised perspective will be offered accompanied by suggestions for research directions.

PREVIOUS CONCEPTUALIZATIONS OF SATISFACTION

Need Gratification

A number of writers have conceived of satisfaction as a cognitive state resulting from need gratification.[6] They perceive people as having basic, inherent needs. Communication has been conceptualized as fulfilling needs such as achievement, affiliation and dominance,[7] physiology, safety, love, esteem and self-actualization,[8] and inclusion, affection, and control.[9] Within the need fulfillment position, then, communication satisfaction results from the use of communication to gratify needs. Gross, for example, studied how groups satisfy primary needs such as love, affection, fellowship, and a sense of belonging.[10] Trow, a little more specific about the process, viewed satisfaction as dependent upon the strength of the need and the degree to which the environment fulfills it.[11] Depending upon the type of need, satisfaction is linked to the elimination of deficits and the fulfillment of pleasure quotas. We fulfill some needs only to avoid the pain of nonfulfillment; we fulfill others to avoid the pain of nonfulfillment *and* to gain the satisfaction derived from fulfillment. Respiration is an example of the former type of need; self-disclosure might be an example of the latter.

The most complete and explicit form of this approach is derived from the work of Maslow[12] as elaborated by Wolf. Wolf's formulation, need gratification theory, was developed to explain job satisfaction but is grounded in the generalized notion of satisfaction as the gratification of need states. The essential premise of this theory is that individuals seek to gratify active needs, i.e., those which have not as yet been gratified.[13] Maslow's hierarchy of needs is assumed, with the individual seeking to fulfill the needs directly above those which have already been gratified. The individual is seen as ignoring previously gratified needs as well as those which exist on levels of Maslow's hierarchy higher than the active needs. For example, having gratified the first level of needs, a person will seek to gratify needs on the second level, ignoring the needs on the first level as well as those on levels three and above. From this perspective dissatisfaction arises when the gratification of active needs is frustrated or the continued gratification of previous needs is threatened or interrupted. Although satisfaction is derived from the gratification of any need, it is greater when a previously unfulfilled need is gratified.

Expectation Fulfillment

A second approach views satisfaction as tied to the process of expectation fulfillment. Basically, the individual envelops a standard against which to compare the outcomes derived from the environment.[14] This standard has been labeled in a number of ways by researchers and theorists. Thibaut and Kelley describe a comparison level which is the average of all one's outcomes experienced directly or vicariously, and therefore the level one anticipates, expects, or believes should come to oneself in a specific situation.[15] Ilgen defines satisfaction as the cognitive comparison between the environment and an internal standard.[16] Smith, Kendall, and Hulin use the term *frame of reference*,[17] and Locke uses *wants*.[18]

Two divergent positions have developed within the expectation approach. The first position, often labeled the "traditional approach,"[19] predicts that satisfaction occurs at the level of expectation and increases linearly as the level of the causal variable increases beyond this point (see Figure 1a). A linear relationship between satisfaction and environmental causal factors is hypothesized. Evidence in support of this position has been reported by Foa,[20] Hulin and Smith,[21] Locke,[22] Klein and Maher,[23] Graen,[24] Verinis, Brandsma, and Cofer,[25] Ilgen,[26] and Ilgen and Hamstra.[27]

The second position predicts a curvilinear relationship between satisfaction and causal variables.[28] This approach predicts satisfaction around the level of expectation, with lesser or diminished satisfaction as the level of the causal factor differs from what is expected (see Figure 1b).

Satisfaction with communication is easily conceived of in expectation fulfillment terms. A recent investigation of self disclosure reveals that people have expectations for judging the appropriateness of disclosing communication.[29] A developmental process is expected in which the conversation evolves from less intimate to more intimate disclosures. Within this framework people expect that intimate communication will occur later in the conversation and will be dissatisfied if it occurs sooner. Further, since disclosure is expected to be reciprocal and incremental, a conversation which evolves from lower to higher levels of disclosure will generally be considered satisfying. Within the expectation fulfillment position, communication satisfaction can be seen as tied to expectations for self, other, relationship, and context.

Equivocality Reduction

Weick developed the notion that environmental equivocality is related to the amount of satisfaction.[30] Operating from a phenomenological perspective, Weick sees a person's primary goal as seeking to give order, structure, and meaning to the environment. Satisfaction is seen as directly related to the removal of equivocality and,

FIGURE 1   Expectation Fulfillment.

1a: Traditional Approach

1b: Curvilinear

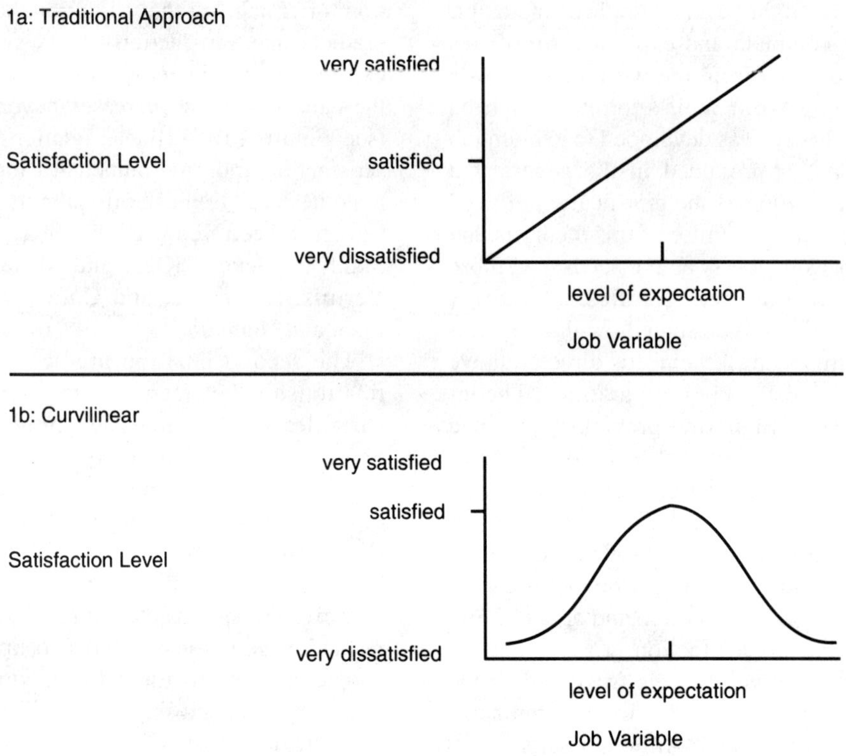

consequently, is associated with increased knowledge or control, accurate predictions, understandings, and success.[31]

Some close parallels exist between the equivocality reduction and the expectation fulfillment positions. Translating Weick's formulation into expectation terms, satisfaction occurs when one successfully expects or anticipates, and thereby functions to control or understand some portion of the environment. The crucial distinction from other expectation positions involves Weick's merger of an expectancy motive (desire for effective behavior) with the phenomenological description of people as seeking to anticipate and give order to the environment. The expectation position maintains that people develop expectations and that an environment which is perceived as meeting those expectations is satisfying. Weick attempts to explain this process by as-

serting that expectations are used to decrease equivocality and therefore anything which allows the reduction of uncertainty is satisfying. Equivocality reduction, not expectation fulfillment, is the crucial determinant of satisfaction. Weick seems to describe a linear relationship between satisfaction and equivocality reduction; the greater the amount of equivocality removed, the greater the satisfaction.

The equivocality reduction approach to communication seems to be closely allied to the theoretical position of information theorists and the psycholinguistic notion of redundancy. Communication is satisfying to the degree to which it removes uncertainty. The insecurity associated with establishing new relationships and the satisfaction felt when the uncertainty is resolved may all be explained by this conceptualization of communication satisfaction.

Constraint-Reinforcement

The constraint-reinforcement position, developed by Shelly[32] and his colleagues, is primarily a stimulus-response approach to satisfaction. A time distinction is utilized to classify types of affects. At the smallest interval of time, simple positive reinforcement is defined as the momentary feeling of pleasantness or well-being and is equated with pleasure. Simple negative reinforcement is the momentary feeling of unpleasantness and is equated with punishment. Collections of pleasures are called satisfaction or reinforcement; collections of punishments are called dissatisfaction or negative reinforcement. Satisfaction and dissatisfaction are seen as existing along separate continua and overall satisfaction is determined by subtracting the total amount of dissatisfaction from the total amount of satisfaction.

A sequence of satisfactions over time is labeled extended satisfaction. When this state exists over a lengthy period it is called happiness. Similarly, a sequence of dissatisfactions is labeled dissatisfaction. When this state exists over a lengthy period it is called unhappiness.

Within this framework, communication behaviors which would maximize satisfaction are assumed to be encouraged and to become more frequent. Communication, however, is constrained by various factors. Constraints are taken to be limitations on the range of possible behaviors. Shelly delineates informational constraints (unknown or forgotten behaviors), environmental constraints (behavior-events which the environment does not support), personal constraints (self-imposed ones as an outcome of previous conditioning), and social constraints (the combination of environmental and personal constraints).

From this viewpoint, then, communication satisfaction is derived from the stimulus characteristics of the environment. Communication behaviors chosen within certain constraints are associated with a greater number of environmental reinforcements than punishments. Communication satisfaction is equated with reinforcement and seen as a cluster of pleasures.

The term becomes synonymous with other positive emotions, all of which are synonymous with reinforcement.

The concept of optimal level and Shelly's notion of over-stimulation lead to a curvilinear view of communication satisfaction. Peak satisfaction occurs at the optimal level of reinforcement. Receiving less than the optimal state is dissatisfying in comparison to peak rewards. Receiving too much of something is also dissatisfying as it results in overstimulation. For example, one may have an optimal level at which one is most satisfied with compliments: Too few or too many compliments are both dissatisfying, although for different reasons. Too few compliments may lead to self-doubt; too many compliments may cause embarrassment.

Herzberg's Two-Factor Theory

The final conceptualization of satisfaction, developed by Herzberg and his associates,[33] deals with job satisfaction. Previous conceptualizations had dealt with satisfaction/dissatisfaction reactions as existing along a single continuum ranging from satisfied to dissatisfied. Herzberg, the first to claim that there are actually separate continua, utilized a content-context dichotomy to discriminate them. Certain factors contribute exclusively to the dissatisfaction continuum, with outcomes ranging from neutral to dissatisfied. He labeled these factors dissatisfiers, or hygiene factors, and postulated that they are part of the work context or environment. A second set of factors contribute exclusively to the satisfaction continuum, with outcomes ranging from neutral to satisfied. He labeled these factors satisfiers, or motivators, and postulated that they are the work content or the actual work performed.

When applied to communication, Herzberg's approach distinguishes the communication content from the communication context. Recent work in the relationship area indicates that when relational considerations have not been worked out denotative meanings of messages take on secondary importance.[34] In these interactions the ''content'' (in Herzberg's sense) is the relational aspect of the message, while the denotative meaning of the message recedes into the context. The primary focus of activity is directed at relationship questions. The denotative meanings are the context within which relationship concerns are dealt with. As relational considerations come to be worked out the denotative meaning becomes the communication content and the relationship recedes into the context. Here the relationship becomes the context within which information is exchanged via denotative meanings. Herzberg's approach leads the researcher to a closer examination of the functions served by aspects of the entire communication event, and proposes that these aspects can be dichotomized into content and the context categories.

Interpretive Summary

As noted previously, satisfaction is a central concept in a variety of major theoretical perspectives. Even though these theories disagree on basic assumptions about causality and relationships, each is elaborated around a satisfaction-type concept. Further, each theory conceptualizes this affect in two stages: a link between the internal state and the environment, and an affect associated with the link. Accordingly, this framework will be utilized to examine the conceptualizations of communication satisfaction.

An examination of the links between the internal state and environment proposed by the various conceptualizations reveals a number of problems. First the expectation fulfillment, equivocality reduction, and need gratification positions all utilize hypothetical variables to explain the link. As a result, no clear parameters are available for establishing a definition of communication satisfaction. In the need gratification position, for example, the physical conditions experienced by the individual when in a certain need state cannot be defined. These physical conditions are common to many other states as well, including states we do not call needs. Further, the use of hypothetical variables precludes direct access to the concept. All access must be indirect, which increases the problems of measurement.

Lacking clear parameters and direct access, we are left with guesses as to the nature and measurement of the key construct (i.e., equivocality, expectation, need). These guesses must then be utilized to estimate the nature and measurement of communication satisfaction. In this way errors are compounded. This process is intensified in the need gratification perspective, which reifies the need construct. All three perspectives fail to ground their construct by reference to observables. Such tenuous processes are to be avoided if sincere attention is to be paid to the law of parsimony.

A second problem involves the cognitive style assumed by the expectation fulfillment, equivocality reduction, and need gratification perspectives. In the expectation and need positions, persons are seen as actively comparing the outcomes derived from the environment with hypothetical internal structures. The equivocality position assumes that uncertainty is salient for the individual and that all people seek to anticipate and structure their environment at all times. It is not clear how the validity of such nebulous conceptions can be established, nor when such complex conceptualizations apply to which people and in which situations.

A third problem concerns Shelly's constraint-reinforcement approach, which, by focusing primarily on the environment, fails to make the necessary link between external and internal states. Communication satisfaction is an internal behavior. In exclusively attending to the environment, Shelly's approach ignores a wide range of information. He does not study satisfaction where it occurs, within the individual, and, consequently, many internal behaviors are not considered in the analysis. While Shelly does examine other emotional reactions to the environment, he does not consider cognitive behaviors such as expectations, equivocality reduction, and dimensions of judgment, which may be part of the emotional reaction called satisfaction.

By addressing themselves to the internal state-environment link, the theories exhibit a number of strengths. The expectation fulfillment position defines communication satisfaction in reference to environmental regularities. The equivocality reduction perspective attempts to examine the establishment of perceived regularities, Herzberg's two-factor approach points to the existence of different types of links. Finally, Shelly's constraint-reinforcement position concretizes his formulation by focusing on observables and thereby lays the groundwork for consensus as to the causes of satisfaction.

As a second stage, each theory must specify how an affect (satisfaction) becomes associated with the link between the internal state and the environment. Again, a number of problems are evident. First, the expectation fulfillment, equivocality reduction, constraint-reinforcement, and need gratification positions assume that all variables cause communication satisfaction by the same process. The need position, for example, assumes that all causal factors produce satisfaction by gratifying needs. Work related to Herzberg's two-factor theory and to the issue of linear or curvilinear relationships between satisfaction and causal variables suggests that this is not the case. It appears likely that the type of perceived environment mediates the association of the affect to the link between internal state and environment. Further, there may be situations in which expectations, needs, and/or equivocality are not relevant or important concerns.

A second problem obtains primarily in the expectation fulfillment and equivocality reduction positions. Neither approach can explain the relationship between communication satisfaction and negative expectation fulfillment or negative equivocality reduction. Negative expectations anticipate undesirable consequences for the individual and are commonly conceived of as insecurity or paranoia. One may, for example, expect to be fired. One cannot, however, expect satisfaction to be associated with the fulfillment of such negative communication expectations. By the same logic, negative equivocality reduction occurs when the degree of uncertainty is reduced by the occurrence of an undesirable event. Persons unsure of retaining employment are generally dissatisfied to be told their job is lost. One

may conclude, therefore, that it is not always satisfying to have expectations fulfilled or equivocality reduced.

A third problem involves the integration of satisfaction and dissatisfaction outcomes. The expectation fulfillment approach, for example, uses an additive model to combine satisfaction and dissatisfaction. As Gergen notes, however, heavy rewards and heavy costs produce conflict.[35] Osgood and Tannenbaum's work in congruity theory lends support to the notion that conflict is not reduced by summation.[36]

A final problem involves the need gratification approach and the equivocality reduction position. Each of these perspectives conceives of communication satisfaction in terms of a deficit state. In the need approach, one fulfills ungratified needs. In the equivocality reduction position, one relieves uncertainty. But do people derive satisfaction when they receive more than they need, or receive more information than is necessary to relieve uncertainty? Continuing, one may ask the need perspective to explain how needs are situationally defined,[37] and how the concept of hierarchy adjusts to situational differences.

In addition to examining the link between the environment and the internal state and the association of an affect with this link, one may ask how the various conceptualizations stand up under the scrutiny of empirical investigation. Empirical evidence damaging to the need gratification approach, for example, was offered by Herman and Hulin,[38] who reported that a need measure of satisfaction (Porter's Need Satisfaction Questionnaire) could not account for differences which were distinguishable by another instrument of established convergent and discriminant validity (Job Description Index). Further, Neeley[39] found no support for hypotheses derived from Wolf's[40] formulation of the theory.

Herzberg's conceptualization[41] has been the subject of a great deal of empirical investigation. Much of this work has challenged Herzberg's assumption that satisfaction and dissatisfaction are independent. Shelly makes the same assumptions.[42] The overwhelming conclusion of the research has been that satisfiers and dissatisfiers each contribute to both satisfaction and dissatisfaction, with satisfiers having a greater impact on both affects.[43] It seems, therefore, that the independence assumption is untenable.

A final area of empirical investigation examines the linear and curvilinear versions of the expectation fulfillment position. The research provides evidence for both types of relationships. The issue, then, becomes one of accounting for both a linear and curvilinear relationship between satisfaction and causal variables. None of the present theories has made this adjustment.

In the final analysis, the expectation fulfillment position comes closest to providing a solid theoretical framework. While utilizing a hypothetical construct for explanatory purposes, it does not reify that construct and the key terms have been operationalized. In addition, the position seems to encompass a fairly wide range of applications. It can straightforwardly embrace Herzberg's two-factor approach as well as the equivocality reduction position. The constraint-reinforcement approach can be utilized to explain the development of certain expectations, and needs can be recast into importance weights. The problems outlined above, however, indicate that even the expectation fulfillment position does not provide a complete and coherent explanation of satisfaction outcomes.

THE DISCRIMINATION FULFILLMENT APPROACH TO COMMUNICATION SATISFACTION

The prevailing conceptualizations of satisfaction do not provide adequate explanatory power nor conceptual clarity. In addition, each conceptualization applies to only a limited range of conditions. Recognition of these shortcomings requires that a new approach be developed.

Any formulation must meet certain criteria. Typical standards are those of parsimony, observability, and the relationship to a general explanation of human behavior; and any conceptualization of communication satisfaction must deal with the present body of empirical findings. The explanation which most parsimoniously encompasses those findings should be accepted. The concept of parsimony is important to the development of science for it tries to insure that the necessary abstractness of theory does not move too far from empirical data. The conceptualization of communication satisfaction proposed here incorporates the evidence provided by those operating from various perspectives within the expectation fulfillment position.

Because satisfaction is an internal behavior, the observability criterion is difficult to meet. This criterion requires that an explanation be grounded in reference to observables in elaborating the development of satisfaction behaviors as well as in exploring the causes of satisfaction. This criterion is accepted in order to provide the greatest area of agreement among researchers investigating satisfaction. Researchers can arrive at greater agreement about a concept defined in terms of observable referents than one defined entirely by abstract, hypothetical constructs.

As indicated above, any explanation of communication satisfaction should take into account the empirical findings of the various expectation fulfillment positions. This position has been the most frequent perspective taken by empirical investigations. Evidence does indicate linear and curvilinear relations between levels of satisfaction and levels of causal variables (see Figure 1). None of the conceptualizations, however, provides the basis for this distinction and, therefore, none provides a complete, coherent conceptualization. In addition, the hypothetical explanatory constructs (i.e., expectation, need, equivocality) are themselves troublesome. As a result, while this paper will take an approach based in the expectation position, an attempt will be made to link it more closely with observables and with Skinnerian behaviorism. The present formulation, however, attempts to expand the Skinnerian system to the study of internal behaviors.

In the Skinnerian paradigm, discriminative stimuli make more probable the manifestation of certain behaviors. Discussing discriminative stimuli, Skinner notes "that a *stimulus* . . . is the occasion upon which a *response* . . . is followed by *reinforcement*."[44] Within the communication process, a discriminative stimulus is communication behavior which makes more likely other communication behavior. To use self-disclosure as an example again, one person's disclosure makes more likely another's disclosure.

Skinner, however, ends his analysis with this point. The present position postulates that once the discrimination is learned and the person begins to manifest behaviors due to the learned association, a secondary reinforcement is set up. Specifically, on those occasions upon which the learned discriminative stimulus leads to the emission of a behavior which is reinforced, the *link* between the stimulus and the behavior is also reinforced. The primary reinforcement of this link gives rise to an affect which is labeled satisfaction. This perspective sees reinforcement as strengthening the link, or association, between the discriminative stimulus and the behavior and, at the same time, giving rise to an affect: satisfaction. Satisfaction and "association strengthening" are part of the same process.

In addition, the internal behavior present when the environment reinforces the discrimination takes on secondary reinforcement properties. As a consequence, the process (the linkage or association) by which behavior is performed based on a discrimination takes on secondary reinforcement properties of its own and may subsequently act as a generalized reinforcer. That is, merely producing a behavior based on the presence of a discriminative stimulus may prove satisfying.

Skinner maintains that when we feel, we feel our behavior.[45] In the study of communication, however, many of the key processes involve internal behaviors. One such internal behavior links discriminative stimuli with external behavior and forms the basis for the discriminative fulfillment approach to satisfaction. This approach applies operant principles to affects by examining the contingencies surrounding the link between discriminative stimuli and behavior.

Self-disclosure again provides an excellent application of this position to the communication situation. Person A discloses to person B. This disclosure acts as a discriminative stimulus for B's own disclosure. If B is reinforced for dis-

closing, the link between another's disclosure and B's own disclosure is also reinforced for B. Therefore, B is satisfied.

In the language of the expectation fulfillment position, the discriminative stimulus acts as the expectation and is "fulfilled" when the environment reinforces the behavior evident due to the discrimination. Linking environmental reinforcement with expectation fulfillment leads to expectation fulfillment taking on secondary reinforcement properties and becoming an internal reinforcer. This internal reinforcer, satisfaction, is then generalized as expectation fulfillment comes to be reinforced in a variety of situations.

In order for expectation fulfillment to be reinforcing, one must expect a minimally positive outcome. If one expects a minimally positive outcome and one's expectations are met, one is reinforced or validated. This is an important modification of previous expectation fulfillment positions, which, as previously discussed, do not explain negative expectations such as the expectation of rejection. The present analysis recasts the notion of expectation in such a way as to avoid this problem. Rejection, for example, acts as a discriminative stimulus for certain communication behaviors. If these behaviors relieve the rejection or produce acceptance, then not only will the communication behaviors be reinforced (negatively or positively, respectively, in the Skinnerian sense), but also the link between the discriminative stimulus and the behavior will be reinforced as well. This latter reinforcement creates an internal reinforcement: a feeling of satisfaction. Dissatisfaction would result from punishing the link between the discriminative stimulus and the resulting behavior.

When translated to a more phenomenological perspective, this analysis indicates that the validation of communication based on an anticipation process gives rise to an affect: satisfaction. As with expectations, the anticipation must be of a positive nature.

To summarize the discriminative fulfillment approach: communication satisfaction is an internal, secondary reinforcer arising from the generalization of environmental reinforcement of behaviors manifested in response to the presence of a discriminative stimulus. This position maintains that persons develop standards by which to judge their world (discriminations, positive expectations, positive anticipations). Such standards represent learning from one's past and are equivalent to one's history of reinforcement with respect to the satisfaction response. From this perspective, *satisfaction* labels a type of response to the environment and is therefore explainable by the conditioning paradigm. One becomes conditioned to deal with the environment. The most frequent and salient experiences (symbolic and behavioral) and the outcomes from these experiences become one's "expectation level." Satisfaction is the reaction to encountering the world one has been conditioned to "expect." It should be clear that the positive expectation standard can also represent a cognitive construct which each individual develops in an attempt to order and structure a personal world. While the presence of the expectation level can be explained from a behavioral paradigm, the development of these standards is not inconsistent with a cognitive approach.

This version of the expectation fulfillment position provides a clear explanation of communication satisfaction. The steps by which the "expectation level" is created minimize the introduction of hypothetical constructs lacking observable referents. The discrimination process is ultimately subject to empirical verification: does the stimulus increase the frequency with which a communication behavior appears? This position provides the researcher with a solid, easily elaborated basis from which to investigate communication satisfaction. It also provides a parsimonious explanation of the expectation research as well as linkage to an approach to the study of all human behavior.

The described approach has other advantages. As in all Skinnerian theory the determination of reinforcement is an empirical question examining the individual. The assessment of which outcomes are reinforcing is made with respect to the individual under study. Therefore the discrepancies between the linear and curvilinear approaches are explainable by individual differences, the type of reinforcement, the reinforcement schedule, and/or the nature of the discriminative stimulus. For example, certain reinforcers may be linearly related to satisfaction, while others are curvilinearly related. A person may become increasingly satisfied with every pay increase received (linear relationship). That person, however, may be maximally satisfied with a certain amount of attention and feel intruded upon with great amounts and neglected with lesser amounts (curvilinear relationship). Similarly, certain types of discriminative stimuli may be linearly related to satisfaction (e.g., cues associated with a behavior I generally perform well), while others are curvilinearly related (e.g., cues associated with behaviors I perform well until I tire).

Expectation research indicates that the state of the individual is an important determinant of the reinforcement properties of stimuli. This is in accord with the Skinnerian position and accounted for by the present approach to communication satisfaction. Factors such as satiation,[46] deprivation, the length of time spent at the level of a variable, previous reinforcement,[47] differences in types of causal factors,[48] and fluctuations in the expectation level[49] are all accounted for by this conceptualization.

Kelly provides a cogent criticism of the motivation field, which is germane to the present discussion.[50] He contends that physicists invented the concept of energy to explain why inert objects move. This hypothetical construct proved a useful paradigm for that field of study. Copying the physicists, social scientists have developed "push" and "pull" theories to explain the "energy" behind the movement of people. Push theories (e.g., Shelly's constraint-reinforcement approach[51]) see people propelled by the environment; pull theories (e.g., need gratification or expectation fulfillment perspectives) see people as being pulled by some internal force. In each instance, Kelly claims, theorists introduce a hypothetical energy concept to explain behavior. Kelly circumvents these problems by assuming that behavior is a fundamental characteristic of people.

The present formulation, adopting a similar orientation, views behavior as a quality of humanness, i.e., people behave. The discriminative fulfillment position is concerned with the outcomes derived from behavior. People are seen as neither "pushed" nor "pulled." Rather, in behaving certain regularities (discriminations) are established. The events surrounding behaviors called forth because of these regularities are seen as determining satisfaction.

In avoiding the problems inherent in previous positions while incorporating their strengths, the discrimination fulfillment approach is potentially superior. The strength of the "pull" theories (expectation fulfillment and equivocality reduction) is their attention to environmental regularities. The discriminative fulfillment position utilizes the discrimination construct to incorporate the process of adjusting to perceived regularities. The strength of the "push" theory (constraint-reinforcement) is its attention to environmental contingencies. This orientation is incorporated in the discrimination fulfillment conceptualization via the reinforcement construct, which focuses the researcher on the perceived environment in order to determine which variables function as reinforcers for a person in a situation.

IMPLICATIONS FOR FUTURE COMMUNICATION RESEARCH

The present discussion implies three areas of primary concern to the communication researcher. First, the researcher should pursue the discovery of salient communication discriminative stimuli or positive expectations and behaviors appropriate to them. These investigations will of necessity be context and relationship bound. However, the search should prove useful in establishing patterns, rules, or laws governing the discriminative stimuli operating in various interactions. Recent investigations explicating personal space expectations[52] and disclosure information sequencing[53] provide examples of this research direction.

A number of the recent approaches to communication competence may also be perceived as attempts to specify salient communication discriminative stimuli. Bienvenu discusses listening (the cues an individual gives off to indicate attention) and clarity of expression as characteristics of effective communication.[54] Hart and Burks stress the flexibility necessary to send discriminative stimuli and the communicator's responsibility to adjust messages to the audience.[55] Finally, Bochner and Kelly suggest descriptiveness, ownership of feelings, and self-disclosure as traits of the effective communicator.[56] All these characteristics may be conceived of in terms of the communicator's ability to send clear and productive discriminative stimuli.

Second, researchers should examine those communication behaviors which serve as reinforcers or validators. Even though there will often be wide latitudes of individual differences in what is considered reinforcing, research in this area can provide a repertoire of possible or common communication reinforcers. The search may most fruitfully begin with an examination of common generalized reinforcers. Sieburg and Larson,[57] for example, investigated verbal behavior associated with satisfying communicators. They isolated such concepts as direct acknowledgment, expression of positive feeling, clarification, agreement, and support as characteristics of enjoyable communicators, and found that responses which are tangential, irrelevant, interrupting, impervious, incoherent, and impersonal are characteristics of unenjoyable communicators. Leathers[58] examined the effects of abstract statements, statements with hidden conclusions, and insincere humor; and Jacobs, Jacobs, Feldman, and Cavior[59] examined types of feedback responses. Others have examined the effects of rate of participation[60] and idiosyncratic behavior.[61]

Third, researchers should assess the skills which facilitate one's ability to recognize the discriminations of others and provide reinforcement, as well as skills which facilitate an awareness of one's own discriminations and maximize reinforcement. This line of research is part of the continuing effort to define communication competence. Bienvenu, for example, isolated a strong self-concept as a dimension of effective communication; those with poor self-concepts tend to distort the messages they receive.[62] In their statement of the rhetorical view of communication competence, Hart and Burks outlined five attitudes of the competent communicator: acceptance of personal complexity, avoidance of communication rigidity, interaction consciousness, knowing what can be communicated and when, and a tolerance for the inventional search.[63] Finally, Bochner and Kelly provided an effective statement of the humanistic view of competent communication, suggesting five skills: empathy, descriptiveness, ownership of feelings, self-disclosure, and flexibility.[64] Both the humanistic and rhetorical positions can be interpreted as statements of skills facilitating awareness of one's own discriminative stimuli and a maximization of reinforcement. Obviously, empirical work in this area is greatly needed. Role taking, perspective taking, congruence, behavior repertoires, dominance, power, conflict, language behavior, and interaction analysis are among the other variables for which investigation might prove fruitful. The use of communication satisfaction as an outcome criterion should facilitate the investigation of these variables and ultimately the development of notions of communication competence.

When combined with the study of other affects, the discriminative fulfillment conceptualization of satisfaction will facilitate a more complete understanding of communication outcomes. Further, when combined with task outcomes this will lead to a clearer perspective on communication competence.

Attraction is an effect to which communication satisfaction should be linked. Such linkage is provided by the classical conditioning conceptualization of attraction developed by Byrne and Krivonos.[65] Attraction is seen as an affect associated with an other who is reinforcing. When this approach to attraction is utilized with the present approach to satisfaction, certain commonalities may be derived.

Byrne and Krivonos maintain that reinforcement is associated with the other who is perceived as attractive. Dealing with all types of reinforcement, the discriminative fulfillment approach goes beyond that provided by the other and associates reinforcement with the link between the discriminative stimulus and communication behavior. The perspectives in combination make it apparent that the attractive other contributes to communication satisfaction. Further, certain environments may not provide contingencies supporting communication. In these environments the reinforcement which the attractive other provides serves to inhibit communication, and satisfaction will be derived from this inhibition.

CONCLUSION

The inadequacies of previous conceptualizations led to the development of the discrimination fulfillment approach to the study of communication satisfaction. This conceptualization avoids many of the pitfalls which detract from previous approaches. Hypothetical constructs have been minimized, lending conceptual clarity and relatively straightforward measurement procedures. The approach is wedded to and extends Skinnerian behaviorism and thereby acquires conceptual strength and clarity. Additionally, this formulation links the internal state of the individual to the environmental contingencies by defining satisfaction in terms of environmental reinforcement of the individual's discrimination of stimuli.

Previous conceptualizations of satisfaction have anchored the affect in the events surrounding the communication interaction: expectations, needs, uncertainty. The discriminative fulfillment approach grounds the satisfaction associated with communication in the communication behavior itself. Rather than basing the conceptualization of communication satisfaction on the fulfillment of mental traits, this new conceptualization emphasizes the way communication functions as discriminative stimuli, behaviors based on discriminations, and reinforcers.

NOTES

1. Dennis S. Gouran, "Response to" 'The Paradox and Promise of Small Group Research,' " *Speech Monographs,* 37 (1970), 217.

2. John DeLamater, "A Definition of 'Group,' " *Small Group Behavior,* 5 (1974), 30–44.

3. Carl E. Larson, "Speech Communication Research on Small Groups," *Speech Teacher,* 20 (1971), 89–107.

4. For examples see Judee K. Burgoon, "The Ideal Source: A Reexamination of Source Credibility Measurement," *Central States Speech Journal,* 27 (1976) 200–06: Judee K. Burgoon and Stephen B. Jones, "Toward a Theory of Personal Space Expectations and Their Violations," *Human Communication Research,* 2 (1976), 131–46; Shirley J. Gilbert and Gale G. Whiteneck, "Toward a Multidimensional Approach to the Study of Self-Disclosure," *Human Communication Research,* 2 (1976), 347–55; and Charles R. Berger, Royce R. Gardner, Glen W. Clatterbuck, and Linda S. Schulman, "Perceptions of Information Sequencing in Relationship Development," *Human Communication Research,* 3 (1976), 29–46.

5. Millard J. Bienvenu, Sr., "An Interpersonal Communication Inventory," *Journal of Communication,* 21 (1971) 381–88; Evelyn Sieburg and Carl Larson, "Dimensions of Interpersonal Response," paper presented at the meeting of the International Communication Association, Phoenix, April, 1971; Roderick P. Hart and Don M. Burks, "Rhetorical Sensitivity and Social Interaction," *Speech Monographs,* 39 (1972), 75–91; Arthur P. Bochner and Clifford W. Kelly, "Interpersonal Competence: Rationale, Philosophy, and Implementation of a Conceptual Framework," *Speech Teacher,* 23 (1974), 279–301; and Roderick P. Hart, William F. Eadie, and Robert E. Carlson, "Rhetorical Sensitivity and Communicative Competence," paper presented at the meeting of the Speech Communication Association, Houston, December, 1975.

6. For examples, see Robert H. Schaffer, "Job Satisfaction as Related to Need Satisfaction in Work," *Psychological Monographs,* 67:14 Whole No. 364 (1953); Edward Gross, "Primary Functions of the Small Group," *American Journal of Sociology,* 60 (1954), 24–29; Ezra Stotland, "Determinants of Attraction to Groups," *Journal of Social Psychology,* 49 (1959), 71–80; Lyman W. Porter, "Job Attitudes in Management: I. Perceived Deficiencies in Need Fulfillment as a Function of Job Level," *Journal of Applied Psychology,* 46 (1962), 375–84; Alvin Zander, "Students' Criteria of Satisfaction in a Classroom Committee Project," *Human Relations,* 22 (1969), 195–207; Ray Wild, "Job Needs, Job Satisfaction, and Job Behavior of Women Manual Workers," *Journal of Applied Psychology,* 54 (1970), 157–62; Martin G. Wolf, "Need Gratification Theory: A Theoretical Reformulation of Job Satisfaction/Dissatisfaction and Job Motivation," *Journal of Applied Psychology,* 54 (1970), 87–94; and James D. Neeley, Jr., "A Test of the Need Gratification Theory of Job Satisfaction," *Journal of Applied Psychology,* 57 (1973), 86–88.

7. Stewart L. Tubbs and Sylvia Moss, *Human Communication,* 2nd ed. (New York: Random House, 1977), pp. 67–71, 236.

8. Gary Cronkhite, *Communication and Awareness* (Menlo Park, Ca.: Cummings, 1976), p. 86.

9. Gail E. Myers and Michele Tolela Myers, *The Dynamics of Human Communication: A Laboratory Approach,* 2nd ed. (New York: McGraw-Hill, 1976), pp. 275–78.

10. Gross, p. 24.

11. Donald B. Trow, "Autonomy and Job Satisfaction in Task-Oriented Groups," *Journal of Abnormal and Social Psychology,* 54 (1957), 204–09.

12. Abraham H. Maslow, *Motivation and Personality,* 2nd ed. (New York: Harper and Row, 1970).

13. Wolf, p. 91.

14. For examples, see Uriel G. Foa, "Relation of Workers Expectation to Satisfaction with Supervisor," *Personnel Psychology,* 10 (1957), 161–68; Martin Patchen, "The Effect of Reference Group Standards on Job Satisfaction," *Human Relations,* 11 (1958), 303–14; Philip E. Slater, "Contrasting Correlates of Group Size," *Sociometry,* 21 (1958), 129–39; Mauk Mulder, "Power and Satisfaction in Task-Oriented Groups." *Acta Psychologica,* 16 (1959), 178–225; John W. Thibaut and Harold H. Kelley, *The Social Psychology of Groups* (New York: Wiley, 1959); Edwin A. Locke, "What is Job Satisfaction?" *Organizational Behavior and Human Performance,* 4 (1969), 309–36; Patricia Cain Smith, Lorne M. Kendall, and Charles L. Hulin, *The Measurement of Satisfaction in Work and Retirement: A Strategy for the Study of Attitudes* (Chicago: Rand-McNally, 1969); and Daniel R. Ilgen, "Satisfaction with Performance as a Function of the Initial Level of Expected Performance and the Deviation from Expectations," *Organizational Behavior and Human Performance,* 6 (1971), 345–61.

15. Thibaut and Kelley, p. 21.

16. Ilgen, pp. 345–46.

17. Smith, Kendall, and Hulin, pp. 12–14.

18. Locke, p. 316.

19. Robert B. Ewen, Patricia Cain Smith, Charles L. Hulin, and Edwin A. Locke. "An Empirical Test of the Herzberg Two-Factor Theory," *Journal of Applied Psychology,* 50 (1966), 544–50; George B. Graen, "Addendum to 'An Empirical Test of the Herzberg Two-Factor Theory,' " *Journal of Applied Psychology,* 50 (1966), 551–55.

20. Foa, pp. 163–67.

21. Charles L. Hulin and Patricia Cain Smith, "A Linear Model of Job Satisfaction," *Journal of Applied Psychology,* 49 (1965), 209–16.

22. Edwin A. Locke, "The Relationship of Task Success to Task Liking and Satisfaction," *Journal of Applied Psychology,* 49 (1965), 379–85.

23. S. M. Klein and J. R. Maher, ''Education Level and Satisfaction with Pay,'' *Personnel Psychology,* 19 (1966), 195–208.
24. Graen.
25. J. Scott Verinis, Jeffrey M. Brandsma, and Charles N. Cofer, ''Discrepancy from Expectation in Relation to Affect and Motivation: Tests of McClelland's Hypothesis,'' *Journal of Personality and Social Psychology,* 9 (1968), 47–58.
26. Ilgen.
27. Daniel R. Ilgen and Bruce W. Hamstra, ''Performance Satisfaction as a Function of the Difference Between Expected and Reported Performance at Five Levels of Reported Performance,'' *Organizational Behavior and Human Performance,* 7 (1972), 359–70.
28. David C. McClelland, John W. Atkinson, Russell A. Clark, and Edgar L. Lowell, *The Achievement Motive* (New York: Appleton-Century-Crofts, 1953); Ralph Norman Haber, ''Discrepancy from Adaptation Level as a Source of Affect,'' *Journal of Experimental Psychology,* 56 (1958), 370–75; Elliot Aronson and J. Merrill Carlsmith, ''Performance Expectancy as a Determinant of Actual Performance,'' *Journal of Abnormal and Social Psychology,* 65 (1962), 178–82; J. Merrill Carlsmith and Elliot Aronson, ''Some Hedonic Consequences of the Confirmation and Disconfirmation of Expectancies,'' *Journal of Abnormal and Social Psychology,* 66 (1963), 151–56; Elliot Aronson, J. Merrill Carlsmith, and John M. Darley, ''The Effects of Expectancy on Volunteering for an Unpleasant Experience,'' *Journal of Abnormal and Social Psychology,* 66 (1963), 220–24.
29. Berger, Gardner, Clatterbuck, and Schulman.
30. Karl E. Weick, *The Social Psychology of Organizing* (Reading, Ma.: Addison-Wesley, 1969).
31. Ibid., p. 99.
32. Maynard W. Shelly, ed., *Analyses of Satisfaction* (New York: M.S.S. Information Corp., 1972), I, II, III.
33. Frederick Herzberg, Bernard Mausner, and Barbara Bloch Synderman, *The Motivation to Work,* 2nd ed. (New York: Wiley, 1959): Frederick Herzberg, ''The Motivation-Hygiene Theory,'' in *Management and Motivation: Selected Readings,* ed. Victor H. Vroom and Edward L. Deci (Baltimore: Penguin Books, 1970), pp. 86–90.
34. W. Barnett Pearce, ''Consensual Rules in Interpersonal Communication: A Reply to Cushman and Whiting,'' *Journal of Communication,* 23 (1973), 160–68.
35. Kenneth J. Gergen, *The Psychology of Behavior Exchange* (Reading, Ma.: Addison-Wesley, 1969), p. 37.
36. Charles E. Osgood and Percy H. Tannenbaum, ''The Principle and Congruity in the Prediction of Attitude Change,'' *Psychological Review,* 62 (1955), 42–55.
37. Neeley, p. 86.
38. Jeanne B. Herman and Charles L. Hulin, ''Managerial Satisfactions and Organizational Roles: An Investigation of Porter's Need Deficiency Scales,'' *Journal of Applied Psychology,* 57 (1973), 118–24.
39. Neeley, p. 87.
40. Wolf.
41. Herzberg, Mausner, and Snyderman; Herzberg.
42. Shelly, I, 3–23.
43. Ronald J. Burke, ''Are Herzberg's Motivators and Hygienes Unidimensional?'' *Journal of Applied Psychology,* 50 (1966), 317–21; Ewen, Smith, Hulin, and Locke; Graen; Robert B. Ewen, ''Weighting Components of Job Satisfaction,'' *Journal of Applied Psychology,* 51 (1967), 68–73; John R. Hinrichs and Louis A. Mischkind, ''Empirical and Theoretical Limitations of the Two-Factor Hypothesis of Job Satisfaction,'' *Journal of Applied Psychology,* 51 (1967), 191–200; L. K. Waters and Carrie Wherry Waters, ''An Empirical Test of Five Versions of the Two-Factor Theory of Job Satisfaction,'' *Organizational Behavior and Human Performance,* 7 (1972), 18–24.
44. B. F. Skinner, *Science and Human Behavior* (New York: Free Press, 1953), p. 108. This concept is somewhat analogous to Weick's phenomenological assumption of the anticipation process. Discrimination is preferred for three reasons. First, the discrimination construct involves fewer assumptions about cognitive processes. Second, when compared to anticipation, discrimination places greater emphasis on the environment while attending to an internal behavior. Third, the anticipation process requires an ad hoc modification to restrict consideration to positive anticipation.
45. Ibid., pp. 160–62.
46. Jacob L. Gewirtz and Donald M. Baer, ''Deprivation and Satiation of Social Reinforcers as Drive Conditions,'' *Journal of Abnormal and Social Psychology,* 57 (1958), 165–72.
47. Elliot Aronson and Darwyn Linder, ''Gain and Loss of Esteem as Determinants of Interpersonal Attractiveness,'' *Journal of Experimental Social Psychology,* 1 (1965), 156–71.
48. Locke, ''What is Job Satisfaction?''
49. Thibaut and Kelley, pp. 82–89.
50. George A. Kelly, *A Theory of Personal Constructs* (New York: Norton, 1963), pp. 34–39.
51. Shelly.
52. Burgoon and Jones.
53. Berger, Gardner, Clatterbuck, and Schulman; Gilbert and Whiteneck.
54. Bienvenu, p. 386.
55. Hart and Burks, pp. 76, et passim.
56. Bochner and Kelly, pp. 289–91.
57. Sieburg and Larson.
58. Dale G. Leathers, ''Process Disruption and Measurement in Small Group Communication,'' *Quarterly Journal of Speech,* 55 (1969), 287–300.
59. Marion Jacobs, Alfred Jacobs, Garry Feldman, and Norman Cavior, ''Feedback II–The 'Credibility Gap': Delivery of Positive and Negative and Emotional and Behavioral Feedback in Groups,'' *Journal of Consulting and Clinical Psychology,* 41 (1973), 215–23.
60. For examples, see Andie L. Knutson, ''Quiet and Vocal Groups,'' *Sociometry,* 23 (1960), 36–49; and Robert N. Bostrom, ''Patterns of Communicative Interaction in Small Groups,'' *Speech Monographs,* 37 (1970), 257–63.

61. Walter Gruen, ''Tolerance for Idiosyncratic Roles in Group Cohesion,'' *Psychological Reports,* 11 (1962), 462.

62. Bienvenu, pp. 384–86.

63. Hart and Burks, pp. 76 et passim.

64. Bochner and Kelly, pp. 289–91.

65. Donn Byrne and Paul D. Krivonos, ''A Reinforcement Affect Theory of Interpersonal Communication,'' paper presented at the meeting of the Speech Communication Association, San Francisco, 1976.

LONELINESS AND RELATIONALLY COMPETENT COMMUNICATION

Brian H. Spitzberg

Daniel J. Canary

Loneliness is seen as a common social experience, best understood through the mechanisms whereby actors attribute causes for their loneliness. From an attributional perspective, the effects of loneliness chronicity on relational, or communicative, competence are delineated in three hypotheses and empirically tested among dyads involved in a conversational exercise. The hypotheses are generally supported, revealing that chronically lonely people generally do not perceive themselves or others as relationally competent and are perceived as incompetent by others as well.

Communication is a fallible method of initiating and sustaining human contact. While communication functions effectively for most people most of the time in providing satisfactory relationships, for many others communication processes are flawed and disappointing. Once the single means of human contact is disparaged, isolation and accompanying loneliness are perpetuated.

The purpose of this study is to examine the connection between the experience of loneliness and relationally competent communication. We find it helpful to define that connection from an attributional orientation. Hence, after brief discussion of loneliness, attribution theory and relational competence, three hypotheses are presented and tested.

Loneliness has been defined as a state of dissatisfaction with achieved, versus desired, relational intimacy (Spitzberg, 1981). Such dissatisfaction exists to the degree that social networks are perceived to be somehow insufficient (Peplau & Perlman, 1979). Self-reported loneliness has been associated with social failure (Horowitz & French, 1979), psychological maladjustment (Putney & Putney, 1964), depression (Beck & Young, 1978), drug abuse, suicide and premature mortality (Sermat, 1980). Loneliness has also been found to be related positively to shyness (Cheek & Busch, 1981), communication apprehension (Spitzberg, 1981), submissiveness or hostility (Moore, 1974), discrepancy between perceived and reflected self-concept (Moore, 1976), and difficulty in being amiable (Horowitz & French, 1979). Inverse relationships have been found to exist between loneliness and positive attributes, including social assertiveness (Sermat, 1980), self-disclosure intimacy (Solano et al., 1982), and supportiveness (Wood, 1979).

Collectively these studies evidence a possible reciprocal cycle that perpetuates loneliness. Shyness and depression may act materially to isolate lonely individuals from the very relationships

Source: The article is taken from the *Journal of Social and Personal Relationships* [2: 387–402, 1985]. © Sage Publications Ltd., 6 Bonhill St., London EC24A 4PU, UK. Reprinted by permission of Sage Publications Ltd.

that could diminish their loneliness. It seems plausible that avoidance and fear of interaction would, over time, lead to the atrophy of important social skills, such as expressiveness and interaction management. Young (1979a), for example, identifies 'common behavioral blocks' among clients who were lonely. These blocks include anxiety in social settings, awkwardness, lack of assertiveness, as well as choice of inappropriate partners. Deficient communicative skills, in turn (when finally utilized), may result in negative social experiences and deeper loneliness. Jones et al. (1982), found that lonely individuals appeared to converse with 'less awareness of or concern for others, with less responsiveness, and in a more self-focused or self-absorbed manner' (p. 685). Thus, for the lonely person, perceptual and communicative processes act to perpetuate the very state they wish to escape.

Despite the theoretical appeal of this depiction, research directly linking loneliness and perceived social communicative skills is inconsistent. After four studies regarding interpersonal consequences of loneliness, Jones et al. (1981) could find only piecemeal support for their hypothesis that lonely subjects would be perceived as socially unskilled. Their most consistent finding was that lonely subjects evaluated *themselves* as lower in social skills and attractiveness than either their conversational partners or third-party raters did (see also Jones et al. 1983). Sloan & Solano (1984) found that lonely subjects talked less than non-lonely subjects but were not particularly self-focused or less self-disclosive than non-lonely subjects. In a similar vein, Chelune et al. (1980) found no relationship between loneliness, self-disclosure flexibility, and either self-rating or other-ratings or social skills.

It is possible that these studies failed to find relationships between loneliness and communication because of imprecise conceptualization and operationalization of loneliness. These studies viewed loneliness as a molar level *state* of perceived discrepancy between actual and desired interpersonal intimacy. It is our contention that loneliness is a phenomenon integrally affected by people's explanations for their suc-

cesses and failures in social and intimate relationships. Failure to take into account people's explanations of loneliness made the predictions of these studies overly simplistic.

Attribution theory is concerned primarily with the ways in which humans perceive, label and act upon causes of social events. One useful attributional approach to studying loneliness has been elaborated by Peplau and colleagues (Peplau & Perlman, 1979; Peplau et al., 1979). Essentially attributions of loneliness are arrayed along three causal dimensions: internality, stability and controllability. Accordingly a person can attribute loneliness to internal causes (e.g. unattractiveness, lack of social skills) or external causes (e.g. impersonal peers, restrictive situation). At the same time, loneliness can be attributed to stable factors (e.g., inability to meet people) or unstable ones (e.g. being new in the neighbourhood). Finally, loneliness can be attributed to controllable causes (e.g. lack of effort in meeting people) or relatively uncontrollable ones (e.g., job transfer).

An attributional approach provides several insights into loneliness. Persons who attribute loneliness to unstable, external and controllable causes are more likely to take steps to remedy their loneliness (e.g. to expend effort to meet people and establish relationships) than are those who attribute loneliness to stable, internal and uncontrollable causes. Furthermore, chronically lonely people are much more likely than situationally lonely people to attribute their loneliness to stable, uncontrollable causes. Loneliness that endures over time regardless of, or despite, efforts to establish satisfying relationships, is likely to be perceived as resistant to change. One probable result of such perceptions is a frustration and dissatisfaction associated with social interaction generally. Since it fails to change things, social interaction is viewed as useless or negatively reinforcing, or both. A person may blame self (internal attribution; e.g. 'I'm so socially inept') or the context (external attribution; e.g. 'It's just too hard to meet people around here', or 'People don't seem very friendly in this area'). Either way, social interaction is devalued. Negative attitudes towards interaction may result in anxiety and social-skill deficits in communicative encounters either from skill atrophy, amotivation or repeated negative reinforcement in social episodes. Spitzberg (1981), for example, found that chronically lonely subjects reported significantly higher communication apprehension than did situationally lonely subjects. Gerson & Perlman (1979) found that situationally lonely subjects were rated as significantly more communicatively expressive than chronically lonely subjects. These findings suggest that the duration of loneliness and communicative skill are related, but the precise nature of this relationship is not clear.

A variety of findings support the view that as the experience of loneliness endures over time, attributions of causes to stable, uncontrollable factors increase; and these causal attributions lead to diminished self-perceived and other-perceived social skills in the view of self and others. Yet, before we can establish our hypotheses based on this approach, the general construct of social skills needs to be recast within a framework specifically tied to interpersonal interaction. In order to better understand the effects of loneliness from an interpersonal perspective, the notion of relational competence should be delineated.

Competence is typically a synonym for ability. When speaking of 'social' competence, theorists are usually referring to the ability to engage in normal or appropriate interaction across a variety of social situations. This general ability, in turn, is thought to depend upon a favourable developmental history and the learning of certain social skills (Argyle, 1980). For example, many researchers view assertiveness as a crucial social skill because it involves achieving or defending one's rights while simultaneously preserving appropriate norms of social interaction. Similarly, many researchers identify empathy, role-taking and the ability to take others' or generalized societal perspectives as central social skills. These skills allow interactants to adapt their behaviour to social expectations, thereby increasing the likelihood of ongoing social reinforcement and goal attainment. Still others have cast social competence as a general cognitive ability to think analytically and to solve problems (for a discussion of these and other relevant approaches, see the chapters in Wine & Smye, 1981). However, despite the variety of approaches to competence, few studies have directly examined the role of such skills in creating the impression of being a good interactant, that is, a competent communicator. Instead, these researchers generally examine the relationship of social skills to psychological health or to other psychological traits. When social skills are examined in actual interaction episodes, the criterion most frequently used is simply a gross level, one-item judgement of 'socially skilled or socially unskilled'.

Communicative competence has also been conceptualized in many diverse ways (see Spitzberg & Cupach, 1984a, for a more detailed discussion). Communicative competence is often viewed and measured as a set of interrelated skills such as self-disclosure, behavioural flexibility, interaction management and relaxation (e.g. Duran, 1983). Still others choose to view communicative competence as an ability to manage meaning (e.g. Pearce & Cronen, 1980) and communicate ideas accurately (Powers & Lowry, 1980). While these perspectives differ considerably in many respects, they all share two common threads: (1) competence is seen as an attribute of an individual and (2) most instruments that have been developed to operationalize these constructs measure it as a trait or generalizable attribute.

In contrast, Spitzberg & Cupach (1984a) have developed the notion of relational competence, conceptualized as the extent to which objectives functionally related to communication are fulfilled through interaction appropriate to the interpersonal context. This definition contains two components of competence—effectiveness and appropriateness. Thus, to be competent, a person's communication needs to be both effective in achieving personal objectives and appropriate to the relationship and social context.

At the dyadic level of analysis, relational competence can be assessed by referencing each interactant's self-rated competence and other-rated competence. In a conversation between persons *A* and *B*, *A's* self-rated competence is *A's* perception of his or her own competence in this particular conversational episode. *A's* other-rated competence, on the other hand, is *B's* assessment of *A's* competence in the same conversation. *A's* self-rated competence has been found to be related significantly to *A's* rating of *B's* competence and both measures have been found to be related substantially and positively to *A's* communication satisfaction, perceived confirmation and perceptions of conversational appropriateness and effectiveness (Spitzberg & Cupach, 1983). Relational competence represents a context-specific, interpersonal conversational construct. It assesses each actor's self-perceptions and allows each to be a participant-observer of the other person's communicative skill as well.

According to the attributional framework of loneliness, several predictions can be made which are relevant to relationally competent communication. Given that stability of loneliness is likely to engender perceptions of self-incompetence, it is expected that: *H1: Loneliness chronicity is negatively related to self-rated competence.* Furthermore, stable attributions of loneliness are presumed to result in attributions of uncontrollability, which, in turn, impair communicative motivation and skills. Thus, *A's* loneliness chronicity should be negatively related to *B's* rating of *A's* communicative competence in a given conversation. More generally, we hypothesize: *H2: Loneliness chronicity is negatively related to other-rated competence.* It appears likely that the increasing hopelessness, despair, and depression accompanying stable attributions of loneliness develop with negative views of self *and* others. For chronically lonely persons who perceive stable and uncontrollable causes of their loneliness, interaction becomes an effort in futility since interaction with another person cannot change things. Because the interaction itself has little reward-value, the partner is also perceived negatively. The prediction suggested by this line of reasoning is that loneliness chronicity is inversely related to perceptions of competence for one's partner in a conversation.

Given the consistent research findings indicating that loneliness is related to negative evaluations of others, it seems reasonable to make such a prediction even controlling for the other person's loneliness. Hence, we expect to find that: *H3: A's loneliness chronicity is related negatively to A's rating of B's competence even when B's loneliness is controlled for.*

Method

Participants were 188 students in communication classes at two private western universities. Samples were combined for statistical analyses. Sixty-three percent of the sample was female, and the ethnic distribution was 70 percent white, 12 percent black, 8 percent Asian and 7 percent Hispanic.

Competence was assessed by four self-report Likert-type instruments. Self-Rated Competence is a twenty-eight-item instrument assessing context-specific impressions of self's interaction management, other-orientation, expressiveness and anxiety in a conversation.

Rating of Alter-Competence is a twenty-seven-item measure assessing context-specific impressions of one's partner's interaction management, other-orientation and expressiveness. Both scales have been found to be unaffected by social desirability biases, and strongly and positively related to such relevant criteria as communication satisfaction, perceived confirmation, perceived appropriateness and effectiveness and positive affect in a particular conversation (see Spitzberg & Cupach, 1983). The scales have also been found to be related to impressions of skills based upon discrete behaviours such as eye contact, vocal variety, topic maintenance and body lean (see Spitzberg & Cupach, 1984b; Spitzberg & Hecht, 1984).

Measures of appropriateness and effectiveness were developed specifically for this study. As we have already mentioned, competent interaction is conceptualized as appropriate and effective communication. Yet only two studies have attempted to validate a competence measure accordingly (Spitzberg & Phelps, 1982). In that paper a twenty-six-item semantic differential instrument displayed an unstable factor structure across studies. The authors suggested that appropriateness and effectiveness might be operationalized more precisely by a Likert-type measure, in which the items reflect more specifiable communication behaviours. Hence, the constructs and adjectives developed in that paper were utilized in the composition of forty Likert-type items tapping appropriateness (twenty items) and effectiveness (twenty items). These measures are exploratory in nature, given that the sample size does not permit extreme confidence in factor analytic procedures. Nevertheless, reliability analysis and the intercorrelation pattern of the appropriateness and effectiveness measures with the known measures in this study should provide sufficient evidence of their suitability. Basically 'appropriateness' refers to perceptions of other's behaviours that violate self's expectations or sense of propriety, and 'effectiveness' to self's sense of reward attainment and dominance in the conversation.

Loneliness was assessed by an instrument developed by Young (1979b). To date, loneliness usually has been assessed by the UCLA loneliness scale (Russell et al., 1980). However, this scale measures only one's immediate or recent state-perception of loneliness. Since our study posits important time elements in the effects of loneliness (i.e. stability and chronicity), it was essential to select a measure sensitive to this. Young's (1979b) measure was specifically constructed for just such a purpose. His loneliness inventory consists of seventeen 'items,' each of which is represented by a graduated sequence of four loneliness stability and intensity 'stem' descriptions. For example, Item 10 reads as follows:

1. I don't miss anyone in particular right now.
2. I miss someone who isn't here now.
3. I often think about a particular person I was close to.
4. I cannot stop thinking about someone I lost.

When the seventeen items are summed, the measure represents a dimension of situational (short-term) versus chronic (long-term) loneliness. The higher the score on the measure, the more it reflects chronic loneliness. Young (1979b) found that his instrument correlated positively with the UCLA loneliness scale ($r = 0.49$ to 0.55), depression ($r = 0.43$ to 0.50), and anxiety ($r = 0.24$ to 0.36). It is important to note that while the Loneliness Chronicity Scale (LCS) is significantly related to the UCLA scale as would be expected, the two constructs are clearly not isomorphic, and appear to measure distinct constructs.

As a validity check on loneliness stability, two forms of the Abbreviated Loneliness Scale (ABLS) developed from the UCLA scale by Ellison & Paloutzian (1979) were included. The ABLS is a six-item Likert-type measure that correlates positively with the UCLA loneliness scale ($r = 0.72$), and is negatively associated with self-reported social skill ($r = -0.55$) and self-esteem ($r = -0.57$). The two forms used were akin to the operationalization used by Spitzberg (1981) in his study of situational and chronic loneliness. Specifically the six items were repeated—but the instructions for the first set required the subject to refer to the previous two weeks, whereas the second set referred to the respondent's lifetime. In this manner, the subject's current and ongoing loneliness was assessed. It was expected that when combined, these measures would be positively correlated with the loneliness inventory.

Student volunteers were solicited in classrooms to participate in a study of 'conversations and interpersonal relationships'. In no instance did a student refuse to participate, although some provided insufficient information on their questionnaires and were excluded from those analyses. Students were paired, and each group was orally instructed to engage in a get-acquainted conversation. This get-acquainted exercise has been used successfully in previous competence research and it was considered particularly relevant to the study of loneliness, since loneliness is perpetuated by the incompetent management of such relationally initiative conversations (Spitzberg & Cupach, 1983). Many (44 percent) labelled their partners as acquaintances, 27 percent rated their relationship as friends, 15 percent considered themselves as colleagues, 4 percent defined themselves as lovers and 9 percent rated the relationship as 'other'.

Overall, the induction appears to have been successful in producing conversations that were moderately involving, fairly normal and relatively typical of other conversations experienced by these subjects. Because the intent of this study is to observe the effect of loneliness on 'normal' conversations, and because the get-acquainted conversation is particularly relevant to the maintenance of loneliness, the induction used in this study appears to possess acceptable internal and external validity. In other words, subjects appeared to utilize their normal repertoire of conversational skills. Indeed, the mean self-rating of competence was high ($\overline{X} = 119.25$, scale range = 28.140, scale mid-point = 84), implying that subjects were motivated sufficiently to call forth their impression management skills to produce what they perceived to be competent performances.

Following 15 minutes of interaction, the participants were asked to stop conversing and complete a questionnaire concerning their reactions to the preceding interaction and general perceptions regarding interpersonal relationships. The questionnaire took about 15 minutes to complete.

Results

Reliability analyses involved assessments of internal consistency by coefficient alpha. The reliability coefficients for each instrument are located in the diagonal of Table 1. As can be seen from the table, the reliabilities are acceptable, with all coefficient alphas 0.75 or higher.

The Loneliness Chronicity Scale did correlate positively (see Table 1) with Two-Week Loneliness ($r = 0.75$, $p < 0.01$) and Lifetime Loneliness

STATISTICAL SUMMARY 1

Correlations were computed to test the relationships among the loneliness variables. A positive correlation means that as the score on one concept increases, the score on the second concept increases as well. A negative correlation means that as the score on one concept increases, the score on the second concept decreases. The closer the correlation is to either $+1.00$ or -1.00 (higher or lower), the more similar the two concepts are.

The Loneliness Chronicity Scale had moderate (.55) to small (.24) relationships to the UCLA scale. This meant that they were somewhat similar in what they were measuring, but there were still some differences between them. The same could be said for the relationships between the Loneliness Chronicity Scale and the Abbreviated Loneliness Scale.

Reliability indicates how accurate and consistent your measures are. If a measure is highly reliable, then you can be confident that the scores are very accurate and consistent. Since the reliabilities in this study ranged from .75 to .94, they were all accurate and consistent.

In addition, the Loneliness Chronicity Scale had moderate (.53) to high (.75) correlations with other loneliness measures. Contrary to predictions, however, the higher correlation was with the measure of short-term (two-week) loneliness than the measure of long-term loneliness.

Next, correlations were computed to see if the appropriateness and effectiveness measures had the expected relationships with the competence measures. These correlations suggested that these measures were operating as expected.

Correlations and analyses of variance were used to test the hypotheses. As indicated above, correlations tell us about relationships between variables. Analysis of variance (ANOVA) is a technique for seeing if three or more groups differ from each other. For example, if you have three groups, you may want to know which one talks the most.

	SRC	RAC	APP	EFF	LCS	TWL	LTL
TABLE 1							
Intercorrelations of All Self and Other Instruments (n = 125)							
SRC	0.90[a]	0.67**	0.51**	0.60**	−0.27**	−0.26**	−0.28**
RAC		0.94	0.67**	0.48**	−0.08	−0.08	−0.15
APP			0.91	0.49**	−0.06	−0.21**	−0.08
EFF				0.85	−0.06	−0.21**	−0.28**
LCS					0.81	0.75**	0.53**
TWL						0.75	0.74**
LTL							0.85
OTHSRC	0.22**	0.20**	0.08	0.19*	−0.19*	−0.17*	−0.08
OTHRAC		0.07	0.07	0.16*	−0.16*	−0.16*	−0.06
OTHAPP			0.19*	0.09	−0.04	−0.15*	−0.08
OTHEFF				0.21**	−0.03	0.03	0.03
OTHLCS					−0.09	−0.03	0.01
OTHTWL						0.04	0.09
OTHLTL							0.15*

* $p < 0.05$; ** $p < 0.01$.

[a] Figures in the upper diagonal represent the coefficient alpha reliabilities for these measures.

SRC	=	Self-Rated Competence	LCS	=	Loneliness Chronicity Scale
RAC	=	Rating of Alter-Competence	TWL	=	Two-Week Loneliness
APP	=	Appropriateness	LTL	=	Lifetime Loneliness
EFF	=	Effectiveness			

($r = 0.53$, $p < 0.01$). The higher coefficient for Two-Week Loneliness was not expected since the Lifetime Loneliness Scale was intended as a closer approximation of chronic loneliness. A possible methodological reason for this result is that the LCS may be measuring an 'intensity' dimension of loneliness more than a duration dimension. The LCS items contain features of both dimensions, but subjects may be responding more to the intensity of their loneliness than to its duration or frequency. Thus subjects may be reporting on how they feel currently rather than how they have felt in the past. For example, the stem 'I am often disturbed about how unsatisfactory my relationships now are compared with other times in my life' may cue subjects to respond more on the nature of the affect involved and less on the time element involved (e.g., 'often' versus 'for several years, . . . '). The

result would be a closer relationship between currently felt loneliness (i.e. two-week loneliness) and the LCS. A compatible, but potentially more troublesome, interpretation is that loneliness is not an experience that is easily or accurately remembered. People may be acutely aware of their current feelings of loneliness and only vaguely aware of how often or how long they have been lonely in the past. This would act to make current or recent reports of loneliness more reliable indicators in comparison to reports of past loneliness. Unfortunately, available research cannot resolve this anomaly. Some studies have found current loneliness to be related to reported frequency and duration of loneliness, while other studies have found no relationship (Schultz & Moore, 1984). Clearly, to resolve this issue, more reliable measures of loneliness duration and frequency need to be developed which do not confound these factors with intensity of loneliness.

As expected, the appropriateness and effectiveness measures were related positively to the competence measures. Appropriateness correlated more strongly with Rating of Alter-Competence ($r = 0.69$) than with Self-Rated Competence ($r = 0.51$); whereas the inverse is true of Effectiveness, which correlated higher with Self-Rated Competence ($r = 0.62$) than with Rating of Alter-Competence ($r = 0.54$).

Hypothesis 1 predicted that loneliness would be related inversely to Self-Rated Competence. This hypothesis is supported, with the Loneliness Chronicity Scale related significantly and negatively to Self-Rated Competence ($r = -0.31$, $p < 0.01$). It is apparent, however, that this is a modest effect size indicating a relatively minor contribution to the impression of Self-Rated Competence.

When exploring relationships such as this, it is desirable to examine 'where' the effect is most pronounced. For example, it may be that moderately chronically lonely people vary randomly in their communicative competence, whereas very chronically lonely people clearly experience communication skill deficits. To explore this possibility further, scores on the LCS were divided into three groups representing high, medium and low loneliness subjects, based on cut-off points one standard of deviation above (>31) and below (<20) the mean. A one-way analysis of variance was then performed with Self-Rated Competence as the dependent measure. The analysis of variance was highly significant ($F = 9.72$, $p > 0.0001$, $\eta^2 = 0.0970$), with post hoc Scheffe contrasts indicating that high lonely subjects differ significantly ($p < 0.05$) from low and medium lonely subjects.

Hypothesis 2 predicted that loneliness chronicity would be related inversely to other-rated competence. As reported in Table 1, this correlation is -0.16 ($p < 0.05$). Thus, while supported, the small amount of shared variance again indicates that caution should accompany interpretation of the association between loneliness and other-competence. Utilizing the procedure previously mentioned, a post hoc one-way analysis of variance was performed with other-

competence as the dependent measure. The results were highly significant ($F = 7.51$, $p < 0.001$, $\eta^2 = 0.1057$) with Scheffe contrasts revealing that high lonely individuals differ as predicted ($p < 0.05$) from low and moderately lonely subjects when rated by their partners.

Hypothesis 3 predicted that A's loneliness would be related inversely to A's rating of B's competence, controlling for B's loneliness. This hypothesis was not supported. The partial correlation between loneliness and Rating of Alter-Competence, controlling for other's loneliness, is non-significant ($r = -0.09$). Examination of Table 1 indicates that these results are not surprising given the non-significant zero-order relationship between loneliness and Rating of Alter-Competence ($r = -0.08$).

Finally, a post hoc analysis of variance reveals a significant difference among high, moderate and low loneliness groups ($F = 4.58$, $p < 0.01$, $\eta^2 = 0.0486$), with high lonely subjects rating their partners significantly ($p < 0.05$) lower in competence than low or moderately lonely subjects, *not* controlling for other's loneliness. Hence B's loneliness does not make an appreciable effect on A's perception of B's competence when A's loneliness is the predictor. It appears, rather, that lonely subjects tend to rate all others as relatively more incompetent in their communication.

Discussion

In this study we examined the effects of loneliness and relational competence from an attributional perspective. There are at least four points that merit discussion at this juncture.

First, the hypotheses were generally supported, lending credence to the attributional framework from which they were derived. The only surprise in terms of our predictions is the finding that lonely, relative to non-lonely, subjects rate all others as more incompetent, not further discriminating against lonely others on the competence measures. Thus we find a picture of a chronically lonely person as someone who devalues both self and others' communicative

STATISTICAL SUMMARY **2**

These analyses indicated that loneliness had a negative or inverse relationship to a person's rating of her/his own competence. That is, the more lonely someone was, the less competent that person felt. This relationship, however, was fairly small. As a second test of this relationship, participants in the study were divided into three groups: high loneliness, medium loneliness, and low loneliness. An analysis of variance was used to compare the competence levels of each group. The highly lonely group rated themselves as the least competent, while the medium and low loneliness groups did not really differ from each other in their amount of competence.

Loneliness also had a negative relationship to ratings of another person's competence, although this relationship was quite small. Thus the more lonely a person was, the less competent that person believed others were. Analyses of variance revealed the same pattern as the test for hypothesis 1, with the most lonely group being different from the other two groups.

Hypothesis 3 predicted that there would be a relationship between a person's loneliness and his/her perceptions of another person's competence regardless of that other person's loneliness. Partial correlations test the relationship between two variables (here, loneliness and ratings of the other's competence) while controlling for or removing the effects of a third variable. This allowed Spitzberg and Canary to see if loneliness and alter competence were related, regardless of how lonely the other person was. The correlations did not support the hypothesis, in that loneliness and alter competence were not significantly related when the other's loneliness was taken into account.

competence and generally is perceived by conversational partners as relationally incompetent. It appears that the stability of chronic loneliness impairs the very tool needed to achieve relational satisfaction.

The forming pattern of results suggests a self-fulfilling prophecy model of loneliness mainte-nance. Results from this study and others consistently support the conclusion that lonely individuals tend to perceive themselves and others negatively (Jones et al., 1981; Jones et al., 1982; Jones et al., 1983). With the onset of loneliness may come such devaluing affects as depression and lowered self-esteem (Schultz & Moore, 1984; Russell et al., 1980). Such affective states may 'filter' the person's view of the social world. Interaction with others loses some of its value since it has not prevented the onset of loneliness. If loneliness continues, interaction becomes discounted as a viable coping response. In the process, lonely people tend to be less involved (Sloan & Solano, 1984), expressive (Gerson & Perlman, 1979), and motivated (Spitzberg, 1981) in interaction. If interactional partners perceive lonely persons as uninvolved and less competent, relationships are less likely to be initiated and maintained. Interaction will in fact become less positively reinforcing. Lonely people will be further isolated, both by self and by others, from the social networks needed to break the cycle. In essence, if lonely people believe and act as if interaction cannot solve their problems, it will not solve their problems. Obviously such a processual cycle is difficult to confirm through standard measurement techniques. It nevertheless poses important concerns for both therapy and research in the future.

Second, although the hypotheses were supported, the overall effect sizes of the loneliness measures were low, when referring only to the intercorrelations (Table 1). There are three apparent reasons for the low correlations. First, and simply, loneliness does not account for all the variance in communicative competence. To be sure, other variables moderate the loneliness-competence link (e.g. non-verbal immediacy, anxiety, self-concept, relationship status, etc.). These relationships need to be explored further. Second, the measures may not be able to identify the transitory nature of loneliness. Although loneliness is a common experience, it is a time-bound and frequently transitory one (Schultz & Moore, 1984; Sermat, 1980). Participants who identified themselves as lonely may have been in a transitional state to or from a more satisfying one. Such transitions could have moderated the effects of loneliness beyond efforts to account for chronicity. The supplementary analyses support this explanation insofar as the high and low loneliness difference scores produced more impressive results. The high, medium and low classifications may have adjusted for many of the peripheral or transitional cases. Third, the correlations may have been restricted by measurement problems, such as the moderate reliability of the LCS (alpha = 0.81). Although the LCS is related to duration and intensity of loneliness, the validity of the scale is by no means proven. The development of valid measures of loneliness chronicity is an important research pursuit for the future.

Third, problems emerged with the instruments used to validate the Loneliness Chronicity Scale. An unexpected finding was that the LCS correlated higher with two-week loneliness ($r = 0.75$) than with lifetime loneliness ($r = 0.53$). There is no obvious reason why the two-week measure provides the stronger correlation, given that the LCS is designed to account for both long and short-term loneliness. It may be that those who are situationally lonely make meaningful responses on the two-week measure because they are focused on the present, but find themselves less able to focus cognitively on their past experience of loneliness. Of course, the chronically lonely can respond more accurately to the two-week and lifetime measures, for what is reported on one's entire lifetime should hold for the past two weeks as well.

Finally, the results of this study suggest that loneliness manifests both behavioural and cognitive characteristics. That is, lonely people devalue communication and are perceived as less competent communicators. Efforts to develop approaches to clinical intervention should be sensitive to both the social skill deficits involved in loneliness and the attributional processes that may be operating to affect perceptions of the social milieu. A situational versus chronic distinction provides a way of adapting the best therapy to the subject. For example, situationally lonely persons may respond best to cognitive inoculation, in which they would be forewarned of the perceptions likely to result from prolonged experience of loneliness and instructed to discount their validity. Chronically lonely persons are more likely to need both cognitive restructuring and social skills training to reinforce productive communicative behaviour. These speculations appear to be useful directions for clinical research.

REFERENCES

Argyle, M. (1980). 'Interaction skills and social competence'. In P. Feldman & J. Orford (eds). *Psychological Problems: The Social Context.* Wiley: New York.

Beck, A. T. & Young, J. E. (1978). 'College blues'. *Psychology Today* (12), 80–97.

Cheek, J. M. & Busch, C. M. (1981). 'Influence of shyness on loneliness in a new situation'. *Personality and Social Psychology Bulletin* (7), 573–7.

Chelune, G. J., Sultan, F. E. & Williams, C. L. (1980). 'Loneliness, self-disclosure and interpersonal effectivenss'. *Journal of Consulting and Clinical Psychology* (27), 462–8.

Duran, R. L. (1983). 'Communicative adaptability: a measure of social communicative competence'. *Communication Quarterly* (31), 320–6.

Ellison, C. W. & Paloutzian, R. F. (1979). 'Developing An Abbreviated Loneliness Scale'. Paper presented at the UCLA Conference on Loneliness, Los Angeles.

Gerson, A. C. & Perlman, D. (1979). 'Loneliness and expressive communication'. *Journal of Abnormal Psychology* (88), 258–61.

Horowitz, L. M. & French, R. D. S. (1979). 'Interpersonal problems of people who describe themselves as lonely'. *Journal of Consulting and Clinical Psychology* (47), 762–4.

Jones, W. H., Freemon, J. E. & Goswick, R. A. (1981). 'The persistence of loneliness: self and other determinants'. *Journal of Personality* (49), 27–48.

Jones, W. H., Hobbs, S. A. & Hockenbury, D. (1982). 'Loneliness and social skill deficits'. *Journal of Personality and Social Psychology* (42), 682–9.

Jones, W.H., Sansone, C. & Helm, B. (1983). 'Loneliness and interpersonal judgements'. *Personality and Social Psychology Bulletin* (9), 437–41.

Moore, J. A. (1974). 'Relationship between loneliness and interpersonal relationships'. *Canadian Counsellor* (8), 84–9.

Moore, J. A. (1976), 'Loneliness: self-discrepancy and sociological variables'. *Canadian Counsellor* (10), 133–5.

Pearce, W. B. & Cronen, V. E. (1980). *Communication, Action and Meaning.* Praeger: New York.

Peplau, L. A. & Perlman, D. (1979). 'Blueprint for a social psychological theory of loneliness'. In M. Cook & G. Wilson (eds). *Love and Attraction: Proceedings of an International Conference*. Pergamon: Oxford.

Peplau, L. A., Russell, D. & Heim, M. (1979). 'The experience of loneliness'. In I. H. Frieze, D. Bar-Tal & J. S. Carroll (eds). *New Approaches to Social Problems: Applications of Attribution Theory*. Jossey-Bass: San Francisco.

Powers, W. G. & Lowry, D. N. (1980). 'Basic communication fidelity: a fundamental approach'. In R. N. Bostrom (ed.). *Competence in Communication: A Multidisciplinary Approach*. Sage: Beverly Hills, CA.

Putney, S. & Putney, G. J. (1964). *The Adjusted American*. Harper & Row: New York.

Russell, D., Peplau, L. A. & Cutrona, C. E. (1980). 'The revised UCLA loneliness scale: concurrent and discriminant validity evidence'. *Journal of Personality and Social Psychology* (39), 472–80.

Schultz, N. R. Jr. & Moore, D. (1984). 'Loneliness: correlates, attributions, and coping among older adults'. *Personality and Social Psychology Bulletin* (10). 67–77.

Sermat, V. (1980). 'Some situational and personality correlates of loneliness'. In J. Hartog, J. R., Audy & Y. A. Cohen (eds). *The Anatomy of Loneliness*. IUP: New York.

Sloan, W. W., Jr. & Solano, C. H. (1984). 'The conversational styles of lonely males with strangers and roommates'. *Personality and Social Psychology Bulletin* (10), 293–301.

Solano, C. H., Batten, P. G. & Parish, E. A. (1982). 'Loneliness and patterns of self-disclosure'. *Journal of Personality and Social Psychology* (43), 524–31.

Spitzberg, B. H. (1981). 'Loneliness and Communication Apprehension'. Paper presented at the Western Speech Communication Association Conference. San José, CA.

Spitzberg, B. H. & Cupach, W. R. (1983). 'The Relational Competence Construct: Development and Validation'. Paper presented at the Speech Communication Association Conference, Washington, DC.

Spitzberg, B. H. & Cupach, W. R. (1984a). *Interpersonal Communication Competence*. Sage: Beverly Hills, CA.

Spitzberg, B. H. & Cupach, W. R. (1984b). 'Conversational Skills and Locus of Perception'. Paper presented at the Speech Communication Association Conference, Chicago, IL.

Spitzberg, B.H. & Hecht, M. L. (1984). 'A component model of relational competence'. *Human Communication Research* (10).

Spitzberg, B.H. & Phelps, L. A. (1982). 'Conversational Appropriateness and Effectiveness: Validation of a Criterion Measure of Relational Competence'. Paper presented at the Western Speech Communication Association Conference, Denver, CO.

Wine, J. D. & Smye, M. D. (eds) (1981). *Social Competence*. Guilford: New York.

Wood, L. A. (1979). 'Social-psychological Correlates of Loneliness: A Preliminary Report'. Paper presented at the UCLA Conference on Loneliness, Los Angeles.

Young, J. (1979a) 'A Cognitive-behavioral Approach to the Treatment of Loneliness'. Paper presented at the UCLA Conference on Loneliness, Los Angeles.

Young, J. (1979b). 'An Instrument for Measuring Loneliness'. Paper presented at the American Psychological Association Conference.

THE EXCHANGE OF NONVERBAL INTIMACY: A CRITICAL REVIEW OF DYADIC MODELS

Peter A. Andersen
Janis F. Andersen

ABSTRACT: *This article examines six different theoretical approaches that attempt to explain the exchange of dyadic immediacy, intimacy, or involvement cues. Affiliative conflict or equilibrium theory, two expectancy norm models, an arousal-labeling model, an arousal valence model, a discrepancy-arousal model, and a sequential functional model are summarized. Advantages and limitations of each of these approaches are discussed, and empirical support for each of these approaches is summarized.*

Source: The article is taken from the *Journal of Nonverbal Behavior* [8: 327–349, 1984]. © Human Science Press, 233 Spring St., New York, NY 10013. Reprinted by permission.

Scholars in a number of disciplines have dramatically increased our knowledge of nonverbal communication during the last decade. This research has established that a primary function of nonverbal behavior is the communication of affect through what commonly have been called intimacy behaviors (Argyle & Dean, 1965: Patterson, 1976, 1978), immediacy behaviors (J. Andersen, P. Andersen, & Jensen, 1979; P. Andersen, in press; Mehrabian, 1971; Patterson 1973) or involvement (Cappella & Greene, 1982; Patterson, 1982, 1983). Even more recently, a number of attempts have been made to build models that explain the numerous empirical findings in this area. Indeed, three of the six sets of models reviewed in this report have been available in published form for just a few years. The purpose here is to summarize these six models briefly and to offer some insights into the strengths and weaknesses of each.

In different ways, each of these models attempts to account for the dyadic exchange of messages that communicate intimacy, immediacy, or involvement. While the authors recognize distinctions among these labels, they will be treated as functionally synonymous in the present paper. Discussions of the merits of these labels are available in a number of recent papers (J. Andersen, 1984; P. Andersen, in press; Cappella & Greene, 1982; Patterson, 1982). The models range from specific and narrow to broad and all-encompassing. The Burgoon (1978) model, for example, was designed to account for the effects of personal space violations, whereas the Patterson (1982) model is an attempt to explain all of the functions of all nonverbal involvement behaviors. Thus the present authors recognize that these models are not entirely comparable. Nonetheless, each of these models examines the exchange of nonverbal intimacy messages in a dyadic setting. It is hoped that this review will contribute to better research and model building in the future.

AFFILIATIVE CONFLICT THEORY

The first and most famous of the intimacy exchange theories is affiliative conflict theory, proposed two decades ago by Argyle and Dean (1965). Affiliative conflict theory, commonly referred to as equilibrium theory, proposes that interactants establish and maintain a comfortable intimacy equilibrium point for every interaction. If both interactants are comfortable with the overall amount of intimacy expressed, they will maintain this equilibrium by continuing to display the same overall amount of intimacy. If an interactant increases or decreases intimacy in one channel, he or she will compensate with an opposite increase or decrease in another channel. Similarly, if one interactant alters the amount of dyadic intimacy, the other interactant will restore equilibrium with a compensatory response.

Argyle and Dean posit that underlying, conflicting approach and avoidance drives are responsible for producing an equilibrium state. Too much approach creates anxiety, and too much avoidance makes it impossible to satisfy affiliation needs. Thus a balance or equilibrium point is maintained through compensatory responses. Patterson (1973) explains the compensatory process as operating like a hydraulic model where the total pressure must remain constant, but can differentially be distributed.

Because the affiliative conflict theory was the earliest of the models, it has been subjected to more scrutiny, both positive and negative, than any of the other models. On the positive side, affiliative conflict theory is an intuitively appealing, parsimonious, and testable explanation for intimacy exchange. The model has stimulated a great deal of research, and there is general support for the compensatory process (see reviews by P. Andersen, 1983, in press; Cappella, 1981; Patterson, 1973). However, many well-conducted studies have failed to support the theory's predictions and these failures lead to the most damaging criticisms.

Several well-conducted investigations (Anderson, 1978; Coutts & Schneider, 1976; Coutts, Irvine, & Schneider, 1977; Russo, 1975; Stephenson, Rutter & Dore, 1972) have failed to find compensatory effects (see P. Andersen, in press; Firestone, 1977; Patterson, 1978, for reviews of these experiments). These failures are noteworthy in that a selection bias for publishing significant results probably means the number of nonsupportive findings is underestimated (Patterson, 1973; P. Andersen, in press). In addition, other researchers have found a reciprocity effect when the theory predicts compensatory effects (Bakken, 1978b; Breed, 1972; Rosenfeld, 1965; Word, Zanna & Cooper, 1974). Furthermore, affiliative conflict theory does not account for reciprocal processes that are both intuitively obvious and have been documented in intimacy exchange (Cappella & Greene, 1982; Patterson, 1982; Patterson, 1983).

Affiliative conflict theory is also vulnerable in its inability to explain individual differences in compensatory responses. For example, Aiello (1972, 1977a, 1977b) has found significant sex differences in compensatory behavior. These findings, together with the absence of an explanatory mechanism for how or why equilibrium levels change (Cappella & Greene, 1982), suggest that there may be numerous individual differences that explain intimacy exchange more fully than a single universal equilibrium response. (See the Rosenfeld et al. paper in this volume for an example of individual and situational differences that affect compensatory reactions.)

In a strong critical stand against affiliative conflict theory's current usefulness. Cappella and Greene (1982) recommend ''respectful internment.'' They acknowledge the theory's historic significance in spawning significant research, but suggest that three major weaknesses in the theory limit its present usefulness: (1) excessive modifications necessary to account for reciprocity, (2) its inapplicability to activity-related or involvement behaviors, and (3) the failure of approach and avoidance forces to provide a priori

predictions and scientific understanding. Affiliative conflict theory is significant today because it was the first theory and, as such, provided the foundation for the other models discussed in this article.

EXPECTANCY-NORM MODELS

One alternative to affiliative conflict theory may be seen in two theories based on interactants expectancies for intimacy. The better formulated and more widely tested of these models is the model of personal space violations proposed by Burgoon and her colleagues (Burgoon & Jones, 1976; Burgoon, 1978; Burgoon, Stacks, & Woodall, 1979; Burgoon & Aho, 1982). Though presently limited to prediction about personal space and conversational distance, the model presents an intriguing alternative to some other approaches. This model proposes that people have well-established expectations about the interaction distances others will adopt. These expectations are primarily a function of cultural norms, but also a result of the known idiosyncrasies of others. Contrary to intuition, the model predicts that if persons are rewarding (high in status, credibility, attractiveness, etc.), they will be perceived more positively by deviating from the norm, unless a threat threshold is reached at close distances. On the other hand, a punishing interactant will create the most positive impressions in receivers at the expected distance and less positive perceptions at either close or farther distances.

A second expectancy-norm model has been offered by Bakken (1978a). Bakken suggests that norms are widely shared expectations about behavior resulting from the fact that most people experience regularity in others' behavior for specific types of interactions. Bakken (1978a) argues that the empirical research on intimacy regulation offers more support for intimacy being a function of social norms than for intrapsychic accounts such as equilibrium or arousal forces. While such intrapsychic forces are central in the Burgoon model, they are tangential to the Bakken model.

The Bakken (1978a) model has not been as widely tested as the Burgoon model.

The Burgoon model is one of the best explicated models of intimacy regulation. Propositions, assumptions, and primitive terms are clearly specified, and empirical tests of the model are clearly derived (Burgoon, 1978; Burgoon & Jones, 1976). Thus it is probably the most testable of the intimacy regulation models. Moreover, it has been subjected to considerable empirical testing (e.g., Burgoon, 1978; Burgoon & Aho, 1982, Burgoon, Stacks, & Burch, 1982; Burgoon, Stacks, & Woodall, 1979; Stacks & Burgoon, 1979). Several tests of the model have established differential effects for the norm violations of low and high reward communicators (Burgoon, 1978; Burgoon, Stacks, & Burch, 1982). However, in a test of the model in a persuasive situation, Stacks and Burgoon (1979) generally failed to support the model. Recent tests of the model have shown patterns of mixed support (Burgoon and Aho, 1982; Burgoon, Stacks, & Woodall, 1979).

While the Burgoon model offers a promising approach to the study of intimacy, it has been limited to tests of distance violations. This is probably not an inherent limitation, but until other nonverbal variables are incorporated, it will remain a model of personal space violations rather than a general model of intimacy violation (P. Andersen, 1983, in press). Finally, recent research on the Burgoon model has found inconsistent patterns of support, numerous confounding or interacting variables, and more complex relationships than originally proposed. These issues have caused Burgoon and Aho (1982) to conclude that the complexities of the communication process require a more complex predictive model than that originally proposed.

THE AROUSAL-LABELING MODEL

A major revision and extension of affiliative conflict theory is Patterson's (1976) arousal model of interpersonal intimacy. It encompasses equilibrium theory and broadens it to explain reciprocity processes in addition to compensatory processes. Using arousal as the explanatory mechanism, Patterson's model proposes that expressed intimacy or immediacy behaviors create arousal change in a dyadic partner that is cognitively labeled as positive or negative. Schachter's (1964) theory of arousal labeling is incorporated into the model to explain how undifferentiated physiological arousal is cognitively interpreted as a positive or negative emotional state. Arousal-labeling theory posits that the cognitive interpretation of the arousal determines compensation or reciprocity. A negative emotional state such as one labeled anxiety, discomfort, or embarrassment will produce a compensatory response, whereas a positive emotion state such as one labeled liking, love, or relief will produce a reciprocity response. Arousal theory also holds that if the expressed intimacy behaviors of one person fail to produce arousal change in the other person, then a reactive behavioral change would not be predicted.

The arousal model can be considered an improvement over equilibrium theory in that it accounts for the compensatory process while also predicting two additional sets of empirical findings not accounted for by equilibrium theory. These findings not explained by equilibrium theory but accounted for by arousal labeling are reciprocity effects and those instances of intimacy manipulation that fail to produce any behavioral adjustments.

Several empirical studies support the predictions of the arousal-labeling model (Anderson, 1978; Chapman & Smith, 1977; Foot, Chapman, & Smith, 1977; Foot, Smith, & Chapman, 1977; Janik, 1980; Schaeffer & Patterson, 1980; Whitcher & Fisher, 1979; see P. Andersen, 1983, for a review of the support). In addition, Patterson's (1976) introduction of the model reviewed previous empirical studies that generally supported the model.

Presently, the most severe critic of the model is Patterson (1983) himself. He claims the model is "too simplistic and mechanical in light of the complexity of nonverbal exchange" (p. 165). Patterson (1982, 1983) also criticizes this model for its focus on arousal as the primary mediator

FIGURE 1 The arousal-labeling model.

From Patterson, M. L. (1976). An arousal model of interpersonal intimacy. *Psychological Review*, 1976, *83*, 235–245.

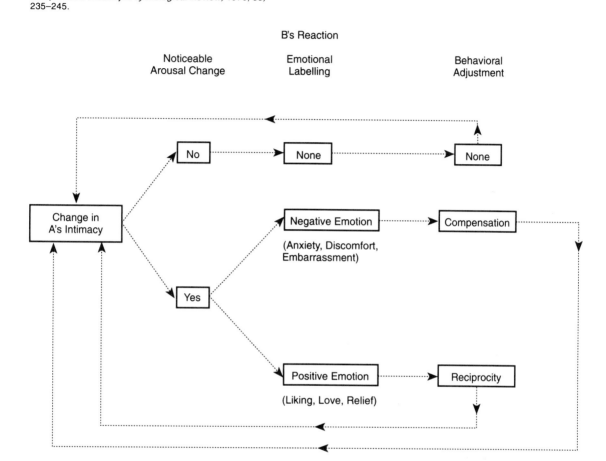

of nonverbal exchange and suggests the cognitive component may be inappropriately directed in typical interactions where people are more concerned with motives of others than they are with their own internal affective states. Cappella and Greene (1982) argue that the labeling component places too heavy a cognitive load and requires too long a reaction time to be compatible with the rapid changes that occur in speaker switches. Patterson (1982) also provides empirical evidence that fails to be explained by the model. Specifically, in one study, a lean-touch manipulation increased arousal when it occurred in the middle of

an interaction, but failed to increase arousal as hypothesized in the beginning of an interaction (Patterson, Jordan, Hogan, & Frecker, 1981). The arousal model cannot easily explain why the same behavior would create different amounts of arousal in different stages of an interaction. In a related criticism, Cappella and Greene (1982) note that the arousal model is incapable of explaining intermittent periods of reciprocity and compensation.

The labeling process itself has attracted the most criticism because it is based on the questionable results of the Schachter and Singer

(1962) studies (Cappella & Greene, 1982; Marshall & Zimbardo, 1979; Maslach, 1979; Schachter & Singer, 1979). However, P. Andersen (in press) suggests that other theories may explain this link in Patterson's model and, consequently, the arousal-labeling component should be evaluated on its own merit rather than on the merits or demerits of its theoretical grandparents.

Additional criticisms of the arousal model include the following observations by Cappella and Greene (1982): (1) the theory's restriction to affiliative behaviors rather than general involvement behavior, (2) the failure to indicate the conditions that produce positive or negative labeling, (3) the failure to specify an upward ceiling on the positive effects of arousal, and (4) the cognitive emphasis of arousal labeling that prevents its extension to infant-adult interaction. The model has also been criticized for beginning in the middle of the intimacy exchange process. That is, the model assumes that immediacy changes are perceived, and this may not always be the case (P. Andersen & Coussoule, 1980). This model and most of the other models of intimacy exchange would be improved by including a decoding component to the model (P. Andersen, in press). In this way, communicative actions that are unnoticed by a receiver would not be expected to trigger the arousal-labeling process.

As previously mentioned, Patterson now criticizes this model as being oversimplified. However, others have criticized the model as being too complex and have suggested that norm theories are more parsimonious explanations (Bakken, 1978a; LaFrance & Mayo, 1978). Despite these criticisms, the arousal model has provided an exciting theoretical framework that continues to stimulate research and controversy. Because the originator and major proponent (Patterson, 1976) is now a leading critic, the model is likely to fall on unfavorable times. However, the original model with appropriate modifications is testable and will continue to be tested. Its eventual worth is to be decided by the future weight of empirical evidence.

THE AROUSAL-VALENCE MODEL

Another recent attempt to explain the exchange of nonverbal intimacy is the arousal-valence model (P. Andersen, 1983, 1984, in press). Like the other models discussed in this article, the arousal-valence model is an attempt to explain the variability in a receiver's responses to changes in the immediacy level of another interactant. The model suggests that when increased immediacy by person A is perceived by person B, arousal in person B occurs. The magnitude of person B's arousal will determine his/her reaction to person A. Very small changes in B's arousal require no changes in B's behavior. Very large changes, including both increases and decreases, in B's arousal are unpleasant and aversive (Berlyne, 1970; Eysenck, 1963, 1967, 1976, 1982; Mehrabian, 1976). Such highly aroused individuals are likely to become startled, fearful, or disoriented and engage in a fight or flight response. The behavioral consequence is withdrawal, compensation, and reduction of immediacy behaviors.

It is at moderate levels of arousal that the most complex and interesting affective and cognitive processes take place. Previous research has demonstrated that moderate arousal is perceived neutrally or positively (Berlyne, 1960; Eyesenck, 1963, 1967, 1976, Mehrabian, 1976). At moderate levels of arousal, P. Andersen (1984) argues that six sets of variables positively or negatively valence the arousal. These valencers include: (1) social or cultural norms, (2) interpersonal relationship history, (3) perceptions of the other person, including interpersonal valence (Garrison, Sullivan, & Pate, 1976) and its components' credibility, attraction, and homophily, (4) environmental context, (5) the temporal, physical, or psychological state of a person, and (6) psychological or communication traits or predispositions. P. Andersen (1984) argues that the valencing process requires little decision-making or cognitive activity. The six valencers act as schemata (Smith, 1982a, 1982b) or scripts (Abelson, 1976, 1981; Berger & Roloff, 1980). Zajonc (1980) suggests these affective reactions

FIGURE 2   The arousal-valence model.

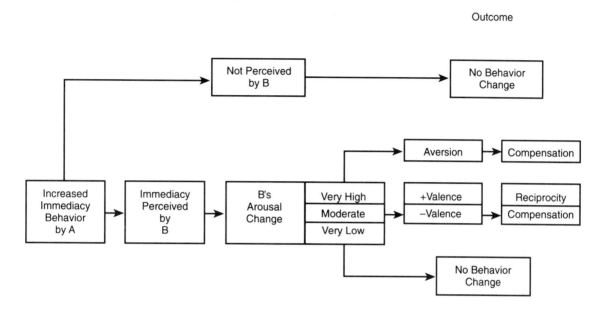

can be invoked in a fraction of a second, sufficient time to produce the reciprocal or compensatory responses characteristic of interpersonal interaction. Thus positively valenced arousal results in reciprocity, whereas negatively valenced arousal results in compensation.

The arousal-valence model represents an improvement over previous approaches in several ways. First it replaces the ambiguous labeling process characteristic of arousal-labeling theory with six clearly specified sets of valencers. Considerable empirical research in both social psychology and communication demonstrates that these valencers are employed by interactants in ongoing interpersonal communication. Second, it is argued that these six sets of valencers create cognitive schema or characteristic responses that can be quickly invoked and, consequently, fit the time demands of the sudden changes that occur in interpersonal interactions. Third, unlike many other models in this article, perception of the other interactant's behavior is included as an important step in the model. Perception is used in a broad sense to refer to the excitation of cells in

the nervous system responsible for processing communication stimuli (Hebb, 1949; Pribram, 1971). If another's communication stimuli fails to evoke a significant neurological response and is not processed by the other interactant, no affective or behavioral changes will result. Finally, the arousal-valence model incorporates the principle that high arousal is perceived aversively. Excessive arousal acts as a warning system that circumvents cognitive processes and results in immediate compensation.

Several criticisms have been launched against the arousal-valence model. First, critics have charged that the arousal-valence model fails to specify clearly the nature of the perception phase of the model. Cappella (1983) argues that the model fails to address whether perception requires knowledge of the change or merely reaction to it. This argument is particularly important in light of research on "mindlessness." Langer's (1978) research on mindlessness demonstrates that behavior can be produced automatically with little or no cognitive activity. A second criticism offered by Cappella (1983) is that the valencing mechanism is unclear. In Andersen's (1984) more fully explicated model, cognitive scripts and schema are the mechanisms by which valencing occurs, but no empirical test of these mechanisms has been conducted. Moreover, the relative impact of these valencers in any interaction is unspecified. Although the arousal-valence model incorporates some of the best aspects of the earlier theories, it still waits the test of empirical research.

THE DISCREPANCY-AROUSAL MODEL

An important alternative to previous models has recently been proposed by Cappella and Greene (1982). Their discrepancy-arousal theory is an attempt to explain patterns of exchange for all communication behaviors, both verbal and nonverbal. This model is an extension of Stern's (1974, 1977) explanation of infant-adult exchanges. Stern's theory proposes that infants develop a schema of objects, persons, and behaviors. When an infant encounters a novel stimulus that fails to conform to her/his expectation, arousal results. At low to moderate levels, Stern argues, this discrepancy becomes a source of stimulation and arousal that produces positive affect and attention. At some threshold, too great a discrepancy becomes unpleasant for the infant and results in avoidance or displeasure.

The Cappella and Greene model suggests that adults have cognitive expectations about other's expressive behavior that result from situational characteristics, social norms, individual's preferences, and past experiences. Increases or decreases in involvement by another individual that violate the person's expectations lead to arousal or cognitive activation. Following the research and theory of Berlyne (1960) and Eysenck (1967), Cappella and Greene (1982) propose that moderate arousal results in positive affect, whereas a large increase in arousal results in negative affect. In turn, the positivity or negativity of the affective response to this experience will determine whether an approach or avoidance response will ensue.

In a number of respects, discrepancy-arousal theory represents a theoretical advance over its predecessors. Perhaps its greatest virtue is its conceptual parsimony in eliminating the need for complex labeling processes or hypothetical equilibrium states as explanations. A second related advantage of the model is that the cognitive "work" occurs in perceiving the magnitude of discrepancy between expressed and expected behavior (P. Andersen, 1983, in press). Cappella and Greene (1982) argue that some accounts of mutual influence are cognitively "top-heavy" and cannot meet the requirements of rapid reaction times during ongoing interaction. For example, the labeling process is perhaps too ponderous a cognitive activity to occur during the rapid moment to moment approaches and withdrawals characteristic of communicative exchanges. The discrepancy-arousal model requires only a comparison between one's expectations and the displayed behavior, a much lighter cognitive load.

A third strength of the discrepancy arousal model is that it gives a strong role to arousal as a direct precursor of affect. The proposition that moderate arousal is perceived neutrally to positively has been repeatedly demonstrated in previous work (Berlyne, 1960; Eysenck, 1963, 1967, 1976, 1982; Mehrabian, 1976). This direct link between arousal and affect proposed in the discrepancy-arousal model replaces the labeling link between arousal and affect characteristic of other models. Indeed, in light of the recent doubts raised over the original research by Schachter and Singer (1962) on the self-labeling process, elimination of the labeling step may be advantageous (see Cappella & Greene, 1982; Marshall & Zimbardo, 1979; Maslach, 1979; Schachter & Singer, 1979).

A final advantage of the discrepancy-arousal model is its comprehensiveness. The model is designed to incorporate a broad range of both verbal and nonverbal behaviors (Patterson, 1983, p. 19). It attempts to explain all involvement behaviors, not just expressions of immediacy and intimacy. Moreover, it provides explanations for expressive behavior for all phases of the life cycle, including infancy.

Despite the fact that discrepancy-arousal theory represents a fresh and promising approach to the question of intimacy exchange, it has also received its share of criticism. One criticism has been aimed at the linkages in the discrepancy-arousal model. The model assumes that discrepancy is a primary precursor of arousal, arousal causes affective states, and affective states cause a reciprocal or compensating response. It is entirely probable that other exogenous variables have substantial impact at each of these linkages. If so, what is the relative impact of these exogenous variables compared with the linkages proposed in the model? The answer to this question is unknown, but prior research has suggested several exogenous variables that may be as important as the links in the discrepancy-arousal model. For example, a number of variables other than discrepancy may produce arousal. Likewise, a number of exogenous precursors of affect other than arousal have been discussed in the psychological literature. Finally, one could easily argue that responses are the result of a number of exogenous variables such as habits or social rules quite independent of affect.

The first questionable link is the crucial discrepancy-arousal link. There is no empirical evidence that the discrepancy-arousal link actually exists, though there is evidence for an immediacy behavior-arousal relationship (P. Andersen, 1983, in press; Patterson, 1976). Moreover, as Andersen (1983, in press) suggests, one can quickly generate a list of arousing cognitions quite independent of discrepancy, including: (1) sexual arousal with a familiar other, (2) racial prejudice, (3) encountering a disliked other, (4) drug induced states, (5) environmental load, and (6) general trait anxiety. It is important to determine the impact of these other arousers relative to that of the discrepancy factor.

The second questionable link is the arousal-affect relationship. In this case, arousal has been empirically linked to affect, but it has been suggested that additional independent precursors of affect may attenuate this relationship (P. Andersen, 1983, in press). It can be argued that learned norms, relational histories, psychological

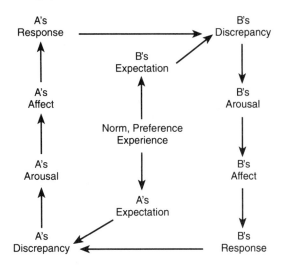

FIGURE 3   A Schematic Representation of the linkages among variables for the discrepancy-arousal model.

From "A discrepancy-arousal explanation of mutual influence in expressive behavior for adult and infant adult interaction," by J. N. Cappella and J. O. Greene, 1982, *Communication Monographs, 49.*

states, and hedonic predispositions are independent, exogenous precursors of affect. If this is the case, the relative contribution of arousal versus those other variables must be ascertained.

The third questionable link is the affect-response relationship (see Figure 3). Although affect is certainly related to approach-avoidance responses, other variables may be antecedents of these responses quite independent of affect. For instance, social norms may require approach or avoidance rituals quite independent of true affective tone. Similarly, relationship or situational constraints may determine approach or avoidance responses that may supercede the effect of interpersonal affect.

Two final criticisms of the discrepancy-arousal model have been reported elsewhere. First, the model assumes that one person's response is perceived by the interactant and accurately processed (P. Andersen, 1983, in press). Such an assumption may be challenged. Some empirical evidence suggests that certain individuals are relatively oblivious to the immediacy and affect displays of others (P. Andersen & Coussoule, 1980; Rosenthal, Hall, DiMatteo, Rogers, & Archer 1979). Finally, though Cappella and Greene's discrepancy-arousal model is one of the broadest and most comprehensive, it has recently been criticized as insufficiently comprehensive (Patterson, 1983, p. 19). Compared to Patterson's (1982, 1983) sequential-functional model, it is true that the discrepancy-arousal model is less than comprehensive. Nevertheless, Cappella and Greene have presented an excellent, parsimonious model with great heuristic value for additional research and theorizing.

THE SEQUENTIAL-FUNCTIONAL MODEL

A recent and ambitious attempt to explain the process of intimacy exchange is Patterson's (1982, 1983) sequential-functional model. This model of nonverbal exchange starts with a set of antecedents, including personal, experiential, and relational-situational factors. Personal factors include variables such as culture, sex differences, and personality that predetermine differential involvement levels. Experiential factors relate to the influence of salient prior experiences on the interactions. Relational-situational influences are those interacting characteristics of relationship type and the setting in which the interaction occurs.

At the time an interaction is initiated, a set of preinteraction mediators acts as links between the antecedents and interaction behaviors. These mediators are behavioral predispositions, potential arousal change, and cognitive affective assessment. Behavioral predispositions are relatively stable characteristics of individuals. Potential arousal change refers to increases or decreases in arousal prior to and in anticipation of the interaction. Cognitive-affective assessments reflect the initiation of cognitive activity through schemas (Markus, 1977) or scripts (Abelson, 1981). These preinteraction mediators limit an individual's involvement and sensitize one to functional judgments about the interaction.

In the interaction phase, nonverbal involvement is a result of preferred involvement level, functional expectancies, and the perceived appropriateness of a behavior. A stable exchange is defined as one in which the discrepancy between the expected and actual involvement of the other person is minimal. When that discrepancy is large, a condition of cognitive instability results (Patterson, 1982). Instability leads to adjustments in nonverbal involvement that may or may not be accompanied by functional reassessment.

A primary advantage of Patterson's (1982) sequential-functional model is that it encompasses multiple functions for nonverbal involvement. Most other models concentrate primarily on exchange of affect or immediacy, to the exclusion of other involvement functions. Moreover, Patterson (1983) points out that the model is not only multifunctional, but provides for reassessments and shifts in the functions of involvement during ongoing interaction and as a result of interaction.

A second related strength of the model is the recognition of the fact that interactants may have incompatible perceptions of the particular function of an interaction. Additionally, these functional perceptions may be unstable within individuals, leading to fluctuating incompatibilities during a given interaction. For example, person A may become involved with another to provide information. During the course of the interaction A may begin to produce behaviors intended to express intimacy or exercise social control. These moment to moment changes in the primary function of A's communication will be different from the moment to moment changes in B's functional behaviors, leading to intermittent and fluctuating compatibilities and incompatibilities.

Another improvement over previous efforts is the recognition of antecedents and preinteraction mediators. Some previous models suggested that behavioral adjustments were simply the reactive product of the other interactant's behavior. The sequential-functional model recognizes that other causes, such as predispositions and scripts, have an impact on the enactment of nonverbal displays.

FIGURE 4   The sequential-functional model.

From Patterson, M. L. (1982). A sequential functional model of
nonverbal exchange. *Psychological Review, 89,* 231–249.

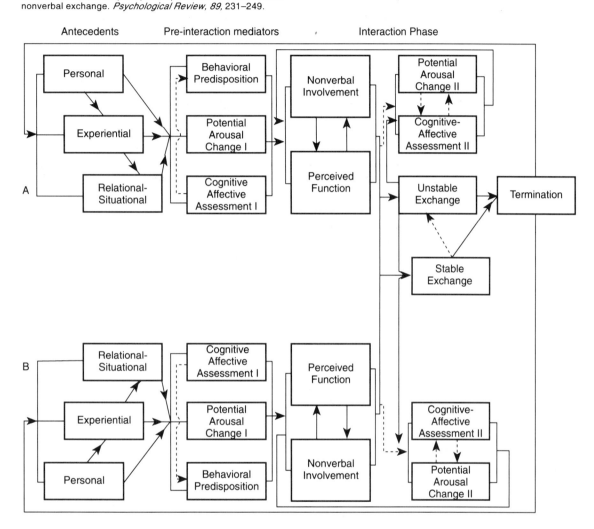

A fourth strength of the model is Patterson's effort to incorporate rather than discard previous models. This is particularly true of both arousal-labeling theory and the discrepancy-arousal model. Important elements of both these approaches are retained and utilized in the sequential-functional approach.

Finally, the cognitive basis of the model is clearly a merit. The sequential-functional model recognizes that interactants have purposes and aims and attempt to direct the effects of their be-

havior. Patterson (1983) argues that this model is less mechanistic than its predecessors and that an individual's involvement behaviors are often part of a larger context of a meaningful coordinated behavioral sequence.

Despite the obvious merits of the sequential-functional model, it is not without problems. First, there is some question as to whether the model is fully testable or disconfirmable. Patterson (1983, p. 167) recognizes this issue and counters that deficiencies in testability might be balanced by the functional model's comprehensiveness. Additionally, Patterson maintains that many parts of the model provide a basis for a variety of important and testable hypotheses.

It is certainly true that the functional model is relatively comprehensive when compared to other models. Nonetheless, it may be the case that it is not comprehensive enough to incorporate all of the relevant functions for nonverbal involvement. Patterson (1982) certainly specifies a number of important functions for nonverbal involvement, including providing information, regulation of interaction, expression of intimacy and involvement, social control, and facilitation of service or task goals. However, no rationale is provided for the exclusion of other functions of involvement behaviors including interactional synchrony and rhythms (Davis, 1982), culture and cultural pride (Hall, 1976), gender appropriateness (LaFrance & Mayo, 1978), inclusion (Schutz, 1960), confirmation (Watzlawick, Beavin, & Jackson, 1967), and manifestation of personality traits and self-definition (LaFrance & Mayo, 1978). Indeed, neither these additions nor Patterson's list is arguably comprehensive. Moreover, people's purposes in communication may be ideographic (Kelly, 1955; Delia, 1977) and individuals may generate numerous unique and idiosyncratic reasons for nonverbal involvement.

A second problem with the sequential-functional model is the lack of justification for the location of behavioral predispositions in the preinteraction phase but not in the interaction phase (P. Andersen, 1984). This gives the impression that behavioral predispositions cease to function during the interaction. The model also fails to distinguish between personal factors (personality) in the antecedent phase and behavioral predispositions (relatively stable characteristics of individuals) in the preinteraction phase. A further distinction needs to be made between these variables, or they should be labeled the same.

Finally, Patterson (1983, p. 166) recognizes that intentionality is still a controversial issue in communication and psychology. Some doubt exists as to whether individuals are consciously aware of their behavior as it is occurring or even whether they can retrospectively verbalize the cognitive processes that guided their behavior (Nisbett & Wilson, 1977). This is a crucial and testable aspect of the sequential-functional model. Future research should certainly address this issue.

CONCLUSION

At this stage in the development of these theories, it is necessary to issue the ubiquitous call for more empirical research on the models. Empirical research on the three most recent models (arousal-valence, discrepancy-arousal, sequential-functional) is certainly needed. Tests of the critical linkages need to be conducted for each of the models. This should culminate in an overall test of each model. This is not an easy task, due to the fact that a number of linkages exist in each model and the arousal and cognitive processes are covert and difficult to measure.

Among the six models reviewed in this article, five of them incorporate arousal as an important construct. Both the Burgoon's (1978) model of personal space violations and the Cappella and Greene (1982) discrepancy-arousal model suggest that deviations from expectations have arousal value. Burgoon maintains that these deviations activate observers' attention and arouse adaptive or defense mechanisms to cope with the deviation. Cappella and Greene (1982) follow others who believe that moderate arousal is pleasing and results in reciprocity whereas extreme arousal is aversive and results in compensation. The Andersen (1983, 1984, in press) arousal-valence model suggests that arousal is a function of changes, particularly increases in immediacy. Like the discrepancy-arousal model, an assumption of the arousal-valence model is that extreme arousal is aversive. However, moderate arousal simply signals a change in state that can be valenced based on one of the six valences described earlier. Arousal-labeling theory also holds that changes in immediacy can be arousing but the verbal labels are employed to determine whether positive or negative responses occur

(Patterson, 1976). The sequential-functional (Patterson, 1982, 1983) model assigns a role to potential arousal changes at both the preinteraction phase and during the interaction phase. Patterson (1982) maintains that arousal changes may motivate behavior adjustment, differentially facilitate dominant adjustment patterns, or serve to initiate an analysis of the meaning associated with the changing circumstances.

As a result of the centrality of arousal as a construct in the five most recent intimacy-exchange models, two research priorities are in order. First, the location or locations of arousal in each model need to be determined. Burgoon (1978) suggests arousal is a consequence of deviation from behavioral expectations and an antecedent of interpersonal evaluations. Cappella and Greene (1982) propose that arousal is a result of deviation from expectancy, but argue that the degree of arousal has a direct relationship with the positivity or negativity of the affective experience. Andersen (1983, 1984, in press) and Patterson (1976) argue that arousal is the result of changes in immediacy, though they differ on the effect of this arousal. Patterson's sequential functional model (1982, 1983) employs arousal as a mediating variable prior to interaction and as a predictor of both adjustments in interpersonal involvement and functional reassessments. A priority for empirical research should be to assess the causal order between arousal and these other variables.

The second priority for empirical research is an unobtrusive or less reactive method of measuring arousal. Andersen (1983, in press) reviews literature that examines behavioral immediacy effects on eight measures of arousal, including galvanic skin response, heart rate, electroencephalograph, nervous movements and self-manipulators, self-reports, palmar sweat, blood pressure, and duration and time to micturition. Similarly Cappella and Green (1982) maintain that arousal may refer to a host of processes, including overt behavioral activity, physiological activity, autonomic arousal, or activation of the cortex.

In the discrepancy-arousal model and most likely the other theories as well, the construct of concern is cognitive activation or activation of the cortex, reticular activating system, and limbic system. It is assumed that most behavioral and physiological measures are indirect measures of cognitive arousal whereas the electroencephalogram and average evoked responses are direct indications of cognitive arousal (Cappella & Greene, 1982, p. 98). Steinfatt and Roberts (1983) also criticize most arousal measures as being too indirect, difficult to interpret, and highly obtrusive. Indeed, prior research indicates arousal may be defined as a metabolic activity that produces heat (Dabbs, 1975). Thus either caloric consumption or temperature would be a good index of arousal. Though the ideal location for such measurements would be at the hypothalamus, this procedure would be unethical and reactive. However, Dabbs (1975) and Steinfatt and Roberts (1983) maintain that hypothalamic temperature is associated with the temperature of the tympanic membrane. Steinfatt and Roberts (1983) report that research has successfully employed an ear probe of soft plastic that was both effective and unobtrusive, though Dabbs (1975) reports it is slightly uncomfortable for some subjects. Future research should examine tympanic temperature, electroencephalographic readings, measures of averaged evoked response, and other indices of cognitive arousal to measure the arousal construct more validly.

What is the present state of research and theory on intimacy exchange? Certainly there is reason for cautious optimism. In less than two decades, substantial strides have been made. The 1960s was a time of beginnings for research and theory in this area. The early 1970s produced a considerable quantity of empirical research but little theory to account for the findings. The late 1970s and early 1980s produced a surge of new theoretical models as well as more empirical research. The viable second-generation models reviewed in this paper are now available for empirical testing. It is likely that none of the current models in its present form will eventually receive consensus as a superior explanation for the dyadic exchange of intimacy behavior. But it is equally likely that future models will incorporate a number of the critical components of the theoretical models discussed in this special issue.

REFERENCES

Abelson, R. P. Script processing in attitude formation and decision making. In J. S. Carroll and J. W. Payne (Eds.). *Cognition and social behavior.* Potomac, Md.: Lawrence Erlbaum, 1976.

Abelson, R. P. Psychological status of the script concept. *American Psychologist,* 1981, *36,* 715–729.

Aiello, J. R. A test of equilibrium theory: Visual interaction in relation to orientation, distance and sex of interactants. *Psychonomic Science,* 1972, 27, 335–336.

Aiello, J. R. A further look at equilibrium theory: Visual interaction as a function of interpersonal distance. *Environmental Psychology and Nonverbal Behavior,* 1977a, *1,* 122–140.

Aiello, J. R. Visual interaction at extended distances. *Personality and Social Psychology Bulletin,* 1977b, *3,* 83–86.

Andersen, J. F., Andersen, P. A., & Jensen, A. D. The measurement of nonverbal immediacy *Journal of Applied Communication Research,* 1979, *7,* 153–180.

Andersen, P. A. Nonverbal immediacy in interpersonal communication. Paper presented at the annual meeting of the International Communication Association, Dallas, Tex., May 1983.

Andersen, P. A. An arousal-valence model of nonverbal immediacy exchange. Paper presented at the annual meeting of the Central States Speech Association, Chicago, Ill., April 1984.

Andersen, P. A. Nonverbal immediacy in interpersonal communication. In A. Seigman & S. Feldstein (Eds.). *Nonverbal communication.* Hillsdale, N.J.: Lawrence Erlbaum, in press.

Andersen, P. A., & Coussoule, A. The perception world of the communication apprehensive. The effect of communication apprehension and interpersonal gaze on interpersonal perception. *Communication Quarterly,* 1980, *28,* 44–53.

Anderson, D. R. Interpersonal relationship and intimacy of social interaction. Re-examining the intimacy-equilibrium model. (Doctoral Dissertation, University of South Dakota, 1977). *Dissertation Abstracts International,* 1978, *38,* 4643B.

Argyle, M., & Dean, J. Eye contact, distance and affiliation. *Sociometry,* 1965, *28,* 289–304.

Bakken, D. Intimacy regulation in social encounters. Paper presented to the meeting of the Eastern Communication Associates, Boston, Mass., April 1978(a).

Bakken, D. Nonverbal immediacy in dyadic interactions: The effects of sex and information about attitude similarity. Paper presented to the Eastern Psychological Association, April 1978b.

Berger, C. R., & Roloff, M. E. Social cognition, self-awareness, and interpersonal communication. In B. Dervin & M. J. Voight (Eds.). *Progress in communication sciences* (Volume II) (pp. 1–49). Norwood, NJ.: Ablex Publishing, 1980.

Berlyne, D. E. *Conflict, arousal, and curiosity.* New York: McGraw-Hill, 1960.

Breed, G. The effect of intimacy: Reciprocity or retreat? *British Journal of Social and Clinical Psychology,* 1972, *11,* 135–142.

Burgoon, J. K. A communication model of personal space violations: Explication and an initial test. *Human Communication Research,* 1978, *4,* 129–142.

Burgoon, J. K., & Aho, L. Three field experiments on the effects of violations of conversational distance. *Communication Monographs,* 1982, *49,* 71–88.

Burgoon, J. K., & Jones, S. B. Toward a theory of personal spaces expectations and their violations. *Human Communication Research,* 1976, *2,* 131–146.

Burgoon, J. K., Stacks, D. W., & Burch, S. A. The role of interpersonal rewards and violations of distancing expectations in achieving influence in small groups. *Communication,* 1982, *11,* 114–128.

Burgoon, J. K., Stacks, D. W., & Woodall, W. G. A communicative model of violations of distancing expectations. *Western Journal of Speech Communication,* 1979, *43,* 153–167.

Cappella, J. N. Mutual influence in expressive behavior: Adult-adult and infant-adult dyadic interaction. *Psychological Bulletin,* 1981, *89,* 101–132.

Cappella, J. N. Remarks on five functional approaches to nonverbal behavior. Paper presented at the annual meeting of the International Communication Association, Dallas, Tex., May 1983.

Cappella, J. N., & Greene, J. O. A discrepancy-arousal explanation of mutual influence in expressive behavior for adult and infant-adult interaction. *Communication Monographs,* 1982, *49,* 89–114.

Coutts, L. M., Irvine, M., & Schneider, F. W. Nonverbal adjustments to changes in gaze and orientation. *Psychology,* 1977, *14,* 28–32.

Coutts, L. M., & Schneider, F. W. Affiliative conflict theory: An investigation of intimacy equilibrium and compensation hypothesis. *Journal of Personality and Social Psychology,* 1976, *34,* 1135–1142.

Dabbs, J. M. Core body temperature and social arousal. *Personality and Social Psychology Bulletin,* 1975, *1,* 517–520.

Davis, M. (Ed.). *Interaction rhythms: Periodicity in communicative behavior.* New York: Human Sciences Press, 1982.

Delia, J. G. Constructivism and the study of human communication. *Quarterly Journal of Speech,* 1977, *63,* 66–83.

Eysenck, H. J. *Experiments with drugs.* Oxford: Pergamon Press, 1963.

Eysenck, H. J. *The biological basis of personality.* Springfield, Ill.: Charles Thomas Publisher, 1967.

Eysenck, H. J. Arousal, learning and memory. *Psychological Bulletin,* 1976, *83,* 389–404.

Eysenck, H.J. *Personality, genetics and behavior.* New York: Praeger, 1982.

Firestone, I. J. Reconciling verbal and nonverbal models of dyadic communication. *Environmental Psychology and Nonverbal Behavior,* 1977, *2,* 30–44.

Foot, H. C., Chapman, A. J., Smith, J. R. Friendship and social responsiveness in boys and girls. *Journal of Personality and Social Psychology,* 1977, *35,* 401–411.

Foot, H. C., Smith, J. R., & Chapman A. J. Individual differences in children's responsiveness in humor situations. In A. J. Chapman & H. C. Foot (Eds.). *It's a funny thing, humor.* London: Pergamon, 1977.

Garrison, J. P., Sullivan, D. L., & Pate, L. E. Interpersonal valence dimensions as discriminators of communication contexts: An empirical assessment of dyadic linkages. Paper presented at the Speech Communication Association Convention, San Francisco, CA, 1976.

Hall, E. T. *Beyond culture.* Garden City, NY.: Anchor Books, 1976.

Hebb, D. O. *The organization of behavior: A neuropsychological theory.* New York: John Wiley, 1949.

Janik, S. W. Visual adjustments to changes in apparent interactive distance. A Test of Patterson's intimacy-arousal model. (Doctoral dissertation, University of Miami, 1979). *Dissertation Abstracts International,* 1980, *41,* 408B–409B.

Kelly, G. A *The psychology of personal constructs.* New York: Norton, 1955.

LaFrance, M., & Mayo, C. *Moving bodies: Nonverbal communication in social relationships.* Monterey, CA: Brooks/Cole, 1978.

Langer, E. J. Rethinking the role of thought in social interaction. In J. H. Harvey, W. Ikes, & R. F. Kidd (eds.). *New Directions in attribution research* (Volume 2) Hillsdale, NJ.: Lawrence Erlbaum Associates, 1978.

Markus, H. Self-schemata and processing information about the self. *Journal of Personality and Social Psychology,* 1977, *35,* 63–78.

Marshall, G. D., & Zimbardo, P. G. Affective consequences of inadequately explained physiological arousal. *Journal of Personality and Social Psychology,* 1979, *37,* 970–988.

Maslach, C. Negative emotional biasing of unexplained arousal. *Journal of Personality and Social Psychology,* 1979, *37,* 953–969.

Mehrabian, A. *Silent messages.* Belmont, CA: Wadsworth Publishing Co., 1971.

Mehrabian, A. *Public places and private spaces.* New York: Basic Books, Inc., 1976.

Nisbett, R. E., & Wilson, T. D. Telling more than we can know. Verbal reports on mental processes. *Psychological Review,* 1977, *84,* 231–259.

Patterson, M. L. Compensation in nonverbal immediacy behaviors. A review. *Sociometry,* 1973, *36,* 237–252.

Patterson, M. L. An arousal model of interpersonal intimacy. *Psychological Review,* 1976, *83,* 235–245.

Patterson, M. L. Arousal change and cognitive labeling. Pursuing the mediators of intimacy exchange. *Environmental Psychology and Nonverbal Behavior,* 1978, *3,* 17–22.

Patterson, M. L. A sequential functional model of nonverbal exchange. *Psychological Review,* 1982, *89,* 231–249.

Patterson, M. L. *Nonverbal behavior: A functional perspective.* New York: Springer-Verlag, 1983.

Patterson, M. L., Jordan, A., Hogan, M., & Frerker, D. Effects of nonverbal intimacy on arousal and behavioral adjustment. *Journal of Nonverbal Behavior,* 1981, *5,* 184–198.

Pribram, K. H. *Languages of the brain: Experimental paradoxes and principles in neuropsychology.* Englewood Cliffs, N.J.: Prentice-Hall, 1971.

Rosenfeld, H. Effect of approval-seeking induction on interpersonal proximity. *Psychological Reports,* 1965, *17,* 120–122.

Rosenthal, R., Hall, J. A., DiMatteo, M. R., Rogers, P. L., & Archer, D. *Sensitivity to nonverbal communication: The pons test.* Baltimore, Md.: Johns Hopkins University Press, 1979.

Russo, N. Eye contact, distance and the equilibrium theory. *Journal of Personality and Social Psychology,* 1975, *31,* 497–502.

Schachter, S. The interaction of cognitive and physiological determinants of emotional state. In L. Berkowitz (ed.). *Advances in experimental social psychology* (Volume 1) New York: Academic Press, 1964.

Schachter, S., & Singer, J. Cognitive, social, and physiological determinants of emotional state. *Psychological Review,* 1962, *69,* 379–399.

Schachter, S., & Singer, J. C. Comments on the Maslach and Marshall-Zimbardo Experiments. *Journal of Personality and Social Psychology,* 1979, *37,* 970–988.

Schaeffer, G. H., & Patterson, M. L. Intimacy, arousal, and small group crowding. *Journal of Personality and Social Psychology,* 1980, *38,* 283, 290.

Schutz, W. C. *FIRO: A three-dimension theory of interpersonal behavior.* New York: Holt, Rinehart, and Winston, 1960.

Smith, M. J. Cognitive schema theory and the perseverance and attentuation of unwarranted empirical beliefs. *Communication Monographs,* 1982a, *4,* 115–126.

Smith, M. J. *Persuasion and human action.* Belmont, CA: Wadsworth Publishing, 1982b.

Stacks, D. W., & Burgoon, J. K. The persuasive effects of violating spatial distance expectations in small groups. Paper presented at the annual convention of the Southern Speech Communication Association, Biloxi, Miss., April 1979.

Steinfatt, T. M., & Roberts, C. V. Source credibility and physiological arousal. An important variable in the credibility-information retention relationship. *Southern Speech Communication Journal,* 1983, *48,* 340–355.

Stephenson, G. M., Rutter, D. R., & Dore, S. R. Visual interaction and distance. *British Journal of Psychology,* 1972, *64,* 251–257.

Stern, D. N. Mother and infant at play: The dyadic interaction involving facial, vocal, and gaze behavior. In M. Lewis & L. A Rosenblum (Eds.). *The effect of the infant on its caregiver.* (pp. 187–213). New York: Wiley, 1974.

Stern, D. *The first relationship: Mother and infant.* Cambridge, Mass., Harvard University Press, 1977.

Storms, M. D., & Thomas, G. C. Reaction to physical closeness. *Journal of Personality and Social Psychology,* 1977, *35,* 412–415.

Watzlawick, P., Beavin, J. H., & Jackson, D. D. *Pragmatics of human communication.* New York: Norton and Company, 1967.

Whitcher, S. J., & Fisher, J. D. Multi-dimensional reaction to therapeutic touch in a hospital setting. *Journal of Personality and Social Psychology,* 1979, *37,* 87–96.

Word, C. O., Zanna, M. P. & Cooper, J. The nonverbal mediation of self-fulfilling prophecies in interracial interaction. *Journal of Experimental Social Psychology,* 1974, *10,* 109–120.

Zajonc, R. B. Feeling and thinking; Preferences need no inferences. *American Psychologist,* 1980, *35,* 151–175.

EMPATHY, COMMUNICATION, AND PROSOCIAL BEHAVIOR

James B. Stiff, James Price Dillard, Lilnabeth Somera, Hyun Kim, and Carra Sleight

Two studies were conducted to examine the relationships among different dimensions of empathy, communication, and prosocial behavior. Study one provides a test of three models hypothesized to explain this process. Results of this study indicated support for altruism as a motivator of prosocial behavior and suggest that the egoism and dual-process models are unlikely explanations. Study two was conducted in hopes of identifying additional support for the model that emerged from study one. The second study fully replicated the findings of the first study. Results from both studies suggest that prosocial behavior is motivated primarily by concern for others. Moreover, emotional reactions to the perceived distress of others are preceded by a concern for others. Together, these findings strongly support an altruistic interpretation of prosocial behavior and suggest that the egoistic model be reformulated.

Empathy, and its associated processes, have been a target of investigation for researchers in social and clinical psychology, child development, counseling, and communication. However, despite this widespread interest and the fact that it has been the topic of scholarly inquiry for well over a century (Smith, 1759; Spencer, 1870), it is only recently that some consensus has begun to emerge regarding the boundaries of the construct and its role in certain affective, cognitive, and behavioral operations.

At this point two generalizations appear warranted. First, there seems to be agreement among researchers regarding the notion that empathy is not one variable but several. Multidimensional conceptualizations are prevalent among empathy theorists in all areas of social science (e.g., Deutsch & Madle, 1975; Feshbach, 1975; Gladstein, 1983). Furthermore, those empirical investigations which have addressed the matter concur on the presence of multiple factors, although they differ in terms of number and content (e.g., Davis, 1983; Johnson, Cheek, & Smither, 1983).

Second, empathy has been broadly implicated in processes which lead to helping and other forms of prosocial behavior. For example, Rogers (1957) contended that empathy was one of the "necessary and sufficient conditions for therapeutic personality change" (p. 99). Batson and his colleagues (Batson, Duncan, Ackerman, Buckley, & Birch, 1981; Coke, Batson, & McDavis, 1978) have emphasized responses to

Source: The article is taken from *Communication Monographs* [55: 198–213, 1988]. Reprinted by permission of the Speech Communication Association, 5105 Backlick Rd., Annandale, VA 22003.

persons in distress such as donating time to help with the completion of academic requirements or volunteering to take the place of a subject who is receiving electrical shocks. Although there seems to be growing agreement about the processual nature of empathically motivated prosocial behavior, there is considerable disagreement about the *specific* causal relationships among variables which produce such behavior.

The present paper operates within the boundaries established by this pair of broad generalizations. Its purpose is (1) to address directly the causal sequencing of certain components of empathy identified by other researchers and (2) to place that process in relation to a specific type of helping behavior, that is, communicative responsiveness.

The Dimensionality of Empathy

Perhaps the aspect of empathy about which there is the greatest consensus is that of *perspective taking*. This cognitive component of the superordinate empathy construct refers to the ability of an individual to adopt the viewpoint of another (Coke et al., 1978; Davis, 1980, 1983; Deutsch & Madle, 1975; Dymond, 1949; Feshbach, 1975; Krebs, 1975; Mead, 1934; Piaget, 1932). By adopting the position of another, persons with this ability report they are able to consider "both sides of an issue."

A second element integral to most current treatments of empathy is *emotional contagion.* Emotional contagion is an explicitly affective aspect of empathy, which occurs when one person experiences an emotional response parallel to, and as a result of, observing another person's actual or anticipated display of emotion (Coke et al., 1978; Davis, 1980, 1983; Deutsch & Madle, 1975; Feshbach, 1975; Stotland, 1969). The "parallel to" portion of the definition suggests that some general correspondence between two persons exists in the substantive nature of an emotion, though perfect correspondence is usually not considered necessary (Hoffman, 1977, 1978).

Empathic concern, a third component, also references an affective component (Davis, 1980, 1983). Efforts to capture the substantive nature of this aspect of empathy can be seen in such terms as "sympathetic arousal" (Hoffman, 1977), "humanistic orientation" (Dillard & Hunter, 1986), "altruistic motivation" (Coke et al., 1978) and "sympathy" (Bennett, 1979). While there is greater variability among definitions of this component than the preceding two, there is considerable common ground among each. The two key features upon which all treatments of empathic concern seem to turn are (1) a general concern and regard for the welfare of others and (2) the stipulation that the affect is *not* parallel to that of the target person. It is this second feature which makes clear the distinction between emotional contagion and empathic concern. Whereas emotional contagion necessitates some degree of correspondence in affect, empathic concern stipulates that the affect of the target and perceiver differ. For example, the observation of a person in distress should activate a parallel, negative response (emotional contagion) and a positive nonparallel response (empathic concern).

While *fictional involvement* is another suggested component of empathy, it has received very little attention. Stotland (1969) recognized its existence years ago when he remarked that when "people read novels, poetry, or just newspaper accounts of emotional experiences, they will often become emotionally aroused" (p. 272). Since then, two data-based studies yielded factors compatible with Stotland's thinking (Davis, 1980; Dillard & Hunter, 1986; see also Stotland, Mathews, Sherman, Hansson, & Richardson, 1978). Because fictional involvements is not yet integrated into the empathy literature and because it appears to bear no relationship to helping behavior, it will not be examined further in this paper. Thus, the three major components of empathy to be considered in this investigation are perspective taking, emotional contagion, and empathic concern.

Empathy Processes

These three components of empathy—perspective taking, emotional contagion, and empathic concern—are viewed by many researchers to be sequentially and causally ordered. In terms of causal sequencing, there is fairly substantial agreement that the cognitive variable, perspective-taking, initiates the process (Coke et al., 1978; Feshbach, 1975; but see Gladstein, 1983). Experimental work such as that of Stotland and Sherman (reported in Stotland, 1969) has emphasized this assumption by instructing study participants to imagine themselves in the situation of the target person (high empathy manipulation) or to simply watch the target person (low empathy manipulation).

Given that the observer assumes the role or perspective of the target, either through innate tendency or experimental manipulation, several things may result. One group of theorists argues that persons who observe the distress of another become emotionally agitated themselves (Gaertner & Dovidio, 1977; Piliavin, Rodin, & Piliavin, 1969). In other words, these theorists contend that perspective taking causes emotional contagion. Emotional contagion motivates persons to reduce the source of unpleasantness to the other because of its indirect effects on themselves. This perspective of empathic helping has been labeled *egoistic* because it assumes that prosocial behavior comes about solely because of a desire to benefit the self.

Another perspective, anchored by the work of Batson and Coke, argues for the existence of *altruistic* motivations for helping others (Batson, Darley, & Coke, 1978; Batson et al., 1981; Batson & Coke, 1981; Coke et al., 1978). This approach suggests that perspective taking causes empathic concern which motivates prosocial behavior. While these researchers do not deny the reality of egoistic motives, they claim that behavior may also be caused by a desire to improve the other's welfare or by a combination of altruistic and egoistic motives.

Empathy and Prosocial Behavior

Traditionally, empathy has been studied in relation to prosocial behavioral responses directed toward some distressed individual in an emergency situation. Much of the recent work in this area has attempted to identify whether such behaviors are altruistically or egoistically motivated (Archer, Diaz-Loving, Gollwitzer, Davis, & Foushee, 1981; Coke, Batson, & McDavis, 1978; Batson, Bolen, Cross, & Neuringer-Benefiel, 1986; Batson et al., 1981; Fultz, Batson, Fortenbach, McCarthy, & Varney, 1986; Toi & Batson, 1982).

Recently, this emphasis has shifted away from the psychological process of offering material aid, and researchers have become increasingly concerned with communicative responses to the perceived emotional states of others. For example, Burleson and his associates (Burleson, 1978, 1982, 1983; Burleson & Delia, 1983; Burleson & Samter, 1983) have focused almost exclusively on the ability to produce comforting messages when interacting with distressed target persons. Stiff (1984) also emphasized the communicative component of empathic responses and developed a measure of communicative responsiveness. This self-report measure focused on perceived ability to listen to and respond effectively to another in distress.

Miller and Steinberg (1975) highlight the importance of overt communicative responses when they argue that vicarious responses and empathic concern are insufficient to produce the impression of empathy. They note, "we do not bestow the title of 'good empathizer' upon someone unless they communicate with us in rewarding ways" (p. 175). Although we prefer to retain the distinction between psychological processes and behavioral outcomes, Miller and Steinberg's argument is sound. Rather than the material aid called for in emergency situations, it is likely that the most frequently expressed responses to empathy are communicative in nature.

Nevertheless, both the psychological process of generating a prosocial response and the re-

FIGURE I   A model of empathy and prosocial behavior.

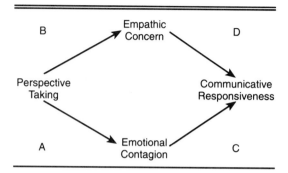

Predicted Sign of Each Path Coefficient				
Theoretical Position	A	B	C	D
Egoistic Model	+	0	+	0
Altruistic Model	0	+	0	+
Dual-Process Model	+	+	+	+

sponse itself are important to understanding empathy. Thus, this paper will compare altruistic and egoistic approaches to explaining communicative responses as a form of prosocial behavior.

Models of Empathy and Prosocial Behavior

The previous discussion of perspective-taking, emotional contagion, empathic concern, and communicative responsiveness suggests the existence of different processes underlying communicative helping behavior. These processes are graphically summarized in Figure 1.

Figure 1 provides a path diagram of the possible relationships among perspective taking, emotional contagion, and empathic concern for generating communicative responses in both altruistically and egoistically motivated processes. Each path can be assigned a coefficient (or weighted value) indicating the strength of the given causal relationship.

If the egoistic position is correct, the matrix of path coefficients which describe the model assumes a certain form. Specifically, the paths for the perspective-taking to emotional contagion link and the emotional contagion to communicative responsiveness link should be positive and significantly different from zero. In addition, the perspective taking to empathic concern and empathic concern to communicative responsiveness paths should be approximately zero.

A purely altruistic model predicts exactly the opposite. That is, the positive links in the egoistic model should be approximately zero, while the perspective-taking to empathic concern and the empathic concern to communicative responsiveness paths should be positive and significantly different from zero.

Finally, a dual-process model is also possible. Batson et al. (1981) have argued that ''motivation for helping may be a mixture of altruism and eogism; it need not be solely altruistic or even primarily altruistic to have an altruistic component'' (p. 291). Because this model hypothesizes that both altruism and egoism motivate prosocial behavior, the coefficients for all four paths in the model could be positive and significantly different from zero.

Rationale

The purpose of this investigation was twofold. First, we wished to examine the operation of altruistic and egoistic processes simultaneously. This approach departs from previous research which has tended to examine the two explanations independently of one another. Our hope was to provide a more thorough picture of the way in which empathy operates by considering all of the relevant pieces of the process together.

Second, while building upon the foundations laid by earlier investigators of prosocial behavior, we sought to extend the theoretical structure to include measures of *communication behavior* designed to benefit distressed individuals. To tie our results to previous efforts, we included a measure of willingness to provide physical assistance to an organization whose purpose is to help children suffering from cancer. In order to carry our inquiry into the underresearched area of communication behavior, we included measures of communicative responsiveness (Stiff, 1984) and of comforting strategies (Burleson, 1978). Two studies were conducted.

STUDY ONE

Method

Participants

A total of 171 students enrolled in introductory communication courses at a large midwestern university served as respondents. Each person received extra course credit for participation.

Procedure

Participants arrived at the laboratory in groups of six to ten and were greeted by one of the investigators. After completing two consent forms, a questionnaire containing measures of empathy and communicative responsiveness was administered. When the participants had completed the surveys, they were informed that the session was over. The study was described as having been designed to test the statistical relationships among several of the personality measures they had completed.

Next, participants were thanked and told that a graduate student from the department was giving a video presentation down the hall and had requested their assistance in evaluating it. They were informed that it would require about ten minutes of their time. The experimenter asked the participants to assist the graduate student by viewing the presentation, but emphasized the voluntary nature of doing so. Following this, participants were again thanked and then shown the way to the room where the graduate student would be making the presentation.

After the participants had arrived at the second lab the graduate student (who was one of the investigators) greeted the participants and read the following statement:

> For the past several months I have been working as a volunteer with an organization that provides social support for families with children who have cancer. This organization's major activity is the operation of a summer camp and two winter weekend camps for the children who have cancer. This is a non-profit organization that relies heavily on the efforts of volunteers. I would like you to view a videotape that introduces the organization and its major activities. Following this, I would like to get some feedback from you about the presentation and the organization.

Following this introduction, participants were shown the videotaped presentation and asked to complete a short questionnaire that assessed their attitudes toward the organization and their willingness to help. The investigator then read the following statement:

> We are currently preparing for the camp this summer. Preparation for an activity like this requires many hours of organization and administrative work and we are looking for volunteers to help with the preparations. Much of the work that we have to do involves collating and mailing information that must be sent to children who would like to attend camp this summer.
>
> All of the work will be completed in this building, so transportation should not be problem. You may volunteer for as little as one hour of time or as many hours as you like. There are many different times next week when we will be holding work sessions; some of these times are during the day and some are at night. This organization and the children it serves could really use your help. If you would like to volunteer, please complete this form (each participant was given a volunteer form) and indicate whether you would like to help.

After they had completed the forms, the graduate student thanked the participants for their cooperation and indicated that those who had volunteered would be contacted by phone to arrange a specific work time.

Stimulus Materials

The videotape used in the experiment was a segment of a news feature about the organization. Because the organization has been operating successfully for a number of years, several local and national news features about the organization exist. The director of the organization granted us permission to use one of these videotaped news features as stimulus material for the project. The segment we chose was approximately nine minutes in length and provided a thorough overview of the organization, camp life, and interviews with some of the young people who attend the camp. Because of its origin, the production quality of the videotape was quite high.

Instrumentation

The first questionnaire was completed by all research participants and contained measures of several dimensions of empathy. Measures of Perspective Taking (Davis, 1983), Emotional Contagion (Dillard & Hunter, 1986), Empathic Concern (Davis, 1983), and Communicative Responsiveness (Stiff, 1984) were included in this questionnaire. Davis (1983) provides evidence of the construct validity and structural quality of the perspective taking and the empathic concern measures. The measure of emotional contagion emerged from Dillard and Hunter's (1986) analysis of the structural qualities of the emotional empathy scale (Mehrabian & Epstein, 1972). Stiff (1984) provided evidence for the construct validity and unidimensionality of the measure of communicative responsiveness. This scale measures a person's ability to listen to and communicate effectively to others who are experiencing distress.

Participants completed a second questionnaire, after viewing the videotape, which measured attitudes toward the organization. Following the appeal for volunteers, participants were asked to indicate if they would like to volunteer to help complete several administrative tasks for the organization. The decision to volunteer served as a measure of their intention to offer help.[1]

Results

Measurement Models

The first step in the analyses was to identify the structural qualities of the self-report measures used in the study. Hunter (1980) identifies three criteria for assessing the unidimensionality of a cluster of items: content homogeneity, internal consistency, and parallelism. Content homogeneity, often termed face validity, suggests that all of the items in a unidimensional cluster should have the same or similar meaning.

Following content analyses, confirmatory factor analyses were conducted on each of the measures using PACKAGE (Hunter, Cohen, & Nicol, 1982). Using theorems provided by Hunter (1980), formal tests of the internal consistency and parallelism of each measure were conducted.

STATISTICAL SUMMARY 1

Measurement Model

Study 1: Confirmatory factor analysis provides a test of the effectiveness of the measures. First, the content of the items is examined and decisions are made about what they measure. Second, the items are tested for internal consistency. Internal consistency means that all of the items measuring a single concept are correlated or consistent with each other. Third, the items are tested for parallelism. Parallelism means the items that measure a single concept should all exhibit similar relationships to other concepts. For example, all of the items measuring perspective taking should have similar relationships to emotional contagion.

As is typical for this type of procedure, not all of the items in each measure fit the criteria for internal consistency and parallelism. Such items are indicators of multidimensionality and were deleted from further analyses before a unidimensional factor could be identified for each measure.

TABLE 1
Factor Loadings and Reliability Estimates of Four Empathy Measures

	Factor Loading	
Perspective Taking	Study I	Study II
1. Before I criticize somebody, I try to imagine how I would feel in their place.	.72	.60
2. If I'm sure I'm right about something, I don't waste much time listening to other people's arguments (R)	.89	.63
3. I believe there are two sides to every question and I try to look at both of them.	.91	.61
4. I sometimes find it difficult to see things from the other person's point of view. (R)	—	.56
5. I try to look at everybody's side of a disagreement before I make a decision.	—	.68
6. When I am upset at someone, I usually try to put myself in his or her "shoes" for a while.	—	.48
Coefficient Alpha	.87	.76
Empathic Concern		
1. When I see someone being taken advantage of, I feel kind of protective toward them.	.57	.57
2. When I see someone being treated unfairly, I sometimes don't feel much pity for them. (R)	.46	.49
3. I often have tender, concerned feelings for people less fortunate than me.	.70	.67
4. I would describe myself as a pretty soft-hearted person.	.65	.71
5. Other people's misfortunes do not usually disturb me a great deal. (R)	.56	.78
6. I am often touched by the things that I see happen.	.71	.61
Coefficient Alpha	.78	.82
Emotional Contagion		
1. I often can remain cool in spite of the excitement around me. (R)	.47	.42
2. I tend to lose control when I am bringing bad news to people.	.43	.36
3. I tend to remain calm even though those around me worry. (R)	.68	.59
4. I cannot continue to feel O.K. if people around me are depressed.	.58	.56
5. I don't get upset just because a friend is acting upset. (R)	.50	.50
6. I become nervous if others around me are nervous.	.52	.44
7. The people around me have a great influence on my moods.	.52	.52
Coefficient Alpha	.73	.68

Table 1—*Continued*

Communicative Responsiveness	Factor Loading	
	Study I	Study II
1. I usually have a knack for saying the right thing to make people feel better when they are upset.	.64	.53
2. I usually respond appropriately to the feelings and emotions of others.	.65	.55
3. Others think of me as a very empathic person.	.36	.57
4. I am the type of person who can say the right thing at the right time.	.55	.42
5. My friends come to me with their problems because I am a good listener.	.59	.42
Coefficient Alpha	.69	.62

Note: Items followed by (R) have been reflected.

T A B L E 2
Correlations among the Four Dimensions of Empathy and the Measure of Helping Behavior in Study One

Perspective Taking	1.00	.30	−.01	.29	.06
Empathic Concern	.25	1.00	.40	.45	.32
Emotional Contagion	−.01	.30	1.00	−.01	.05
Communicative Responsiveness	.23	.33	−.01	1.00	.21
Helping Behavior	.05	.28	.04	.17	1.00

Note: Correlations below the diagonal are not corrected for attenuation due to measurement error. Correlations above the diagonal are corrected for attenuation due to error in measurement. The corrected correlations were used for all path analyses.

Three of the seven items developed by Davis (1983) survived this analysis and formed a unidimensional factor labeled perspective taking. Seven items identified by Dillard (1983) formed a measure of emotional contagion. Six items identified by Davis (1983) were used to measure empathic concern, and five items developed by Stiff (1984) measured communicative responsiveness. The alpha coefficients for these four measures ranged from .69 to .87. The items and reliability estimate for each measure are presented in Table 1. Sixty-five of the 171 research participants who viewed the stimulus tape volunteered to help the organization. Whether or not an individual volunteered was used as the measure of helping behavior.

STATISTICAL SUMMARY 2

Coefficient alpha is a measure of reliability which tells us how accurate a measure is. If a measure is highly reliable, then you can be confident that the scores are very accurate. The measures in this study varied from moderate (.69) to high (.87) accuracy.

Theoretical Models

Correlations among the four dimensions of empathy and the measure of volunteering were computed. Table 2 gives these correlations corrected and uncorrected for measurement error. To test the altruistic, egoistic, and dual-process models of empathy, path analyses were conducted on the corrected correlations using LISREL V (Joreskog & Sorbom, 1981). Communicative responsiveness and volunteering were treated as separate indices of prosocial behavior.[2]

The path coefficients for the dual-process model are given in Figure 2. A cursory inspection of the results would seem to support the altruistic explanation, but not the egoistic one. However, an omnibus test revealed that the model as a whole failed to fit the data. The chi-square goodness of fit test for the overall model indicated that the matrix of correlations predicted by the model deviated from the observed matrix of correlations by more than could be expected from sampling error alone. X^2 (4) = 38.75, $p < .001$.

STATISTICAL SUMMARY 3

Theoretical Model

Correlations are used to see if two concepts are related to each other. A positive correlation means that as the score on one concept increases, the score on the second concept increases as well. A negative correlation means that as the score on one concept increases, the score on the second concept decreases. The closer the correlation is to either +1.00 or −1.00 (higher or lower), the more similar the two concepts are. Correlations that are corrected for measurement error are really estimates of what the correlation would be if measured with perfect reliability (accuracy).

The correlation in this study were then tested using path analysis. Path analysis is a way of testing a series of relationships or a model. For example, the model presented in Figure 1 predicts that perspective taking will cause both empathic concern and emotional contagion, each of which will cause communicative responsiveness. In this way a system or collection of relationships can be tested.

The predicted model did not work well. However, a revised model did work well and is presented in Figure 3. This model shows that perspective taking caused empathic concern which, in turn, caused volunteering behavior.

FIGURE 2   Results of a test of the hypothesized model.

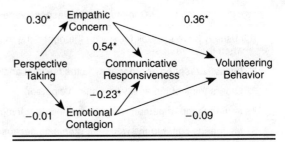

Note: Path coeffecients with asterisks differ significantly from zero.

Micro analyses showed three modifications that would improve the overall fit of the model. Inspection of the matrix of deviations revealed two deviations that were larger than one would expect by sampling error and two others that were relatively large. Diagnostics produced by LISREL V suggested that the deletion of two paths and the addition of another would reduce the size of these deviations and provide a better fit of the model.

The revised model deleted the paths from perspective taking to emotional contagion and from emotional contagion to volunteering. The final modification was the addition of a path from empathic concern to emotional contagion. Analysis of the revised model indicated that the data fit this model well (Figure 3). The test for the overall goodness of fit of the model indicated that the matrix of deviations did not differ from zero, X^2 (5) = 10.51, $p > .05$. In addition to this global assessment, micro analyses indicated a good fit of the model. All of the path coefficients differed substantively and significantly from zero. None of the reproduced correlations predicted by the model deviated from the observed correlations by more than one would expect due to sampling error alone. The sum of squared deviations was relatively small (.05), as was the average absolute deviation (.094). In sum, both the micro and macro analyses indicate that the revised model fits the data well.

FIGURE 3   Results of a test of the revised model (study one).

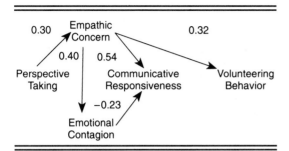

Note: All paths differ significantly from zero.

Discussion

Two issues are highlighted by the revised model. First, although the revised model is compatible with current theorizing regarding the operation of altruistic processes, it suggests that a radical reformulation of the egoistic position is necessary. The lack of a relationship between emotional contagion and volunteering and the negative path from contagion to communicative responsiveness are both incompatible with the claim that persons offer aid to suffering others in order to relieve their own distress. The fact that the data called for a link from empathic concern to emotional contagion, rather than the expected path from perspective taking to emotional contagion, also contributes to the overall disconfirmation of the egoistic hypothesis.

Second, it is important to note that with the absence of a link from emotional contagion to volunteering, the two measures of prosocial behavior have different causal antecedents. This suggests the possible existence of different classes of prosocial variables.

In short, study one yielded findings which were quite surprising for the egoistic model and inconsistent across the two measures of prosocial behavior. In order to test the durability of these findings another study was conducted. It mirrored the first investigation in every way but one: A measure of comforting behavior was substituted for volunteering. This measure was chosen be-

cause (1) like volunteering, it indexed a specific class of prosocial behavior, and (2) like communication responsiveness, it tapped a form of communication. We reasoned that if the difference between specific indices and trait-like measures accounted for the variation in findings between the two measures of prosocial response, then study two would replicate the study one findings by showing no path between emotional contagion and (helping) behavior. In contrast, if the common, communication aspects of the two measures was predominant then both should manifest similar relationships with empathic concern and with emotional contagion.

Method

Research Participants

Research participants were 126 students enrolled in communication courses at the same large midwestern university. Again, participation was voluntary and students who agreed to act as respondents received extra credit for participation.

Procedure

Students were assembled in large groups and asked to complete a questionnaire containing measures of perspective-taking, emotional contagion, empathic concern, and communicative responsiveness. Next, participants were asked to respond to Burleson's (1984) measure of comforting behavior. When everyone had completed this second questionnaire, the group was debriefed concerning the nature of the study and thanked for their participation.

Instrumentation

The first questionnaire contained the same measures of perspective taking (Davis, 1983) emotional contagion (Dillard & Hunter, 1986), empathic concern (Davis, 1983; Dillard & Hunter, 1986) and communicative responsiveness (Stiff, 1984) that were used in study one.

The second questionnaire contained two role-play scenarios designed to assess an individual's ability to comfort a distressed other (Burleson, 1984). One scenario asked respondents to imagine that a close friend had just flunked a class that was important to him or her to perform well in. Respondents were asked to think about this friend for a few minutes before listing the things they would say to this person to make him or her feel better. The second scenario asked respondents to imagine that their friend had recently "broken up" with a long time boyfriend or girlfriend. Once again, respondents were asked to think about this person before listing the things they would say to make him or her feel better.

Two graduate students trained to use Burleson's (1984) coding scheme categorized the comforting responses. Although respondents were asked to provide several responses to each scenario, the highest level response offered by each participant served as the indicator of their comforting response for the scenario. This approach is consistent with the one adopted by Burleson (1984). He argued that the highest level message produced by an individual is an indicator of his or her comforting competence. Hence, this treatment of the data emphasizes the respondent's level of social skill over his or her social motivation. Because we had data from two situations, the average of the highest response in each situation was used to estimate competence.[3]

Twenty-five percent of the comforting responses were rated by both raters. There was considerable uniformity in the raters' evaluations of the comforting messages for both the exam scenario ($r = .85$) and the boyfriend/girlfriend scenario ($r = .72$). The remaining 75 percent of the strategies were rated by one person.

STATISTICAL SUMMARY 4

Study 2

Correlations (r) were computed to test the accuracy of the coding. They proved to be moderately accurate.

Results

Measurement Models

Once again, the first step in the analysis was to identify the structural features of the measures used in the study. Using the procedures outlined in the initial study, confirmatory factor analyses were performed on each of the measures of empathy. These analyses were conducted on the complete list of items used in study one. The results of those analyses were very similar to those in study one. The only difference was the Davis (1983) measure of perspective taking. In that study three items were used to assess this construct. Results of the factor analyses for study two indicated that six of the seven original items developed by Davis (1983) formed a unidimensional measure of perspective taking. Other than the addition of three items to the perspective taking measure, the measures were used in the second study were identical to those used in study one. The factor loadings for each of the items and the reliability estimates for these measures are presented in Table 1.

STATISTICAL SUMMARY 5

Measurement Model

Again, confirmatory factor analysis was used to test the measures. Results were generally consistent with the first study.

Theoretical model

The major focus of this study was to test the model of empathy which emerged from study one. To do this, correlations among the measures of perspective taking, empathic concern, emotional contagion, communicative responsiveness and comforting behavior were computed and corrected for error in measurement (Table 3).

These correlations were then subjected to path analysis using LISREL V (Joreskog & Sorbom, 1981). Results from this analysis indicated that

T A B L E 3
Correlations among the Four Dimensions of Empathy and the Measure
of Helping Behavior in Study Two

Perspective Taking	1.00	.47	.13	.34	.26
Empathic Concern	.37	1.00	.34	.55	.22
Emotional Contagion	.09	.26	1.00	.01	−.07
Communicative Responsiveness	.24	.39	.01	1.00	.20
Comforting Behavior	.14	.12	−.04	.09	1.00

Note: Correlations below the diagonal are not corrected for attenuation due to measurement error. Correlations above the diagonal are corrected for attenuation due to error in measurement. The corrected correlations were used for all path analysis.

FIGURE 4   Results of a test of the hypothesized model (study two).

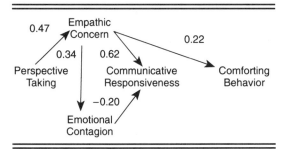

Note: All paths differ significantly from zero.

the model fit the data very well (Figure 4). Although the overall test of the goodness of fit of the model indicated that the observed matrix of deviations differed from zero, X^2 (5) = 12.27, $p < .05$, Fink and Monge (1985) argue that this test is very sensitive. That is, very small deviations can often produce statistically significant differences. Instead, they offer the chi-squared to degrees of freedom ratio as a better indicator of overall goodness of fit. This ratio was computed for the present data and was lower (2.45) than the value (5.00) Fink and Monge recommend as a "rule of thumb" upper limit for the fit of a model.

STATISTICAL SUMMARY 6

Theoretical Model

Path analysis was then used to test the model derived from study 2. Results indicated that the model worked well.

In addition to the overall test, micro analyses indicated that the model fit the data well. All of the observed paths differed significantly from zero and none of the individual correlations in the deviation matrix was larger than one would expect due to sampling error alone. In fact, the sum of squared deviations was small (.08), as was the average absolute deviation (.098).

Perhaps most important is the extent to which the observed paths in this model are similar to the observed paths in the model that emerged from study one. In this respect the data fit the hypothesized form very well. None of the observed paths in this model differed significantly from the corresponding paths in the model that emerged from study one. In short, the observed relationships in this study fully replicated the findings of study one.

DISCUSSION

In light of the near-perfect replication we can have considerable confidence that the structure of the data in two studies is not simply an aberration produced by sampling error. Rather, the fact that both data sets fit the same model well suggests that this hypothesized set of relationships may be an accurate depiction of the empathy process. The model indicates that perspective taking leads to empathic concern which influences emotional contagion, communicative responsiveness, and particular prosocial behaviors, i.e., volunteering and comforting. The implications of this model are numerous.

First of all, the role of empathic concern in this model strongly underscores the centrality of altruistic motivation in all forms of empathic responding. Empathic concern was shown to have a substantial impact on three different outcomes of the empathy process: communicative responsiveness, comforting behavior, and volunteering. Although the pair of studies reported here might be criticized for their reliance on static data to make causal claims, it should be noted that this sequencing of the various components of empathy is specified by existing theory and is corroborated by several experimental studies (Batson, Fultz, Schoenrade, & Paduano, 1987; Batson et al., 1981, 1986). In conjunction with the extant literature it would seem safe to conclude that the existence of an altruistic motivation for prosocial behavior is no longer in question (see also Eisenberg, 1983; Eisenberg & Miller, 1987).

Equally important are the conclusions which must be drawn concerning egoistic processes. Twice the data fit a model in which the influence of perspective taking was mediated by empathic concern. The presence of this intervening variable indicates that a wholly new conception of the functioning of emotional contagion is needed. It appears that a concern for other people is a necessary precursor to the personal distress produced by emotional contagion. This finding is diametrically opposed to the egoistic position which emphasizes the importance of the welfare of self over that of others.

In addition, the observed impact of emotional contagion was shown to be sharply at odds with expectations derived from egoistic theory. Its negative influence on communicative responsiveness implies that emotional contagion may actually interfere with empathic responding. Although our original predictions were consistent with the conclusions of a number of previous researchers, a closer examination of the data in these prior studies suggests that our "counterintuitive" finding should have been expected.

Three recent studies (Batson et al., 1986; Fultz et al., 1986; Toi & Batson, 1982) measured the effect of personal distress (emotional contagion) on some empathic response (helping behavior). In each of these studies, the simple correlations between personal distress and helping behavior were relatively small and nonsignificant. However, these correlations may have been suppressed by "other factors" which were not considered by the researchers. In fact, when Fultz et al. (1986) partialled out the effect of empathic concern, they found that the correlations between personal distress and helping behavior changed substantially (from $\tau = .40$ to $\tau = -.31$ in study one and from $\tau = .21$ to $\tau = .04$ in study two). Thus, despite our surprise at uncovering the negative link from emotional contagion to communicative responsiveness, findings from earlier experimental work are congruent with the results of the present study one and study two.

Also of interest is the fact that communication responsiveness was the result of both empathic concern and emotional contagion while volunteering and comforting were related only to empathic concern. Communication responsiveness is a trait measure which addresses a broad range of encoding and decoding skills as well as tapping into the motivation to employ those skills. By contrast, comforting competence and volunteering are more narrow indices. What seems abundantly evident is that there are multiple outcomes to the empathy process. Some appear to be the result of caring about others (empathic concern) while others are a function of both empathic concern and emotional contagion. Specifying the contents of these two classes of prosocial behaviors is certainly a task worthy of future inquiry.

One other, more general conclusion also emerges from this research. Because the correlations among the *predictor* variables in the present study and in previous research are sizeable, the effect of one factor on another cannot be fully estimated with a simple correlation. Without systematically controlling for the influence of suppressor variables, it is impossible to identify correctly the relationships among the various components of the empathy process.

In the present study, the use of path analytic techniques helped identify an important suppressor effect. Although the correlation in the first study between emotional contagion and communicative responsiveness was −.01, the path coefficient was −.23, indicating a significant, negative relationship. The relationship between empathic concern and emotional contagion served to suppress the true nature of the relationship. In sum, careful consideration of the influence of suppressor effects on causal relationships is critical to the development and testing of models of empathic responsiveness. Only by studying the empathy process in its entirety can we hope to advance our understanding of this important area of inquiry.

NOTES

1. We intended to give all participants who indicated their intent to volunteer the opportunity to return to the lab and volunteer time for the organization. Because the first wave of volunteers were able to complete all the work the organization asked us to do, we canceled the remaining work sessions and did not schedule additional sessions. As a result, we were not able to observe actual volunteering behaviors of everyone who indicated an intent to volunteer.
   Thirty-five of the 65 people who indicated an intent to volunteer were contacted in the first wave of phone calls. Twenty-seven of these 35 people were willing to be scheduled for a work session later this week. The remaining eight people indicated their desire to work at a later point in time. Eighteen of the 27 people who were scheduled to work were given the opportunity to volunteer time. Work sessions for the remaining nine people were canceled. Of the 18 people who were scheduled and given the opportunity to work, 14 actually volunteered time. The remaining four people did not show up at the scheduled time. Thus, 77% (27 out of 35) of the people who initially indicated they would volunteer were willing to be scheduled for a work time later in the week. Of the people who were

scheduled and given the opportunity to volunteer 78% (14 out of 18) actually showed up to work for the organization. These limited data suggest that, although not perfect, the measure of intent to volunteer was a good predictor of actual volunteering behavior.

2. The test of all theoretical models required the specification of the Beta, Gamma, and Psi matrices. The Beta and Gamma matrices consisted of free elements for the path coefficients being estimated. All other elements of these matrices were fixed at zero. The Psi matrix was specified as diagonal and free.

3. The ratings for the average score in the two situations were not highly correlated ($\tau = .19$), indicating a considerable amount of situational variance in people's comforting message development. As a result, this two-item mesure of comforting behavior was not highly reliable. Findings involving this factor should be interpreted with caution.

REFERENCES

Archer, R. L., Diaz-Loving, R., Gollwitzer, P. M., Davis, M. H., & Fousher, H. C. (1981). The role of dispositional empathy and social evaluation in the empathic mediation of helping. *Journal of Personality and Social Psychology, 40,* 786–796.

Azjen, I., & Fishbein, M. (1977). Attitude-behavior relation: A theoretical analysis and review of empirical research. *Psychological Bulletin, 84,* 888–918.

Batson, C. D., Bolen, M.H., Cross, J. A., & Neuringer-Benefiel, H. E. (1986). Where is the altruism in the altruistic personality? *Journal of Personality and Social Psychology, 50,* 212–220.

Batson, C. D., & Coke, J. S. (1981). *Empathy: A source of altruistic motivation for helping behavior.* Hillsdale, NJ: Erlbaum.

Batson, C. D., Darley, J. M., & Coke, J. S. (1978). Altruism and human kindness: Internal and external determinants of helping behavior. In L. Pervin & M. Lewis (Eds.), *Perspectives in interactional psychology.* New York: Plenum.

Batson, C. D., Duncan, B. D., Ackerman, P., Buckley, T., & Birch, K. (1981). Is empathic emotion a source of altruistic motivation? *Journal of Personality and Social Psychology, 40,* 290–302.

Batson, C. D., Fultz, J., Schoenrade, P. A., & Paduano, A. (1987). Critical self-reflection and self-perceived altruism. When self-reward fails, *Journal of Personaity and Social Psychology, 53,* 594–602.

Bennett, M. J. (1979). Overcoming the golden rules: Sympathy and empathy. In D. Nimmo (Ed.), *Communication yearbook 3.* New Brunswick: Transaction Books.

Bentler, P. N., & Bonnett, D. G. (1980). Significance tests and goodness of fit in the analysis of covariance structures. *Psychological Bulletin, 88,* 585–606.

Burleson, B. R. (1978, November). *Relationally oriented construct system content and messages directed to an affectively distressed listener: Two exploratory studies.* Paper presented at the annual meeting of the Speech Communication Association, Minneapolis.

Burleson, B. R. (1982). The affective perspective-taking process: A test of Turiel's role-taking model. In M. Burgoon (Ed.), *Communication yearbook 6,* New Brunswick: Transaction Books.

Burleson, B. R. (1983). Social cognition, empathic motivation, and adults' comforting strategies. *Human Communication Research,* 10, 295–304.

Burleson, B. R. (1984). Age, social-cognitive development, and the use of comforting strategies. *Communication Monographs,* 51, 140–153.

Burleson, B. R., & Delia, J.G. (1983, April). *Adaptive communication skills in childhood: A unitary construct?* Paper presented at the biennial meeting of the Society for Research in Child Development, Detroit.

Burleson, B. R., & Samter, W. (1983, September). *Social, cognitive and personality influences on prosocial behavior: A model of comforting determinants and an empirical test.* Paper presented at the Conference on Social Cognition and Interpersonal Behavior, University of Kansas, Lawrence.

Coke, J. S., Batson, C. D., & McDavis, K. (1978). Empathic mediation of helping: A two-stage model. *Journal of Personality and Social Psychology,* 36, 752–766.

Davis, M. H. (1980). Multidimensional approach to individual differences in empathy. *JSAS Catalog of Selected Documents in Psychology,* 10, 75.

Davis, M. H. (1983). Measuring individual differences in empathy: Evidence for a multidimensional approach. *Journal of Personality and Social Psychology,* 44, 113–126.

Deutsch, F., & Madle, R. A. (1975). Empathy: Historic and current conceptualizations, measurements, and a cognitive theoretical approach. *Human Development,* 18, 267–287.

Dillard, J. P. (1984). Empathy in instrumental communication: Tests of a theory. (Doctoral dissertation, Michigan State University, 1983). *Dissertation Abstracts International,* 45, 16A.

Dillard, J. P., & Hunter, J. E. (1986). Questions about the construct solidity of three scales: Emotional empathy, self-consciousness scales, and self-monitoring. Unpublished manuscript, Department of Communication Arts, University of Wisconsin–Madison.

Dymond, R. (1949). A scale for the measurement of empathic ability. *Journal of Consulting Psychology,* 13, 127–133.

Eisenberg, N. (1983). The relation between empathy and altruism: Conceptual and methodological issues. *Academic Psychology Bulletin, 5,* 195–208.

Eisenberg, N., & Miller, P. A. (1987). Empathy and prosocial behavior. *Psychological Bulletin,* 101, 91–119.

Feshbach, N. D., (1975). Empathy in children: Some theoretical and empirical considerations. *Counseling Psychologist, 5,* 25–29.

Fink, E. L., & Monge, P. R. (1985). An exploration of confirmatory factor analysis. In B. Dervin & M. J. Voigt (Eds.), *Progress in Communication Sciences* (Vol. 6, pp. 167–197). Norwood, NJ: Ablex.

Fultz, J., Batson, C. D., Fortenbach, V. A., McCarthy, P. M., & Varney, L. L. (1986). Social evaluation and the empathy-altruism hypothesis. *Journal of Personality and Social Psychology, 50,* 761–768.

Gaertner, S. L., & Dovidio, J. F. (1977). The subtlety of white racism, arousal, and helping behavior. *Journal of Personality and Social Psychology, 50,* 761–769.

Gladstein, G. A. (1983). Understanding empathy: Integrating counseling, developmental and social psychological perspectives. *Journal of Counseling Behavior, 34,* 467–482.

Hoffman, M. L. (1977). *Sex differences in empathy and related behaviors.* Psychological Bulletin, 84, 712–722.

Hoffman, M. L. (1978). Toward a theory of empathic arousal and its development. In M. Lewis & L. Rosenblum (Eds.), *Affect development.* New York: Plenum.

Hunter, J. E. (1980). Factor analysis. In P. R. Monge & J. N. Capella (Eds.), *Multivariate techniques in human communication research* (pp. 229–258). New York: Academic Press.

Hunter, J. E., Cohen, S. H., & Nicol, T. S. (1982). *PACKAGE: A system of routines to do correlational analysis, including path analysis, confirmatory factor analysis, and exploratory factor analysis.* Unpublished manuscript, Department of Psychology, Michigan State University.

Johnson, J. A., Cheek, J. M., & Smither, R. (1983). The structure of empathy. *Journal of Personality and Social Psychology, 45,* 1299–1312.

Joreskog, K. G., & Sorbom, D. (1981). *Lisrel V: Analysis of linear structural relationships by maximum likelihood and least squares methods.* Chicago: International Education Services.

Krebs, D. (1975). Empathy and altruism. *Journal of Personality and Social Psychology, 32,* 1134–1146.

Mead, G. H. (1934). *Mind, self and society.* Chicago: University of Chicago Press.

Mehrabian, A., & Epstein, N. (1972). A measure of emotional empathy, *Journal of Personality, 50,* 525–543.

Miller, G. R., & Steinberg, M. (1975). *Between people: A new analysis of interpersonal communication.* Chicago: Science Research Associates.

Piaget, J. (1932). *The moral judgment of the child.* New York: Harcourt, Brace & World.

Piliavin, I. M., Rodin, J., & Piliavin, J. A. (1969). Good samaritanism: An underground phenomenon? *Journal of Personality and Social Psychology, 13,* 289–299.

Rogers, C. R. (1957). The necessary and sufficient conditions of therapeutic personality change. *Journal of Consulting Psychology, 21,* 95–103.

Smith, A. (1759). *Theory of moral sentiments*. London: A. Miller.

Spencer, H. (1870). *The principles of psychology*. London: Williams & Norgate.

Stiff, J.B. (1984). *Construct validity of two measures of empathy*. Unpublished manuscript, Department of Communication, Michigan State University.

Stotland, E. (1969). Exploratory investigations of empathy. In L. Berkowitz (Ed.), *Advances in experimental social psychology, Vol. 4* (pp. 271–314). New York: Academic Press.

Stotland, E., Mathews, K. E., Sherman, S. E. Hannson, R. O., & Richardson, B. E. (1978). *Empathy, fantasy, and helping*. Beverly Hills, CA: Sage.

Toi, M., & Batson, C. D. (1982). More evidence that empathy is a source of altruistic motivation. *Journal of Personality and Social Psychology, 43,* 281–292.

Glossary of Methods of Statistical Analysis

Analysis of Variance (ANOVA) is a technique for examining if three or more groups differ from one another. For example, if you have three groups (children, adolescents, and adults), ANOVA allows you to discover which one talks the most. The test used to compare the groups is called an F-test.

Chi-Square Analysis establishes whether two variables are associated (or related) to one another (e.g., complaint type and response type).

Cluster/Factor Analysis is a method for grouping variables together into a smaller number of categories. If you have a large number of variables, you may want to see if two or more of them actually combine or work together.

Confirmatory Factor Analysis is used to validate the grouping of items. For example, if you have twenty items on a survey of relational satisfaction and you think they will group into four variables (e.g., communication, conflict, decision making, and support), you can use confirmatory factor analysis to test this.

Correlations are used to determine if two or more variables are related to each other. A high correlation (e.g., .90 or 1.00) means they are very much related while a zero correlation may mean they are independent of each other (that is, unrelated). A positive correlation means that as the scores of one variable increase, the scores on the second variable also increase. Thus, if a person scores high on one variable (e.g., talkativeness), she or he is likely also to score high on the other variable (e.g., eye contact). A negative correlation means that as the score on one variable increases, the score on the second decreases. The closer the correlation is to either +1.00 or −1.00 (higher or lower), the more related the two variables are.

F-Test: See Analysis of Variance.

Log-Linear Analysis tests whether three or more variables are associated (or related) to one another. It reveals whether categories of each variable tend to occur together more frequently. For example, in a study of ethnicity, gender and income, one might determine that the variables Mexican-American, male, and medium income occur together more frequently.

Multiple Regression can be used to see if an outcome variable is related to another group of variables. For example, you might want to know how someone becomes highly satisfied with a conversation. Using multiple regression you can discover if the variables of topic, length of conversation, nonverbal contact, and empathy affect satisfaction.

Multivariate Analysis (MANOVA) tells us if groups differ on two or more variables. Thus if you have three groups (children, adolescents, and adults), you could determine who talks the most and which group maintains more eye contact during conversation.

Path Analysis is a way of testing a series of relationships on a model. For example, a model might predict that perspective taking will cause both empathic concern and emotional contagion, each of which will cause communicative responsiveness. In this way a system or collection of relationships can be tested.

Reliability represents how accurate a measure is. If a measure is highly reliable, then one can be confident that the scores are very accurate.

T-Tests tell if there is a difference between two groups. For example, you might want to determine if one group (e.g., males) had more eye contact during conversation than another group (e.g., females).

Validity represents the degree to which the method one uses to measure something actually measures it.

Bibliography of Interpersonal Communication

This bibliography is a biased sample of theory and research in interpersonal communication. It is presented to you as a resource for your work, but it is not all-inclusive. Items were selectively chosen.

The bibliography is divided into two main sections. Section 1 contains Theories of Interpersonal Communication and Section 2 contains Research in Interpersonal and Relationship Communication. Topics within each section are listed alphabetically.

Section 1: Theories of Interpersonal Communication

Section 2: Research in Interpersonal and Relationship Communication

SECTION 1: THEORIES OF INTERPERSONAL COMMUNICATION

Dialectic Approach

Altman, I., Vinsel, A., & Brown, B. (1981). Dialectic conceptions in social psychology: An application to social penetration and privacy regulation. In L. Berkowitz (Ed.), *Advances in experimental social psychology* (Vol. 14, pp. 76–100). New York: Academic Press.

Baxter, L. A. (1988). A dialectic perspective on communication strategies in relationship development. In S. W. Duck (Ed.), *A handbook of personal relationships.* New York: John Wiley & Sons.

Berelson, B. (1971). *Content analysis in communication research.* NY: Hafner.

Berger, P., & Kellner, H. (1964). Marriage and the construction of reality: An exercise in the microsociology of knowledge. *Diogenes, 46,* 12–13.

Bochner, A. P. (1981). Forming warm ideas. In C. Wilder-Mott & J. H. Weakland (Eds.), *Rigor and imagination: Essays from the legacy of Gregory Bateson.* New York: Praeger.

Holzner, B. (1968). *Reality construction in society.* Cambridge, MA: Schenkman.

Lofland, L. (1976). *Doing social life.* New York: John Wiley & Sons.

Masheter, C., & Harris, L. (1986). From divorce to friendship: A study of dialectic relationship development. *Journal of Social and Personal Relationships, 3,* 177–189.

Rawlins, W. K. (1983a). Negotiating close friendship: The dialectic of conjunctive freedoms. *Human Communication Research, 9,* 255–266.

Rawlins, W. K. (1983b). Openness as problematic in ongoing relationships: Two conversational dilemmas. *Communication Monographs, 50,* 1–13.

Rawlins, W. K., & Holl, M. (1987). The communicative achievement of friendship during adolescence: Predicaments of trust and violation. *Western Journal of Speech Communication, 51,* 345–363.

Rawlins, W. K., & Holl, M. R. (1988). Adolescents' interaction with parents and friends: Dialectics of temporal perspective and evaluation. *Journal of Social and Personal Relationships, 5,* 27–46.

Rawlins, W. K., Leibowitz, K., & Bochner, A. P. (1986). Affective and instrumental dimensions of best, equal, and unequal friendships. *Central States Speech Journal, 37,* 90–101.

Wiseman, J. P. (1986). Friendship: Bonds and binds in a voluntary relationship. *Journal of Social and Personal Relationships, 3,* 191–211.

Exchange Approach

Altman, I., & Taylor, D. A. (1973). *Social penetration: The development of interpersonal relationships.* New York: Holt, Rinehart and Winston.

Banks, S. P., Altendorf, D. M., Greene, J. O., & Cody, M. (1987). An examination of relationship disengagement: Perceptions, breakup strategies, and outcomes. *Western States Speech Journal, 51,* 19–41.

Berg, J. H., & McQuinn, R. D. (1986). Attraction and exchange in continuing and noncontinuing dating relationships. *Journal of Personality and Social Psychology, 50,* 942–952.

Clark, M. S., & Waddell, B. (1985). Perceptions of exploitation in communal and exchange relationships. *Journal of Social and Personal Relationships, 2,* 403–418.

Cline, R. J., & Musolf, K. E. (1985). Disclosure as social exchange: Anticipated length of relationship, sex roles, and disclosure intimacy. *Western Journal of Speech Communication, 49,* 43–56.

Cody, M. (1982). A typology of disengagement strategies and an examination of the role intimacy, reactions to inequity, and relational problems play in strategy selection. *Communication Monographs, 49,* 148–170.

Foa, U. G., & Foa, E. B. (1974). *Societal structures of the mind.* Springfield, IL: Charles Thomas.

Gergen, K. J. (1969). *The psychology of behavior exchange.* Reading, MA: Addison-Wesley.

Gudykunst, W. B., Yoon, Y-C, & Nishida, T. (1987). The influence of individualism-collectivism on perceptions of communication in ingroup and outgroup relationships. *Communication Monographs, 54,* 295–306.

Hays, R. B. (1984). The development and maintenance of friendship. *Journal of Social and Personal Relationships, 1,* 75–98.

Homans, G. (1961). *Social behavior: Its elementary forms.* New York: Harcourt, Brace & World.

Kayser, E., Schwinger, T., & Cohen, R. L. (1984). Laypersons' conceptions of social relationships: A test of contract theory. *Journal of Social and Personal Relationships, 1,* 433–459.

Kelley, H. H., & Thibaut, J. W. (1978). *Interpersonal relations.* New York: John Wiley & Sons.

Knapp. M. (1978). *Social intercourse: From greeting to goodbye.* Boston: Allyn & Bacon.

Lund, M. (1985). The development of investment and commitment scales for predicting continuity of personal relationships. *Journal of Social and Personal Relationships, 2,* 3–24.

O'Connell, L. (1984). An exploration of exchange in three social relationships: Kinship, friendship, and the marketplace. *Journal of Social and Personal Relationships, 1,* 333–346.

Roloff, M. E. (1981). *Interpersonal communication: The social exchange approach.* Beverly Hills, CA: Sage.

Shea, L., Thompson, L., & Blieszner, R. (1988). Resources in older adults' old and new friendships. *Journal of Social and Personal Relationships, 5,* 83–96.

Sunnafrank, M. (1986). Predicted outcome value during initial interactions: A reformulation of uncertainty reduction theory. *Human Communication Research, 13,* 3–33.

Thibaut, J. W., & Kelley, H. H. (1959). *The social psychology of groups.* New York: John Wiley & Sons.

Utne, M. K., Hatfield, E., Traupman, J., & Greenberger, D. (1984). Equity, marital satisfaction, and stability. *Journal of Social and Personal Relationships, 1,* 323–332.

Wilmot, W. W. (1980). *Dyadic communication: A transactional perspective* (2nd ed.). Reading, MA: Addison-Wesley.

Wright, P. H. (1984). Self-referent motivation and the intrinsic quality of friendship. *Journal of Social and Personal Relationships, 1,* 115–130.

Interpretive Approaches

Phenomenological Approaches

Ehrenhaus, P. (1988). Silence and symbolic expression. *Communication Monographs, 55,* 41–57.

McLeod, R. B. (1964). Phenomenology: A challenge to experimental psychology. In T. W. Wann (Ed.), *Behaviorism and phenomenology* (pp. 47–78). Chicago: University of Chicago Press.

Phillipson, M. (1973). Phenomenological philosophy and sociology. In P. Filmer, M. Phillipson, D. Silverman, & D. Walsh (Eds.), *New directions in sociological theory* (pp. 119–153). Cambridge, MA: MIT Press.

Rules

Argyle, M., & Henderson, M. (1984). The rules of friendship. *Journal of Social and Personal Relationships, 1,* 211–237.

Baxter, L. A. (1986). Gender differences in the heterosexual relationship rules embedded in break-up accounts. *Journal of Social and Personal Relationships, 3,* 289–306.

Brenders, D. A. (1987). Fallacies in the coordinated management of meaning: A philosophy of language critique of the hierarchical organization of coherent conversation and related theory. *Quarterly Journal of Speech, 73,* 329–348.

Collier, M. J. (1988). A comparison of conversations among and between domestic culture groups: How intra- and intercultural competencies vary. *Communication Quarterly, 36,* 122–144.

Collier, M. J., Ribeau, S., & Hecht, M. L. (1986). Intracultural rules and outcomes within three domestic cultural groups. *International Journal of Intercultural Relations, 10,* 439–457.

Cronen, V. E., Pearce, W. B., & Harris, L. (1982). The coordinated management of meaning: A theory of communication. In F.E.X. Dance (Ed.), *Human communication theory* (pp. 61–89). New York: Harper & Row.

Cronen, V. E., Pearce, W. B., & Snavely, L. M. (1979). A theory of rules-structure and types of episodes and a study of perceived enmeshment in undesired repetitive patterns (URPs). In D. Nimmo (Ed.), *Communication yearbook 3* (pp. 225–240). Beverly Hills, CA: Sage.

Cushman, D. P., Valentinsen, D., & Dietrich, D. (1982). A rules theory of interpersonal relationships. In F.E.X. Dance (Ed.), *Human communication theory* (pp. 90–120). New York: Harper & Row.

Duncan, S. (1973). Toward a grammar for dyadic conversation. *Semiotica, 9,* 29–46.

Fairhust, G. T., Green, S. G., & Snavely, B. K. (1984). Face support in controlling poor performance. *Human Communication Research, 11,* 272–295.

Fisher, D. V. (1986). Decision-making and self-disclosure. *Journal of Social and Personal Relationships, 3,* 323–336.

Gauld, A., & Shotter, J. (1977). *Human action and its psychological investigation.* London: Routledge and Kegan Paul.

Gergen, K. J. (1985). The social construction movement in modern psychology. *American Psychologist, 40,* 266–275.

Harre, R., & Secord, P. F. (1972). *The explanation of social behavior.* Oxford: Blackwell.

Harris, L. M. (1974). Why a perfect knowledge of all the rules one must know to act like a native cannot lead to the knowledge of how natives act. *Journal of Anthropological Research, 30,* 242–252.

Harris, L. M., & Sadeghi, A. R. (1987). Realizing: How facts are created in human interaction. *Journal of Social and Personal Relationships, 4,* 481–495.

Jones, S. E. (1986). Sex differences in touch communication. *Western Journal of Speech Communication, 50,* 227–241.

Knepprath, H. E. (1985). A test of Shimanoff's procedures for determining communication rules from behavior. *Central States Speech Journal, 36,* 201–207.

Krippendorff, K. (1971). Communication and the genesis of structure. *General Systems, 16,* 171–185.

Littlejohn, S. W. (1983). *Theories of human communication* (2nd ed., pp. 60–71). Belmont, CA: Wadsworth.

Morris, G. H. (1985). The remedial episode as a negotiation of rules. In R. L. Street & J. N. Cappella (Eds.), *Sequence and pattern in communicative behavior* (pp. 70–84). London: Edward Arnold.

Nofsinger, R. E. (1976). On answering questions indirectly: Some rules in the grammar of doing conversation. *Human Communication Research, 2,* 172–181.

Pearce, W. B. (1976). The coordinated management of meaning: A rules based theory of interpersonal communication. In G. R. Miller (Ed.), *Explorations in human communication* (pp. 9–16). Beverly Hills, CA: Sage.

Pearce, W. B., & Conklin, F. (1979). A model of hierarchical meanings in coherent conversations and a study of 'indirect responses.' *Communication Monographs, 46,* 75-87.

Pearce, W. B., & Cronen, V. E. (1980). *Communication, action, and meaning: The creation of social realities.* NY: Praeger.

Rabinow, P., & Sullivan, L. T. (Eds.). (1979). *Interpretive social science: A reader.* Berkeley: University of California Press.

Ricoeur, P. (1976). *Interpretation theory: Discourse and the surplus of meaning.* New Haven, CT: Yale University Press.

Sacks, H., Schegloff, E. A., & Jefferson, G. (1974). A simplest systematics for the organization of turn-taking for conversation. *Language, 50,* 696–735.

Sarbin, T. R., & Allen, V. L. (1968). Role theory. In G. Lindzey & E. Aronson (Eds.), *The handbook of social psychology* (Vol. 1, pp. 223–258). Reading, MA: Addison-Wesley.

Schall, M. S. (1983). A communication-rules approach to organizational communication. *Administrative Science Quarterly, 28,* 557–581.

Shimanoff, S. (1980). *Communication rules.* Beverly Hills, CA: Sage.

Shimanoff, S. B. (1987). Types of emotional disclosures and request compliance between spouses. *Communication Monographs, 54,* 85–100.

Wiemann, J. M., & Knapp, M. (1975). Turn-taking in conversations. *Journal of Communication, 25,* 75–92.

Cultural Approaches

Bantz, C. R. (1983). Naturalistic research traditions. In L. L. Putnam & M. E. Pacanowsky (Eds.), *Communication and organizations: An interpretive approach* (pp. 55–71). Beverly Hills, CA: Sage.

Berelson, B. (1971). *Content analysis in communication research*. New York: Hafner Publishing Co.

Black, M. (1962). *Models and metaphors*. Ithaca, NY: Cornell University Press.

Blumer, H. (1969). The methodological position of symbolic interactionism. *Symbolic Interactionism* (pp. 1–21). Englewood Cliffs, NJ: Prentice-Hall.

Bochner, A. P. (1981). Forming warm ideas. In C. Wilder-Mott & J. H. Weakland (Eds.), *Rigor and imagination: Essays from the legacy of Gregory Bateson* (pp. 65–81). New York: Praeger.

Brockreide, W. (1975). Where is argument? *Journal of the American Forensics Association, 11,* 179–182.

Burke, K. (1969). *A grammar of motives*. Berkeley: Univ. of California Press.

Geertz, C. (1973). Thick description: Toward an interpretive theory of culture. *The interpretation of cultures* (Ch. 1). New York: Basic Books.

Geertz, C. (1983). *Local knowledge*. New York: Basic Books.

Glaser, B. G., & Strauss, A. L. (1967). *The discovery of grounded theory*. Chicago: Aldine.

Goffman, E. (1959). *The presentation of self in everyday life*. Garden City, NY: Anchor.

Goffman, E. (1967). *Interaction ritual*. Garden City, NY: Anchor Book.

Honeck, R. P., & Hoffman, R. R. (1980). *Cognition and figurative language*. Hillsdale, NJ: Erlbaum.

Jick, T. (1983). Mixing qualitative and quantitative methods: Triangulation in action. In J. Van Maanen (Ed.), *Qualitative methodology* (pp. 135–148). Beverly Hills, CA: Sage.

Katriel, T., & Philipsen, G. (1981). "What we need is communication": "Communication" as a cultural category in some American speech. *Communication Monographs, 48,* 301–318.

Kuhn, T. S. (1979). *The structure of scientific revolutions* (2nd ed.). Chicago: University of Chicago Press.

Lakoff, G., & Johnson, M. (1980). *Metaphors we live by*. Chicago: University of Chicago Press.

Langer, S. K. (1979). *Philosophy in a new key*. Cambridge, MA: Harvard University Press.

Leiter, K. (1980). *A primer on ethnomethodology*. New York: Oxford University Press.

Lofland, J. (1976). *Doing social life*. New York: John Wiley & Sons.

O'Keefe, D. J. (1975). Logical positivism and the study of human communication. *Speech Monographs, 42,* 169–183.

Ortnoy, A. (1979). *Metaphor and thought*. Cambridge, MA: Harvard University Press.

Putnam, L. L. (1983). The interpretive perspective: An alternative to functionalism. In L. L. Putnam & M. E. Pacanowsky (Eds.), *Communication and organizations: An interpretive approach* (pp. 31–54). Beverly Hills, CA: Sage.

Richards, I. A. (1936). *The philosophy of rhetoric*. New York: Oxford University Press.

Van Maanen, J. (Ed.). (1983). *Qualitative methodology*. Beverly Hills, CA: Sage.

Interpretive Approaches to Interpersonal Relationships

Baxter, L. A. (1987). Symbols of relationship identity in relationship cultures. *Journal of Social and Personal Relationships, 4,* 261–280.

Bell, R. A., Buerkel-Rothfuss, N. L., & Gore, K. E. (1987). Did you bring the yarmulke for the cabbage patch kid?: The idiomatic communication of young lovers. *Human Communication Research, 14,* 47–68.

Berger, P., & Kellner, H. (1964). Marriage and the construction of reality: An exercise in the microsociology of knowledge. *Diogenes, 46,* 12–13.

Deetz, S., & Mumby, D. (1985). Metaphors, information, and power. *Information and Behavior, 1,* 369–386.

Hecht, M. L. (1984). Satisfying communication and relationship labels: Intimacy and length of relationship as perceptual frames of naturalistic conversations. *Western Journal of Speech Communication, 48,* 201–216.

Hecht, M. L., & Ribeau, S. (1987). Afro-American identity labels and communication effectiveness. *Journal of Language and Social Psychology, 6,* 319–326.

Hecht, M. L., & Ribeau, S. (in press). Socio-cultural roots of ethnic identity: A look at Black America. *Journal of Black Studies*.

Hoffman, L. (1981). *Foundations of family therapy*. NY: Basic Books.

Hopper, R., Knapp, M. L., & Scott, L. (1981). Couples' personal idioms: Exploring intimate talk. *Journal of Communication, 31,* 23–33.

Marston, P. J., Hecht, M. L., & Robers, T. (1987). 'True love ways': The subjective experience and communication of romantic love. *Journal of Social and Personal Relationships, 4,* 387–407.

McCall, G., & Simmons, J. (1982). *Social psychology: A sociological approach*. New York: Free Press.

Oring, E. (1984). Dyadic traditions. *Journal of Folklore Research, 21,* 19–28.

Owen, W. F. (1985). Thematic metaphors in relational communication: A conceptual framework. *Western Journal of Speech Communication, 49,* 1–13.

Reis, D. (1981). *The family's construction of reality*. Cambridge, MA: Harvard University Press.

Stephen, T., & Enholm, D. K. (1987). On linguistic and social forms: Correspondences between metaphoric and intimate relationships. *Western Journal of Speech Communication, 51,* 329–344.

Weick, K. E. (1983). Organizational communication: Toward a research agenda. In L. L. Putnam & M. Pacanowsky (Eds.), *Communication and organizations: An interpretive approach* (pp. 12–39). Beverly Hills, CA: Sage.

Wood, J. (1982). Communication and relational culture: Bases for the study of human relationships. *Communication Quarterly, 30,* 75–83.

Interpretive Approaches to Organizations and Groups

Berg, P. (1985). Organizational change as a symbolic transformation process. In P. Frost, L. Moore, M. Louis, C. Lundberg, & J. Martin (Eds.), *Organizational culture* (pp. 281–300). Beverly Hills, CA: Sage.

Borman, E. G. (1983). Symbolic convergence: Organizational communication and culture. In L. L. Putnam & M. E. Pacanowsky (Eds.), *Communication and organizations: An interpretive approach* (pp. 99–122). Beverly Hills, CA: Sage.

Carbaugh, D. (1985). Cultural communication and organizing. In W. B. Gudykunst, L. P. Stewart, & S. Ting Toomey (Eds.), *Communication, culture and organizational processes* (pp. 30–47). Newbury Park, CA: Sage.

Carbaugh, D. (1988). Cultural terms and tensions in the speech at a television station. *Western Journal of Speech Communication, 52,* 216–237.

Eisenberg, E. M. (1986). Meaning and interpretation in organizations. *Quarterly Journal of Speech, 72,* 88–97.

Eisenberg, E. M., & Riley, P. A. (in press). Organizational symbolism and sense-making. In G. Goldhaber & G. Barnett (Eds.), *Handbook of organizational communication.* Norwood, NJ: Ablex.

Fine, G. (1979). Small groups and culture creation: The idioculture of little league baseball teams. *American Sociological Review, 44,* 733–745.

Fine, G. A. (1986). Friendships in the work place. In V. J. Derlega & B. A. Winstead (Eds.), *Friendship and social interaction* (pp. 185–206). New York: Springer-Verlag.

Frost, P., Moore, L., Louis, M., Lundberg, C., & Martin, J. (Eds.). (1985). *Organizational culture.* Beverly Hills, CA: Sage.

Hebden, J. E. (1975). Patterns of work identification. *Sociology of Work and Occupations, 2,* 107–132.

Koch, S., & Deetz, S. (1981). Metaphor analysis of social reality in organizations. *Journal of Applied Communication, 9,* 1–15.

Pacanowsky, M. E., & O'Donnell-Trujillo, N. (1983). Organizational communication as cultural performance. *Communication Monographs, 50,* 126–147.

Pettigrew, A. M. (1979). On studying organizational cultures. *Administrative Science Quarterly, 24,* 570–581.

Pondy, L. R. (1978). Leadership is a language game. In M. M. Lombardo & M. W. McCall, Jr. (Eds.), *Leadership: Where else can we go?* (pp. 87–99). Durham, NC: Duke University Press.

Putnam, L. L. (1983). The interpretive perspective: An alternative to functionalism. In L. L. Putnam & M. E. Pacanowsky (Eds.), *Communication and organizations: An interpretive approach* (pp. 31–54). Beverly Hills, CA: Sage.

Putnam, L. L., & Pacanowsky, M. E. (Eds.). (1983). *Communication and organizations: An interpretive approach.* Beverly Hills, CA and London: Sage.

Putnam, L. L., & Poole, M. S. (1987). Conflict and negotiation. In F. M. Jablin, L. L. Putnam, K. H. Roberts, & L. W. Porter (Eds.), *Handbook of organizational communication.* Newbury Park, CA: Sage.

Smircich, L. (1983). Implications for management theory. In L. L. Putnam & M. E. Pacanowsky (Eds.), *Communication and organizations: An interpretive approach* (pp. 221–241). Beverly Hills, CA: Sage.

Smircich, L., & Calas, M. B. (1987). Organizational culture: A critical assessment. In F. M. Jablin, L. L. Putnam, K. H. Roberts, & L. W. Porter (Eds.), *Handbook of organizational communication.* Newbury Park, CA: Sage.

Tomkins, P. K., & Cheney, G. (1983). Account analysis of organizations: Decision making and identification. In L. L. Putnam & M. E. Pacanowsky (Eds.), *Communication and organizations: An interpretive approach* (pp. 123–146). Beverly Hills, CA: Sage.

Trujillo, N. (1983). ''Performing'' Mintzberg's roles: The nature of managerial communication. In L. L. Putnam & M. E. Pacanowsky (Eds.), *Communication and organizations: An interpretive approach* (pp. 73–97). Beverly Hills, CA: Sage.

Social Cognition

Abbott, V., & Black, J. B. (1986). Goal-related inferences in comprehension. In J. A. Galambos, R. P. Abelson, & J. B. Black (Eds.), *Knowledge structures* (pp. 123–142). Hillsdale, NJ: Erlbaum.

Abelson, R. (1981). Psychological status of the script concept. *American Psychologist, 136,* 715–729.

Allen, J. J. (1986). A developmental approach to self-monitoring behavior. *Communication Monographs, 53,* 277–288.

Andersen, J. R. (1982). Acquisition of cognitive skill. *Psychological Review, 89,* 369–406.

Andrews, P. A. (1987). Gender differences in persuasive communication and attribution of success and failure. *Human Communication Research, 13,* 372–385.

Bandura, A. (1982). Self-efficacy mechanisms in human agency. *American Psychologist, 37,* 122–147.

Bandura, A. (1986). *Social foundations of thought and action: A social cognitive theory.* Englewood Cliffs, NJ: Prentice-Hall.

Baxter, L., & Philpott, J. (1982). Attribution-based strategies for initiating and terminating friendships. *Communication Quarterly, 30,* 217–224.

Berger, C. R. (1987). Planning and scheming: Strategies for initiating relationships. In R. Burnett, P. McGhee, & D. Clarke (Eds.), *Accounting for relationships: Social representations of interpersonal links* (pp. 158–174). London: Metheun.

Berger, C. R. (1988). Planning, affect and social action generation. In R. L. Donohew, H. Sypher, & E. T. Higgins (Eds.), *Communication, social cognition, and affect* (pp. 93–116). Hillsdale, NJ: Erlbaum.

Berger, C. R., & Bell, R. A. (1988). Plans and the initiation of social relationships. *Human Communication Research, 15,* 217–235.

Berger, C. R., & Douglas, W. (1981). Studies in interpersonal epistemology III: Anticipated interaction, self-monitoring, and observational context selection. *Communication Monographs, 48,* 183–196.

Berley, R. A., & Jacobson, N. S. (1984). Causal attributions in intimacy relationships: Toward a model of cognitive-behavioral therapy. In P. Kendall (Ed.), *Advances in cognitive-behavioral research and therapy* (Vol. 3, pp. 2–60). New York: Academic Press.

Booth-Butterfield, S. (1987). Action assembly theory and communication apprehension: A psychophysiological study. *Human Communication Research, 13,* 386–398.

Brand, M. (1984). *Intending and acting: Toward a naturalized action theory.* Cambridge, MA: MIT Press.

Burgoon, J. K., & Hale, J. L. (1988). Nonverbal expectancy violations: Model elaboration and application to immediacy behaviors. *Communication Monographs, 55,* 58–79.

Buttney, R. (1985). Accounts as a reconstruction of an event's context. *Communication Monographs, 52,* 57–77.

Cappella, J. M. (1979). Talk-silence sequences in informal conversations I. *Human Communication Research, 6,* 3–17.

Crocker, J., Fiske, S. T., & Taylor, S. F. (1984). Schematic basis of belief change. In J. R. Eiser (Ed.), *Attitudinal judgment* (pp. 197–226). New York: Springer-Verlag.

Dillard, J. P. (1987). Close relationships at work: Perceptions of the motives and performance of relational participants. *Journal of Social and Personal Relationships, 4,* 179–194.

Dillard, J. P. (1989). Types of influence goals in personal relationships. *Journal of Social and Personal Relationships, 6,* 293–308.

Doelger, J. A., Hewes, D. E., & Graham, M. L. (1986). Knowing when to 'second guess': The mindful analysis of messages. *Human Communication Research, 12,* 301–338.

Douglas, W. (1983). Scripts & self-monitoring: When does being a high self-monitor really make a difference? *Human Communication Research, 10,* 81–96.

Douglas, W. (1984). Initial interaction scripts: When knowing is behaving. *Human Communication Research, 11,* 203–220.

Douglas, W. (1985). Anticipated interaction and information seeking. *Human Communication Research, 12,* 243–258.

Douglas, W. (1987). Question-asking in same- and opposite-sex initial interactions: The effects of anticipated future interaction. *Human Communication Research, 14,* 230–245.

Erenhaus, P. (1982). Attribution theory: Implications for intercultural communication. In M. Burgoon (Ed.), *Communication yearbook 6* (pp. 721–734). Beverly Hills, CA: Sage.

Fehr, B. (in press). Prototype analysis of the concepts of love and commitment. *Journal of Personality and Social Psychology.*

Fenigstein, A., Scheier, M., & Buss, A. (1975). Public and private self-consciousness: Assessment and theory. *Journal of Consulting and Clinical Psychology, 43,* 522–527.

Fincham, F. D. (1985). Attributions in close relationships. In J. H. Harvey & G. Weary (Eds.), *Attribution: Basic issues and applications* (pp. 203–234). Orlando, FL: Academic Press.

Fincham, F. D., & Bradbury, T. N. (1987). The impact of attributions in marriage: A longitudinal analysis. *Journal of Personality and Social Psychology, 53,* 510–517.

Fischoff, B., Slovic, P., & Lichtenstein, S. (1977). Knowing with certainty: The appropriateness of extreme confidence. *Journal of Experimental Psychology: Human Perceptions and Performance, 3,* 552–564.

Fiske, S. T., & Linville, T. (1980). What does the schema concept buy us? *Personality and Social Psychology Bulletin, 6,* 543–557.

Fiske, S. T., & Taylor, S. E. (1984). *Social cognition.* Reading, MA: Addison-Wesley.

Fletcher, G.J.O., Danilovics, P., Fernandez, G., Peterson, D., & Reeder, G. D. (1986). Attributional complexity: An individual difference measure. *Journal of Personality and Social Psychology, 51,* 875–884.

Fletcher, G.J.O., Fincham, F. D., Carmer, L., & Heron, N. (1987). The role of attributions in the development of dating relationships. *Journal of Personality and Social Psychology, 53,* 481–489.

Folger, J. P., & Woodall, W. G. (1982). Nonverbal cues as linguistic context: An information-processing view. In M. Burgoon (Ed.), *Communication yearbook 6* (pp. 63–91). Beverly Hills, CA: Sage.

Franzoi, S. L., Davis, M. H., & Young, R. D. (1985). The effects of private self-consciousness and perspective taking on satisfaction in close relationships. *Journal of Personality and Social Psychology, 48,* 1584–1594.

Greene, J. O. (1984). Evaluating cognitive explanations of communication phenomena. *Quarterly Journal of Speech, 70,* 241–254.

Greene, J. O., & Cody, M. J. (1985). On thinking and doing: Cognitive science and the production of social behavior. *Journal of Language and Social Psychology, 4,* 157–170.

Greene, J. O., O'Hair, D., Cody, M. J., & Yen, K. (1985). Planning and control of behavior during deception. *Human Communication Research, 11,* 335–364.

Greene, J. O., & Sparks, G. G. (1983). Explication and test of a cognitive model of communication apprehension: A new look at an old construct. *Human Communication Research, 9,* 349–366.

Gudykunst, W. B. (1985). The influence of cultural similarity, type of relationship, and self-monitoring on uncertainty reduction processes. *Communication Monographs, 52,* 203–217.

Harvey, J. H., Wells, G. L., & Alvarez, M. D. (1978). Attribution in the context of conflict and separation in close relationships. In J. Harvey, W. Ickes, & R. Kidd (Eds.), *New directions in attribution research* (Vol. 2, pp. 235–260). Hillsdale, NJ: Erlbaum.

Helgeson, V. S., Shaver, P., & Dyer, M. (1987). Prototypes of intimacy and distance in same-sex and opposite-sex relationships. *Journal of Social and Personal Relationships, 4,* 195–233.

Hewes, D. E., Graham, M. L., Doelger, J., & Pavitt, C. (1985). 'Second guessing': Message interpretation in social networks. *Human Communication Research, 11,* 299–334.

Hewes, D. E., & Planalp, S. (1982). There is nothing as useful as a good theory . . . : The influence of social knowledge on interpersonal communication. In M. E. Roloff & C. R. Berger (Eds.), *Social cognition and communication* (pp. 107–150). Newbury Park, CA: Sage.

Hewes, D. E., & Planalp, S. (1987). The place of the individual in communication science. In C. R. Berger & S. H. Chaffee (Eds.), *Handbook of communication science* (pp. 146–183). Newbury Park, CA: Sage.

Hobbs, J. R., & Evans, D. A. (1980). Conversation as planned behavior. *Cognitive Science, 3,* 275–310.

Holzworth-Munroe, A., & Jacobson, N. S. (1985). Causal attributions of married couples: When do they search for causes? What do they conclude when they do? *Journal of Personality and Social Psychology, 48,* 1398–1412.

Kellerman, K. (1986). Anticipation of future interaction and information exchange in initial interaction. *Human Communication Research, 13,* 41–75.

Klinger, E. (1985). Missing links in action theory. In M. Frese & J. Sabini (Eds.), *Goal directed behavior.* Hillsdale, NJ: Erlbaum.

Lindsey, A. E., & Greene, J. O. (1987). Social tendencies and social knowledge: Self-monitoring differences in the representation and recall of social knowledge. *Communication Monographs, 54,* 381–395.

Lloyd, S. A., & Cate, R. M. (1985). Attributions associated with significant turning points in premarital relationship development and dissolution. *Journal of Social and Personal Relationships, 2,* 419–436.

Locke, E., & Pennington, D. (1982). Reasons and other causes: Their role in attribution processes. *Journal of Personality and Social Psychology, 42,* 212–243.

Miller, G. A., Galanter, E., & Pribram, K. H. (1960). *Plans and the structure of behavior.* New York: Holt, Rinehart, and Winston.

Miller, G. R., deTurck, M. A. & Kalbfleisch, P. J. (1983). Self-monitoring, rehearsal, and deceptive communication. *Human Communication Research, 10,* 97–118.

Morgan, D. L. (1986). Personal relationships as an interface between social networks and social cognitions. *Journal of Social and Personal Relationships, 3,* 403–422.

Nesbitt, R., & Wilson, T. (1977). Telling more than we know: Verbal reports on mental processes. *Psychological Review, 84,* 231–259.

Owen, W. F. (1985). Thematic metaphors in relational communication: A conceptual framework. *Western Journal of Speech Communication, 49,* 1–13.

Pavitt, C., & Haight, L. (1985). The 'competent communicator' as a cognitive prototype. *Human Communication Research, 12,* 225–242.

Pavitt, C., & Haight, L. (1986a). Implicit theories of communicative behavior: The semantics of social behavior. *Central State Speech Journal, 37,* 204–219.

Pavitt, C., & Haight, L. (1986b). Implicit theories of communicative competence: Situational and competence level differences in judgments of prototype and target. *Communication Monographs, 53,* 221–235.

Pettigrew, T. F. (1979). The ultimate attribution error. *Journal of Personality and Social Psychology, 42,* 1051–1068.

Planalp, S. (1985). Relational schemata: A test of alternative forms of relational knowledge as guides to communication. *Human Communication Research, 12,* 3–29.

Planalp, S., & Hewes, D. (1982). A cognitive approach to communication theory: Cognito ergo dico? In M. Burgoon (Ed.), *Communication yearbook 5* (pp. 49–77). New Brunswick, NJ: Transaction-International Communication Association.

Planalp, S., Rutherford, D. K., & Honeycutt, J. M. (1988). Events that increase uncertainty in personal relationships II: Replication and extension. *Human Communication Research, 14,* 516–547.

Ray, G. B. (1986). Vocally cued personality prototypes: An implicit personality theory approach. *Communication Monographs, 53,* 266–276.

Roloff, M. E., & Berger, C. R. (Eds.). (1982). *Social cognition and communication.* Newbury Park, CA: Sage.

Rule, B. G., Bisanz, G. L., & Kohn, M. (1985). Anatomy of a persuasive schema: Target, goals, and strategies. *Journal of Personality and Social Psychology, 48,* 1127–1140.

Schank, R. C., & Abelson, R. P. (1977). *Scripts, plans, goals, and understanding.* Hillsdale, NJ: Erlbaum.

Schneider, D. J., Hastorf, A. H., & Ellsworth, P. C. (1979). *Person perception* (2nd ed.). Reading, MA: Addison-Wesley.

Shaver, P., Schwartz, J. Kirson, D., & O'Connor, C. (1987). Emotion knowledge: Further exploration of a prototype approach. *Journal of Personality and Social Psychology, 52,* 1061–1086.

Sillars, A. L. (1982). Attribution and communication: Are people "naive" scientists or just naive? In M. E. Roloff & C. R. Berger (Eds.), *Social cognition and communication* (pp. 73–106). Beverly Hills, CA: Sage.

Smith, M. J. (1982). Cognitive schema theory and the perseverance and attenuation of unwarranted empirical beliefs. *Communication Monographs, 49,* 115–126.

Sparks, G. (1986). An action assembly approach to predicting emotional responses to frightening mass media. *Central States Speech Journal, 37,* 102–112.

Stafford, L., Burggraf, C. S., & Sharkley, W. F. (1987). Conversational memory: The effects of time, recall mode, and memory expectancies on remembrances of natural conversations. *Human Communication Research, 14,* 203–229.

Stafford, L., & Daly, J. A. (1984). Conversation memory: The effects of recall mode and memory expectancies on remembrances of natural conversations. *Human Communication Research, 10,* 379–402.

Stephen, T. (1987). Attribution and adjustment to relationship termination. *Journal of Social and Personal Relationships, 4,* 47–61.

Tracy, K. (1982). On getting the point: Distinguishing 'issues' from 'events,' an aspect of conversational coherence. In M. Burgoon (Ed.), *Communication yearbook 5* (pp. 279–301). New Brunswick, NJ: Transaction-International Communication Association.

Tracy, K. (1984). The effect of multiple goals on conversational relevance and topic shift. *Communication Monographs, 51,* 274–287.

Weber, R., & Crocker, J. (1983). Cognitive processes in the revision of stereotypic beliefs. *Journal of Personality and Social Psychology, 45,* 961–977.

Weiner, B. (1985). "Spontaneous" causal thinking. *Psychological Bulletin, 97,* 74–84.

Wilson, S. R., & Kramer, K. K. (1986). Attitude object prototypicality, attitudinal confidence, and attitude-behavioral intention consistency: A cognitive view of the attitude-behavior relationship. *Central States Speech Journal, 37,* 225–238.

Woodall, W. G., & Folger, J. P. (1985). Nonverbal cue context and episodic memory: On the availability and endurance of nonverbal behaviors as retrieval cues. *Communication Monographs, 52,* 319–333.

Wyer, R. S., & Srull, T. K. (Eds.). (1984). *Handbook of social cognition.* Hillsdale, NJ: Erlbaum.

Constructivism

Applegate, J. L. (1982). The impact of construct system development in communication and impression formation in persuasive contexts. *Communication Monographs, 49,* 277–289.

Bannister, D., & Mair, M. (1968). *Evaluation of personal constructs.* London: Academic Press.

Beatty, M. J. (1987). Erroneous assumptions underlying Burleson's critique. *Communication Quarterly, 35,* 329–333.

Beatty, M. J., & Payne, S. K. (1984). Loquacity and quantity of constructs as predictors of social perspective-taking. *Communication Quarterly, 32,* 207–210.

Burleson, B. A., Applegate, J. L., & Neuwirth, C. M. (1981). Is cognitive complexity loquacity?: A reply to Powers, Jordan & Street. *Human Communication Research, 7,* 212, 225.

Burleson, B. R. (1984). Role-taking and communication skills in childhood: Why they *aren't* related and what can be done about it. *Western Journal of Speech Communication, 48,* 155–170.

Burleson, B. R., & Samter, W. (1985). Consistencies in theoretical and naive evaluations of comforting messages. *Communication Monographs, 52,* 103–123.

Burleson, B. R., Waltman, M. S., & Samter, W. (1987). More evidence that cognitive complexity is *not* loquacity: A reply to Beatty and Payne. *Communication Quarterly, 35,* 317–328.

Carrocci, N. M. (1987). Perceiving and responding to interpersonal conflict. *Central States Speech Journal, 36,* 215–229.

Chandler, M. J. (1973). Egocentrism and antisocial behavior. *Developmental Psychology, 9,* 326–32.

Clark, R. A., O'Dell, L. L., & Willinganz, S. (1986). The development of compromising as an alternative to persuasion. *Central States Speech Journal, 37,* 220–224.

Daly, J. A., Bell, R. A., Glenn, P. J., & Lawrence, S. (1985). Conceptualizing conversational complexity. *Human Communication Research, 12,* 30–53.

Delia, J. G. (1975). Constructivism and the study of human communication. *Quarterly Journal of Speech, 63,* 66–83.

Delia, J. G., & Clark, R. A. (1977). Cognitive complexity, social perception, and the development of listener-adapted communication in six-, eight-, ten-, and twelve-year old boys. *Communication Monographs, 44,* 326–345.

Delia, J. G., Kline, S. L., & Burleson, B. R. (1979). The development of persuasive communication strategies in kindergartners through twelfth-graders. *Communication Monographs, 46,* 241–256.

Delia, J. G., O'Keefe, B. J., & O'Keefe, D. J. (1982). The constructivist approach to communication. In F.E.X. Dance (Ed.), *Human communication theory* (pp. 147–191). New York: Harper and Row.

Duck, S. (1973). *Personal relationships and personal constructs: A study of friendship formation.* London: John Wiley & Sons.

Duck, S. W., & Spencer, C. (1972). Personal constructs and friendship formation. *Journal of Personality and Social Psychology, 23,* 40–45.

Feffer, M. H., & Suchotliff, L. (1966). Decentering implications of social interaction. *Journal of Personal and Social Psychology, 4,* 415–422.

Flavell, J. (1968). *The development of role-taking and communication skills in children,* New York: John Wiley & Sons.

Hale, C. L. (1982). An investigation of the relationship between cognitive complexity and listener-adapted communication. *Central States Speech Journal, 33,* 339–344.

Kelly, G. (1963). *A theory of personality.* New York: Norton.

Matefy, R. (1972). Attitude change induced by role playing as a function of improvisation and role-taking skill. *Journal of Personal and Social Psychology, 24,* 343–350.

Neimeyer, G. J. (1984). Cognitive complexity and marital satisfaction. *Journal of Social and Clinical Psychology, 2,* 258–263.

Neimeyer, G. J., & Neimeyer, R. A. (1981). Personal constructs perspectives on cognitive assessment. In T. Merluzzi, C. Glass, & M. Genest (Eds.), *Cognitive assessment* (pp. 188–232). New York: Guilford.

Neimeyer, G. J., & Neimeyer, R. A. (1985). Relational trajectories: A personal construct contribution. *Journal of Social and Personal Relationships, 2,* 325–350.

Neimeyer, R. A., & Mitchell, K. A. (1988). Similarity and attraction: A longitudinal study. *Journal of Social and Personal Relationships, 5,* 131–148.

Neuliep, J. W., & Hazelton, V., Jr. (1986). Enhanced conversational recall and reduced conversational interference as a function of cognitive complexity. *Human Communication Research, 13,* 211–224.

O'Keefe, D. J., & Delia, J. G. (1981). Construct differentiation and the relationship of attitudes and behavioral intentions, *Communication Monographs, 48,* 146–157.

O'Keefe, D. J., & Sypher, H. E. (1981). Cognitive complexity measures and the relationship of cognitive complexity to communication. *Human Communication Research, 8,* 72–92.

Powers, W. G., Jordan, W. J., Gurley, K., & Linstrom, E. (1986). Attributions toward cognitively complex sources based on message samples. *Communication Research Reports, 3,* 110–114.

Powers, W. G., Jordan, W. J., & Street, R. L. (1979). Language indices in the measurement of cognitive complexity: Is complexity loquacity? *Human Communication Research, 6,* 69–73.

Rubin, K. H. (1973). Egocentrism in child: A unitary construct. *Child Development, 44,* 102–110.

Rubin, R. B., & Henzl, S. A. (1984). Cognitive complexity, communication competence, and verbal ability. *Communication Quarterly, 32,* 263–270.

Samter, W., & Burleson, B. R. (1984). Cognitive and motivational influences on spontaneous comforting behavior. *Human Communication Research, 11,* 231–260.

Samter, W., Burleson, B. R., & Murphy, L. B. (1987). Comforting conversations: The effects of strategy type on evaluations of messages and message producers. *Southern Speech Communication Journal, 3,* 263–284.

Shantz, C. U., & Wilson, K. E. (1972). Training communication skills in young children. *Child Development, 43,* 693–698.

Stiff, J. B., Dillard, J. P., Somera, L., Kim, H., & Sleight, C. (1988). Empathy, communication, and prosocial behavior. *Communication Monographs, 55,* 198–213.

Uncertainty Reduction

Berger, C. R. (1979). Beyond initial interactions. In H. Giles & R. St. Claire (Eds.), *Language and social psychology* (pp. 122–144). Oxford: Basil Blackwell.

Berger, C. R. (1986). Response: Uncertain outcome values in predicted relationships: Uncertainty reduction theory then and now. *Human Communication Research, 13,* 34–38.

Berger, C. R., & Bradac, J. J. (1982). *Language and social knowledge: Uncertainty in interpersonal relations.* London: Edward Arnold.

Berger, C. R., & Calabrese, R. J. (1975). Some explorations in initial interactions and beyond: Toward a developmental theory of interpersonal communication. *Human Communication Research, 1,* 99–112.

Gudykunst, W. B. (1985). The influence of cultural similarity, type of relationship, and self-monitoring on uncertainty reduction processes. *Communication Monographs, 52,* 203–217.

Gudykunst, W. B., & Hammer, M. (1988). The influence of social identity and intimacy of interethnic relationships on uncertainty reduction processes. *Human Communication Research, 14,* 569–601.

Gudykunst, W. B., & Nishida, T. (1986). Attributional confidence in low- and high-context cultures. *Human Communication Research, 12,* 525–550.

Gudykunst, W. B., Nishida, T., & Chua, E. (1986). Uncertainty reduction in Japanese-North American dyads. *Communication Research Reports, 3,* 39–46.

Gudykunst, W. B., Sodetani, L. L., & Sonoda, K. T. (1987). Uncertainty reduction in Japanese-American/Caucasian relationships in Hawaii. *Western Journal of Speech Communication, 51,* 256–278.

Gudykunst, W. B., Yang, S-M., & Nishida, T. (1985). A cross-cultural test of uncertainty reduction theory: Comparisons of acquaintance, friends, and dating relationships in Japan, Korea, and the United States. *Human Communication Research, 11,* 407–454.

Kellerman, K. (1986). Anticipation of future interaction and information exchange in initial interaction. *Human Communication Research, 13,* 41–75.

Livingston, K. R. (1980). Love as a process of reducing uncertainty-cognitive theory. In K. Pope (Ed.), *On love and loving* (pp. 133–151). San Francisco: Jossey Bass.

Parks, M. R., & Adelman, M. B. (1983). Communication networks and the development of romantic relationships: An expansion of uncertainty reduction theory. *Human Communication Research, 10,* 55–79.

Planalp, S., & Honeycutt, J. M. (1985). Events that increase uncertainty in personal relationships. *Human Communication Research, 11*, 593–604.

Planalp, S., Rutherford, D. K., & Honeycutt, J. M. (1988). Events that increase uncertainty in personal relationships II: Replication and extension. *Human Communication Research, 14*, 516–547.

Sunnafrank, M. (1986a). Predicted outcome value during initial interactions: A reformulation of uncertainty reduction theory. *Human Communication Research, 13*, 3–33.

Sunnafrank, M. (1986b). Rejoinder: Predicted outcome values: Just now and then? *Human Communication Research, 13*, 39–40.

Systems Theory

Antill, J. K. (1983). Sex role complementarity versus similarity in married couples. *Journal of Personality and Social Psychology, 45*, 145–155.

Bateson, G. (1935). Culture, contact, and schismogenesis. *Man, 35*, 178–183.

Bavelas, J. B., & Smith, B. J. (1982). A method for scaling verbal disqualification. *Human Communication Research, 8*, 214–227.

Bernal, G., & Baker, J. (1979). Toward a metacommunicational framework of couple interaction. *Family Process, 18*, 293–302.

Collier, M. J., Ribeau, S., & Hecht, M. L. (1986). Intracultural rules and outcomes within three domestic cultural groups. *International Journal of Intercultural Relations, 10*, 439–457.

Courtright, J. A., Millar, F. E., & Rogers-Millar, L. E. (1979). Domineeringness and dominance: Replication and expansion. *Communication Monographs, 46*, 179–192.

Cusella, L. P. (1987). Feedback, motivation, and performance. In F. M. Jablin, L. L. Putnam, K. H. Roberts, & L. W. Porter (Eds.), *Handbook of organizational communication: An interdisciplinary perspective* (pp. 624–678). Newbury Park, CA: Sage.

Dansereau, F., & Markham, S. E. (1987). Superior-subordinate communication: Multiple levels of analysis. In F. M. Jablin, L. L. Putnam, K. H. Roberts, & L. W. Porter (Eds.), *Handbook of organizational communication: An interdisciplinary perspective* (pp. 343–388). Newbury Park, CA: Sage.

Ellis, D. G. (1979). Relational control in two group systems. *Communication Monographs, 46*, 153–166.

Fine, G. A. (1986). Friendships in the workplace. In V. L. Derlega & B. A. Winstead (Eds.), *Friendship and social interaction* (pp. 185–206). New York: Springer-Verlag.

Fisher, B. A. (1982). The pragmatic perspective of human communication. In F.E.X. Dance (Ed.), *Human communication theory* (pp. 192–219). New York: Harper and Row.

Fisher, B. A. (1983). Differential effects of sexual composition and interactional context on interactional patterns in dyads. *Human Communication Research, 9*, 225–238.

Fisher, B. A., & Drecksel, G. L. (1983). A cyclical model of developing relationships: A study of relational control interaction. *Communication Monographs, 50*, 66–78.

Gottman, J. (1979). *Marital interaction: Experimental investigations.* New York: Academic Press.

Hawes, L. C. (1973). Elements of a model for communication processes. *Quarterly Journal of Speech, 59*, 11–21.

Huber, G. P., & Daft, R. L. (1987). The information environments of organizations. In F. M. Jablin, L. L. Putnam, K. H. Roberts, & L. W. Porter (Eds.), *Handbook of organizational communication: An interdisciplinary perspective* (pp. 130–164). Newbury Park, CA: Sage.

Jablin, F. M. (1987). Formal organizational structure. In F. M. Jablin, L. L. Putnam, K. H. Roberts, & L. W. Porter (Eds.), *Handbook of organizational communication: An interdisciplinary perspective* (pp. 389–419). Newbury Park, CA: Sage.

Johnson, M. P., & Leslie, L. (1982). Couple involvement and network structure: A test of the dyadic withdrawal hypothesis. *Social Psychology Quarterly, 45*, 34–43.

Katz, D., & Kahn, R. L. (1978a). Communication, feedback processes, and evaluation research. *The social psychology of organizations* (2nd ed., Ch. 14, pp. 427–473). New York: John Wiley & Sons.

Katz, D., & Kahn, R. L. (1978b). Organizations and the systems concept. *The social psychology of organizations* (2nd ed., Ch. 2, pp. 17–34). New York: John Wiley & Sons.

Korkoff, L. J., Gottman, J. M., & Roy, A. K. (1988). Blue-collar and white-collar marital interaction and communication orientation. *Journal of Social and Personal Relationships, 5*, 201–221.

Milardo, R. M. (1982). Friendship networks in developing relationships: Converging and diverging social environments. *Social Psychology Quarterly, 45*, 162–172.

Monge, P. R. (1973). Theory construction in the study of human communication: The systems paradigm. *Journal of Communication, 23*, 5–16.

Monge, P. R. (1977). The systems perspective as a theoretical basis for the study of human communication. *Communication Quarterly, 25*, 19–29.

Monge, P. R. (1982). Systems theory and research in the study of organizational communication: The correspondence problem. *Human Communication Research, 8*, 245–261.

Monge, P. R., & Eisenberg, E. M. (1987). Emergent communication networks. In F. M. Jablin, L. L. Putnam, K. H. Roberts, & L. W. Porter (Eds.), *Handbook of organizational communication: An interdisciplinary perspective* (pp. 304–342). Newbury Park, CA: Sage.

Morgan, D. L. (1986). Personal relationships as an interface between social networks and social cognitions. *Journal of Social and Personal Relationships, 3*, 403–422.

O'Donnell-Trujillo, N. (1981). Relational communication: A comparison of coding systems. *Communication Monographs, 48*, 91–105.

O'Reilly, C. A., Chatman, J. A., & Anderson, J. C. (1987). Message flow and decision making. In F. M. Jablin, L. L. Putnam, K. H. Roberts, & L. W. Porter (Eds.), *Handbook of organizational communication: An interdisciplinary perspective* (pp. 600–623). Newbury Park, CA: Sage.

Parks, M. R., & Adelman, M. B. (1984). Communication networks and the development of romantic relationships: An expansion of uncertainty reduction theory. *Human Communication Research, 10,* 55–79.

Parks, M. R., Stan, C., & Eggert, L. (1983). Romantic involvement and social network involvement. *Social Psychology Quarterly, 46,* 116–131.

Rogers, E. M., & Agarwala-Rogers, R. (1976). Communication networks in organizations. *Communication in organizations* (Ch. 5). New York: Free Press.

Rogers-Millar, L. E., & Farace, R. V. (1975). Analysis of relational communication in dyads: New measurement procedures. *Human Communication Research, 1,* 222–239.

Rogers-Millar, L. E., & Millar, F. E. (1979). Domineeringness and dominance: A transactional view. *Human Communication Research, 5,* 238–246.

Stohl, C., & Redding, W. C. (1987). Messages and message exchange processes. In F. M. Jablin, L. L. Putnam, K. H. Roberts, & L. W. Porter (Eds.), *Handbook of organizational communication: An interdisciplinary perspective* (pp. 451–502). Newbury Park, CA: Sage.

Watzlawick, P., Beavin, J., & Jackson, D. (1967). *Pragmatics of human communication.* New York: Norton.

Wilder, C. (1979). The Palo Alto group: Difficulties and directions of the interactional view for human communication research. *Human Communication Research, 5,* 171–186.

Section 2:1 Research in Interpersonal and Relationship Communication

Attraction

Bell, R. A., & Daly, J. (1984). The affinity-seeking function of communication. *Communication Monographs, 51,* 91–115.

Bell, R. A., & Gonzalez, M. C. (1988). Loneliness, negative life events, and the provisions of social relationships. *Communication Quarterly, 36,* 1–15.

Bell, R. A., Tremblay, S. W., & Buerkel-Rothfuss, N. L. (1987). Interpersonal attraction as a communication accomplishment: Development of a measure of affinity-seeking competence. *Western Journal of Speech Communication, 51,* 1–18.

Berg, J. H., & McQuinn, R. D. (1986). Attraction and exchange in continuing and noncontinuing dating relationships. *Journal of Personality and Social Psychology, 50,* 942–952.

Berscheid, E. (1985). Interpersonal attraction. In G. Lindzey & E. Aronson (Eds.), *The handbook of social psychology* (pp. 413–484). New York: Random House.

Broome, B. J. (1983). The attraction paradigm revisited: Responses to dissimilar others. *Human Communication Research, 10,* 137–153.

Canary, D. J., & Spitzberg, B. H. (1987). Appropriateness and effectiveness perceptions of conflict strategies. *Human Communication Research, 14,* 93–118.

Dillard, J. P., & Witteman, H. (1985). Romantic relationships at work: Organizational and personal influences. *Human Communication Research, 12,* 99–116.

Doyle, M. V. (1985). The rhetoric of romance: A fantasy theme analysis of Barbara Cartland novels. *Southern States Speech Journal, 51,* 24–48.

Duran, R. L., & Kelly, L. (1988). The influence of communicative competence on perceived task, social, and physical attraction. *Communication Quarterly, 36,* 41–49.

Erwin, P. G., & Calev, A. (1984). Beauty: More than skin deep? *Journal of Social and Personal Relationships, 1,* 359–362.

Koester, R., & Wheeler, L. (1988). Self-presentation in personal advertisements: The influence of implicit notions of attraction and role expectations. *Journal of Social and Personal Relationships, 5,* 149–160.

Montgomery, B. M. (1986). Interpersonal attraction as a function of open communication and gender. *Communication Research Reports, 3,* 140–145.

Murstein, B. (1980). Mate selection in the 1970s. *Journal of Marriage and the Family, 42,* 777–792.

Powers, W. G., Jordon, W. J., Gurley, K., & Lindstrom, E. (1986). Attributions toward communicatively complex sources based upon message samples. *Communication Research Reports, 3,* 110–114.

Riggio, R. E., & Woll, S. B. (1984). The role of nonverbal cues and physical attractiveness in the selection of dating partners. *Journal of Social and Personal Relationships, 1,* 347–358.

Sprecher, S. (1987). The effects of self-disclosure given and received on affection for an intimate partner and stability of the relationship. *Journal of Social and Personal Relationships, 4,* 115–127.

Sunnafrank, M. (1983). Attitude similarity and interpersonal attraction in communication processes: In pursuit of an ephemeral influence. *Communication Monographs, 50,* 273–284.

Sunnafrank, M. (1985). Communicative influences on perceived similarity and attraction: An expansion of the interpersonal goals perspective. *Western Journal of Speech Communication, 50,* 158–170.

Communication Satisfaction

Allen, A., & Thompson, T. (1984). Agreement, understanding, realization, and feeling understood as predictors of communication satisfaction in marital dyads. *Journal of Marriage and the Family, 46,* 915–921.

Buller, M., & Buller, D. (1987). Physicians' communication style and patient satisfaction. *Journal of Health and Social Behavior, 28,* 375–388.

Canary, D. J., & Spitzberg, B. H. (1988). Relational and episodic characteristics associated with conflict tactics. *Journal of Social and Personal Relationships, 5,* 305–325.

Daniels, T., & Logan, L. (1983). Communication in women's career development relationships. In R. N. Bostrom (Ed.), *Communication yearbook 7,* (pp. 532–553). Beverly Hills, CA: Sage.

Daniels, T. D., & Spiker, B. K. (1983). Social exchange and the relationship between information adequacy and relational satisfaction. *Western Journal of Speech Communication, 47,* 118–137.

Duran, R. L., & Zakahi, W. R. (1987). Communication performance and communication satisfaction: What do we teach our students? *Communication Education, 36,* 13–22.

Duran, R. L., & Zakahi, W. (1988). The influence of communicative competence upon roommate satisfaction. *Western Journal of Speech Communication, 52,* 135–146.

Hecht, M. L. (1978a). The conceptualization and measurement of interpersonal communication satisfaction. *Human Communication Research, 4,* 253–264.

Hecht, M. L. (1978b). Toward a conceptualization of communication satisfaction. *Quarterly Journal of Speech, 64,* 47–62.

Hecht, M. L. (1984a). An investigation of the effects of sex of self and other on perceptions of communication satisfaction. *Sex Roles: A Journal of Research, 10,* 733–741.

Hecht, M. L. (1984b). Persuasive efficacy: A study of the relationships among types of change, message strategies, and satisfying communication. *Western Journal of Speech Communication, 48,* 373–389.

Hecht, M. L. (1984c). Satisfying communication and relationship labels: Intimacy and length of relationship as perceptual frames of naturalistic conversations. *Western Journal of Speech Communication, 48,* 201–216.

Hecht, M. L., & Marston, P. (1987). Communication satisfaction and the temporal development of conversations. *Communication Research Reports, 4,* 60–65.

Hecht, M. L., & Ribeau, S. (1984). Ethnic communication: A comparative analysis of satisfying communication. *International Journal of Intercultural Relations, 8,* 135–151.

Hecht, M. L., & Ribeau, S. (1987). Afro-American identity labels and communicative effectiveness. *Journal of Language and Social Psychology, 6,* 319–326.

Hecht, M. L., Ribeau, S., & Alberts, J. K. (1989). An Afro-American perspective on interethnic communication. *Communication Monographs, 56,* 385–410.

Hecht, M. L., Ribeau, S., & Sedano, M. V. (1990). A Mexican-American perspective on interethnic communication. *International Journal of Intercultural Relations, 14,* 31–55.

Hecht, M. L., & Riley, P. (1985). A three factor model of group satisfaction and consensus. *Communication Research Reports, 2,* 178–181.

Hecht, M. L., & Sereno, K., (1985). Interpersonal communication satisfaction: Relationship to satisfaction with self and other. *Communication Research Reports, 2,* 141–148.

Hecht, M. L., Sereno, K. K., & Spitzberg, B. H. (1984). The relevance of relationship level and topic level to the relationship between communication satisfaction and satisfaction with self and other. *Personality and Social Psychology Bulletin, 10,* 376–384.

Hecht, M. L., Shepherd, T., & Hall, M. J. (1979). Multivariate indices of the effects of self-disclosure: Communication satisfaction, reciprocity of valence and intimacy, and response repertoires. *Western Journal of Speech Communication, 43,* 235–245.

Korzenny, F., & Bauer, C. (1981). Testing the theory of electronic propinquity: Organizational teleconferencing. *Communication Research, 8,* 479–498.

Kraut, R. E., Lewis, S. H., & Swezey, L. W. (1982). Listener responsiveness and the coordination of conversation. *Journal of Personality and Social Psychology, 43,* 718–731.

Lamude, K., Daniels, T., & Graham, E. (1988). The paradoxical influence of sex on communication rules coorientation and communication satisfaction in superior-subordinate relationships. *Western Journal of Speech Communication, 52,* 122–134.

McLaughlin, M. L., & Cody, M. J. (1982). Awkward silences: Behavioral antecedents and consequences of conversational lapses. *Human Communication Research, 8,* 299–317.

Pacanowsky, M. E., & O'Donnell-Trujillo, N. (1982). Communication and organizational cultures. *Western Journal of Speech Communication, 46,* 115–130.

Powell, L. (1986). Participant satisfaction in second-language conversations. *Communication Research Reports, 3,* 135–139.

Prisbell, M. (1985). Interpersonal perception variables and communication satisfaction in the classroom. *Communication Research Reports, 2,* 90–96.

Spitzberg, B. H., & Hecht, M. L. (1984). A component model of relational competence. *Human Communication Research, 10,* 575–600.

Vause, C. J., & Weimann, J. M. (1981). Communication strategies for role invention. *Western Journal of Speech Communication, 45,* 241–251.

Wheeless, L. R., Wheeless, V. E., & Baus, R. (1984). Sexual communication, communication satisfaction, and solidarity in the developmental stages of intimate relationships. *Western Journal of Speech Communication, 48,* 217–230.

Wheeless, V., Wheeless, L., & Howard, R. (1983). An analysis of the contribution of participative decision making and communication with supervisor as predictors of job satisfaction. *Research in Higher Education, 18,* 145–150.

Culture

Andersen, P. A., Lustig, M. W., & Andersen, J. F. (1987). Regional patterns of communication in the United States: A theoretical perspective. *Communication Monographs, 54,* 128–144.

Beebe, L. M., & Giles, H. (1984). Speech accommodation theories: A discussion in terms of second language acquisition. *International Journal of the Sociology of Language, 46,* 5–32.

Chua, E. G., & Gudykunst, W. B. (1987). Conflict resolution styles in high and low context cultures. *Communication Research Reports, 4,* 32–37.

Collier, M. J. (1988). A comparison of conversations among and between domestic culture groups: How intra- and intercultural competencies vary. *Communication Quarterly, 36,* 122–144.

Collier, M. J., Hecht, M. L., & Ribeau, S. (1986). Intracultural rules and outcomes within three domestic cultural groups. *International Journal of Intercultural Relations, 10,* 439–457.

Foeman, A. K., & Pressley, G. (1987). Ethnic culture and corporate culture: Using black styles in organizations. *Communication Quarterly, 35,* 293–307.

Garner, T. (1987). Instrumental interactions: Speech acts in daily life. *Central States Speech Journal, 36,* 229–238.

Gudykunst, W. B. (1985a). An exploratory comparison of closer intracultural and intercultural friendships. *Communication Quarterly, 33,* 270–283.

Gudykunst, W. B. (1985b). The influence of cultural similarity, type of relationship, and self-monitoring on uncertainty reduction processes. *Communication Monographs, 52,* 203–217.

Gudykunst, W. B., & Nishida, T. (1986). The influence of cultural variability on perceptions of communication behavior associated with relationship terms. *Human Communication Research, 13,* 147–166.

Gudykunst, W. B., Nishida, T., & Chua, E. (1986). Uncertainty reduction in Japanese-North American dyads. *Communication Research Reports, 3,* 39–46.

Gudykunst, W. B., Yang, S-M., & Nishida, T. (1985). A cross-cultural test of uncertainty reduction theory: Comparisons of acquaintance, friends, and dating relationships in Japan, Korea, and the United States. *Human Communication Research, 11,* 407–454.

Hecht, M. L., Andersen, P. A., & Ribeau, S. (1989). The cultural dimensions of nonverbal communication. In M. K. Asante & W. B. Gudykunst (Eds.), *Handbook of intercultural communication* (pp. 163–185). Beverly Hills, CA: Sage.

Hecht, M. L., & Ribeau, S. (1984). Ethnic communication: A comparative analysis of satisfying communication. *International Journal of Intercultural Relations, 8,* 135–151.

Hecht, M. L., & Ribeau, S. (1987). Afro-American identity labels and communicative effectiveness. *Journal of Language and Social Psychology, 4,* 387–407.

Hecht, M. L., & Ribeau, S. (in press). Socio-cultural roots of ethnic identity: A look at Black America. *Journal of Black Studies.*

Hecht, M. L., Ribeau, S., & Alberts, J. K. (1989). An Afro-American perspective on interethnic communication. *Communication Monographs, 56,* 385–410.

Hecht, M. L., Ribeau, S., & Sedano, M. V. (1990). A Mexican-American perspective on interethnic communication. *International Journal of Intercultural Communication, 14,* 31–55.

McCann, L. D., Hecht, M. L., & Ribeau, S. (1986). Communication apprehension and second language acquisition among Vietnamese and Mexican immigrants: A test of the Affect Filter Hypothesis. *Communication Research Reports, 3,* 33–38.

Miller, M. D., Reynolds, R. A., & Cambra, R. E. (1987). The influence of gender and culture on language intensity. *Communication Monographs, 54,* 101–105.

Nakanishi, M. (1986). Perceptions of self-disclosure in initial interaction. *Human Communication Research, 13,* 167–190.

Philipsen, G. (1987). The prospect for cultural communication. In D. L. Kincaid (Ed.), *Communication theory: Eastern and Western perspectives* (pp. 245–254). San Diego, CA: Academic Press.

Powell, L. (1986). Participant satisfaction in second-language conversations. *Communication Research Reports, 3,* 135–139.

Wheeless, L. R., Erickson, K. V., & Behrens, J. S. (1986). Cultural differences in disclosiveness as a function of locus of control. *Communication Monographs, 53,* 36–46.

Won-Doornick, M. J. (1985). Self-disclosure reciprocity in conversation: A cross-national study. *Social Psychology Quarterly, 48,* 97–107.

Emotion

Bailey, F. G. (1983). *The tactical uses of passion.* Ithaca, New York: Cornell University Press.

Beebe, S. A., & Biggers, T. (1986). Trait emotion and emotional response. *Communication Research Reports, 3,* 47–52.

Biggers, T. (1987). Trait emotion and communication apprehension. *Communication Research Reports, 4,* 20–25.

Bowers, J. W., Metts, S. M., & Duncanson, W. T. (1985). Emotion and interpersonal communication. In M. L. Knapp & G. R. Miller (Eds.), *Handbook of interpersonal communication* (pp. 500–550). Beverly Hills, CA: Sage.

Buunk, B., & Bringle, R. G. (1987). Jealousy in love relationships. In D. Perlman & S. W. Duck (Eds.), *Intimate relationships: Development, dynamics, and deterioration* (pp. 123–147). Beverly Hills, CA: Sage.

Campos, J. J., & Barrett, K. C. (1984). Toward a new understanding of emotions and their development. In C. E. Izard, J. Kagan, & R. B. Zajonc (Eds.), *Emotions, cognition and behavior* (pp. 229–263). Cambridge: Cambridge University Press.

Christ, W. G. (1985). The construct of arousal in communication research. *Human Communication Research, 11*, 575–592.

Clark, M. S., & Fiske, S. T. (Eds.). (1982). *Affect and cognition*. Hillsdale, NJ: Erlbaum.

Clynes, M. (1978). *Sentics: The touch of emotions*. Garden City, NY: Anchor Books.

DeLongis, A., Coyne, J. C., Dakof, G., Folkman, S., & Lazarus, R. S. (1982). Relationship of daily hassles, uplifts, and major life events to health status. *Health Psychology, 1*, 119–136.

Eckenrode, J. (1984). Impact of chronic and acute stressors on daily reports of mood. *Journal of Personality and Social Psychology, 46*, 902–918.

Folkman, S., Lazarus, R. S., Gruen, R. J., & DeLongis, A. (1986). Appraisal, coping, health status and psychological symptoms. *Journal of Personality and Social Psychology, 50*, 571–579.

Frijda, N. H. (1986). *The emotions*. Cambridge: Cambridge University Press.

Greene, J. O., & Sparks, G. O. (1983). Explication and test of a cognitive model of communication apprehension: A new look at an old construct. *Human Communication Research, 9*, 349–366.

Hyde, M. J. (1984). Emotion and human communication: A rhetorical, scientific, and philosophical picture. *Communication Quarterly, 32*, 120–132.

Izard, C. E. (1977). *Human emotions*. New York: Plenum Press.

Izard, C. E., Kagan, J., & Zajonc, R. B. (Eds.). (1984). *Emotions, cognition and behavior*. Cambridge: Cambridge University Press.

Kelley, H. H. (1984). Affect in interpersonal relations. In P. Shaver (Ed.), *Review of personality and social psychology: Emotions, relationships, and health*. Beverly Hills, CA: Sage.

Kemper, T. D. (1978). *A social interactional theory of emotions*. New York: John Wiley & Sons.

Plutchik, R., & Kellerman, H. (Eds.). (1980). *Emotions: Theory, research and experience. Vol. 1: Theories of emotion*. New York: Academic Press.

Radecki Bush, C., Bush, J., & Jennings, J. (1988). Effects of jealousy threats on relationship perceptions and emotions. *Journal of Social and Personal Relationships, 5*, 285–303.

Sarbin, T. R. (in press). Emotions as narrative employments. In M. J. Parker & R. B. Addison (Eds.), *Interpretive investigations: Contributions to psychological research*. Albany, New York: State University of New York Press.

Shaver, P., Schwartz, J., Kirson, D., & O'Connor, C. (1987). Emotional knowledge: Further exploration of a prototype approach. *Journal of Personality and Social Psychology, 52*, 1061–1086.

Shimanoff, S. B. (1984). Commonly named emotions in everyday conversations. *Perceptual and Motor Skills, 58*, 514.

Shimanoff, S. B. (1985). Rules governing the verbal expression of emotions between married couples. *Western Journal of Speech Communication, 49*, 147–165.

Shimanoff, S. B. (1987). Types of emotional disclosures and request compliance between spouses. *Communication Monographs, 54*, 85–100.

Sparks, G. (1986). An action assembly approach to predicting emotional responses to frightening mass media. *Central States Speech Journal, 37*, 102–112.

Issues in Interpersonal Communication Research

Awareness

Acitelli, L. K. (1988). When spouses talk to each other about their relationship. *Journal of Social and Personal Relationships, 5*, 185–199.

Acitelli, L. K., & Duck, S. W. (1987). Intimacy as the proverbial elephant. In D. Perlman & S. W. Duck (Eds.), *Intimate relationships: Development, dynamics, and deterioration* (pp. 297–308). Beverly Hills, CA: Sage.

Andersen, P. A. (1986). Consciousness, cognition, and communication. *Western Journal of Speech Communication, 50*, 87–101.

Bailey, W. (1986). Consciousness and action/motion theories of communication. *Western Journal of Speech Communication, 50*, 64–73.

Berger, C. R. (1980). Self-consciousness and the adequacy of theory and research into relationship development. *Western Journal of Speech Communication, 50*, 97–103.

Berger, C. R., & Douglas, W. (1982). Thought and talk: 'Excuse me but have I been talking to myself?' In F.E.X. Dance (Ed.), *Human communication theory* (pp. 42–60). New York: Harper and Row.

Bochner, A. P. (1978). On taking ourselves seriously: An analysis of some persistent problems and promising directions in interpersonal research. *Human Communication Research, 4*, 178–191.

Camden, C., & Verba, S. (1986). Communication and consciousness: Applications in marketing. *Western Journal of Speech Communication, 50*, 64–73.

Douglas, W. (1983). Scripts and self-monitoring: When does being a high self-monitor really make a difference? *Human Communication Research, 10*, 81–96.

Duck, S. (1985). Social and personal relationships. In M. L. Knapp & G. R. Miller (Eds.), *Handbook of interpersonal communication* (pp. 685–686). Beverly Hills, CA: Sage.

Greene, J. O. (1984). A cognitive approach to human communication: An action assembly theory. *Communication Monographs, 51,* 289–306.

Hample, D. (1986). Logic, conscious and unconscious. *Western Journal of Speech Communication, 50,* 24–40.

Langer, E., Blank, A., & Chanowitz, B. (1978). The mindlessness of essentially thoughtful action: The role of 'placebo' information in interpersonal interaction. *Journal of Personality and Social Psychology, 37,* 635–642.

Locke, E., & Pennington, D. (1982). Reasons and other causes: Their role in attribution processes. *Journal of Personality and Social Psychology, 42,* 212–243.

Miller, G. R., & Steinberg, M. (1975). *Between people: A new analysis of interpersonal communication.* Chicago: Science Research Associates.

Motley, M. (1986). Consciousness and intentionality in communication: A preliminary model and methodological approaches. *Western Journal of Speech Communication, 50,* 23–33.

Nesbitt, R., & Ross, L. (1980). *Human inference strategies and shortcoming of social judgment.* Englewood Cliffs, NJ: Prentice-Hall.

Nesbitt, R., & Wilson, T. (1977). Telling more than we know: Verbal reports on mental processes. *Psychological Reports, 84,* 231–259.

Nofsinger, R. E. (1986). Becoming of (un)consciousness: An introductory note to a special section on communication and consciousness. *Western Journal of Speech Communication, 50,* 1–2.

Shimanoff, S. (1980). *Communication rules theory and research.* Beverly Hills, CA: Sage.

Sigman, S. J. (1980). On communication rules from a social perspective. *Human Communication Research, 7,* 37–51.

Spitzberg, B. H., & Cupach, W. R. (1984). *Interpersonal communication competence.* Beverly Hills, CA: Sage.

Zeller, E. (1983). *A history of eclecticism.* London: Longman, Green, and Co.

Cross-Situational Consistency

Allport, G. W. (1966). Traits revisited. *American Psychologist, 21,* 1–10.

Bem, D. J. (1983). Further déjà vu in the search for cross-situational consistency: A response to Mischel and Peake. *Psychological Review, 90,* 390–393.

Bem, D. J., & Allen, A. (1974). On predicting some of the people some of the time: The search for cross-situational consistencies in behavior. *Psychological Review, 81,* 506–520.

Block, J. (1981). Some enduring and consequential structures of personality. In A. I. Rabin, J. Arnoff, A. M. Barclay, & R. A. Zucker (Eds.), *Further explorations in personality* (pp. 27–43). New York: John Wiley & Sons.

Cappella, J. N. (1984). The relationship of the microstructure of interaction to relationship change. *Journal of Social and Personal Relationships, 1,* 239–264.

Epstein, S., & O'Brien, E. J. (1985). The person-situation debate in historical and current perspective. *Psychological Bulletin, 98,* 513–537.

Farley, F. (1986). World of the T personality. *Psychology Today, 20,* 46–51.

Funder, D. C. (1983a). Three issues in predicting more of the people: A reply to Mischel and Peake. *Psychological Review, 90,* 283–289.

Funder, D. C. (1983b). The "consistency" controversy and the accuracy of personality judgments. *Journal of Personality, 51,* 346–359.

Hewes, D., & Haight, L. (1979). The cross-situational consistency of communication behaviors. *Communication Research, 6,* 243–270.

Infante, D. A. (1987). Enhancing the prediction of response to a communication situation from communication traits. *Communication Quarterly, 35,* 308–317.

Kenrick, D. T. (1986). How strong is the case against contemporary social and personality psychology? *Journal of Personality and Social Psychology, 50,* 839–844.

Mischel, W., & Peake, P. K. (1982). Beyond déjà vu in the search for cross-situational consistency. *Psychological Review, 89,* 730–755.

Mischel, W., & Peake, P. K. (1983). Some facets of consistency: Replies to Epstein, Funder, and Bem. *Psychological Review, 90,* 394–402.

Moskowitz, D. S. (1988). Cross-situational consistency in the laboratory: Dominance and friendliness. *Journal of Personality and Social Psychology, 54,* 829–839.

Sherman, S. J., & Fazio, R. H. (1983). Parallels between attitudes and traits as predictors of behavior. *Journal of Personality, 51,* 308–345.

Small, S. A., Zeldin, R. S., & Savin-Williams, R. C. (1983). In search of personality traits: A multimethod analysis of naturally occurring prosocial and dominance behavior. *Journal of Personality, 51,* 1–16.

Street, R. L., & Murphy, T. L. (1987). Interpersonal orientation and speech behavior. *Communication Monographs, 54,* 42–62.

Eclecticism

Allport, G. (1968). Fruits of eclecticism: Bitter or sweet? In G. Allport (Ed.), *The person in psychology: Selected essays* (pp. 3–27). Boston: Beacon Press.

Blumer, H. (1960). Sociological analysis and the variable. In H. Blumer, *Symbolic interactionism: Perspective and method* (pp. 127–139). Englewood Cliffs, NJ: Prentice-Hall.

Henle, M. (1961). Some problems of eclecticism. In M. Henle (Ed.), *Documents of Gestalt psychology* (pp. 76–89). Berkeley, CA: University of California Press.

Sykes, G. (1962). *The hidden remnant.* New York: Harper & Row.

Level of Analysis

Ambert, A. M. (1988). Relationships between ex-spouses: Individual and dyadic perspectives. *Journal of Social and Personal Relationships, 5,* 327–346.

Burggraf, C. S., & Sillars, A. L. (1987). A critical examination of sex differences in marital communication. *Communication Monographs, 54,* 276–294.

Canary, D. J., & Spitzberg, B. H. (1988). Relational and episodic characteristics associated with conflict tactics. *Journal of Social and Personal Relationships, 5,* 305–325.

Cappella, J. N. (1984). The relevance of the microstructure of interaction to relationship change. *Journal of Social and Personal Relationships, 1,* 239–264.

Duck, S. W., & Sants, H.K.A. (1983). On the origin of the specious: Are personal relationships really interpersonal states? *Journal of Social and Clinical Psychology, 1,* 27–41.

Fincham, F. D., & Bradbury, T. N. (1989). The impact of attribution in marriage: An individual difference analysis. *Journal of Social and Personal Relationships, 6,* 69–85.

Fitzpatrick, M. A., & Indvik, J. (1986). On alternative conceptions of relational communication. *Communication Quarterly, 34,* 19–23.

Glick, W. H., & Roberts, K. H. (1984). Hypothesized interdependence, assumed interdependence. *Academy of Management Review, 9,* 722–735.

Gottman, J. M. (1979). *Marital interaction.* London: Academic Press.

Hauser, R. M. (1974). Contextual effects revisited. *Sociological Methods and Research, 2,* 365–375.

Indvik, J., & Fitzpatrick, M. A. (1986). Perceptions of inclusion, affiliation and control in five interpersonal relationships. *Communication Quarterly, 34,* 1–13.

Jacobson, N. S., & Moore, D. (1981). Spouses as observers of the events in their relationships. *Journal of Consulting and Clinical Psychology, 49,* 269–277.

Kenny, D. A. (1988). Interpersonal perception: A social relations analysis. *Journal of Social and Personal Relationships, 5,* 247–261.

Kenny, D. A. (1990). What makes a relationship special? In T. W. Draper & A. C. Marcos (Eds.), *Family variables: Conceptualization, measurement, and use* (pp. 161–178). Newbury Park, CA: Sage.

Kenny, D. A., & La Voie, L. (1982). Reciprocity of attraction: A confirmed hypothesis. *Social Psychological Quarterly, 45,* 54–58.

Kenny, D. A., & La Voie, L. (1984). The social relations model. In L. Berkowitz (Ed.), *Advances in experimental social psychology* (Vol. 18, pp. 141–182). Orlando, FL: Academic Press.

Kenny, D. A., & La Voie, L. (1985). Separating individual and group effects. *Journal of Personality and Social Psychology, 48,* 339–348.

Kenny, D. A., & Nasby, W. (1980). Splitting the reciprocity correlation. *Journal of Personality and Social Psychology, 38,* 249–256.

Kessler, R. C., Price, R. H., & Wortman, C. B. (1985). Social factors in psychopathology: Stress, social support, and coping processes. *Annual Review of Psychology, 36,* 531–572.

Miller, L. C., & Kenny, D. A. (1986). Reciprocity of self-disclosure at the individual and dyadic levels: A social relations analysis. *Journal of Personality and Social Psychology, 50,* 713–719.

Montgomery, B. M. (1984). Individual differences and relational interdependencies in social interaction. *Human Communication Research, 11,* 33–60.

Montgomery, B. M. (1986). A commentary on Indvik and Fitzpatrick's study of relationship defining communication. *Communication Quarterly, 34,* 14–18.

Morgan, D. L. (1986). Personal relationships as an interface between social networks and social cognitions. *Journal of Social and Personal Relationships, 3,* 403–423.

Linearity/Process/Transaction

Andersen, K. (1968). Variant views on the communication act. In H. H. Martin & K. B. Andersen (Eds.), *Speech communication: Analysis and readings* (pp. 2–23). Boston: Allyn & Bacon.

Barnlund, D. (1962). Toward a meaning-centered philosophy of communication. *Journal of Communication, 12,* 198–202.

Berlo, D. (1960). *Process of communication.* New York: Holt, Rinehart, and Winston.

Rogers-Millar, L. E., & Millar, F. E. (1979). Domineeringness and dominance: A transactional view. *Human Communication Research, 5,* 238–246.

Smith, D. (1972). Communication research and the idea of process. *Speech Monographs, 39,* 174–182.

Subject Variables

Underwood, B. J. (1957). *Psychological research.* New York: Appleton-Century-Crofts.

Wright, P. H. (1988). Interpreting research on gender differences in friendship: A case for moderation and a plea for caution. *Journal of Social and Personal Relationships, 5,* 367–373.

Miscellaneous

Baron, R. M., & Kenny, D. A. (1986). The moderator-mediator variable distinction in social psychological research: Conceptual, strategic, and statistical considerations. *Journal of Personal and Social Psychology, 51,* 1173–1182.

Bradac, J. J. (1983). On generalizing cabbages, messages, kings and several other things: The virtues of multiplicity. *Human Communication Research, 9,* 181–187.

Hewes, D. E. (1983). Confessions of a methodological puritan: A response to Jackson and Jacobs. *Human Communication Research, 9,* 187–191.

Hewes, D. E., & Haight, L. (1980). Multiple-act criteria in the validation of communication traits: What do we gain and what do we lose? *Human Communication Research, 6,* 352–366.

Jaccard, J., & Daly, J. (1980). Personality traits and multiple-act criteria. *Human Communication Research, 6,* 367–377.

Jackson, S., & Jacobs, S. (1983). Generalizing about messages: Suggestions for design and analysis of experiments. *Human Communication Research, 9,* 169–181.

O'Keefe, D. (1975). Logical empiricism and the study of human communication. *Speech Monographs, 42,* 169–183.

Rychlak, J. F. (1984). Relationship theory: An historical development in psychology leading to a teleological image of humanity. *Journal of Social and Personal Relationships, 1,* 363–386.

Spitzberg, B. H., & Cupach, W. R. (1984). *Interpersonal communication competence.* Beverly Hills, CA: Sage.

Stacks, D. W., & Sellers, D. E. (1986). Toward a holistic approach to communication: The effect of 'pure' hemispheric reception on message acceptance. *Communication Quarterly, 34,* 266–285.

Whiffen, V. E., & Gotlib, I. H. (1989). Stress and coping in maritally distressed and nondistressed couples. *Journal of Social and Personal Relationships, 6,* 327–344.

Wright, P. H. (1984). Self-referent motivation and the intrinsic quality of friendship. *Journal of Social and Personal Relationships, 1,* 115–130.

Love

Aron, A., & Aron, E. N. (1986). *Love and the expansion of self: Understanding attraction and satisfaction.* Washington, DC: Hemisphere.

Aron, A., Dutton, D. G., Aron, E. N., & Iverson, A. (1989). Experiences of falling in love. *Journal of Social and Personal Relationships, 6,* 243–258.

Baxter, L. A. (1987). Symbols of relationship identity in relationship cultures. *Journal of Social and Personal Relationships, 4,* 261–280.

Belove, L. (1980). First encounters of the close kind (FECK): The use of the story of the first interaction as an early recollection of a marriage. *Journal of Individual Psychology, 36,* 191–208.

Berscheid, E., & Frei, J. (1977). Romantic love and sexual jealousy. In G. Clanton & L. G. Smith (Eds.), *Jealousy* (pp. 101–109). Englewood Cliffs, NJ: Prentice-Hall.

Bradac, J. J. (1983). The language of lovers, flovers, and friends: Communicating in social and personal relationships. *Journal of Language and Social Psychology, 2,* 141–162.

Brehm, S. S. (1988). Passionate love. In R. Sternberg & M. L. Barnes (Eds.), *The psychology of love* (pp. 232–263). New Haven, CT: Yale University Press.

Buunk, B., & Bringle, R. G. (1987). Jealousy in love relationships. In D. Perlman & S. W. Duck (Eds.), Intimate relationships: Development, dynamics, and deterioration (pp. 123–147). Beverly Hills, CA: Sage.

Critelli, J., Myers, E., & Loos, V. (1986). The components of love: Romantic attraction and sex role orientation. *Journal of Personality, 54,* 354–369.

Davis, K. E., & Latty-Mann, H. (1987). Love styles and relationship quality: A contribution to validation. *Journal of Social and Personal Relationships, 4,* 409–428.

Davis, K. E., & Todd, M. J. (1982). Friendship and love relationships. In K. E. Davis & T. O. Mitchell (Eds.), *Advances in descriptive psychology* (Vol. 2, pp. 79–122). Greenwich, CT: JAI Press.

Davis, K. E., & Todd, M. J. (1985). Assessing friendship: Prototypes, paradigm cases, and relationship assessment. In S. W. Duck & D. Perlman (Eds.), *Understanding personal relationships: An interdisciplinary approach* (pp. 17–34). Beverly Hills, CA: Sage.

D'Hondt, W., & Vandewiele, M. (1983). Attitudes of West African students toward love and marriage. *Psychological Reports, 53,* 615–621.

Grant, V. W. (1986). *Falling in love: The psychology of the romantic emotion.* New York: Springer.

Hatfield, E. (1988). Passionate and companionate love. In R. Sternberg & M. L. Barnes (Eds.), *The psychology of love* (pp. 191–217). New Haven, CT: Yale University Press.

Hatfield, E., & Rapson, R. L. (1987). Passionate love: New directions in research. In W. H. Jones & D. Perlman (Eds.), *Advances in personal relationships* (Vol. 1, pp. 109–139). Greenwich, CT: JAI Press.

Hatfield, E., & Walster, G. W. (1981). *A new look at love.* Reading, MA: Addison-Wesley.

Hazen, C., & Shaver, P. (1987). Romantic love conceptualized as an attachment process. *Journal of Personality and Social Psychology, 42,* 511–524.

Hendrick, C., & Hendrick, S. (1983). *Liking, loving, and relating.* Monterey, CA: Brooks/Cole.

Hendrick, C., & Hendrick, S. (1986). A theory and method of love. *Journal of Social and Personal Relationships, 50,* 392–402.

Hendrick, C., & Hendrick, S. S. (1988). Lovers wear rose colored glasses. *Journal of Social and Personal Relationships, 5,* 161–183.

Hendrick, C., Hendrick, S., Foote, F. H., & Slapion-Foote, M. J. (1984). Do men and women love differently? *Journal of Social and Personal Relationships, 1,* 177–195.

Hendrick, S., & Hendrick, C. (1987a). Love and sexual attitudes, self disclosure, and sensation seeking. *Journal of Social and Personal Relationships, 4,* 281–297.

Hendrick, S. S., & Hendrick, C. (1987b). Love and sex attitudes: A close relationship. In W. H. Jones & D. Perlman (Eds.), *Advances in personal relationships* (Vol. 1, pp. 141–169). Greenwich, CT: JAI Press.

Hill, C., Peplau, L., & Rubin, Z. (1976). Break-ups before marriage: The end of 103 affairs. *Journal of Social Issues, 32,* 147–168.

Kelley, H. H. (1983). Love and commitment. In H. H. Kelley et al. (Eds.), *Close relationships* (pp. 265–314). New York: W. H. Freeman.

King, C. E., & Christensen, A. (1983). The relationship events scale: A Guttman scaling of progress through courtship. *Journal of Marriage and the Family, 45,* 671–678.

Lee, J. A. (1973). *The colors of love: An exploration of the ways of loving.* Toronto: New Press.

Lee, J. A. (1977). A typology of styles of loving. *Personality and Social Psychology Bulletin, 3,* 173–182.

Leibowitz, M. R. (1983). *The chemistry of love.* New York: Berkeley Books.

Levy, M. B., & Davis, K. E. (1988). Lovestyles and attachment styles compared: Their relations to each other and to various relationship characteristics. *Journal of Social and Personal Relationships, 5,* 439–471.

Livingston, K. R. (1980). Love as a process of reducing uncertainty-cognitive theory. In K. Pope (Ed.), *On love and loving* (pp. 133–151). San Francisco: Jossey Bass.

Marston, P. J., Hecht, M. L., & Robers, T. (1987). 'True love ways': The subjective experience and communication of romantic love. *Journal of Social and Personal Relationships, 4,* 387–408.

Mathes, E., & Sevena, N. (1981). Jealousy, romantic love, and liking: Theoretical considerations and preliminary scale development. *Psychological Reports, 49,* 23–31.

Maxwell, G. M. (1985). Behavior of lovers: Measuring the closeness of relationships. *Journal of Social and Personal Relationships, 2,* 215–238.

Money, J. (1980). *Love and lovesickness: The science of sex, gender difference, and pair-bonding.* Baltimore, MD: The Johns Hopkins University Press.

Morse, S. J. (1983). Requirements for love and friendship in Australia and Brazil. *Australian Journal of Psychology, 35,* 469–476.

Pope, K. S. (Ed.). (1980). *On love and loving.* San Francisco: Jossey Bass.

Rubin, Z. (1970). Measurement of romantic love. *Journal of Personality and Social Psychology, 16,* 265–273.

Rubin, Z. (1974). From liking to love: Patterns of attraction in dating relationships. In T. Huston (Ed.), *Foundations of interpersonal attraction* (pp. 383–402). New York: Academic Press.

Shaver, P., Hazen, C., & Bradshaw, D. (1988). Love as attachment: The integration of three behavioral systems. In R. J. Sternberg & M. Barnes (Eds.), *The anatomy of love* (pp. 68–99). New Haven, CT: Yale University Press.

Shaver, P., Schwartz, J., Kirson, D., & O'Connor, C. (1987). Emotion knowledge: Further explorations of a prototype approach. *Journal of Personality and Social Psychology, 52,* 1061–1086.

Shea, J. A., & Adams, G. R. (1984). Correlates of romantic attachment: A path analysis study. *Journal of Youth and Adolescence, 13,* 27–44.

Siegel, B. S. (1986). *Love, medicine, and miracles.* New York: Harper & Row.

Simpson, J. A., Campbell, G., & Berscheid, E. (1986). The association between romantic love and marriage: Kephart (1967) twice revisited. *Personality and Social Psychology Bulletin, 12,* 363–372.

Sperling, M. B. (1985). Discriminant measures for desperate love. *Journal of Personality Assessment, 49,* 324–328.

Steck, L., Leviton, D., McLane, D., & Kelley, H. H. (1982). Care, need, and conceptions of love. *Journal of Personality and Social Psychology, 43,* 481–491.

Sternberg, R. J. (1986). A triangular theory of love. *Psychological Review, 93,* 119–135.

Sternberg, R. J. (1987). Liking versus loving: A comparative evaluation of theories. *Psychological Bulletin, 102,* 331–345.

Sternberg, R. J., & Barnes, M. L. (1985). Real and ideal others in romantic relationships: Is four a crowd? *Journal of Personality and Social Psychology, 49,* 1586–1608.

Sternberg, R. J., & Barnes, M. (Eds.). (1988). *The psychology of love.* New Haven, CT: Yale University Press.

Sternberg, R. J., & Grajek, S. (1984). The nature of love. *Journal of Personality and Social Psychology, 47,* 312–329.

Tennov, D. (1979). *Love and limerance: The experience of being in love.* New York: Stein and Day.

Thompson, B., & Borrello, G. M. (1987). Concurrent validity of a love relationships scale. *Educational and Psychological Measurement, 47,* 985–995.

White, G. (1984). A comparison of 4 jealousy scales. *Journal of Research in Personality, 18,* 115–130.

Overviews of Relationship Communication

Altman, I., & Taylor, D. (1973). *Social penetration: The development of interpersonal relationships.* New York: Holt, Rinehart and Winston.

Altman, I., Vinsel, A., & Brown, B. B. (1981). Dialectic conceptions in social psychology: An application to social penetration and privacy regulation. In L. Berkowitz (Ed.), *Advances in experimental social psychology* (Vol. 14, pp. 107–160). Orlando, FL: Academic Press.

Burgoon, J. K., & Hale, J. L. (1984). The fundamental topoi of relational communication. *Communication Monographs, 51,* 193–214.

Burgoon, J. K., & Hale, J. L. (1987). Validation and measurement of the fundamental themes of relational communication. *Communication Monographs, 54,* 19–41.

Duck, S. A. (1985). Social and personal relationships. In M. L. Knapp & G. R. Miller (Eds.), *Handbook of interpersonal communication* (pp. 655–686). Beverly Hills, CA: Sage.

Duck, S. W., Hays, D. F., Hobfoll, S. E., Ickes, W., & Montgomery, B. (1988). *Handbook of personal relationships*. London: John Wiley & Sons.

Hinde, R. A. (1981). The basis of a science of interpersonal relationships. In S. Duck & R. Gilmour (Eds.), *Personal relationships 1: Studying personal relationships* (pp. 1–22). London: Academic Press.

Kelley, H. H., Berscheid, E., Christensen, A., Harvey, J. H., Huston, T. L., Levinger, G., McClintock, E., Peplau, L. A., & Peterson, D. R. (1983). Analyzing close relationships. In H. H. Kelley, et al. (Eds.), *Close relationships* (pp. 20–67). New York: W. H. Freeman.

McCarthy, B. (1981). Studying personal relationships. In S. Duck & R. Gilmour (Eds.), *Personal relationships 1: Studying personal relationships* (pp. 23–46). London: Academic Press.

Owen, W. F. (1984). Interpretive themes in relational communication. *Quarterly Journal of Speech, 70,* 274–286.

Relationship Development

Ainsworth, M.D.S., Blehar, M. D., Waters, E., & Wall, S. (1978). *Patterns of attachment: A psychological study of the strange situation*. Hillsdale, NJ: Erlbaum.

Argyle, M., & Henderson, M. (1984). The rules of friendship. *Journal of Social and Personal Relationships, 1,* 211–238.

Ayres, J. (1983). Strategies to maintain relationships: Their identification and perceived usage. *Communication Quarterly, 31,* 62–67.

Banks, S. P., Altendorf, D. M., Greene, J. O., & Cody, M. J. (1987). An examination of relationship disengagement: Perceptions, breakup strategies and outcomes. *Western Journal of Speech Communication, 51,* 19–41.

Baxter, L. (1982). Strategies for ending relationships: Two studies. *Western Journal of Speech Communication, 46,* 233–242.

Baxter, L. (1983). Relationship disengagement: An examination of the reversal hypothesis. *Western Journal of Speech Communication, 47,* 85–98.

Baxter, L. (1984). Trajectories of relationship disengagement. *Journal of Social and Personal Relationships, 1,* 29–48.

Baxter, L. (1985). Accomplishing relationship disengagement. In S. W. Duck & D. Perlman (Eds.), *Understanding personal relationships*. London: Sage.

Baxter, L. (1986). Gender differences in the heterosexual relationship rules embedded in break-up accounts. *Journal of Social and Personal Relationships, 3,* 289–306.

Baxter, L. (1987). Cognition and communication in the relationship process. In R. Burnett, P. McGhee, & D. Clark (Eds.), *Accounting for relationships: Explanation, representation and knowledge*. London: Methuen.

Baxter, L., & Bullis, C. (1986). Turning points in developing romantic relationships. *Human Communication Research, 12,* 469–493.

Baxter, L., & Philpott, J. (1982). Attribution-based strategies for initiating and terminating friendships. *Communication Quarterly, 30,* 217–224.

Baxter, L. A., & Wilmot, W. W. (1983). Communication characteristics of relationships with differential growth rates. *Communication Monographs, 50,* 264–272.

Bell, R. A., Buerkel-Rothfuss, N. L., & Gore, K. E. (1987). Did you bring the yarmulke for the cabbage patch kid?: The idiomatic communication of young lovers. *Human Communication Research, 14,* 47–68.

Berg, J. H., & McQuinn, R. D. (1986). Attraction and exchange in continuing and noncontinuing dating relationships. *Journal of Personality and Social Psychology, 50,* 942–952.

Bowlby, J. (1969). *Attachment and loss: Vol. 1 Attachment*. New York: Basic Books.

Bowlby, J. (1979). *The making and breaking of affectional bonds*. London: Tavistock.

Bronfenbrenner, U. (1986). Ecology of family as a context for human development: Research perspectives. *Developmental Psychology, 22,* 723–742.

Cappella, J. N. (1984). The relevance of the microstructure of interaction to relationship change. *Journal of Social and Personal Relationships, 1,* 239–264.

Cody, M. (1982). A typology of disengagement strategies and an examination of the role intimacy, reactions to inequity and relational problems play in strategy selection. *Communication Monographs, 49,* 148–170.

Cupach, W., & Metts, S. (1986). Accounts for relational dissolution: A comparison of marital and non-marital relationships. *Communication Monographs, 53,* 311–334.

Derlega, V. J., Winstead, B. A., Wong, P.T.P., & Hunter, S. (1985). Gender effects in an initial encounter: A case where men exceed women in disclosure. *Journal of Social and Personal Relationships, 2,* 25–44.

Dindia, K., & Baxter, L. A. (1987). Strategies for maintaining and repairing marital relationships. *Journal of Social and Personal Relationships, 4,* 143–158.

Douglas, W. (1987). Affinity-testing in initial interactions. *Journal of Social and Personal Relationships, 4,* 1–15.

Duck, S. (Ed.). (1983). *Personal relationships #4: Dissolving personal relationships*. London: Academic Press.

Duck, S. (1983). A topography of relationship disengagement and dissolution. In S. W. Duck (Ed.), *Personal relationships #4: Dissolving personal relationships* (pp. 1–30). London: Academic Press.

Duck, S. W. (1984). A perspective on the repair of personal relationships: Repair of what? when? In S. W. Duck (Ed.), *Personal relationships #5: Repairing personal relationships* (pp. 163–184). London: Academic Press.

Duck, S. W. (1986). *Human relationships: An introduction to social psychology.* London: Sage.

Duck, S., & Gilmour, R. (Eds.). (1981). *Personal relationships #3: Personal relationships in disorder.* London: Academic Press.

Fisher, B. A., & Drecksel, G. L. (1983). A cyclical model of developing relationships: A study of relational control interaction. *Communication Monographs, 50,* 66–78.

Fletcher, G.J.O., Fincham, F. D., Carmer, L., & Heron, N. (1987). The role of attributions in the development of dating relationships. *Journal of Personality and Social Psychology, 53,* 481–489.

Hanson, R. O. (1986). Relational competence: Relationships and adjustments. *Journal of Personality and Social Psychology, 50,* 1050–1058.

Harvey, J. H., Wells, G. L., & Alvarez, M. D. (1978). Attribution in the context of conflict and separation in close relationships. In J. Harvey, W. Ickes, & R. Kidd (Eds.), *New directions in attribution research* (Vol. 2, pp. 235–260). Hillsdale, NJ: Erlbaum.

Hays, R. B. (1984). The development and maintenance of friendship. *Journal of Social and Personal Relationships, 1,* 75–98.

Hays, R. B. (1985). A longitudinal study of friendship development. *Journal of Personality and Social Psychology, 48,* 909–924.

Hays, R. B. (1989). The day-to-day functioning of close versus casual friendships. *Journal of Social and Personal Relationships, 6,* 21–37.

Hill, C., Rubin, Z., & Peplau, L. A. (1976). Breakups before marriage: The end of 103 affairs. *Journal of Social Issues, 32,* 147–168.

Johnson, M. P., & Leslie, L. (1982). Couple involvement and network structure: A test of the dyadic withdrawal hypothesis. *Social Psychology Quarterly, 45,* 34–43.

Juhasz, A. M. (1979). A concept of divorce: Not busted bond but severed strand. *Alternative Lifestyles, 2,* 471–482.

Kelley, H. H. (1979). *Personal relationships.* Hillsdale, NJ: Erlbaum.

Kelley, H. H., Berscheid, E., Christensen, A., Harvey, J. H., Huson, L., Levinger, G., McClintock, E., Peplau, L. A., & Peterson, D. R. (1983). *Close relationships.* Chicago: Aldine.

King, C. E., & Christensen, A. (1983). The relationship events scale: A Guttman scaling of progress through courtship. *Journal of Marriage and the Family, 45,* 671–678.

Kingsbury, N. M., & Minda, R. B. (1988). An analysis of three expected intimate relationship states: Commitment, maintenance, and termination. *Journal of Social and Personal Relationships, 5,* 405–422.

Lee, L. (1984). Sequences in separation: A framework for investigating endings of the personal (romantic) relationships. *Journal of Social and Personal Relationships, 1,* 49–74.

Levinger, G. (1980). Toward the analysis of close relationships. *Journal of Experimental Social Psychology, 16,* 510–544.

Levinger, G. (1983). Development and change. In H. H. Kelley et al. (Eds.), *Close relationships* (pp. 315–359). New York: W. H. Freeman.

Livingston, K. R. (1980). Love as a process of reducing uncertainty-cognitive theory. In K. Pope (Ed.), *On love and loving* (pp. 133–151). San Francisco: Jossey Bass.

Lloyd, S. A., & Cate, R. M. (1985). Attributions associated with significant turning points in premarital relationship development and dissolution. *Journal of Social and Personal Relationships, 2,* 419–436.

Masheter, D. W., & Harris, L. M. (1986). From divorce to friendship: A study of dialectic relationship development. *Journal of Social and Personal Relationships, 3,* 177–189.

Maxwell, G. M. (1985). Behavior of lovers: Measuring the closeness of relationships. *Journal of Social and Personal Relationships, 2,* 215–239.

Miell, D., & Duck, S. (1986). Strategies in developing friendships. In V. Derlega & B. Winstead (Eds.), *Friendship and social interaction* (pp. 129–143). New York: Springer-Verlag.

Milardo, R. M. (1982). Friendship networks in developing relationships: Converging and diverging social environments. *Social Psychology Quarterly, 45,* 162–172.

Morris, G. H., & Hopper, R. (1980). Remediation and legislation in everyday talk: How communicators achieve consensus. *Quarterly Journal of Speech, 66,* 266–274.

Morton, T. L., & Douglas, M. A. (1981). Growth of relationships. In S. Duck & R. Gilmour (Eds.), *Personal relationships 2: Developing personal relationships* (pp. 3–26). London: Academic Press.

Neimeyer, G. J., & Neimeyer, R. A. (1985). Relational trajectories: A personal construct contribution. *Journal of Social and Personal Relationships, 2,* 325–349.

Parks, M. R., & Adelman, M. B. (1983). Communication networks and the development of romantic relationships: An expansion of uncertainty reduction theory. *Human Communication Research, 10,* 55–79.

Planalp, S., & Honeycutt, J. (1985). Events that increase uncertainty in personal relationships. *Human Communication Research, 11,* 593–604.

Rawlins, W. (1983a). Negotiating close friendship: The dialectic of conjunctive freedoms. *Human Communication Research, 9,* 255–266.

Rawlins, W. (1983b). Openness as problematic in ongoing friendships: Two conversational dilemmas. *Communication Monographs, 50,* 1–13.

Rawlins, W. K., & Holl, M. (1987). The communicative achievement of friendship during adolescence: Predicaments of trust and violation. *Western Journal of Speech Communication, 51,* 345–363.

Richmond, V. P., Gorham, J. S., & Furio, B. J. (1987). Affinity-seeking communication in collegiate female-male relationships. *Communication Quarterly, 35,* . 334–348.

Rose, S. M. (1984). How friendships end: Patterns among young adults. *Journal of Social and Personal Relationships, 1,* 267–277.

Rose, S., & Serafica, F. C. (1986). Keeping and ending casual, close and best friendships. *Journal of Social and Personal Relationships, 3,* 275–288.

Rosenbaum, M. E. (1986). The repulsion hypothesis: On the nondevelopment of relationships. *Journal of Personality and Social Psychology, 51,* 1156–1166.

Rusbult, C. E. (1987). Responses to dissatisfaction in close relationships: The exit-voice-loyalty-neglect model. In D. Perlman & S. W. Duck (Eds.), *Intimate relationships: Development, dynamics, and deterioration.* Beverly Hills, CA: Sage.

Schultz, N. R., Jr., & Moore, D. (1988). Loneliness: Differences across three age levels. *Journal of Social and Personal Relationships, 5,* 275–284.

Shea, B. C., & Pearson, J. C. (1986). The effect of relationship type, partner intent, and gender on the selection of relationship maintenance strategies. *Communication Monographs, 53,* 352–364.

Snyder, M., Berscheid, E., & Glick, P. (1985). Focusing on the exterior and the interior: Two investigations of the initiation of personal relationships. *Journal of Personality and Social Psychology, 48,* 1427–1439.

Sprecher, S. (1987). The effects of self-disclosure given and received on affection for an intimate partner and stability of the relationship. *Journal of Social and Personal Relationships, 4,* 115–127.

Stephen, T. (1987). Attribution and adjustment to relationship termination. *Journal of Social and Personal Relationships, 4,* 47–61.

Stephen, T., & Markman, H. (1983). Assessing the development of relationships: A new measure. *Family Processes, 22,* 15–25.

Surra, C. A. (1985a). Courtship types: Variations in interdependence between partners and social networks. *Journal of Social and Personal Relationships, 49,* 357–375.

Surra, C. A. (1985b). Reasons for changes in commitment: Variations by courtship type. *Journal of Social and Personal Relationships, 4,* 17–33.

Tolhuizen, J. H. (1986). Perceived communication indicators of evolutionary changes in friendship. *Southern Speech Communication Journal, 52,* 69–91.

VanLear, C. A., Jr. (1987). The formation of social relationships: A longitudinal study of social penetration. *Human Communication Research, 13,* 299–322.

VanLear, C. A., Jr., & Trujillo, N. (1986). On becoming acquainted: A longitudinal study of social judgment processes. *Journal of Social and Personal Relationships, 3,* 375–392.

Walster, E., Walster, G. W., & Berscheid, E. (1978). *Equity: Theory and research.* Boston: Allyn & Bacon.

Wilmot, W. W. (1987). *Dyadic communication* (3rd ed.). New York: Random House.

Wilmot, W. W., Carbaugh, D. A., & Baxter, L. A. (1985). Communicative strategies used to terminate romantic relationships. *Western Journal of Speech Communication, 49,* 204–216.

Zietlow, P. H., & Sillars, A. L. (1988). Life-stage differences in communication during marital conflicts. *Journal of Social and Personal Relationships, 5,* 223–245.

Relationship Quality

Argyle, M., & Hendersen, M. (1984). The rules of friendship. *Journal of Social and Personal Relationships, 1,* 211–237.

Davis, K. E., & Latty-Mann, H. (1987). Love styles and relationship quality: A contribution to validation. *Journal of Social and Personal Relationships, 4,* 409–428.

Davis, K. E., & Todd, M. J. (1982). Friendship and love relationships. In K. E. Davis & T. O. Mitchell (Eds.), *Advances in descriptive psychology* (Vol. 2, pp. 79–122). Greenwich, CT: JAI Press.

Davis, K. E., & Todd, M. J. (1985). Assessing friendships: Prototypes, paradigm cases, and relationship assessment. In S. W. Duck & D. Perlman (Eds.), *Understanding personal relationships: An interdisciplinary approach* (pp. 17–34). Beverly Hills, CA: Sage.

Eidelson, R. J., & Epstein, N. (1982). Cognition and relationship maladjustment: Development of a measure of dysfunctional relational beliefs. *Journal of Consulting and Clinical Psychology, 50,* 715–720.

Fletcher, G.J.O., Fincham, F. D., Carmer, L., & Heron, N. (1987). The role of attributions in the development of dating relationships. *Journal of Personality and Social Psychology, 53,* 481–489.

Folkman, S., & Lazarus, R. S. (1985). If it changes it must be a process: A study of emotion and coping during three stages of a college examination. *Journal of Personality and Social Psychology, 48,* 150–170.

Hecht, M. L. (1978a). The conceptualization and measurement of interpersonal communication satisfaction. *Human Communication Research, 4,* 253–264.

Hecht, M. L. (1978b). Measures of communication satisfaction. *Human Communication Research, 4,* 350–368.

Hecht, M. L. (1978c). Toward a conceptualization of interpersonal communication satisfaction. *Quarterly Journal of Speech, 64,* 47–62.

Hecht, M. L. (1984a). Persuasive efficacy: A study of the relationship among type of change and degree of change, message strategies and satisfying communication. *Western Journal of Speech Communication, 48,* 373–389.

Hecht, M. L. (1984b). An investigation of the effects of sex of self and other on perceptions of communication satisfaction. *Sex Roles: A Journal of Research, 10,* 733–741.

Hecht, M. L. (1984c). Satisfying communication and relationship labels: Intimacy and length of relationship as perceptual frames of naturalistic conversations. *Western Journal of Speech Communication, 48,* 201–216.

Hecht, M. L., & Marston, P. J. (1987). Communication satisfaction and the temporal development of conversations. *Communication Research Reports, 4,* 60–65.

Hecht, M. L., & Riley, P. (1985). A three factor model of group satisfaction and consensus. *Communication Research Reports, 2,* 178–181.

Hecht, M. L., & Sereno, K. K. (1985). Interpersonal communication satisfaction: Relationship to satisfaction with self and other. *Communication Research Reports, 2,* 141–148.

Hecht, M. L., Sereno, K. K., & Spitzberg, B. H. (1984). The relevance of relationship level and topic level to the relationship between communication satisfaction and satisfaction with self and other. *Personality and Social Psychology Bulletin, 10,* 376–384.

Hendrick, C., & Hendrick, S. S. (1988). Lovers wear rose colored glasses. *Journal of Social and Personal Relationships, 5,* 161–183.

Hendrick, S. S. (1981). Self-disclosure and marital satisfaction. *Journal of Personality and Social Psychology, 40,* 1150–1159.

Hendrick, S. S. (1988). The relationship assessment scale: A generic measure of relationship quality. *Journal of Marriage and the Family, 50,* 93–98.

Kurdek, L. A. (1989). Relationship quality in gay and lesbian cohabiting couples: A 1-year follow-up study. *Journal of Social and Personal Relationships, 6,* 39–59.

Lewis, R. (1979). A longitudinal test of a developmental framework for premarital dyadic formation. *Journal of Marriage and the Family, 35,* 16–25.

Locke, H., & Wallace, K. (1959). Short marital adjustment and prediction tests: Their reliability and validity. *Marriage and Family Living, 21,* 251–255.

Lund, M. (1985). The development of investment and commitment scales for predicting continuity of personal relationships. *Journal of Social and Personal Relationships, 2,* 3–23.

Maxwell, G. M. (1985). Behavior of lovers: Measuring the closeness of relationships. *Journal of Social and Personal Relationships, 2,* 215–238.

Parmelee, P. A. (1987). Sex role identity, role performance and marital satisfaction of newly-wed couples. *Journal of Social and Personal Relationships, 4,* 429–444.

Petronio, S. (1982). The effect of interpersonal communication on the women's family role satisfaction. *Western Journal of Speech Communication, 46,* 208–222.

Rubin, Z. (1974). From liking to love: Patterns of attraction in dating relationships. In T. Huston (Ed.), *Foundations of interpersonal attraction* (pp. 383–402). New York: Academic Press.

Spanier, G. B. (1976). Measuring dyadic adjustment: New scales for assessing the quality of marriage and similar dyads. *Journal of Marriage and the Family, 38,* 15–28.

Steck, L., Leviton, D., McLane, D., & Kelley, H. H. (1982). Care, need, and conceptions of love. *Journal of Personality and Social Psychology, 43,* 481–491.

Stephen, T., & Markman, H. (1983). Assessing the development of relationships: A new measure. *Family Processes, 22,* 15–25.

Sternberg, R. J., & Grajek, S. (1984). The nature of love. *Journal of Personality and Social Psychology, 47,* 312–329.

Wolf, M. H., Putnam, S. M., James, S. M., & Wright, D. D. (1978). The medical interview satisfaction scale: Development of a scale to measure patients' perceptions of physician behavior. *Journal of Behavioral Medicine, 1,* 391–401.

Relationship Satisfaction

Baxter, L. A., & Bullis, C. (1986). Turning points in developing romantic relationships. *Human Communication Research, 12,* 469–493.

Berg, J., & McQuinn, R. (1986). Attraction and exchange in continuing and noncontinuing dating relationships. *Journal of Personality and Social Psychology, 50,* 942–952.

Canary, D. J., & Spitzberg, B. H. (1988). Relational and episodic characteristics associated with conflict tactics. *Journal of Social and Personal Relationships, 5,* 305–325.

Davis, K. E., & Latty-Mann, H. (1987). Love styles and relationship quality: A contribution to validation. *Journal of Social and Personal Relationships, 4,* 409–428.

Davis, K. E., & Todd, M. J. (1982). Friendship and love relationships. In K. E. Davis & T. O. Mitchell (Eds.), *Advances in descriptive psychology* (Vol. 2). Greenwich, CT: JAI Press.

Davis, K. E., & Todd, M. J. (1985). Assessing friendship: Prototypes, paradigm cases, and relationship assessment. In S. W. Duck & D. Perlman (Eds.), *Understanding personal relationships: An interdisciplinary approach* (pp. 17–34). Beverly Hills, CA: Sage.

Eidelson, R. J. (1980). Interpersonal satisfaction and level of involvement: A curvilinear relationship. *Journal of Personality and Social Psychology, 39,* 460–470.

Fitzpatrick, M. A., & Winke, J. (1979). You always hurt the one you love: Strategies and tactics in interpersonal conflict. *Communication Quarterly, 27,* 3–11.

Franzoi, S. L., Davis, M. H., & Young, R. D. (1985). The effects of private self-consciousness and perspective taking on satisfaction in close relationships. *Journal of Personality and Social Psychology, 48,* 1584–1594.

Gottman, J. M. (1979). *Martial interaction: Experimental investigations.* New York: Academic Press.

Gottman, J. M. (1982). Emotional responsiveness in marital conversations. *Journal of Communication, 32,* 108–120.

Grigg, F., Fletcher, G.J.O., & Fitness, J. (1989). Spontaneous attributions in happy and unhappy dating relationships. *Journal of Social and Personal Relationships, 6*, 61–68.

Hatfield, E., Utne, M., & Traupmann, J. (1979). Equity theory and intimate relationships. In R. Burgess & T. Huston (Eds.), *Social exchange in developing relationships*. New York: Academic Press.

Hendrick, S. (1981). Self disclosure and marital satisfaction. *Journal of Personality and Social Psychology, 48*, 1158–1159.

Hill, C., Peplau, L., & Rubin, Z. (1976). Break-ups before marriage: The end of 103 affairs. *Journal of Social Issues, 32*, 147–168.

Kingsbury, N. M., & Minda, R. B. (1988). An analysis of three expected intimate relationship states: Commitment, maintenance and termination. *Journal of Social and Personal Relationships, 5*, 405–422.

Kirchler, E. (1988). Marital happiness and interaction in everyday surroundings: A time-sample diary approach for couples. *Journal of Social and Personal Relationships, 5*, 375–382.

Metts, S. (1989). An exploratory investigation of deception in close relationships. *Journal of Social and Personal Relationships, 6*, 159–179.

Morton, T., & Douglas, M. (1981). Growth of relationships. In S. W. Duck & R. Gilmour (Eds.), *Personal relationships 2: Developing personal relationships* (pp. 3–26). London: Academic Press.

Wheeler, L., Reis, H. T., & Nezlek, J. (1983). Loneliness, social interaction, and sex roles. *Journal of Personality and Social Psychology, 45*, 943–953.

Wong, H. (1981). Typologies of intimacy. *Psychology of Women Quarterly, 5*, 435–445.

Relationship Turning Points

Baxter, L., & Bullis, C. (1986). Turning points in developing romantic relationships. *Human Communication Research, 12*, 469–493.

Duck, S. W. (1986). *Human relationships: An introduction to social psychology*. London: Sage.

Levinger, G. (1980). Toward the analysis of close relationships. *Journal of Experimental Social Psychology, 16*, 510–544.

Lloyd, S. A., & Cate, R. M. (1985). Attributions associated with significant turning points in premarital relationship development and dissolution. *Journal of Social and Personal Relationships, 2*, 419–436.

Masheter, D. W., & Harris, L. M. (1986). From divorce to friendship: A study of dialectic relationship development. *Journal of Social and Personal Relationships, 3*, 177–189.

Morris, G. H., & Hopper, R. (1980). Remediation and legislation in everyday talk: How communicators achieve consensus. *Quarterly Journal of Speech, 66*, 266–274.

Planalp, S., & Honeycutt, J. (1985). Events that increase uncertainty in personal relationships. *Human Communication Research, 11*, 593–604.

Surra, C. A. (1985a). Courtship types: Variations in interdependence between partners and social networks. *Journal of Social and Personal Relationships, 2*, 357–375.

Surra, C. A. (1985b). Reasons for changes in commitment: Variations by courtship type. *Journal of Social and Personal Relationships, 2*, 17–33.

Wilmont, W. W. (1987). *Dyadic communication* (3rd ed.). New York: Random House.

Relationship Types

Argyle, M., & Henderson, M. (1984). The rules of friendship. *Journal of Social and Personal Relationships, 1*, 211–237.

Baxter, L. A. (1987). Symbols of relationship identity in relationship cultures. *Journal of Social and Personal Relationships, 4*, 261–280.

Baxter, L. A., & Wilmot, W. W. (1984). 'Secret tests': Social strategies for acquiring information about the state of the relationship. *Human Communication Research, 11*, 171–201.

Bell, R. A., Buerkel-Rothfuss, N. L., & Gore, K. E. (1987). Did you bring the yarmulke for the cabbage patch kid?: The idiomatic communication of young lovers. *Human Communication Research, 14*, 47–46.

Berger, C. R., Weber, M. B., & Dixon, J. T. (1977). Interpersonal relationship levels and interpersonal attraction. In B. D. Ruben (Ed.), *Communication yearbook 1* (pp. 245–261). New Brunswick, NJ: Transaction Books.

Bradac, J. J., Tardy, C. H., & Hosman, L. A. (1980). Disclosure styles and a hint at their genesis. *Human Communication Research, 6*, 228–238.

Burggraf, C. S., & Sillars, A. L. (1987). A critical examination of sex differences in marital communication. *Communication Monographs, 54*, 276–294.

Clark, M. S., & Waddell, B. (1985). Perceptions of exploitation in communal and exchange relationships. *Journal of Social and Personal Relationships, 2*, 403–419.

Fitzpatrick, M. A. (1977). A typological approach to communication in relationships. In B. Ruben (Ed.), *Communication yearbook 1* (pp. 263–274). New Brunswick, NJ: Transaction Books.

Gudykunst, W. B. (1985). The influence of cultural similarity, type of relationship, and self-monitoring on uncertainty reduction processes. *Communication Monographs, 52*, 203–217.

Gudykunst, W. B., & Nishida, T. (1986). The influence of cultural variability on perceptions of communication behavior associated with relationship terms. *Human Communication Research, 13*, 147–166.

Gudykunst, W. B., Sodetani, L. L., & Sonoda, K. T. (1987). Uncertainty reduction in Japanese-American/Caucasian relationships in Hawaii. *Western Journal of Speech Communication, 51,* 256–278.

Gudykunst, W. B., Yang, S-M., & Nishida, T. (1985). A cross-cultural test of uncertainty reduction theory: Comparisons of acquaintances, friends, and dating relationships in Japan, Korea, and the United States. *Human Communication Research, 11,* 407–454.

Hays, R. B. (1984). The development and maintenance of friendship. *Journal of Social and Personal Relationships, 1,* 75–98.

Hecht, M. L. (1984). Satisfying communication and relationship labels: Intimacy and length of relationship as perceptual frames of naturalistic conversations. *Western Journal of Speech Communication, 48,* 201–216.

Kayser, E., Schwinger T., & Cohen, R. L. (1984). Laypersons' conceptions of social relationships: A test of contract theory. *Journal of Social and Personal Relationships, 1,* 433–458.

Knapp, M. L., Ellis, D. G., & Williams, B. A. (1980). Perceptions of communication behavior associated with relationship terms. *Communication Monographs, 47,* 262–278.

Montgomery, B. M. (1984). Communication in intimate relationships: A research challenge. *Communication Quarterly, 32,* 318–327.

Neimeyer, G. J., & Neimeyer, R. A. (1985). Relational trajectories: A personal construct contribution. *Journal of Social and Personal Relationships, 2,* 325–349.

O'Connell, L. (1984). An exploration of exchange in three social relationships: Kinship, friendship and the marketplace. *Journal of Social and Personal Relationships, 1,* 333–346.

Planalp, S., & Honeycutt, J. M. (1985). Events that increase uncertainty in personal relationships. *Human Communication Research, 11,* 593–604.

Ragan, S. L., & Hopper, R. (1984). Ways to leave your lover: A conversational analysis of literature. *Communication Quarterly, 32,* 310–317.

Rawlins, W. E. (1983). Openness as problematic in ongoing friendships: Two conversational dilemmas. *Communication Monographs, 50,* 1–13.

Rawlins, W. E., Leibowitz, K., & Bochner, A. P. (1986). Affective and instrumental dimensions of best, equal, and unequal friendships. *Central States Speech Journal, 37,* 90–101.

Rose, S., & Serfica, F. C. (1986). Keeping and ending casual, close and best friendships. *Journal of Social and Personal Relationships, 3,* 275–288.

Sillars, A. L., & Scott, M. D. (1983). Interpersonal perception between intimates: An integrative review. *Human Communication Research, 10,* 153–176.

Sykes, R. E. (1983). Initial interaction between strangers and acquaintances: A multivariate analysis of factors affecting choice of communication partners. *Human Communication Research, 10,* 27–54.

Wilmot, W. W., & Baxter, L. A. (1983). Reciprocal framing of relationship definitions and episodic interaction. *Western Journal of Speech Communication, 47,* 205–217.

Wiseman, J. P. (1986). Friendship: Binds and bonds in a voluntary relationship. *Journal of Social and Personal Relationships, 3,* 191–211.

Wright, P. H. (1984). Self-referent motivation and the intrinsic quality of friendship. *Journal of Social and Personal Relationships, 1,* 115–130.

Reviews of Interpersonal Communication

Ayers, J. (1984). Four approaches to interpersonal communication: Review, observation, prognosis. *Western Journal of Speech Communication, 48,* 408–440.

Berger, C. R. (1977). Interpersonal communication: Contemporary issues and directions in theory and research. In B. D. Ruben (Ed.), *Communication yearbook 1* (pp. 217–228). New Brunswick, NJ: Transaction Books.

Bochner, A. (1978). On taking ourselves seriously: An analysis of some persistent problems and promising directions in interpersonal research. *Human Communication Research, 4,* 179–191.

Bochner, A. P. (1983). Functions of communication in interpersonal bonding. In C. A. Arnold & J. W. Bowers (Eds.), *Handbook of rhetoric and communication* (pp. 554–621). Boston: Allyn & Bacon.

Bochner, A. P., & Krueger, D. (1979). Interpersonal communication theory and research: An overview of inscrutable epistemologies and muddled concepts. In D. Nimmo (Ed.), *Communication yearbook 3* (pp. 197–211). New Brunswick, NJ: Transaction Books.

Miller, G. R. (1978). The current status of theory and research in interpersonal communication. *Human Communication Research, 4,* 164–178.

Miller, G. R. (1981). 'Tis the season to be jolly': A yuletide 1980 assessment of communication research. *Human Communication Research, 7,* 371–377.

Miller, G. R. (1983). Taking stock of the discipline. *Journal of Communication, 33,* 31–41.

Miller, G. R., & Sunnafrank, M. J. (1982). All is for one but one is not for all: A conceptual perspective on interpersonal communication. In F.E.X. Dance (Ed.), *Human communication theory* (pp. 220–242). New York: Harper & Row.

Parks, M. (1982). Ideology in interpersonal communication: Off the couch and into the world. In M. Burgoon (Ed.), *Communication yearbook 5* (pp. 89–92). New Brunswick, NJ: Transaction Books.

Phillips, G. M. (1981). Science and the study of human communication: An inquiry from the other side of two cultures. *Human Communication Research, 7,* 361–370.

Studies of Interpersonal Communication

Acitelli, L. K. (1988). When spouses talk to each other about their relationship. *Journal of Social and Personal Relationships, 5,* 185–199.

Acitelli, L. K., & Duck, S. W. (1987). Intimacy as the proverbial elephant. In D. Perlman & S. W. Duck (Eds.), *Intimate relationships: Development, dynamics, and deterioration* (pp. 297–308). Beverly Hills, CA: Sage.

Alberts, J. K. (1986). The role of couples' conversations in relational development: A content analysis of courtship talk in Harlequin romance novels. *Communication Quarterly, 34,* 127–142.

Alberts, J. K. (1988). An analysis of couples' conversational complaints. *Communication Monographs, 55,* 184–197.

Andrews, P. A. (1987). Gender differences in persuasive communication and attribution of success and failure. *Human Communication Research, 13,* 372–385.

Aron, A., Dutton, D. G., Aron, E. N., & Iverson, A. (1989). Experiences of falling in love. *Journal of Social and Personal Relationships, 6,* 243–258.

Barbatis, G. S., Wong, M. R., & Herek, G. M. (1983). A struggle for dominance: Relational communication patterns in television drama. *Communication Quarterly, 31,* 148–155.

Baxter, L. A., & Bullis, C. (1986). Turning points in developing romantic relationships. *Human Communication Research, 12,* 469–493.

Baxter, L. A., & Wilmot, W. W. (1984). 'Secret test's: Social strategies for acquiring information about the state of the relationship. *Human Communication Research, 11,* 171–202.

Baxter, L. A., & Wilmot, W. W. (1985). Taboo topics in close relationships. *Journal of Social and Personal Relationships, 2,* 253–270.

Bell, R. A. (1986). The multivariate structure of communication avoidance. *Communication Monographs, 53,* 365–375.

Bell, R. A., Buerkel-Rothfuss, N. L., & Gore, K. E. (1987). Did you bring the yarmulke for the cabbage patch kid?: The idiomatic communication of young lovers. *Human Communication Research, 14,* 47–68.

Bell, R. A., & Daly, J. A. (1984). The affinity-seeking function of communication. *Communication Monographs, 51,* 91–115.

Bell, R. A., Tremblay, S. W., & Buerkel-Rothfuss, N. L. (1987). Interpersonal attraction as a communication accomplishment: Development of a measure of affinity-seeking competence. *Western Journal of Speech Communication, 51,* 1–18.

Berger, C. R. (1985). Social power and interpersonal communication. In M. L. Knapp & G. R. Miller (Eds.), *Handbook of interpersonal communication* (pp. 439–499). Beverly Hills, CA: Sage.

Berger, C. R., & Bell, R. A. (1988). Plans and the initiation of social relationships. *Human Communication Research, 15,* 217–235.

Berger, C. R., & Calabrese, R. J. (1975). Some explorations in initial interactions and beyond: Toward a developmental theory of interpersonal communication. *Human Communication Research, 1,* 99–112.

Berscheid, E., Dion, K., Walster, E., & Walster, G. W. (1971). Physical attractiveness and dating choice: A test of the matching hypothesis. *Journal of Experimental Social Psychology, 7,* 173–189.

Bradac, J. J. (1983). The language of lovers, flovers, and friends: Communicating in social and personal relationships. *Journal of Language and Social Psychology, 2,* 141–162.

Buller, D. B., & Burgoon, J. K. (1986). The effects of vocalics and nonverbal sensitivity on compliance: A replication and extension. *Human Communication Research, 13,* 126–144.

Burggraf, C. S., & Sillars, A. L. (1987). A critical examination of sex differences in marital communication. *Communication Monographs, 54,* 276–294.

Burgoon, J. K. (1982). Privacy and communication. In M. Burgoon (Ed.), *Communication yearbook 6* (pp. 206–249). Beverly Hills, CA: Sage.

Burgoon, J. K. (1985). Nonverbal signals. In M. L. Knapp & G. R. Miller (Eds.), *Handbook of interpersonal communication* (pp. 344–392). Beverly Hills, CA: Sage.

Burgoon, J. K., Buller, D. B., Hale, J. L., & deTurck, M. A. (1984). Relational messages associated with nonverbal behavior. *Human Communication Research, 10,* 351–378.

Burgoon, J. K., & Hale, J. L. (1988). Nonverbal expectancy violations: Model elaboration and application to immediacy behaviors. *Communication Monographs, 55,* 58–79.

Burgoon, J. K., Parrot, R., LePoire, B. A., Kelley, D. L., Walther, J. B., & Perry, D. (1989). Maintaining and restoring privacy through communication in different types of relationships. *Journal of Social and Personal Relationships, 6,* 131–158.

Burgoon, J. K., Pfau, M., Parrott, R., Birk, T., Coker, R., & Burgoon, M. (1987). Relational communication, satisfaction, compliance-gaining strategies, and compliance in communication between physicians and patients. *Communication Monographs, 54,* 307–324.

Burleson, B. R., Wilson, S. R., Waltman, M. S., Goering, E. M., Ely, T. K., & Whaley, B. B. (1988). Item desirability effects in compliance-gaining research: Seven studies documenting artifacts in the strategy selection procedure. *Human Communication Research, 14,* 429–486.

Bush, C. R., Bush, J., & Jennings, J. (1988). Effects of jealousy threats on relationship perceptions and emotions. *Journal of Social and Personal Relationships, 5,* 285–303.

Canary, D. J., & Spitzberg, B. H. (1987). Appropriateness and effectiveness perceptions of conflict strategies. *Human Communication Research, 14,* 93–118.

Carrocci, N. M. (1985). Perceiving and responding to interpersonal conflict. *Central States Speech Journal, 36*, 215–228.

Cheek, J. M., & Buss, A. H. (1981). Shyness and sociability. *Journal of Personality and Social Psychology, 41*, 330–339.

Chelune, G. J. (1977). Sex differences, repression-sensitization, and self-disclosure: A behavioral look. *Psychological Reports, 40*, 667–670.

Clarke, D. D., Allen, C.M.B., & Salinas, M. (1986). Conjoint time budgeting: Investigating behavioural accommodation in marriage. *Journal of Social and Personal Relationships, 3*, 53–70.

Cline, R. J. (1983). The acquaintance process as relational communication. In R. Bostrom (Ed.), *Communication yearbook 7* (pp. 396–413). Beverly Hills, CA: Sage.

Cline, R.J.W. (1988). The politics of intimacy: Costs and benefits determining disclosure intimacy in male-female dyads. *Journal of Social and Personal Relationships, 6*, 5–20.

Cody, M. J., Woefel, M. L., & Jordan, W. J. (1983). Dimensions of compliance-gaining situations. *Human Communication Research, 9*, 99–113.

Cody, M. L., & McLaughlin, M. L. (1985). The situation as a construct in interpersonal communication. In M. L. Knapp & G. R. Miller (Eds.), *Handbook of interpersonal communication* (pp. 263–312). Beverly Hills, CA: Sage.

Conville, R. L. (1988). Relational transitions: An inquiry into their structure and function. *Journal of Social and Personal Relationships, 5*, 423–437.

Coopersmith, S. (1967). *The antecedents of self-esteem.* New York: W. H. Freeman.

Cramer, D. (1985). An item factor analysis of the original Relationship Inventory. *Journal of Social and Personal Relationships, 3*, 121–127.

Deal, J. E., & Wampler, K. S. (1986). Dating violence: The primacy of previous experience. *Journal of Social and Personal Relationships, 3*, 457–472.

Dillard, J. P. (1987). Close relationships at work: Perceptions of the motives and performance of relational participants. *Journal of Social and Personal Relationships, 4*, 179–194.

Dillard, J. P. (1988). Compliance-gaining message-selection: What is our dependent variable? *Communication Monographs, 5*, 162–183.

Dillard, J. P. (1989). Types of influence goals in personal relationships. *Journal of Social and Personal Relationships, 6*, 293–308.

Dindia, K. (1987). The effects of sex of subject and sex of partner on interruptions. *Human Communication Research, 13*, 345–371.

Edelmann, R. J. (1985). Social embarrassment: An analysis of the process. *Journal of Social and Personal Relationships, 2*, 215–238.

Eidelson, R. J., & Epstein, N. (1982). Cognition and relationship maladjustment: Development of a measure of relationship beliefs. *Journal of Consulting and Clinical Psychology, 50*, 715–720.

Ekman, P. (1985). *Telling lies.* New York: Norton.

Fischoff, B., Slovic, P., & Lichtenstein, S. (1977). Knowing with certainty: The appropriateness of extreme confidence. *Journal of Experimental Psychology: Human Perceptions and Performance, 3*, 552–564.

Fisher, D. V. (1986). Decision-making and self-disclosure. *Journal of Social and Personal Relationships, 3*, 323–336.

Fitzpartrick, M. A. (1985). All in the family: Interpersonal communication in kin relationships. In M. L. Knapp & G. R. Miller (Eds.), *Handbook of interpersonal communication* (pp. 687–732). Beverly Hills, CA: Sage.

Gerstein, L. H., & Tesser, A. (1987). Antecedents and responses associated with loneliness. *Journal of Social and Personal Relationships, 4*, 329–363.

Giles, H., & Street, R. L., Jr. (1985). Communicator characteristics and behavior. In M. L. Knapp & G. R. Miller (Eds.), *Handbook of interpersonal communication* (pp. 205–262). Beverly Hills, CA: Sage.

Goffman, E. (1959). *The presentation of self in everyday life.* Garden City, NY: Anchor.

Gottlieb, B. H. (1985). Social support and the study of personal relationships. *Journal of Social and Personal Relationships, 2*, 351–376.

Gudykunst, W. B. (1976). Attributional confidence in low- and high-context cultures. *Human Communication Research, 12*, 525–549.

Gudykunst, W. B. (1985). An exploratory comparison of closer intracultural and intercultural friendships. *Communication Quarterly, 33*, 270–283.

Gudykunst, W. B., Yoon, Y-C., & Nishida, T. (1987). The influence of individualism-collectivism on perceptions of communication in ingroup and outgroup relationships. *Communication Monographs, 54*, 295–306.

Harris, L. M., Gergen, K. J., & Lannaman, J. W. (1986). Aggression rituals. *Communication Monographs, 53*, 252–265.

Hatfield, E. (1984). The dangers of intimacy. In V. J. Derlega (Ed.), *Communication, intimacy and close relationships* (pp. 207–220). New York: Academic Press.

Hays, R. B. (1989). The day-to-day functioning of close versus casual friendships. *Journal of Social and Personal Relationships, 6*, 21–37.

Helgeson, V. S., Shaver, P., & Dyer, M. (1987). Prototypes of intimacy and distance in same-sex and opposite sex relationships. *Journal of Social and Personal Relationships, 4*, 195–233.

Hendrick, C., Hendrick, S., Foote, F. H., & Slapion-Foote, M. J. (1984). Do men and women love differently? *Journal of Social and Personal Relationships, 1*, 177–196.

Hinde, R. A. (1984). Why do the sexes behave differently in close relationships? *Journal of Social and Personal Relationships, 1*, 471–502.

Hinsz, V. B. (1989). Facial resemblance in engaged and married couples. *Journal of Social and Personal Relationships, 6*, 223–229.

Hollingshead, A., & Redlich, F. (1958). *Social class and mental illness*. New York: John Wiley & Sons.

Hopper, R., & Bell, R. A. (1984). Broadening the deception construct. *Quarterly Journal of Speech, 70,* 288–302.

Hopper, R., Knapp, M. L., & Scott, L. (1981). Couples' personal idiom: Exploring intimate talk. *Journal of Communication, 31,* 23–33.

Hornstein, G. A. (1985). Intimacy in conversational style as a function of the degree of closeness between members of a dyad. *Journal of Personality and Social Psychology, 49,* 671–681.

Hortacsu, N. (1989). Current and dissolved relationships: Descriptive and attributional dimensions and predictors of involvement. *Journal of Social and Personal Relationships, 6,* 373–383.

Hosman, L. (1987). The evaluative consequences of topic reciprocity and self-disclosure reciprocity. *Communication Monographs, 54,* 420–435.

Hosman, L. A. (1989). The evaluative characteristics of hedges, hesitations, and intensifiers: Powerful and powerless speech styles. *Human Communication Research, 15,* 383–406.

Infante, D. A., & Rancer, A. S. (1982). A conceptualization and measurement of argumentativeness. *Journal of Personality Assessment, 46,* 72–80.

Infante, D. A., & Wigley, C. J., III (1986). Verbal aggressiveness: An interpersonal model and measure. *Communication Monographs, 53,* 61–69.

Jablin, F. M. (1985). Task/work relationships: A life-span perspective. In M. L. Knapp & G. R. Miller (Eds.), *Handbook of interpersonal communication* (pp. 615–654). Beverly Hills, CA: Sage.

Jacobs, S. (1985). Language. In M. L. Knapp & G. R. Miller (Eds.), *Handbook of interpersonal communication* (pp. 313–343). Beverly Hills, CA: Sage.

Kelly, L. (1982). A rose by any other name is still a rose: A comparative analysis of reticence, communication apprehension, unwillingness to communicate, and shyness. *Human Communication Research, 8,* 99–113.

Kurdek, L. A. (1989). Relationship quality in gay and lesbian cohabiting couples: A 1-year follow-up study. *Journal of Social and Personal Relationships, 6,* 39–59.

Marangoni, C., & Ickes, W. (1989). Loneliness: A theoretical review with implications for measurement. *Journal of Social and Personal Relationships, 6,* 93–128.

Maynard, D. W., & Zimmerman, D. H. (1984). Topical talk, ritual and the social organization of relationships. *Social Psychology Quarterly, 47,* 301–316.

McCroskey, J. C. (1982). Oral communication apprehension: A reconceptualization. In M. Burgoon (Ed.), *Communication yearbook 6* (pp. 136–170). Beverly Hills, CA: Sage.

McFarlane, A. H., Norman, G. R., Streiner, D. L., Ray, R., & Scott, D. J. (1980). A longitudinal study of the influence of the psychosocial environment on health status: A preliminary report. *Journal of Health and Social Behavior, 21,* 124–133.

McLeroy, K. R., DeVellis, R., DeVellis, B., Kaplan, B., & Toole, J. (1984). Social support and physical recovery in a stroke population. *Journal of Social and Personal Relationships, 1,* 395–414.

Metts, S. (1989). An exploratory investigation of deception in close relationships. *Journal of Social and Personal Relationships, 6,* 159–179.

Metts, S., Cupach, W. R., & Bejlovec, R. A. (1989). 'I love you too much to ever start liking you': Redefining romantic relationships. *Journal of Social and Personal Relationships, 6,* 259–274.

Miller, G. R., Mongeau, P. A., & Sleight, C. (1986). Fudging with friends and lying to lovers: Deceptive communication in personal relationships. *Journal of Social and Personal Relationships, 3,* 495–512.

Miller, L. C., Berg, J. H., & Archer, R. L. (1983). Openers: Individuals who elicit intimate self-disclosure. *Journal of Personality and Social Psychology, 44,* 1234–1244.

Miller, L. C., & Kenny, D. A. (1986). Reciprocity of self-disclosure at the individual and dyadic levels: A social relations analysis. *Journal of Personality and Social Psychology, 50,* 713–719.

Miller, M. D., Reynolds, R. A., & Cambra, R. E. (1987). The influence of gender and culture on language intensity. *Communication Monographs, 54,* 101–105.

Montgomery, B. M. (1984). Individual differences and relational interdependencies in social interaction. *Human Communication Research, 11,* 33–60.

Morgan, D. L. (1986). Personal relationships as an interface between social networks and social cognition. *Journal of Social and Personal Relationships, 3,* 403–422.

Morris, G. H. (1985). The remedial episode as a negotiation of rules. In R. L. Street & J. N. Cappella (Eds.), *Sequence and pattern in communicative behavior* (pp. 70–84). London: Edward Arnold.

Mulac, A., Studley, L. B., Wiemann, J. M., & Bradac, J. J. (1987). Male/female gaze in same-sex and mixed-sex dyads: Gender-linked differences and mutual influence. *Human Communication Research, 13,* 323–343.

Notarius, C. I., & Herrick, L. R. (1988). Listener response strategies to a distressed other. *Journal of Social and Personal Relationships, 5,* 97–108.

Nussbaum, J. F. (1983). Relational closeness of elderly interaction. *Western Journal of Speech Communication, 47,* 229–243.

O'Connor, P., & Brown, G. W. (1984). Supportive relationships: Fact or fantasy? *Journal of Social and Personal Relationships, 1,* 159–176.

O'Hair, D., & Cody, M. J. (1987). Machiavellian beliefs and social influence. *Western Journal of Speech Communication, 51,* 279–303.

O'Hair, D., Cody, M. J., Goss, B., & Krayer, K. J. (1988). The effect of gender, deceit orientation and communicator style on macro-assessments of honesty. *Communication Quarterly, 36,* 77–93.

Owen, W. F. (1987). Mutual interaction of discourse structures and relational pragmatics in conversational influence attempts. *Southern Speech Communication Journal, 52,* 103–127.

Parks, M. R., & Adelman, M. B. (1983). Communication networks and the development of romantic relationships: An expansion of uncertainty reduction theory. *Human Communication Research, 10*, 55–79.

Parks, M. R., Stan, C., & Eggert, L. (1983). Romantic involvement and social network involvement. *Social Psychology Quarterly, 46*, 116–131.

Peplau, L. A., & Cochran, S. D. (1981). Value orientations in the intimate relationships of gay men. *Journal of Homosexuality, 6*, 1–9.

Petronio, S. (1984). Communication strategies to reduce embarrassment: Differences between men and women. *Western Journal of Speech Communication, 48*, 28–38.

Pfeiffer, S. M., & Wong, P. T. (1989). Multidimensional jealousy. *Journal of Social and Personal Relationships, 6*, 181–196.

Pilkington, C. J., & Richardson, D. R. (1988). Perception of risk in intimacy. *Journal of Social and Personal Relationships, 5*, 503–508.

Planalp, S. (1985). Relational schemata: A test of alternative forms of relational knowledge as guide to communication. *Human Communication Research, 12*, 3–29.

Planalp, S., & Honeycutt, J. M. (1985). Events that increase uncertainty in personal relationships. *Human Communication Research, 11*, 593–604.

Planalp, S., Rutherford, D. K., & Honeycutt, J. M. (1988). Events that increase uncertainty in personal relationships II: Replication and extension. *Human Communication Research, 14*, 516–547.

Prisbell, M. (1986). The relationship between assertiveness and dating behavior among college students. *Communication Research Reports, 3*, 9–12.

Rempel, J. K., Holmes, J. G., & Zanna, M. P. (1985). Trust in close relationships. *Journal of Personality and Social Psychology, 49*, 95–112.

Rosecrance, J. (1986). Racetrack buddies' relations: Compartmentalized and satisfying. *Journal of Social and Personal Relationships, 3*, 441–456.

Sapadin, L. A. (1988). Friendship and gender: Perspectives of professional men and women. *Journal of Social and Personal Relationships, 5*, 387–403.

Sarason, I. G., Sarason, B. R., Shearin, E. N., & Pierce, G. R. (1987). A brief measure of social support: Practical and theoretical implications. *Journal of Social and Personal Relationships, 4*, 497–510.

Schaeffer, M., & Olson, D. (1981). Assessing intimacy: The pair inventory. *Journal of Marriage and Family Therapy, 7*, 47–60.

Schmidt, T. O., & Cornelius, R. R. (1987). Self-disclosure in everyday life. *Journal of Social and Personal Relationships, 4*, 365–373.

Schultz, N. R., Jr., & Moore, D. (1988). Loneliness: Differences across three age levels. *Journal of Social and Personal Relationships, 5*, 275–284.

Sherer, M., Maddux, J. E., Mercandante, B., Prentice-Dunn, S., Jacobs, B., & Rogers, R. W. (1982). The self-efficacy scale: Construction and validation. *Psychological Reports, 51*, 663–671.

Spitzberg, B. H., & Canary, D. J. (1985). Loneliness and relationally competent communication. *Journal of Social and Personal Relationships, 2*, 387–402.

Stephen, T. (1986). Communication and interdependence in geographically separate relationships. *Human Communication Research, 13*, 191–210.

Stephen, T., & Enholm, D. K. (1987). On linguistic and social forms: Correspondences between metaphoric and intimate relationships. *Western Journal of Speech Communication, 51*, 329–344.

Stephen, T., & Markman, H. (1983). Assessing the development of relationships: A new measure. *Family Processes, 22*, 15–25.

Stiff, J. B., Dillard, J. P., Somera, L., Kim, H., & Sleight, C. (1988). Empathy, communication, and prosocial behavior. *Communication Monographs, 55*, 198–213.

Swap, W. C., & Rubin, J. Z. (1983). Measurement of interpersonal orientation. *Journal of Personality and Social Psychology, 44*, 208–219.

Tesch, S. A. (1985). The psychosocial intimacy questionnaire: Validation studies and an investigation of sex roles. *Journal of Social and Personal Relationships, 2*, 471–488.

Thelan, M. H., Fishbein, M. D., & Tatten, H. (1985). Interspousal similarity: A new approach to an old question. *Journal of Social and Personal Relationships, 2*, 437–446.

Thoits, P. A. (1982). Life stress, social support, and psychological vulnerability: Epidemiological considerations. *Journal of Community Psychology, 10*, 341–362.

Tschann, J. M. (1988). Self-disclosure in adult friendship: Gender and marital status differences. *Journal of Social and Personal Relationships, 5*, 65–81.

Turner, R. E., Edgeley, C., & Olmstead, G. (1975). Information control in conversations: Honesty is not always the best policy. *Kansas Journal of Sociology, 11*, 69–89.

Utne, M. K., Hatfield, E., Traupmann, J., & Greenberger, D. (1984). Equity, marital satisfaction, and stability. *Journal of Social and Personal Relationships, 1*, 323–332.

Werner, C. M., & Haggard, L. M. (1985). Temporal qualities of interpersonal relationships. In M. L. Knapp & G. R. Miller (Eds.), *Handbook of interpersonal communication* (pp. 59–99). Beverly Hills, CA: Sage.

Wheeler, L., Reis, H. T., & Nezlek, J. (1983). Loneliness, social interaction, and sex roles. *Journal of Personality and Social Psychology, 45*, 943–953.

Wheeless, L. R. (1978). A follow-up study of the relationships among trust, disclosure, and interpersonal solidarity. *Human Communication Research, 4*, 143–157.

Wheeless, L. R., Erickson, K. V., & Behrens, J. S. (1986). Cultural differences in disclosiveness as a function of locus of control. *Communication Monographs, 53*, 36–46.

Wittemann, H., & Fitzpatrick, M. A. (1986). Compliance-gaining in marital interaction: Power bases, processes, and outcomes. *Communication Monographs, 53,* 130–143.

Won-Doornick, M. J. (1985). Self-disclosure reciprocity in conversation: A cross-national study. *Social Psychology Quarterly, 48,* 97–107.

Zakahi, W. R. (1986). The effects of loneliness on perceptions of interaction: A cross-lag panel study. *Communication Research Reports, 3,* 94–99.

Zuckerman, M., Eysenck, S., & Eysenck, H. J. (1978). Sensation seeking in England and America: Cross-cultural, age and sex comparisons. *Journal of Consulting and Clinical Psychology, 46,* 139–149.

Zuckerman, M., Kolin, E. A., Price, L., & Zoob, I. (1964). Development of a sensation seeking scale. *Journal of Consulting Psychology, 28,* 477–482.

Author Index

Subject Index